DIONYSIUS OF HALICARNASSUS

I

LCL 319

DIONYSIUS OF HALICARNASSUS

THE ROMAN ANTIQUITIES

BOOKS I–II

WITH AN ENGLISH TRANSLATION BY
EARNEST CARY

ON THE BASIS OF THE VERSION OF
EDWARD SPELMAN

HARVARD UNIVERSITY PRESS
CAMBRIDGE, MASSACHUSETTS
LONDON, ENGLAND

First published 1937
Reprinted 1948, 1960, 1968, 1990, 2001

LOEB CLASSICAL LIBRARY® is a registered trademark
of the President and Fellows of Harvard College

ISBN 0-674-99352-7

Printed in Great Britain by St Edmundsbury Press Ltd,
Bury St Edmunds, Suffolk, on acid-free paper.
Bound by Hunter & Foulis Ltd, Edinburgh, Scotland.

CONTENTS

41587

INTRODUCTION

Life of Dionysius

THE few facts known about the life of Dionysius are virtually all given us by the author himself. At the close of the preface to the *Roman Antiquities* (chap. 8) he announces himself as Dionysius, the son of Alexander, and a native of Halicarnassus. He also informs us (chap. 7) that he had come to Italy at the time when Augustus Caesar put an end to the civil war in the middle of the 187th Olympiad (late in 30 B.C. or in 29), and that he had spent the following twenty-two years in acquainting himself with the language and the literature of the Romans, in gathering his materials, and in writing his History. The preface is dated (chap. 3) in the consulship of Nero and Piso (7 B.C.), and the first part, at least, of the work must have been published at that time. It is generally assumed that the entire History appeared then ; but in Book VII. (70, 2) Dionysius refers to Book I. as having been already published. This leaves it an open question in how many instalments and at what intervals he issued the work. We do not know the exact date of his birth : but two casual statements in the History enable us to fix it within certain limits. He cites the disastrous campaign of Crassus against the Parthians as an event of his own lifetime (ii. 6, 4) ; and in describing the erection of the original Capitol he states that the new edifice, ' built in the days of our fathers,' stood on the same foundations as the old (iv. 61, 4). The first of these passages shows that he was born at least as early as 53, and perhaps as early as 54 or 55, since the reference may very well be to the whole Parthian expedition. The second allusion is more indefinite. The new Capitol, begun by Sulla shortly after the burning of the old structure in 83, was formally dedicated by Catulus in 69 ; nevertheless, as late as the beginning of 62 Caesar, in bringing charges of embezzlement against Catulus, claimed that many parts of the temple were still but half-finished and accordingly wished to have Pompey entrusted with the completion of the work.[1] We do not know how much justification there was for Caesar's action, though it is evident that it was primarily a political move ; in any case, he was unsuccessful, and Catulus' name remained on the pediment of the temple. Whether Dionysius knew of Caesar's charges or attached any importance to them we can only conjecture. Egger,[2] taking these charges seriously, argued that Dionysius must have been born after 63 ; yet it is just as natural to believe that the historian dated the temple by the official dedication. The two passages, then, give as extreme limits for the date of Dionysius' birth 69 and 53, with some possibility of the narrower limits of 62 and 55. Modern scholars have generally

---

[1] Dio Cassius, xxxvii. 44 ; cf. xliii. 14, 6.
[2] Max. Egger, *Denys d' Halicarnasse*, p. 3.

INTRODUCTION

assumed a date between 60 and 55, from the feeling that Dionysius must have been a fairly young man when he came to Rome and undertook to master a new language and literature. The only other reference in an ancient author to the time when Dionysius lived is even more indefinite than those just quoted. Strabo (*ca.* 63 B.C.—*ca.* 21 A.D.), in speaking of Halicarnassus, names, as authors who claimed that city as their birthplace, Herodotus, Heracleitus the poet, and, ' in our time,' Dionysius the historian (xiv. 2, 16).

Halicarnassus had declined greatly in importance after the time of Maussolus, and finally suffered grievously at the hands of the pirates not far from the time when Dionysius was born. It was given a new lease of life by Quintus Cicero while he was serving as governor of Asia (61-58), if we may believe the enthusiastic tribute paid him by his brother.[1] Such was the city in which Dionysius apparently spent his youth and early manhood. Whether he composed any of his rhetorical treatises while still residing there is uncertain ; but it is generally held that they were all written at Rome.

In Rome Dionysius was a teacher of rhetoric, probably giving private lessons ; in one of his treatises addressed to a pupil he refers to ' our daily exercises.' [2] From these shorter works which took the form of letters addressed to friends, patrons

---

[1] Cicero, *ad Quint. frat.* i. 1, 8 : *urbes complures dirutas ac paene desertas, in quibus unam Ioniae nobilissimam, alteram Cariae, Samum et Halicarnassum, per te esse recreatas.*

[2] *On the Arrangement of Words,* chap. 20.

or pupils, we learn the names of a number of his friends and associates ; but unfortunately they are, with one or two exceptions, otherwise unknown to us. Aelius Tubero may have been the historian and jurist who was consul in 11 B.C., the same historian who is praised in the *Antiquities* (i. 80, 1). Melitius Rufus, a pupil, and his father, whom Dionysius calls a most valued friend, were evidently Romans. Cn. Pompeius Geminus may well have been a Greek, in spite of his name ; Ammaeus also was probably a Greek, and so almost certainly were Demetrius and Zeno. Caecilius of Calacte, who is styled a dear friend, was a rhetorician and historian of whom a good deal is known In the introduction to the History (chap. 7) Dionysius states that he gained some of his information orally from most learned men (Romans by implication) with whom he came in contact. It would be interesting indeed to know the names of some of these men and how intimately he associated with them ; but, with the possible exception of Aelius Tubero, he nowhere names a contemporary Roman author, although he pays tribute to the many excellent works that were being produced in his day,—histories, speeches and philosophical treatises,—by both Romans and Greeks.[1] From the circumstance that he gives particular credit to the ruling classes of Rome for the recent purification of literary taste, Roberts suggests that he may have been ' influenced more directly . . . by the Roman men of affairs with whom (or with whose sons) his vocation brought him

On the Ancient Orators, chap. 3.

INTRODUCTION

into contact than by any Roman man of letters.'[1]
One avowed purpose in writing his History was to
make a grateful return to Rome for the education
and other advantages he had enjoyed there ;[2] and
this certainly suggests that he felt he had been
made welcome in Rome.

We have no information regarding the date of
his death. If he was the author of the summary
of his History in five books which Photius (Cod. 84)
attributes to him, he doubtless wrote this after the
publication of the large work, and so must have
lived for some little time at least after 7 B.C. There
are several passages in his shorter works in which
he promises to discuss this or that topic ' if I have
the time,' or ' if it is possible,' or ' if Heaven
keeps us safe and sound.' These have sometimes
been taken to indicate that he was already an old
man or in poor health ; but it is by no means
necessary to put such a construction upon his words.

THE ROMAN ANTIQUITIES

The work which Dionysius undoubtedly regarded
as his masterpiece and the practical embodiment
of his theories regarding historical writing was the
Roman Antiquities.[3] It treated the history of Rome
from the earliest legendary times down to the

[1] W. Rhys Roberts, *Dionysius of Halicarnassus : The
Three Literary Letters*, p. 35.
[2] *Antiq.* i. 6, 5.
[3] This is the traditional English rendering of the Greek
title ; if we were translating it to-day for the first time
we should probably render it *Early History* (or *Ancient
Lore*) *of Rome*.

beginning of the First Punic War, the point at which
Polybius' history began. The work was in twenty
books,[1] of which the first ten are preserved, together
with the greater part of the eleventh. Of the remaining books we have fragments amounting all
told to a little more than the average length of one
of the earlier books. Most of these fragments come
from the great collection of historical extracts
made at the direction of the emperor Constantine
Porphyrogennetus in the tenth century.

In his preface Dionysius lays down two principles
as fundamental for historians, first, that they should
choose subjects noble and lofty and of great utility
to their readers, and, second, that they should use
the greatest care and discrimination in gathering
their materials. He then proceeds to justify his
own choice of subject and to describe the careful
preparation he had made for his task. In two chapters, obviously imitated from Polybius' introduction, he gives a brief survey of the empires of the
past, from the Assyrian to the Macedonian, with a
glance at the Greek hegemonies, and points out
how greatly Rome had surpassed them all, both in
the extent of her dominion and in the length of
time it had already endured. He then undertakes
to answer the anticipated criticism of those who
might censure him for choosing the humble beginnings of Rome as his particular theme when there
were so many glorious periods in her later history

[1] Photius, *Cod.* 83. Stephanus of Byzantium cited
numerous Italian place-names from the *Antiquities*, often
giving the number of the book ; the last book he names
is the nineteenth.

that would furnish excellent subjects. He declares that the Greeks for the most part were ignorant of Rome's early history, having been misled by baseless reports that attributed the founding of the city to some homeless wanderers, at once barbarians and slaves, and hence were inclined to rail at Fortune for unfairly bestowing the heritage of the Greeks upon the basest of barbarians. He promises to correct these erroneous impressions and to prove that Rome's founders were in reality Greeks, and Greeks from no mean tribes; he will also show that Rome from the very beginning produced countless instances of men as pious, just and brave as any other city ever did, and that it was due to these early leaders and to the customs and institutions handed down by them that their descendants advanced to so great power. Thus he hopes to reconcile his Greek readers to their subjection to Rome. He points out that there had been no accurate history of Rome written by Greeks, but only summary accounts, and even the Romans who had written histories of their country in Greek had passed lightly over events occurring before their own days. He feels, therefore, that in this earlier period of Rome's history he has found a noble theme virtually untouched as yet. By treating this period adequately he will confer immortal glory upon those worthy men of early Rome and encourage their descendants to emulate them in leading honourable and useful lives; at the same time he will have the opportunity of showing his goodwill toward all good men who delight in the contemplation of great and noble deeds, and also of

INTRODUCTION

making a grateful return to Rome for the cultural advantages and other blessings that he had enjoyed while residing there. He declares, however, that it is not for the sake of flattering the Romans that he has turned his attention to this subject, but out of regard for truth and justice, the proper objects of every history. He then describes his preparation for his task,—the twenty-two years he had spent in familiarizing himself with the language and literature of the Romans, the oral information he had received from the most learned men, and the approved Roman histories that he had read. Finally, he announces the period of Roman history to be covered in his work [1] and the topics to be treated. He will relate the wars waged by Rome with other peoples and the seditions at home, her various forms of government, the best of her customs and the most important of her laws ; in short, he will picture the whole life of the ancient city. As regards the form of his History, it will not be like the works of those who write of wars alone or treat solely of political constitutions, nor will it be monotonous and tiresome like the annalistic histories of Athens ; but it will be a combination of every style, so as to appeal

[1] He does not explicitly state why he terminated his History with the beginning of the First Punic War, but the reasons are not far to seek. With this war Rome emerged from the relative obscurity of her own peninsula and entered upon her struggle for the supremacy of the Mediterranean. There were already histories in Greek, notably that of Polybius, recounting her achievements from this time onward ; but for the period preceding the Punic Wars Dionysius could feel that he was virtually a pioneer in his undertaking.

alike to statesmen and to philosophers as well as to those who desire mere undisturbed entertainment in their reading of history.

More than once in the course of his History (v. 56, xi. 1 ; cf. vii. 66) Dionysius interrupts his narrative to insist on the importance of acquainting the reader not only with the mere outcome of events, but also with the causes, remote as well as proximate, that led up to them, the circumstances in which the events occurred and the motives of the chief participants,—in fact, the whole background of the action. Such information, he says, is of the utmost importance to statesmen, in order that they may have precedents for the various situations that may confront them and may thus be able to persuade their fellow-citizens when they can adduce numerous examples from the past to show the advantage or the harm of a given course of action. Dionysius here shows an understanding of the true function of history, as he does also, in a measure, in his various protestations of devotion to the truth, though he nowhere sets up such a strict standard of absolute impartiality as did Polybius (i. 14, 4).

Unfortunately, in spite of these high ideals which Dionysius tried to keep before him, his *Antiquities* is an outstanding example of the mischievous results of that unnatural alliance between rhetoric and history which was the vogue after the time of Thucydides. The rhetoricians regarded a history as a work of art whose primary purpose was to give pleasure. Events in themselves seem to have been considered as of less importance than the manner in which they were presented. Hence various liberties could be taken with the facts in order to produce a more telling effect ; and as long as this was done not out of fear or favour, but simply from the desire to make the account more effective, the writer was not conscious of violating the truth. Dionysius doubtless thought that he was living up to his high ideals ; but he was first and foremost a rhetorician and could see history only through a rhetorician's eyes. The desire to please is everywhere in evidence ; there is a constant straining after rhetorical and dramatic effects.

In conformity with the rhetorical tradition, he interlarded his narrative with speeches which he managed to insert on every possible occasion from the third book onward. One technical purpose which they were intended to serve—to give variety to the narrative—is clear from the very circumstance that there are scarcely any speeches at all in Books I. and II., which have a sufficiently diversified narrative to require no further efforts at variety, whereas from Book III. onward the speeches occupy very nearly one-third of the total text. Dionysius himself occasionally felt the need of some justification of his insertion of so many speeches and argued that, inasmuch as the crisis under consideration was settled by discussion, it was therefore important for the reader to know the arguments that were advanced on both sides (vii. 66 ; xi. 1). Yet he had no adequate conception of the talents required for carrying out this ambitious programme successfully. Possessing neither the historical sense nor psychological insight, nor even any special gift of imagination, he undertook to compose speeches for any and all occasions by the simple process of following certain stereotyped rhetorical rules. The main argument of many of his speeches he doubtless found already expressed in his sources, either in some detail or in the form of a brief résumé, while in other cases there was probably a mere form of statement that implied a speech at that point ; numerous instances of each of these methods can be seen in Livy (who was not one of his sources) on the occasions where Dionysius inserts a speech. But it was little more than the main argument at best that he took over from his sources in most of the speeches of any length. The speeches were the part of a history in which the author was expected to give the freest reign to his rhetorical talents ; and that Dionysius did not fail to make full use of this opportunity is evident from the many imitations of the classical Attic prose writers that are found in his speeches. One of his fundamental principles for the acquiring of a good style was the imitating of classical models, and in the speeches of the *Antiquities* we see how it was to be done. Not only do we find single phrases and sentences from Demosthenes, Thucydides and Xenophon paraphrased and amplified, but even the tenor of entire passages in those authors is imitated.[1] It is not at all surprising, therefore, that these speeches fail almost completely to perform their true function of

---

[1] His imitations of the authors named have been analysed by Flierle, *Ueber Nachahmungen des Demosthenes, Thucydides und Xenophon in den Reden der Röm. Archäologie des Dionysius von Halicarnass*, Leipzig, 1890. The investigation should be continued to include Lysias and other orators.

revealing the character and the motives of the different speakers. Nor are they redeemed by any profound thoughts, unless in the imitated passages, or by any original sentiments ; for the most part they are little more than a succession of cheap platitudes and rhetorical commonplaces. Indeed, we might almost believe at times that we were reading the declamations of Dionysius' own pupils.

It has generally been suspected that Dionysius invented a good many of his speeches outright, inserting them at points where there was no indication of any speech in his sources. One fairly clear instance of the sort is found in his account of Coriolanus (viii. 5-8). After giving much the same account as Livy does of the trick played on the Romans by Attius Tullus at Coriolanus' suggestion in order to provoke them into giving the Volscians a just cause for going to war, Dionysius then represents Coriolanus as summoned by the Volscian leaders to advise them how best to prosecute the war. Coriolanus, in a speech clearly modelled upon the one addressed to the Spartans by the exiled Alcibiades (Thuc. vi. 89 ff.), says much by way of self-justification, and finally offers a fresh plan for providing the Volscians with a just ground for war. There is no valid excuse for this second plan, the first one having already proved successful ; Dionysius clearly wished to offer a parallel in his History to the famous episode in Thucydides. It is quite probable that several other speeches in this long account of Coriolanus also originated with Dionysius. Yet it must be remembered that he drew largely on the late annalists, some of whose

histories were very voluminous ; and he may have
found at least hints of speeches more frequently
than has generally been supposed.

Quite in keeping with the tiresome speeches of
the *Antiquities* are the long, circumstantial accounts
of such events as Dionysius chose to emphasize in
his narrative, and the cumulation of pathetic or
gruesome details in tragic situations. His account
of the combat between the Horatii and the Curiatii,
followed by Horatius' slaying of his sister, occupies
ten chapters (iii. 13-22) as against but three in Livy
(i. 24-26) ; and there is even a greater disproportion
in the length of their accounts of the events leading up to the combat (Dionys. iii. 2-12, Livy i.
22 f.) due in part to several long speeches in Dionysius. The outstanding instance of prolixity in
the *Antiquities* is the account of Coriolanus. The
events leading up to his exile (including 15 speeches)
require 48 chapters (vii. 20-67), whereas Livy
relates them in one-half of a single chapter (ii. 34,
7-12) ; the remaining events to the end of his life
are told by Dionysius in 62 chapters (viii. 1-62),
and by Livy in 6 (ii. 35-40). Almost everywhere
in the extant portions of Dionysius his account is
longer than that of Livy ; but this relative fullness
of detail was not maintained to the end of the
History. To the struggle between the orders and
to the Samnite wars he devoted less than four books
(part of xiv. and xv.-xvii), where Livy has more
than six (vi.-xi. and part of xii.). In other words,
for events nearer his own day, for which the traditions should have been fuller and more reliable, he
contented himself with a briefer narrative than for

the earlier periods, which for most historians had been full of doubt and uncertainty, thereby exactly reversing the logical procedure of Livy. An exception is seen in his detailed account of the war with Pyrrhus, a war which aroused his special interest for more reasons than one. Nowhere is his fondness for minute detail more out of place than in his accounts of tragic events, such as the encounter of the triumphant Horatius with his sister, Tullia's behaviour when she forces the driver of her car to continue on his way over the dead body of her father, the grief of Lucretius when his daughter slays herself, Verginius' slaying of his own daughter, and Veturia's visit to the camp of her son Coriolanus. By his constant effort to make us realize the full pathos or horror of the scene he defeats his own purpose. The dignified restraint shown by Livy in relating these same events is far more impressive.

Dionysius perhaps felt that he was making a distinct contribution toward the solidarity of the Graeco-Roman world when he undertook to prove, as his principal thesis, the Greek origin of Rome's founders. Not only did he trace the Aborigines back through the Oenotrians to Arcadia, but he even showed that the ancestors of the Trojans had come originally from that same district of Greece; other Greek elements represented in the population of early Rome were the Pelasgians, naturally of Greek origin, Evander and his company from Arcadia, and some Peloponnesian soldiers in the following of Hercules, who had remained behind in Italy when that hero passed through the peninsula on his return from Spain to Argos. None of the

various details of this theory was original with
Dionysius, for he cites his authorities at every step ;
but he may have been the first to combine these
separate strands of tradition into a single, compre-
hensive argument. The entire first book is devoted
to the proving of this thesis ; and the argument is
further strengthened at the end of Book VII. by a
detailed comparison of the ceremonies at the Ludi
Romani with early Greek religious observances.
As we saw from his introduction, he hoped by this
demonstration to reconcile his fellow Greeks to
Rome's supremacy ; at the same time, he obviously
understood the Romans of his day well enough to
realize that, far from regarding Rome's glory as
thereby diminished in any way, they would feel
flattered by the thought of such a connexion with
the heroic age of Greece. Incidentally, the proving
of his thesis afforded him an excellent opportunity
for dealing with the legendary period and thus
giving greater variety to his work. But the accept-
ance of this theory was bound to give him an
inverted view of the course of Roman history.
Instead of recognizing the gradual evolution of
the people and their institutions from very rude
beginnings, he sees an advanced stage of civilization
existing from the very first ; and Rome's kings and
later leaders are in such close contact with the
Greek world that they borrow thence most of the
new institutions that they establish from time to
time. Thus he assumes that the *celeres*, the senate,
the two consuls with joint powers, and the custom
whereby the members of each *curia* dined together
on holy days, were all based on Spartan models ;

that the division of the citizens into patricians and plebeians followed a similar division at Athens; that Servius Tullius organized a Latin League on the analogy of the Amphictyonic League of Greece, and that even the dictatorship was suggested by the practice followed in various Greek cities of appointing an *aisymnetes* to deal with a particular emergency. Dionysius probably found most, if not all, of these institutions thus explained in his sources; in about half of the instances he qualifies his statement by the words ' in my opinion,' but this does not seem a sufficient criterion for deciding the authorship of these views.

Dionysius is so ready to praise Rome's ancient heroes and institutions on every occasion, with never a word of disapprobation, that his impartiality may well be questioned. On a number of occasions he praises the piety and other virtues of the early Romans, which secured for them the special favour of Heaven; once (xx. 6) he styles them the most holy and just of Greeks. A number of their laws and practices, especially some of those said to have been instituted by Romulus, are declared to be superior to those in vogue among the Greeks. Thus, Romulus' policy of colonizing captured cities and sometimes even granting them the franchise is contrasted with the ruthless practices of the leading Greek states and their narrow-minded policy of withholding the rights of citizenship from outsiders (ii. 16 f., xiv. 6); and his laws regarding marriage and the *patria potestas* are described as better than the corresponding Greek practices (ii. 24-27). Romulus is praised also for rejecting such of the

myths as attributed any unseemly conduct to the
gods and all grosser forms of religious worship
(ii. 18 f.). Indeed, our historian even approves of
the Roman censorship, the inquisitorial powers of
which were not limited, as in Athens and Sparta,
to the public behaviour of the citizens, but extended
even inside the walls of private homes (xx. 13).
But it is not the Greeks alone who are contrasted
unfavourably with the old Romans ; Dionysius is
just as ready to point out to the Romans of his own
day their failure to maintain the high standards
set by their ancestors. He contrasts the spirit of
mutual helpfulness and forbearance that character-
ized the relations of the plebeians and patricians in
the early days with the era of bloodshed that began
under Gaius Gracchus (ii. 11) ; similarly, he praises
the simplicity of the first triumph (ii. 34), the
excellent grounds on which Servius Tullius granted
the franchise to manumitted slaves (iv. 24), the
deference shown by the early consuls to the authority of the senate (v. 60), and the lawful and
modest behaviour of the dictators down to the
time of Sulla (v. 77), contrasting each of these
practices and institutions with the evil forms they
assumed in later days. In one instance (viii. 80) he
leaves it to the reader to decide whether the traditional Roman practice or the practice of the Greeks
which some had recently wished to introduce at
Rome, was the better. The pointing of all these contrasts is part of the historian's function as moralist,
the function which he had in mind when in his *Letter
to Pompeius* (chap. 3) he said that the attitude of
Herodotus toward the events he was describing was

everywhere fair, showing pleasure in those that were good and grief at those that were bad. Dionysius doubtless endeavoured to be fair and sincere in his judgments; but he was, nevertheless, biased in favour of the Romans and in favour of the senatorial party, the Optimates of his own day. He even attempts to palliate one or two of the less savoury incidents associated with Rome's beginnings: he pictures Romulus as plunged into the depths of grief and despair at the death of Remus; and again, as addressing words of comfort and cheer to the captured Sabine maidens, assuring them that their seizure was in accordance with a good old Greek custom, and that it was the most distinguished way for women to be married! Livy makes no attempt to save the character of Romulus in the first instance, and in the second stops far short of Dionysius.

In the matter of religion, also, Dionysius makes no concealment of his attitude. He frequently refers to a divine providence. He speaks scornfully of the professors of atheistic philosophies, ' if philosophies they should be called,' who deny that the gods concern themselves with the affairs of mortals (ii. 68, 2 ; viii. 56, 1). He, for his part, is assured that the gods do sometimes intervene on behalf of the righteous (ii. 68 f.) and also to punish the wicked, as in the case of Pyrrhus (xx. 9 f.). The Romans, in particular, because of their piety and other virtues, had frequently been the recipients of divine favour, while the designs of their enemies were brought to naught (v. 54, 1 ; vi. 13 ; vii. 12, 4 ; viii. 26, 3). The gods, he holds, manifest their will through portents, and the disregarding of these may be severely punished, as in the case of Crassus (ii. 6, 4). Hence he recorded from time to time a goodly number of portents which he regarded as particularly noteworthy. With respect to the myths, he looked upon many of them, in which the gods played shameful parts, as blasphemous (ii. 18, 3) ; and, though he recognized that some of the Greek myths had a certain value as allegorical interpretations of natural phenomena, or as consolations in misfortune or other similar ways, he nevertheless felt that for the ignorant mass of mankind they did more harm than good, and he was more inclined himself to accept the Roman religion (ii. 20). It is to be observed that in relating myths he nowhere implies his own belief in them, but generally introduces them with some qualifying phrase, such as ' it is said,' ' they say,' etc.

Dionysius doubtless made what he considered to be a thorough study of Roman political institutions ; but his narrative constantly shows that he came far short of a real understanding of many of them. His failure to distinguish accurately between patricians and senators and between the *patrum auctoritas* and a *senatus consultum* is a source of no little confusion ; but, worse still, he often uses the Attic term προβούλευμα (preliminary decree) both for *senatus consultum* and for *patrum auctoritas*. His frequent use of ' patricians ' for ' senators ' is easily explained when we compare Livy, who constantly uses the word *patres* for both patricians and senators. This ambiguous term was doubtless found by both historians in their sources ; indeed, in a few instances Dionysius carelessly retained the word as ' fathers ' (v. 33, 2 ; vi. 69, 2). In making his choice between the renderings ' patricians ' and ' senators ' he seems to have adopted the former wherever the *patres* seemed to be opposed as a class to the plebeians (*e.g.*, iv. 8, 2 ; viii. 82, 4 ; ix. 42, 3). The term *patrum auctoritas* was apparently no better understood by Livy than by Dionysius ; even for the early period he several times represents the *auctoritas* as preceding the vote of the comitia, and after the Publilian law of 339, which required the *auctoritas* to be given before the people voted, he uses *patrum auctoritas* and *senatus consultum* indiscriminately. There is, in fact, every reason for believing that the term *patrum auctoritas* had become obsolete even in the time of the older annalists who were Livy's chief sources. But Dionysius, with sources before him that probably showed no greater misunderstanding of this term than does Livy, made matters much worse as the result of his assumption that the *patrum auctoritas*, and indeed any decree of the senate, was usually a preliminary decree to be ratified by the people. This view justified him in using the word προβούλευμα, the name given to the programme of business prepared by the Athenian Boulê for the consideration of the Ecclesia. It can hardly have been the desire to use the word προβούλευμα that led him to adopt its essential implications ; for he often uses δόγμα or ψήφισμα in the same way for a decree of the senate that was to be ratified by the people. He must have had some reason in the first place for believing that the *patrum auctoritas* was a necessary preliminary to action by the people. We know that it was customary for the consuls, as a matter of practical convenience, to ask the senate's advice and secure its approval before bringing any important matter before the people, inasmuch as the action taken in the comitia would have to receive the *patrum auctoritas* later in order to be valid. If Dionysius was aware of this custom but not of its purpose, he might well reason that it was absurd for the senate to give its approval more than once to the same business, and hence, since he knew the *patrum auctoritas* was required for all votes of the people, he would naturally identify this term with the preliminary approval of the senate. It is true this view of the matter seems to be directly opposed to an important statement which he makes at the very outset. When defining the powers of the senate and of the people as established by Romulus, he states that the senate was to ratify the decisions of the people, but adds that in his own day the reverse principle was followed, the decrees of the senate then requiring the approval of the people (ii. 14, 3). The natural implication of his statement is that the change had come about in fairly late times, but he nowhere in the extant books has anything more definite to say on the subject. In a very few instances he speaks of the ' patricians ' (doubtless to him identical with the senators) as ratifying a vote of the people afterwards, *e.g.*, in the case of the election of Numa (ii. 60, 3) and the appointment of the first tribunes (vi. 90, 2) ; but as early as the election of Ancus Marcius he represents the people as ratifying the choice of the senators (iii. 36, 1), and a little later speaks of this as the normal procedure (iv. 40, 2 ; 80, 2). In the last passage he is more explicit, declaring it to be the duty of the senate to consider in advance (προβουλεύειν) all matters relating to the general welfare, and the duty of the people to ratify their decision. It is fairly evident, then, that Dionysius' own theory was that a προβούλευμα of the senate had been necessary from the beginning. If his narrative occasionally violates this theory in practice, it is probably either because his sources were so explicit in particular instances that he felt he could not contradict them, or because he was negligent now and then and forgot to make his practice conform consistently to his theory. Another important matter in which he failed to make theory and practice coincide at all times will be mentioned a little later. It is not clear whether he believed the *plebiscita*, also, required a προβούλευμα ; his language is at times ambiguous and his accounts of the procedure in the case of various *plebiscita* are inconsistent with one another. He held the mistaken view that all senators were patricians, even under the republic ; for he believed that plebeians were made patricians before being admitted to the senate (ii. 47, 1 ; v. 13, 2). But it is not in constitutional matters only that he made serious errors ; there is confusion also in his account of religious matters. Thus, he uses ' haruspex ' for ' augur ' in ii. 22, 3, and his account of the duties of the pontifices (ii. 73) contains many errors.[1]

[1] On the subject of this paragraph see Edw. Schwartz in the *Real-Enc.*, *s.v.* Dionysius, pp. 940 ff., and E. Bux, *Das Probuleuma bei Dionys.*

INTRODUCTION

A few words must be said about Dionysius' chronology. His date for the founding of Rome was 751 B.C., two years later than that adopted by Varro; and this difference between the two chronologies remains constant for the first 304 years of the city down to the time of the decemvirs (the period covered by Books I.-X.). At that point the gap widens : Dionysius represents the decemviral rule as continuing for a third year, while Varro assigned to it only two years. Accordingly, for the half-dozen years covered by Book XI. Dionysius' dates are three years later than those of Varro. The fragments of the last nine books do not give any dates ; but three sporadic references in the earlier books to events of the third and first centuries B.C. show that for this late period his dates are the same as Varro's.[1] Dionysius devotes two chapters (i. 74 f.) to explaining how he arrived at the date 751 for the founding of the city, and for fuller information refers the reader to a separate work [2] that he had published to show how the Roman chronology was to be reduced to the Greek. There are other passages also which bear witness to the particular interest he felt in matters of chronology.[3] Notwithstanding all the attention he devoted to this side of his work, modern scholars have for the most

---

[1] i. 8, 1 (265 B.C.) ; ii. 25, 7 (231 B.C.); i. 3, 4 (7 B.C.). See O. Leuze, *Die röm. Jahrzählung*, pp. 189-93, for a plausible explanation of the closing of the gap between the two chronologies before the end of the fourth century.

[2] Χρόνοι, or Περὶ Χρόνων, cited by Clemens Alexandr., *Strom*. i. 102.

[3] i. 63 ; ii. 59 ; iv. 6 f., 30, 64 ; vi. 11 ; vii. 1.

part been very harsh in their judgments of him in
this very regard, accusing him of carelessness generally in the matter of his dates and, in particular, of
following one system of chronology for the period
treated in his History and another for events nearer
his own day. Our historian had to wait long for
his vindication ; but one of the most recent investi-
gators in the field of Roman chronology, Oscar
Leuze, has come ably to his defence and shown that
at least the more important of these charges of in-
accuracy rest upon misunderstanding of Dionysius'
real meaning or of his usage.[1]

Like most of the later Greek historians, Dionysius
uses the reckoning by Olympiads, usually adding
the name of the Athenian archon. From the
beginning of the republic he normally gives the
Greek date only for the first year of each Olympiad,
identifying the intervening years merely by the
names of the Roman magistrates. As the Athenian
official year began in mid-summer and the Olympiadic year of the historians either in mid-summer or
early autumn, whereas the Roman consular year
began, in later times, on January 1, though in

[1] *Die röm. Jahrzählung,* pp. 177-99. Of particular
interest is his defence of Dionysius' date for the beginning
of the First Punic War (pp. 184-87). Leuze argues that
Dionysius is here following a usage of Polybius and
Diodorus, who in a number of instances regard as the
beginning of a war, not the formal declaration of war or
the first armed clash, but the event that was the immediate
cause of the conflict. In the case in question this was
Rome's decision to aid the Mamertines, apparently at the
end of the year 265. The *Antiquities* naturally included
the events of the year 265 up to the sending of the
Mamertine embassy to Rome.

INTRODUCTION

earlier times at various seasons of the year, the Greek historians were confronted with an awkward problem in synchronizing Roman and Greek dates. The solution apparently followed by Dionysius, and probably by Polybius and Diodorus also, was to adopt the later Roman year of uniform length for all periods of Roman history, and to identify a given Roman year with the Olympiadic year in the course of which it began, rather than with that in which it ended (as is the modern practice). The dates given in the notes of the present edition follow this principle, only a single year being indicated as the modern equivalent of the Greek year, instead of parts of two years. Thus Olymp. 7, 1 is identified as 751 B.C. instead of 752/1. The only exceptions are a few dates of non-Roman events, where Dionysius was probably not concerned with the exact Roman equivalent.

Dionysius was in theory opposed to the annalistic method of writing history. In his *Letter to Pompeius* (chap. 3) he criticized Thucydides' chronological arrangement of events, by winters and summers, as seriously interrupting the continuity of the narrative, and praised Herodotus for adopting the topical order. Yet when he himself was to write a history of Rome he evidently found it impracticable to avoid following the annalistic method in vogue among the Romans. For the regal period, it is true, he arranges the events of each reign under the two headings of wars and peaceful achievements. But beginning with the establishment of the republic, he treats the events of each year by themselves, first naming the consuls or other chief magistrates. For the greater part of the period that he covers this method could cause no confusion, as the military campaigns were of short duration ; and it had the further advantage of avoiding monotony, since the narrative was constantly alternating between wars abroad and dissensions at home.

As regards his sources, Dionysius states in his preface (chap. 7) that he had consulted the works of the approved Roman historians,—Cato, Fabius Maximus (Servilianus ?), Valerius Antias, Licinius Macer, Aelius (Tubero), Gellius, Calpurnius (Piso) and many others,—and that he had also derived information from conversations with the most learned men. And at the end of Book I. (chap. 89) he refers to his careful reading of many works by both Greek and Roman writers on the subject of the origin of the Romans. His claim certainly appears to be justified, so far at least as Book I. is concerned. In this one book he cites no fewer than thirty Greek authors, most of them historians or logographers, and seven Roman writers, — Cato, Tubero and Piso, of those named above, and Fabius Pictor, Lucius Alimentus, C. Sempronius (Tuditanus) and Varro. To the last-named he owns his indebtedness for his account of the old cities of the Aborigines (chaps. 14 f.) ; but he probably owes considerable more to him in this book in places where he has not named his source. After the birth of Romulus and Remus there was scarcely any further occasion for using Greek sources ; and he usually mentioned the Roman historians only in cases where there were divergent traditions. He

naturally considered it to be his task as a historian
to reconcile the different traditions so far as possible
and present a smooth, uninterrupted narrative;
and in the main he has succeeded very well in doing
so.[1] But now and then he found such divergences
among his sources that he could not ignore them.
In such cases he presents the two or more versions
and either expresses his own preference or, quite
often, leaves the decision to the reader. At times
he makes the decision with the greatest confidence,
especially in matters of chronology. He is prompt
to discover anachronisms, and rebukes rather
sharply the historians who have carelessly per-
petuated them; Licinius Macer and Cn. Gellius
are thus censured on two occasions (vi. 11, 2; vii.
1, 4), also Fabius Pictor (iv. 6 f.; 30, 2 f.), while
Calpurnius Piso Frugi is named in one instance
(iv. 7, 5) as the only one to give the correct version.
It is generally recognized that he followed the late
annalists as his principal sources; their histories
were generally very voluminous, and in them he
could find the full, detailed accounts which he
frequently gives. His political orientation is that
of the annalists of Sulla's time, who were strong
champions of the senate's supremacy. They wrote
their annals as propaganda, deliberately falsifying
their account of events from time to time in order
to make it appear that the senate had held from
the first, or at least from the beginning of the
republic, the same dominant position in the State

[1] A number of contradictions that appear in the History
are probably due to his using first one source and then
another.

that it held in the second and first centuries before Christ. They did this by representing the senate as having been consulted in early times on various occasions where tradition made no mention of any action on its part.[1] Dionysius seems to have held the extreme view that even under the monarchy the senate had played a dominant part, the king's power being limited much as at Sparta (ii. 14, 1 f. ; cf. vi. 66, 3). This was his theory ; but in actual practice his narrative mentions very few specific occasions where the senate was consulted by the king, and we gain the impression that the power of the latter was virtually supreme. But from the moment of the establishing of the republic his account of events is in strict agreement with his theory. His failure to reconcile practice and theory earlier argues a lack of inventiveness either on his part or on that of his sources ; it probably did not seem worth the trouble to work out the details. This view of the senate's original supremacy was the view taken also by Cicero in his *De Republica;* but it was not the view of Livy, who followed earlier annalists and rightly held that the senate had only gradually gained its wide powers. It is just such differences in orientation as this that make it fairly certain that Dionysius was not using Livy as his source in the numerous passages where their accounts seem at first sight strikingly similar.[2] Besides the authors cited by Dionysius, he also

[1] A number of instances of this sort are discussed by Bux, *Das Probuleuma*, pp. 83-122.

[2] See Schwartz, *Real-Enc.*, pp. 946-57, for an analysis of some of these passages.

mentions a number of inscriptions, both at Rome and elsewhere, and there are sporadic references to the *annales maximi*, the records of the censors, etc. ; but he does not say that he had seen any of these himself, and it is probable that he found the references in the annalists.

The first historian to cite Dionysius was Plutarch, who modelled his style upon that of the *Antiquities*.[1] Schwartz held that Dionysius was Plutarch's sole source for his *Coriolanus*, but this view is opposed by Bux. The *Romulus* and *Numa* may each contain a little from the *Antiquities*, the *Camillus* is chiefly based on Livy.[2] Dionysius is twice quoted in the *Pyrrhus*, but not enough of his account is preserved to enable us to make any accurate comparison between the two.

SCRIPTA RHETORICA

The shorter works of Dionysius have generally gone under the name of *Scripta Rhetorica ;* but they contain more of literary criticism than of technical rhetoric. They are all in the form of letters addressed to some literary friend, patron or pupil. There is no internal evidence to show whether they were composed before or after the History was published ; but it is generally assumed that Dionysius wrote them from time to time during the years that he was engaged upon his great work. Although no absolute dates can be assigned to these several treatises, the relative order in which

---

[1] Goetzler, *Einfluss des Dionys*, p. 194.
[2] So Schwartz, *Real-Enc.*, pp. 943-45.

they were composed can be determined in most cases by means of the frequent references in one to what the writer has already discussed or proposes to discuss in another. The order in which Roberts arranges them is as follows:

1. *First Letter to Ammaeus.*
2. *On the Arrangement of Words.*
3. *On the Ancient Orators.*
4. *On the Style of Demosthenes.*
5. *On Imitation :* Books I., II.
6. *Letter to Cn. Pompeius.*
7. *On Imitation :* Book III.
8. *On Dinarchus.*
9. *On Thucydides.*
10. *Second Letter to Ammaeus.*

Egger would transpose the second and third items, seeing a greater maturity of judgment in the treatise on the *Arrangement of Words.* As regards the *Dinarchus*, he says we can be sure only that it was later than the *Ancient Orators.*

The treatise on *Imitation* is known to us only from fragments. Only the first half of the study of the *Ancient Orators* is preserved, treating of Lysias, Isocrates and Isaeus ; in the second part Demosthenes, Hyperides and Aeschines were discussed. The treatise on the *Style of Demosthenes* is thought to be an enlarged edition of the discussion of Demosthenes in the earlier series. Other Works which have been lost were on the *Choice of Words*, on *Figures*, and on *Political Philosophy*, the latter a defence of the rhetoric of Isocrates and his school

INTRODUCTION

against its Epicurean detractors. The early editions attributed to Dionysius an *Ars Rhetorica*, but this is no longer held to be his work.

For a detailed account of the *Scripta Rhetorica* the reader is referred to Max. Egger, *Denys d' Halicarnasse*, pp. 20-246 ; a brief survey of these works may be found in W. Rhys Roberts, *Dionysius of Halicarnassus : The Three Literary Letters*, pp. 4-34. Roberts also gives (pp. 209-19) a bibliography of the *Scripta Rhetorica* down to the year 1900.

To his labours as literary critic Dionysius brought a wide and thorough acquaintance with the works of the Attic prose writers, a discriminating taste, and great industry and zeal. His chief merit as a critic lies in his purity of taste ; he rejoiced in the recent triumph of Atticism over Asianism and did his best to strengthen that victory. His rhetorical works have much in common with those of Cicero, due to their both using many of the same sources. Like Cicero, Dionysius held Demosthenes in the greatest admiration ; but this excessive admiration for one man seems to have made him unfair in his judgment of others : he tended to judge all the prose writers by the standards he set up for the orators. In other respects as well he is often narrow and superficial in his criticisms, and his manner is too dogmatic.

The first reference to Dionysius as a rhetorician in any extant author is in Quintilian, who merely names him three times in lists of rhetoricians. In the third century the circle of Libanius paid some attention to him. From the fifth century onward he was regarded by the Byzantines as the supreme authority on rhetoric.

MANUSCRIPTS

The manuscripts used by Jacoby for the first ten books of the *Antiquities* are as follows :

A. Chisianus 58, 10th cent.
B. Urbinas 105, 10th–11th cent.
C. Coislinianus 150, 16th cent.
D. Regius Parisinus 1654 and 1655, 16th cent.
E. Vaticanus 133, 15th cent.
F. Urbinas 106, 15th cent.

C and E also contain Book XI. ; F contains only I.-V.

The MSS. used for Book XI. and those for the Fragments of XII.-XX. will be listed in Vol. VII.

A and B are by far the best of the MSS. ; the others are all late, and some of them, especially C and D, contain numerous interpolations. The *editio princeps* was based on D. B was first used by Hudson, but he contented himself with giving its readings in his notes. The translators Bellanger and Spelman were prompt to adopt most of the good readings of B, and many were taken into the text by Reiske. Ritschl was the first to make a comparative study of A and B. As a result of his first investigation, based on insufficient evidence, he was inclined to rate A much higher than B ; but later he showed a better appreciation of the good readings found only in B, and concluded that a sound text must rest upon a judicious use of both

INTRODUCTION

A and B,[1]—a conclusion in which Jacoby heartily
concurred. Kiessling based his edition on B so far
as possible.

The individual symbols of the late MSS. appear
very infrequently in Jacoby's (and the present)
critical apparatus, since these MSS. are rarely of
any service in establishing the text. An occasional
good reading found only in the margin of D (Dmg)
may have been entered by R. Stephanus himself; in
any event such readings are evidently based on
conjecture rather than on the authority of any
manuscript.

Editions

The important editions of the *Antiquities* follow :
Robert Estienne (Stephanus), Paris, 1546. The
editio princeps of the Greek text, Books I.-XI.
Based on the very inferior Cod. Reg. Paris. 1654-55.

Friedrich Sylburg, Frankfort, 1586. Books I.-XI.
and the *Excerpta de Legationibus*, translation
(Gelenius' version revised) and notes. Sylburg
made use, chiefly in his notes, of two MSS., a
Romanus (not to be identified) and a Venetus (272).
Reprinted in careless form at Leipzig in 1691.

John Hudson, Oxford, 1704. Books I.-XI. with
the *Excerpta de Legationibus* and *Excerpta de
Virtutibus et Vitiis*, a revision of Portus' Latin
translation, and notes of various scholars. Hudson
was the first to use the Urbinas (which he called

---

[1] His monographs on Dionysius were reprinted in his
Opuscula, Vol. i., pp. 471-540.

Cod. Vaticanus), but cited its readings only in the notes.

J. J. Reiske, Leipzig, 1774-75. The text and translation of Hudson's edition with Reiske's own notes added. Too late to accomplish much in Vol. I., Reiske discovered that the printer was faithfully reproducing all the typographical errors of Hudson's edition ; but from Book III. 21 onward he corrected the proof sheets and also for the first time inserted the good readings of B in the text. Dionysius is often cited by the pages of this edition.

Adolf Kiessling, Leipzig (Teubner), 1860-70. Based on B, so far as possible.

Carl Jacoby, Leipzig (Teubner), 1885-1905 ; Index, 1925.

Adolf Kiessling-Victor Prou, Paris (Didot), 1886. Greek text and Latin translation (Portus revised). An unfortunate edition. Kiessling, after getting the work fairly started, dropped it completely ; and Prou, who was called upon to complete the task, was far from possessing Kiessling's critical ability. Jacoby recognized the hand of Kiessling through the greater part of Books I.-III. ; from that point on the edition has virtually no critical value.

Besides these complete editions of the *Antiquities*, selected chapters were edited by D. C. Grimm (*Archaeologiae Romanae quae ritus Romanos explicat Synopsis*), Leipzig, 1786 ; J. J. Ambrosch (i. 9-38 ; ii. 1-29 ; ii. 30-56 ; ii. 64-74) in four academic Festschriften, Breslau, 1840-46 ; Fr. Ritschl (i. 1-30), Bonn, 1846. Angelo Mai published at Milan, in 1816, some fragments from an epitome contained in a Milan MS., Cod. Ambrosianus Q 13 sup., and its copy, A 80 sup. These are now included (as the *Excerpta Ambrosiana*) among the Fragments of Books XII.-XX.

TRANSLATIONS

The first Latin translation of the *Antiquities* (Books I.-XI.) was that of Lapus (or Lappus) Biragus, published at Treviso in 1480, three-quarters of a century before the first edition of the Greek text appeared. It possesses a special interest because it was based on two MSS., not as yet identified with any now extant, which were placed at the translator's disposal by Pope Paul II. Ritschl argued that one of these must have belonged to the better class of MSS. now represented by A and B, since the translation contains most of the additions to the text of the *editio princeps* that are found in one or both of the older MSS.[1] Lapus'

[1] *Opuscula*, i. pp. 489, 493. Since some of the interpolations now found in C and D are included by Lapus, Ritschl concluded that he now and then consulted his later MS. for help (p. 530). Had Ritschl carried his investigation a little farther, he would have discovered that Lapus made diligent use of his older MS., closely related to B, only for Books I., II. and the first third of III., after which he practically ignored it. (The good readings which he has in common with B in the later books are in virtually every instance found also in C.) Down to iii. 23 he has most of the good readings of B, including a goodly number that appear in no other MS., but he avoids nearly all of B's errors; he also ignores the interpolations of C. From iii. 24 through Book XI. he nearly always agrees with C's readings, including a number of the marginal interpolations; in a

INTRODUCTION

translation was reprinted, ' with corrections,' but also with a multitude of fresh typographical errors, at Paris in 1529, and again, as revised by Glareanus, at Basle in 1532. A fresh translation of Books I.-X. by Gelenius, based on the text of the *princeps*, appeared at Basle in 1549 ; for Book XI. he merely reprinted Lapus' translation. Sylburg (1586) revised the translation of Gelenius and added his own version of Book XI. Aemilius Portus brought out a new translation (Lausanne, 1588) ; and this translation was adopted in the editions of Hudson and Reiske, and, with numerous corrections, in that of Kiessling-Prou.

An Italian translation by Francesco Venturi appeared at Venice in 1545, one year before the *editio princeps*. The translator names as his sources a Greek copy, very difficult to read, and a Latin translation [Lapus] full of errors. Apparently no serious use was made of the manuscript ; it may well have proved to be generally inferior to Lapus' reading. In any case, Venturi's translation, with the exception of a few minor changes which were probably due to conjecture, presupposes the same Greek text as that of Lapus. Another Italian translation was published by M. Mastrofini, Rome, 1812-13.

very few cases he supplies a few words missing in both B and C, so that one or the other of his MSS. must have been better than its present representative. Since he refers to the confused order of the text in both his MSS. at the end of Book XI., his older MS. cannot have been B ; and the interpolated one cannot have been C, if C is correctly assigned to the sixteenth century.

INTRODUCTION

A French version by G. F. le Jay (Paris, 1722) was loudly acclaimed by the admirers of the translator as representing perfection itself; but the two men who next translated the *Antiquities*, Bellanger and Spelman, showed that it was a servile translation of Portus' Latin version, errors and all. The following year Bellanger brought out, anonymously, his own translation, based on Hudson's text and the good readings of B contained in Hudson's notes. It is a smooth, fluent translation, but often rather free and at times little more than a paraphrase. It was reprinted later under Bellanger's own name.

In German there have been translations by J. L. Benzler (1752; reprinted 1771-72) and by G. J. Schaller and A. H. Christian (Stuttgart, 1827-50). Benzler's version was quite free, that of Schaller (Books I.-IV.) accurate and scholarly; the part translated by Christian has not been seen by the present translator.

The only English version to appear hitherto is that of Edward Spelman, which was published with notes and dissertations at London in 1758. It is a good and, for the most part, fairly close translation of Hudson's text (Books I.-XI.) as improved by the good readings of the Urbinas and occasional conjectural emendations. See further on p. xlv.

The Greek text here presented is based on the edition of Jacoby, but departs rather frequently from his text. All significant departures are indicated in the critical notes, but not, as a rule, minor details of orthography, elision and crasis, or corrections of obvious typographical errors that appear in his edition. Jacoby was fairly consistent in following out the principles which he had established with greater or less probability in two preliminary studies of Dionysian usage.[1] But in the case of some phrases and combinations of vowels for which he could not show that elision or crasis is normally to be expected, he vacillated in his attitude toward the MSS., sometimes following them in permitting hiatus and at other times emending; the present edition follows the MSS. (or some MS.) in all such cases. The MSS. are likewise followed in their spelling of the various forms of adjectives such as χαλκοῦς and χρυσοῦς, which appear in the contracted and the uncontracted forms with about equal frequency; Jacoby occasionally emended an uncontracted form. He adopted the late spellings ἐπαύσθην and ἠλάσθην wherever they have the authority of any MS.,[2] and occasionally elsewhere; in the present text the Attic forms ἐπαύθην and ἠλάθην are everywhere restored.

The present editor has permitted himself the liberty of spelling a few Latin proper names in the Greek text in the manner that many an editor would have liked to spell them, but as only a few of the earlier editors ventured to do in actual

[1] (a) *Observationes criticae in Dionysii Hal. Antiquitates Romanas*, in *Acta Societatis Philol. Lipsiensis*, i. (1871), 287-344. (b) *Ueber die Sprache des Dionysios von Halikarnassos in der Röm. Archäologie*, Aarau, 1874.

[2] In one instance C alone seems to show the σ; elsewhere the only MS. giving it is B (about half the time), but even in this MS. the σ has usually been deleted by a correcting hand.

practice, and then only in the case of part of the names. It is hard to believe that Dionysius would have written such forms, for example, as Φαιστύλος for Φαυστύλος (compare his correct form Φαυστῖνος), Λωρεντόν (in Book I.) for Λαύρεντον (the form found in Book V.; cf. Λαυρεντῖνοι and Λαυρεντία), or Λαῦνα for Λαοϋινία in such a context as i. 59, 3 (and if he wrote the correct form here, he must have used it elsewhere).

The critical apparatus lists only the more important variants and emendations; many simple emendations made by the early editors and adopted in subsequent editions are passed over in silence. No fresh collations of the MSS. have been available; but here and there an obvious error in Jacoby's report has been corrected or a suspicious entry queried.

The present translation is based on that of Spelman. His rendering of numerous passages, more especially in the speeches, is so spirited and so idiomatic, and often requires so few changes to make it seem thoroughly modern in tone, that it seemed desirable to use what was best of it in preparing this version for the Loeb Classical Library. If Spelman had been at his best more uniformly, a mild revision, to bring his translation into accord with the present Greek text, would have been all that was required. But the quality of his English is very uneven. He constructs a good many long, cumbersome sentences, in imitation of the Greek, shows an excessive fondness for the absolute use of the participle, and at times uses a vocabulary that seems more Latin than English. Where he thus departs from a good English style, and wherever his rendering is not sufficiently close to the Greek for the present purpose, changes have been freely made, some of them very drastic. No attempt has been made to preserve the antique flavour that character-izes Spelman's rendering, as a whole, inasmuch as the passages which he has rendered most successfully from other points of view are usually the most modern in diction. He did not translate the frag-ments ; they appear here in English for the first time. The notes with which Spelman accom-panied his version were scholarly and useful in their day, but have not the same interest now ; accord-ingly, an entirely new set of notes has been prepared for this edition.

For the convenience of the reader parallel passages from Livy have been indicated in the notes, beginning with i. 64.

BIBLIOGRAPHY

A BIBLIOGRAPHY of the *Roman Antiquities* covering the period from 1774 to 1876 was published by Jacoby in *Philologus*, xxxvi. (1877), pp. 129-31, 152-54. It was continued in the introductions to the several volumes of his edition, including the Index (1925). To the lists there given should be added :

Edw. Schwartz, in Pauly-Wissowa, *Real-Encyclopädie*, *s.v.* Dionysius, cols. 934-61.

Max. Egger, *Denys d'Halicarnasse* (Paris, 1902) pp. 1-19, 247-98. An excellent study of Dionysius, more particularly as rhetorician.

H. Liers, *Die Theorie der Geschichtsschreibung des Dionys von Halikarnass*, Waldenburg, 1886.

Eiliv Skard, *Epigraphische Formeln bei Dionys von Halikarnass*, in *Symbolae Osloenses* xi. (1932), 55-60.

E. Gaida, *Die Schlachtschilderungen in den Antiquitates Romanae des Dionys von Halikarnass*, Breslau, 1934.

SIGLA

A = Chisianus 58.
B = Urbinas 105.
C = Coislinianus 150.
D = Regius Parisinus 1654 and 1655.
E = Vaticanus 133.
F = Urbinas 106.
O = All [1] the MSS.
R = All [1] the MSS. not otherwise cited.

a, b, and occasionally c, added to the symbol of a MS. indicate the successive hands; mg denotes a marginal entry.

Steph. = *editio princeps* of R. Stephanus.
Steph.[2] = notes of H. Stephanus.

[1] But there is good reason for suspecting that Jacoby usually ignored E and F; in fact, he nowhere seems to cite the latter individually.

THE ROMAN ANTIQUITIES
OF
DIONYSIUS OF HALICARNASSUS

ΔΙΟΝΥΣΙΟΥ

ΑΛΙΚΑΡΝΑΣΕΩΣ

ΡΩΜΑΙΚΗΣ ΑΡΧΑΙΟΛΟΓΙΑΣ

ΛΟΓΟΣ ΠΡΩΤΟΣ

I. Τοὺς εἰωθότας ἀποδίδοσθαι ἐν[1] τοῖς προ-
οιμίοις τῶν ἱστοριῶν λόγους ἥκιστα βουλόμενος
ἀναγκάζομαι περὶ ἐμαυτοῦ προειπεῖν, οὔτ' ἐν τοῖς
ἰδίοις μέλλων πλεονάζειν ἐπαίνοις, οὓς ἐπαχθεῖς
οἶδα φαινομένους τοῖς ἀκούουσιν, οὔτε διαβολὰς
καθ' ἑτέρων ἐγνωκὼς ποιεῖσθαι συγγραφέων,
ὥσπερ Ἀναξιμένης[2] καὶ Θεόπομπος ἐν τοῖς προ-
οιμίοις τῶν ἱστοριῶν ἐποίησαν, ἀλλὰ τοὺς ἐμαυτοῦ
λογισμοὺς ἀποδεικνύμενος, οἷς ἐχρησάμην ὅτε ἐπὶ
ταύτην ὥρμησα τὴν πραγματείαν, καὶ περὶ τῶν
ἀφορμῶν ἀποδιδοὺς λόγον, ἐξ ὧν τὴν ἐμπειρίαν
2 ἔλαβον τῶν γραφησομένων. ἐπείσθην γὰρ ὅτι δεῖ
τοὺς προαιρουμένους μνημεῖα τῆς ἑαυτῶν ψυχῆς

[1] ἐν Steph. [2]: om. O, Jacoby.
[2] C. Müller, Usener : ἀναξίλαος O.

---

[1] Anaximenes of Lampsacus wrote a history of Greece
(down to the battle of Mantinea) and a history of Philip

THE ROMAN ANTIQUITIES

OF

DIONYSIUS OF HALICARNASSUS

BOOK I

I. Although it is much against my will to indulge
in the explanatory statements usually given in the
prefaces to histories, yet I am obliged to prefix
to this work some remarks concerning myself. In
doing this it is neither my intention to dwell too
long on my own praise, which I know would be
distasteful to the reader, nor have I the purpose
of censuring other historians, as Anaximenes and
Theopompus[1] did in the prefaces to their histories but I shall only show the reasons that induced me to undertake this work and give an
accounting of the sources from which I gained the
knowledge of the things I am going to relate. For
I am convinced that all who propose to leave such
monuments of their minds to posterity as time shall

of Macedon ; also an epic on Alexander. Theopompus
in his *Hellenica* continued the history of Thucydides from
411 down to the battle of Cnidus in 394; his *Philippica,*
in 58 books, treated not only of Philip but of contemporary
events elsewhere.

τοῖς ἐπιγιγνομένοις καταλιπεῖν, ἃ μὴ συναφανι-
σθήσεται τοῖς σώμασιν αὐτῶν ὑπὸ τοῦ χρόνου,
καὶ πάντων μάλιστα τοὺς ἀναγράφοντας ἱστορίας,
ἐν αἷς καθιδρῦσθαι τὴν ἀλήθειαν ὑπολαμβάνομεν [1]
ἀρχὴν φρονήσεώς τε καὶ σοφίας οὖσαν, πρῶτον
μὲν ὑποθέσεις προαιρεῖσθαι καλὰς καὶ μεγαλο-
πρεπεῖς καὶ πολλὴν ὠφέλειαν τοῖς ἀναγνωσομένοις
φερούσας, ἔπειτα παρασκευάζεσθαι τὰς ἐπιτηδείους
εἰς τὴν ἀναγραφὴν τῆς ὑποθέσεως ἀφορμὰς μετὰ
3 πολλῆς ἐπιμελείας τε καὶ φιλοπονίας. οἱ μὲν γὰρ
ὑπὲρ ἀδόξων πραγμάτων ἢ πονηρῶν ἢ μηδεμιᾶς
σπουδῆς ἀξίων ἱστορικὰς καταβαλόμενοι πραγματείας, εἴτε τοῦ προελθεῖν εἰς γνῶσιν ὀρεγόμενοι
καὶ τυχεῖν ὁποιουδήποτε ὀνόματος, εἴτε περιουσίαν
ἐπιδείξασθαι [2] τῆς περὶ λόγους δυνάμεως βουλόμενοι, οὔτε τῆς γνώσεως ζηλοῦνται παρὰ τοῖς
ἐπιγιγνομένοις οὔτε τῆς δυνάμεως ἐπαινοῦνται,
δόξαν ἐγκαταλιπόντες τοῖς ἀναλαμβάνουσιν αὐτῶν
τὰς ἱστορίας ὅτι τοιούτους ἐζήλωσαν αὐτοὶ βίους,
οἵας ἐξέδωκαν τὰς γραφάς· ἐπιεικῶς γὰρ ἅπαντες
νομίζουσιν εἰκόνας εἶναι τῆς ἑκάστου ψυχῆς τοὺς
4 λόγους. οἱ δὲ προαιρούμενοι μὲν τὰς κρατίστας
ὑποθέσεις, εἰκῇ δὲ καὶ ῥαθύμως αὐτὰς συντιθέντες
ἐκ τῶν ἐπιτυχόντων ἀκουσμάτων, οὐδένα ὑπὲρ τῆς
προαιρέσεως ἔπαινον κομίζονται· οὐ γὰρ ἀξιοῦμεν
αὐτοσχεδίους οὐδὲ ῥαθύμους εἶναι τὰς περί τε
πόλεων ἐνδόξων καὶ ἀνδρῶν ἐν δυναστείᾳ γεγονό-
των ἀναγραφομένας ἱστορίας   ταῦτα δὴ νομίσας
ἀναγκαῖα καὶ πρῶτα θεωρήματα τοῖς ἱστορικοῖς

---

[1] ὑπολαμβάνομεν B: ὑπολαμβάνομεν πάντες A.

not involve in one common ruin with their bodies, and particularly those who write histories, in which we have the right to assume that Truth, the source of both prudence and wisdom, is enshrined, ought, first of all, to make choice of noble and lofty subjects and such as will be of great utility to their readers, and then, with great care and pains, to provide themselves with the proper equipment for the treatment of their subject. For those who base historical works upon deeds inglorious or evil or unworthy of serious study, either because they crave to come to the knowledge of men and to get a name of some sort or other, or because they desire to display the wealth of their rhetoric, are neither admired by posterity for their fame nor praised for their eloquence; rather, they leave this opinion in the minds of all who take up their histories, that they themselves admired lives which were of a piece with the writings they published, since it is a just and a general opinion that a man's words are the images of his mind. Those, on the other hand, who, while making choice of the best subjects, are careless and indolent in compiling their narratives out of such reports as chance to come to their ears gain no praise by reason of that choice; for we do not deem it fitting that the histories of renowned cities and of men who have held supreme power should be written in an offhand or negligent manner. As I believe these considerations to be necessary and of the first importance to historians

---

² Schwartz: ἀποδείξασθαι O, Jacoby.

εἶναι καὶ πολλὴν ποιησάμενος ἀμφοτέρων ἐπιμέλειαν οὔτε παρελθεῖν τὸν ὑπὲρ αὐτῶν λόγον
ἐβουλήθην οὔτε ἐν ἄλλῳ τινὶ τόπῳ καταχωρίσαι
μᾶλλον ἢ τῷ προοιμίῳ τῆς πραγματείας.

II. Τὴν μὲν οὖν ὑπόθεσιν ὅτι καλὴν εἴληφα καὶ
μεγαλοπρεπῆ καὶ πολλοῖς ὠφέλιμον οὐ μακρῶν
οἶμαι δεήσειν λόγων τοῖς γε δὴ μὴ παντάπασιν
ἀπείρως ἔχουσι τῆς κοινῆς ἱστορίας. εἰ γάρ τις
ἐπιστήσας τὴν διάνοιαν ἐπὶ τὰς παραδεδομένας ἐκ
τοῦ παρεληλυθότος χρόνου πόλεών τε καὶ ἐθνῶν
ἡγεμονίας, ἔπειτα χωρὶς ἑκάστην σκοπῶν καὶ παρ'
ἀλλήλας ἐξετάζων διαγνῶναι βουληθείη τίς αὐτῶν
ἀρχήν τε μεγίστην ἐκτήσατο καὶ πράξεις ἀπεδείξατο
λαμπροτάτας ἐν εἰρήνῃ τε καὶ κατὰ πολέμους,
μακρῷ δή τινι τὴν Ῥωμαίων ἡγεμονίαν ἁπάσας
ὑπερβεβλημένην ὄψεται τὰς πρὸ αὐτῆς μνημονευο-
μένας, οὐ μόνον κατὰ τὸ μέγεθος τῆς ἀρχῆς καὶ
κατὰ τὸ κάλλος τῶν πράξεων, ἃς οὔπω κεκόσμηκε
λόγος οὐδεὶς ἀξίως, ἀλλὰ καὶ κατὰ τὸ μῆκος τοῦ
περιειληφότος αὐτὴν χρόνου μέχρι τῆς καθ' ἡμᾶς
2 ἡλικίας. ἡ μὲν γὰρ Ἀσσυρίων ἀρχὴ παλαιά τις
οὖσα καὶ εἰς τοὺς μυθικοὺς ἀναγομένη χρόνους
ὀλίγου τινὸς ἐκράτησε τῆς Ἀσίας μέρους. ἡ δὲ
Μηδικὴ καθελοῦσα τὴν Ἀσσυρίων καὶ μείζονα
δυναστείαν περιβαλομένη χρόνον οὐ πολὺν κατέσχεν, ἀλλ' ἐπὶ τῆς τετάρτης κατελύθη γενεᾶς.
Πέρσαι δὲ οἱ Μήδους καταγωνισάμενοι τῆς μὲν
Ἀσίας ὀλίγου δεῖν πάσης τελευτῶντες ἐκράτησαν,
ἐπιχειρήσαντες δὲ καὶ τοῖς Εὐρωπαίοις ἔθνεσιν οὐ

6

and as I have taken great care to observe them
both, I have felt unwilling either to omit mention
of them or to give it any other place than in the
preface to my work.

II. That I have indeed made choice of a subject
noble, lofty and useful to many will not, I think,
require any lengthy argument, at least for those
who are not utterly unacquainted with universal
history. For if anyone turns his attention to the
successive supremacies both of cities and of nations,
as accounts of them have been handed down from
times past, and then, surveying them severally and
comparing them together, wishes to determine which
of them obtained the widest dominion and both in
peace and war performed the most brilliant achievements, he will find that the supremacy of the Romans
has far surpassed all those that are recorded from
earlier times, not only in the extent of its dominion and in the splendour of its achievements—which
no account has as yet worthily celebrated—but also
in the length of time during which it has endured
down to our day. For the empire of the Assyrians,
ancient as it was and running back to legendary
times, held sway over only a small part of Asia.
That of the Medes, after overthrowing the Assyrian
empire and obtaining a still wider dominion, did not
hold it long, but was overthrown in the fourth
generation.[1] The Persians, who conquered the
Medes, did, indeed, finally become masters of almost
all Asia ; but when they attacked the nations of
Europe also, they did not reduce many of them to

[1] In 550 B.C., in the reign of Astyages, the fourth
Median king according to Herodotus.

πολλὰ ὑπηγάγοντο, χρόνον τε οὐ πολλῷ πλείονα
3 διακοσίων ἐτῶν ἔμειναν ἐπὶ τῆς ἀρχῆς. ἡ δὲ
Μακεδονικὴ δυναστεία τὴν Περσῶν καθελοῦσα
ἰσχὺν μεγέθει μὲν ἀρχῆς ἁπάσας ὑπερεβάλετο τὰς
πρὸ αὐτῆς, χρόνον δὲ οὐδὲ αὕτη¹ πολὺν ἤνθησεν,
ἀλλὰ μετὰ τὴν Ἀλεξάνδρου τελευτὴν ἐπὶ τὸ χεῖρον
ἤρξατο φέρεσθαι. διασπασθεῖσα γὰρ εἰς πολλοὺς
ἡγεμόνας εὐθὺς ἀπὸ τῶν διαδόχων καὶ μετ' ἐκείνους
ἄχρι τῆς δευτέρας ἢ τρίτης ἰσχύσασα προελθεῖν
γενεᾶς, ἀσθενὴς αὐτὴ δι' ἑαυτῆς ἐγένετο καὶ
4 τελευτῶσα ὑπὸ Ῥωμαίων ἠφανίσθη. καὶ οὐδὲ
αὕτη¹ μέντοι πᾶσαν ἐποιήσατο γῆν τε καὶ θάλασσαν
ὑπήκοον· οὔτε γὰρ Λιβύης, ὅτι μὴ τῆς πρὸς
Αἰγύπτῳ οὐ² πολλῆς οὔσης, ἐκράτησεν οὔτε τὴν
Εὐρώπην ὅλην ὑπηγάγετο, ἀλλὰ τῶν μὲν βορείων
αὐτῆς μερῶν μέχρι Θρᾴκης προῆλθε, τῶν δ'
ἑσπερίων μέχρι τῆς Ἀδριανῆς κατέβη θαλάσσης.

III. Αἱ μὲν οὖν ἐπιφανέσταται τῶν πρόσθεν ἡγε-
μονιῶν, ἃς παρειλήφαμεν ἐκ τῆς ἱστορίας, τοσαύτην
ἀκμήν τε καὶ ἰσχὺν λαβοῦσαι κατελύθησαν· τὰς γὰρ
Ἑλληνικὰς δυνάμεις οὐκ ἄξιον αὐταῖς ἀντιπαρεξετά-
ζειν, οὔτε μέγεθος ἀρχῆς οὔτε χρόνον ἐπιφανείας
2 τοσοῦτον ὅσον ἐκεῖναι λαβούσας. Ἀθηναῖοι μέν
γε αὐτῆς μόνον ἦρξαν τῆς παραλίου δυεῖν δέοντα
ἑβδομήκοντα ἔτη καὶ οὐδὲ ταύτης ἁπάσης, ἀλλὰ

---

¹ αὕτη Bücheler : αὐτὴ O.　　　² οὐ added by Casaubon.

---

¹ 550-330 B.C.
² i.e. "Successors," the term applied to the generals

8

submission, and they continued in power not much above two hundred years.[1] The Macedonian dominion, which overthrew the might of the Persians, did, in the extent of its sway, exceed all its predecessors, yet even it did not flourish long, but after Alexander's death began to decline; for it was immediately partitioned among many commanders from the time of the Diadochi,[2] and although after their time it was able to go on to the second or third generation, yet it was weakened by its own dissensions and at the last destroyed by the Romans.[3] But even the Macedonian power did not subjugate every country and every sea; for it neither conquered Libya, with the exception of the small portion bordering on Egypt, nor subdued all Europe, but in the North advanced only as far as Thrace and in the West down to the Adriatic Sea.

III. Thus we see that the most famous of the earlier supremacies of which history has given us any account, after attaining to so great vigour and might, were overthrown. As for the Greek powers, it is not fitting to compare them to those just mentioned, since they gained neither magnitude of empire nor duration of eminence equal to theirs. For the Athenians ruled only the sea coast, during the space of sixty-eight years,[4] nor did their sway extend even over all that, but only to the part

of Alexander who divided his empire among themselves after his death.

[3] By the overthrow of Perseus in 168, or possibly by the defeat of Philip V in 197, followed by that of Antiochus in 190. Compare chap. 3 (end).

[4] From *ca.* 472 to 404.

τῆς ἐντὸς Εὐξείνου τε πόντου καὶ τοῦ Παμφυλίου πελάγους, ὅτε μάλιστα ἐθαλασσοκράτουν. Λακεδαιμόνιοι δὲ Πελοποννήσου καὶ τῆς ἄλλης κρατοῦντες Ἑλλάδος ἕως Μακεδονίας τὴν ἀρχὴν προὐβίβασαν, ἐπαύθησαν δὲ ὑπὸ Θηβαίων οὐδὲ

3 ὅλα τριάκοντα ἔτη τὴν ἀρχὴν κατασχόντες. ἡ δὲ Ῥωμαίων πόλις ἁπάσης μὲν ἄρχει γῆς ὅση μὴ ἀνέμβατός ἐστιν, ἀλλ' ὑπ' ἀνθρώπων κατοικεῖται, πάσης δὲ κρατεῖ θαλάσσης, οὐ μόνον τῆς ἐντὸς Ἡρακλείων στηλῶν, ἀλλὰ καὶ τῆς Ὠκεανίτιδος ὅση πλεῖσθαι μὴ ἀδύνατός ἐστι, πρώτη καὶ μόνη τῶν ἐκ τοῦ παντὸς αἰῶνος μνημονευομένων ἀνατολὰς καὶ δύσεις ὅρους ποιησαμένη τῆς δυναστείας· χρόνος τε αὐτῇ τοῦ κράτους οὐ βραχύς, ἀλλ' ὅσος οὐδεμιᾷ τῶν ἄλλων οὔτε πόλεων οὔτε βασιλειῶν.

4 εὐθὺς μὲν γὰρ ἐξ ἀρχῆς μετὰ τὸν οἰκισμὸν τὰ πλησίον ἔθνη πολλὰ καὶ μάχιμα ὄντα προσήγετο καὶ προὔβαινεν ἀεὶ πᾶν δουλουμένη τὸ ἀντίπαλον· ταῦτα δὲ πέντε καὶ τετταράκοντα ἤδη πρὸς ἑπτακοσίοις ἔτεσίν ἐστιν εἰς ὑπάτους Κλαύδιον Νέρωνα τὸ δεύτερον ὑπατεύοντα[1] καὶ Πείσωνα Καλπούρνιον, οἳ κατὰ τὴν τρίτην ἐπὶ ταῖς ἐνενήκοντα καὶ ἑκατὸν

5 ὀλυμπιάσιν ἀπεδείχθησαν. ἐξ οὗ δὲ ὅλης ἐκράτησεν Ἰταλίας καὶ ἐπὶ τὴν ἁπάντων ἐθάρρησεν ἀρχὴν

---

[1] ὑπατεύοντα deleted (with Suidas) by Reudler, Jacoby.

---

[1] This statement is puzzling, since the period actually extended from the surrender of Athens in 404 to the battle of Leuctra in 371. The text may be corrupt.

[2] Dionysius may have had in mind Pytheas' report of a πεπηγυῖα θάλασσα (a sea filled with floating ice ?) in the far

between the Euxine and the Pamphylian seas, when
their naval supremacy was at its height. The Lacedaemonians, when masters of the Peloponnesus and
the rest of Greece, advanced their rule as far as
Macedonia, but were checked by the Thebans before
they had held it quite thirty years.[1] But Rome
rules every country that is not inaccessible or uninhabited, and she is mistress of every sea, not only
of that which lies inside the Pillars of Hercules but
also of the Ocean, except that part of it which is
not navigable [2]; she is the first and the only State
recorded in all time that ever made the risings and
the settings of the sun the boundaries of her dominion. Nor has her supremacy been of short duration,
but more lasting than that of any other commonwealth or kingdom. For from the very beginning, immediately after her founding, she began to
draw to herself the neighbouring nations, which
were both numerous and warlike, and continually
advanced, subjugating every rival. And it is now
seven hundred and forty-five years from her foundation down to the consulship of Claudius Nero, consul
for the second time, and of Calpurnius Piso, who
were chosen in the one hundred and ninety-third
Olympiad.[3] From the time that she mastered the
whole of Italy she was emboldened to aspire to

north. From Eratosthenes we learn also that that other
early navigator, the Carthaginian Hanno, who sailed far
south along the west coast of Africa, was finally forced by
many difficulties (of what sort we are not told) to turn
back.

[3] Nero and Piso were consuls in 7 B.C. This was the
year 745 of the City according to Dionysius, who assigns
its founding to the year 751. See chap. 74.

προελθεῖν, ἐκβαλοῦσα μὲν ἐκ τῆς θαλάττης Καρχηδονίους, οἳ πλείστην ἔσχον ναυτικὴν δύναμιν, ὑπο-
χείριον δὲ λαβοῦσα Μακεδονίαν, ἣ τέως ἐδόκει
μέγιστον ἰσχύειν κατὰ γῆν, οὐδὲν ἔτι ἀντίπαλον
ἔχουσα οὔτε βάρβαρον φῦλον οὔτε Ἑλληνικὸν γενεὰν ἑβδόμην ἤδη τὴν ἐπ᾽ ἐμοῦ διαμένει παντὸς
ἄρχουσα τόπου· ἔθνος δὲ οὐδὲν ὡς εἰπεῖν ἐστιν ὃ
περὶ τῆς κοινῆς ἡγεμονίας ἢ τοῦ μὴ ἄρχεσθαι πρὸς
6 αὐτὴν διαφέρεται. ἀλλὰ γὰρ ὅτι μὲν οὔτε τὴν
ἐλαχίστην τῶν ὑποθέσεων προῄρημαι, καθάπερ
ἔφην, οὔτε περὶ φαύλας καὶ ἀσήμους πράξεις
ἔγνωκα διατρίβειν, ἀλλὰ περί τε πόλεως γράφω
τῆς περιφανεστάτης καὶ περὶ πράξεων ὧν οὐκ ἂν
ἔχοι τις ἑτέρας ἐπιδείξασθαι λαμπροτέρας, οὐκ οἶδ᾽
ὅ τι δεῖ πλείω λέγειν.

IV. Ὅτι δ᾽ οὐκ ἄνευ λογισμοῦ καὶ προνοίας
ἔμφρονος ἐπὶ τὰ παλαιὰ τῶν ἱστορουμένων περὶ
αὐτῆς ἐτραπόμην, ἀλλ᾽ ἔχων εὐλογίστους ἀποδοῦναι
τῆς προαιρέσεως αἰτίας, ὀλίγα βούλομαι προειπεῖν,
ἵνα μή τινες ἐπιτιμήσωσί μοι τῶν πρὸς ἅπαντα
φιλαιτίων, οὐδέν πω[1] τῶν μελλόντων δηλοῦσθαι
προακηκοότες, ὅτι τῆς ἀοιδίμου γενομένης καθ᾽
ἡμᾶς πόλεως ἀδόξους καὶ πάνυ ταπεινὰς τὰς
ἡρώτας ἀφορμὰς λαβούσης καὶ οὐκ ἀξίας ἱστορικῆς
ἀναγραφῆς, οὐ πολλαῖς δὲ γενεαῖς πρότερον εἰς
ἐπιφάνειαν καὶ δόξαν ἀφιγμένης, ἐξ οὗ τάς τε

[1] πω Cobet: οὔπω O.

---

[1] This would normally mean six full generations plus
part of another. If Dionysius was counting from the battle
of Pydna (168), he must have reckoned a generation here

govern all mankind, and after driving from off the sea the Carthaginians, whose maritime strength was superior to that of all others, and subduing Macedonia, which until then was reputed to be the most powerful nation on land, she no longer had as rival any nation either barbarian or Greek; and it is now in my day already the seventh generation [1] that she has continued to hold sway over every region of the world, and there is no nation, as I may say, that disputes her universal dominion or protests against being ruled by her. However, to prove my statement that I have neither made choice of the most trivial of subjects nor proposed to treat of mean and insignificant deeds, but am undertaking to write not only about the most illustrious city but also about brilliant achievements to whose like no man could point, I know not what more I need say.

IV. But before I proceed, I desire to show in a few words that it is not without design and mature premeditation that I have turned to the early part of Rome's history, but that I have well-considered reasons to give for my choice, to forestall the censure of those who, fond of finding fault with everything and not as yet having heard of any of the matters which I am about to make known, may blame me because, in spite of the fact that this city, grown so famous in our days, had very humble and inglorious beginnings, unworthy of historical record, and that it was but a few generations ago, that is,

at less than twenty-eight years (his usual estimate); but he may have felt that the Macedonian power was broken at Cynoscephalae (197). Or the seven generations may have been actually counted in some important family.

Μακεδονικὰς καθεῖλε δυναστείας καὶ τοὺς Φοινικικοὺς κατώρθωσε πολέμους, ἐξόν μοι τῶν ἐνδόξων
τινὰ λαβεῖν αὐτῆς ὑποθέσεων, ἐπὶ τὴν οὐδὲν ἔχουσαν
2 ἐπιφανὲς ἀρχαιολογίαν ἀπέκλινα. ἔτι γὰρ ἀγνοεῖ-
ται παρὰ τοῖς Ἕλλησιν ὀλίγου δεῖν πᾶσιν ἡ παλαιὰ
τῆς Ῥωμαίων πόλεως ἱστορία, καὶ δόξαι τινὲς οὐκ
ἀληθεῖς ἀλλ' ἐκ τῶν ἐπιτυχόντων ἀκουσμάτων τὴν
ἀρχὴν λαβοῦσαι τοὺς πολλοὺς ἐξηπατήκασιν, ὡς
ἀνεστίους μέν τινας καὶ πλάνητας καὶ βαρβάρους
καὶ οὐδὲ τούτους ἐλευθέρους οἰκιστὰς εὑρομένης,[1]
οὐ δι' εὐσέβειαν δὲ καὶ δικαιοσύνην καὶ τὴν ἄλλην
ἀρετὴν ἐπὶ τὴν ἁπάντων ἡγεμονίαν σὺν χρόνῳ
παρελθούσης, ἀλλὰ δι' αὐτοματισμόν τινα καὶ
τύχην ἄδικον εἰκῆ δωρουμένην τὰ μέγιστα τῶν
ἀγαθῶν τοῖς ἀνεπιτηδειοτάτοις· καὶ οἵ γε κα-
κοηθέστεροι κατηγορεῖν εἰώθασι τῆς τύχης κατὰ
τὸ φανερὸν ὡς βαρβάρων τοῖς πονηροτάτοις τὰ
3 τῶν Ἑλλήνων χαριζομένης[2] ἀγαθά. καίτοι[3] τί
δεῖ περὶ τῶν ἄλλων λέγειν, ὅπου γε καὶ τῶν
συγγραφέων τινὲς ἐτόλμησαν ἐν ταῖς ἱστορίαις
ταῦτα γράψαντες καταλιπεῖν, βασιλεῦσι βαρβάροις
μισοῦσι τὴν ἡγεμονίαν, οἷς δουλεύοντες αὐτοὶ καὶ
τὰ καθ' ἡδονὰς ὁμιλοῦντες διετέλεσαν, οὔτε δικαίας
οὔτε ἀληθεῖς ἱστορίας χαριζόμενοι;

[1] εὑρομένης Sauppe, παρεχομένης Steph.[2], κεκτημένης or
δεχομένης Reiske : εὐχομένης AB, Jacoby.
[2] Schwartz : ποριζομένης O, Jacoby.
[3] καίτοι Capps : καὶ O, Jacoby.

[1] Sylburg suggested that Hieronymus and Timaeus
(see beginning of chap. 6) were among the writers

since her overthrow of the Macedonian powers
and her success in the Punic wars, that she arrived
at distinction and glory, nevertheless, when I was at
liberty to choose one of the famous periods in her
history for my theme, I turned aside to one so
barren of distinction as her antiquarian lore. For
to this day almost all the Greeks are ignorant of
the early history of Rome and the great majority
of them have been imposed upon by sundry false
opinions grounded upon stories which chance has
brought to their ears and led to believe that, having
come upon various vagabonds without house or
home and barbarians, and even those not free men,
as her founders, she in the course of time arrived at
world domination, and this not through reverence
for the gods and justice and every other virtue, but
through some chance and the injustice of Fortune,
which inconsiderately showers her greatest favours
upon the most undeserving. And indeed the more
malicious are wont to rail openly at Fortune for
freely bestowing on the basest of barbarians the
blessings of the Greeks. And yet why should I
mention men at large, when even some historians
have dared to express such views in the writings
they have left, taking this method of humouring
barbarian kings who detested Rome's supremacy,—
princes to whom they were ever servilely devoted
and with whom they associated as flatterers,—by
presenting them with "histories" which were neither
just nor true ?[1]

Dionysius here had in mind and that Pyrrhus was one of
the kings.

15

V. Ταύτας δὴ τὰς πεπλανημένας, ὥσπερ ἔφην,
ὑπολήψεις ἐξελέσθαι τῆς διανοίας τῶν πολλῶν[1]
προαιρούμενος καὶ ἀντικατασκευάσαι τὰς ἀληθεῖς,
περὶ μὲν τῶν οἰκισάντων τὴν πόλιν, οἵτινες ἦσαν
καὶ κατὰ τίνας ἕκαστοι καιροὺς συνῆλθον καὶ τίσι
τύχαις χρησάμενοι τὰς πατρίους οἰκήσεις ἐξέλιπον,
ἐν ταύτῃ δηλώσω τῇ γραφῇ, δι' ἧς Ἕλληνάς τε
αὐτοὺς ὄντας ἐπιδείξειν ὑπισχνοῦμαι καὶ οὐκ ἐκ
τῶν ἐλαχίστων ἢ φαυλοτάτων ἐθνῶν συνεληλυθότας.
2 περὶ δὲ τῶν πράξεων, ἃς μετὰ τὸν οἰκισμὸν εὐθέως
ἀπεδείξαντο, καὶ περὶ τῶν ἐπιτηδευμάτων, ἐξ ὧν
εἰς τοσαύτην ἡγεμονίαν προῆλθον οἱ μετ' αὐτούς,
ἀπὸ τῆς μετὰ ταύτην ἀρξάμενος ἀναγραφῆς ἀφηγήσομαι, παραλιπὼν οὐδὲν ὅση μοι δύναμις τῶν
ἀξίων ἱστορίας, ἵνα τοῖς γε[2] μαθοῦσι τὴν ἀλήθειαν
ἃ προσήκει περὶ τῆς πόλεως τῆσδε παραστῇ
φρονεῖν, εἰ μὴ παντάπασιν ἀγρίως καὶ δυσμενῶς
διάκεινται πρὸς αὐτήν, καὶ μήτε ἄχθεσθαι τῇ
ὑποτάξει κατὰ τὸ εἰκὸς γενομένῃ (φύσεως γὰρ δὴ
νόμος ἅπασι κοινός, ὃν οὐδεὶς καταλύσει χρόνος,
ἄρχειν ἀεὶ τῶν ἡττόνων τοὺς κρείττονας) μήτε
κατηγορεῖν τῆς τύχης, ὡς οὐκ ἐπιτηδείῳ πόλει
τηλικαύτην ἡγεμονίαν καὶ τοσοῦτον ἤδη χρόνον
3 προῖκα δωρησαμένης· μαθοῦσί γε δὴ παρὰ τῆς
ἱστορίας, ὅτι μυρίας ἤνεγκεν ἀνδρῶν ἀρετὰς εὐθὺς
ἐξ ἀρχῆς μετὰ τὸν οἰκισμόν, ὧν οὔτ' εὐσεβεστέρους
οὔτε δικαιοτέρους οὔτε σωφροσύνῃ πλείονι παρὰ

---

[1] πολλῶν B : πολιτῶν R.

V. In order, therefore, to remove these erroneous impressions, as I have called them, from the
minds of the many and to substitue true ones in their
room, I shall in this Book show who the founders
of the city were, at what periods the various groups
came together, and through what turns of fortune
they left their native countries. By this means I
engage to prove that they were Greeks and came
together from nations not the smallest nor the least
considerable. And beginning with the next Book
I shall tell of the deeds they performed immediately
after their founding of the city and of the customs
and institutions by virtue of which their descendants
advanced to so great dominion ; and, so far as I am
able, I shall omit nothing worthy of being recorded
in history, to the end that I may instil in the minds
of those who shall then be informed of the truth the
fitting conception of this city,—unless they have
already assumed an utterly violent and hostile
attitude toward it, —and also that they may neither
feel indignation at their present subjection, which is
grounded on reason (for by an universal law of Nature, which time cannot destroy, it is ordained that
superiors shall ever govern their inferiors), nor rail at
Fortune for having wantonly bestowed upon an undeserving city a supremacy so great and already of
so long continuance, particularly when they shall
have learned from my history that Rome from the
very beginning, immediately after its founding,
produced infinite examples of virtue in men whose
superiors, whether for piety or for justice or for

---

[2] τοῖς γε Ritschl, τοῖς Kiessling : τότε O.

πάντα τὸν βίον χρησαμένους οὐδέ γε τὰ πολέμια
κρείττους ἀγωνιστὰς οὐδεμία πόλις ἤνεγκεν οὔτε
Ἑλλὰς οὔτε βάρβαρος, εἰ δὴ ἀπέσται τοῦ λόγου τὸ
ἐπίφθονον· ἔχει γάρ τι καὶ τοιοῦτον ἡ τῶν παρα-
4 δόξων καὶ θαυμαστῶν ὑπόσχεσις. οἱ δὲ σύμπαντες οἱ τοσοῦτο περιθέντες αὐτῇ δυναστείας μέγεθος
ἀγνοοῦνται πρὸς Ἑλλήνων, οὐ τυχόντες ἀξιολόγου
συγγραφέως· οὐδεμία γὰρ ἀκριβὴς ἐξελήλυθε περὶ
αὐτῶν Ἑλληνὶς ἱστορία μέχρι τῶν καθ᾽ ἡμᾶς χρόνων, ὅτι μὴ κεφαλαιώδεις ἐπιτομαὶ πάνυ βραχεῖαι,

VI. πρῶτου μέν, ὅσα κἀμὲ εἰδέναι, τὴν Ῥωμαϊκὴν ἀρχαιολογίαν ἐπιδραμόντος Ἱερωνύμου τοῦ
Καρδιανοῦ συγγραφέως ἐν τῇ περὶ τῶν Ἐπιγόνων
πραγματείᾳ· ἔπειτα Τιμαίου τοῦ Σικελιώτου τὰ
μὲν ἀρχαῖα τῶν ἱστοριῶν ἐν ταῖς κοιναῖς ἱστορίαις
ἀφηγησαμένου, τοὺς δὲ πρὸς Πύρρον τὸν Ἠπειρώτην
πολέμους εἰς ἰδίαν καταχωρίσαντος πραγματείαν·
ἅμα δὲ τούτοις Ἀντιγόνου τε καὶ Πολυβίου καὶ
Σιληνοῦ καὶ μυρίων ἄλλων τοῖς αὐτοῖς πράγμασιν
οὐχ ὁμοίως ἐπιβαλόντων, ὧν ἕκαστος ὀλίγα καὶ
οὐδὲ ἀκριβῶς αὐτῷ διεσπουδασμένα, ἀλλ᾽ ἐκ τῶν
2 ἐπιτυχόντων ἀκουσμάτων συνθεὶς ἀνέγραψεν. ὁμοίας δὲ τούτοις καὶ οὐδὲν διαφόρους ἐξέδωκαν ἱστορίας καὶ Ῥωμαίων ὅσοι τὰ παλαιὰ ἔργα τῆς πόλεως Ἑλληνικῇ διαλέκτῳ συνέγραψαν, ὧν εἰσι πρε-

---

[1] Hieronymus wrote a history of the Diadochi (the immediate successors of Alexander) and of their sons, sometimes called the Epigoni (cf. Diodorus i. 3), covering the
period down to the war of Pyrrhus in Italy.

[2] Timaeus' great work was his history of Sicily down to
the overthrow of Agathocles in 289. It included the

life-long self-control or for warlike valour, no city, either Greek or barbarian, has ever produced. This, I say, is what I hope to accomplish, if my readers will but lay aside all resentment ; for some such feeling is aroused by a promise of things which run counter to received opinion or excite wonder. And it is a fact that all those Romans who bestowed upon their country so great a dominion are unknown to the Greeks for want of a competent historian. For no accurate history of the Romans written in the Greek language has hitherto appeared, but only very brief and summary epitomes.

VI. The first historian, so far as I am aware, to touch upon the early period of the Romans was Hieronymus of Cardia, in his work on the Epigoni.[1] After him Timaeus of Sicily related the beginnings of their history in his general history and treated in a separate work the wars with Pyrrhus of Epirus.[2] Besides these, Antigonus, Polybius, Silenus [3] and innumerable other authors devoted themselves to the same themes, though in different ways, each of them recording some few things compiled without accurate investigation on his own part but from reports which chance had brought to his ears. Like to these in all respects are the histories of those Romans, also, who related in Greek the early achievements of the

histories of Italy and Carthage ; hence Dionysius describes it as a " general history."

[3] Antigonus, cited by Plutarch on early Roman history, is otherwise unknown. Polybius is too well known to require comment here. Silenus was one of the historians in the suite of Hannibal ; his history of the Second Punic War was praised by Cicero and Nepos.

σβύτατοι Κόιντός τε Φάβιος καὶ Λεύκιος Κίγκιος,
ἀμφότεροι κατὰ τοὺς Φοινικικοὺς ἀκμάσαντες πολέμους. τούτων δὲ τῶν ἀνδρῶν ἑκάτερος, οἷς μὲν
αὐτὸς ἔργοις παρεγένετο, διὰ τὴν ἐμπειρίαν ἀκριβῶς ἀνέγραψε, τὰ δὲ ἀρχαῖα τὰ μετὰ τὴν κτίσιν
τῆς πόλεως γενόμενα κεφαλαιωδῶς ἐπέδραμεν.
3 διὰ ταύτας μὲν δὴ τὰς αἰτίας ἔδοξέ μοι μὴ παρελθεῖν καλὴν ἱστορίαν ἐγκαταλειφθεῖσαν ὑπὸ τῶν
πρεσβυτέρων ἀμνημόνευτον, ἐξ ἧς ἀκριβῶς γρα-
φείσης συμβήσεται τὰ κράτιστα καὶ δικαιότατα
τῶν ἔργων· τοῖς μὲν ἐκπεπληρωκόσι τὴν ἑαυτῶν
μοῖραν ἀνδράσιν ἀγαθοῖς δόξης αἰωνίου τυχεῖν καὶ
πρὸς τῶν ἐπιγιγνομένων ἐπαινεῖσθαι, ἃ ποιεῖ τὴν
θνητὴν φύσιν ὁμοιοῦσθαι τῇ θείᾳ καὶ μὴ συναπο-
4 θνήσκειν τὰ[1] ἔργα τοῖς σώμασι· τοῖς δὲ ἀπ᾽ ἐκείνων
τῶν ἰσοθέων ἀνδρῶν νῦν τε οὖσι καὶ ὕστερον ἐσομένοις μὴ τὸν ἥδιστόν τε καὶ ῥᾷστον αἱρεῖσθαι τῶν
βίων, ἀλλὰ τὸν εὐγενέστατον καὶ φιλοτιμότατον,
ἐνθυμουμένους ὅτι τοὺς εἰληφότας καλὰς τὰς πρώ-
τας ἐκ τοῦ γένους ἀφορμὰς μέγα ἐφ᾽ ἑαυτοῖς
προσήκει φρονεῖν καὶ μηδὲν ἀνάξιον ἐπιτηδεύειν
5 τῶν προγόνων· ἐμοὶ δέ, ὃς οὐχὶ κολακείας χάριν
ἐπὶ ταύτην ἀπέκλινα τὴν πραγματείαν, ἀλλὰ τῆς
ἀληθείας καὶ τοῦ δικαίου προνοούμενος, ὧν δεῖ
στοχάζεσθαι πᾶσαν ἱστορίαν, πρῶτον μὲν ἀποδείξασθαι[2] τὴν ἐμαυτοῦ διάνοιαν, ὅτι χρηστὴ πρὸς
ἅπαντάς[3] ἐστι τοὺς ἀγαθοὺς καὶ φιλοθεώρους τῶν

---

[1] τὰ B: αὐτῆς τὰ A, αὐτοῖς τὰ R.
[2] Ritschl: ἐπιδείξασθαι O, Jacoby.
[3] ἅπαντας B: ἅπαντας ἀνθρώπους R.

city ; the oldest of these writers are Quintus Fabius [1] and Lucius Cincius,[2] who both flourished during the Punic wars. Each of these men related the events at which he himself had been present with great exactness, as being well acquainted with them, but touched only in a summary way upon the early events that followed the founding of the city. For these reasons, therefore, I have determined not to pass over a noble period of history which the older writers left untouched, a period, moreover, the accurate portrayal of which will lead to the following most excellent and just results : In the first place, the brave men who have fulfilled their destiny will gain immortal glory and be extolled by posterity, which things render human nature like unto the divine and prevent men's deeds from perishing together with their bodies. And again, both the present and future descendants of those godlike men will choose, not the pleasantest and easiest of lives, but rather the noblest and most ambitious, when they consider that all who are sprung from an illustrious origin ought to set a high value on themselves and indulge in no pursuit unworthy of their ancestors. And I, who have not turned aside to this work for the sake of flattery, but out of a regard for truth and justice, which ought to be the aim of every history, shall have an opportunity, in the first place, of expressing my attitude of goodwill toward all good men and toward all who take pleasure in the

[1] Q. Fabius Pictor.
[2] L. Cincius Alimentus.

καλῶν ἔργων καὶ μεγάλων· ἔπειτα χαριστηρίους
ἀμοιβάς, ἃς ἐμοὶ δύναμις ἦν, ἀποδοῦναι τῇ πόλει,
παιδείας τε μεμνημένῳ καὶ τῶν ἄλλων ἀγαθῶν
ὅσων ἀπέλαυσα διατρίψας ἐν αὐτῇ.

VII. Ἀποδεδωκὼς δὲ τὸν ὑπὲρ τῆς προαιρέσεως
λόγον ἔτι βούλομαι καὶ περὶ τῶν ἀφορμῶν εἰπεῖν,
αἷς ἐχρησάμην ὅτ᾽ ἔμελλον ἐπιχειρεῖν τῇ γραφῇ·
ἴσως γὰρ οἱ προανεγνωκότες Ἱερώνυμον ἢ Τίμαιον
ἢ Πολύβιον ἢ τῶν ἄλλων τινὰ συγγραφέων, ὑπὲρ
ὧν ἐποιησάμην λόγον ὀλίγῳ πρότερον ὡς ἐπι-
σεσυρκότων τὴν γραφήν, πολλὰ τῶν ὑπ᾽ ἐμοῦ
γραφομένων οὐχ εὑρηκότες παρ᾽ ἐκείνοις κείμενα
σχεδιάζειν ὑπολήψονταί με καὶ πόθεν ἡ τούτων
γνῶσις εἰς ἐμὲ παραγέγονεν ἀξιώσουσι μαθεῖν.
ἵνα δὴ μὴ τοιαύτη δόξα παραστῇ τισι περὶ ἐμοῦ,
βέλτιον ἀφ᾽ ὧν ὡρμήθην λόγων τε καὶ ὑπομνη-
2 ματισμῶν προειπεῖν. ἐγὼ καταπλεύσας εἰς Ἰταλίαν
ἅμα τῷ καταλυθῆναι τὸν ἐμφύλιον πόλεμον ὑπὸ τοῦ
Σεβαστοῦ Καίσαρος ἑβδόμης καὶ ὀγδοηκοστῆς καὶ
ἑκατοστῆς ὀλυμπιάδος μεσούσης, καὶ τὸν ἐξ ἐκείνου
χρόνον ἐτῶν δύο καὶ εἴκοσι μέχρι τοῦ παρόντος
γενόμενον ἐν Ῥώμῃ διατρίψας, διάλεκτόν τε τὴν
Ῥωμαϊκὴν ἐκμαθὼν καὶ γραμμάτων τῶν [1] ἐπιχωρίων λαβὼν ἐπιστήμην, ἐν παντὶ τούτῳ τῷ [2]
χρόνῳ τὰ συντείνοντα πρὸς τὴν ὑπόθεσιν ταύτην
3 διετέλουν πραγματευόμενος. καὶ τὰ μὲν παρὰ τῶν
λογιωτάτων ἀνδρῶν, οἷς εἰς ὁμιλίαν ἦλθον, διδαχῇ
παραλαβών, τὰ δ᾽ ἐκ τῶν ἱστοριῶν ἀναλεξάμενος,

[1] τῶν added by Reiske.   [2] τῷ added by Ritschl.

contemplation of great and noble deeds ; and, in the second place, of making the most grateful return that I may to the city in remembrance of the education and other blessings I have enjoyed during my residence in it.

VII. Having thus given the reason for my choice of subject, I wish now to say something concerning the sources I used while preparing for my task. For it is possible that those who have already read Hieronymus, Timaeus, Polybius, or any of the other historians whom I just now mentioned as having slurred over their work, since they will not have found in those authors many things mentioned by me, will suspect me of inventing them and will demand to know how I came by the knowledge of these particulars. Lest anyone, therefore, should entertain such an opinion of me, it is best that I should state in advance what narratives and records I have used as sources. I arrived in Italy at the very time that Augustus Caesar put an end to the civil war, in the middle of the one hundred and eighty-seventh Olympiad [1] ; and having from that time to this present day, a period of twenty-two years, lived at Rome, learned the language of the Romans and acquainted myself with their writings, I have devoted myself during all that time to matters bearing upon my subject. Some information I received orally from men of the greatest learning, with whom I associated ; and the rest I gathered from

---

[1] Perhaps late in 30 B.C., if Dionysius wrote this preface *early* in the year 7 (chap. 3, 4) ; but the closing of the temple of Janus in January, 29, or Octavian's triumph in August may have marked for him the end of the war.

ἃς οἱ πρὸς αὐτῶν ἐπαινούμενοι ῾Ρωμαίων συνέγραψαν Πόρκιός τε Κάτων καὶ Φάβιος Μάξιμος
καὶ Οὐαλέριος ὁ[1] Ἀντιεὺς καὶ Λικίννιος[2] Μάκερ
Αἴλιοί τε καὶ Γέλλιοι καὶ Καλπούρνιοι καὶ ἕτεροι
συχνοὶ πρὸς τούτοις ἄνδρες οὐκ ἀφανεῖς, ἀπ᾽ ἐκείνων ὁρμώμενος τῶν πραγματειῶν (εἰσὶ δὲ ταῖς
῾Ελληνικαῖς χρονογραφίαις ἐοικυῖαι), τότε ἐπεχεί-
4 ρησα τῇ γραφῇ. ταῦτα μὲν οὖν ὑπὲρ ἐμαυτοῦ
διείλεγμαι. λοιπὸν δ᾽ ἔτι[3] μοι καὶ περὶ τῆς
ἱστορίας αὐτῆς προειπεῖν, τίσι τε αὐτὴν περιλαμ-
βάνω χρόνοις καὶ περὶ τίνων ποιοῦμαι πραγμάτων
τὴν διήγησιν καὶ ποταπὸν ἀποδίδωμι τὸ σχῆμα τῇ
πραγματείᾳ.

VIII. Ἄρχομαι μὲν οὖν τῆς ἱστορίας ἀπὸ τῶν
παλαιοτάτων μύθων, οὓς παρέλιπον οἱ πρὸ ἐμοῦ
γενόμενοι συγγραφεῖς χαλεποὺς ὄντας ἄνευ πραγ-
2 ματείας μεγάλης ἐξευρεθῆναι · καταβιβάζω δὲ τὴν
διήγησιν ἐπὶ τὴν ἀρχὴν τοῦ πρώτου Φοινικικοῦ
πολέμου τὴν γενομένην ἐνιαυτῷ τρίτῳ τῆς ὀγδόης
καὶ εἰκοστῆς ἐπὶ ταῖς ἑκατὸν ὀλυμπιάσιν. ἀφη-
γοῦμαι δὲ τούς τε ὀθνείους πολέμους τῆς πόλεως
ἅπαντας ὅσους[4] ἐν ἐκείνοις τοῖς χρόνοις ἐπολέμησε,
καὶ τὰς ἐμφυλίους στάσεις ὁπόσας ἐστασίασεν, ἐξ

---

[1] ὁ added by Bücheler.
[2] λικίννιος O (and so nearly always): Λικίνιος Jacoby (here only).
[3] δ᾽ ἔτι Cary: ἔτι δέ B, Jacoby, ἐστι δέ R; δέ Pflugk.
[4] ὅσους Krüger: οὓς O.

24

histories written by the approved Roman authors—
Porcius Cato, Fabius Maximus,[1] Valerius Antias,
Licinius Macer, the Aelii, Gellii and Calpurnii,[2] and
many others of note ; with these works, which are
like the Greek annalistic accounts, as a basis, I set
about the writing of my history. So much, then,
concerning myself. But it yet remains for me to
say something also concerning the history itself—to
what periods I limit it, what subjects I describe,
and what form I give to the work.

VIII. I begin my history, then, with the most
ancient legends, which the historians before me have
omitted as a subject difficult to be cleared up without diligent study ; and I bring the narrative down
to the beginning of the First Punic War, which fell
in the third year of the one hundred and twenty-
eighth Olympiad.[3] I relate all the foreign wars
that the city waged during that period and all
the internal seditions with which she was agitated,

---

[1] Probably Q. Fabius Maximus Servilianus (cos. 142);
but we have very little evidence to go on. See Schanz-
Hosius, *Röm. Litteraturgesch.* i. p. 174.

[2] As Niebuhr pointed out (*Röm. Gesch.* ii. note 11),
these plurals are not to be taken literally, but in the sense
of " men like Aelius," etc. We read of two Aelii, it is true,
who were engaged in writing history—L. Aelius Tubero,
a boyhood friend of Cicero, and his son, Quintus ; but it
is doubtful whether the father ever published his work,
whereas the son's history is quoted several times. The
only Gellius and the only Calpurnius known to have been
historians were Cn. Gellius and L. Calpurnius Piso Frugi,
sometimes styled Censorius (the ex-censor). Both lived in
the time of the Gracchi and both wrote histories of Rome
from the beginning down to their own day.

[3] 265 B.C., the date of the *casus belli.*

οἴων αἰτιῶν ἐγένοντο καὶ δι᾽ οἴων τρόπων τε καὶ
λόγων κατελύθησαν· πολιτειῶν τε ἰδέας διέξειμι
πάσας ὅσαις ἐχρήσατο βασιλευομένη τε καὶ μετὰ
τὴν κατάλυσιν τῶν μονάρχων, καὶ τίς ἦν αὐτῶν
ἑκάστης ὁ κόσμος· ἔθη τε τὰ κράτιστα καὶ νόμους
τοὺς ἐπιφανεστάτους διηγοῦμαι καὶ συλλήβδην ὅλον
3 ἀποδείκνυμι τὸν ἀρχαῖον βίον τῆς πόλεως. σχῆμα
δὲ ἀποδίδωμι τῇ πραγματείᾳ οὔθ᾽ ὁποῖον οἱ τοὺς
πολέμους μόνους [1] ἀναγράψαντες ἀποδεδώκασι ταῖς
ἱστορίαις οὔθ᾽ ὁποῖον οἱ τὰς πολιτείας αὐτὰς ἐφ᾽
ἑαυτῶν διηγησάμενοι οὔτε ταῖς χρονικαῖς παραπλήσιον, ἃς ἐξέδωκαν οἱ τὰς Ἀτθίδας πραγματευ-
σάμενοι· μονοειδεῖς τε γὰρ ἐκεῖναι [2] καὶ ταχὺ
προσιστάμεναι τοῖς ἀκούουσιν· ἀλλ᾽ ἐξ ἁπάσης
ἰδέας μικτὸν ἐναγωνίου τε καὶ θεωρητικῆς καὶ
διηγηματικῆς,[3] ἵνα καὶ τοῖς περὶ τοὺς πολιτικοὺς
διατρίβουσι λόγους καὶ τοῖς περὶ τὴν φιλόσοφον
ἐσπουδακόσι θεωρίαν καὶ εἴ τισιν ἀοχλήτου δεήσει
διαγωγῆς ἐν ἱστορικοῖς ἀναγνώσμασιν ἀποχρώντως
4 ἔχουσα φαίνηται. ἡ μὲν οὖν ἱστορία περὶ τοιούτων
τε γενήσεται πραγμάτων καὶ τοιούτου τεύξεται
σχήματος· ὁ δὲ συντάξας αὐτὴν Διονύσιός εἰμι
Ἀλεξάνδρου Ἁλικαρνασεύς· ἄρχομαι δ᾽ ἐνθένδε.

[1] μόνους added by Steph.[2].
[2] τε γὰρ ἐκεῖναι Pflugk : γὰρ ἐκεῖναί τε O, Jacoby; γὰρ
ἐκεῖναί γε Reiske.
[3] καὶ διηγηματικῆς added by Cary, καὶ ἡδείας by Steph.[2],
Jacoby.

showing from what causes they sprang and by what
methods and by what arguments they were brought
to an end. I give an account also of all the forms of
government Rome used, both during the monarchy
and after its overthrow, and show what was the
character of each. I describe the best customs and
the most remarkable laws; and, in short, I show the
whole life of the ancient Romans. As to the form
I give this work, it does not resemble that which the
authors who make wars alone their subject have
given to their histories, nor that which others who
treat of the several forms of government by themselves have adopted, nor is it like the annalistic
accounts which the authors of the *Atthides*[1] have
published (for these are monotonous and soon grow
tedious to the reader), but it is a combination of
every kind, forensic, speculative and narrative,
to the intent that it may afford satisfaction both
to those who occupy themselves with political de-
bates and to those who are devoted to philosophical
speculations,[2] as well as to any who may desire mere
undisturbed entertainment in their reading of history.
Such things, therefore, will be the subjects of my
history and such will be its form. I, the author, am
Dionysius of Halicarnassus, the son of Alexander.
And at this point I begin.

[1] *Atthis* (an adjective meaning " Attic ") was the name
given to histories of Attica; there were many of these
written in the fourth and third centuries. They made no
pretension to literary style.

[2] A comparison of the introductory chapter of Book XI
(§§ 1 and 4) makes it probable that the first group mentioned here were those who took an active part in public
affairs, the second the political philosophers or theorists.

IX. Τὴν ἡγεμόνα γῆς καὶ θαλάσσης ἁπάσης πόλιν, ἣν νῦν κατοικοῦσι Ῥωμαῖοι, παλαιότατοι τῶν μνημονευομένων λέγονται κατασχεῖν βάρβαροι Σικελοί, ἔθνος αὐθιγενές· τὰ δὲ πρὸ τούτων οὔθ᾽ ὡς κατείχετο πρὸς ἑτέρων οὔθ᾽ ὡς ἔρημος ἦν οὐδεὶς ἔχει βεβαίως εἰπεῖν. χρόνῳ δὲ ὕστερον Ἀβοριγῖνες αὐτὴν παραλαμβάνουσι πολέμῳ μακρῷ 2 τοὺς ἔχοντας ἀφελόμενοι· οἳ τὸ μὲν πρότερον ἐπὶ τοῖς ὄρεσιν ᾤκουν ἄνευ τειχῶν κωμηδὸν καὶ σποράδες, ἐπεὶ δὲ Πελασγοί τε καὶ τῶν ἄλλων Ἑλλήνων τινὲς ἀναμιχθέντες αὐτοῖς συνήραντο τοῦ πρὸς τοὺς ὁμοτέρμονας πολέμου, τὸ Σικελικὸν γένος ἀναστήσαντες ἐξ αὐτῆς πόλεις περιεβάλοντο συχνὰς καὶ παρεσκεύασαν ὑπήκοον αὐτοῖς γενέσθαι πᾶσαν ὅσην ὁρίζουσι ποταμοὶ δύο Λῖρις καὶ Τέβερις·[1] οἳ τὰς μὲν ἀρχὰς λαμβάνουσι τῆς ῥύσεως ἐκ τῆς ὑπωρείας τῶν Ἀπεννίνων ὀρῶν, ὑφ᾽ ὧν δίχα τέμνεται πᾶσα ἐπὶ μῆκος ἡ Ἰταλία, διαστάντες δὲ κατὰ τὰς ἐκβολὰς ὀκτακόσιά που στάδια ἀπ᾽ ἀλλήλων εἰς τὸ Τυρρηνικὸν ἐξερεύγονται πέλαγος, ἀπὸ μὲν τῶν βορείων μερῶν ὁ Τέβερις Ὠστίας πόλεως πλησίον ἐκδιδούς, ἀπὸ δὲ τοῦ μεσημβρινοῦ κλίματος ὁ Λῖρις Μίντουρναν παραμειβόμενος· Ῥωμαίων δέ εἰσιν αἱ πόλεις 3 ἀμφότεραι ἄποικοι. καὶ διέμειναν ἐπὶ τῆς αὐτῆς οἰκήσεως οὐκέτι πρὸς ἑτέρων ἐξελαθέντες, ὀνομάτων ἀλλαγαῖς[2] διτταῖς[3] οἱ αὐτοὶ ἄνθρωποι προσαγορευόμενοι, μέχρι μὲν τοῦ Τρωικοῦ πολέμου τὴν ἀρχαίαν

---

[1] Τέβερις Ritschl: τίβερις O (and so just below; but in later passages τέβερις is the more common form).

IX. This city, mistress of the whole earth and sea, which the Romans now inhabit, is said to have had as its earliest known occupants the barbarian Sicels, a native race. As to the condition of the place before their time, whether it was occupied by others or uninhabited, none can certainly say. But some time later the Aborigines gained possession of it, having taken it from the occupants after a long war. These people had previously lived on the mountains in unwalled villages and scattered groups; but when the Pelasgians,[1] with whom some other Greeks had united, assisted them in the war against their neighbours, they drove the Sicels out of this place, walled in many towns, and contrived to subjugate all the country that lies between the two rivers, the Liris and the Tiber. These rivers spring from the foot of the Apennine mountains, the range by which all Italy is divided into two parts throughout its length, and at points about eight hundred stades from one another discharge themselves into the Tyrrhenian Sea, the Tiber to the north, near the city of Ostia, and the Liris to the south, as it flows by Minturnae, both these cities being Roman colonies. And these people remained in this same place of abode, being never afterwards driven out by any others; but, although they continued to be one and the same people, their name was twice changed. Till the time of the Trojan war they preserved their ancient name

[1] As will be seen a little later (chap. 17), Dionysius regarded the Pelasgians as a Greek nation.

---

[2] ἀλλαγαῖς Dmg., Steph.: ἀλλὰ ταῖς O.
[3] διτταῖς Kiessling: αὐταῖς O.

τῶν Ἀβοριγίνων ὀνομασίαν ἔτι σώζοντες, ἐπὶ δὲ
Λατίνου βασιλέως, ὃς κατὰ τὸν Ἰλιακὸν πόλεμον
4 ἐδυνάστευε, Λατῖνοι ἀρξάμενοι καλεῖσθαι. ʽΡω-
μύλου δὲ τὴν ἐπώνυμον αὐτοῦ πόλιν οἰκίσαντος [1]
ἑκκαίδεκα γενεαῖς τῶν Τρωικῶν ὕστερον, ἣν νῦν
ἔχουσιν ὀνομασίαν μεταλαβόντες, ἔθνος τε μέγιστον
ἐξ ἐλαχίστου γενέσθαι σὺν χρόνῳ παρεσκεύασαν
καὶ περιφανέστατον ἐξ ἀδηλοτάτου, τῶν τε δεομένων οἰκήσεως παρὰ σφίσι φιλανθρώπῳ ὑποδοχῇ
καὶ πολιτείας μεταδόσει τοῖς μετὰ τοῦ γενναίου
ἐν πολέμῳ κρατηθεῖσι, δούλων τε ὅσοι παρ᾽ αὐτοῖς
ἐλευθερωθεῖεν ἀστοῖς εἶναι συγχωρήσει, τύχης τε
ἀνθρώπων οὐδεμιᾶς εἰ μέλλοι τὸ κοινὸν ὠφελεῖν
ἀπαξιώσει· ὑπὲρ ταῦτα δὲ πάντα κόσμῳ τοῦ
πολιτεύματος, ὃν ἐκ πολλῶν κατεστήσαντο παθη-
μάτων, ἐκ παντὸς καιροῦ λαμβάνοντές τι χρήσιμον.

X. Τοὺς δὲ Ἀβοριγῖνας, ἀφ᾽ ὧν ἄρχει ʽΡωμαίοις
τὸ γένος, οἱ μὲν αὐτόχθονας Ἰταλίας, γένος αὐτὸ
καθ᾽ ἑαυτὸ γενόμενον,[2] ἀποφαίνουσιν· Ἰταλίαν δὲ
καλῶ τὴν ἀκτὴν σύμπασαν, ὅσην Ἰόνιός τε κόλπος
καὶ Τυρρηνικὴ θάλασσα καὶ τρίται περιέχουσιν ἐκ
γῆς Ἄλπεις. καὶ τὴν ὀνομασίαν αὐτοῖς τὴν πρώτην
φασὶ τεθῆναι διὰ τὸ γενέσεως τοῖς μετ᾽ αὐτοὺς

---

[1] Steph.: οἰκήσαντος O.
[2] γένος . . . γενόμενον deleted by Garrer.

---

[1] This clause is added, possibly by a scribe, as a defini-
tion of the well-known Greek word *autochthones*, here
rendered " natives." The word means literally " sprung
from the land itself," corresponding to the Latin *indigenae*.

of Aborigines ; but under Latinus, their king, who reigned at the time of that war, they began to be called Latins, and when Romulus founded the city named after himself sixteen generations after the taking of Troy, they took the name which they now bear. And in the course of time they contrived to raise themselves from the smallest nation to the greatest and from the most obscure to the most illustrious, not only by their humane reception of those who sought a home among them, but also by sharing the rights of citizenship with all who had been conquered by them in war after a brave resistance, by permitting all the slaves, too, who were manumitted among them to become citizens, and by disdaining no condition of men from whom the commonwealth might reap an advantage, but above everything else by their form of government, which they fashioned out of their many experiences, always extracting something useful from every occasion.

X. There are some who affirm that the Aborigines, from whom the Romans are originally descended, were natives of Italy, a stock which came into being spontaneously [1] (I call Italy all that peninsula which is bounded by the Ionian Gulf [2] and the Tyrrhenian Sea and, thirdly, by the Alps on the landward side) ; and these authors say that they were first called Aborigines because they were the founders of the

It was the proud boast of the Athenians that they were *autochthones*.

[2] "The Ionian Gulf" or simply "the Ionian" is Dionysius' usual term for the Adriatic, or more particularly perhaps for the entrance to this sea.

ἄρξαι, ὥσπερ ἂν ἡμεῖς εἴποιμεν γενεάρχας ἢ πρωτο-
2 γόνους ἔτεροι δὲ λέγουσιν ἀνεστίους τινὰς καὶ
πλάνητας ἐκ πολλῶν συνελθόντας χωρίων κατὰ
δαίμονα περιτυχεῖν ἀλλήλοις αὐτόθι καὶ τὴν οἴκησιν
ἐπὶ τοῖς ἐρύμασι καταστήσασθαι, ζῆν δὲ ἀπὸ λῃστείας
καὶ νομῆς. παραλλάττουσι δὲ καὶ τὴν ὀνομασίαν
αὐτῶν ἐπὶ τὸ ταῖς τύχαις οἰκειότερον, Ἀβερριγῖνας[1]
λέγοντες, ὥστε δηλοῦσθαι αὐτοὺς πλάνητας. κιν-
δυνεύει δὴ κατὰ τούτους μηδὲν διαφέρειν τὸ τῶν
Ἀβοριγίνων φῦλον ὧν ἐκάλουν οἱ παλαιοὶ Λελέγων·[2]
τοῖς γὰρ ἀνεστίοις καὶ μιγάσι καὶ μηδεμίαν γῆν
βεβαίως ὡς πατρίδα κατοικοῦσι ταύτην ἐτίθεντο[3]
3 τὴν ὀνομασίαν ὡς τὰ πολλά. ἄλλοι δὲ Λιγύων
ἀποίκους μυθολογοῦσιν αὐτοὺς γενέσθαι τῶν ὁμορούντων Ὀμβρικοῖς· οἱ γὰρ Λίγυες οἰκοῦσι μὲν
καὶ τῆς Ἰταλίας πολλαχῇ, νέμονται δέ τινα καὶ τῆς
Κελτικῆς. ὁποτέρα δ᾽ αὐτοῖς ἐστι γῆ πατρίς,
ἄδηλον· οὐ γὰρ ἔτι λέγεται περὶ αὐτῶν προσωτέρω
σαφὲς οὐδέν.

XI. Οἱ δὲ λογιώτατοι τῶν Ῥωμαϊκῶν συγγραφέων, ἐν οἷς ἐστι Πόρκιός τε Κάτων ὁ τὰς
γενεαλογίας τῶν ἐν Ἰταλίᾳ πόλεων ἐπιμελέστατα

---

[1] Ἀβερριγῖνας Steph.: ἀβορριγῖνας B, ἀβοριγίνας A.
[2] Λελέγων Dmg., Steph.[2]: δὴ λέγω O.
[3] Schwartz: ἐπετίθεντο O, Jacoby.

---

[1] "Founders of families" and "first-born" respectively.
[2] From the Latin *aberrare* ("wander").
[3] Strabo cites (vii. 7, 2) some verses of Hesiod in which the Leleges are described as λεκτοὺς ἐκ γαίης λαούς, "peoples gathered out of earth," an etymological word-play which

families of their descendants, or, as we should call them, *genearchai* or *prôtogonoi*.[1] Others claim that certain vagabonds without house or home, coming together out of many places, met one another there by chance and took up their abode in the fastnesses, living by robbery and grazing their herds. And these writers change their name, also, to one more suitable to their condition, calling them Aberrigines,[2] to show that they were wanderers ; indeed, according to these, the race of the Aborigines would seem to be no different from those the ancients called Leleges ; for this is the name they generally gave to the homeless and mixed peoples who had no fixed abode which they could call their country.[3] Still others have a story to the effect that they were colonists sent out by those Ligurians who are neighbours of the Umbrians. For the Ligurians inhabit not only many parts of Italy but some parts of Gaul as well , but which of these lands is their native country is not known, since nothing certain is said of them further.

XI. But the most learned of the Roman historians, among whom is Porcius Cato, who compiled with the greatest care the " origins "[4] of the Italian cities,

he thinks shows that Hesiod regarded them as having been from the beginning a collection of mixed peoples. This derivation of the name from the root λεγ (" gather ") is the only one the ancients have handed down.

[4] Cato's history seems to have consisted at first of one book, in which Rome's beginnings and the regal period were recounted, followed by two books devoted to the origin of the various Italian cities ; hence the title *Origines*. Later he added four more books, in which an account was given of the Punic Wars and subsequent events.

συναγαγὼν καὶ Γάϊος Σεμπρώνιος καὶ ἄλλοι συχνοί,
Ἕλληνας αὐτοὺς εἶναι λέγουσι τῶν ἐν Ἀχαΐᾳ ποτὲ
οἰκησάντων, πολλαῖς γενεαῖς πρότερον τοῦ πολέμου
τοῦ Τρωικοῦ μεταναστάντας. οὐκέτι μέντοι διο-
ρίζουσιν οὔτε φῦλον Ἑλληνικὸν οὗ μετεῖχον, οὔτε
πόλιν ἐξ ἧς ἀπανέστησαν, οὔτε χρόνον οὔθ᾽ ἡγεμόνα
τῆς ἀποικίας, οὔθ᾽ ὁποίαις τύχαις χρησάμενοι τὴν
μητρόπολιν ἀπέλιπον· Ἑλληνικῷ τε μύθῳ χρησάμενοι οὐδένα τῶν τὰ Ἑλληνικὰ γραψάντων βε-
βαιωτὴν παρέσχοντο. τὸ μὲν οὖν ἀληθὲς ὅπως
ποτ᾽ ἔχει, ἄδηλον· εἰ δ᾽ ἐστὶν ὁ τούτων λόγος
ὑγιής, οὐκ ἂν ἑτέρου τινὸς εἴησαν ἄποικοι γένους
2 ἢ τοῦ καλουμένου νῦν Ἀρκαδικοῦ. πρῶτοι γὰρ
Ἑλλήνων οὗτοι περαιωθέντες τὸν Ἰόνιον κόλπον
ᾤκησαν Ἰταλίαν, ἄγοντος αὐτοὺς Οἰνώτρου τοῦ
Λυκάονος· ἦν δὲ πέμπτος ἀπό τε Αἰζειοῦ καὶ
Φορωνέως τῶν πρώτων ἐν Πελοποννήσῳ δυναστευ-
σάντων. Φορωνέως μὲν γὰρ Νιόβη γίνεται· ταύτης
δὲ υἱὸς καὶ Διός, ὡς λέγεται, Πελασγός· Αἰζειοῦ δὲ
υἱὸς Λυκάων· τούτου δὲ Δηιάνειρα θυγάτηρ· ἐκ δὲ
Δηιανείρας καὶ Πελασγοῦ Λυκάων ἕτερος· τούτου
δὲ Οἴνωτρος, ἑπτακαίδεκα γενεαῖς πρότερον τῶν
ἐπὶ Τροίαν στρατευσάντων. ὁ μὲν δὴ χρόνος, ἐν
ᾧ τὴν ἀποικίαν ἔστειλαν Ἕλληνες εἰς Ἰταλίαν,
3 οὗτος ἦν. ἀπανέστη δὲ τῆς Ἑλλάδος Οἴνωτρος οὐκ
ἀρκούμενος τῇ μοίρᾳ· δύο γὰρ καὶ εἴκοσι παίδων
Λυκάονι γενομένων εἰς τοσούτους ἔδει κλήρους
νεμηθῆναι τὴν Ἀρκάδων χώραν. ταύτης μὲν δὴ
τῆς αἰτίας ἕνεκα Πελοπόννησον Οἴνωτρος ἐκλιπὼν

Gaius Sempronius [1] and a great many others, say
that they were Greeks, part of those who once dwelt
in Achaia, and that they migrated many generations
before the Trojan war. But they do not go on
to indicate either the Greek tribe to which they
belonged or the city from which they removed, or
the date or the leader of the colony, or as the result
of what turns of fortune they left their mother country; and although they are following a Greek legend,
they have cited no Greek historian as their authority. It is uncertain, therefore, what the truth of
the matter is. But if what they say is true, the
Aborigines can be a colony of no other people but of
those who are now called Arcadians; for these were
the first of all the Greeks to cross the Ionian
Gulf, under the leadership of Oenotrus, the son of
Lycaon, and to settle in Italy. This Oenotrus was
the fifth from Aezeius and Phoroneus, who were the
first kings in the Peloponnesus. For Niobê was
the daughter of Phoroneus, and Pelasgus was the
son of Niobê and Zeus, it is said; Lycaon was
the son of Aezeius, and Deïanira was the daughter of
Lycaon; Deïanira and Pelasgus were the parents
of another Lycaon, whose son Oenotrus was born
seventeen generations before the Trojan expedition.
This, then, was the time when the Greeks sent the
colony into Italy. Oenotrus left Greece because
he was dissatisfied with his portion of his father's
land; for, as Lycaon had twenty-two sons, it was
necessary to divide Arcadia into as many shares.
For this reason Oenotrus left the Peloponnesus,

[1] C. Sempronius Tuditanus (cos. 129). Besides his *liber
magistratuum* he seems to have written a historical work.

καὶ κατασκευασάμενος ναυτικὸν διαίρει τὸν Ἰόνιον[1]
καὶ σὺν αὐτῷ Πευκέτιος τῶν ἀδελφῶν εἷς. εἵποντο
δὲ αὐτοῖς τοῦ τε οἰκείου λαοῦ συχνοί, πολυάνθρωπον
γὰρ δὴ τὸ ἔθνος τοῦτο λέγεται κατ' ἀρχὰς γενέσθαι,
καὶ τῶν ἄλλων Ἑλλήνων ὅσοι χώραν εἶχον ἐλάττω
4 τῆς ἱκανῆς. Πευκέτιος μὲν οὖν, ἔνθα τὸ πρῶτον
ὡρμίσαντο τῆς Ἰταλίας, ὑπὲρ ἄκρας Ἰαπυγίας
ἐκβιβάσας τὸν λεὼν αὐτοῦ καθιδρύεται, καὶ ἀπ'
αὐτοῦ οἱ περὶ ταῦτα τὰ χωρία οἰκοῦντες Πευκέτιοι
ἐκλήθησαν. Οἴνωτρος δὲ τὴν πλείω τοῦ στρατοῦ
μοῖραν ἀγόμενος εἰς τὸν ἕτερον ἀφικνεῖται κόλπον
τὸν ἀπὸ τῶν ἑσπερίων μερῶν παρὰ τὴν Ἰταλίαν
ἀναχεόμενον, ὃς τότε μὲν Αὐσόνιος ἐπὶ τῶν προσοικούντων Αὐσόνων ἐλέγετο, ἐπεὶ δὲ Τυρρηνοὶ
θαλασσοκράτορες ἐγένοντο, μετέλαβεν[2] ἣν ἔχει νῦν
προσηγορίαν.

XII. Εὑρὼν δὲ χώραν πολλὴν μὲν εἰς νομάς,
πολλὴν δὲ εἰς ἀρότους εὔθετον, ἔρημον δὲ τὴν
πλείστην καὶ οὐδὲ τὴν οἰκουμένην πολυάνθρωπον,
ἀνακαθήρας τὸ βάρβαρον ἐκ μέρους τινὸς αὐτῆς
ᾤκισε πόλεις μικρὰς καὶ συνεχεῖς ἐπὶ τοῖς ὄρεσιν,
ὅσπερ ἦν τοῖς παλαιοῖς τρόπος οἰκήσεως συνήθης.
ἐκαλεῖτο δὲ ἥ τε χώρα πᾶσα πολλὴ οὖσα ὅσην
κατέσχεν Οἰνωτρία, καὶ οἱ ἄνθρωποι πάντες ὅσων
ἦρξεν Οἴνωτροι, τρίτην μεταλαβόντες ὀνομασίαν
ταύτην. ἐπὶ μὲν γὰρ Αἰζειοῦ βασιλεύοντος Αἰζειοὶ
ἐλέγοντο, Λυκάονος δὲ παραλαβόντος τὴν ἀρχὴν
ἀπ' ἐκείνου αὖθις Λυκάονες ὠνομάσθησαν, Οἰνώτρου

prepared a fleet, and crossed the Ionian Gulf with Peucetius, one of his brothers. They were accompanied by many of their own people—for this nation is said to have been very populous in early times—and by as many other Greeks as had less land than was sufficient for them. Peucetius landed his people above the Iapygian Promontory, which was the first part of Italy they made, and settled there; and from him the inhabitants of this region were called Peucetians. But Oenotrus with the greater part of the expedition came into the other sea that washes the western regions along the coast of Italy; it was then called the Ausonian Sea, from the Ausonians who dwelt beside it, but after the Tyrrhenians became masters at sea its name was changed to that which it now bears.

XII. And finding there much land suitable for pasturage and much for tillage, but for the most part unoccupied, and even that which was inhabited not thickly populated, he cleared some of it of the barbarians and built small towns contiguous to one another on the mountains, which was the customary manner of habitation in use among the ancients. And all the land he occupied, which was very extensive, was called Oenotria, and all the people under his command Oenotrians, which was the third name they had borne. For in the reign of Aezeius they were called Aezeians, when Lycaon succeeded to the rule, Lycaonians, and after Oenotrus

---

[1] Ἰόνιον Kiessling, Ἰόνιον κόλπον Reiske: ἰόνιον πόρον B, ἰόνιον πόντον R.
[2] Steph.[2]: μετέβαλεν O.

δὲ κομίσαντος αὐτοὺς εἰς Ἰταλίαν Οἴνωτροι χρόνον
2 τινὰ ἐκλήθησαν. μαρτυρεῖ δέ μοι[1] τῷ λόγῳ
Σοφοκλῆς μὲν ὁ τραγῳδοποιὸς ἐν Τριπτολέμῳ
δράματι· πεποίηται γὰρ αὐτῷ Δημήτηρ διδάσκουσα
τὸν Τριπτόλεμον ὅσην χώραν ἀναγκασθήσεται σπεί-
ρων τοῖς δοθεῖσιν ὑπ' αὐτῆς καρποῖς διεξελθεῖν·
μνησθεῖσα δὲ τῆς ἑῴου πρῶτον Ἰταλίας, ἥ ἐστιν
ἀπ' ἄκρας Ἰαπυγίας μέχρι πορθμοῦ Σικελικοῦ,
καὶ μετὰ τοῦτο τῆς ἀντικρυς[2] ἀψαμένη Σικελίας,
ἐπὶ τὴν ἑσπέριον Ἰταλίαν αὖθις ἀναστρέφει καὶ τὰ
μέγιστα τῶν οἰκούντων τὴν παράλιον ταύτην ἐθνῶν
διεξέρχεται, τὴν ἀρχὴν ἀπὸ τῆς Οἰνώτρων οἰκήσεως
ποιησαμένη. ἀπόχρη δὲ ταῦτα μόνα λεχθέντα τῶν
ἰαμβείων, ἐν οἷς φησι·

τὰ δ' ἐξόπισθε, χειρὸς εἰς τὰ δεξιά,
Οἰνωτρία τε πᾶσα καὶ Τυρρηνικὸς
κόλπος Λιγυστική τε γῆ σε δέξεται.

3 Ἀντίοχος δὲ ὁ Συρακούσιος, συγγραφεὺς πάνυ
ἀρχαῖος, ἐν Ἰταλίας οἰκισμῷ τοὺς παλαιοτάτους
οἰκήτορας διεξιών, ὡς ἕκαστοί τι μέρος αὐτῆς
κατεῖχον, Οἰνώτρους λέγει πρώτους τῶν μνημονευομένων ἐν αὐτῇ κατοικῆσαι, εἰπὼν ὧδε·
"Ἀντίοχος Ξενοφάνεος τάδε συνέγραψε περὶ Ἰταλίης
ἐκ τῶν ἀρχαίων λόγων τὰ πιστότατα καὶ σαφέστατα·

---

[1] Jacoby: μου O.
[2] Kiessling: ἀντικρὺ O, Jacoby.

led them into Italy they were for a while called Oenotrians. What I say is supported by the testimony
of Sophocles, the tragic poet, in his drama entitled
Triptolemus ; for he there represents Demeter as
informing Triptolemus how large a tract of land he
would have to travel over while sowing it with the
seeds she had given him. For, after first referring
to the eastern part of Italy, which reaches from
the Iapygian Promontory to the Sicilian Strait, and
then touching upon Sicily on the opposite side,
she returns again to the western part of Italy and
enumerates the most important nations that inhabit this coast, beginning with the settlement of
the Oenotrians. But it is enough to quote merely
the iambics in which he says :

" And after this,—first, then, upon the right,
    Oenotria wide-outstretched and Tyrrhene Gulf,
    And next the Ligurian land shall welcome thee." [1]

And Antiochus of Syracuse,[2] a very early historian,
in his account of the settlement of Italy, when
enumerating the most ancient inhabitants in the
order in which each of them held possession of
any part of it, says that the first who are reported
to have inhabited that country are the Oenotrians.
His words are these : " Antiochus, the son of
Xenophanes, wrote this account of Italy, which
comprises all that is most credible and certain out of

---

[1] Nauck, *Trag. Graec. Frag.*[2], p. 262, frg. 541.
[2] Antiochus (latter half of fifth century) wrote a history
of Sicily and a history of Italy. The former was used by
Thucydides, and the latter is frequently cited by Strabo.
The quotation here given is frg. 3 in Müller, *Frag. Hist.
Graec.* i. p. 181.

τὴν γῆν ταύτην, ἥτις νῦν Ἰταλίη¹ καλεῖται, τὸ παλαιὸν εἶχον Οἴνωτροι." ἔπειτα διεξελθὼν ὃν τρόπον ἐπολιτεύοντο, καὶ ὡς βασιλεὺς ἐν αὐτοῖς Ἰταλὸς ἀνὰ χρόνον ἐγένετο, ἀφ' οὗ μετωνομάσθησαν Ἰταλοί, τούτου δὲ τὴν ἀρχὴν Μόργης διεδέξατο, ἀφ' οὗ Μόργητες ἐκλήθησαν, καὶ ὡς Σικελὸς ἐπιξενωθεὶς Μόργητι ἰδίαν πράττων ἀρχὴν διέστησε τὸ ἔθνος, ἐπιφέρει ταυτί· "οὕτω δὲ Σικελοὶ καὶ Μόργητες ἐγένοντο καὶ Ἰταλίητες ἐόντες Οἴνωτροι."

XIII. Φέρε δὴ καὶ τὸ γένος ὅθεν² ἦν τὸ τῶν Οἰνώτρων ἀποδείξωμεν, ἕτερον ἄνδρα τῶν ἀρχαίων συγγραφέων παρασχόμενοι μάρτυρα, Φερεκύδην τὸν Ἀθηναῖον,³ γενεαλόγων οὐδενὸς δεύτερον. πεποίηται γὰρ αὐτῷ περὶ τῶν ἐν Ἀρκαδίᾳ βασιλευσάντων ὅδε⁴ ὁ λόγος· "Πελασγοῦ καὶ Δηιανείρης γίνεται Λυκάων· οὗτος γαμεῖ Κυλλήνην, Νηΐδα νύμφην, ἀφ' ἧς τὸ ὄρος ἡ Κυλλήνη καλεῖται." ἔπειτα τοὺς ἐκ τούτων γεννηθέντας διεξιὼν καὶ τίνας ἕκαστοι τόπους ᾤκησαν, Οἰνώτρου καὶ Πευκετίου μιμνήσκεται λέγων ὧδε· "καὶ Οἴνωτρος, ἀφ' οὗ Οἴνωτροι καλέονται οἱ ἐν Ἰταλίῃ οἰκέοντες, καὶ Πευκέτιος, ἀφ' οὗ Πευκέτιοι καλέονται οἱ ἐν τῷ Ἰονίῳ κόλπῳ."

2 τὰ μὲν οὖν ὑπὸ τῶν παλαιῶν εἰρημένα ποιητῶν τε καὶ μυθογράφων περί τε οἰκήσεως καὶ γένους τῶν Οἰνώτρων τοιαῦτά ἐστιν· οἷς ἐγὼ πειθόμενος, εἰ

---

¹ Cobet : ἰταλία O.
³ Casaubon : τῶν ἀθηναίων O.
² Dobree : ὅσον O.
⁴ Krüger : ὧδε O.

---

¹ Pherecydes (fifth century) was one of the more prominent of the early logographers and the first prose writer of Athens. His great work was a mythological history,

the ancient tales; this country, which is now called Italy, was formerly possessed by the Oenotrians." Then he relates in what manner they were governed and says that in the course of time Italus came to be their king, after whom they were named Italians; that this man was succeeded by Morges, after whom they were called Morgetes, and that Sicelus, being received as a guest by Morges and setting up a kingdom for himself, divided the nation. After which he adds these words: "Thus those who had been Oenotrians became Sicels, Morgetes and Italians."

XIII. Now let me also show the origin of the Oenotrian race, offering as my witness another of the early historians, Pherecydes of Athens,[1] who was a genealogist inferior to none. He thus expresses himself concerning the kings of Arcadia: "Of Pelasgus and Deïanira was born Lycaon; this man married Cyllenê, a Naiad nymph, after whom Mount Cyllenê is named." Then, having given an account of their children and of the places each of them inhabited, he mentions Oenotrus and Peucetius, in these words: "And Oenotrus, after whom are named the Oenotrians who live in Italy, and Peucetius, after whom are named the Peucetians who live on the Ionian Gulf." Such, then, are the accounts given by the ancient poets and writers of legends concerning the places of abode and the origin of the Oenotrians; and on their authority

beginning with a brief theogony, but largely devoted to the genealogies of the great families of the heroic age. The following quotations appear as frg. 85 in Müller, *F.H.G.* i. p. 92.

τῷ ὄντι Ἑλληνικὸν φῦλον ἦν τὸ τῶν Ἀβοριγίνων,
ὡς Κάτωνι καὶ Σεμπρωνίῳ καὶ πολλοῖς ἄλλοις
εἴρηται, τούτων ἔγγονον αὐτὸ [1] τῶν Οἰνώτρων
τίθεμαι.[2] τὸ γὰρ δὴ Πελασγικὸν καὶ τὸ Κρητικὸν
καὶ ὅσα ἄλλα ἐν Ἰταλίᾳ ᾤκησεν, ὑστέροις εὑρίσκω
χρόνοις ἀφικόμενα· παλαιότερον δὲ τούτου στόλον
ἀπαναστάντα τῆς Ἑλλάδος εἰς τὰ προσεσπέρια τῆς
3 Εὐρώπης οὐδένα δύναμαι καταμαθεῖν. τοὺς δὲ
Οἰνώτρους τῆς τ' ἄλλης Ἰταλίας πολλὰ χωρία
οἴομαι κατασχεῖν, τὰ μὲν ἔρημα, τὰ δὲ φαύλως
οἰκούμενα καταλαβόντας, καὶ δὴ καὶ τῆς Ὀμβρικῶν
γῆς ἔστιν ἣν ἀποτεμέσθαι, κληθῆναι δὴ Ἀβοριγῖνας
ἐπὶ τῆς ἐν τοῖς ὄρεσιν οἰκήσεως (Ἀρκαδικὸν γὰρ
τὸ φιλοχωρεῖν ὄρεσιν [3]), ὡς ὑπερακρίους τινὰς καὶ
4 παραλίους Ἀθήνησιν. εἰ δέ τινες πεφύκασι μὴ
ταχεῖς εἶναι περὶ πραγμάτων παλαιῶν ἀβασανίστως
τὰ λεγόμενα δέχεσθαι, μὴ ταχεῖς ἔστωσαν μηδὲ
Λίγυας ἢ Ὀμβρικοὺς ἢ ἄλλους τινὰς βαρβάρους
αὐτοὺς νομίσαι, περιμείναντες δὲ καὶ τὰ λοιπὰ
μαθεῖν κρινέτωσαν ἐξ ἁπάντων τὸ πιθανώτατον.

XIV. Τῶν δὲ πόλεων, ἐν αἷς τὸ πρῶτον ᾤκησαν
Ἀβοριγῖνες, ὀλίγαι περιῆσαν ἐπ' ἐμοῦ· αἱ δὲ πλεῖσται
ὑπό τε πολέμων καὶ ἄλλων κακῶν οἰκοφθορηθεῖσαι
ἔρημοι ἀφεῖνται. ἦσαν δ' ἐν τῇ Ῥεατίνῃ γῇ τῶν

---

[1] τούτων ἔγγονον αὐτὸ R : τοῦτο· ἔγγονον αὐτῶν B ; τούτων
ἔγγονον αὐτῶν Jacoby.
[2] τίθεμαι Reiske, ὑποτίθεμαι Jacoby : πείθομαι O.
[3] ὄρεσιν O : ἐν ὄρεσιν Jacoby.

I assume that if the Aborigines were in reality a Greek nation, according to the opinion of Cato, Sempronius and many others, they were descendants of these Oenotrians. For I find that the Pelasgians and Cretans and the other nations that lived in Italy came thither afterwards; nor can I discover that any other expedition more ancient than this came from Greece to the western parts of Europe. I am of the opinion that the Oenotrians, besides making themselves masters of many other regions in Italy, some of which they found unoccupied and others but thinly inhabited, also seized a portion of the country of the Umbrians, and that they were called Aborigines from their dwelling on the mountains [1] (for it is characteristic of the Arcadians to be fond of the mountains), in the same manner as at Athens some are called *Hyperakrioi*,[2] and others *Paralioi*.[3] But if any are naturally slow in giving credit to accounts of ancient matters without due examination, let them be slow also in believing the Aborigines to be Ligurians, Umbrians, or any other barbarians, and let them suspend their judgment till they have heard what remains to be told and then determine which opinion out of all is the most probable.

XIV. Of the cities first inhabited by the Aborigines few remained in my day; the greatest part of them, having been laid waste both by wars and other calamities, are abandoned. These cities were in the Reatine territory, not far from the Apennine

---

[1] A hybrid etymology : *ab* + ὄρος (mountain).
[2] People of the highlands.   [3] People of the coast.

Ἀπεννίνων ὀρῶν οὐ μακράν, ὡς Οὐάρρων¹ Τερέντιος
ἐν ἀρχαιολογίαις γράφει, ἀπὸ τῆς Ῥωμαίων πόλεως
αἳ τὸ βραχύτατον ἀπέχουσαι ἡμερήσιον διάστημα
ὁδοῦ · ὧν ἐγὼ τὰς ἐπιφανεστάτας, ὡς ἐκεῖνος
2 ἱστορεῖ, διηγήσομαι. Παλάτιον μὲν πέντε πρὸς
τοῖς εἴκοσι σταδίοις ἀφεστῶσα Ῥεάτου, πόλεως
οἰκουμένης ² ὑπὸ Ῥωμαίων ἔτι καὶ εἰς ἐμέ, Κοϊντίας
ὁδοῦ πλησίον. Τριβόλα ³ δὲ ἀμφὶ τοὺς ἑξήκοντα
σταδίους τῆς αὐτῆς πόλεως ἀφεστῶσα, λόφον ἐπι-
καθημένη σύμμετρον. Συεσβόλα ⁴ δὲ τὸ αὐτὸ
διάστημα τῆς Τριβόλας ἀπέχουσα, τῶν Κεραυνίων
ὀρῶν πλησίον. ἀπὸ δὲ ταύτης τετταράκοντα
σταδίοις διηρημένη πόλις ἐπιφανὴς Σούνα,⁵ ἔνθα
3 νεὼς πάνυ ἀρχαῖός ἐστιν Ἄρεος. Μήφυλα δὲ ὡς
τριάκοντα σταδίους ⁶ ἄπωθεν τῆς Σούνης · δείκνυται δὲ αὐτῆς ἐρείπιά τε καὶ τείχους ἴχνη.
τετταράκοντα δὲ σταδίους ἀπέχουσα Μηφύλης
Ὀρουΐνιον, εἰ καί τις ἄλλη τῶν αὐτόθι πόλεων
ἐπιφανὴς καὶ μεγάλη · δῆλοι γάρ εἰσιν αὐτῆς οἵ τε
θεμέλιοι τῶν τειχῶν καὶ τάφοι τινὲς ἀρχαιοπρεπεῖς
καὶ πολυανδρίων ἐν ὑψηλοῖς χώμασι μηκυνομένων

---

¹ Jacoby : βάρρων O.   ² πόλις οἰκουμένη Bunsen.
³ Τρηβούλα Cluver.
⁴ συεσβόλα AB : Συεσσόλα Sylburg.
⁵ Σοάνα Sylburg.   ⁶ Kiessling : σταδίοις O.

---

¹ This monumental work of antiquarian lore is no longer
extant. Varro was a native of Reate (49 Roman miles
north-east of Rome), and may well have taken a particular
interest in these old sites of the Aborigines. The latest
discussion of this chapter is to be found in Nissen, *Italische
Landeskunde*, ii. 1, pp. 471-6 ; Bunsen's article appeared

mountains, as Terentius Varro writes in his *Antiqui-*
ties,[1] the nearest being one day's journey distant from
Rome. I shall enumerate the most celebrated of
them, following his account. Palatium, twenty-five
stades distant from Reate (a city that was still inhabited by Romans down to my time),[2] near the
Quintian Way.[3] Tribula, about sixty stades from
Reate and standing upon a low hill. Suesbula, at
the same distance from Tribula, near the Ceraunian
Mountains. Suna, a famous city forty stades from
Suesbula ; in it there is a very ancient temple of
Mars. Mefula, about thirty stades from Suna ; its
ruins and traces of its walls are pointed out. Or-
vinium, forty stades from Mefula, a city as famous
and large as any in that region ; for the foundations of its walls are still to be seen and some tombs
of venerable antiquity, as well as the circuits of
burying-places [4] extending over lofty mounds ; and

in the *Annali dell' Instituto di Corrispondenza Archeologica*,
vi. (1834), pp. 129 ff. See also Smith's *Dict. of Greek and
Roman Geography*, *s.v.* Aborigines.

[2] Bunsen emended the text so as to make the clause
here included in parentheses refer to Palatium ; he held
that Reate was too well known to call for such an explanation.

[3] The Via Quintia is not elsewhere mentioned, but seems
to have been the more direct of two roads leading down
the valley to the north-west of Reate. The names of the
towns that immediately follow are probably corruptions
of Trebula and Suessula. The Ceraunian Mountains are
tentatively identified by Nissen with the Monte Rotondo
of to-day.

[4] The word *polyandrion* usually means a place where
many are buried together ; it is contrasted, as here, with
individual tombs by Aelian, *Var. Hist.* xii. 21, and Pausanias ii. 22, 9.

DIONYSIUS OF HALICARNASSUS

περίβολοι· ἔνθα καὶ νεὼς Ἀθηνᾶς ἐστιν ἀρχαῖος,
ἱδρυμένος ἐπὶ τῆς ἄκρας.

4 Ἀπὸ δὲ σταδίων ὀγδοήκοντα Ῥεάτου τοῖς
ἰοῦσι διὰ τῆς Κουρίας¹ ὁδοῦ παρὰ Κόρητον² ὄρος
Κόρσουλα³ νεωστὶ διεφθαρμένη. δείκνυται δέ τις
καὶ νῆσος, Ἴσσα αὐτῇ ὄνομα, λίμνη περίρρυτος, ἣν
χωρὶς ἐρύματος ποιητοῦ κατοικῆσαι λέγονται τοῖς
τέλμασι τῆς λίμνης ὁπόσα τείχεσι χρώμενοι.
πλησίον δὲ τῆς Ἴσσης Μαρούιον ἐπὶ τῷ μυχῷ
τῆς αὐτῆς λίμνης κειμένη, τετταράκοντα σταδίους
ἀπέχουσα τῶν καλουμένων Ἑπτὰ ὑδάτων.

5 Ἀπὸ δὲ Ῥεάτου πάλιν τοῖς⁴ τὴν ἐπὶ Λιστίνην⁵
ὁδὸν ἰοῦσι⁶ Βατία μὲν ἀπὸ τριάκοντα σταδίων,
Τιῶρα δὲ ἀπὸ τριακοσίων, ἡ καλουμένη Ματιήνη.

¹ Κουρίας Chaupy, Ἰουλίας Portus, Οὐαλερίας Sylburg,
Σαλαρίας Gelenius: ἰουρίας O.
² Κόριτον Cluver.
³ Καρσούλα Cluver.
⁴ τοῖς Kiessling: om. O, Jacoby.
⁵ Nissen: λιτίνην A, λατίνην R; λίμνην Bunsen.
⁶ ἰοῦσι Kiessling: ἰοῦσιν ἡ O.

¹ The Via Curia is thought to have been a second road
leading north-west from Reate but running round the
east and north sides of the chain of small lakes called by
the collective name of Lacus Velinus or Palus Reatina.
M'. Curius Dentatus in 272 drained the lowlands at the
northern end of the valley, and he may well have constructed this road at that time. Mount Coretus is unknown. The Maruvium here named is not to be confused
with the Marsian capital on the Fucine Lake. Cicero
mentions the Septem Aquae in a letter to Atticus (iv. 15, 5).

² This reading is due to Nissen, who believes that Listina
(the district of Lista) was an earlier name for the district of
Amiternum. In view of the story related at the end of the

there is also an ancient temple of Minerva built on the summit.

At the distance of eighty stades from Reate, as one goes along the Curian Way [1] past Mount Coretus, stood Corsula, a town but recently destroyed. There is also pointed out an island, called Issa, surrounded by a ake; the Aborigines are said to have lived on this island without any artificial fortification, relying on the marshy waters of the lake instead o: walls. Near Issa is Maruvium, situated on an arm of the same lake and distant forty stades from what they call the Septem Aquae.

Again, as one goes from Reate by the road towards the Listine district,[2] there is Batia,[3] thirty stades distant; then Tiora, called Matiene, at a distance of

chapter Lista must have been fairly close to Amiternum, which was 33 miles east of Reate. The vulgate reading with Λατίνην, "the road to Latium" or possibly "to the Latin Way," has been taken to mean a road leading south-east from Reate towards the Fucine Lake, and Bunsen's emendation λίμνην was designed to make that direction still plainer. But the site, a few miles north-west of that lake, which various scholars have selected for Lista is more than 20 miles distant from Amiternum across a mountain pass; moreover, it lies in the country of the Aequians, which is not reported to have been occupied by the Sabines at any time. Nissen's view likewise places Lista distinctly outside the Reatine territory. But it is quite possible that the distance of 300 stades assigned to Tiora is seriously in error; we might then look for Tiora and Lista a little east of Interocreum, or somewhat more than half-way from Reate to Amiternum. Nissen unjustifiably assumes that in this entire section Dionysius is counting the stade as only one-tenth of a Roman mile, instead of one-eighth of a mile, as he usually does.

[3] Or Vatia.

DIONYSIUS OF HALICARNASSUS

ἐν ταύτῃ λέγεται χρηστήριον Ἄρεος γενέσθαι πάνυ
ἀρχαῖον. ὁ δὲ τρόπος αὐτοῦ παραπλήσιος ἦν ὡς
φασι τῷ παρὰ Δωδωναίοις μυθολογουμένῳ ποτὲ
γενέσθαι· πλὴν ὅσον ἐκεῖ μὲν ἐπὶ δρυὸς ἱερᾶς
πέλεια¹ καθεζομένη θεσπιῳδεῖν ἐλέγετο, παρὰ δὲ
τοῖς Ἀβοριγῖσι θεόπεμπτος ὄρνις, ὃν αὐτοὶ μὲν
πῖκον, Ἕλληνες δὲ δρυοκολάπτην καλοῦσιν, ἐπὶ
6 κίονος ξυλίνου φαινόμενος τὸ αὐτὸ ἔδρα. τέτταρας δ' ἐπὶ τοῖς εἴκοσι σταδίοις ἀπέχουσα τῆς
εἰρημένης πόλεως Λίστα, μητρόπολις Ἀβοριγίνων,
ἣν παλαίτερον ἔτι Σαβῖνοι νύκτωρ ἐπιστρατεύσαντες
ἐκ πόλεως Ἀμιτέρνης ἀφύλακτον αἱροῦσιν· οἱ δ' ἐκ
τῆς ἁλώσεως περισωθέντες ὑποδεξαμένων αὐτοὺς
Ῥεατίνων, ὡς πολλὰ πειραθέντες οὐχ οἷοί τε ἦσαν
ἀπολαβεῖν, ἱερὰν ἀνῆκαν ὡς σφετέραν ἔτι τὴν γῆν,
ἐξαγίστους ποιήσαντες ἀραῖς τοὺς καρπωσομένους
αὐτὴν ὕστερον.

XV. Ἀπὸ δὲ σταδίων ἑβδομήκοντα Ῥεάτου
Κοτυλία πόλις ἐπιφανὴς πρὸς ὄρει κειμένη· ἧς
ἔστιν οὐ πρόσω λίμνη τεττάρων πλέθρων ἔχουσα
τὴν διάστασιν, αὐθιγενοῦς πλήρης νάματος ἀπορ-
ρέοντος ἀεί, βάθος ὡς λέγεται ἄβυσσος. ταύτην

¹ πέλεια added here by Jacoby, after καθεζομένη by
Sintenis; περιστερὰ added by Steph.

---

¹ At Dodona the god was said to dwell in the stem of an
oak and to reveal his will from the branches of the tree,
probably by the rustling of the leaves. In the time of
Herodotus the oracles were interpreted by two or three
aged women called πελειάδες or πέλειαι, both terms
meaning "pigeons." According to some it was actually
a pigeon that delivered the oracles.

48

three hundred stades. In this city, they say there was a very ancient oracle of Mars, the nature of which was similar to that of the oracle which legend says once existed at Dodona; only there a pigeon was said to prophesy, sitting on a sacred oak,[1] whereas among the Aborigines a heaven-sent bird, which they call *picus* and the Greeks *dryokolaptês*,[2] appearing on a pillar of wood, did the same. Twenty-four stades from the afore-mentioned city[3] stood Lista, the mother-city of the Aborigines, which at a still earlier time the Sabines had captured by a surprise attack, having set out against it from Amiternum by night. Those who survived the taking of the place, after being received by the Reatines, made many attempts to retake their former home, but being unable to do so, they consecrated the country to the gods, as if it were still their own, invoking curses against those who should enjoy the fruits of it.

XV. Seventy stades from Reate stood Cutilia,[4] a famous city, beside a mountain. Not far from it there is a lake, four hundred feet in diameter, filled by everflowing natural springs and, it is said, bottomless. This lake, as having something divine about

[2] Both the Greek and Latin words mean "woodpecker."

[3] The context certainly suggests Tiora as the city referred to; but Holstenius understood Reate, and thus brought Lista between Cutilia and Reate, where the name Monte di Lesta is found to-day.

[4] Also called Cutiliae. Its approximate site is determined by the remains of Aquae Cutiliae near by, a watering-place that was especially favoured by the Flavian emperors. It lay east of Reate, on the road last mentioned, if Nissen's identification of that road is correct. He suggests that the place is mentioned last, out of its natural order, in view of the important rôle the lake was to play later (see chap. 19).

ἔχουσάν τι θεοπρεπὲς ἱερὰν τῆς Νίκης οἱ ἐπιχώριοι
νομίζουσι καὶ περιείρξαντες κύκλῳ σταυρώμασι[1]
τοῦ μηδένα τῷ νάματι πελάζειν ἄβατον φυλάττουσιν,
ὅτι μὴ καιροῖς τισιν ἐτησίοις,[2] ἐν οἷς ἱερὰ θύουσιν ἃ
νόμος ἐπιβαίνοντες τῆς ἐν αὐτῇ νησῖδος οἷς ὅσιον.
2 ἡ δὲ νῆσός ἐστι μὲν ὡσπερὰν πεντήκοντα ποδῶν
τὴν διάμετρον, ὑπερανέστηκε δὲ τοῦ νάματος οὐ
πλεῖον ἢ ποδιαῖον ὕψος· ἀνίδρυτος δ' ἐστὶ καὶ
περινήχεται πολλαχῇ δινοῦντος αὐτὴν ἄλλοτε κατ'
ἄλλους τόπους ἠρέμα τοῦ πνεύματος. χλόη δέ τις
ἐν αὐτῇ φύεται βουτόμῳ προσεμφερὴς καὶ θάμνοι
τινὲς οὐ μεγάλοι, πρᾶγμα κρεῖττον λόγου τοῖς
ἀθεάτοις ὧν ἡ φύσις δρᾷ καὶ θαυμάτων οὐδενὸς
δεύτερον.

XVI. Τὴν μὲν δὴ πρώτην οἴκησιν οἱ Ἀβοριγῖνες
ἐν τούτοις λέγονται ποιήσασθαι τοῖς τόποις, ἐξελά-
σαντες ἐξ αὐτῶν Ὀμβρικούς. ἐντεῦθεν δὲ ὁρμώμενοι τοῖς τε ἄλλοις βαρβάροις καὶ πάντων μάλιστα
Σικελοῖς ὁμοτέρμοσιν οὖσιν ὑπὲρ τῆς χώρας ἐπολέμουν, τὸ μὲν πρῶτον ἱερά τις ἐξελθοῦσα νεότης,
ἄνδρες ὀλίγοι κατὰ βίου ζήτησιν ὑπὸ τῶν γειναμένων
ἀποσταλέντες, ἔθος ἐκπληροῦντες ἀρχαῖον, ᾧ πολλοὺς βαρβάρων τε καὶ Ἑλλήνων ἐπίσταμαι χρησα-
2 μένους. ὁπότε γὰρ εἰς ὄχλου πλῆθος ἐπίδοσιν
αἱ πόλεις τισὶ λάβοιεν ὥστε μηκέτι τὰς οἰκείας

---

[1] Smit : στέμμασι O, Jacoby.
[2] τισιν ἐτησίοις B : τισι διετησίοις R, Jacoby.

it, the inhabitants of the country look upon as sacred
to Victory; and surrounding it with a palisade, so
that no one may approach the water, they keep it
inviolate; except that at certain times each year
those whose sacred office it is go to the little island
in the lake and perform the sacrifices required by
custom. This island is about fifty feet in diameter
and rises not more than a foot above the water;
it is not fixed, and floats about in any direction,
according as the wind gently wafts it from one
place to another. An herb grows on the island
like the flowering rush and also certain small shrubs,
a phenomenon which to those who are unacquainted
with the works of Nature seems unaccountable and
a marvel second to none.[1]

XVI. The Aborigines are said to have settled first
in these places after they had driven out the
Umbrians. And making excursions from there,
they warred not only upon the barbarians in general
but particularly upon the Sicels, their neighbours,
in order to dispossess them of their lands. First,
a sacred band of young men went forth, consisting
of a few who were sent out by their parents to seek
a livelihood, according to a custom which I know
many barbarians and Greeks have followed.[2] For
whenever the population of any of their cities
increased to such a degree that the produce of their

---

[1] The fullest account and explanation of this strange
islet is given by Seneca (*Nat. Quaest.* iii. 25, 8). The lake
is still to be seen, but the islet has disappeared.

[2] The only recorded instance from the Greek world is that
of the Chalcidians, who dedicated to Apollo one man in
every ten and sent them to Delphi; these men later
founded Rhegium (Strabo vi. 1, 6). Compare chap. 24 and
note.

τροφὰς ἅπασιν εἶναι διαρκεῖς, ἢ κακωθεῖσα ταῖς
οὐρανίοις μεταβολαῖς ἡ γῆ σπανίους τοὺς εἰωθότας
καρποὺς ἐξενέγκειεν,[1] ἢ τοιόνδε τι πάθος ἄλλο τὰς
πόλεις κατασχὸν εἴτε ἄμεινον εἴτε χεῖρον ἀνάγκην
ἐπιστήσειε μειώσεως τοῦ πλήθους, θεῶν ὅτῳ δὴ
καθιεροῦντες ἀνθρώπων ἐτείους γονὰς ἐξέπεμπον
ὅπλοις κοσμήσαντες ἐκ τῆς σφετέρας· εἰ μὲν ὑπὲρ
εὐανδρίας ἢ νίκης ἐκ πολέμου χαριστήρια θεοῖς
ἀποδιδοῖεν, προθύοντες ἱερὰ τὰ νομιζόμενα, εὐφήμοις
οἰωνοῖς τὰς ἀποικίας προπέμποντες· εἰ δ' ἐπὶ μηνί-
μασι δαιμονίοις ἀπαλλαγὰς αἰτούμενοι τῶν κατεχόντων σφᾶς κακῶν τὸ παραπλήσιον δρῷεν, αὐτοί
τε ἀχθόμενοι καὶ συγγνώμονας ἀξιοῦντες γενέσθαι
3 τοὺς ἀπελαυνομένους. οἱ δὲ ἀπαναστάντες ὡς
οὐκέτι τῆς πατρῴας γῆς μεταληψόμενοι, εἰ μὴ
κτήσαιντο ἑτέραν, τὴν ὑποδεξαμένην αὐτοὺς εἴτε
πρὸς φιλίαν εἴτε ἐν πολέμῳ κρατηθεῖσαν πατρίδα
ἐποιοῦντο· ὅ τε θεός, ᾧ κατονομασθεῖεν ἀπελαυνό-
μενοι, συλλαμβάνειν αὐτοῖς ὡς τὰ πολλὰ ἐδόκει καὶ
παρὰ τὴν ἀνθρωπίνην δόξαν κατορθοῦν τὰς ἀποικίας.
4 τούτῳ δὴ τῷ νόμῳ χρώμενοι καὶ τότε τῶν Ἀβοριγίνων τινὲς ἀνθούντων ἀνδράσι τῶν χωρίων (κτείνειν
γὰρ οὐδένα τῶν ἐκγόνων ἠξίουν, ἄγος [2] οὐδενὸς ἔλαττον τοῦτο τιθέμενοι), θεῶν ὅτῳ δὴ καθιερώσαντες
ἐνιαυσίους γονὰς ἀνδρωθέντας ἀποικίζουσι τοὺς
παῖδας ἐκ τῆς σφετέρας, οἳ τοὺς Σικελοὺς ἄγοντές
τε καὶ φέροντες διετέλουν, ἐπειδὴ τὴν ἑαυτῶν ἐξέ-

---

[1] Jacoby: ἐξήνεγκεν O.
[2] ἄγος R: ἄγους B, Jacoby.

52

lands no longer sufficed for them all, or the earth, injured by unseasonable changes of the weather, brought forth her fruits in less abundance than usual, or any other occurrence of like nature, either good or bad, introduced a necessity of lessening their numbers, they would dedicate to some god or other all the men born within a certain year, and providing them with arms, would send them out of their country. If, indeed, this was done by way of thanksgiving for populousness or for victory in war, they would first offer the usual sacrifices and then send forth their colonies under happy auspices; but if, having incurred the wrath of Heaven, they were seeking deliverance from the evils that beset them, they would perform much the same ceremony, but sorrowfully and begging forgiveness of the youths they were sending away. And those who departed, feeling that henceforth they would have no share in the land of their fathers but must acquire another, looked upon any land that received them in friendship or that they conquered in war as their country. And the god to whom they had been dedicated when they were sent out seemed generally to assist them and to prosper the colonies beyond all human expectation. In pursuance, therefore, of this custom some of the Aborigines also at that time, as their places were growing very populous (for they would not put any of their children to death, looking on this as one of the greatest of crimes), dedicated to some god or other the offspring of a certain year and when these children were grown to be men they sent them out of their country as colonists; and they, after leaving their own land, were

5 λιπον. ὡς δ᾽ ἅπαξ οὗτοι χωρίων τινῶν τῆς πολε-
μίας ἐκράτησαν, ἐκ τοῦ ἀσφαλεστέρου ἤδη καὶ οἱ
λοιποὶ Ἀβοριγῖνες οἱ δεόμενοι γῆς κατὰ σφᾶς
ἕκαστοι ἐπεχείρουν τοῖς ὁμόροις καὶ πόλεις ἔκτισαν
ἄλλας τέ τινας καὶ τὰς μέχρι τοῦδε οἰκουμένας,
Ἀντεμνάτας καὶ Τελληνεῖς καὶ Φικολνέους τοὺς
πρὸς τοῖς καλουμένοις Κορνίκλοις ὄρεσι καὶ Τιβουρ-
τίνους, παρ᾽ οἷς ἔτι καὶ εἰς τόδε χρόνου μέρος τι
τῆς πόλεως ὀνομάζεται Σικελικόν· καὶ ἦσαν ἁπάντων μάλιστα τῶν προσοικούντων λυπηροὶ τοῖς
Σικελοῖς. ἀνίσταται δὲ ἐκ τούτων τῶν διαφορῶν
τοῖς ἔθνεσιν ὅλοις πόλεμος ὅσος οὐδεὶς τῶν πρότερον γενομένων ἐν Ἰταλίᾳ, καὶ προῆλθεν ἄχρι
πολλοῦ χρόνου[1] μηκυνόμενος.

XVII. Ἔπειτα Πελασγῶν τινες τῶν οἰκούντων
ἐν τῇ καλουμένῃ νῦν Θετταλίᾳ τὴν ἑαυτῶν ἀναγ-
κασθέντες ἐκλιπεῖν σύνοικοι γίνονται τοῖς Ἀβοριγῖσι
καὶ κοινῇ μετ᾽ ἐκείνων ἐπολέμουν πρὸς τοὺς Σικελούς. ἐδέξαντο δὲ αὐτοὺς οἱ Ἀβοριγῖνες, ἴσως μὲν
καὶ κατὰ τὴν τοῦ ὠφεληθήσεσθαι ἐλπίδα, ὡς δ᾽
2 ἐγὼ πείθομαι κατὰ τὸ συγγενὲς μάλιστα. ἦν
γὰρ δὴ καὶ τὸ τῶν Πελασγῶν γένος Ἑλληνικὸν ἐκ
Πελοποννήσου τὸ ἀρχαῖον, ἐχρήσατο δὲ τύχαις
δυσπότμοις εἰς πολλὰ μὲν καὶ ἄλλα, μάλιστα δ᾽
εἰς τὴν πολύπλανόν τε καὶ οὐδενὸς τόπου βέβαιον
οἴκησιν· πρῶτον μὲν γὰρ περὶ τὸ καλούμενον νῦν
Ἀχαϊκὸν Ἄργος ᾤκησαν αὐτόχθονες ὄντες, ὡς οἱ
πολλοὶ περὶ αὐτῶν λέγουσι. τὴν δὲ ἐπωνυμίαν
ἔλαβον ἐξ ἀρχῆς ταύτην ἐπὶ Πελασγοῦ[2] βασιλέως.

[1] πολλοῦ χρόνου Kiessling: πόρρω χρόνῳ O.

54

continually plundering the Sicels. And as soon as they became masters of any places in the enemy's country the rest of the Aborigines, also, who needed lands now attacked each of them their neighbours with greater security and built various cities, some of which are inhabited to this day—Antemnae, Tellenae, Ficulea, which is near the Corniculan mountains, as they are called, and Tibur, where a quarter in the city is even to this day called the Sicel quarter [1]; and of all their neighbours they harassed the Sicels most. From these quarrels there arose a general war between the nations more important than any that had occurred previously in Italy, and it went on extending over a long period of time.

XVII. Afterwards some of the Pelasgians who inhabited Thessaly, as it is now called, being obliged to leave their country, settled among the Aborigines and jointly with them made war upon the Sicels. It is possible that the Aborigines received them partly in the hope of gaining their assistance, but I believe it was chiefly on account of their kinship; for the Pelasgians, too, were a Greek nation originally from the Peloponnesus. They were unfortunate in many ways but particularly in wandering much and in having no fixed abode. For they first lived in the neighbourhood of the Achaean Argos, as it is now called, being natives of the country, according to most accounts. They received their name originally from Pelasgus, their king. Pelasgus was the

[2] Cary : τοῦ Πελασγοῦ O, Jacoby.

---

[1] This would presumably be *vicus Siculus* or *regio Sicula* in Latin ; no mention of the quarter is found elsewhere.

3 ἦν δὲ ὁ Πελασγὸς ἐκ Διός, ὡς λέγεται, καὶ
Νιόβης τῆς Φορωνέως, ᾗ πρώτῃ γυναικὶ θνητῇ
μίσγεται ὁ Ζεὺς ὡς ὁ μῦθος ἔχει. ἕκτῃ δ᾽ ὕστερον
γενεᾷ Πελοπόννησον ἐκλιπόντες εἰς τὴν τότε μὲν
Αἱμονίαν, νῦν δὲ Θετταλίαν ὀνομαζομένην μετανέ-
στησαν· ἡγοῦντο δὲ τῆς ἀποικίας Ἀχαιὸς καὶ Φθῖος
καὶ Πελασγὸς οἱ Λαρίσης καὶ Ποσειδῶνος υἱοί
ἀφικόμενοι δ᾽ εἰς τὴν Αἱμονίαν τούς τε κατοικοῦντας
ἐν αὐτῇ βαρβάρους ἐξελαύνουσι καὶ νέμονται τὴν
χώραν τριχῇ, τοῖς ἡγεμόσι ποιήσαντες ὁμωνύμους
τὰς μοίρας, Φθιῶτιν καὶ Ἀχαΐαν καὶ Πελασγιῶτιν.
πέντε δὲ μείναντες αὐτόθι γενεάς, ἐν αἷς ἐπὶ μήκιστον εὐτυχίας ἤλασαν τὰ κράτιστα τῶν ἐν τῇ
Θετταλίᾳ πεδίων καρπούμενοι, περὶ τὴν ἕκτην
γενεὰν ἐξελαύνονται Θετταλίας ὑπό τε Κουρήτων
καὶ Λελέγων, οἳ νῦν Αἰτωλοὶ καὶ Λοκροὶ καλοῦνται,
καὶ συχνῶν ἄλλων τῶν περὶ τὸν Παρνασὸν οἰκούντων, ἡγουμένου τῶν πολεμίων Δευκαλίωνος τοῦ
Προμηθέως, μητρὸς δὲ Κλυμένης τῆς Ὠκεανοῦ.

XVIII. Σκεδασθέντες δὲ κατὰ τὴν φυγὴν οἱ μὲν
εἰς Κρήτην ἀπῆλθον, οἱ δὲ τῶν Κυκλάδων νήσων
τινὰς κατέσχον, οἱ δὲ τὴν[1] περὶ τὸν Ὄλυμπόν τε
καὶ τὴν Ὄσσαν, καλουμένην δὲ Ἑστιαιῶτιν ᾤκισαν,
ἄλλοι δὲ εἴς τε Βοιωτίαν καὶ Φωκίδα καὶ Εὔβοιαν
διεκομίσθησαν· οἱ δ᾽ εἰς τὴν Ἀσίαν περαιωθέντες
τῆς περὶ τὸν Ἑλλήσποντον παραλίου πολλὰ χωρία
κατέσχον καὶ τῶν παρακειμένων αὐτῇ νήσων ἄλλας
τε συχνὰς καὶ τὴν νῦν καλουμένην Λέσβον, ἀναμιχθέντες τοῖς ἐκ τῆς Ἑλλάδος στέλλουσι τὴν πρώτην

[1] τὴν added by Ritschl.

son of Zeus, it is said, and of Niobê, the daughter of Phoroneus, who, as the legend goes, was the first mortal woman Zeus had knowledge of. In the sixth generation afterwards, leaving the Peloponnesus, they removed to the country which was then called Haemonia and now Thessaly. The leaders of the colony were Achaeus, Phthius and Pelasgus, the sons of Larisa and Poseidon. When they arrived in Haemonia they drove out the barbarian inhabitants and divided the country into three parts, calling them, after the names of their leaders, Phthiotis, Achaia and Pelasgiotis. After they had remained there five generations, during which they attained to the greatest prosperity while enjoying the produce of the most fertile plains in Thessaly, about the sixth generation they were driven out of it by the Curetes and Leleges, who are now called Aetolians and Locrians, and by many others who lived near Parnassus, their enemies being commanded by Deucalion, the son of Prometheus and Clymenê, the daughter of Oceanus.

XVIII. And dispersing themselves in their flight, some went to Crete, others occupied some of the islands called the Cyclades, some settled in the region called Hestiaeotis near Olympus and Ossa, others crossed into Boeotia, Phocis and Euboea; and some, passing over into Asia, occupied many places on the coast along the Hellespont and many of the adjacent islands, particularly the one now called Lesbos, uniting with those who composed the first colony that was sent thither from Greece under

57

ἀποικίαν εἰς αὐτὴν ἄγοντος Μάκαρος τοῦ Κρινάκου.[1]
2 τὸ δὲ πλεῖον αὐτῶν μέρος διὰ τῆς μεσογείου τραπόμενοι πρὸς τοὺς ἐν Δωδώνῃ κατοικοῦντας σφῶν
συγγενεῖς, οἷς οὐδεὶς ἠξίου πόλεμον ἐπιφέρειν ὡς
ἱεροῖς, χρόνον μέν τινα σύμμετρον αὐτόθι διέτριψαν·
ἐπεὶ δὲ λυπηροὶ αὐτοῖς ὄντες ᾐσθάνοντο οὐχ ἱκανῆς
οὔσης ἅπαντας τρέφειν τῆς γῆς, ἐκλείπουσι τὴν
χώραν χρησμῷ πειθόμενοι κελεύοντι πλεῖν εἰς
3 Ἰταλίαν, ἣ τότε Σατορνία ἐλέγετο. κατασκευασάμενοι δὲ ναῦς πολλὰς περαιοῦνται τὸν Ἰόνιον,
σπουδὴν μὲν ποιούμενοι τῶν ἔγγιστα τῆς Ἰταλίας
ἅψασθαι χωρίων· ὑπὸ δὲ νοτίου πνεύματος καὶ
ἀγνοίας τῶν τόπων μετεωρότεροι ἐνεχθέντες καὶ
πρὸς ἑνὶ τῶν τοῦ Πάδου στομάτων ὁρμισάμενοι
Σπινῆτι καλουμένῳ τὰς [2] ναῦς μὲν αὐτοῦ ταύτῃ
καταλείπουσι καὶ τὸν ἥκιστα δυνάμενον ταλαιπωρεῖν
ὄχλον, φυλακὴν ἐπ' αὐταῖς [3] καταστήσαντες, ὡς
ἔχοιεν εἰ μὴ προχωροίη σφίσι τὰ πράγματα κατα-
4 φυγήν. καὶ οἱ μὲν ὑπομείναντες ἐν τούτῳ τῷ
χωρίῳ, τεῖχος τῷ στρατοπέδῳ περιβαλόμενοι καὶ
ταῖς ναυσὶν εἰσκομίσαντες τὰς εἰς τὸν βίον εὐπορίας,
ἐπειδὴ κατὰ γνώμην ἐδόκει χωρεῖν αὐτοῖς τὰ πράγματα, πόλιν ἔκτισαν ὁμώνυμον τῷ στόματι τοῦ
ποταμοῦ· εὐτύχησάν τε [4] μάλιστα τῶν περὶ τὸν
Ἰόνιον οἰκούντων θαλαττοκρατοῦντες ἄχρι πολλοῦ,

---

[1] Κρινάκου Wesseling, Κριάσου Sylburg, Jacoby: κιρασίου
B, κριασίου R.
[2] τὰς ναῦς Hertlein: ναῦς O, Jacoby.
[3] ἐπ' αὐταῖς Madvig: ἐπ' αὐτοὺς A, αὐτοῦ B.
[4] εὐτύχησάν τε Steph.: εὐτυχήσαντες O.

Macar, the son of Crinacus.[1] But the greater part
of them, turning inland, took refuge among the
inhabitants of Dodona, their kinsmen, against
whom, as a sacred people, none would make war ;
and there they remained for a reasonable time.
But when they perceived they were growing burden-
some to their hosts, since the land could not support
them all, they left it in obedience to an oracle that
commanded them to sail to Italy, which was then called
Saturnia. And having prepared a great many ships
they set out to cross the Ionian Gulf, endeavouring
to reach the nearest parts of Italy. But as the wind
was in the south and they were unacquainted with
those regions, they were carried too far out to sea
and landed at one of the mouths of the Po called
the Spinetic mouth. In that very place they left their
ships and such of their people as were least able
to bear hardships, placing a guard over the ships,
to the end that, if their affairs did not prosper,
they might be sure of a retreat. Those who were
left behind there surrounded their camp with a
wall and brought in plenty of provisions in their
ships ; and when their affairs seemed to prosper
satisfactorily, they built a city and called it by the
same name as the mouth of the river.[2] These
people attained to a greater degree of prosperity
than any others who dwelt on the Ionian Gulf ; for
they had the mastery at sea for a long time, and

[1] This is the form of the name given by Diodorus
(v. 81) and others ; the son's name usually appears as
Macareus.
[2] In reality it was, of course, the town Spina that gave
its name to the ostium Spineticum.

καὶ δεκάτας εἰς Δελφοὺς ἀνῆγον τῷ θεῷ[1] τῶν ἀπὸ
τῆς θαλάττης ὠφελειῶν, εἴπερ τινὲς καὶ ἄλλοι,
5 λαμπροτάτας. ὕστερον μέντοι μεγάλῃ χειρὶ τῶν
προσοικούντων βαρβάρων ἐπιστρατευσάντων αὐτοῖς
ἐξέλιπον τὴν πόλιν· οἱ δὲ βάρβαροι μετὰ χρόνον
ἀνέστησαν ὑπὸ Ῥωμαίων. καὶ τὸ μὲν ἐν τῷ
Σπινῆτι καταλειφθὲν γένος τῶν Πελασγῶν οὕτως
ἐφθάρη.

XIX. Οἱ δὲ διὰ τῆς μεσογείου τραπόμενοι, τὴν
ὀρεινὴν τῆς Ἰταλίας ὑπερβαλόντες, εἰς τὴν Ὀμβρικῶν ἀφικνοῦνται χώραν τῶν ὁμορούντων Ἀβοριγῖσι.
πολλὰ δὲ καὶ ἄλλα χωρία τῆς Ἰταλίας ᾤκουν Ὀμ-
βρικοί, καὶ ἦν τοῦτο τὸ ἔθνος ἐν τοῖς πάνυ μέγα τε
καὶ ἀρχαῖον. τὸ μὲν οὖν κατ' ἀρχὰς ἐκράτουν οἱ
Πελασγοὶ τῶν χωρίων ἔνθα τὸ πρῶτον ἱδρύσαντο
καὶ πολισμάτια τῶν Ὀμβρικῶν κατελάβοντό τινα·
συνελθόντος δ' ἐπ' αὐτοὺς μεγάλου στρατοῦ δεί-
σαντες τῶν πολεμίων τὸ πλῆθος εἰς τὴν Ἀβοριγί-
2 νων ἀπιόντες τρέπονται. καὶ οἱ μὲν Ἀβοριγῖνες
ἅτε πολεμίοις ἐδικαίουν αὐτοῖς προσφέρεσθαι καὶ
συνῄεσαν ἐκ τῶν ἔγγιστα χωρίων διὰ τάχους ὡς
ἐξαναστήσοντες αὐτούς. οἱ δὲ Πελασγοί (τυγχάνουσι γὰρ ἐν τούτῳ τῷ χρόνῳ κατὰ δαίμονα περὶ
Κοτυλίαν πόλιν Ἀβοριγίνων αὐλισάμενοι πλησίον
τῆς ἱερᾶς λίμνης) ὡς δὴ[2] τήν τε νησῖδα τὴν ἐν
αὐτῇ περιδινουμένην κατέμαθον καὶ παρὰ τῶν
αἰχμαλώτων, οὓς ἐκ τῶν ἀγρῶν ἔλαβον, ἤκουσαν
τὸ τῶν ἐπιχωρίων ὄνομα, τέλος ἔχειν σφίσι τὸ

---

[1] καὶ after θεῷ deleted by Reiske.
[2] δὴ Ambrosch : δὲ O, Jacoby ; deleted by Reudler.

out of their revenues from the sea they used to send tithes to the god at Delphi, which were among the most magnificent sent by any people. But later, when the barbarians in the neighbourhood made war upon them in great numbers, they deserted the city ; and these barbarians in the course of time were driven out by the Romans. So perished that part of the Pelasgians that was left at Spina.

XIX. Those, however, who had turned inland crossed the mountainous part of Italy and came to the territory of the Umbrians who were neighbours to the Aborigines. (The Umbrians inhabited a great many other parts of Italy also and were an exceeding great and ancient people.) At first the Pelasgians made themselves masters of the lands where they first settled and took some of the small towns belonging to the Umbrians. But when a great army came together against them, they were terrified at the number of their enemies and betook themselves to the country of the Aborigines. And these, seeing fit to treat them as enemies, made haste to assemble out of the places nearest at hand, in order to drive them out of the country. But the Pelasgians luckily chanced to be encamped at that time near Cutilia, a city of the Aborigines hard by the sacred lake, and observing the little island circling round in it and learning from the captives they had taken in the fields the name of the inhabitants, they concluded that their oracle was now fulfilled.

3 θεοπρόπιον ὑπέλαβον. ὁ γὰρ ἐν Δωδώνῃ γενόμενος αὐτοῖς χρησμός, ὃν φησι Λεύκιος Μάλλιος[1]
ἀνὴρ οὐκ ἄσημος αὐτὸς ἰδεῖν ἐπί τινος τῶν ἐν τῷ
τεμένει τοῦ Διὸς κειμένων τριπόδων γράμμασιν
ἀρχαίοις ἐγκεχαραγμένον, ὡδὶ εἶχε·

στείχετε μαιόμενοι Σικελῶν[2] Σατόρνιον[3] αἶαν
ἠδ' Ἀβοριγινέων Κοτύλην, οὗ νᾶσος ὀχεῖται·
οἷς ἀναμιχθέντες δεκάτην ἐκπέμψατε Φοίβῳ
καὶ κεφαλὰς Κρονίδῃ[4] καὶ τῷ πατρὶ πέμπετε φῶτα.

XX. Ἐλθοῦσι δὴ τοῖς Ἀβοριγῖσι σὺν πολλῇ
στρατιᾷ ἱκετηρίας οἱ Πελασγοὶ προτείνοντες ὁμόσε
χωροῦσιν ἄνοπλοι φράζοντές τε τὰς ἑαυτῶν τύχας
καὶ δεόμενοι πρὸς φιλίαν δέξασθαι σφᾶς συνοίκους
οὐ λυπηροὺς ἐσομένους, ἐπεὶ καὶ τὸ δαιμόνιον
αὐτοὺς εἰς τήνδε μόνην ἄγει τὴν χώραν, ἐξηγού-
2 μενοι τὸ λόγιον. τοῖς δὲ Ἀβοριγῖσι ταῦτα πυθομένοις ἐδόκει πείθεσθαι τῷ θεοπροπίῳ καὶ λαβεῖν
συμμαχίαν Ἑλληνικὴν κατὰ τῶν διαφόρων σφίσι
βαρβάρων, καταπονουμένοις[5] τῷ πρὸς τοὺς Σικελοὺς
πολέμῳ. σπένδονταί τε δὴ πρὸς τοὺς Πελασγοὺς

[1] Sylburg : μάμιος AB.   [2] σικελοὶ AB.
[3] Sylburg, σατούρνιον Macrobius : σατορνίαν A, σατουρνίαν B.
[4] κρονίδη O : ᾄδη Macrobius.
[5] Cobet : πονουμένοις O.

---

[1] Or Manlius. Nothing is known of the man beyond
what may be inferred from the present passage.

[2] A poetic variant of Cotylia, the Greek form of Cutilia.

[3] Varro's version of this story is quoted by Macrobius
(i. 7, 28 ff.). In the last verse of the oracle he has Ἅιδῃ for

For this oracle, which had been delivered to them in Dodona and which Lucius Mallius,[1] no obscure man, says he himself saw engraved in ancient characters upon one of the tripods standing in the precinct of Zeus, was as follows :

" Fare forth the Sicels' Saturnian land to seek,
    Aborigines' Cotylê,[2] too, where floats an isle ;
  With these men mingling, to Phoebus send a
      tithe,
    And heads to Cronus' son, and send to the sire
      a man." [3]

XX. When, therefore, the Aborigines advanced with a numerous army, the Pelasgians approached unarmed with olive branches in their hands, and telling them of their own fortunes, begged that they would receive them in a friendly manner to dwell with them, assuring them that they would not be troublesome, since Heaven itself was guiding them into this one particular country according to the oracle, which they explained to them. When the Aborigines heard this, they resolved to obey the oracle and to gain these Greeks as allies against their barbarian enemies, for they were hard pressed by their war with the Sicels. They accordingly made a treaty with the Pelasgians and assigned to them

Κρονίδῃ. He says the oracle was at first taken to call for human heads as an offering to Dis and the sacrifice of men to Saturn. But several generations later Hercules taught the people a more humane interpretation : to Dis they should offer little images made in the likeness of men and Saturn should be honoured with lighted candles, since φῶτα meant " light " as well as " man."

καὶ διδόασιν αὐτοῖς χωρία τῆς ἑαυτῶν ἀποδασά-
μενοι τὰ περὶ τὴν ἱερὰν λίμνην, ἐν οἷς ἦν τὰ πολλὰ
ἑλώδη, ἃ νῦν κατὰ τὸν ἀρχαῖον τῆς διαλέκτου τρόπον
3 Οὐέλια ὀνομάζεται. σύνηθες γὰρ ἦν τοῖς ἀρχαίοις
Ἕλλησιν ὡς τὰ πολλὰ προτιθέναι τῶν ὀνομάτων,
ὁπόσων αἱ ἀρχαὶ ἀπὸ φωνηέντων ἐγίνοντο, τὴν ου
συλλαβὴν ἑνὶ στοιχείῳ γραφομένην. τοῦτο δ᾽ ἦν
ὥσπερ γάμμα διτταῖς ἐπὶ μίαν ὀρθὴν ἐπιζευγνύμενον
ταῖς πλαγίοις, ὡς Ϝελένη καὶ Ϝάναξ καὶ Ϝοῖκος
4 καὶ Ϝέαρ [1] καὶ πολλὰ τοιαῦτα. ἔπειτα μοῖρά τις
αὐτῶν οὐκ ἐλαχίστη, ὡς ἡ γῆ πᾶσιν οὐκ ἀπέχρη,
πείσαντες τοὺς Ἀβοριγῖνας συνάρασθαί σφισι τῆς
ἐξόδου στρατεύουσιν ἐπὶ τοὺς Ὀμβρικοὺς καὶ πόλιν
αὐτῶν εὐδαίμονα καὶ μεγάλην ἄφνω προσπεσόντες
αἱροῦσι Κρότωνα· ταύτῃ φρουρίῳ καὶ ἐπιτειχίσματι
κατὰ τῶν Ὀμβρικῶν χρώμενοι, κατεσκευασμένῃ τε
ὡς ἔρυμα εἶναι πολέμου ἀποχρώντως καὶ χώραν
ἐχούσῃ τὴν πέριξ εὔβοτον, πολλῶν καὶ ἄλλων
ἐκράτησαν χωρίων τοῖς τε Ἀβοριγῖσι τὸν πρὸς τοὺς
Σικελοὺς πόλεμον ἔτι συνεστῶτα πολλῇ προθυμίᾳ
συνδιέφερον, ἕως ἐξήλασαν αὐτοὺς ἐκ τῆς σφετέ-
5 ρας. καὶ πόλεις πολλάς, τὰς μὲν οἰκουμένας καὶ
πρότερον ὑπὸ τῶν Σικελῶν, τὰς δ᾽ αὐτοὶ κατασκευάσαντες, ᾤκουν οἱ Πελασγοὶ κοινῇ μετὰ τῶν
Ἀβοριγίνων, ὧν ἐστιν ἥ τε Καιρητανῶν πόλις,
Ἄγυλλα δὲ τότε καλουμένη, καὶ Πῖσα καὶ Σατορνία

---

[1] Ϝέαρ Cary, Ϝαρήν Naber: Ϝὰήρ B(?), Jacoby, Ϝάνήρ A.

---

[1] This letter, vau, later called digamma, has actually
been found in numerous early inscriptions from various

some of their own lands that lay near the sacred
lake ; the greater part of these were marshy and
are still called Velia, in accordance with the ancient
form of their language. For it was the custom of
the ancient Greeks generally to place before those
words that began with a vowel the syllable ου,
written with one letter (this was like a gamma,
formed by two oblique lines joined to one upright
line), as Ϝελένη, Ϝάναξ, Ϝοῖκος, Ϝέαρ and many
such words.[1] Afterwards, a considerable part of the
Pelasgians, as the land was not sufficient to support
them all, prevailed on the Aborigines to join them in
an expedition against the Umbrians, and marching
forth, they suddenly fell upon and captured Croton, a
rich and large city of theirs. And using this place
as a stronghold and fortress against the Umbrians,
since it was sufficiently fortified as a place of defence in time of war and had fertile pastures lying
round it, they made themselves masters also of a
great many other places and with great zeal assisted
the Aborigines in the war they were still engaged
in against the Sicels, till they drove them out of
their country. And the Pelasgians in common
with the Aborigines settled many cities, some of
which had been previously inhabited by the Sicels
and others which they built themselves ; among these
are Caere, then called Agylla, and Pisae, Saturnia,

parts of Greece ; its value was that of the Latin *v*, or
English *w*. See Kühner-Blass, *Griech. Gram.* i. 1, § 16 f.
Dionysius assumes that Velia is an early form of ἔλεια
(" marshy "). In his day the Latin *v* was usually represented in Greek by ου, sometimes by β.

καὶ Ἄλσιον καὶ ἄλλαι τινὲς, ἃς ἀνὰ χρόνον ὑπὸ Τυρρηνῶν ἀφῃρέθησαν.

XXI. Φαλέριον δὲ καὶ Φασκέννιον ἔτι καὶ εἰς ἐμὲ ἦσαν οἰκούμεναι ὑπὸ Ῥωμαίων, μίκρ' ἄττα δια- σώζουσαι ζώπυρα τοῦ Πελασγικοῦ γένους, Σικελῶν ὑπάρχουσαι πρότερον. ἐν ταύταις διέμεινε πολλὰ τῶν ἀρχαίων διαιτημάτων, οἷς τὸ Ἑλληνικόν ποτ' ἐχρήσατο, ἐπὶ μήκιστον χρόνον, οἷον ὅ τε τῶν ὅπλων τῶν πολεμιστηρίων κόσμος, ἀσπίδες Ἀργο- λικαὶ καὶ δόρατα, καὶ ὁπότε πολέμου ἄρχοντες ἢ τοὺς ἐπιόντας ἀμυνόμενοι στρατὸν ὑπερόριον [1] ἀπο- στέλλοιεν ἱεροί τινες ἄνδρες ἄνοπλοι πρὸ τῶν ἄλλων ἰόντες σπονδοφόροι, τῶν τε ἱερῶν αἱ κατασκευαὶ καὶ τὰ ἕδη τῶν θεῶν ἁγισμοί τε καὶ θυσίαι καὶ 2 πολλὰ τοιαῦτα ἕτερα· πάντων δὲ περιφανέστατον μνημεῖον τῆς ἐν Ἄργει ποτὲ οἰκήσεως τῶν ἀνθρώ- πων ἐκείνων οἳ τοὺς Σικελοὺς ἐξήλασαν, ὁ τῆς Ἥρας νεὼς ἐν Φαλερίῳ κατεσκευασμένος ὡς ἐν Ἄργει, ἔνθα καὶ τῶν θυηπολιῶν ὁ τρόπος ὅμοιος ἦν καὶ γυναῖκες ἱεραὶ θεραπεύουσαι τὸ τέμενος ἥ τε λεγομένη κανηφόρος ἁγνὴ γάμων παῖς καταρ- χομένη τῶν θυμάτων χοροί τε παρθένων ὑμνουσῶν 3 τὴν θεὸν ᾠδαῖς πατρίοις. ἔσχον δέ τινα καὶ οὗτοι τῶν καλουμένων Καμπανῶν εὐβότων πάνυ καὶ τὴν ὄψιν ἡδίστων πεδίων οὐκ ἐλαχίστην μοῖραν, ἔθνος τι βαρβαρικὸν Αὐρωνίσσους [2] ἐκ μέρους ἀνα-

---

[1] ὑπερόριον Kiessling: ὑπὲρ τῶν ὅρων O.
[2] Αὐρώγκους or Αὐρούγ:ους Sylburg, Portus.

---

[1] The *fetiales* ; see ii. 72.

Alsium and some others, of which they were in the course of time dispossessed by the Tyrrhenians.

XXI. But Falerii and Fescennium were even down to my day inhabited by Romans and preserved some small remains of the Pelasgian nation, though they had earlier belonged to the Sicels. In these cities there survived for a very long time many of the ancient customs formerly in use among the Greeks, such as the fashion of their arms of war, like Argolic bucklers and spears; and whenever they sent out an army beyond their borders, either to begin a war or to resist an invasion, certain holy men, unarmed, went ahead of the rest bearing the terms of peace [1]; similar, also, were the structure of their temples, the images of their gods, their purifications and sacrifices and many other things of that nature. But the most conspicuous monument which shows that those people who drove out the Sicels once lived at Argos is the temple of Juno at Falerii, built in the same fashion as the one at Argos; here, too, the manner of the sacrificial ceremonies was similar, holy women served the sacred precinct, and an unmarried girl, called the *canephorus* or "basket-bearer," performed the initial rites of the sacrifices, and there were choruses of virgins who praised the goddess in the songs of their country. These people also possessed themselves of no inconsiderable part of the Campanian plains, as they are called, which afford not only very fertile pasturage but most pleasing prospects as well, having driven the Auronissi,[2] a barbarous

[2] The name occurs nowhere else and is very probably a corruption of Aurunci.

στήσαντες αὐτῶν καὶ πόλεις αὐτόθι κατεσκεύασαν
ἄλλας τε καὶ Λάρισαν,[1] ἐπὶ τῆς ἐν Πελοποννήσῳ
4 σφῶν μητροπόλεως ὄνομα θέμενοι αὐτῇ. τῶν μὲν
οὖν ἄλλων πολισμάτων ἔστιν ἃ καὶ μέχρις ἐμοῦ
ὀρθὰ ἦν, διαμείψαντα πολλάκις τοὺς οἰκήτορας· ἡ
δὲ Λάρισα ἐκ πολλῶν πάνυ χρόνων ἐρημωθεῖσα
οὐδ' εἰ πώποτε ᾠκήθη[2] γνώρισμα φανερὸν οὐδὲν
ἔχει τοῖς νῦν ὅτι μὴ τοὔνομα, καὶ οὐδὲ τοῦτο πολλοὶ
ἴσασιν· ἦν δὲ ἀγορᾶς Ποπιλίας καλουμένης οὐ
πρόσω. πολλὰ δὲ καὶ ἄλλα τῆς τε παραθαλαττίου
καὶ ἐν τῇ μεσογείῳ χωρία κατέσχον ἀφελόμενοι
τοὺς Σικελούς.

XXII. Οἱ δὲ Σικελοὶ (οὐ γὰρ ἔτι ἀντέχειν οἷοί
τε ἦσαν ὑπό τε Πελασγῶν καὶ Ἀβοριγίνων πολεμού-
μενοι) τέκνα καὶ γυναῖκας καὶ τῶν χρημάτων ὅσα
χρυσὸς ἢ ἄργυρος ἦν ἀνασκευασάμενοι μεθίενται
αὐτοῖς ἁπάσης τῆς γῆς. τραπόμενοι δὲ διὰ τῆς
ὀρεινῆς ἐπὶ τὰ νότια καὶ διεξελθόντες ἅπασαν
Ἰταλίαν τὴν κάτω, ἐπειδὴ πανταχόθεν ἀπηλαύνοντο, σὺν χρόνῳ κατασκευασάμενοι σχεδίας ἐπὶ
τῷ πορθμῷ καὶ φυλάξαντες κατιόντα τὸν ῥοῦν
ἀπὸ τῆς Ἰταλίας διέβησαν ἐπὶ τὴν ἔγγιστα νῆσον.
2 κατεῖχον δ' αὐτὴν Σικανοί, γένος Ἰβηρικόν, οὐ
πολλῷ πρότερον ἐνοικισάμενοι[3] Λίγυας φεύγοντες,
καὶ παρεσκεύασαν ἀφ' ἑαυτῶν Σικανίαν κληθῆναι
τὴν νῆσον, Τρινακρίαν πρότερον ὀνομαζομένην ἐπὶ

---

[1] Ritschl: λάρισσαν O (and similarly elsewhere).
[2] Kiessling: ᾠκίσθη O.
[3] Cobet: συνοικησάμενοι AB.

nation, out of part of them. There they built various other cities and also Larisa, which they named after their mother-city in the Peloponnesus. Some of these cities were standing even to my day, having often changed their inhabitants. But Larisa has been long deserted and shows to the people of to-day no other sign of its ever having been inhabited but its name,[1] and even this is not generally known. It was not far from the place called Forum Popilii.[2] They also occupied a great many other places, both on the coast and in the interior, which they had taken from the Sicels.

XXII. The Sicels, being warred upon by both the Pelasgians and the Aborigines, found themselves incapable of making resistance any longer, and so, taking with them their wives and children and such of their possessions as were of gold or silver, they abandoned all their country to these foes. Then, turning their course southward through the mountains, they proceeded through all the lower part of Italy, and being driven away from every place, they at last prepared rafts at the Strait and, watching for a downward current, passed over from Italy to the adjacent island. It was then occupied by the Sicanians, an Iberian nation, who, fleeing from the Ligurians, had but lately settled there and had caused the island, previously named Trinacria, from its

---

[1] Larisa originally meant " citadel." Places with this name, of which there were several in Greece and Asia, seem to have been of Pelasgic origin.

[2] This Forum Popilii was in the Falernian district at the northern end of the Campanian plain, a few miles south of Teanum.

DIONYSIUS OF HALICARNASSUS

τοῦ τριγώνου σχήματος. ἦσαν δὲ οὐ πολλοὶ νὲ
μεγάλῃ αὐτῇ οἰκήτορες, ἀλλ' ἡ πλείων τῆς χώρας
ἔτι ἦν ἔρημος. καταχθέντες οὖν εἰς αὐτὴν Σικελοὶ
τὸ μὲν πρῶτον ἐν τοῖς ἑσπερίοις μέρεσιν ᾤκησαν,
ἔπειτα καὶ ἄλλῃ πολλαχῇ, καὶ τοὔνομα ἡ νῆσος ἐπὶ
3 τούτων ἤρξατο Σικελία καλεῖσθαι. τὸ μὲν δὴ
Σικελικὸν γένος οὕτως ἐξέλιπεν Ἰταλίαν, ὡς μὲν
Ἑλλάνικος ὁ Λέσβιός φησι, τρίτῃ γενεᾷ πρότερον
τῶν Τρωικῶν Ἀλκυόνης ἱερωμένης ἐν Ἄργει κατὰ
τὸ ἕκτον καὶ εἰκοστὸν ἔτος. δύο δὲ [1] ποιεῖ στόλους
Ἰταλικοὺς διαβάντας εἰς Σικελίαν· τὸν μὲν πρότερον Ἐλύμων, οὓς φησιν ὑπ' Οἰνώτρων ἐξαναστῆναι, τὸν δὲ μετὰ τοῦτον ἔτει πέμπτῳ γενόμενον
Αὐσόνων Ἰάπυγας φευγόντων· βασιλέα δὲ τούτων
ἀποφαίνει Σικελόν, ἀφ' οὗ τοὔνομα τοῖς τε ἀνθρώ-
4 ποις καὶ τῇ νήσῳ τεθῆναι. ὡς δὲ Φίλιστος ὁ
Συρακούσιος γράφει,[2] χρόνος μὲν τῆς διαβάσεως
ἦν ἔτος ὀγδοηκοστὸν πρὸ τοῦ Τρωικοῦ πολέμου,
ἔθνος δὲ τὸ διακομισθὲν ἐξ Ἰταλίας οὔτε Αὐσόνων [3] οὔτ' Ἐλύμων, ἀλλὰ Λιγύων, ἄγοντος αὐτοὺς

---

[1] δὲ added by Ritschl.   [2] Kiessling: ἔγραψε O, Jacoby.
[3] Before οὔτε Αὐσόνων Stephanus inserted οὔτε Σικελῶν.
Kiessling was the first editor to bracket these words, which
appear in none of the MSS. By a strange inadvertence
Jacoby replaced them in the text, attributing them to
Kiessling !

---

[1] Hellanicus (fifth century), the most prominent of the
logographers, wrote histories of various Greek lands, including an *Atthis* for Attica and a *Phoronis* for Argos
(*cf.* chap. 28, 3), as well as accounts of the Trojan expedition and the Persian invasion.   He also compiled some
chronological lists, such as *The Priestesses of Hera at Argos*

70

triangular shape, to be called Sicania, after themselves. There were very few inhabitants in it for so
large an island, and the greater part of it was as yet
unoccupied. Accordingly, when the Sicels landed
there they first settled in the western parts and
afterwards in several others ; and from these people
the island began to be called Sicily. In this manner
the Sicel nation left Italy, according to Hellanicus of Lesbos,[1] in the third generation before the
Trojan war, and in the twenty-sixth year of the
priesthood of Alcyonê at Argos.[2] But he says that
two Italian expeditions passed over into Sicily, the
first consisting of the Elymians, who had been
driven out of their country by the Oenotrians, and
the second, five years later, of the Ausonians, who
fled from the Iapygians. As king of the latter
group he names Sicelus, from whom both the people
and the island got their name. But according to
Philistus of Syracuse[3] the date of the crossing was
the eightieth year before the Trojan war[4] and the
people who passed over from Italy were neither
Ausonians nor Elymians, but Ligurians, whose

(cf. chap. 72, 2), with the apparent purpose of devising
a scientific chronology. The present quotation appears
as frg. 53 in Müller, *F.H.G.* i. p. 52.

[2] Probably in the second quarter of the thirteenth century B.C. ; but it is not certain that Hellanicus is here
using the generation as a definite measure of time (usually
reckoned as one-third of a century). Unfortunately the
date of Alcyonê's priesthood is not known.

[3] Philistus (first half of fourth century) stood high in the
counsels of the elder Dionysius, for a time, and particularly
of the younger Dionysius. He was famous for his history
of Sicily, which closely imitated the style of Thucydides.
Müller, *F.H.G.* i. p. 185, frg. 2.   [4] *ca.* 1263 B.C.

Σικελοῦ· τοῦτον δ' εἶναί φησιν υἱὸν Ἰταλοῦ,
καὶ τοὺς ἀνθρώπους ἐπὶ τούτου δυναστεύοντος
5 ὀνομασθῆναι Σικελούς· ἐξαναστῆναι δ' ἐκ τῆς
ἑαυτῶν τοὺς Λίγυας ὑπό τε Ὀμβρικῶν καὶ Πελασγῶν. Ἀντίοχος δὲ ὁ Συρακούσιος χρόνον μὲν οὐ
δηλοῖ τῆς διαβάσεως, Σικελοὺς δὲ τοὺς μεταναστάντας ἀποφαίνει βιασθέντας ὑπό τε Οἰνώτρων
καὶ Ὀπικῶν, Στράτωνα¹ δ'² ἡγεμόνα τῆς ἀποικίας
ποιησαμένους. Θουκυδίδης δὲ Σικελοὺς μὲν εἶναι
γράφει τοὺς μεταναστάντας, Ὀπικοὺς δὲ τοὺς
ἐκβαλόντας, τὸν δὲ χρόνον πολλοῖς ἔτεσι τῶν
Τρωικῶν ὕστερον. τὰ μὲν δὴ περὶ Σικελῶν λεγόμενα τῶν ἐξ Ἰταλίας μετενεγκαμένων τὴν οἴκησιν
εἰς Σικελίαν ὑπὸ τῶν λόγου ἀξίων τοιάδε ἐστίν.

XXIII. Οἱ δὲ Πελασγοὶ πολλῆς καὶ ἀγαθῆς
χώρας κρατήσαντες, πόλεις τε πολλὰς μὲν παραλαβόντες,³ ἄλλας δ' αὐτοὶ κατασκευάσαντες, μεγάλην καὶ ταχεῖαν ἐπίδοσιν ἔλαβον εἰς εὐανδρίαν
καὶ πλοῦτον καὶ τὴν ἄλλην εὐτυχίαν, ἧς οὐ πολὺν
ὤναντο χρόνον· ἀλλ' ἡνίκα μάλιστα τοῖς σύμπασιν
ἀνθεῖν ἐδόκουν, δαιμονίοις τισὶ χόλοις ἐλαστρη-
θέντες οἱ μὲν ὑπὸ τῶν θείων συμφορῶν, οἱ δὲ ὑπὸ
τῶν προσοικούντων βαρβάρων ἐξεφθάρησαν, τὸ δὲ
πλεῖστον αὐτῶν μέρος εἰς τὴν Ἑλλάδα καὶ τὴν
βάρβαρον αὖθις ἐσκεδάσθη (περὶ ὧν πολὺς ἂν εἴη
λόγος, εἰ βουλοίμην τὴν ἀκρίβειαν γράφειν), ὀλίγον

---

¹ Στράτωνα Urlichs, Πάτρωνα Bernays, Συράκωνα Reiske:
στρατῶν O.
² δ' added by Reiske.
³ πόλεις . . . παραλαβόντες Ambrosch: πόλεις τε παρέλαβον
(προσέλαβον A) BA.

leader was Sicelus; this Sicelus, he says, was
the son of Italus and in his reign the people were
called Sicels, and he adds that these Ligurians had
been driven out of their country by the Umbrians
and Pelasgians. Antiochus of Syracuse[1] does not
give the date of the crossing, but says the people
who migrated were the Sicels, who had been forced
to leave by the Oenotrians and Opicans, and that
they chose Straton[2] as leader of the colony. But
Thucydides writes[3] that the people who left Italy
were the Sicels and those who drove them out the
Opicans, and that the date was many years after
the Trojan war. Such, then, are the reports
given by credible authorities concerning the Sicels
who changed their abode from Italy to Sicily.

XXIII. The Pelasgians, after conquering a large
and fertile region, taking over many towns and
building others, made great and rapid progress,
becoming populous, rich and in every way prosperous. Nevertheless, they did not long enjoy their
prosperity, but at the moment when they seemed
to all the world to be in the most flourishing condition they were visited by divine wrath, and some
of them were destroyed by calamities inflicted by
the hand of Heaven, others by their barbarian
neighbours; but the greatest part of them were
again dispersed through Greece and the country of
the barbarians (concerning whom, if I attempted
to give a particular account, it would make a very

[1] See p. 39, n. 2. Müller, *F.H.G.* i. p. 181, frg. 1.
[2] The name rests on conjecture. See critical note.
[3] vi. 2.

δὲ κατέμεινεν ἐν Ἰταλίᾳ τῶν Ἀβοριγίνων προνοίᾳ.
2 πρῶτον μὲν οὖν τῆς οἰκοφθορίας ταῖς πόλεσιν
ἐδόκει αὐχμῷ ἡ γῆ κακωθεῖσα ἄρξαι, ἡνίκα οὔτ᾽
ἐπὶ τοῖς δένδρεσι καρπὸς οὐδεὶς ὡραῖος γενέσθαι
διέμεινεν, ἀλλ᾽ ὠμοὶ κατέρρεον, οὔθ᾽ ὁπόσα σπερ-
μάτων ἀνέντα βλαστοὺς ἀνθήσειεν ἕως στάχυος
ἀκμῆς τοὺς κατὰ νόμον ἐξεπλήρου χρόνους, οὔτε
πόα κτήνεσιν ἐφύετο διαρκής, τῶν τε ναμάτων τὰ
μὲν οὐκέτι πίνεσθαι σπουδαῖα ἦν, τὰ δ᾽ ὑπελίμπανε
3 θέρους, τὰ δ᾽ εἰς τέλος ἀπεσβέννυτο. ἀδελφὰ δὲ
τούτοις ἐγίνετο περί τε προβάτων καὶ γυναικῶν
γονάς· ἢ γὰρ ἐξημβλοῦτο τὰ ἔμβρυα ἢ κατὰ τοὺς
τόκους διεφθείρετο ἔστιν ἃ καὶ τὰς φερούσας συν-
διαλυμηνάμενα. εἰ δέ τι διαφύγοι τὸν ἐκ τῶν
ὠδίνων κίνδυνον, ἔμπηρον ἢ ἀτελὲς ἢ δι᾽ ἄλλην τινὰ
τύχην βλαφθὲν τρέφεσθαι χρηστὸν οὐκ ἦν· ἔπειτα
καὶ τὸ ἄλλο πλῆθος τὸ ἐν ἀκμῇ μάλιστα ἐκακοῦτο
νόσοις καὶ θανάτοις παρὰ τὰ εἰκότα συχνοῖς.
4 μαντευομένοις δ᾽ αὐτοῖς τίνα θεῶν ἢ δαιμόνων
παραβάντες τάδε πάσχουσι καὶ τί ποιήσασιν αὐτοῖς
λωφῆσαι τὰ δεινὰ ἐλπίς, ὁ θεὸς ἀνεῖλεν ὅτι τυχόντες
ὧν ἐβούλοντο οὐκ ἀπέδοσαν ἃ εὔξαντο, ἀλλὰ προσ-
5 οφείλουσι τὰ πλείστου ἄξια. οἱ γὰρ Πελασγοὶ
ἀφορίας αὐτοῖς γενομένης ἐν τῇ γῇ πάντων χρημάτων εὔξαντο τῷ τε Διὶ καὶ τῷ Ἀπόλλωνι καὶ τοῖς

---

[1] Similar calamities are mentioned, much more briefly,
in Sophocles, Oed. Rex 25-27.

long story), though some few of them remained
in Italy through the care of the Aborigines. The first
cause of the desolation of their cities seemed to be
a drought which laid waste the land, when neither
any fruit remained on the trees till it was ripe,
but dropped while still green, nor did such of the
seed corn as sent up shoots and flowered stand for
the usual period till the ear was ripe, nor did sufficient grass grow for the cattle; and of the waters
some were no longer fit to drink, others shrank during
the summer, and others were totally dried up.
And like misfortunes attended the offspring both of
cattle and of women.[1] For they were either abortive
or died at birth, some by their death destroying
also those that bore them; and if any got safely
past the danger of their delivery, they were either
maimed or defective or, being injured by some other
accident, were not fit to be reared. The rest of the
people, also, particularly those in the prime of life,
were afflicted with many unusual diseases and un-
common deaths. But when they asked the oracle
what god or divinity they had offended to be thus
afflicted and by what means they might hope for
relief, the god answered that, although they had
obtained what they desired, they had neglected to
pay what they had promised, and that the things
of greatest value were still due from them. For the
Pelasgians in a time of general scarcity in the land
had vowed to offer[2] to Jupiter, Apollo and the

[2] The verbs καταθύσειν (here) and ἀπέθυσαν (just below) are
rendered by the ambiguous word " offer "; for, though
both are compounds of θύω (" sacrifice "), they sometimes
mean merely " dedicate " or " devote."

DIONYSIUS OF HALICARNASSUS

Καβείροις καταθύσειν δεκάτας τῶν προσγενησο-
μένων ἁπάντων, τελεσθείσης δὲ τῆς εὐχῆς ἐξελό-
μενοι καρπῶν τε καὶ βοσκημάτων ἁπάντων τὸ
λάχος ἀπέθυσαν τοῖς θεοῖς, ὡς δὴ κατὰ τούτων
μόνων εὐξάμενοι. ταῦτα δὴ Μυρσίλος ὁ Λέσβιος
ἱστόρηκεν ὀλίγου δεῖν τοῖς αὐτοῖς ὀνόμασι γράφων
οἷς ἐγὼ νῦν, πλὴν ὅσον οὐ Πελασγοὺς καλεῖ τοὺς
ἀνθρώπους. ἀλλὰ Τυρρηνούς· τὴν δ᾽ αἰτίαν ὀλίγον
ὕστερον ἐρῶ.

XXIV. Ὡς δὲ ἀπενεχθέντα τὸν χρησμὸν ἔμαθον,
οὐκ εἶχον τὰ λεγόμενα συμβαλεῖν. ἀμηχανοῦσι δὲ
αὐτοῖς τῶν γεραιτέρων τις λέγει συμβαλὼν τὸ
λόγιον, ὅτι τοῦ παντὸς ἡμαρτήκασιν, εἰ οἴονται
τοὺς θεοὺς ἀδίκως αὐτοῖς ἐγκαλεῖν. χρημάτων
μὲν γὰρ ἀποδεδόσθαι τὰς ἀπαρχὰς αὐτοῖς ἁπάσας
ὀρθῶς τε καὶ σὺν δίκῃ, ἀνθρώπων δὲ γονῆς τὸ
λάχος, χρῆμα παντὸς μάλιστα θεοῖς τιμιώτατον,
ὀφείλεσθαι· εἰ δὲ δὴ καὶ τούτων λάβοιεν τὴν δικαίαν
2 μοῖραν, τέλος ἕξειν σφίσι τὸ λόγιον. τοῖς μὲν
δὴ ὀρθῶς ἐδόκει λέγεσθαι ταῦτα, τοῖς δὲ ἐξ ἐπιβουλῆς συγκεῖσθαι ὁ λόγος· εἰσηγησαμένου δέ
τινος τὴν γνώμην τὸν θεὸν ἐπερέσθαι, εἰ αὐτῷ
φίλον ἀνθρώπων δεκάτας ἀπολαμβάνειν, πέμπουσι
τὸ δεύτερον θεοπρόπους, καὶ ὁ θεὸς ἀνεῖλεν οὕτω

---

[1] Myrsilus (first half of third century) composed a history
of Lesbos. This quotation is frg. 2 in Müller, *F.H.G.* iv.
pp. 456 f. [2] In chaps. 25 and 29.

[3] In a similar story related by Strabo (v. 4, 12) the Sabines
had vowed to dedicate all their increase of the year, and
learning, as the result of a famine that later befell them,
that they should have included their children, they dedi-

Cabeiri tithes of all their future increase; but when their prayer had been answered, they set apart and offered to the gods the promised portion of all their fruits and cattle only, as if their vow had related to them alone. This is the account related by Myrsilus of Lesbos,[1] who uses almost the same words as I do now, except that he does not call the people Pelasgians, but Tyrrhenians, of which I shall give the reason a little later.[2]

XXIV. When they heard the oracle which was brought to them, they were at a loss to guess the meaning of the message. While they were in this perplexity, one of the elders, conjecturing the sense of the saying, told them they had quite missed its meaning if they thought the gods complained of them without reason. Of material things they had indeed rendered to the gods all the first-fruits in the right and proper manner, but of human offspring, a thing of all others the most precious in the sight of the gods, the promised portion still remained due; if, however, the gods received their just share of this also, the oracle would be satisfied. There were, indeed, some who thought that he spoke aright, but others felt that there was treachery behind his words. And when some one proposed to ask the god whether it was acceptable to him to receive tithes of human beings, they sent their messengers a second time, and the god ordered them so to do.[3]

cated these to Mars, and when the children had grown up, sent them out as colonists. Dionysius has already narrated (in chap. 16) a like procedure on the part of the Aborigines. This form of vow, when it involved the increase of a particular year, was called a *ver sacrum*, as we

[Note continued on p. 79.

ποιεῖν. ἐκ δὲ τούτου στάσις αὐτοὺς καταλαμβάνει
περὶ τοῦ τρόπου τῆς δεκατεύσεως. καὶ ἐν ἀλλήλοις οἱ προεστηκότες τῶν πόλεων τὸ[1] πρῶτον
3 ἐταράχθησαν· ἔπειτα καὶ τὸ λοιπὸν πλῆθος δι᾽
ὑποψίας τοὺς ἐν τέλει ἐλάμβανεν. ἐγίνοντό τε
οὐδενὶ κόσμῳ ἀπαναστάσεις,[2] ἀλλ᾽ ὥσπερ εἰκὸς
οἴστρῳ καὶ θεοβλαβείᾳ ἀπελαυνόμεναι, καὶ πολλὰ
ἐφέστια ὅλα ἐξηλείφθη μέρους αὐτῶν μεθισταμένου·
οὐ γὰρ ἐδικαίουν οἱ προσήκοντες τοῖς ἐξιοῦσιν ἀπο-
λείπεσθαί τε τῶν φιλτάτων καὶ ἐν τοῖς ἐχθίστοις
4 ὑπομένειν. πρῶτοι μὲν δὴ οὗτοι μεταναστάντες
ἐξ Ἰταλίας εἴς τε τὴν Ἑλλάδα καὶ τῆς βαρβάρου
πολλὴν ἐπλανήθησαν. μετὰ δὲ τοὺς πρώτους ἕτεροι
τὸ αὐτὸ[3] ἔπαθον, καὶ τοῦτο διετέλει γινόμενον ὅσ᾽ ἔτη.
οὐ γὰρ ἀνίεσαν οἱ δυναστεύοντες ἐν ταῖς πόλεσι τῆς
ἀνδρουμένης ἀεὶ νεότητος ἐξαιρούμενοι τὰς ἀπαρχάς,
τοῖς τε θεοῖς τὰ δίκαια ὑπουργεῖν ἀξιοῦντες καὶ
στασιασμοὺς ἐκ τῶν διαλαθόντων[4] δεδιότες. ἦν
δὲ πολὺ καὶ τὸ πρὸς ἔχθραν σὺν προφάσει εὐπρεπεῖ

----

[1] τὸ Sintenis : τότε O.
[2] ἀπαναστάσεις A : αἱ ἐπαναστάσεις B ; αἱ ἀπαναστάσεις
Jacoby.
[3] τὸ αὐτὸ O : ταὐτὸν Jacoby.
[4] διαλαθόντων O : διαλαχόντων Sylburg, ἀεὶ λαχόντων Cobet.

Thereupon strife arose among them concerning the manner of choosing the tithes, and those who had the government of the cities first quarrelled among themselves and afterwards the rest of the people held their magistrates in suspicion. And there began to be disorderly emigrations, such as might well be expected from a people driven forth by a frenzy and madness inflicted by the hand of Heaven. Many households disappeared entirely when part of their members left; for the relations of those who departed were unwilling to be separated from their dearest friends and remain among their worst enemies. These, therefore, were the first to migrate from Italy and wander about Greece and many parts of the barbarian world ; but after them others had the same experience, and this continued every year. For the rulers in the cities ceased not to select the first-fruits of the youth as soon as they arrived at manhood, both because they desired to render what was due to the gods and also because they feared uprisings on the part of lurking enemies. Many, also, under specious

learn from Paulus Diaconus in his abridgment of Festus, p. 379. He states that it was a custom of the Italian peoples in times of dire peril to vow to sacrifice (*immolaturos*) all the living things that should be born to them during the following spring ; but that, since it seemed to them cruel to slay innocent boys and girls, they reared these and then drove them forth, with their heads veiled, beyond the boundaries. It is not altogether clear in the case of the Pelasgians what the fate of the human tithes was, whether mere expulsion or actual sacrifice. In favour of the former view may be urged the fact of their respite until they had grown up ; yet the violent disturbances that accompanied the selection of the tithes would seem to point to a more cruel fate.

ἀπελαυνόμενον ὑπὸ τῶν διαφόρων· ὥστε πολλαὶ αἱ
ἀπαναστάσεις[1] ἐγίνοντο καὶ ἐπὶ πλεῖστον γῆς τὸ
Πελασγικὸν γένος διεφορήθη.

XXV. Ἦσαν δὲ τά τε[2] πολέμια ἐκ τοῦ μετὰ
κινδύνων πεποιῆσθαι τὰς μελέτας ἐν ἔθνεσι φιλο-
πολέμοις ζῶντες πολλῶν ἀμείνους καὶ τῆς κατὰ τὰ
ναυτικὰ ἐπιστήμης διὰ τὴν μετὰ Τυρρηνῶν οἴκησιν
ἐπὶ πλεῖστον ἐληλακότες·[3] ἥ τε ἀνάγκη ἱκανὴ
οὖσα τοῖς ἀπορουμένοις βίου τόλμαν παρασχεῖν
ἡγεμών τε καὶ διδάσκαλος τοῦ παντὸς κινδυνεύματος αὐτοῖς ἐγίνετο, ὥστε οὐ χαλεπῶς ὅπῃ
2 ἐπέλθοιεν ἐπεκράτουν. ἐκαλοῦντο δὲ ὑπὸ τῶν
ἄλλων ἀνθρώπων τῆς τε χώρας ἐπικλήσει ἀφ' ἧς
ἐξανέστησαν καὶ τοῦ παλαιοῦ γένους μνήμῃ οἱ
αὐτοὶ Τυρρηνοὶ καὶ Πελασγοί. ὧν ἐγὼ λόγον
ἐποιησάμην τοῦ μή τινα θαῦμα ποιεῖσθαι, ἐπειδὰν
ποιητῶν ἢ συγγραφέων ἀκούῃ τοὺς Πελασγοὺς
καὶ Τυρρηνοὺς ὀνομαζόντων, πῶς ἀμφοτέρας ἔσχον
3 τὰς ἐπωνυμίας οἱ αὐτοί. ἔχει γὰρ περὶ αὐτῶν[4]
Θουκυδίδης μὲν ἐναργῆ Ἀκτῆς[5] τῆς Θρᾳκίας
μνήμην[6] καὶ τῶν ἐν αὐτῇ κειμένων πόλεων, ἃς
οἰκοῦσιν ἄνθρωποι δίγλωττοι. περὶ δὲ τοῦ Πελασγικοῦ ἔθνους ὅδε ὁ λόγος· '' ἔνι δέ τι καὶ Χαλκιδι-
κόν, τὸ δὲ πλεῖστον Πελασγικὸν τῶν καὶ Λῆμνόν

---

[1] ἀπαναστάσεις A: ἐπαναστάσεις B.
[2] τε placed after τά by Kiessling: after κινδύνων in B;
A omits.
[3] Steph.[2]: ἀπολελαυκότες O.
[4] περὶ αὐτῶν A: καὶ περὶ αὐτῶν B; περ. αὐτῶν καὶ Ritschl,
Jacoby.

pretences were being driven away by their enemies through hatred; so that there were many emigrations and the Pelasgian nation was scattered over most of the earth.

XXV. Not only were the Pelasgians superior to many in warfare, as the result of their training in the midst of dangers while they lived among warlike nations, but they also rose to the highest proficiency in seamanship, by reason of their living with the Tyrrhenians; and Necessity, which is quite sufficient to give daring to those in want of a livelihood, was their leader and director in every dangerous enterprise, so that wherever they went they conquered without difficulty. And the same people were called by the rest of the world both Tyrrhenians and Pelasgians, the former name being from the country out of which they had been driven and the latter in memory of their ancient origin. I mention this so that no one, when he hears poets or historians call the Pelasgians Tyrrhenians also, may wonder how the same people got both these names. Thus, with regard to them, Thucydides has a clear account [1] of the Thracian Actê and of the cities situated in it, which are inhabited by men who speak two languages. Concerning the Pelasgian nation these are his words: " There is also a Chalcidian element among them, but the largest element is Pelasgian.

[1] iv. 109.

---

[5] ἐναργῆ ἀκτῆς Jacoby: ἐν ἀρκτηι A, ἐν ἀρκτῆι $\overset{\chi\eta}{B}$.

[6] μνήμην Steph.: μνήμηι A, μνήμη B; λέγει γὰρ . . . ἐν 'Ακτῆς τ. Θ. μνήμῃ Sauppe.

4 ποτε καὶ Ἀθήνας οἰκησάντων Τυρρηνῶν." Σο-
φοκλεῖ δ' ἐν Ἰνάχῳ δράματι ἀνάπαιστον ὑπὸ τοῦ
χοροῦ λεγόμενον πεποίηται ὧδε

Ἴναχε νᾶτορ,[1] παῖ τοῦ κρηνῶν
πατρὸς, Ὠκεανοῦ, μέγα πρεσβεύων
Ἄργους τε γύαις Ἥρας τε πάγοις
καὶ Τυρσηνοῖσι[2] Πελασγοῖς.

5 Τυρρηνίας μὲν γὰρ δὴ ὄνομα τὸν χρόνον ἐκεῖνον
ἀνὰ τὴν Ἑλλάδα ἦν, καὶ πᾶσα ἡ προσεσπέριος
Ἰταλία τὰς κατὰ τὸ ἔθνος ὀνομασίας ἀφαιρεθεῖσα
τὴν[3] ἐπίκλησιν ἐκείνην ἐλάμβανεν, ὥσπερ καὶ[4] τῆς
Ἑλλάδος ἄλλη τε πολλαχῇ καὶ περὶ τὴν καλουμένην
νῦν Πελοπόννησον ἐγένετο· ἐπὶ γὰρ ἑνὸς τῶν
οἰκούντων ἐν αὐτῇ ἐθνῶν, τοῦ Ἀχαϊκοῦ, καὶ ἡ
σύμπασα χερρόνησος, ἐν ᾗ καὶ τὸ Ἀρκαδικὸν καὶ
τὸ Ἰωνικὸν καὶ ἄλλα συχνὰ ἔθνη ἔνεστιν, Ἀχαΐα
ὠνομάσθη.

XXVI. Ὁ δὲ χρόνος ἐν ᾧ τὸ Πελασγικὸν κα-
κοῦσθαι ἤρξατο δευτέρα γενεᾷ[5] σχεδὸν πρὸ τῶν
Τρωικῶν ἐγένετο· διέτεινε δὲ καὶ μετὰ τὰ Τρωικά,
ἕως εἰς ἐλάχιστον συνεστάλη τὸ ἔθνος. ἔξω γὰρ
Κρότωνος τῆς ἐν Ὀμβρικοῖς πόλεως ἀξιολόγου,
καὶ εἰ δή τι ἄλλο ἐν τῇ Ἀβοριγίνων οἰκισθὲν
ἐτύγχανε, τὰ λοιπὰ τῶν Πελασγῶν διεφθάρη πολί-
σματα. ἡ δὲ Κρότων ἄχρι πολλοῦ διαφυλάξασα
τὸ παλαιὸν σχῆμα χρόνος οὐ πολὺς ἐξ οὗ τήν τε

[1] Meineke : νάτορ Ba, γεννάτορ ABb.
[2] Meineke : τυρρηνοῖς AB.
[3] τὴν Ambrosch : καὶ τὴν O.
[4] καὶ added by Reiske.   [5] δευτέρα γενεᾶ B.

belonging to the Tyrrhenians who once inhabited
Lemnos and Athens." And Sophocles makes the
chorus in his drama *Inachus* speak the following
anapaestic verses :

" O fair-flowing Inachus, of Ocean begot,
   That sire of all waters, thou rulest with might
   O'er the Argive fields and Hera's hills
   And Tyrrhene Pelasgians also." [1]

For the name of Tyrrhenia was then known throughout Greece, and all the western part of Italy was
called by that name, the several nations of which
it was composed having lost their distinctive appel-
lations. The same thing happened to many parts of
Greece also, and particularly to that part of it which
is now called the Peloponnesus ; for it was after one
of the nations that inhabited it, namely the Achaean,
that the whole peninsula also, in which are comprised
the Arcadian, the Ionian and many other nations,
was called Achaia.

XXVI. The time when the calamities of the
Pelasgians began was about the second generation
before the Trojan war ; and they continued to
occur even after that war, till the nation was
reduced to very inconsiderable numbers. For,
with the exception of Croton, the important city in
Umbria,[2] and any others that they had founded in
the land of the Aborigines, all the rest of the Pelasgian towns were destroyed. But Croton long preserved its ancient form, having only recently changed

---

[1] Nauck, *T.G.F.*[2], p. 189, frg. 248.
[2] See chap. 20, 4.

ὀνομασίαν καὶ τοὺς οἰκήτορας ἤλλαξε· καὶ νῦν ἐστι
2 Ῥωμαίων ἀποικία, καλεῖται δὲ Κορθωνία. οἱ
δὲ τῶν ἐκλιπόντων τὴν χώραν Πελασγῶν κατασχόντες τὰς πόλεις ἄλλοι τε πολλοὶ ἦσαν, ὡς
ἕκαστοί τισιν ἔτυχον ὁμοτέρμονας τὰς οἰκήσεις
ἔχοντες, καὶ ἐν τοῖς μάλιστα πλείστας τε καὶ
ἀρίστας Τυρρηνοί. τοὺς δὲ Τυρρηνοὺς οἱ μὲν
αὐτόχθονας Ἰταλίας ἀποφαίνουσιν, οἱ δὲ ἐπήλυδας·
καὶ τὴν ἐπωνυμίαν αὐτοῖς ταύτην οἱ μὲν αὐθιγενὲς
τὸ ἔθνος ποιοῦντες ἐπὶ τῶν ἐρυμάτων, ἃ πρῶτοι
τῶν τῇδε οἰκούντων κατεσκευάσαντο, τεθῆναι λέ-
γουσι· τύρσεις γὰρ καὶ παρὰ Τυρρηνοῖς αἱ ἐν-
τείχιοι καὶ στεγαναὶ οἰκήσεις ὀνομάζονται ὥσπερ
παρ᾽ Ἕλλησιν   ἀπὸ δὴ τοῦ συμβεβηκότος αὐτοῖς
ἀξιοῦσι τεθῆναι τοὔνομα, ὥσπερ καὶ τοῖς ἐν Ἀσίᾳ
Μοσσυνοίκοις·[1] οἰκοῦσι μὲν γὰρ δὴ κἀκεῖνοι ἐπὶ
ξυλίνοις ὡσπερὰν πύργοις ὑψηλοῖς σταυρώμασι,
μόσσυνας[2] αὐτὰ καλοῦντες.

XXVII. Οἱ δὲ μετανάστας μυθολογοῦντες αὐτοὺς
εἶναι Τυρρηνὸν ἀποφαίνουσιν ἡγεμόνα τῆς ἀποικίας
γενόμενον ἀφ᾽ ἑαυτοῦ θέσθαι τῷ ἔθνει τοὔνομα·
τοῦτον δὲ Λυδὸν εἶναι τὸ γένος ἐκ τῆς πρότερον
Μηονίας καλουμένης, παλαιὸν δή τινα μετανάστην
ὄντα·[3] εἶναι δ᾽ αὐτὸν πέμπτον ἀπὸ Διός, λέγοντες
ἐκ Διὸς καὶ Γῆς Μάνην[4] γενέσθαι πρῶτον ἐν τῇ γῇ
ταύτῃ βασιλέα· τούτου δὲ καὶ Καλλιρρόης[5] τῆς

[1] τοῖς . . μοσσυνοίκοις B: τοὺς . . . μοσυνοίκους A.
[2] μόσσυνας B: μόσυνας R.
[3] μετανάστην ὄντα Sintenis: μεταναστάντα O.
[4] Sylburg: μάνην O (and similarly in § 3).
[5] Cary: Καλλιρόης O, Jacoby.

both its name and inhabitants ; it is now a Roman
colony, called Corthonia.[1] After the Pelasgians left
the country their cities were seized by the various
peoples which happened to live nearest them in
each case, but chiefly by the Tyrrhenians, who made
themselves masters of the greatest part and the best
of them. As regards these Tyrrhenians, some declare them to be natives of Italy, but others call
them foreigners. Those who make them a native
race say that their name was given them from the
forts, which they were the first of the inhabitants
of this country to build ; for covered buildings
enclosed by walls are called by the Tyrrhenians as
well as by the Greeks *tyrseis* or " towers." [2] So they
will have it that they received their name from this
circumstance in like manner as did the Mossynoeci [3]
in Asia ; for these also live in high wooden palisades
resembling towers, which they call *mossynes*.

XXVII. But those who relate a legendary tale
about their having come from a foreign land say
that Tyrrhenus, who was the leader of the colony,
gave his name to the nation, and that he was a Lydian
by birth, from the district formerly called Maeonia,
and migrated in ancient times. They add that he
was the fifth in descent from Zeus ; for they say the
son of Zeus and Gê was Manes, the first king of that
country, and his son by Callirrhoê, the daughter

[1] *i.e.* Cortona. Compare the name Corythus used by
Virgil (*Aen.* iii. 170).

[2] The form *Tyrrhênoi* is the Attic development of
Tyrsênoi, the form used by most of the Greeks.

[3] This people lived on the shore of the Euxine, a short
distance west of Trapezus. Xenophon mentions them in
the *Anabasis* (v. 4).

DIONYSIUS OF HALICARNASSUS

Ὠκεανοῦ θυγατρὸς γεννηθῆναι Κότυν· τῷ δὲ Κότυϊ
γήμαντι θυγατέρα Τύλλου τοῦ γηγενοῦς Ἁλίην δύο
2 γενέσθαι παῖδας Ἀσίην καὶ Ἄτυν· ἐκ δὲ Ἄτυος
καὶ Καλλιθέας τῆς Χωραίου Λυδὸν φῦναι καὶ Τυρ-
ρηνόν· καὶ τὸν μὲν Λυδὸν αὐτοῦ καταμείναντα τὴν
πατρῴαν ἀρχὴν παραλαβεῖν καὶ ἀπ' αὐτοῦ Λυδίαν
τὴν γῆν ὀνομασθῆναι· Τυρρηνὸν δὲ τῆς ἀποικίας
ἡγησάμενον πολλὴν κτήσασθαι τῆς Ἰταλίας καὶ
τοῖς συναραμένοις τοῦ στόλου ταύτην θέσθαι τὴν
3 ἐπωνυμίαν. Ἡροδότῳ δὲ εἴρηνται[1] Ἄτυος τοῦ
Μάνεω παῖδες οἱ περὶ Τυρρηνόν, καὶ ἡ μετανάστασις
τῶν Μηόνων εἰς Ἰταλίαν οὐχ ἑκούσιος. φησὶ γὰρ
ἐπὶ τῆς Ἄτυος ἀρχῆς ἀφορίαν καρπῶν ἐν τῇ γῇ
Μηόνων γενέσθαι, τοὺς δὲ ἀνθρώπους τέως μὲν
ὑπὸ τῆς φιλοχωρίας κρατουμένους πολλὰ διαμη-
χανήσασθαι πρὸς τὴν συμφορὰν ἀλεξητήρια, τῇ μὲν
ἑτέρᾳ τῶν ἡμερῶν μέτρια σιτία προσφερομένους,
τῇ δ' ἑτέρᾳ διακαρτεροῦντας· χρονίζοντος δὲ τοῦ
δεινοῦ δεινείμαντας ἅπαντα τὸν δῆμον διχῇ[2] κλήρους[3] ταῖς μοίραις ἐπιβαλεῖν, τὸν μὲν ἐπ' ἐξόδῳ
τῆς χώρας, τὸν δ' ἐπὶ μονῇ, καὶ τῶν Ἄτυος παίδων
4 τὸν μὲν τῇ προσνεῖμαι, τὸν δὲ τῇ.[4] λαχούσης δὲ
τῆς ἅμα Λυδῷ μοίρας τὴν τοῦ μεῖναι τύχην,[5] ἐκ-
χωρῆσαι τὴν ἑτέραν ἀπολαχοῦσαν τῶν χρημάτων

---

[1] Reiske: εἴρηται O; εἴρηται ὡς . . . ἑκούσιος γέγονεν Sylburg.
[2] διχῇ BmgCD, διὰ AB.
[3] κλήρους Steph.: κλήρου O.
[4] τὸν μὲν τῇ προσνεῖμαι τὸν δὲ τῇ B : τὸν μὲν προσμεῖναι τὸν δὲ
μὴ R.
[5] τὴν τοῦ μεῖναι (or μένειν) τύχην Casaubon : τὴν μὲν ἀμείνω
τύχην O.

of Oceanus, was Cotys, who by Haliê, the daughter
of earth-born Tyllus, had two sons, Asies and Atys,
from the latter of whom by Callithea, the daughter
of Choraeus, came Lydus and Tyrrhenus. Lydus,
they continue, remaining there, inherited his father's
kingdom, and from him the country was called
Lydia ; but Tyrrhenus, who was the leader of the
colony, conquered a large portion of Italy and gave
his name to those who had taken part in the expedition. Herodotus, however, says[1] that Tyrrhenus
and his brother were the sons of Atys, the son of
Manes, and that the migration of the Maeonians to
Italy was not voluntary. For he says that in the
reign of Atys there was a dearth in the country of
the Maeonians and that the inhabitants, inspired
by love of their native land, for a time contrived a
great many methods to resist this calamity, one day
permitting themselves but a moderate allowance of
food and the next day fasting. But, as the mischief
continued, they divided the people into two groups
and cast lots to determine which should go out of
the country and which should stay in it ; of the
sons of Atys one was assigned to the one group and
the other to the other. And when the lot fell to that
part of the people which was with Lydus to remain
in the country, the other group departed after receiving their share of the common possessions ; and

[1] i. 94. But the quotation is inaccurate in two important details : Herodotus mentions only one son of Atys,
Tyrrhenus, and says that Atys joined himself to the group
destined to remain at home, but assigned his son to the
other.

τὰ μέρη, ὁρμισαμένην δ' ἐπὶ τοῖς ἑσπερίοις μέρεσι
τῆς Ἰταλίας, ἔνθα ἦν Ὀμβρικοῖς ἡ οἴκησις, αὐτοῦ
καταμεῖναι ἱδρύσασθαι πόλεις τὰς ἔτι καὶ κατ'
αὐτὸν ἐκεῖνον οὔσας.

XXVIII. Τούτῳ τῷ λόγῳ πολλοὺς καὶ ἄλλους
συγγραφεῖς [1] περὶ τοῦ Τυρρηνῶν γένους χρησαμένους ἐπίσταμαι, τοὺς μὲν κατὰ ταὐτά, τοὺς δὲ
μεταθέντας τὸν οἰκισμὸν καὶ τὸν χρόνον. ἔλεξαν
γὰρ δή τινες Ἡρακλέους υἱὸν εἶναι τὸν Τυρρηνὸν
ἐξ Ὀμφάλης τῆς Λυδῆς γενόμενον· τοῦτον δ'
ἀφικόμενον εἰς Ἰταλίαν ἐκβαλεῖν τοὺς Πελασγοὺς
ἐκ τῶν πόλεων οὐχ ἁπασῶν, ἀλλ' ὅσαι πέραν ἦσαν
τοῦ Τεβέριος ἐν τῷ βορείῳ μέρει. ἕτεροι δὲ Τηλέ-
φου παῖδα τὸν Τυρρηνὸν ἀποφαίνουσιν, ἐλθεῖν δὲ
2 μετὰ [2] Τροίας ἅλωσιν εἰς Ἰταλίαν. Ξάνθος δὲ ὁ
Λυδὸς ἱστορίας παλαιᾶς εἰ καί τις ἄλλος ἔμπειρος
ὤν, τῆς δὲ πατρίου καὶ βεβαιωτὴς ἂν οὐδενὸς ὑπο-
δεέστερος νομισθείς, οὔτε Τυρρηνὸν ὠνόμακεν οὐ-
δαμοῦ τῆς γραφῆς δυνάστην Λυδῶν οὔτε ἀποικίαν
Μηόνων εἰς Ἰταλίαν κατασχοῦσαν ἐπίσταται Τυρρηνίας τε μνήμην ὡς Λυδῶν ἀποκτίσεως [3] ταπει-
νοτέρων ἄλλων μεμνημένος οὐδεμίαν πεποίηται·
Ἄτυος δὲ παῖδας γενέσθαι λέγει Λυδὸν καὶ Τόρηβον,
τούτους δὲ μερισαμένους τὴν πατρῴαν ἀρχὴν ἐν
Ἀσίᾳ καταμεῖναι ἀμφοτέρους· καὶ τοῖς ἔθνεσιν ὧν
ἦρξαν ἐπ' ἐκείνων φησὶ τεθῆναι τὰς ὀνομασίας,
λέγων ὧδε· " ἀπὸ Λυδοῦ μὲν γίνονται Λυδοί, ἀπὸ

---

[1] συγγραφεῖς Ambrosch: ἐν γραφῇ O.
[2] μετὰ O: μετὰ τὴν Jacoby.
[3] ἀποκτίσεως Ba (?): ἀποικήσεως R.

landing in the western parts of Italy where the
Umbrians dwelt, they remained there and built the
cities that still existed even in his time.

XXVIII. I am aware that many other authors
also have given this account of the Tyrrhenian
race, some in the same terms, and others changing
the character of the colony and the date. For some
have said that Tyrrhenus was the son of Herakles
by Omphalê, the Lydian, and that he, coming into
Italy, dispossessed the Pelasgians of their cities,
though not of all, but of those only that lay beyond
the Tiber toward the north. Others declare that
Tyrrhenus was the son of Telephus and that after
the taking of Troy he came into Italy. But Xanthus
of Lydia,[1] who was as well acquainted with ancient
history as any man and who may be regarded as
an authority second to none on the history of his
own country, neither names Tyrrhenus in any part
of his history as a ruler of the Lydians nor knows
anything of the landing of a colony of Maeonians
in Italy; nor does he make the least mention of
Tyrrhenia as a Lydian colony, though he takes
notice of several things of less importance. He
says that Lydus and Torebus were the sons of Atys;
that they, having divided the kingdom they had
inherited from their father, both remained in Asia,
and from them the nations over which they reigned
received their names. His words are these: " From
Lydus are sprung the Lydians, and from Torebus

---

[1] Xanthus, an older contemporary of Herodotus, was
the first barbarian to write the history of his country in
Greek. The passage here cited is given as frg. 1 in Müller,
F.H.G. i. p. 36.

Τορήβου δὲ Τόρηβοι. τούτων ἡ γλῶσσα ὀλίγον παραφέρει, καὶ νῦν ἔτι σιλλοῦσιν[1] ἀλλήλους[2] ῥή-ματα οὐκ ὀλίγα, ὥσπερ Ἴωνες καὶ Δωριεῖς."

3 Ἑλλάνικος δὲ ὁ Λέσβιος τοὺς Τυρρηνούς φησι Πελασγοὺς πρότερον καλουμένους, ἐπειδὴ κατῴ-κησαν ἐν Ἰταλίᾳ, παραλαβεῖν ἣν νῦν ἔχουσι προση-γορίαν. ἔχει δὲ αὐτῷ ἐν Φορωνίδι ὁ λόγος ὧδε·
" τοῦ Πελασγοῦ τοῦ βασιλέος[3] αὐτῶν καὶ Μενίππης τῆς Πηνειοῦ ἐγένετο Φράστωρ, τοῦ δὲ Ἀμύντωρ, τοῦ δὲ Τευταμίδης, τοῦ δὲ Νάνας. ἐπὶ τούτου βασιλεύοντος οἱ Πελασγοὶ ὑπ᾽ Ἑλλήνων ἀνέστησαν, καὶ ἐπὶ Σπινῆτι ποταμῷ ἐν τῷ Ἰονίῳ[4] κόλπῳ τὰς νῆας καταλιπόντες Κρότωνα πόλιν ἐν μεσογείῳ εἷλον καὶ ἐντεῦθεν ὁρμώμενοι τὴν νῦν καλεομένην

4 Τυρσηνίην ἔκτισαν." Μυρσίλος δὲ τὰ ἔμπαλιν ἀποφαίνων[5] Ἑλλανίκῳ τοὺς Τυρρηνούς φησιν, ἐπειδὴ τὴν ἑαυτῶν ἐξέλιπον, ἐν τῇ πλάνῃ μετο-νομασθῆναι Πελαργούς, τῶν ὀρνέων τοῖς καλου-μένοις πελαργοῖς εἰκασθέντας, ὡς κατ᾽ ἀγέλας ἐφοίτων εἴς τε τὴν Ἑλλάδα καὶ τὴν βάρβαρον καὶ

---

[1] σιλλοῦσιν A, σίλλουσιν B: συλῶσιν Ritschl, ὁμολογοῦσιν Sintenis, συνᾴδουσιν Jacoby (in note), ξυνοῦσιν Meineke, ξυνιᾶσιν Naber.
[2] ἀλλήλους O: ἀλλήλοις Sintenis, Meineke, Jacoby (in note), ἀλλήλων Naber. The construction required by the rare verb σιλλόω is uncertain, but the double accusative is very questionable; probably either ἀλλήλων ῥήματα or ἀλλή-λους εἰς ῥήματα should be read.

the Torebians. There is little difference in their language and even now each nation scoffs at many words used by the other,[1] even as do the Ionians and Dorians." Hellanicus of Lesbos says that the Tyrrhenians, who were previously called Pelasgians, received their present name after they had settled in Italy. These are his words in the *Phoronis* :[2] " Phrastor was the son of Pelasgus, their king, and Menippê, the daughter of Peneus ; his son was Amyntor, Amyntor's son was Teutamides, and the latter's son was Nanas. In his reign the Pelasgians were driven out of their country by the Greeks, and after leaving their ships on the river Spines [3] in the Ionian Gulf, they took Croton, an inland city ; and proceeding from there, they colonized the country now called Tyrrhenia." But the account Myrsilus gives is the reverse of that given by Hellanicus. The Tyrrhenians, he says,[4] after they had left their own country, were in the course of their wanderings called Pelargoi or " Storks," from their resemblance to the birds of that name, since they swarmed in flocks both into Greece and into the barbarian

[1] In other words, they simply spoke different dialects of a common language and each nation jested at the " provincialisms " of the other. This explanation obviates the numerous emendations that have been offered for the rare word σιλλοῦσιν.
[2] Müller, *F.H.G.* i. p. 45, frg. 1.
[3] The Spinetic mouth of the Po. See chap. 18, **3**.
[4] Müller, *F.H.G.* iv. p. 457 frg. **3**.

---

[3] Cobet : βασιλέως O. To Cobet are also due the other Ionic forms in the quotation.
[4] Sylburg : ἰονικῷ AB.
[5] ἀποφαινόμενος O, Jacoby.

τοῖς Ἀθηναίοις τὸ τεῖχος τὸ περὶ τὴν ἀκρόπολιν,
τὸ Πελαργικὸν καλούμενον, τούτους περιβαλεῖν.

XXIX. Ἐμοὶ μέντοι δοκοῦσιν ἅπαντες ἁμαρ-
τάνειν οἱ πεισθέντες ἓν καὶ τὸ αὐτὸ ἔθνος εἶναι τὸ
Τυρρηνικὸν καὶ τὸ Πελασγικόν. τῆς μὲν γὰρ ὀνομασίας ἀπολαῦσαί ποτε αὐτοὺς τῆς ἀλλήλων οὐδὲν
θαυμαστὸν ἦν, ἐπεὶ καὶ ἄλλα δή τινα ἔθνη, τὰ μὲν
Ἑλλήνων, τὰ δὲ βαρβάρων, ταὐτὸ [1] ἔπαθεν, ὥσπερ
τὸ Τρωικὸν καὶ τὸ Φρυγικὸν ἀγχοῦ οἰκοῦντα ἀλλήλων (πολλοῖς γέ τοι γένος ἓν ἄμφω ταῦτ' ἐνομίσθη,
κλήσει διαλλάττον, οὐ φύσει) καὶ οὐχ ἥκιστα τῶν
ἄλλοθί που συνωνυμίαις ἐπικερασθέντων καὶ τὰ ἐν
2 Ἰταλίᾳ ἔθνη.[2] ἦν γὰρ δὴ χρόνος ὅτε καὶ Λατῖνοι
καὶ Ὀμβρικοὶ καὶ Αὔσονες καὶ συχνοὶ ἄλλοι Τυρρηνοὶ ὑφ' Ἑλλήνων ἐλέγοντο, τῆς διὰ μακροῦ τῶν
ἐθνῶν οἰκήσεως ἀσαφῆ ποιούσης τοῖς πρόσω τὴν
ἀκρίβειαν· τήν τε Ῥώμην αὐτὴν πολλοὶ τῶν συγγραφέων Τυρρηνίδα πόλιν εἶναι ὑπέλαβον. ὀνομάτων
μὲν οὖν ἐναλλαγήν, ἐπεὶ καὶ βίων, πείθομαι τοῖς
ἔθνεσι γενέσθαι· κοινοῦ δὲ ἄμφω μετειληφέναι γένους οὐ πείθομαι, πολλοῖς τε ἄλλοις καὶ μάλιστα
ταῖς φωναῖς αὐτῶν διηλλαγμέναις καὶ οὐδεμίαν
3 ὁμοιότητα σωζούσαις τεκμαιρόμενος. "καὶ [3] γὰρ

---

[1] ταὐτὸ O: ταὐτὸν Jacoby.
[2] τὸ αὐτὸ ἔπαθον after ἔθνη deleted by Garrer.
[3] καὶ Herodotus: ἢ AB.

lands; and they built the wall round the citadel of Athens which is called the Pelargic wall.[1]

XXIX. But in my opinion all who take the Tyrrhenians and the Pelasgians to be one and the same nation are mistaken. It is no wonder they were sometimes called by one another's names, since the same thing has happened to certain other nations also, both Greeks and barbarians,—for example, to the Trojans and Phrygians, who lived near each other (indeed, many have thought that those two nations were but one, differing in name only, not in fact). And the nations in Italy have been confused under a common name quite as often as any nations elsewhere. For there was a time when the Latins, the Umbrians, the Ausonians and many others were all called Tyrrhenians by the Greeks, the remoteness of the countries inhabited by these nations making their exact distinctions obscure to those who lived at a distance. And many of the historians have taken Rome itself for a Tyrrhenian city. I am persuaded, therefore, that these nations changed their name along with their place of abode, but can not believe that they both had a common origin, for this reason, among many others, that their languages are different and preserve not the least resemblance to one another. " For neither the

[1] *Pelargikon* was the earlier form of the word, perhaps meaning "Stork's Nest"; but its close resemblance to *Pelasgikon* gave rise in time to the belief that the latter was the true form. The tradition that Pelasgians once dwelt in Athens and built this wall on the Acropolis does not appear to be much older than the time of Herodotus. The next step was to show that even the form *Pelargikon* had reference to the Pelasgians.

δὴ οὔτε Κροτωνιῆται," [1], ὥς φησιν Ἡρόδοτος,
"οὐδαμοῖσι [2] τῶν νῦν σφεας περιοικεόντων εἰσὶν
ὁμόγλωσσοι οὔτε Πλακιηνοί, σφίσι δ' ὁμόγλωσσοι.
δηλοῦσι δὲ ὅτι, τὸν ἠνείκαντο γλώσσης χαρακτῆρα
μεταβαίνοντες ἐς ταῦτα τὰ χωρία, τοῦτον ἔχουσιν
ἐν φυλακῇ." καίτοι θαυμάσειεν ἄν τις, εἰ Πλακια-
νοῖς μὲν τοῖς περὶ τὸν Ἑλλήσποντον οἰκοῦσιν ὁμοίαν
διάλεκτον εἶχον οἱ Κροτωνιᾶται, ἐπειδὴ Πελασγοὶ
ἦσαν ἀμφότεροι ἀρχῆθεν, Τυρρηνοῖς δὲ τοῖς ἔγγιστα
οἰκοῦσι μηδὲν ὁμοίαν. εἰ γὰρ τὸ συγγενὲς τῆς
ὁμοφωνίας αἴτιον ὑποληπτέον, θάτερον δή που τῆς
4 διαφωνίας· οὐ γὰρ δὴ κατά γε τὸ αὐτὸ ἐγχωρεῖ
νομίζειν τἀμφότερα. καὶ γὰρ δὴ τὸ μὲν ἕτερον
καὶ λόγον τιν' ἂν [3] εἶχε γενόμενον, τὸ δὴ τοὺς πρόσω
τὰς οἰκήσεις ἀπ' ἀλλήλων ποιησαμένους ὁμοεθνεῖς
μηκέτι διασώζειν τὸν αὐτὸν τῆς διαλέκτου χαρακτῆρα διὰ τὰς πρὸς τοὺς πέλας ὁμιλίας· τὸ δὲ τοὺς
ἐν τοῖς αὐτοῖς οἰκοῦντας χωρίοις μηδ' ὁτιοῦν κατὰ
τὴν φωνὴν ἀλλήλοις ὁμολογεῖν ἐκ ταὐτοῦ φύντας
γένους οὐδένα λόγον ἔχει.

XXX. Τούτῳ μὲν δὴ τῷ τεκμηρίῳ χρώμενος
ἑτέρους εἶναι πείθομαι τῶν Τυρρηνῶν τοὺς Πελασ-

---

[1] Jacoby: κροτωνιάταις A, κροτωνίταις B: κρηστωνιῆται
MSS. of Herodotus.
[2] οὐδαμοῖσι Ambrosch, οὐδαμοῖς Reiske: οὐδ' ἄλλοις O.
[3] τιν' ἂν Jacoby, ἄν τινα Reiske: τινὰ O.

Crotoniats," says Herodotus,[1] " nor the Placians agree in language with any of their present neighbours, although they agree with each other ; and it is clear that they preserve the fashion of speech which they brought with them into those regions." However, one may well marvel that, although the Crotoniats had a speech similar to that of the Placians, who lived near the Hellespont,[2] since both were originally Pelasgians, it was not at all similar to that of the Tyrrhenians, their nearest neighbours. For if kinship is to be regarded as the reason why two nations speak the same language, the contrary must, of course, be the reason for their speaking a different one, since surely it is not possible to believe that both these conditions arise from the same cause. For, although it might reasonably happen, on the one hand, that men of the same nation who have settled at a distance from one another would, as the result of associating with their neighbours, no longer preserve the same fashion of speech, yet it is not at all reasonable that men sprung from the same race and living in the same country should not in the least agree with one another in their language.

XXX. For this reason, therefore, I am persuaded that the Pelasgians are a different people from the

[1] i. 57. Since Niebuhr first championed (*Röm. Gesch.* i. note 89, p. 39) the form of the name given by Dionysius as against Crestoniats (and Creston) found in Herodotus, the belief has steadily gained ground that the MSS. of Herodotus are in error. The latest editor of Herodotus, Legrand (1932), restores Κροτωνιῆται (and Κρότωνα) in the text.

[2] Placia lay to the east of Cyzicus, at the foot of Mt. Olympus. It disappeared at an early date.

γούς. οὐ μὲν δὴ οὐδὲ Λυδῶν τοὺς Τυρρηνοὺς ἀποίκους οἶμαι γενέσθαι· οὐδὲ γὰρ ἐκείνοις ὁμόγλωσσοι
εἰσίν, οὐδ' ἔστιν εἰπεῖν ὡς φωνῇ μὲν οὐκέτι χρῶνται
παραπλησίᾳ, ἄλλα δέ τινα διασῴζουσι τῆς μητροπόλεως [1] μηνύματα. οὔτε γὰρ θεοὺς Λυδοῖς τοὺς
αὐτοὺς νομίζουσιν οὔτε νόμοις οὔτ' ἐπιτηδεύμασι
κέχρηνται παραπλησίοις, ἀλλὰ κατά γε ταῦτα πλέον
2 Λυδῶν διαφέρουσιν ἢ Πελασγῶν. κινδυνεύουσι
γὰρ τοῖς ἀληθέσι μᾶλλον ἐοικότα λέγειν οἱ [2] μηδα-
μόθεν ἀφιγμένον, ἀλλ' ἐπιχώριον τὸ ἔθνος ἀποφαίνοντες, ἐπειδὴ ἀρχαῖόν τε πάνυ καὶ οὐδενὶ ἄλλῳ
γένει οὔτε ὁμόγλωσσον οὔτε ὁμοδίαιτον ὂν [3] εὑρίσκεται. ὠνομάσθαι δ' ὑφ' Ἑλλήνων αὐτὸ τῇ
προσηγορίᾳ ταύτῃ οὐδὲν κωλύει, καὶ διὰ τὰς ἐν
ταῖς τύρσεσιν οἰκήσεις καὶ ἀπ' ἀνδρὸς δυνάστου.
3 Ῥωμαῖοι μέντοι ἄλλαις αὐτὸ προσαγορεύουσιν
ὀνομασίαις· καὶ γὰρ ἐπὶ τῆς χώρας, ἐν ᾗ ποτε
ᾤκησαν, Ἐτρουρίας προσαγορευομένης Ἐτρούσκους
καλοῦσι τοὺς ἀνθρώπους· καὶ ἐπὶ τῆς ἐμπειρίας
τῶν περὶ τὰ θεῖα σεβάσματα λειτουργιῶν, δια-
φέροντας εἰς αὐτὴν ἑτέρων, νῦν μὲν Τούσκους [4]
ἀσαφέστερον, πρότερον δ' ἀκριβοῦντες τοὔνομα
ὥσπερ Ἕλληνες Θυοσκόους ἐκάλουν   αὐτοὶ μέντοι
σφᾶς αὐτοὺς ἐπὶ τῶν ἡγεμόνων τινὸς Ῥασέννα [5]

[1] γῆς after μητροπόλεως deleted by Madvig.
[2] οἱ added by Reiske.   [3] ὂν added by Cobet.
[4] μὲν Τούσκους Sintenis, μέντοι Τούσκους Ritschl : μέν τοι O.
[5] Ταρασένα or Ταρσένα Lepsius.

Tyrrhenians. And I do not believe, either, that the Tyrrhenians were a colony of the Lydians; for they do not use the same language as the latter, nor can it be alleged that, though they no longer speak a similar tongue, they still retain some other indications of their mother country. For they neither worship the same gods as the Lydians nor make use of similar laws or institutions, but in these very respects they differ more from the Lydians than from the Pelasgians. Indeed, those probably come nearest to the truth who declare that the nation migrated from nowhere else, but was native to the country, since it is found to be a very ancient nation and to agree with no other either in its language or in its manner of living. And there is no reason why the Greeks should not have called them by this name, both from their living in towers and from the name of one of their rulers. The Romans, however, give them other names: from the country they once inhabited, named Etruria, they call them Etruscans, and from their knowledge of the ceremonies relating to divine worship, in which they excel others, they now call them, rather inaccurately, Tusci,[1] but formerly, with the same accuracy as the Greeks, they called them Thyoscoï.[2] Their own name for themselves, however, is the same as that of one of their

[1] The prevailing view to-day is that *Tusci* is for *Tursci*, *turs* being the same element that is seen in Τυρσηνός. *Etrusci* may be simply a lengthened form of *Tursci*, with *u* and *r* interchanged.

[2] This statement is not borne out by information we have from any other source. It is merely an attempt to find a Greek etymology for Tusci. Θυοσκόοι were sacrificing priests.

DIONYSIUS OF HALICARNASSUS

4 τὸν αὐτὸν ἐκείνῳ τρόπον ὀνομάζουσι. πόλεις
δὲ ἅστινας ᾤκισαν[1] οἱ Τυρρηνοί, καὶ πολιτευμάτων
οὕστινας κατεστήσαντο κόσμους, δύναμίν τε ὁπόσην
ἐκτήσαντο[2] καὶ ἔργα εἴ τινα μνήμης ἄξια διεπρά-
ξαντο, τύχαις τε ὁποίαις ἐχρήσαντο, ἐν ἑτέρῳ
5 δηλωθήσεται λόγῳ. τὸ δ' οὖν Πελασγικὸν φῦλον,
ὅσον μὴ διεφθάρη τε καὶ κατὰ τὰς ἀποικίας
διεσπάσθη, διέμεινε δὲ ὀλίγον ἀπὸ πολλοῦ, μετὰ
τῶν Ἀβοριγίνων πολιτευόμενον ἐν τούτοις ὑπελείφθη
τοῖς χωρίοις, ὅπου σὺν χρόνῳ τὴν Ῥώμην οἱ ἔκ-
γονοι αὐτῶν σὺν τοῖς ἄλλοις[3] ἐπολίσαντο. καὶ
τὰ μὲν ὑπὲρ τοῦ Πελασγικοῦ γένους μυθολογούμενα
τοιάδε ἐστί.

XXXI. Μετὰ δὲ οὐ πολὺν χρόνον στόλος ἄλλος
Ἑλληνικὸς εἰς ταῦτα τὰ χωρία τῆς Ἰταλίας κατάγεται, ἑξηκοστῷ μάλιστα ἔτει πρότερον τῶν Τρωικῶν, ὡς αὐτοὶ Ῥωμαῖοι λέγουσιν, ἐκ Παλλαντίου
πόλεως Ἀρκαδικῆς ἀναστάς. ἡγεῖτο δὲ τῆς ἀποικίας Εὔανδρος Ἑρμοῦ λεγόμενος καὶ νύμφης τινὸς
Ἀρκάσιν ἐπιχωρίας, ἣν οἱ μὲν Ἕλληνες Θέμιν εἶναι
λέγουσι καὶ θεοφόρητον ἀποφαίνουσιν, οἱ δὲ τὰς
Ῥωμαϊκὰς συγγράψαντες ἀρχαιολογίας τῇ πατρίῳ[4]
γλώσσῃ Καρμέντην[5] ὀνομάζουσιν· εἴη δ' ἂν Ἑλλάδι
φωνῇ Θεσπιῳδὸς τῇ νύμφῃ τοὔνομα· τὰς μὲν γὰρ
ᾠδὰς καλοῦσι Ῥωμαῖοι κάρμινα,[b] τὴν δὲ γυναῖκα
ταύτην ὁμολογοῦσι δαιμονίῳ πνεύματι κατάσχετον

[1] Portus: ᾤκησαν O.
[2] ἐκτήσαντο Garrer: οἱ σύμπαντες O, Jacoby; οἱ σύμπαντες
ἐκέκτηντο Reiske.
[3] ἄλλοις O: Ἀλβανοῖς Kiessling.
[4] Meineke: πατρώῳ AB.

98

leaders, Rasenna. In another book [1] I shall show what cities the Tyrrhenians founded, what forms of government they established, how great power they acquired, what memorable achievements they performed, and what fortunes attended them. As for the Pelasgian nation, however, those who were not destroyed or dispersed among the various colonies (for a small number remained out of a great many) were left behind as fellow citizens of the Aborigines in these parts, where in the course of time their posterity, together with others, built the city of Rome. Such are the legends told about the Pelasgian race.

XXXI. Soon after, another Greek expedition landed in this part of Italy, having migrated from Pallantium, a town of Arcadia, about the sixtieth year before the Trojan war,[2] as the Romans themselves say. This colony had for its leader Evander, who is said to have been the son of Hermes and a local nymph of the Arcadians. The Greeks call her Themis and say that she was inspired, but the writers of the early history of Rome call her, in the native language, Carmenta. The nymph's name would be in Greek *Thespiôdos* or " prophetic singer " ; for the Romans call songs *carmina*, and they agree that this woman, possessed by divine inspiration, fore-

---

[1] Nothing of the sort is found in the extant portions of the *Antiquities*. It is hardly probable that Dionysius intended to devote a separate work to the Etruscans.

[2] *ca.* 1243 B.C.

---

[5] Urlichs: καρμένταν A, καρμετῖνον B.
[6] Steph.: καρμίανα B, θερμίανα A.

γενομένην τὰ μέλλοντα συμβαίνειν τῷ πλήθει δι᾽
2 ᾠδῆς προλέγειν. ὁ δὲ στόλος οὗτος οὐκ ἀπὸ
τοῦ κοινοῦ τῆς γνώμης ἐπέμφθη, ἀλλὰ στασιάσαν-
τος τοῦ δήμου τὸ ἐλαττωθὲν μέρος ἑκούσιον [1]
ὑπεξῆλθεν. ἐτύγχανε δὲ τότε τὴν βασιλείαν τῶν
Ἀβοριγίνων παρειληφὼς Φαῦνος, Ἄρεος ὥς φασιν
ἀπόγονος, ἀνὴρ μετὰ τοῦ δραστηρίου καὶ συνετός,
καὶ αὐτὸν ὡς τῶν ἐπιχωρίων τινὰ Ῥωμαῖοι δαιμόνων θυσίαις καὶ ᾠδαῖς γεραίρουσιν. οὗτος ὁ
ἀνὴρ δεξάμενος κατὰ πολλὴν φιλότητα τοὺς Ἀρκάδας ὀλίγους ὄντας, δίδωσιν αὐτοῖς τῆς αὑτοῦ
3 χώρας ὁπόσην ἐβούλοντο. οἱ δὲ Ἀρκάδες, ὡς
ἡ Θέμις αὐτοῖς ἐπιθειάζουσα ἔφραζεν, αἱροῦνται
λόφον ὀλίγον ἀπέχοντα τοῦ Τεβέριος, ὅς ἐστι νῦν
ἐν μέσῳ μάλιστα τῆς Ῥωμαίων πόλεως, καὶ κατα-
σκευάζονται πρὸς αὐτῷ κώμην βραχεῖαν, δυσὶ
ναυτικοῖς [2] πληρώμασιν ἐν οἷς ἀπανέστησαν τῆς
Ἑλλάδος ἀποχρῶσαν, ἣν ἔμελλε τὸ πεπρωμένον
σὺν χρόνῳ θήσειν ὅσην οὔθ᾽ Ἑλλάδα πόλιν οὔτε
βάρβαρον κατά τε οἰκήσεως μέγεθος καὶ κατὰ
δυναστείας ἀξίωσιν καὶ τὴν ἄλλην ἅπασαν εὐτυχίαν,
χρόνον τε ὁπόσον ἂν ὁ θνητὸς αἰὼν ἀντέχῃ πόλεων
4 μάλιστα πασῶν μνημονευθησομένην. ὄνομα δὲ
τῷ πολίσματι τούτῳ τίθενται Παλλάντιον ἐπὶ τῆς
ἐν Ἀρκαδίᾳ σφῶν μητροπόλεως· νῦν μέντοι Παλάτιον ὑπὸ Ῥωμαίων λέγεται συγχέαντος τοῦ χρόνου
τὴν ἀκρίβειαν καὶ παρέχει πολλοῖς ἀτόπων ἐτυμο-
λογιῶν ἀφορμάς·

[1] Ambrosch : ἑκούσιον μέρος O.

100

told to the people in song the things that would come to pass. This expedition was not sent out by the common consent of the nation, but, a sedition having arisen among the people, the faction which was defeated left the country of their own accord. It chanced that the kingdom of the Aborigines had been inherited at that time by Faunus, a descendant of Mars, it is said, a man of prudence as well as energy, whom the Romans in their sacrifices and songs honour as one of the gods of their country. This man received the Arcadians, who were but few in number, with great friendship and gave them as much of his own land as they desired. And the Arcadians, as Themis by inspiration kept advising them, chose a hill, not far from the Tiber, which is now near the middle of the city of Rome, and by this hill built a small village sufficient for the complement of the two ships in which they had come from Greece. Yet this village was ordained by fate to excel in the course of time all other cities, whether Greek or barbarian, not only in its size, but also in the majesty of its empire and in every other form of prosperity, and to be celebrated above them all as long as mortality shall endure. They named the town Pallantium after their mother-city in Arcadia; now, however, the Romans call it Palatium, time having obscured the correct form, and this name has given occasion to many to suggest absurd etymologies.

---

[2] δυσὶ ναυτικοῖς Steph.: δυσὶν (δυσὶ B) ἀλτικοῖς AB, δυσὶν ἀλητικοῖς Ca, Madvig; δυσὶν ἀλιευτικοῖς Kiessling.

DIONYSIUS OF HALICARNASSUS

XXXII. ὡς δέ τινες ἱστοροῦσιν, ὧν ἐστι καὶ
Πολύβιος ὁ Μεγαλοπολίτης, ἐπί τινος μειρακίου
Πάλλαντος αὐτόθι τελευτήσαντος· τοῦτον δὲ Ἡρακλέους εἶναι παῖδα καὶ Λαουϊνίας[1] τῆς Εὐάνδρου
θυγατρός· χώσαντα δ᾽ αὐτῷ τὸν μητροπάτορα
τάφον ἐπὶ τῷ λόφῳ Παλλάντιον ἐπὶ τοῦ μειρακίου
2 τὸν τόπον ὀνομάσαι. ἐγὼ μέντοι οὔτε τάφον
ἐθεασάμην ἐν Ῥώμῃ Πάλλαντος οὔτε χοὰς ἔμαθον
ἐπιτελουμένας οὔτε ἄλλο τῶν τοιουτοτρόπων οὐδὲν
ἠδυνήθην ἰδεῖν,[2] καίτοι γε οὐκ ἀμνήστου τῆς οἰκίας
ταύτης ἀφειμένης οὐδ᾽ ἀμοίρου τιμῶν αἷς τὸ δαιμόνιον γένος ὑπ᾽ ἀνθρώπων γεραίρεται. καὶ γὰρ
Εὐάνδρῳ θυσίας ἔμαθον ὑπὸ Ῥωμαίων ἐπιτελουμένας ὁσέτη δημοσίᾳ καὶ Καρμέντῃ, καθάπερ τοῖς
λοιποῖς ἥρωσι καὶ δαίμοσι, καὶ βωμοὺς ἐθεασάμην
ἱδρυμένους, Καρμέντῃ μὲν ὑπὸ τῷ καλουμένῳ
Καπιτωλίῳ παρὰ ταῖς Καρμεντίσι πύλαις, Εὐάνδρῳ
δὲ πρὸς ἑτέρῳ τῶν λόφων Αὐεντίνῳ λεγομένῳ τῆς
Τριδύμου πύλης οὐ πρόσω· Πάλλαντι δὲ οὐδὲν
3 οἶδα τούτων γινόμενον. οἱ δ᾽ οὖν Ἀρκάδες ὑπὸ
τῷ λόφῳ συνοικισθέντες τά τε ἄλλα διεκόσμουν τὸ
κτίσμα[3] τοῖς οἴκοθεν νομίμοις χρώμενοι καὶ ἱερὰ
ἱδρύονται, πρῶτον μὲν τῷ Λυκαίῳ Πανὶ τῆς Θέμιδος ἐξηγουμένης (Ἀρκάσι γὰρ θεῶν ἀρχαιότατός
τε καὶ τιμιώτατος ὁ Πάν) χωρίον ἐξευρόντες ἐπιτήδειον, ὃ καλοῦσι Ῥωμαῖοι Λουπερκάλιον, ἡμεῖς
4 δ᾽ ἂν εἴποιμεν Λύκαιον. νῦν μὲν οὖν συμπεπολι-

---

[1] Λαουϊνίας Cary (see p. 196, n. 2), Λαύνας Ambrosch :
δύνας O.   [2] ἰδεῖν B, μαθεῖν R.
[3] διεκόσμουν τὸ κτίσμα Kiessling : διεκοσμοῦντο κτίσματα O.

XXXII. But some writers, among them Polybius of Megalopolis, relate that the town was named after Pallas, a lad who died there; they say that he was the son of Hercules and Lavinia, the daughter of Evander, and that his maternal grandfather raised a tomb to him on the hill and called the place Pallantium, after the lad. But I have never seen any tomb of Pallas at Rome nor have I heard of any drink-offerings being made in his honour nor been able to discover anything else of that nature, although this family has not been left unremembered or without those honours with which divine beings are worshipped by men. For I have learned that public sacrifices are performed yearly by the Romans to Evander and to Carmenta in the same manner as to the other heroes and minor deities; and I have seen two altars that were erected, one to Carmenta under the Capitoline hill near the Porta Carmentalis, and the other to Evander by another hill, called the Aventine, not far from the Porta Trigemina; but I know of nothing of this kind that is done in honour of Pallas. As for the Arcadians, when they had joined in a single settlement at the foot of the hill, they proceeded to adorn their town with all the buildings to which they had been accustomed at home and to erect temples. And first they built a temple to the Lycaean Pan by the direction of Themis (for to the Arcadians Pan is the most ancient and the most honoured of all the gods), when they had found a suitable site for the purpose. This place the Romans call the Lupercal, but we should call it *Lykaion* or " Lycaeum." Now, it is true, since the district about

103

σμένων τῷ τεμένει τῶν πέριξ χωρίων δυσείκαστος
γέγονεν ἡ παλαιὰ τοῦ τόπου φύσις, ἦν δὲ τὸ ἀρχαῖον
ὡς λέγεται σπήλαιον ὑπὸ τῷ λόφῳ μέγα, δρυμῷ
λασίῳ κατηρεφές, καὶ κρηνῖδες ὑπὸ ταῖς πέτραις
ἐμβύθιοι, ἥ τε προσεχὴς τῷ κρημνῷ[1] νάπη πυκνοῖς
5 καὶ μεγάλοις δένδρεσιν ἐπίσκιος. ἔνθα βωμὸν
ἱδρυσάμενοι τῷ θεῷ τὴν πάτριον θυσίαν ἐπετέλεσαν,
ἣν μέχρι τοῦ καθ᾽ ἡμᾶς χρόνου ῾Ρωμαῖοι θύουσιν
ἐν μηνὶ Φεβρουαρίῳ μετὰ τὰς χειμερίους τροπάς,
οὐδὲν τῶν τότε γενομένων μετακινοῦντες· ὁ δὲ
τρόπος τῆς θυσίας ἐν τοῖς ἔπειτα λεχθήσεται. ἐπὶ
δὲ τῇ κορυφῇ τοῦ λόφου τὸ τῆς Νίκης τέμενος
ἐξελόντες θυσίας καὶ ταύτῃ κατεστήσαντο διε-
τησίους, ἃς καὶ ἐπ᾽ ἐμοῦ ῾Ρωμαῖοι ἔθυον.

[1] τῷ κρημνῷ Kiessling : τῶν κρημνῶν O.

---

[1] The Lupercal was situated at the foot of the Palatine,
probably at the south-west corner ; it is further described
in chap. 79, 8, and the Lupercalia in 80, 1. For a discussion of the various theories respecting the origin of the
Lupercalia the reader is referred to Sir James Frazer's
note on Ovid, *Fasti* ii. 267 (vol. ii. pp. 327 ff. = pp. 389 ff.
in his *L.C.L.* edition). When once the adjective Λυκαῖος
(really " of Mt. Lycaeus," in Arcadia) was taken as the
equivalent of *Lupercalis* and Lycaean Pan identified with
the god worshipped at the Lupercalia, Λύκαιον and Λύκαια
would naturally be equated with Lupercal and Lupercalia,
in spite of the fact that these words as used in Greece
meant the shrine and games of Zeus Lycaeus.

[2] With the present passage should be compared three
others in the *Antiquities* where Dionysius, for the benefit
of his Greek public, indicates the season of the year in
which a Roman date fell. Just below, in chap. 38, 3, he
speaks of the Ides of May as being a little after the vernal
equinox ; in chap. 88, 3, he places the Parilia (April 21) in

the sacred precinct has been united with the city, it has become difficult to make out by conjecture the ancient nature of the place. Nevertheless, at first, we are told, there was a large cave under the hill overarched by a dense wood; deep springs issued from beneath the rocks, and the glen adjoining the cliffs was shaded by thick and lofty trees.[1] In this place they raised an altar to the god and performed their traditional sacrifice, which the Romans have continued to offer up to this day in the month of February, after the winter solstice,[2] without altering anything in the rites then performed. The manner of this sacrifice will be related later. Upon the summit of the hill they set apart the precinct of Victory and instituted sacrifices to her also, lasting throughout the year, which the Romans performed even in my time.

the beginning of spring; and in ix. 25, 1, he says the new consuls assumed office near the summer solstice in the month of Sextilis (probably on the Calends of August). At first sight it might be thought that he was following an early Roman calendar that was a month or a little more in advance of the seasons. But the only calendar with which he can have had any personal acquaintance at Rome was the calendar as reformed by Julius Caesar, in effect since the year 46; and in three of the four passages he is describing a festival as it was still celebrated in his own day. We are almost forced, then, to one of two conclusions, either that he was content to define the season very roughly, or else that he was using the term " solstice " loosely for the middle of winter or summer and " equinox " for a period midway between—a usage that it would be hard to parallel—and even delaying " spring " correspondingly. Yet when it came to a Greek date as far back as the fall of Troy he could write with the greatest precision (chap. 63, 1).

DIONYSIUS OF HALICARNASSUS

XXXIII. Ταύτην δὲ Ἀρκάδες μυθολογοῦσι Πάλλαντος εἶναι θυγατέρα τοῦ Λυκάονος· τιμὰς δὲ παρ' ἀνθρώπων ἃς ἔχει νῦν Ἀθηνᾶς βουλήσει λαβεῖν, γενομένην τῆς θεοῦ σύντροφον. δοθῆναι γὰρ εὐθὺς ἀπὸ γονῆς τὴν Ἀθηνᾶν Πάλλαντι ὑπὸ Διὸς καὶ παρ' ἐκείνῳ τέως εἰς ὥραν[1] ἀφίκετο τραφῆναι. ἱδρύσαντο δὲ καὶ Δήμητρος ἱερὸν καὶ τὰς θυσίας αὐτῇ διὰ γυναικῶν τε καὶ νηφαλίους ἔθυσαν, ὡς Ἕλλησι νόμος, ὧν οὐδὲν ὁ καθ' ἡμᾶς ἤλλαξε 2 χρόνος. ἀπέδειξαν δὲ καὶ Ποσειδῶνι τέμενος Ἱππίῳ καὶ τὴν ἑορτὴν Ἱπποκράτεια μὲν ὑπ' Ἀρκάδων, Κωνσουάλια δὲ ὑπὸ Ῥωμαίων λεγόμενα κατεστήσαντο, ἐν ᾗ παρὰ Ῥωμαίοις ἐξ ἔθους ἐλινύουσιν ἔργων ἵπποι καὶ ὀρεῖς καὶ στέφονται 3 τὰς κεφαλὰς ἄνθεσι. πολλὰ δὲ καὶ ἄλλα τεμένη καὶ βωμοὺς καὶ βρέτη θεῶν καθωσίωσαν, ἁγισμούς τε καὶ θυσίας κατεστήσαντο πατρίους, αἳ μέχρι τῶν κατ' ἐμὲ χρόνων τὸν αὐτὸν ἐγίνοντο τρόπον. οὐ θαυμάσαιμι δ' ἂν εἰ καὶ παρεῖναί τινες διαφυγοῦσαι τὴν τῶν ἐπιγινομένων μνήμην ὑπὸ[2] τοῦ πάνυ ἀρχαίου ἀλλ' ἀποχρῶσί γε αἱ[3] νῦν ἔτι γινόμεναι τεκμήρια εἶναι τῶν Ἀρκαδικῶν ποτε νομίμων· λεχθήσεται δὲ περὶ αὐτῶν ἐπὶ πλεῖον ἐν ἑτέροις.

[1] ὥραν A : οὐρανοὺς B.   [2] ὑπὸ Cobet : ἀπὸ O.
[3] αἱ Ambrosch, αἱ καὶ Reiske : καὶ O.

---

[1] Poseidon Hippios of the Greeks.
[2] See note on ii. 31, 2.
[3] Dionysius perhaps is thinking particularly of the passage in Book VII (72, 14-18), where he points out the

106

XXXIII. The Arcadians have a legend that this goddess was the daughter of Pallas, the son of Lycaon, and that she received those honours from mankind which she now enjoys at the desire of Athena, with whom she had been reared. For they say that Athena, as soon as she was born, was handed over to Pallas by Zeus and that she was reared by him till she grew up. They built also a temple to Ceres, to whom by the ministry of women they offered sacrifices without wine, according to the custom of the Greeks, none of which rites our time has changed. Moreover, they assigned a precinct to the Equestrian Neptune [1] and instituted the festival called by the Arcadians Hippocrateia and by the Romans Consualia, [2] during which it is customary among the latter for the horses and mules to rest from work and to have their heads crowned with flowers. They also consecrated many other precincts, altars and images of the gods and instituted purifications and sacrifices according to the customs of their own country, which continued to be performed down to my day in the same manner. Yet I should not be surprised if some of the ceremonies by reason of their great antiquity have been forgotten by their posterity and neglected ; however, those that are still practised are sufficient proofs that they are derived from the customs formerly in use among the Arcadians, of which I shall speak more at length elsewhere. [3] The Arcadians

close agreement even in details between a Roman and a Greek sacrifice. See also i. 80, 1 (the Lupercalia) and i. 34, 4 ; 38, 2-3 ; 40, 3-5.

4 λέγονται δὲ καὶ γραμμάτων Ἑλληνικῶν χρῆσιν
εἰς Ἰταλίαν πρῶτοι διακομίσαι νεωστὶ φανεῖσαν
Ἀρκάδες καὶ μουσικὴν τὴν δι' ὀργάνων, ἃ δὴ λύραι
τε καὶ τρίγωνα καὶ αὐλοὶ [1] καλοῦνται, τῶν προτέρων
ὅτι μὴ σύριγξι ποιμενικαῖς οὐδενὶ ἄλλῳ μουσικῆς
τεχνήματι χρωμένων, νόμους τε θέσθαι καὶ τὴν
δίαιταν ἐκ τοῦ θηριώδους ἐπὶ πλεῖστον εἰς ἡμερό-
τητα μεταγαγεῖν τέχνας τε καὶ ἐπιτηδεύματα καὶ
ἄλλα πολλά τινα ὠφελήματα εἰς τὸ κοινὸν κατα-
θεῖναι, καὶ διὰ ταῦτα πολλῆς ἐπιμελείας τυγχάνειν
5 πρὸς τῶν ὑποδεξαμένων. τοῦτο δεύτερον ἔθνος
Ἑλληνικὸν μετὰ Πελασγοὺς ἀφικόμενον εἰς Ἰταλίαν
κοινὴν ἔσχε μετὰ τῶν [2] Ἀβοριγίνων οἴκησιν ἐν τῷ
κρατίστῳ τῆς Ῥώμης ἱδρυσάμενον χωρίῳ.

XXXIV. Ὀλίγοις δ' ὕστερον ἔτεσι μετὰ τοὺς
Ἀρκάδας ἄλλος εἰς Ἰταλίαν ἀφικνεῖται στόλος
Ἑλληνικὸς ἄγοντος Ἡρακλέους, ὃς Ἰβηρίαν καὶ
τὰ μέχρι δυσμῶν ἡλίου πάντα χειρωσάμενος ἧκεν.[3]
ἐξ ὧν τινες Ἡρακλέα παραιτησάμενοι τῆς στρατείας [4] ἀφεθῆναι, περὶ ταῦτα τὰ χωρία ὑπέμειναν
καὶ πολίζονται λόφον ἐπιτήδειον εὑρόντες, τρι-
σταδίῳ δὲ μάλιστα μήκει τοῦ Παλλαντίου διειργό-
μενον, ὃς νῦν μὲν Καπιτωλῖνος ὀνομάζεται, ὑπὸ
δὲ τῶν τότε ἀνθρώπων Σατόρνιος ἐλέγετο, ὥσπερ
2 ἂν εἴποι τις Ἑλλάδι φωνῇ Κρόνιος. τῶν δὲ
ὑπολειφθέντων οἱ μὲν πλείους ἦσαν Πελοποννήσιοι,

---

[1] αὐλοὶ Camerarius : λυδοὶ O.
[2] μετὰ τῶν Bb (?), Steph. : μετὰ τὴν ABa ; μετὰ τὴν τῶν (sic)
Jacoby, who probably meant to print μετὰ τῶν Ἀ. τὴν οἴκησιν.
[3] ἧκεν Kiessling : ἦν O.

are said also to have been the first to introduce into
Italy the use of Greek letters, which had lately
appeared among them, and also music performed
on such instruments as lyres, trigons [1] and flutes ;
for their predecessors had used no musical invention
except shepherd's pipes.   They are said also to have
established laws, to have transformed men's mode
of life from the prevailing bestiality to a state of
civilization, and likewise to have introduced arts
and professions and many other things conducive
to the public good, and for these reasons to have been
treated with great consideration by those who had
received them.   This was the next Greek nation
after the Pelasgians to come into Italy and to take
up a common residence with the Aborigines, establishing itself in the best part of Rome.

XXXIV. A few years after the Arcadians another Greek expedition came into Italy under the
command of Hercules, who had just returned from
the conquest of Spain and of all the region that ex-
tends to the setting of the sun.   It was some of his
followers who, begging Hercules to dismiss them from
the expedition, remained in this region and built
a town on a suitable hill, which they found at a
distance of about three stades from Pallantium.
This is now called the Capitoline hill, but by the
men of that time the Saturnian hill, or, in Greek,
the hill of Cronus.   The greater part of those who
stayed behind were Peloponnesians — people of

[1] The trigon was a triangular harp.

---

[4] στρατείας Naber : πραγματείας O, Jacoby.

DIONYSIUS OF HALICARNASSUS

Φενεᾶταί τε καὶ Ἐπειοὶ οἱ[1] ἐξ Ἤλιδος, οἷς οὐκέτι πόθος ἦν τῆς οἴκαδε ὁδοῦ διαπεπορθημένης αὐτοῖς τῆς πατρίδος ἐν τῷ πρὸς Ἡρακλέα πολέμῳ, ἐμέμικτο δέ τι καὶ Τρωικὸν αὐτοῖς τῶν ἐπὶ Λαομέδοντος αἰχμαλώτων ἐξ Ἰλίου γενομένων ὅτε τῆς πόλεως Ἡρακλῆς ἐκράτησε. δοκεῖ δέ μοι καὶ τοῦ ἄλλου στρατοῦ πᾶν, εἴ τι καματηρὸν ἢ τῇ πλάνῃ ἀχθόμενον ἦν, ἄφεσιν τῆς στρατείας αἰτησάμενον 3 ἐν τῷ χωρίῳ τῷδε ὑπομεῖναι. τὸ δὲ ὄνομα τῷ λόφῳ τινὲς μὲν ὥσπερ ἔφην ἀρχαῖον οἴονται εἶναι, καὶ δι' αὐτὸ τοὺς Ἐπειοὺς οὐχ ἥκιστα φιλοχωρῆσαι τῷ λόφῳ μνήμῃ τοῦ ἐν Ἤλιδι Κρονίου λόφου, ὅς ἐστιν ἐν τῇ Πισάτιδι γῇ ποταμοῦ πλησίον Ἀλφειοῦ, καὶ αὐτὸν ἱερὸν τοῦ Κρόνου νομίζοντες Ἠλεῖοι θυσίαις καὶ ἄλλαις τιμαῖς συνιόντες γε- 4 ραίρουσιν ἐν ὡρισμένοις χρόνοις. Εὔξενος[2] δὲ ποιητὴς[3] ἀρχαῖος καὶ ἄλλοι τινὲς τῶν Ἰταλικῶν μυθογράφων ὑπ' αὐτῶν οἴονται Πισατῶν διὰ τὴν ὁμοιότητα τοῦ παρὰ σφίσι Κρονίου τεθῆναι τῷ τόπῳ τοὔνομα, καὶ τὸν βωμὸν τῷ Κρόνῳ τοὺς Ἐπειοὺς ἱδρύσασθαι μεθ' Ἡρακλέους, ὃς ἔτι καὶ νῦν διαμένει παρὰ τῇ ῥίζῃ τοῦ λόφου κατὰ τὴν ἄνοδον τὴν ἀπὸ τῆς ἀγορᾶς φέρουσαν εἰς τὸ Καπιτώλιον, τήν τε θυσίαν, ἣν καὶ ἐπ' ἐμοῦ Ῥωμαῖοι ἔθυον φυλάττοντες τὸν Ἑλληνικὸν νόμον, ἐκείνους 5 εἶναι τοὺς καταστησαμένους. ὡς δ' ἐγὼ συμ-

[1] οἱ O : om. Reudler, Jacoby.
[2] Ἔννιος Sylburg. [3] Kiessling : ὁ ποιητὴς O.

---

[1] No poet of this name is known, and Sylburg was perhaps right in proposing to read Ennius. Strictly speaking,

Pheneus and Epeans of Elis, who no longer had any desire to return home, since their country had been laid waste in the war against Hercules. There was also a small Trojan element mingled with these, consisting of prisoners taken from Ilium in the reign of Laomedon, at the time when Hercules conquered the city. And I am of the opinion that all the rest of the army, also, who were either wearied by their labours or irked by their wanderings, obtained their dismissal from the expedition and remained there. As for the name of the hill, some think it was an ancient name, as I have said, and that consequently the Epeans were especially pleased with the hill through memory of the hill of Cronus in Elis. This is in the territory of Pisa, near the river Alpheus, and the Eleans, regarding it as sacred to Cronus, assemble together at stated times to honour it with sacrifices and other marks of reverence. But Euxenus,[1] an ancient poet, and some others of the Italian mythographers think that the name was given to the place by the men from Pisa themselves, from its likeness to their hill of Cronus, that the Epeans together with Hercules erected the altar to Saturn which remains to this day at the foot of the hill near the ascent that leads from the Forum to the Capitol, and that it was they who instituted the sacrifice which the Romans still performed even in my time, observing the Greek ritual. But from the

Ennius was an Italian rather than a Roman, though it may be questioned whether Dionysius would have made this distinction. In the extant fragments of Ennius there is no reference to Hercules' visit, to say nothing of the Epeans.

111

βαλλόμενος εὑρίσκω, καὶ πρὶν Ἡρακλέα ἐλθεῖν εἰς
Ἰταλίαν ἱερὸς ἦν ὁ τόπος τοῦ Κρόνου καλούμενος
ὑπὸ τῶν ἐπιχωρίων Σατόρνιος, καὶ ἡ ἄλλη δὲ ἀκτὴ
σύμπασα ἡ νῦν Ἰταλία καλουμένη τῷ θεῷ τούτῳ
ἀνέκειτο, Σατορνία πρὸς τῶν ἐνοικούντων ὀνομαζο-
μένη, ὡς ἔστιν εὑρεῖν ἔν τε Σιβυλλείοις τισὶ λογίοις[1]
καὶ ἄλλοις χρηστηρίοις ὑπὸ τῶν θεῶν δεδομένοις
εἰρημένον, ἱερά τε πολλαχῇ τῆς χώρας ἐστὶν ἱδρυ-
μένα τῷ θεῷ καὶ πόλεις τινὲς οὕτως ὥσπερ ἡ
σύμπασα τότε ἀκτὴ ὀνομαζόμεναι χωροί τε πολλοὶ
τοῦ δαίμονος ἐπώνυμοι καὶ μάλιστα οἱ σκόπελοι
καὶ τὰ μετέωρα·

XXXV. Ἰταλία δὲ ἀνὰ χρόνον ὠνομάσθη ἐπ'
ἀνδρὸς δυνάστου ὄνομα Ἰταλοῦ. τοῦτον δέ φησιν
Ἀντίοχος ὁ Συρακούσιος ἀγαθὸν καὶ σοφὸν γεγενη-
μένον καὶ τῶν πλησιοχώρων τοὺς μὲν λόγοις ἀνα-
πείθοντα, τοὺς δὲ βίᾳ προσαγόμενον, ἅπασαν ὑφ'
ἑαυτῷ ποιήσασθαι τὴν γῆν ὅση ἐντὸς ἦν τῶν κόλ-
πων τοῦ τε Ναπητίνου[2] καὶ τοῦ Σκυλλητίνου·[3]
ἦν δὴ πρώτην κληθῆναι Ἰταλίαν ἐπὶ τοῦ Ἰταλοῦ.
ἐπεὶ δὲ ταύτης καρτερὸς ἐγένετο καὶ ἀνθρώπους
πολλοὺς εἶχεν ὑπηκόους αὐτίκα[4] τῶν ἐχομένων
ἐπορέγεσθαι καὶ πόλεις ὑπάγεσθαι[5] πολλάς· εἶναι
2 δ' αὐτὸν Οἴνωτρον τὸ γένος. Ἑλλάνικος δὲ ὁ

---

[1] Reiske: λόγοις O.
[2] Ναπητίνου O: Λαμητικοῦ Aristotle, *Pol.* vii. 9, 2.
[3] Σκυλλητικοῦ Hudson.
[4] αὐτίκα R: αὐτῶ καὶ B; αὐτῷ, αὐτίκα Jacoby.
[5] Usener: συνάγεσθαι O, Jacoby.

best conjectures I have been able to make, I find that even before the arrival of Hercules in Italy this place was sacred to Saturn and was called by the people of the country the Saturnian hill, and all the rest of the peninsula which is now called Italy was consecrated to this god, being called Saturnia [1] by the inhabitants, as may be found stated in some Sibylline prophecies and other oracles delivered by the gods. And in many parts of the country there are temples dedicated to this god ; certain cities bear the same name by which the whole peninsula was known at that time, and many places are called by the name of the god, particularly headlands and eminences.

XXXV. But in the course of time the land came to be called Italy, after a ruler named Italus. This man, according to Antiochus of Syracuse,[2] was both a wise and good prince, and persuading some of his neighbours by arguments and subduing the rest by force, he made himself master of all the land which lies between the Napetine and Scylacian bays,[3] which was the first land, he says, to be called Italy, after Italus. And when he had possessed himself of this district and had many subjects, he immediately coveted the neighbouring peoples and brought many cities under his rule. He says further that Italus was an Oenotrian by birth.

---

[1] Compare Virgil's use of *Saturnia tellus* (*Georg.* ii. 173, *Aen.* viii. 329) and *Saturnia arva* (*Aen.* i. 569) for Italy.

[2] For Antiochus see p. 39, n. 2. This quotation is frg. 4 in Müller, *F.H.G.* i. pp. 181 f.

[3] In other words, nearly all the " toe " of Italy south of the latitude of the Lacinian promontory.

Λέσβιός φησιν Ἡρακλέα τὰς Γηρυόνου βοῦς ἀπε-
λαύνοντα εἰς Ἄργος, ἐπειδή τις αὐτῷ δάμαλις
ἀποσκιρτήσας τῆς ἀγέλης ἐν Ἰταλίᾳ ἐόντι ἤδη
φεύγων διῆρε τὴν ἀκτὴν καὶ τὸν μεταξὺ διανηξάμενος πόρον τῆς θαλάττης εἰς Σικελίαν ἀφίκετο,
ἐρόμενον ἀεὶ τοὺς ἐπιχωρίους καθ' οὓς ἑκάστοτε
γίνοιτο διώκων τὸν δάμαλιν, εἴ πή τις αὐτὸν
ἑωρακὼς εἴη, τῶν τῇδε ἀνθρώπων Ἑλλάδος μὲν
γλώττης ὀλίγα συνιέντων, τῇ δὲ πατρίῳ φωνῇ
κατὰ τὰς μηνύσεις τοῦ ζῴου καλούντων τὸν δάμαλιν οὐίτουλον, ὥσπερ καὶ νῦν λέγεται, ἐπὶ τοῦ
ζῴου τὴν χώραν ὀνομάσαι πᾶσαν ὅσην ὁ δάμαλις
3 διῆλθεν Οὐιτουλίαν. μεταπεσεῖν δὲ ἀνὰ χρόνον
τὴν ὀνομασίαν εἰς τὸ νῦν σχῆμα οὐδὲν θαυμαστόν,
ἐπεὶ καὶ τῶν Ἑλληνικῶν πολλὰ τὸ παραπλήσιον
πέπονθεν ὀνομάτων. πλὴν εἴτε ὡς Ἀντίοχός φησιν
ἐπ' ἀνδρὸς ἡγεμόνος, ὅπερ ἴσως καὶ πιθανώτερόν
ἐστιν, εἴθ' ὡς Ἑλλάνικος οἴεται ἐπὶ τοῦ ταύρου τὴν
ὀνομασίαν ταύτην ἔσχεν, ἐκεῖνό γε ἐξ ἀμφοῖν δῆλον,
ὅτι κατὰ τὴν Ἡρακλέους ἡλικίαν ἢ μικρῷ πρόσθεν
οὕτως ὠνομάσθη. τὰ δὲ πρὸ τούτων Ἕλληνες μὲν
Ἑσπερίαν καὶ Αὐσονίαν αὐτὴν ἐκάλουν, οἱ δ' ἐπιχώριοι Σατορνίαν, ὡς εἴρηταί μοι πρότερον.

XXXVI. Ἔστι δέ τις καὶ ἕτερος λόγος ὑπὸ
τῶν ἐπιχωρίων μυθολογούμενος, ὡς πρὸ τῆς Διὸς
ἀρχῆς ὁ Κρόνος ἐν τῇ γῇ ταύτῃ δυναστεύσειε, καὶ
ὁ λεγόμενος ἐπ' ἐκείνου βίος ἅπασι δαψιλὴς ὁπόσοις

---

[1] For Hellanicus see p. 71, n. 1. The quotation that
follows is frg. 97 in Müller, *F.H.G.* i. p. 58.

But Hellanicus of Lesbos [1] says that when Hercules was driving Geryon's cattle to Argos and was come to Italy, a calf escaped from the herd and in its flight wandered the whole length of the coast and then, swimming across the intervening strait of the sea, came into Sicily. Hercules, following the calf, inquired of the inhabitants wherever he came if anyone had seen it anywhere, and when the people of the island, who understood but little Greek and used their own speech when indicating the animal, called it *vitulus* (the name by which it is still known), he, in memory of the calf, called all the country it had wandered over Vitulia.[2] And it is no wonder that the name has been changed in the course of time to its present form, since many Greek names, too, have met with a similar fate. But whether, as Antiochus says, the country took this name from a ruler, which perhaps is more probable, or, as Hellanicus believes, from the bull, yet this at least is evident from both their accounts, that in Hercules' time, or a little earlier, it received this name. Before that it had been called Hesperia and Ausonia by the Greeks and Saturnia by the natives, as I have already stated.

XXXVI. There is another legend related by the inhabitants, to the effect that before the reign of Jupiter Saturn was lord in this land and that the celebrated manner of life [3] in his reign, abounding

---

[2] Hesychius cites the Greek word ἰταλός (originally Ϝιταλός) for " bull," and Timaeus, Varro and Festus state that *Italia* came from this root.

[3] In Greek ὁ ἐπὶ Κρόνου βίος was proverbial for the Golden Age ; compare the Latin *Saturnia regna*.

115

DIONYSIUS OF HALICARNASSUS

ὧραι φύουσιν οὐ παρ᾽ ἄλλοις μᾶλλον ἢ παρὰ σφίσι
2 γένοιτο. καὶ εἴ τις[1] ἀφελὼν τὸ μυθῶδες τοῦ
λόγου χώρας ἀρετὴν ἐξετάζειν ἐθελήσειεν, ἐξ ἧς
γένος τὸ ἀνθρώπων πλείστας εὐφροσύνας ἐκαρπώ-
σατο γενόμενον εὐθύς, εἴτ᾽ ἐκ γῆς ὡς ὁ παλαιὸς
ἔχει λόγος, εἴτ᾽ ἄλλως πως, οὐκ ἂν εὕροι ταύτης
τινὰ ἐπιτηδειοτέραν. ὡς γὰρ μία γῆ πρὸς ἑτέραν
κρίνεσθαι τοσαύτην τὸ μέγεθος, οὐ μόνον τῆς
Εὐρώπης ἀλλὰ καὶ τῆς ἄλλης ἁπάσης κρατίστη
3 κατ᾽ ἐμὴν δόξαν ἐστὶν Ἰταλία. καίτοι με οὐ
λέληθεν ὅτι πολλοῖς οὐ πιστὰ δόξω λέγειν, ἐνθυμου-
μένοις Αἴγυπτόν τε καὶ Λιβύην καὶ Βαβυλῶνα καὶ
εἰ δή τινες ἄλλοι χῶροί εἰσιν εὐδαίμονες· ἀλλ᾽ ἐγὼ
τὸν ἐκ γῆς πλοῦτον οὐκ ἐν μιᾷ τίθεμαι καρπῶν
ἰδέᾳ οὐδ᾽ εἰσέρχεταί με ζῆλος οἰκήσεως, ἐν ᾗ μόνον
εἰσὶν ἄρουραι πίονες, τῶν δ᾽ ἄλλων οὐδὲν ἢ βραχύ
τι χρησίμων,[2] ἀλλ᾽ ἥτις ἂν εἴη πολυαρκεστάτη τε
καὶ τῶν ἐπεισάκτων ἀγαθῶν ἐπὶ τὸ πολὺ ἐλάχιστον δεομένη, ταύτην κρατίστην εἶναι λογίζομαι.
τοῦτο δὲ τὸ παμφόρον καὶ πολυωφελὲς παρ᾽ ἥν-
τινοῦν ἄλλην γῆν Ἰταλίαν ἔχειν πείθομαι.

XXXVII. Οὐ γὰρ ἀρούρας μὲν ἀγαθὰς ἔχει καὶ
πολλάς, ἄδενδρος δ᾽ ἐστὶν ὡς σιτοφόρος· οὐδ᾽ αὖ
φυτὰ μὲν ἱκανὴ παντοῖα θρέψασθαι, σπείρεσθαι δ᾽
ὡς δενδρῖτις ὀλιγόκαρπος· οὐδ᾽ ἄμφω μὲν ταῦτα
παρέχειν δαψιλής, προβατεύεσθαι δ᾽ ἀνεπιτήδειος·
οὐδ᾽ ἄν τις αὐτὴν φαίη πολύκαρπον μὲν εἶναι καὶ

---

[1] εἴ τις B: εἴ τις ἄλλος R; εἴ τις ἄλλως Sylburg, Jacoby.
[2] Bücheler: χρήσιμον O.

in the produce of every season, was enjoyed by none more than by them. And, indeed, if anyone, setting aside the fabulous part of this account, will examine the merit of any country from which mankind received the greatest enjoyments immediately after their birth, whether they sprang from the earth, according to the ancient tradition, or came into being in some other manner, he will find none more beneficent to them than this. For, to compare one country with another of the same extent, Italy is, in my opinion, the best country, not only of Europe, but even of all the rest of the world. And yet I am not unaware that I shall not be believed by many when they reflect on Egypt, Libya, Babylonia and any other fertile countries there may be. But I, for my part, do not limit the wealth derived from the soil to one sort of produce, nor do I feel any eagerness to live where there are only rich arable lands and little or nothing else that is useful; but I account that country the best which is the most self-sufficient and generally stands least in need of imported commodities. And I am persuaded that Italy enjoys this universal fertility and diversity of advantages beyond any other land.

XXXVII. For Italy does not, while possessing a great deal of good arable land, lack trees, as does a grain-bearing country; nor, on the other hand, while suitable for growing all manner of trees, does it, when sown to grain, produce scanty crops, as does a timbered country; nor yet, while yielding both grain and trees in abundance, is it unsuitable for the grazing of cattle; nor can anyone say that, while it bears rich produce of crops and timber

117

DIONYSIUS OF HALICARNASSUS

πολύδενδρον¹ καὶ πολύβοτον, ἐνδιαίτημα δ' ἀνθρώ
ποις ὑπάρχειν ἄχαρι· ἀλλ' ἔστι πάσης ὡς εἰπεῖν
2 ἡδονῆς τε καὶ ὠφελείας ἔκπλεως. ποίας μὲν
γὰρ λείπεται σιτοφόρου μὴ ποταμοῖς, ἀλλὰ τοῖς
οὐρανίοις ὕδασιν ἀρδομένης τὰ καλούμενα Καμ
πανῶν πεδία, ἐν οἷς ἐγὼ καὶ τρικάρπους ἐθεασάμην
ἀρούρας θερινὸν ἐπὶ χειμερινῷ καὶ μετοπωρινὸν ἐπὶ
θερινῷ σπόρον ἐκτρεφούσας² ; ποίας δ' ἐλαιοφόρου
τὰ Μεσσαπίων καὶ Δαυνίων καὶ Σαβίνων καὶ
πολλῶν ἄλλων γεώργια ; ποίας δ' οἰνοφύτου Τυρ
ρηνία καὶ Ἀλβανὴ³ καὶ τὰ⁴ Φαλερίνων χωρία
θαυμαστῶς ὡς φιλάμπελα καὶ δι' ἐλαχίστου πόνου
πλείστους ἅμα καὶ κρατίστους καρποὺς ἐξενεγκεῖν
3 εὔπορα ; χωρὶς δὲ τῆς ἐνεργοῦ πολλὴν μὲν ἄν
τις εὕροι τὴν εἰς ποίμνας ἀνειμένην αὐτῆς, πολλὴν
δὲ τὴν αἰγίνομον, ἔτι δὲ πλείω καὶ θαυμασιωτέραν
τὴν ἱπποφορβόν τε καὶ βουκολίδα· ἡ γὰρ ἕλειος καὶ
λειμωνία βοτάνη δαψιλὴς οὖσα τῶν τε ὀργάδων ἡ
δροσερὰ καὶ κατάρρυτος ἄπειρος ὅση⁵ θέρει τε καὶ
χειμῶνι⁶ νέμεται καὶ παρέχει διὰ παντὸς εὐθενούσας
4 τὰς ἀγέλας. πάντων δ' εἰσὶν οἱ δρυμοὶ θαυ
μασιώτατοι περί τε τὰ κρημνώδη χωρία καὶ τὰς
νάπας καὶ τοὺς ἀγεωργήτους λόφους, ἐξ ὧν ὕλης⁷
πολλῆς μὲν εὐποροῦσι καὶ καλῆς ναυπηγησίμου,⁸
πολλῆς δὲ τῆς εἰς τὰς ἄλλας ἐργασίας εὐθέτου·

---

¹ καὶ πολύδενδρον added by Bücheler.
² ἐκτρεφούσας O : ἐκφερούσας Meineke, Jacoby.
³ Sylburg : ἀλβανοὶ O.　⁴ τὰ added by Ambrosch.
⁵ ὅση Sylburg : ἢ ABa, ἦ Bb.
⁶ τε καὶ χειμῶνι Meutzner : om. O, Jacoby.
⁷ ὕλης added here by Krüger, after καλῆς by Casaubon, Jacoby.

118

and herds, it is nevertheless disagreeable for men to live in. Nay, on the contrary, it abounds in practically everything that affords either pleasure or profit. To what grain-bearing country, indeed, watered, not with rivers, but with rains from heaven, do the plains of Campania yield, in which I have seen fields that produce even three crops in a year, summer's harvest following upon that of winter and autumn's upon that of summer ? To what olive orchards are those of the Messapians, the Daunians, the Sabines and many others inferior ? To what vineyards those of Tyrrhenia and the Alban and the Falernian districts, where the soil is wonderfully kind to vines and with the least labour produces the finest grapes in the greatest abundance ? And besides the land that is cultivated one will find much that is left untilled as pasturage for sheep and goats, and still more extensive and more wonderful is the land suitable for grazing horses and cattle; for not only the marsh and meadow grass, which is very plentiful, but the dewy and well-watered grass of the glades, infinite in its abundance, furnish grazing for them in summer as well as in winter and keep them always in good condition. But most wonderful of all are the forests growing upon the rocky heights, in the glens and on the uncultivated hills, from which the inhabitants are abundantly supplied with fine timber suitable for the building of ships as well as for all other purposes. Nor are

---

[8] ναυπηγησίμου R : εἰς ναυπήγησιν B.

καὶ τούτων οὐδὲν οὔτε δυσπόριστόν ἐστιν οὔτε
πρόσω τῆς ἀνθρωπίνης χρείας κείμενον, ἀλλ' εὐ-
κατέργαστα καὶ ῥᾴδια παρεῖναι πάντα διὰ πλῆθος
τῶν ποταμῶν, οἳ διαρρέουσιν ἅπασαν τὴν ἀκτὴν
καὶ ποιοῦσι τάς τε κομιδὰς καὶ τὰς ἀμείψεις τῶν
5 ἐκ γῆς φυομένων λυσιτελεῖς. ἔχει δὲ ἡ γῆ καὶ
νάματα θερμῶν ὑδάτων ἐν πολλοῖς εὑρημένα
χωρίοις, λουτρὰ παρασχεῖν ἥδιστα καὶ νόσους
ἰάσασθαι χρονίους ἄριστα, καὶ μέταλλα παντοδαπὰ
καὶ θηρίων ἄγρας ἀφθόνους καὶ θαλάττης φύσιν
πολύγονον ἄλλα τε μυρία, τὰ μὲν εὔχρηστα, τὰ δὲ
θαυμάσια, πάντων δὲ κάλλιστον, ἀέρα κεκραμένον
ταῖς ὥραις συμμέτρως, οἷον ἥκιστα πημαίνειν
κρυμῶν ὑπερβολαῖς ἢ[1] θάλπεσιν ἐξαισίοις καρπῶν
τε γένεσιν καὶ[2] ζῴων φύσιν.

XXXVIII. Οὐδὲν δὴ θαυμαστὸν ἦν τοὺς πα-
λαιοὺς ἱερὰν ὑπολαβεῖν τοῦ Κρόνου τὴν χώραν ταύτην, τὸν μὲν δαίμονα τοῦτον οἰομένους εἶναι πάσης
εὐδαιμονίας δοτῆρα καὶ πληρωτὴν ἀνθρώποις, εἴτε
Κρόνον[3] αὐτὸν δεῖ καλεῖν, ὡς Ἕλληνες ἀξιοῦσιν,
εἴτε Σάτορνον,[4] ὡς Ῥωμαῖοι, πᾶσαν δὲ περιειλη-
φότα τὴν τοῦ κόσμου φύσιν, ὁποτέρως ἄν τις
ὀνομάσῃ, τὴν δὲ χώραν ταύτην ὁρῶντας ἔκπλεω
πάσης εὐπορίας καὶ χάριτος, ἧς τὸ θνητὸν ἐφίεται
γένος, ἀξιοῦντας δὲ καὶ θείῳ καὶ θνητῷ γένει τὸ
πρόσφορον εἶναι[5] πάντων χωρίων ἁρμοδιώτατον,
ὄρη μὲν καὶ νάπας Πανί,[6] λειμῶνας δὲ καὶ τεθηλότα

[1] ἢ Ambrosch: καὶ O.   [2] καὶ Reiske: ἢ O.
[3] Κρόνον Sylburg: χρόνον O.
[4] Σάτορνον Sylburg (after Lapus), Σάτουρνον Jacoby,
Οὐρανὸν Usener: κρόνον AB.   [5] ἀνεῖναι Kiessling.

any of these materials hard to come at or at a distance from human need, but they are easy to handle and readily available, owing to the multitude of rivers that flow through the whole peninsula and make the transportation and exchange of everything the land produces inexpensive. Springs also of hot water have been discovered in many places, affording most pleasant baths and sovereign cures for chronic ailments. There are also mines of all sorts, plenty of wild beasts for hunting, and a great variety of sea fish, besides innumerable other things, some useful and others of a nature to excite wonder. But the finest thing of all is the climate, admirably tempered by the seasons, so that less than elsewhere is harm done by excessive cold or inordinate heat either to the growing fruits and grains or to the bodies of animals.

XXXVIII. It is no wonder, therefore, that the ancients looked upon this country as sacred to Saturn, since they esteemed this god to be the giver and accomplisher of all happiness to mankind,—whether he ought to be called Cronus, as the Greeks deem fitting, or Saturn, as do the Romans,—and regarded him as embracing the whole universe, by whichever name he is called, and since they saw this country abounding in universal plenty and every charm mankind craves, and judged those places to be most agreeable both to divine and to human beings that are suited to them—for example, the mountains and woods to Pan, the meadows and

---

[6] νεῖμαι added after Πανὶ by Reiske.

χωρία νύμφαις, ἀκτὰς δὲ καὶ νήσους πελαγίοις δαίμοσι, τῶν δ' ἄλλων, ὡς ἑκάστῳ τι θεῷ καὶ δαίμονι
2 οἰκεῖον. λέγουσι δὲ καὶ τὰς θυσίας ἐπιτελεῖν
τῷ Κρόνῳ τοὺς παλαιούς, ὥσπερ ἐν Καρχηδόνι
τέως ἡ πόλις διέμεινε καὶ παρὰ Κελτοῖς εἰς τόδε
χρόνου γίνεται καὶ ἐν ἄλλοις τισὶ τῶν ἑσπερίων
ἐθνῶν, ἀνδροφόνους, Ἡρακλέα δὲ παῦσαι τὸν νόμον
τῆς θυσίας βουληθέντα τόν τε βωμὸν ἱδρύσασθαι
τὸν ἐπὶ τῷ Σατορνίῳ καὶ κατάρξασθαι θυμάτων
ἁγνῶν ἐπὶ καθαρῷ πυρὶ ἁγιζομένων,[1] ἵνα δὲ μηδὲν
εἴη τοῖς ἀνθρώποις ἐνθύμιον,[2] ὡς πατρίων ἠλογηκόσι
θυσιῶν, διδάξαι τοὺς ἐπιχωρίους ἀπομειλιττομένους
τὴν τοῦ θεοῦ μῆνιν ἀντὶ τῶν ἀνθρώπων, οὓς
συμποδίζοντες καὶ τῶν χειρῶν ἀκρατεῖς ποιοῦντες
ἐρρίπτουν εἰς τὸ τοῦ Τεβέριος ῥεῖθρον, εἴδωλα
ποιοῦντας ἀνδρείκελα κεκοσμημένα τὸν αὐτὸν ἐκείνοις τρόπον ἐμβαλεῖν εἰς τὸν ποταμόν, ἵνα δὴ τὸ
τῆς ὀττείας ὅ τι δή ποτε ἦν ἐν ταῖς ἁπάντων
ψυχαῖς παραμένον ἐξαιρεθῇ τῶν εἰκόνων τοῦ
3 παλαιοῦ πάθους[3] ἔτι σωζομένων. τοῦτο δὲ καὶ
μέχρις ἐμοῦ ἔτι διετέλουν Ῥωμαῖοι δρῶντες[4]
ὁσέτη[5] μικρὸν ὕστερον τῆς[6] ἐαρινῆς ἰσημερίας ἐν
μηνὶ Μαΐῳ ταῖς καλουμέναις εἰδοῖς, διχομήνιδα
βουλόμενοι ταύτην εἶναι τὴν ἡμέραν, ἐν ᾗ προθύ-
σαντες ἱερὰ τὰ κατὰ τοὺς νόμους οἱ καλούμενοι
ποντίφικες, ἱερέων οἱ διαφανέστατοι, καὶ σὺν αὐ-

---

[1] ἁγιζομένων Ambrosch (from Eusebius), σφαζομένων
Reiske : ἀζομένων AB.
[2] ἐνθύμιον A : δέος ἢ ἐνθύμιον B, δέους ἐνθύμιον Eusebius.
[3] πάθους B : ἔθους A.   [4] δρῶντες A : om. B.

verdant places to the nymphs, the shores and islands
to the sea-gods, and all the other places to the god
or genius to whom each is appropriate. It is
said also that the ancients sacrificed human victims
to Saturn, as was done at Carthage while that city
stood and as is still done to this day among the
Gauls [1] and certain other western nations, and that
Hercules, desiring to abolish the custom of this
sacrifice, erected the altar upon the Saturnian hill
and performed the initial rites of sacrifice with un-
blemished victims burning on a pure fire. And lest
the people should feel any scruple at having neglected
their traditional sacrifices, he taught them to appease
the anger of the god by making effigies resembling
the men they had been wont to bind hand and foot
and throw into the stream of the Tiber, and dressing
these in the same manner, to throw them into the
river instead of the men, his purpose being that any
superstitious dread remaining in the minds of all
might be removed, since the semblance of the ancient
rite would still be preserved. This the Romans
continued to do every year even down to my
day a little after the vernal equinox, in the month
of May,[2] on what they call the Ides (the day they
mean to be the middle of the month); on this
day, after offering the preliminary sacrifices according to the laws, the *pontifices*, as the most
important of the priests are called, and with

---

[1] Dionysius regularly uses the word Celts for Gauls;
but it seems preferable to follow the English usage in the
translation. [2] See p. 105, n. 2.

---

[5] ὁσέτη (ὅσα ἔτη) Ambrosch: ὅσοντι B, om. A, Jacoby.
[6] τῆς Ambrosch: om. O, Jacoby.

τοῖς αἱ τὸ ἀθάνατον πῦρ διαφυλάττουσαι παρθένοι
στρατηγοί τε καὶ τῶν ἄλλων πολιτῶν οὓς παρεῖναι
ταῖς ἱερουργίαις θέμις εἴδωλα μορφαῖς ἀνθρώπων
εἰκασμένα, τριάκοντα τὸν ἀριθμόν, ἀπὸ τῆς ἱερᾶς
γεφύρας βάλλουσιν εἰς τὸ ῥεῦμα τοῦ Τεβέριος,
4 Ἀργείους αὐτὰ καλοῦντες. ἀλλὰ γὰρ περὶ μὲν
τῶν θυσιῶν καὶ τῶν ἄλλων ἱερουργιῶν, ἃς ἡ
Ῥωμαίων πόλις συντελεῖ κατά τε τὸν Ἑλληνικὸν
καὶ τὸν ἐπιχώριον τρόπον, ἐν ἑτέρῳ λόγῳ δηλώ-
σομεν, ἀπαιτεῖν δὲ ὁ παρὼν καιρὸς ἔοικε καὶ περὶ
τῆς Ἡρακλέους ἀφίξεως εἰς Ἰταλίαν μετ᾽ ἐπιστά-
σεως πλείονος διελθεῖν καὶ εἴ τι λόγου ἄξιον ἔδρασεν
αὐτόθι μὴ παραλιπεῖν.

XXXIX. Ἔστι δὲ τῶν ὑπὲρ τοῦ δαίμονος τοῦδε
λεγομένων τὰ μὲν μυθικώτερα, τὰ δ᾽ ἀληθέστερα.
ὁ μὲν οὖν μυθικὸς περὶ τῆς παρουσίας αὐτοῦ λόγος
ὧδ᾽ ἔχει· ὡς δὴ κελευσθεὶς ὑπ᾽ Εὐρυσθέως Ἡρακλῆς
σὺν τοῖς ἄλλοις ἄθλοις καὶ τὰς Γηρυόνου βοῦς ἐξ
Ἐρυθείας εἰς Ἄργος ἀπελάσαι, τελέσας τὸν ἆθλον
καὶ τὴν οἴκαδε πορείαν ποιούμενος ἄλλη τε πολλαχῇ
τῆς Ἰταλίας ἀφίκετο καὶ τῆς Ἀβοριγίνων γῆς εἰς
2 τὸ προσεχὲς τῷ Παλλαντίῳ χωρίον. εὑρὼν δὲ
πόαν ἐν αὐτῷ βουκολίδα πολλὴν καὶ καλήν, τὰς
μὲν βοῦς ἀνῆκεν εἰς νομήν,[1] αὐτὸς δὲ βαρυνόμενος
ὑπὸ κόπου κατακλιθεὶς ἔδωκεν αὐτὸν ὕπνῳ. ἐν δὲ

[1] νομήν L. Dindorf : ἐκνομὴν O.

---

[1] According to Varro the number of these effigies, made
of bulrushes, was twenty-seven, equal to the number of
the chapels, also called *Argei*, situated in various parts of
the city. The number thirty given by Dionysius would

them the virgins who guard the perpetual fire, the praetors, and such of the other citizens as may lawfully be present at the rites, throw from the sacred bridge into the stream of the Tiber thirty effigies made in the likeness of men, which they call *Argei*.[1] But concerning the sacrifices and the other rites which the Roman people perform according to the manner both of the Greeks and of their own country I shall speak in another book.[2] At present, it seems requisite to give a more particular account of the arrival of Hercules in Italy and to omit nothing worthy of notice that he did there.

XXXIX. Of[3] the stories told concerning this god some are largely legend and some are nearer the truth. The legendary account of his arrival is as follows : Hercules, being commanded by Eurystheus, among other labours, to drive Geryon's cattle from Erytheia[4] to Argos, performed the task, and having passed through many parts of Italy on his way home, came also to the neighbourhood of Pallantium in the country of the Aborigines ; and there, finding much excellent grass for his cattle, he let them graze, and being overcome with weariness, lay down and gave himself over to sleep. Thereupon a robber

mean one for each *curia ;* but this does not seem so probable. The sacred bridge was the *pons sublicius.* For a full discussion of the *Argei* see Sir James Frazer's note on Ovid, *Fasti* v. 621 (vol. iv. pp. 74 ff., condensed in his *L.C.L.* edition, pp. 425 ff.). [2] In vii. 72, 14-18.

[3] For chaps. 39-40 *cf.* Livy i. 7, 4-14.

[4] Erytheia ("Red" Island) was perhaps originally the fabulous land of the sunset glow. Later it was usually placed somewhere near the Pillars of Hercules.

τούτῳ λῃστής τις ἐπιχώριος ὄνομα Κάκος περι-
τυγχάνει ταῖς βουσὶν ἀφυλάκτοις νεμομέναις καὶ
αὐτῶν ἔρωτα ἴσχει. ὡς δὲ τὸν Ἡρακλέα κοιμώ-
μενον αὐτοῦ κατέμαθεν, ἁπάσας μὲν οὐκ ἂν ᾤετο
δύνασθαι λαθεῖν ἀπελάσας, καὶ ἅμα οὐδὲ ῥᾴδιον
ὂν[1] τὸ πρᾶγμα κατεμάνθανεν· ὀλίγας δέ τινας ἐξ
αὐτῶν εἰς τὸ ἄντρον, ἐν ᾧ πλησίον ὄντι ἐτύγχανε
τὴν δίαιταν ποιούμενος, ἀποκρύπτεται ἔμπαλιν τῆς
κατὰ φύσιν τοῖς ζῴοις πορείας ἐπισπώμενος ἑκάστην κατ' οὐράν. τοῦτο δὲ αὐτῷ τῶν ἐλέγχων
ἀφανισμὸν ἐδύνατο παρασχεῖν ἐναντίας φανησο-
3 μένης[2] τοῖς ἴχνεσι τῆς ὁδοῦ. ἀναστὰς δὲ μετ'
ὀλίγον ὁ Ἡρακλῆς καὶ τὸν ἀριθμὸν ἐπιλεξάμενος
τῶν βοῶν, ὡς ἔμαθέ τινας[3] ἐκλειπούσας, τέως μὲν
ἠπόρει ποῦ κεχωρήκασι καὶ ὡς πεπλανημένας ἀπὸ
τῆς νομῆς ἐμάστευεν ἀνὰ τὸν χῶρον·[4] ὡς δ' οὐχ
εὕρισκεν ἐπὶ τὸ σπήλαιον ἀφικνεῖται τοῖς μὲν
ἴχνεσι διαρτώμενος, οὐδὲν δὲ ἧττον οἰόμενος δεῖν[5]
διερευνήσασθαι τὸν χῶρον. τοῦ δὲ Κάκου πρὸ τῆς
θύρας ἑστῶτος καὶ οὔτ' ἰδεῖν τὰς βοῦς φάσκοντος
ἐρομένῳ οὔτ' ἐρευνᾶσθαι ἐπιτρέποντος αἰτουμένῳ
τούς τε πλησίον ὡς δεινὰ πάσχοι ὑπὸ τοῦ ξένου
ἐπιβοῶντος, ἀμηχανῶν ὁ Ἡρακλῆς ὅ τι χρήσεται
τῷ πράγματι εἰς νοῦν βάλλεται προσελάσαι τῷ
σπηλαίῳ τὰς ἄλλας βοῦς. ὡς δὲ ἄρα τῆς συν-
νόμου φωνῆς τε καὶ ὀσμῆς αἱ ἔντοσθεν ᾔσθοντο,
ἀντεμυκῶντο ταῖς ἔκτοσθεν καὶ ἐγεγόνει ἡ φωνὴ

---

[1] ὂν added by Usener, Cobet.
[2] φανησομένης A : φαινομένης B.
[3] τινας Cobet : τὰς O.

of that region, named Cacus, chanced to come upon the cattle feeding with none to guard them and longed to possess them. But seeing Hercules lying there asleep, he imagined he could not drive them all away without being discovered and at the same time he perceived that the task was no easy one, either. So he secreted a few of them in the cave hard by, in which he lived, dragging each of them thither by the tail backwards. This might have destroyed all evidence of his theft, as the direction in which the oxen had gone would be at variance with their tracks. Hercules, then, arising from sleep soon afterwards, and having counted the cattle and found some were missing, was for some time at a loss to guess where they had gone, and supposing them to have strayed from their pasture, he sought them up and down the region ; then, when he failed to find them, he came to the cave, and though he was deceived by the tracks, he felt, nevertheless, that he ought to search the place. But Cacus stood before the door, and when Hercules inquired after the cattle, denied that he had seen them, and when the other desired to search the cave, would not suffer him to do so, but called upon his neighbours for assistance, complaining of the violence offered to him by the stranger. And while Hercules was puzzled to know how he should act in the matter, he hit upon the expedient of driving the rest of the cattle to the cave. And thus, when those inside heard the lowing and perceived the smell of their companions outside, they bellowed to them in turn and thus their lowing

---

⁴τὸν χῶρον B : τὴν χώραν R.　　⁵δεῖν Schmitz : εἶναι O.

4 αὐτῶν κατήγορος τῆς κλοπῆς. ὁ μὲν οὖν Κάκος,
ἐπειδὴ περιφανὴς ἐγένετο κακουργῶν, τρέπεται
πρὸς ἀλκὴν καὶ τοὺς εἰωθότας αὐτῷ συναγραυλεῖν
ἀνεκάλει· Ἡρακλῆς δὲ ἀλοιῶν[1] αὐτὸν τῷ ῥοπάλῳ
κτείνει, καὶ τὰς βοῦς ἐξαγαγών, ἐπειδὴ κακούργων
ὑποδοχαῖς εὔθετον ἑώρα τὸ χωρίον, ἐπικατασκάπτει
τῷ κλωπὶ[2] τὸ σπήλαιον. ἁγνίσας δὲ τῷ ποταμῷ
τὸν φόνον ἱδρύεται πλησίον τοῦ τόπου Διὸς Εὑρεσίου
βωμόν, ὅς ἐστι τῆς Ῥώμης παρὰ τῇ Τριδύμῳ πύλῃ,
καὶ θύει τῷ θεῷ δάμαλιν ἕνα τῆς εὑρέσεως τῶν βοῶν
χαριστήριον. ταύτην ἔτι καὶ εἰς ἐμὲ τὴν θυσίαν ἡ Ῥωμαίων πόλις συνετέλει, νομίμοις Ἑλληνικοῖς ἅπασιν
ἐν αὐτῇ χρωμένη, καθάπερ ἐκεῖνος κατεστήσατο.

XL. Οἱ δὲ Ἀβοριγῖνες καὶ τῶν Ἀρκάδων οἱ τὸ
Παλλάντιον κατοικοῦντες, ὡς τοῦ τε Κάκου τὸν
θάνατον ἔγνωσαν καὶ τὸν Ἡρακλέα εἶδον, τῷ μὲν
ἀπεχθόμενοι διὰ τὰς ἁρπαγάς, τοῦ δὲ τὴν ὄψιν ἐκ-
παγλούμενοι θεῖόν τι χρῆμα ἐνόμισαν ὁρᾶν καὶ τοῦ
λῃστοῦ μέγα εὐτύχημα τὴν ἀπαλλαγὴν[3] ἐποιοῦντο.
οἱ δὲ πένητες αὐτῶν κλάδους δρεψάμενοι δάφνης, ἣ
πολλὴ περὶ τὸν τόπον ἐφύετο, ἐκεῖνόν τε καὶ
αὐτοὺς ἀνέστεφον, ἧκον δὲ οἱ βασιλεῖς αὐτῶν ἐπὶ
ξένια τὸν Ἡρακλέα καλοῦντες. ὡς δὲ καὶ τοὔνομα
καὶ τὸ γένος αὐτοῦ καὶ τὰς πράξεις διεξιόντος
ἔμαθον, ἐνεχείριζον αὐτῷ τήν τε χώραν καὶ σφᾶς
2 αὐτοὺς ἐπὶ φιλίᾳ. Εὔανδρος δὲ παλαίτερον ἔτι τῆς
Θέμιδος ἀκηκοὼς διεξιούσης, ὅτι πεπρωμένον εἴη

---

[1] ἀλοιῶν R : ἀλύων Bb ; ἀλοῶν Reudler.
[2] τῷ κλωπὶ Bb, τῷ κάλωπι Ba : τῇ καλαύροπι A, Jacoby.
[3] Schwartz : ἀποβολὴν O, Jacoby.

betrayed the theft. Cacus, therefore, when his thievery was thus brought to light, put himself upon his defence and began to call out to his fellow herdsmen. But Hercules killed him by smiting him with his club and drove out the cattle ; and when he saw that the place was well adapted to the harbouring of evil-doers, he demolished the cave, burying the robber under its ruins. Then, having purified himself in the river from the murder, he erected an altar near the place to Jupiter the Discoverer,[1] which is now in Rome near the Porta Trigemina, and sacrificed a calf to the god as a thank-offering for the finding of his cattle. This sacrifice the city of Rome continued to celebrate even down to my day, observing in it all the ceremonies of the Greeks just as he instituted them.

XL. When the Aborigines and the Arcadians who lived at Pallantium learned of the death of Cacus and saw Hercules, they thought themselves very fortunate in being rid of the former, whom they detested for his robberies, and were struck with awe at the appearance of the latter, in whom they seemed to see something divine. The poorer among them, plucking branches of laurel which grew there in great plenty, crowned both him and themselves with it ; and their kings also came to invite Hercules to be their guest. But when they heard from him his name, his lineage and his achievements, they recommended both their country and themselves to his friendship. And Evander, who had even before this heard Themis relate that it was ordained

[1] Jupiter Inventor.

τὸν ἐκ Διὸς καὶ Ἀλκμήνης γενόμενον Ἡρακλέα
διαμείψαντα τὴν θνητὴν φύσιν ἀθάνγατον ἐνέσθαι
δι' ἀρετήν, ἐπειδὴ τάχιστα ὅστις ἦν ἐπύθετο,
φθάσαι βουλόμενος ἅπαντας ἀνθρώπους Ἡρακλέα
θεῶν τιμαῖς πρῶτος ἱλασάμενος, βωμὸν αὐτοσχέδιον
ὑπὸ σπουδῆς ἱδρύεται καὶ δάμαλιν ἄζυγα θύει πρὸς
αὐτῷ, τὸ θέσφατον ἀφηγησάμενος Ἡρακλεῖ καὶ
3 δεηθεὶς τῶν ἱερῶν κατάρξασθαι. ἀγασθεὶς δὲ
τοὺς ἀνθρώπους τῆς φιλοξενίας Ἡρακλῆς, τὸν μὲν
δῆμον ἑστιάσει ὑποδέχεται θύσας τῶν βοῶν τινας
καὶ τῆς ἄλλης λείας τὰς δεκάτας ἐξελών· τοὺς δὲ
βασιλεῖς χώρᾳ πολλῇ δωρεῖται Λιγύων τε καὶ τῶν
ἄλλων προσοίκων, ἧς μέγα ἐποιοῦντο ἄρχειν, παρα-
νόμους τινὰς ἐξ αὐτῆς ἐκβαλὼν ἀνθρώπους. λέγεται
δὲ πρὸς τούτοις, ὡς καὶ δέησίν τινα ποιήσαιτο τῶν
ἐπιχωρίων, ἐπειδὴ πρῶτοι θεὸν αὐτὸν ἐνόμισαν,
ὅπως ἀθανάτους αὐτῷ διαφυλάττωσι τὰς τιμάς,
θύοντες μὲν ἄζυγα δάμαλιν ἀνὰ πᾶν ἔτος, ἁγιστεύ-
οντες δὲ τὴν ἱερουργίαν ἔθεσιν Ἑλληνικοῖς· καὶ ὡς
διδάξειεν αὐτὸς [1] τὰς θυσίας, ἵνα διὰ παντὸς αὐτῷ
κεχαρισμένα θύοιεν, οἴκους δύο τῶν ἐπιφανῶν.[2]
4 εἶναι δὲ τοὺς μαθόντας τότε τὴν Ἑλληνικὴν ἱερουργίαν Ποτιτίους τε καὶ Πιναρίους, ἀφ' ὧν τὰ γένη
διαμεῖναι μέχρι πολλοῦ τὴν ἐπιμέλειαν ποιούμενα
τῶν θυσιῶν, ὡς ἐκεῖνος κατεστήσατο, Ποτιτίων μὲν
ἡγουμένων τῆς ἱερουργίας καὶ τῶν ἐμπύρων ἀπαρ-
χομένων, Πιναρίων δὲ σπλάγχνων τε μετουσίας
εἰργομένων καὶ ὅσα ἄλλα ἐχρῆν ὑπ' ἀμφοῖν γίνεσθαι

---

[1] αὐτὸς Reiske : αὐτοὺς O, Jacoby.
[2] ἐπιφανῶν B, Reiske : ἐπιφανῶν παραλαβών R, Jacoby.

by fate that Hercules, the son of Jupiter and Alcmena, changing his mortal nature, should become immortal by reason of his virtue, as soon as he learned who the stranger was, resolved to forestall all mankind by being the first to propitiate Hercules with divine honours, and he hastily erected an improvised altar and sacrificed upon it a calf that had not known the yoke, having first communicated the oracle to Hercules and asked him to perform the initial rites. And Hercules, admiring the hospitality of these men, entertained the common people with a feast, after sacrificing some of the cattle and setting apart the tithes of the rest of his booty ; and to their kings he gave a large district belonging to the Ligurians and to some others of their neighbours, the rule of which they very much desired, after he had first expelled some lawless people from it. It is furthermore reported that he asked the inhabitants, since they were the first who had regarded him as a god, to perpetuate the honours they had paid him by offering up every year a calf that had not known the yoke and performing the sacrifice with Greek rites ; and that he himself taught the sacrificial rites to two of the distinguished families, in order that their offerings might always be acceptable to him. Those who were then instructed in the Greek ceremony, they say, were the Potitii and the Pinarii, whose descendants continued for a long time to have the superintendence of these sacrifices, in the manner he had appointed, the Potitii presiding at the sacrifice and taking the first part of the burnt-offerings, while the Pinarii were excluded from tasting the inwards and held second rank in those ceremonies which had to be performed by both of

131

τὴν δευτέραν τιμὴν ἐχόντων. ταύτην δὲ αὐτοῖς
προστεθῆναι τὴν ἀτιμίαν ὀψίμου τῆς παρουσίας
ἕνεκα, ἐπειδὴ ἔωθεν αὐτοῖς κελευσθὲν ἥκειν ἐσπλαγ-
5 χνευμένων ἤδη τῶν ἱερῶν ἀφίκοντο. νῦν μέντοι
οὐκέτι τοῖς γένεσι τούτοις ἡ περὶ τὰς ἱερουργίας
ἐπιμέλεια ἀνάκειται, ἀλλὰ παῖδες ἐκ τοῦ δημοσίου
ὠνητοὶ δρῶσιν αὐτάς.[1] δι' ἃς δὲ αἰτίας τὸ ἔθος
μετέπεσε καὶ τίς ἡ τοῦ δαίμονος ἐπιφάνεια περὶ
τὴν ἀλλαγὴν τῶν ἱεροποιῶν ἐγένετο, ἐπειδὰν κατὰ
τοῦτο γένωμαι τοῦ λόγου τὸ μέρος, διηγήσομαι.
6 ὁ δὲ βωμός, ἐφ' οὗ τὰς δεκάτας ἀπέθυσεν[2]
Ἡρακλῆς, καλεῖται μὲν ὑπὸ Ῥωμαίων Μέγιστος,
ἔστι δὲ τῆς[3] Βοαρίας λεγομένης ἀγορᾶς πλησίον,
ἁγιστευόμενος εἰ καί τις ἄλλος ὑπὸ τῶν ἐπιχωρίων·
ὅρκοι τε γὰρ ἐπ' αὐτῷ καὶ συνθῆκαι τοῖς βουλομένοις βεβαίως τι διαπράττεσθαι καὶ δεκατεύσεις
χρημάτων γίνονται συχναὶ κατ' εὐχάς· τῇ μέντοι
κατασκευῇ πολὺ τῆς δόξης ἐστὶ καταδεέστερος·
πολλαχῇ δὲ καὶ ἄλλῃ τῆς Ἰταλίας ἀνεῖται τεμένη
τῷ θεῷ καὶ βωμοὶ κατὰ πόλεις τε ἵδρυνται καὶ
παρ' ὁδούς, καὶ σπανίως ἂν εὕροι τις Ἰταλίας
χῶρον ἔνθα μὴ τυγχάνει τιμώμενος ὁ θεός. ὁ
μὲν οὖν μυθικὸς λόγος ὑπὲρ αὐτοῦ τοιόσδε παραδέδοται.

XLI. Ὁ δ' ἀληθέστερος, ᾧ πολλοὶ τῶν ἐν
ἱστορίας σχήματι τὰς πράξεις αὐτοῦ διηγησαμένων
ἐχρήσαντο, τοιόσδε· ὡς στρατηλάτης γενόμενος

---

[1] αὐτὰς Bb : αὐταῖς Ba, αὐτοῖς A.
[2] Krüger : ἐπέθυσεν O.
[3] τῆς added by Kiessling.

them together. It is said that this disgrace was
fixed upon them for having been late in arriving;
for though they had been ordered to be present
early in the morning, they did not come till the entrails had been eaten. To-day, however, the superintendence of the sacrifices no longer devolves on
these families, but slaves purchased with the public
money perform them. For what reasons this
custom was changed and how the god manifested
himself concerning the change in his ministers, I
shall relate when I come to that part of the history.[1]
The altar on which Hercules offered up the tithes is
called by the Romans the Greatest Altar.[2] It stands
near the place they call the Cattle Market[3] and no
other is held in greater veneration by the inhabitants;
for upon this altar oaths are taken and agreements
made by those who wish to transact any business
unalterably and the tithes of things are frequently
offered there pursuant to vows. However, in its
construction it is much inferior to its reputation.
In many other places also in Italy precincts are
dedicated to this god and altars erected to him,
both in cities and along highways; and one could
scarcely find any place in Italy in which the god
is not honoured. Such, then, is the legendary
account that has been handed down concerning him.

XLI. But the story which comes nearer to the
truth and which has been adopted by many who
have narrated his deeds in the form of history
is as follows: Hercules, who was the greatest

[1] In a portion of the work now lost.
[2] *Ara maxima.*
[3] *Forum boarium.*

ἁπάντων κράτιστος τῶν καθ' ἑαυτὸν Ἡρακλῆς καὶ
δυνάμεως πολλῆς ἡγούμενος ἅπασαν ἐπῆλθε τὴν
ἐντὸς Ὠκεανοῦ, καταλύων μὲν εἴ τις εἴη τυραννὶς
βαρεῖα καὶ λυπηρὰ τοῖς ἀρχομένοις ἢ πόλις ὑβρί-
ζουσα καὶ λωβωμένη τὰς πέλας ἢ ἡγεμονία[1] ἀνθρώπων ἀνημέρῳ διαίτῃ καὶ ξενοκτονίαις ἀθεμίτοις[2]
χρωμένων, καθιστὰς δὲ νομίμους βασιλείας καὶ
σωφρονικὰ πολιτεύματα καὶ βίων ἔθη φιλάνθρωπα
καὶ κοινοπαθῆ· πρὸς δὲ τούτοις Ἕλλησί τε βαρβάρους συγκεραννύμενος καὶ θαλαττίοις ἠπειρώτας,
οἳ τέως ἀπίστους καὶ ἀσυναλλάκτους εἶχον ὁμιλίας,
ἐρήμῳ τε γῇ πόλεις ἐνιδρυόμενος καὶ ποταμοὺς
ἐκτρέπων ἐπικλύζοντας πεδία καὶ τρίβους ἐκτέμνων
ἀβάτοις ὄρεσι καὶ τἆλλα μηχανώμενος, ὡς ἅπασα
γῆ καὶ θάλαττα κοινὴ ταῖς ἁπάντων χρείαις γενή-
2 σοιτο. ἀφίκετο δὲ εἰς Ἰταλίαν οὐ μονόστολος
οὐδὲ ἀγέλην[3] βοῶν ἐπαγόμενος[4] (οὔτε γὰρ ὁ
χῶρος ἐν τρίβῳ τοῖς εἰς Ἄργος ἐξ Ἰβηρίας ἀνακομιζομένοις,[5] οὔτε τοῦ διελθεῖν ἕνεκα τὴν χώραν
τοσαύτης ἂν ἠξιώθη τιμῆς) ἀλλ' ἐπὶ δουλώσει καὶ
ἀρχῇ τῶν τῇδε ἀνθρώπων στρατὸν ἄγων πολὺν
Ἰβηρίαν ἤδη κεχειρωμένος· διατρῖψαί τε αὐτόθι
πλείω χρόνον ἠναγκάσθη τοῦ τε ναυτικοῦ τῇ
ἀπουσίᾳ, ἢ ἐγένετο χειμῶνος ἐπιλαβόντος,[6] καὶ τῷ

---

[1] ἢ ἡγεμονία Kiessling, ἢ ἡγεμὼν Sintenis, ἢ μοναὶ Meineke :
ἡγεμονίας R, ἡγεμονείας B.
[2] Steph. : ἀθεμίστοις AB, Jacoby.
[3] ἀγέλην R ; ἀγέλη B.
[4] ἐπαγόμενος Ab : ἐπάμενος Aa, σπόμενος B ; ἑπόμενος
Kiessling.

commander of his age, marched at the head of a large
force through all the country that lies on this side
of the Ocean, destroying any despotisms that were
grievous and oppressive to their subjects, or common-
wealths that outraged and injured the neighbouring states, or organized bands of men who lived in
the manner of savages and lawlessly put strangers
to death, and in their room establishing lawful
monarchies, well-ordered governments and humane
and sociable modes of life. Furthermore, he mingled
barbarians with Greeks, and inhabitants of the
inland with dwellers on the sea coast, groups which
hitherto had been distrustful and unsocial in their
dealings with each other ; he also built cities in
desert places, turned the course of rivers that overflowed the fields, cut roads through inaccessible
mountains, and contrived other means by which
every land and sea might lie open to the use of all
mankind. And he came into Italy not alone nor
yet bringing a herd of cattle (for neither does this
country lie on the road of those returning from
Spain to Argos nor would he have been deemed
worthy of so great honour merely for passing through
it), but at the head of a great army, after he had
already conquered Spain, in order to subjugate and
rule the people in this region ; and he was obliged
to tarry there a considerable time both because of
the absence of his fleet, due to stormy weather that

---

⁵ ἀνακομιζομένοις Steph.², ἀνασκευαζομένοις Steph.², Jacoby:
ἀναγκαζομένοις AB.

⁶ ἐπιλαβόντος Cmg, Sintenis: ἐπιβαλόντος AB.

μὴ πάντα τὰ ἔθνη τὰ κατέχοντα Ἰταλίαν προσ-
3 χωρῆσαι αὐτῷ ἑκούσια· χωρὶς γὰρ τῶν ἄλλων
βαρβάρων τὸ Λιγύων γένος πολὺ καὶ μάχιμον, ἐπὶ
ταῖς παρόδοις τῶν Ἀλπείων ὀρῶν ἱδρυμένον, ἀπο-
κωλύειν ὅπλοις τὰς εἰσβολὰς αὐτοῦ τὰς εἰς Ἰταλίαν
ἐπεχείρησεν, ἔνθα μέγιστος ἀγὼν τοῖς Ἕλλησιν
ἐγένετο πάντων αὐτοὺς ἐπιλειπόντων ἐν τῇ μάχῃ
τῶν βελῶν. δηλοῖ δὲ τὸν πόλεμον τόνδε τῶν
ἀρχαίων ποιητῶν Αἰσχύλος ἐν Προμηθεῖ λυομένῳ.
πεποίηται γὰρ αὐτῷ ὁ Προμηθεὺς Ἡρακλεῖ τά τε
ἄλλα προλέγων, ὡς ἕκαστον αὐτῷ τι συμβήσεσθαι
ἔμελλε κατὰ τὴν ἐπὶ Γηρυόνην στρατείαν, καὶ δὴ
καὶ περὶ τοῦ Λιγυστικοῦ πολέμου ὡς οὐ ῥᾴδιος ὁ
ἀγὼν ἔσται διηγούμενος. τὰ δὲ ποιήματα ὧδ' ἔχει·

ἥξεις δὲ Λιγύων εἰς ἀτάρβητον στρατόν,
ἔνθ' οὐ μάχης, σάφ' οἶδα, καὶ θοῦρός περ ὢν
μέμψει. πέπρωται γάρ σε καὶ βέλη λιπεῖν.

XLII. Ἐπειδὴ δὲ τούτους καταστρεψάμενος τῶν
παρόδων ἐκράτησεν, οἱ μέν τινες ἑκούσιοι παρεδίδοσαν αὐτῷ τὰς πόλεις, μάλιστα δὲ ὅσοι ἀπὸ τοῦ
Ἑλληνικοῦ γένους ἦσαν ἢ δυνάμεις οὐκ εἶχον
ἀξιοχρέους, οἱ δὲ πλείους ἐκ πολέμου καὶ πολι-
2 ορκίας παρίσταντο. ἐν δὴ τούτοις τοῖς[1] μάχῃ
κρατηθεῖσι καὶ τὸν ὑπὸ Ῥωμαίων μυθολογούμενον
Κάκον, δυνάστην τινὰ κομιδῇ βάρβαρον καὶ ἀνθρώπων ἀνημέρων ἄρχοντα, γενέσθαι φασὶν αὐτῷ διάφορον, ἐρυμνοῖς χωρίοις ἐπικαθήμενον καὶ διὰ ταῦτα

---

[1] τοῖς added by Reiske.

detained it, and because not all the nations of Italy willingly submitted to him. For, besides the other barbarians, the Ligurians, a numerous and warlike people seated in the passes of the Alps, endeavoured to prevent his entrance into Italy by force of arms, and in that place so great a battle was fought by the Greeks that all their missiles gave out in the course of the fighting. This war is mentioned by Aeschylus, among the ancient poets, in his *Prometheus Unbound*; for there Prometheus is represented as foretelling to Hercules in detail how everything else was to befall him on his expedition against Geryon and in particular recounting to him the difficult struggle he was to have in the war with the Ligurians. The verses are these :

" And thou shalt come to Liguria's dauntless host,
  Where no fault shalt thou find, bold though thou
      art,
  With the fray : 'tis fated thy missiles all shall
      fail." [1]

XLII. After Hercules had defeated this people and gained the passes, some delivered up their cities to him of their own accord, particularly those who were of Greek extraction or who had no considerable forces ; but the greatest part of them were reduced by war and siege. Among those who were conquered in battle, they say, was Cacus, who is celebrated in the Roman legend, an exceedingly barbarous chieftain reigning over a savage people, who had set himself to oppose Hercules ; he was established in the fastnesses and on that account

[1] Nauck, *T.G.F.*[2], p. 66, frg. 199.

τοῖς πλησιοχώροις ὄντα λυπηρόν. ὃς ἐπειδὴ κατα-
στρατοπεδεύσαντα τὸν Ἡρακλέα ἔμαθεν ἐν τῷ
προσεχεῖ πεδίῳ, ληστρικῶς διασκευασάμενος ἐπι-
δρομῇ αἰφνιδίῳ ἐχρήσατο κατακοιμωμένου[1] τοῦ
στρατοῦ καὶ τῆς λείας ὅσῃ ἐπέτυχεν ἀφυλάκτῳ
3 περιβαλόμενος ἀπήλασεν. ὕστερον δὲ κατακλει-
σθεὶς ὑπὸ τῶν Ἑλλήνων εἰς πολιορκίαν, τά τε
φρούρια κατὰ κράτος ἁλόντ᾽[2] ἐπεῖδε[3] καὶ αὐτὸς ἐν
τοῖς ἐρύμασιν[4] ἀνῃρέθη. τῶν δὲ φρουρίων αὐτοῦ
κατασκαφέντων τὰ πέριξ χωρία οἱ συνεξελθόντες
Ἡρακλεῖ κατὰ σφᾶς ἑκάτεροι[5] παρέλαβον, Ἀρκάδες
τέ τινες οἱ σὺν Εὐάνδρῳ καὶ Φαῦνος ὁ τῶν Ἀβοριγίνων βασιλεύς. εἰκάσειε δ᾽ ἄν τις καὶ τοὺς
ὑπομείναντας αὐτόθι τῶν Ἑλλήνων Ἐπειοὺς καὶ
τοὺς ἐκ Φενεοῦ Ἀρκάδας καὶ Τρῶας ἐπὶ φυλακῇ
4 τῆς χώρας καταλειφθῆναι. στρατηγικὸν γὰρ δὴ
καὶ τοῦτο τῶν Ἡρακλέους ἔργων καὶ οὐδενὸς
ἧττον θαυμάζεσθαι ἐπιτήδειον, τὸ δὴ τοὺς ἀνασπά-
στους ἐκ τῶν κεκρατημένων πόλεων τέως μὲν
ἐπάγεσθαι κατὰ τὰς στρατείας, ἐπεὶ δὲ προθύμως
τοὺς πολέμους συνδιενέγκαιεν εἰς τὰ δορίκτητα
κατοικίζειν καὶ[6] τοῖς παρ᾽ ἑτέρων ἐπιχορηγηθεῖσι
δωρεῖσθαι πλούτοις. διὰ μὲν δὴ ταῦτα μέγιστον
ὄνομα καὶ κλέος Ἡρακλέους ἐν Ἰταλίᾳ γεγένηται,[7]
καὶ οὐ τῆς παρόδου χάριν, ᾗ σεμνὸν οὐδὲν προσῆν.

[1] Kiessling : καὶ κοιμωμένου O.
[2] Meutzner : ἑλόντων O.   [3] Reiske : ἐπειδὴ O.
[4] ἐν τοῖς ἐρύμασιν B : ἀμυνόμενος A.
[5] ἑκάτεροι Reiske, ἑταῖροι Schmitz : ἕτεροι O.
[6] καὶ added by Meineke.
[7] Madvig : γεγενῆσθαι R, Jacoby, γενέσθαι A.

was a pest to his neighbours. He, when he heard that Hercules lay encamped in the plain hard by, equipped his followers like brigands and making a sudden raid while the army lay sleeping, he surrounded and drove off as much of their booty as he found unguarded. Afterwards, being besieged by the Greeks, he not only saw his forts taken by storm, but was himself slain amid his fastnesses. And when his forts had been demolished, those who had accompanied Hercules on the expedition (these were some Arcadians with Evander, and Faunus, king of the Aborigines) took over the districts round about, each group for itself. And it may be conjectured that those of the Greeks who remained there, that is, the Epeans and the Arcadians from Pheneus, as well as the Trojans, were left to guard the country. For among the various measures of Hercules that bespoke the true general none was more worthy of admiration than his practice of carrying along with him for a time on his expeditions the prisoners taken from the captured cities, and then, after they had cheerfully assisted him in his wars, settling them in the conquered regions and bestowing on them the riches he had gained from others. It was because of these deeds that Hercules gained the greatest name and renown in Italy, and not because of his passage through it, which was attended by nothing worthy of veneration.

DIONYSIUS OF HALICARNASSUS

XLIII. Λέγουσι δέ τινες αὐτὸν καὶ παῖδας ἐν τοῖς χωρίοις τούτοις, ἃ νῦν Ῥωμαῖοι κατοικοῦσιν, ἐκ δύο γυναικῶν γενομένους καταλιπεῖν· Πάλλαντα μὲν ἐκ τῆς Εὐάνδρου θυγατρός, ᾗ Λαουϊνίαν ὄνομά φασιν εἶναι, Λατῖνον δὲ ἔκ τινος ὑπερβορίδος κόρης, ἣν πατρὸς εἰς ὁμηρείαν δόντος ἐπήγετο καὶ αὐτὴν μέχρι μέν τινος ἁγνὴν γάμων ἐφύλαττεν, ἐπεὶ δὲ εἰς Ἰταλίαν ἔπλει ἐρασθεὶς ἐγκύμονα ποιεῖ, καὶ[1] ὅτε δὴ ἀπαίρειν εἰς Ἄργος ἔμελλε τῷ βασιλεῖ τῶν Ἀβοριγίνων Φαύνῳ γυναῖκα ποιήσασθαι δίδωσι· δι' ἣν αἰτίαν τοὺς πολλοὺς τὸν Λατῖνον τούτου υἱὸν 2 νομίζειν, οὐχ Ἡρακλέους. Πάλλαντα μὲν οὖν πρὶν ἡβῆσαι λέγουσιν ἀποθανεῖν, Λατῖνον δὲ ἀνδρωθέντα τὴν Ἀβοριγίνων ἀρχὴν παραλαβεῖν. τούτου δὲ ἄπαιδος ἀρρένων παίδων τελευτήσαντος ἐν τῇ πρὸς τοὺς ὁμόρους Ῥοτόλους μάχῃ περιστῆναι τὴν ἀρχὴν εἰς Αἰνείαν τὸν Ἀγχίσου κηδεστὴν αὐτοῦ γενόμενον. ἀλλὰ ταῦτα μὲν ἐν ἑτέροις χρόνοις ἐγένετο.

XLIV. Ἡρακλῆς δ' ἐπεὶ τά τε κατὰ τὴν Ἰταλίαν ἅπαντα ὡς ἐβούλετο κατεστήσατο καὶ ὁ ναυτικὸς αὐτῷ στρατὸς σῶος ἐξ Ἰβηρίας ἀφίκετο, θύσας τοῖς θεοῖς τὰς δεκάτας τῶν λαφύρων καὶ πολίχνην ἐπώνυμον αὐτοῦ κτίσας, ἔνθα ὁ στόλος αὐτῷ ἐναυλοχεῖτο,[2] ᾗ καὶ νῦν ὑπὸ Ῥωμαίων οἰκουμένη Νέας Πόλεως καὶ Πομπηίας ἐν μέσῳ κεῖται[3] λιμένας ἐν παντὶ καιρῷ βεβαίους ἔχουσα, δόξης τε καὶ ζήλου καὶ τιμῶν ἰσοθέων παρὰ πᾶσι τοῖς οἰκοῦσιν ἐν

[1] καὶ Kiessling: ἣν καὶ O.
[2] ἐναυλοχεῖτο (ἐναυτολοχεῖτο Aa) O: ἐναυλόχει Cobet, Jacoby.

140

XLIII. Some say that he also left sons by two women in the region now inhabited by the Romans. One of these sons was Pallas, whom he had by the daughter of Evander, whose name, they say, was Lavinia ; the other, Latinus, whose mother was a certain Hyperborean girl whom he brought with him as a hostage given to him by her father and preserved for some time untouched ; but while he was on his voyage to Italy, he fell in love with her and got her with child. And when he was preparing to leave for Argos, he married her to Faunus, king of the Aborigines ; for which reason Latinus is generally looked upon as the son of Faunus, not of Hercules. Pallas, they say, died before he arrived at puberty ; but Latinus, upon reaching man's estate, succeeded to the kingdom of the Aborigines, and when he was killed in the battle against the neighbouring Rutulians, without leaving any male issue, the kingdom devolved on Aeneas, the son of Anchises, his son-in-law. But these things happened at other times.

XLIV. After Hercules had settled everything in Italy according to his desire and his naval force had arrived in safety from Spain, he sacrificed to the gods the tithes of his booty and built a small town named after himself [1] in the place where his fleet lay at anchor (it is now occupied by the Romans, and lying as it does between Neapolis and Pompeii, has at all times secure havens) ; and having gained fame and glory and received divine honours from

[1] Herculaneum.

---

[2] Bücheler : κειμένη Bb, space left blank in ABa.

DIONYSIUS OF HALICARNASSUS

2 Ἰταλίᾳ τυχὼν ἀπῆρεν εἰς Σικελίαν. οἱ δὲ καταλειφθέντες ὑπ᾽ αὐτοῦ φρουροὶ καὶ οἰκήτορες Ἰταλίας
οἱ περὶ τὸν Σατόρνιον ὄχθον ἱδρυμένοι τέως μὲν
ἐπολιτεύοντο καθ᾽ ἑαυτούς, χρόνῳ δ᾽ ὕστερον οὐ
μακρῷ δίαιτάν τε καὶ νόμους καὶ θεῶν ἱερὰ συνενεγκάμενοι τὰ σφέτερα τοῖς Ἀβοριγίνων ὥσπερ Ἀρκάδες
καὶ ἔτι πρότερον Πελασγοὶ πόλεώς τε τῆς αὐτῆς τοῖς
Ἀβοριγῖσι κοινωνήσαντες συνέβη ταν ὁμοεθνεῖς νομί-
ζεσθαι. Ἡρακλέους μὲν δὴ στρατείας πέρι καὶ Πελοποννησίων ὑπομονῆς ἐν Ἰταλίᾳ τοσαῦτα[1] εἰρήσθω.
3 Δευτέρᾳ δ᾽ ὕστερον γενεᾷ μετὰ τὴν Ἡρακλέους
ἄπαρσιν, ἔτει δὲ πέμπτῳ καὶ πεντηκοστῷ μάλιστα,
ὡς αὐτοὶ Ῥωμαῖοι λέγουσι, βασιλεὺς μὲν Ἀβοριγίνων ἦν Λατῖνος ὁ Φαύνου, γόνος δὲ Ἡρακλέους,
πέμπτον δὲ καὶ τριακοστὸν ἔτος ἔχων τὴν ἀρχήν.

XLV Κατὰ δὲ τὸν χρόνον τοῦτον Τρῶες οἱ σὺν
Αἰνείᾳ διαφυγόντες ἐξ Ἰλίου τῆς πόλεως ἁλούσης
κατέσχον εἰς Λαύρεντον,[2] αἰγιαλὸν Ἀβοριγίνων ἐπὶ
τῷ Τυρρηνικῷ πελάγει κείμενον, οὐ πρόσω τῶν
ἐκβολῶν τοῦ Τεβέριος· λαβόντες δὲ παρὰ τῶν
Ἀβοριγίνων χωρίον εἰς οἴκησιν καὶ ὅσα ἠξίουν,
πολίζονται μικρὸν ἀποσχόντες ἀπὸ θαλάττης ἐπὶ
λόφῳ τινὶ Λαουΐνιον ὄνομα τῇ πόλει θέμενοι.
2 ὀλίγῳ δ᾽ ὕστερον χρόνῳ τὴν ἀρχαίαν ἀλλάξαντες
ὀνομασίαν ἅμα τοῖς Ἀβοριγῖσιν ἀπὸ τοῦ βασιλέως
τῆς χώρας Λατῖνοι ὠνομάσθησαν· καὶ μεταναστάντες ἐκ τοῦ Λαουΐνιου κοινῇ μετὰ τῶν ἐπι-

---

[1] Reiske: τοιαῦτα AB.
[2] Cary (cf. Λαυρέντου, v. 54, Λαυρεντίνων, v. 61): Λωρεντὸν
O, Jacoby (and so in i. 53, 55, 63).

all the inhabitants of Italy, he set sail for Sicily.
Those who were left behind by him as a garrison to
dwell in Italy and were settled around the Saturnian
hill lived for some time under an independent
government ; but not long afterwards they adapted
their manner of life, their laws and their religious
ceremonies to those of the Aborigines, even as the
Arcadians and, still earlier, the Pelasgians had done,
and they shared in the same government with them,
so that in time they came to be looked upon as of
the same nation with them. But let this suffice
concerning the expedition of Hercules and concerning the Peloponnesians who remained behind in
Italy.

In the second generation after the departure of
Hercules, and about the fifty-fifth year, according to
the Romans' own account, the king of the Aborigines
was Latinus, who passed for the son of Faunus, but
was actually the son of Hercules ; he was now in the
thirty-fifth year of his reign.

XLV. At that time the Trojans who had fled
with Aeneas from Troy after its capture landed at
Laurentum, which is on the coast of the Aborigines
facing the Tyrrhenian sea, not far from the mouth of
the Tiber. And having received from the Aborigines
some land for their habitation and everything else
they desired, they built a town on a hill not far from
the sea and called it Lavinium. Soon after this they
changed their ancient name and, together with the
Aborigines, were called Latins, after the king of that
country. And leaving Lavinium, they joined with
the inhabitants of those parts in building a larger

χωρίων μείζονα περιβάλλονται πόλιν, ἣν Ἄλβαν
ἐκάλεσαν, ἐξ ἧς ὁρμώμενοι πολλὰς μὲν καὶ ἄλλας
πόλεις ἔκτισαν τῶν κληθέντων Πρίσκων Λατίνων,
ἐξ ὧν αἱ πλεῖσται ἔτι καὶ εἰς ἐμὲ ἦσαν οἰκούμεναι,
3 γενεαῖς δ' ὕστερον ἐκκαίδεκα μετ'[1] Ἰλίου ἅλωσιν
ἐκπέμψαντες ἀποικίαν εἰς τὸ Παλλάντιόν τε καὶ
τὴν Σατορνίαν, ἔνθα Πελοποννήσιοί τε καὶ Ἀρκάδες
τὴν πρώτην οἴκησιν ἐποιήσαντο καὶ ἦν ἔτι[2] ζώπυρ'
ἄττα περιλειπόμενα τοῦ παλαιοῦ γένους, οἰκίζουσι
τοὺς τόπους περιλαβόντες τείχεσι τὸ Παλλάντιον,
ὥστε λαβεῖν πόλεως σχῆμα τότε πρῶτον. τίθενται
δὲ τῷ κτίσματι Ῥώμην ὄνομα ἀπὸ τοῦ στείλαντος
τὴν ἀποικίαν Ῥωμύλου, ὃς ἦν ἕβδομος καὶ δέκατος
4 ἀπ' Αἰνείου γεγονώς. βούλομαι δὲ καὶ περὶ τῆς
Αἰνείου παρουσίας εἰς Ἰταλίαν, ἐπεὶ τῶν συγγραφέων τοῖς μὲν ἠγνόηται, τοῖς δὲ διαπεφώνηται ὁ
περὶ αὐτοῦ λόγος, μὴ παρέργως διελθεῖν τάς τε
τῶν Ἑλλήνων καὶ τὰς Ῥωμαίων τῶν μάλιστα
πιστευομένων ἱστορίας παραβαλών.[3] ἔχει δὲ τὰ
περὶ αὐτοῦ λεγόμενα ὧδε.

XLVI. Ἰλίου κρατηθέντος ὑπ' Ἀχαιῶν, εἴτε
τοῦ δουρείου ἵππου τῇ ἀπάτῃ, ὡς Ὁμήρῳ πεποίηται,
εἴτε τῇ προδοσίᾳ τῶν Ἀντηνοριδῶν εἴτε ἄλλως πως,

---

[1] μετὰ O : μετὰ τὴν Jacoby.
[2] ἔτι B : ἔτι ἐπ' αὐτῶν R.
[3] Reiske : παραλαβών O.

city, surrounded by a wall, which they called Alba ; and setting out thence, they built many other cities, the cities of the so-called Prisci Latini, of which the greatest part were inhabited even to my day. Then, sixteen generations after the taking of Troy,[1] sending out a colony to Pallantium and Saturnia, where the Peloponnesians and the Arcadians had made their first settlement and where there were still left some remains of the ancient race, they settled these places and surrounded Pallantium with a wall, so that it then first received the form of a city. This settlement they called Rome, after Romulus, who was the leader of the colony and the seventeenth in descent from Aeneas. But also concerning the arrival of Aeneas in Italy, since some historians have been ignorant of it and others have related it in a different manner, I wish to give more than a cursory account, having compared the histories of those writers, both Greek and Roman, who are the best accredited. The stories concerning him are as follows :

XLVI. When Troy had been taken by the Achaeans, either by the stratagem of the wooden horse, as Homer represents, or by the treachery of the

---

[1] See chap. 74, 2, and notes. We learn just below how the sixteen generations were reckoned : Romulus is declared to be seventeenth in descent from Aeneas. A comparison of the list of the Alban kings given in chaps. 70 f. shows that, strictly speaking, he was only sixteenth in descent, counting inclusively ; but inasmuch as Ascanius' half-brother Silvius belonged in point of time to the following generation, he was evidently counted as third in the line of descent.

τὸ μὲν ἄλλο πλῆθος ἐν τῇ πόλει Τρωικόν τε καὶ
συμμαχικὸν ἐν ταῖς εὐναῖς ἔτι καταλαμβανόμενον
ἐφονεύετο (νυκτὸς γὰρ δὴ τὸ δεινὸν ἀφυλάκτοις
αὐτοῖς ἐπιστῆναι ἔοικεν), Αἰνείας δὲ καὶ οἱ σὺν
αὐτῷ παρόντες Ἰλιεῦσιν ἐπίκουροι Τρῶες ἐκ Δαρδάνου τε πόλεως καὶ Ὀφρυνίου τῶν τε ἄλλων ὅσοι
τῆς κάτω πόλεως ἁλισκομένης ἔφθασαν αἴσθησιν
τοῦ δεινοῦ λαβεῖν, ἐπὶ τὰ καρτερὰ τοῦ Περγάμου
συμφυγόντες τὴν ἀκρόπολιν ἰδίῳ τείχει φρουρουμένην καταλαμβάνονται, ἐν ᾗ καὶ ἱερὰ τὰ πατρῷα
τοῖς Τρωσὶν ἦν καὶ χρημάτων ὁ πολὺς πλοῦτος,
οἷα εἰκὸς ἐν ἐχυρῷ, καὶ τοῦ στρατιωτικοῦ τὸ κρά-
2 τιστον· ἔνθα ὑπομένοντες ἀπεκρούοντο τοὺς πειρω-
μένους ἐπιβαίνειν τῆς ἄκρας καὶ τὸ διαπῖπτον ὑπὸ
τῆς ἁλώσεως πλῆθος ἐμπειρίᾳ στενωπῶν ὑποθέον-
τες ἀνελάμβανον·[1] καὶ ἐγένετο τοῦ καταληφθέντος
πλεῖον τὸ διαφυγόν. τὴν μὲν δὴ αὐτίκα ὁρμὴν τῶν
πολεμίων ἦν εἶχον, ὅλην διαχρήσασθαι τὴν πόλιν,
καὶ τὸ μὴ πᾶν ἐξ ἐφόδου καταληφθῆναι τὸ ἄστυ
τοῦτο τὸ μηχάνημα ἐξευρὼν Αἰνείας ἐπέσχε.
λογισμὸν δὲ τὸν εἰκότα περὶ τοῦ μέλλοντος λαμβάνων, ὡς ἀμήχανον εἴη πρᾶγμα σῶσαι πόλιν

[1] Pflugk : ἀπελάμβανον AB.

---

[1] The tradition that Antenor proved a traitor to his
country is late, appearing first in Lycophron's *Alexandra*
(verse 340), where the scholiast explains the cryptic words
as meaning that Antenor raised a signal fire to the Greeks
waiting at Tenedos and also released the Greek warriors
from the wooden horse. Dictys relates (v. 8) that Antenor,

146

Antenoridae,[1] or by some other means, the greatest
part of the Trojans and of their allies then in the
city were surprised and slain in their beds ; for it
seems that this calamity came upon them in the
night, when they were not upon their guard. But
Aeneas and his Trojan forces which he had brought
from the cities of Dardanus and Ophrynium to the
assistance of the people of Ilium, and as many others
as had early notice of the calamity, while the Greeks
were taking the lower town, fled together to the
stronghold of Pergamus,[2] and occupied the citadel,
which was fortified with its own wall ; here were
deposited the holy things of the Trojans inherited
from their fathers and their great wealth in valuables, as was to be expected in a stronghold, and
here also the flower of their army was stationed.
Here they awaited and repulsed the enemy who were
endeavouring to gain a foothold on the acropolis,
and by making secret sallies they were able, through
their familiarity with the narrow streets, to rescue
the multitude which was seeking to escape at the
taking of the city ; and thus a larger number
escaped than were taken prisoner. By hitting upon
this plan Aeneas checked the immediate purpose of
the enemy, which was to put all the citizens to the
sword, and prevented them from taking the whole
city by storm. But with respect to the future he
reasoned very properly that it would be impossible to

with the aid of his wife Theano, handed over the Palladium
to Odysseus and Diomed; and Dares (41) represents
Antenor and Aeneas as opening the Scaean gate to the
enemy.

   [2] Pergamus was the citadel of Troy (*Iliad* iv. 508; vi.
512).

ἧς τὰ πλείω ἤδη ἐκρατεῖτο, εἰς νοῦν βάλλεται τοῦ
μὲν τείχους ἐρήμου παραχωρῆσαι τοῖς πολεμίοις,
3 τὰ δὲ σώματα αὐτὰ καὶ τὰ ἱερὰ τὰ πατρῷα καὶ
χρήματα ὁπόσα φέρειν δύναιτο διασώσασθαι. δόξαν
δὲ αὐτῷ, παῖδας μὲν καὶ γυναῖκας καὶ τὰ γηραιὰ
σώματα καὶ ὁπόσοις ἄλλοις βραδείας ἔδει φυγῆς
προεξελθεῖν κελεύει τῆς πόλεως κατὰ τὰς ἐπὶ τὴν
Ἴδην φερούσας ὁδούς, ἕως Ἀχαιοὶ τὴν ἄκραν ἑλεῖν
προθυμούμενοι διώξεως τοῦ διαπίπτοντος ἐκ τῆς
πόλεως πλήθους οὐδὲν προεμηχανῶντο, τοῦ δὲ
στρατιωτικοῦ τὸ μὲν ἐπὶ φυλακῇ τῶν ἐξιόντων
ἔταξεν, ὡς ἀσφαλής τε καὶ ἀταλαίπωρος ἐκ τῶν
ἐνόντων ἥ[1] φυγὴ αὐτοῖς γένοιτο, εἴρητο δὲ τούτοις
τὰ καρτερώτατα καταλαβέσθαι τῆς Ἴδης· τὸ δὲ
λοιπόν, ὃ δὴ κράτιστον ἦν, αὐτὸς ἔχων ὑπέμενεν
ἐπὶ τοῦ τείχους καὶ παρεῖχε τοῖς προεξελθοῦσιν
ἧττον ἐπιπόνους διηρτημένων τειχομαχίᾳ τῶν
4 πολεμίων τὰς φυγάς. Νεοπτολέμου δὲ σὺν τοῖς
ἀμφ' αὐτὸν ἐπιβάντος μέρους τινὸς τῆς ἄκρας
καὶ προσβοηθησάντων αὐτοῖς Ἀχαιῶν ἁπάντων
τῆς μὲν ἄκρας μεθίεται, ἀνοίξας δὲ τὰς πύλας[2]
ἀπῄει συντεταγμένους ἔχων τοὺς λοιποὺς φυγάδας,
ἀγόμενος ἐπὶ ταῖς κρατίσταις συνωρίσι τόν τε πατέρα
καὶ θεοὺς τοὺς πατρῴους γυναῖκά τε καὶ τέκνα καὶ
τῶν ἄλλων εἴ τι πλείστου ἄξιον ἦν σῶμα ἢ χρῆμα.

XLVII. Ἐν δὲ τούτῳ κατὰ κράτος εἰλήφεσαν
Ἀχαιοὶ τὴν πόλιν καὶ περὶ τὰς ἁρπαγὰς ἐσπουδα-

---

[1] ἥ added by Sintenis.
[2] τὰς πύλας . . . φυγάδας Kiessling: τὰς φυγάδας πύλας O;
τὰς φηγάδας π. Meineke, τὰς φυγαδικὰς π. Madvig.

save a city the greater part of which was already in the possession of the enemy, and he therefore decided to abandon the wall, bare of defenders, to the enemy and to save the inhabitants themselves as well as the holy objects inherited from their fathers and all the valuables he could carry away. Having thus resolved, he first sent out from the city the women and children together with the aged and all others whose condition required much time to make their escape, with orders to take the roads leading to Mount Ida, while the Achaeans, intent on capturing the citadel, were giving no thought to the pursuit of the multitude who were escaping from the city. Of the army, he assigned one part to escort the inhabitants who were departing, in order that their flight might be as safe and free from hardships as the circumstances would permit; and they were ordered to take possession of the strongest parts of Mount Ida. With the rest of the troops, who were the most valiant, he remained upon the wall of the citadel and, by keeping the enemy occupied in assaulting it, he rendered less difficult the flight of those who had gone on ahead. But when Neoptolemus and his men gained a foothold on part of the acropolis and all the Achaeans rallied to their support, Aeneas abandoned the place; and opening the gates, he marched away with the rest of the fugitives in good order, carrying with him in the best chariots his father and the gods of his country, together with his wife and children and whatever else, either person or thing, was most precious.

XLVII. In the meantime the Achaeans had taken the city by storm, and being intent on plunder,

κότες πολλὴν ἄδειαν σώζεσθαι τοῖς φεύγουσι παρῆ-
καν. οἱ δὲ ἀμφὶ τὸν Αἰνείαν ἔτι καθ' ὁδὸν εὑρόντες
τοὺς σφετέρους καὶ καθ' ἓν ἅπαντες γενόμενοι τὰ
2 ὀχυρώτατα καταλαμβάνονται τῆς Ἴδης. ἦλθον δ'
ὡς αὐτοὺς οἵ τ' ἐν Δαρδάνῳ τότε οἰκοῦντες, ὡς
εἶδον φλόγα πολλὴν παρὰ τὰ εἰωθότα φερομένην
ἐξ Ἰλίου, νύκτωρ καταλιπόντες τὴν πόλιν ἔρημον,
χωρὶς ἢ ὅσοι σὺν Ἐλύμῳ καὶ Αἰγέστῳ ναυτικόν
τι συνεσκευασμένοι ἔτυχον προεξεληλυθότες τῆς
πόλεως, καὶ ἐξ Ὀφρυνίου πόλεως ὁ δῆμος ἅπας
καὶ ἐκ τῶν ἄλλων Τρωικῶν πόλεων τῆς ἐλευθερίας
οἱ¹ περιεχόμενοι· δύναμίς τε αὕτη δι' ἐλαχίστου
3 χρόνου μεγίστη τῶν Τρωικῶν ἐγένετο. οἱ μὲν οὖν
σὺν Αἰνείᾳ διασωθέντες ἐκ τῆς καταλήψεως ἐν τούτοις ὑπομένοντες τοῖς χωρίοις οὐ διὰ μακροῦ πάλιν
ἐπὶ τὰ σφέτερα κατελεύσεσθαι ἤλπιζον τῶν πολεμίων ἀποπλευσάντων, Ἀχαιοὶ δὲ ἀνδραποδισάμενοι
τὴν πόλιν καὶ τὰ σύνεγγυς χωρία καὶ φρούρια δῃώ-
σαντες παρεσκευάζοντο μὲν ὡς καὶ τοὺς ἐν τοῖς
4 ὄρεσι χειρωσόμενοι. πεμψάντων δὲ κήρυκας αὐτῶν
περὶ διαλύσεων καὶ δεομένων μὴ σφᾶς εἰς ἀνάγκην
καταστῆσαι πολέμου, συνελθόντες εἰς ἐκκλησίαν
ἐπὶ τοῖσδε ποιοῦνται πρὸς αὐτοὺς τὰς διαλύσεις·
Αἰνείαν μὲν καὶ τοὺς σὺν αὐτῷ τὰ χρήματα φέροντας ὅσα διεσώσαντο κατὰ τὴν φυγὴν ἐν ὡρισμένοις
τισὶ χρόνοις ἐκ τῆς Τρωάδος ἀπελθεῖν, παραδόντας
Ἀχαιοῖς τὰ φρούρια· Ἀχαιοὺς δὲ παρασχεῖν αὐτοῖς
τὴν ἀσφάλειαν ἐξ ἁπάσης ὅσης ἐκράτουν γῆς καὶ
5 θαλάττης ἀπιοῦσι κατὰ τὰς ὁμολογίας. δεξά-

¹ οἱ added by Sintenis.

gave those who fled abundant opportunity of making their escape. Aeneas and his band overtook their people while still on the road, and being united now in one body, they seized the strongest parts of Mount Ida. Here they were joined not only by the inhabitants of Dardanus, who, upon seeing a great and unusual fire rising from Ilium, had in the night left their city undefended,—all except the men with Elymus and Aegestus, who had got ready some ships and had departed even earlier,—but also by the whole populace of Ophrynium and by those of the other Trojan cities who clung to their liberty ; and in a very short time this force of the Trojans became a very large one. Accordingly, the fugitives who had escaped with Aeneas from the taking of the city and were tarrying on Mount Ida were in hopes of returning home soon, when the enemy should have sailed away ; but the Achaeans, having reduced to slavery the people who were left in the city and in the places near by and having demolished the forts, were preparing to subdue those also who were in the mountains. When, however, the Trojans sent heralds to treat for peace and begged them not to reduce them to the necessity of making war, the Achaeans held an assembly and made peace with them upon the following terms : Aeneas and his people were to depart from the Troad with all the valuables they had saved in their flight within a certain fixed time, after first delivering up the forts to the Achaeans ; and the Achaeans were to allow them a safe-conduct by land and sea throughout all their dominions when they departed in pursuance of these terms. Aeneas, having accepted these

DIONYSIUS OF HALICARNASSUS

μενος δὲ ταῦτα Αἰνείας καὶ νομίσας ἐκ τῶν ἐνόντων κράτιστα εἶναι Ἀσκάνιον μὲν τὸν πρεσβύτατον τῶν παίδων ἔχοντα τοῦ συμμαχικοῦ τινα μοῖραν, ἧς Φρύγιον ἦν τὸ πλεῖστον, εἰς τὴν Δασκυλῖτιν καλουμένην γῆν, ἔνθα ἐστὶν ἡ Ἀσκανία λίμνη, μετάπεμπτον ὑπὸ τῶν ἐγχωρίων γενόμενον ἐπὶ βασιλείᾳ τοῦ ἔθνους ἀποπέμπει· καὶ ᾤκησεν Ἀσκάνιος αὐτόθι χρόνον τινὰ οὐ πολύν. ἐλθόντων δὲ ὡς αὐτὸν Σκαμανδρίου τε καὶ τῶν ἄλλων Ἑκτοριδῶν ἀφειμένων [1] ἐκ τῆς Ἑλλάδος ὑπὸ Νεοπτολέμου, κατάγων αὐτοὺς ἐπὶ τὴν πατρῴαν ἀρχὴν εἰς Τροίαν 6 ἀφικνεῖται. καὶ περὶ μὲν Ἀσκανίου τοσαῦτα λέγεται· τοὺς δὲ ἄλλους παῖδας Αἰνείας παραλαβὼν καὶ τὸν πατέρα καὶ τὰ ἔδη τῶν θεῶν, ἐπειδὴ παρεσκευάσθη τὸ ναυτικὸν αὐτῷ, διαπλεῖ τὸν Ἑλλήσποντον ἐπὶ τῆς ἔγγιστα κειμένης χερρονήσου τὸν πλοῦν ποιούμενος, ἣ πρόκειται μὲν τῆς Εὐρώπης, καλεῖται δὲ Παλλήνη. ἔθνος δ᾽ εἶχεν αὐτὴν [2]

[1] ἀφειμένων Sylburg : ἀφιγμένων ABb, ἀφιγμένον Ba.
[2] αὐτὴν Sintenis : αὕτη A, ἐν αὐτῇ B.

---

[1] This was the region about Dascylium on the Propontis, near the Mysian Olympus. The Ascanian lake actually lay some 50 miles to the east, being just west of Nicaea.
[2] Scamandrius was Hector's name for Astyanax (Il. vi. 402). According to the usual tradition, he was slain upon the capture of Troy. But the early logographers represented him as surviving and being carried off to Greece by Neoptolemus. And they usually spoke also of other sons

conditions, which he looked upon as the best possible
in the circumstances, sent away Ascanius, his eldest
son, with some of the allies, chiefly Phrygians, to the
country of Dascylitis,[1] as it is called, in which lies
the Ascanian lake, since he had been invited by the
inhabitants to reign over them. But Ascanius did
not tarry there for any great length of time ; for when
Scamandrius and the other descendants of Hector [2]
who had been permitted by Neoptolemus to return
home from Greece, came to him, he went to Troy, in
order to restore them to their ancestral kingdom.
Regarding Ascanius, then, this is all that is told.
As for Aeneas, after his fleet was ready, he embarked
with the rest of his sons and his father, taking with
him the images of the gods, and crossing the Hellespont, sailed to the nearest peninsula, which lies in
front of Europe and is called Pallenê.[3] This country

of Hector (*cf.* Euripides, *Androm.* 224). There were
various accounts of their return to the neighbourhood of
Troy, or eventually to Troy itself, of which we have but a
few brief fragments preserved. Two of these are found in
Strabo (xiii. 1, 52 f. ; xiv. 5, 29).

[3] This is certainly a strange way of describing Pallenê,
the westernmost of the three Chalcidic peninsulas, but the
description evidently goes back to Hellanicus (see chap.
48, 1) or even earlier ; before the Peloponnesian war this
region was often regarded as part of Thrace. Furthermore,
Aeneia, the town the Trojans were said to have built during
their stay there (chap. 49, 4), was not in Pallenê at all, but
lay only a few miles south of Thessalonica, in the north-
west corner of Chalcidicê. It would seem as if Pallenê
were used loosely here for the whole eastern shore of the
Thermaic gulf. This is not the part of Thrace that Virgil
had in mind as the first stopping-place of the Trojans
(*Aen.* iii. 13-68) ; for the tomb of Polydorus was shown at
Aenus, at the mouth of the Hebrus.

DIONYSIUS OF HALICARNASSUS

Θράκιον σύμμαχον Κρουσαῖον καλούμενον ἁπάντων προθυμότατον τῶν συναραμένων αὐτοῖς τοῦ πολέμου.

XLVIII. Ὁ μὲν οὖν πιστότατος τῶν λόγων, ᾧ κέχρηται τῶν παλαιῶν συγγραφέων Ἑλλάνικος ἐν τοῖς Τρωικοῖς, περὶ τῆς Αἰνείου φυγῆς τοιόσδε ἐστίν. εἴρηνται δὲ καὶ ἄλλοις τισὶ περὶ τῶν αὐτῶν οὐ κατὰ ταὐτὰ ἔχοντες λόγοι, οὓς ἧττον ἔγωγε τούτου πιθανοὺς εἶναι νομίζω. κρινέτω δὲ ὡς 2 ἕκαστος τῶν ἀκουόντων βούλεται. Σοφοκλῆς μὲν ὁ τραγῳδοποιὸς ἐν Λαοκόωντι δράματι μελλούσης ἁλίσκεσθαι τῆς πόλεως πεποίηκε τὸν Αἰνείαν ἀνασκευαζόμενον εἰς τὴν Ἴδην, κελευσθέντα ὑπὸ τοῦ πατρὸς Ἀγχίσου κατὰ τὴν μνήμην ὧν Ἀφροδίτη ἐπέσκηψε καὶ ἀπὸ τῶν νεωστὶ γενομένων περὶ τοὺς Λαοκοωντίδας σημείων τὸν μέλλοντα ὄλεθρον τῆς πόλεως συντεκμηραμένου. ἔχει δ' ἐν αὐτῷ τὰ ἰαμβεῖα ἐν ἀγγέλου[1] προσώπῳ λεγόμενα ὧδε·

νῦν δ' ἐν πύλαισιν Αἰνέας ὁ τῆς θεοῦ
πάρεστ' ἐπ' ὤμων πατέρ' ἔχων κεραυνίου
νώτου καταστάζοντα βύσσινον φάρος,
κύκλῳ[2] δὲ πᾶσαν οἰκετῶν παμπληθίαν·

---

[1] ἐν ἀγγέλου (or ἐξαγγέλου) Kiessling : ἐν ἀγγέλῳ B, ἐν ἄλλῳ R.
[2] κύκλῳ B : κυκλεῖ R.

---

[1] Müller, *F.H.G.* i. pp. 61 f., frg. 127. For Hellanicus see p. 71, n. 2.

[2] It is not certain whether καταστάζοντα is to be taken here literally ("dripping") or figuratively ("letting drop"); the construction of the sentence is without exact parallel, but there are analogies for interpreting it to mean simply "letting his robe stream, or fall, down his back." Plutarch (*De Virtute et Vitio*, 2) took the participle in a literal sense

was occupied by a Thracian people called Crusaeans, who were allies of the Trojans and had assisted them during the war with greater zeal than any of the others.

XLVIII. This, then, is the most credible account concerning the flight of Aeneas and is the one which Hellanicus, among the ancient historians, adopts in his *Troica*.[1] There are different accounts given of the same events by some others, which I look upon as less probable than this. But let every reader judge as he thinks proper. Sophocles, the tragic poet, in his drama *Laocoön* represents Aeneas, just before the taking of the city, as removing his household to Mount Ida in obedience to the orders of his father Anchises, who recalled the injunctions of Aphroditê and from the omens that had lately happened in the case of Laocoön's family conjectured the approaching destruction of the city. His iambics, which are spoken by a messenger, are as follows :

" Now at the gates arrives the goddess' son,
Aeneas, his sire upon his shoulders borne
Aloft, while down that back by thunderbolt
Of Zeus once smit the linen mantle streams ; [2]
Surrounding them the crowd of household slaves.

(" bedewing the robe down his back ") and adds the explanation that the body of Anchises gave off a foul exudation. Whether he had any evidence before him, other than this passage of Sophocles, we can only conjecture. We are told that Anchises was struck, or grazed, by lightning because he foolishly boasted of his intimacy with Aphroditê. There were various stories concerning the permanent disability suffered by him in consequence, but the early tradition represented him as lamed.

155

συμπλάζεται δὲ πλῆθος οὐχ ὅσον δοκεῖς,
οἳ¹ τῆσδ᾽ ἐρῶσι τῆς ἀποικίας Φρυγῶν.

3 Μενεκράτης δὲ ὁ Ξάνθιος προδοῦναι τοῖς Ἀχαιοῖς
αὐτὸν ἀποφαίνει τὴν πόλιν τῆς πρὸς Ἀλέξανδρον
ἔχθρας ἕνεκα, καὶ διὰ τὴν εὐεργεσίαν ταύτην
Ἀχαιοὺς αὐτῷ συγχωρῆσαι διασώσασθαι τὸν οἶκον.
σύγκειται δὲ αὐτῷ ὁ λόγος ἀρξαμένῳ ἀπ᾽² Ἀχιλ-
λέως ταφῆς τὸν τρόπον τόνδε· " Ἀχαιοὺς δ᾽ ἀνίη
εἶχε καὶ ἐδόκεον τῆς στρατιῆς τὴν κεφαλὴν ἀπ-
ηράχθαι. ὅμως δὲ τάφον αὐτῷ δαίσαντες ἐπολέμεον
βίῃ³ πάσῃ, ἄχρις Ἴλιος ἑάλω Αἰνείεω ἐνδόντος.
Αἰνείης γὰρ ἄτιτος ἐὼν ὑπὸ Ἀλεξάνδρου καὶ ἀπὸ
γερέων⁴ ἐξειργόμενος ἀνέτρεψε Πρίαμον· ἐργασά-
4 μενος δὲ ταῦτα εἰς Ἀχαιῶν ἐγεγόνει." ἄλλοι δέ τινες
ἐπὶ τοῦ ναυστάθμου τοῦ Τρωικοῦ τυχεῖν αὐτὸν τηνι-
καῦτα διατρίβοντα λέγουσιν, οἱ δ᾽ εἰς Φρυγίαν ἀπ-
εσταλμένον ὑπὸ Πριάμου μετὰ δυνάμεως ἐπί τινα
χρείαν στρατιωτικήν· εἰσὶ δ᾽ οἳ μυθωδεστέραν αὐτοῦ
ποιοῦσι τὴν ἔξοδον. ἐχέτω δ᾽ ὅπῃ τις αὐτὸν πείθει.

XLIX. Τὰ δὲ μετὰ τὴν ἔξοδον ἔτι πλείω παρέχει
τοῖς πολλοῖς τὴν ἀπορίαν. οἱ μὲν γὰρ ἕως Θρᾴκης
ἀγαγόντες αὐτὸν ἐκεῖ λέγουσι τελευτῆσαι τὸν βίον,
ὧν ἐστι Κεφάλων τε ὁ Γεργίθιος καὶ Ἡγήσιππος

---

¹ δοκεῖς, οἳ Reiske: δοκεῖ σοί O.
² ἀπὸ O: ἀπὸ τῆς Reiske, Jacoby.
³ βίῃ Schaller, τῇ Reiske: γῇ AB.
⁴ ἱερῶν deleted after γερέων by Kiessling.

---

¹ Nauck, *T.G.F.*², p. 212, frg. 344.
² Menecrates (fourth century ?), a Lycian, wrote the
history of his own country.

There follows a multitude beyond belief
Who long to join this Phrygian colony." [1]

But Menecrates of Xanthus [2] says that Aeneas betrayed the city to the Achaeans out of hatred for Alexander and that because of this service he was permitted by them to save his household. His account, which begins with the funeral of Achilles, runs on this wise : " The Achaeans were oppressed with grief and felt that the army had had its head lopped off. However, they celebrated his funeral feast and made war with all their might till Ilium was taken by the aid of Aeneas, who delivered it up to them. For Aeneas, being scorned by Alexander and excluded from his prerogatives, overthrew Priam ; and having accomplished this, he became one of the Achaeans." Others say that he chanced to be tarrying at that time at the station where the Trojan ships lay ; and others that he had been sent with a force into Phrygia by Priam upon some military expedition. Some give a more fabulous account of his departure. But let the case stand according to each man's convictions.

XLIX. What happened after his departure creates still greater difficulty for most historians. For some, after they have brought him as far as Thrace, say he died there ; of this number are Cephalon of Gergis [3] and Hegesippus,[4] who wrote concerning

---

[3] A fictitious author under whose name Hegesianax of Alexandria in the Troad published some of his own works, especially his *Troica* (Athenaeus ix. 393d). Dionysius cites him again in chap. 72, 1.

[4] Hegesippus of Mecyberna in Chalcidicê probably lived in the fourth or third century.

ὁ[1] περὶ Παλλήνης γράψας, ἄνδρες ἀρχαῖοι καὶ
λόγου ἄξιοι. ἔτεροι δὲ ἐκ Θράκης ἀναστήσαντες
αὐτὸν ἕως Ἀρκαδίας παρακομίζουσιν, οἰκῆσαι δὲ
λέγουσιν ἐν Ὀρχομενῷ τε τῷ Ἀρκαδικῷ, καὶ
Νήσῳ δὲ[2] λεγομένῃ, καίπερ[3] οὔσῃ μεσόχθονι,
ἀπὸ[4] τελμάτων καὶ ποταμοῦ· τάς τε καλουμένας
Καπύας Αἰνείου τε καὶ Τρώων ἀπόκτισιν εἶναι,
Καπύας[5] ὀνομασθείσας ἀπὸ τοῦ Τρωικοῦ Κάπυος.
λέγεται δὲ ταῦτα ἄλλοις τε καὶ Ἀριαίθῳ τῷ[6]
2 γράψαντι τὰ Ἀρκαδικά. εἰσὶ δὲ καὶ οἳ δεῦρο μὲν
ἀφικέσθαι τὸν Αἰνείαν μυθολογοῦσιν, οὐ μέντοι τήν
γε τελευτὴν αὐτῷ τοῦ βίου συμπεσεῖν ἐν τοῖσδε
τοῖς χωρίοις, ἀλλ' ἐν Ἰταλίᾳ, ὡς ἄλλοι τε πολλοὶ
δηλοῦσι καὶ Ἀγάθυλλος Ἀρκὰς ὁ ποιητὴς ἐν ἐλεγείῳ
λέγων ὧδε·

ἵκετο δ' Ἀρκαδίην, Νήσῳ δ' ἐγκάτθετο παῖδας
δοιάς, Κωδώνης λέκτρα καὶ Ἀνθεμόνης.
αὐτὸς δ' Ἑσπερίην ἔσυτο χθόνα, γείνατο δ' υἷα
Ῥωμύλον.

3 Τῆς δ' εἰς Ἰταλίαν Αἰνείου καὶ Τρώων ἀφίξεως
Ῥωμαῖοί τε πάντες βεβαιωταὶ καὶ τὰ δρώμενα ὑπ'

---

[1] ὁ added by Kiessling.
[2] καὶ νήσω δὲ A: καὶ νήσω B; καὶ omitted by Sauppe.
[3] καίπερ Steph.: καὶ O.
[4] Bücheler, Meineke· ὑπὸ O.
[5] Καφύας Sylburg.
[6] τῷ added by Kiessling.

Pallenê, both of them ancient and reputable men.
Others make him leave Thrace and take him to
Arcadia, and say that he lived in the Arcadian
Orchomenus, in a place which, though situated inland, yet by reason of marshes and a river, is called
Nesos or " Island " ; [1] and they add that the town
called Capyae [2] was built by Aeneas and the Trojans
and took its name from Capys the Trojan. This is
the account given by various other writers and by
Ariaethus, the author of *Arcadica*.[3] And there are
some who have the story that he came, indeed, to
Arcadia and yet that his death did not occur there,
but in Italy ; this is stated by many others and
especially by Agathyllus of Arcadia, the poet, who
writes thus in an elegy :

" Then to Arcadia came and in Nesos left his two
    daughters,
    Fruit of his love for Anthemonê fair and for
        lovely Codonê ;
Thence made haste to Hesperia's land and begat
    there male offspring,
    Romulus named."

The arrival of Aeneas and the Trojans in Italy is
attested by all the Romans and evidences of it are
to be seen in the ceremonies observed by them both

[1] The city of Orchomenus, built on a hill between two
plains, one of which was often a lake, and with a deep
gorge on a third side, may perhaps answer this description.
Or Nesos may have been in the northern plain (to-day a
lake) near Caphyae.

[2] More correctly Caphyae (Pausan. viii. 23, 2).

[3] A history of Arcadia. We know nothing more about
Ariaethus (Araethus ?) and Agathyllus than is told here.

αὐτῶν ἔν τε θυσίαις καὶ ἑορταῖς μηνύματα, Σιβύλλης
τε λόγια καὶ χρησμοὶ Πυθικοὶ καὶ ἄλλα πολλά,
ὧν οὐκ ἄν τις ὡς εὐπρεπείας ἕνεκα συγκειμένων
ὑπερίδοι   πολλὰ δὲ καὶ παρ' Ἕλλησι γνωρίσματα
καὶ φανερὰ εἰς τόδε χρόνου περιλείπεται, ἔνθα
ὡρμίσαντο καὶ παρ' οἷς διατριβὴν ἀπλοίας ἕνεκεν
ἐποιήσαντο· ὧν ἐγὼ μνήμην ὡς ἂν οἷός τε ὦ
4 πολλῶν ὄντων βραχυτάτην ποιήσομαι.   πρῶτον
μὲν εἰς Θρᾴκην ἀφικόμενοι κατὰ τὴν χερρόνησον,
ἣ καλεῖται Παλλήνη, ὡρμίσαντο.   εἶχον δὲ αὐτὴν
ὥσπερ ἔφην βάρβαροι Κρουσαῖοι καλούμενοι καὶ
παρέσχον αὐτοῖς τὰς καταγωγὰς ἀσφαλεῖς.   μείναντες δὲ τὴν χειμερινὴν ὥραν αὐτόθι νεὼν Ἀφροδίτης
ἱδρύσαντο ἐπὶ τῶν ἀκρωτηρίων ἑνὸς καὶ πόλιν

----

[1] In the " digression," as Dionysius calls it (chap. 53, 4),
which begins at this point, he gives a confident, straight-
forward account of the wanderings of Aeneas from Troy to
Lavinium, without once naming a source or hinting at
any variations in the legend.   Kiessling (*De Dionysi Hal.
Antiquitatum auctoribus Latinis*, p. 40) argued that he was
here following Varro as his authority, as he does silently in
various other places, and many scholars have accepted
his conclusions ; but unfortunately, for our knowledge of
Varro's account, we have to depend on a few scattered
quotations, found chiefly in Servius' commentary on the
Aeneid.   The route of Aeneas as traced by Virgil agrees
so closely for the most part with that given by Dionysius
as to suggest that both authors were drawing largely on
the same source.   The differences in their accounts can
easily be explained when we bear in mind that one was a
historian who prided himself on his chronological studies
(chap. 74, 2) and the other a poet who gave free rein to
his imagination.   Thus, Dionysius was bound to reject the
visit of Aeneas to Carthage if, as seems probable, he

in their sacrifices and festivals, as well as in the
Sibyl's utterances, in the Pythian oracles, and in
many other things, which none ought to disdain
as invented for the sake of embellishment. Among
the Greeks, also, many distinct monuments remain
to this day on the coasts where they landed and
among the people with whom they tarried when
detained by unfavourable weather. In mentioning
these, though they are numerous, I shall be as brief
as possible.[1] They first went to Thrace and landed
on the peninsula called Pallenê. It was inhabited, as
I have said,[2] by barbarians called Crusaeans, who
offered them a safe refuge. There they stayed the
winter season and built a temple to Aphroditê on one
of the promontories, and also a city called Aeneia,

accepted Timaeus' date for the founding of that city
(813 ; see chap. 74, 1). Chronological considerations may
also account in part for Dionysius' silence concerning
Cumae and Crete, though the Cumaean episode is evidently
a late addition to the legend, perhaps due to Virgil himself ;
we shall see (chap. 55, 4) that Dionysius connected another
Sibyl, living in the neighbourhood of Mt. Ida, with the
destiny of the Trojan exiles, and this is doubtless the
original form of the legend. One very important difference
between the stories of Dionysius and Virgil is seen in the
length of time assigned to the voyage from Troy to
Lavinium ; the historian allows just two years, the poet
seven. For brief discussions of the growth of the Aeneas
legend see Glover, *Vergil*, chap. iv. ; Nettleship, *Virgil*,
pp. 47-50 ; Prescott, *Development of Virgil's Art*, pp. 153-
168. A detailed comparison of the accounts of Dionysius
and Virgil may be found in Wörner, *Die Sage von den
Wanderungen des Aeneas bei Dionysios und Vergilius*, and
also in his article on Aineias in Roscher's *Lexikon der
griech. und röm. Mythologie*, i. pp. 165-78.

[2] Chap. 47, end.

Αἰνείαν ἔκτισαν, ἐν ᾗ τούς τε ὑπὸ καμάτων ἀδυνά-
τους πλεῖν καὶ ὅσοις αὐτοῦ μένειν βουλομένοις ἦν,
ὡς ἐν οἰκείᾳ γῇ τὸ λοιπὸν ἐσομένους, ὑπελίποντο.
αὕτη διέμεινεν ἕως τῆς Μακεδόνων δυναστείας τῆς
κατὰ τοὺς διαδόχους τοὺς Ἀλεξάνδρου γενομένης·
ἐπὶ δὲ τῆς Κασάνδρου βασιλείας καθῃρέθη, ὅτε
Θεσσαλονίκη πόλις ἐκτίζετο, καὶ οἱ Αἰνεᾶται σὺν
ἄλλοις πολλοῖς εἰς τὴν νεόκτιστον μετῴκησαν.

L. Ἐκ δὲ τῆς Παλλήνης ἄραντες οἱ Τρῶες εἰς
Δῆλον ἀφικνοῦνται βασιλεύοντος αὐτῆς Ἀνίου· καὶ
ἦν πολλὰ σημεῖα ἐν Δήλῳ τῆς Αἰνείου τε καὶ
Τρώων παρουσίας, ἕως [1] ἤνθει τε καὶ ᾠκεῖτο [2] ἡ
νῆσος. ἔπειτα εἰς Κύθηρα νῆσον ἑτέραν, ἣ πρόκειται Πελοποννήσου, παραγενόμενοι ἱερὸν Ἀφρο-
2 δίτης ἱδρύονται. ἀπὸ δὲ Κυθήρων ποιούμενοι τὸν
πλοῦν οὐ πρόσω τῆς Πελοποννήσου τελευτήσαντα
τῶν ἑταίρων τινὰ τῶν Αἰνείου Κίναιθον ἐπὶ τῶν
ἀκρωτηρίων τινὸς θάπτουσιν, ὃ νῦν ἀπ' ἐκείνου
Κιναίθιον καλεῖται· καὶ τὴν πρὸς Ἀρκάδας συγγένειαν ἀνανεωσάμενοι, περὶ ἧς ἐν ὑστέρῳ λόγῳ
διηγήσομαι, χρόνον τε ὀλίγον περὶ ταῦτα τὰ χωρία
διατρίψαντες καὶ ὑπολιπόμενοί τινας σφῶν αὐτῶν
3 εἰς Ζάκυνθον ἀφικνοῦνται. δεξαμένων δ' αὐτοὺς
καὶ τῶν Ζακυνθίων πρὸς φιλίαν διὰ τὸ συγγενές
(Δαρδάνῳ γὰρ τῷ Διὸς καὶ Ἠλέκτρας τῆς Ἀτλαν-
τίδος δύο γενέσθαι φασὶν ἐκ Βατείας παῖδας,
Ζάκυνθόν τε καὶ Ἐριχθόνιον, ὧν ὁ μὲν Αἰνείου

---

[1] ἕως added by Sylburg.
[2] Madvig: ὠκίσθη AB; ᾤκήθη Reiske, ᾤκισθ' Jacoby.

where they left all those who from fatigue were
unable to continue the voyage and all who chose to
remain there as in a country they were henceforth
to look upon as their own. This city existed down
to that period of the Macedonian rule which came
into being under the successors of Alexander, but
it was destroyed in the reign of Cassander, when
Thessalonica was being founded; and the inhabitants of Aeneia with many others removed to
the newly-built city.[1]

L. Setting sail from Pallenê, the Trojans came to
Delos, of which Anius was king. Here there were
many evidences of the presence of Aeneas and the
Trojans as long as the island was inhabited and
flourished. Then, coming to Cythera, another island,
lying off the Peloponnesus, they built a temple there
to Aphroditê. And while they were on their voyage from Cythera and not far from the Peloponnesus, one of Aeneas' companions, named Cinaethus,
died and they buried him upon one of the promontories, which is now called Cinaethion after him.
And having renewed their kinship with the Arcadians,
concerning which I shall speak in a later chapter,[2]
and having stayed a short time in those parts, they
left some of their number there and came to
Zacynthus. The Zacynthians, also, received them
in a friendly manner on account of their kinship;
for Dardanus, the son of Zeus and Electra, the
daughter of Atlas, had, as they say, by Bateia two
sons, Zacynthus and Erichthonius of whom the

---

[1] But Aeneia is mentioned by Livy (xliv. 10, 7) as still
in existence at a later time.

[2] Chap. 61.

πρόγονος ἦν, Ζάκυνθος δὲ τῆς νήσου κτίστης),
ταύτης τε δὴ τῆς συγγενείας ἀναμνήσει καὶ φιλο-
φροσύνῃ τῶν ἐπιχωρίων διατρίβοντες αὐτόθι καὶ
ἅμα ἀπλοίᾳ κατειργόμενοι θύουσιν Ἀφροδίτῃ πρὸς
τῷ κατασκευασθέντι ἱερῷ θυσίαν, ἣν εἰς τόδε
χρόνου συντελοῦσι κοινῇ Ζακύνθιοι, καὶ ἀγῶνα
ποιοῦσιν ἐφήβοις τῶν τε ἄλλων ἀγωνισμάτων καὶ
δρόμου· τὸ δὲ νικητήριον ὁ πρῶτος ἐλθὼν εἰς τὸν
νεὼν λαμβάνει· λέγεται δὲ Αἰνείου καὶ Ἀφροδίτης
ὁ δρόμος, καὶ ξόανα τούτων ἕστηκεν ἀμφοτέρων.
4 ἐκεῖθεν δὲ πελάγιον ποιησάμενοι τὸν πλοῦν εἰς
Λευκάδα κατάγονται, κατεχόντων ἔτι τὸ χωρίον
Ἀκαρνάνων. κἂν ταύτῃ πάλιν ἱερὸν Ἀφροδίτης
ἱδρύονται τοῦτο, ὃ νῦν ἐστιν ἐν τῇ νησῖδι τῇ μεταξὺ
τοῦ Διορύκτου τε καὶ τῆς πόλεως, καλεῖται δὲ
Ἀφροδίτης Αἰνειάδος. ἄραντες δὲ αὐτόθεν ἐπί
τε Ἄκτιον ἐλθόντες ὁρμίζονται τοῦ Ἀμβρακικοῦ
κόλπου πρὸς τὸ ἀκρωτήριον. κἀκεῖθεν εἰς Ἀμ-
βρακίαν ἀφικνοῦνται πόλιν, ἧς ἐβασίλευεν Ἄμβραξ
ὁ Δεξαμενοῦ τοῦ Ἡρακλέους, καὶ ὑπολείπονται
ἑκατέρωθι μνημεῖα τῆς ἀφίξεως· ἐν Ἀκτίῳ μὲν
Ἀφροδίτης Αἰνειάδος ἱερὸν καὶ πλησίον αὐτοῦ θεῶν

---

[1] Dioryctus (literally, a place " dug through ") usually
means the canal which made Leucas an island. But as
Oberhummer has pointed out (*Akarnanien*, . . . *Leukas im
Altertum*, p. 10, n. 1) the only place for the little island
here named would seem to have been in the canal ; hence
Dioryctus was evidently the name also of a place on the
canal, probably on the Acarnanian side, at the end of the
bridge mentioned by Strabo (x. 2, 8).

latter was the ancestor of Aeneas, and Zacynthus
was the first settler of the island. In memory,
therefore, of this kinship and by reason of the
kindness of the inhabitants they stayed there some
time, being also detained by unfavourable weather ;
and they offered to Aphroditê at the temple they
had built to her a sacrifice which the entire population of Zacynthus performs to this day, and instituted games for young men, consisting among other
events of a foot-race in which the one who comes
first to the temple gains the prize. This is called the
course of Aeneas and Aphroditê, and wooden statues
of both are erected there. From there, after a
voyage through the open sea, they landed at Leucas,
which was still in the possession of the Acarnanians.
Here again they built a temple to Aphroditê, which
stands to-day on the little island between Dioryctus [1]
and the city ; it is called the temple of Aphroditê
Aeneias.[2] And departing thence, they sailed to
Actium and anchored off the promontory of the
Ambracian Gulf ; and from there they came to the
city of Ambracia, which was then ruled by Ambrax,
the son of Dexamenus, the son of Herakles. Monuments of their coming are left in both places : at
Actium, the temple of Aphroditê Aeneias, and near
to it that of the Great Gods, both of which existed

[2] This cult-title of Aphroditê has been variously explained.
See Farnell, *Cults of the Greek States*, ii. 638 ff., and Rossbach
in Pauly-Wissowa, *Real-Enc.*, *s.v.* Aineias, pp. 1018 f. Malten,
the latest to discuss the problem (*Archiv für Religionswissen-
schaft*, xxix. (1931), pp. 33-59), regards this goddess as the
mother of the race of the Aeneadae, and identifies her with
the Mater Idaea, a variant form of the Great Mother ; she
is not to be confused with the Phoenician Astartê.

μεγάλων, ἃ καὶ εἰς ἐμὲ ἦν· ἐν δὲ Ἀμβρακίᾳ ἱερόν
τε τῆς αὐτῆς θεοῦ καὶ ἡρῷον Αἰνείου πλησίον τοῦ
μικροῦ θεάτρου, ἐν ᾧ καὶ ξόανον μικρὸν ἀρχαϊκὸν
Αἰνείου λεγόμενον, καὶ αὐτὸ θυσίαις ἐγέραιρον αἱ
καλούμεναι παρ' αὐτοῖς ἀμφίπολοι.

LI. Ἐκ δὲ Ἀμβρακίας Ἀγχίσης μὲν τὰς ναῦς
ἔχων παρὰ γῆν κομιζόμενος εἰς Βουθρωτὸν λιμένα
τῆς Ἠπείρου κατάγεται, Αἰνείας δὲ καὶ οἱ ἀκμαιό-
τατοι σὺν αὐτῷ τοῦ στρατοῦ διανύσαντες ἡμερῶν
δυεῖν ὁδὸν εἰς Δωδώνην ἀφικνοῦνται χρησόμενοι
τῷ θεῷ καὶ καταλαμβάνουσιν αὐτόθι Τρῶας τοὺς
σὺν Ἑλένῳ. ἀνελόμενοι δὲ χρησμοὺς περὶ τῆς
ἀποικίας καὶ τὸν θεὸν ἀναθήμασι δωρησάμενοι
Τρωικοῖς ἄλλοις τε καὶ κρατῆρσι χαλκοῖς, ὧν
τινες ἔτι περίεισιν ἐπιγραφαῖς πάνυ ἀρχαίαις δη-
λοῦντες τοὺς ἀναθέντας, ἐπὶ τὸ ναυτικὸν ἀφικνοῦνται τεττάρων μάλιστα ἡμερῶν διελθόντες ὁδόν.
δηλοῖ[1] δὲ καὶ τὴν εἰς Βουθρωτὸν τῶν Τρώων
παρουσίαν λόφος τις, ᾧ τότε[2] στρατοπέδῳ ἐχρή-
2 σαντο, Τροία καλούμενος. ἐκ δὲ Βουθρωτοῦ παρὰ
γῆν κομισθέντες ἄχρι λιμένος Ἀγχίσου μὲν τότε
ὀνομασθέντος, νῦν δ' ἀσαφεστέραν ἔχοντος ὀνομασίαν, ἱερὸν καὶ αὐτόθι τῆς Ἀφροδίτης ἱδρυσάμενοι
διαίρουσι τὸν Ἰόνιον ἡγεμόνας ἔχοντες τῆς ναυτιλίας,[3] οἳ συνέπλευσαν αὐτοῖς ἐθελούσιοι συνεπι-
σπόμενοι,[4] τοὺς σὺν Πάτρωνι τῷ Θουρίῳ[5]· καὶ

---

[1] δηλοῖ . . . καλούμενος B : om. R.   [2] Kiessling : ποτὲ B.
[3] Ἀκαρνᾶνας added after ναυτιλίας by Kiessling.
[4] Reiske : συνεπισπώμενοι O, Kiessling.
[5] Θουρίῳ Meineke.

even to my time ; and in Ambracia, a temple of
the same goddess and a hero-shrine of Aeneas near
the little theatre. In this shrine there was a small
archaic statue of wood, said to be of Aeneas, that
was honoured with sacrifices by the priestesses they
called *amphipoloi* or " handmaidens."

LI. From Ambracia Anchises, sailing with the
fleet along the coast, came to Buthrotum, a seaport
of Epirus. But Aeneas with the most vigorous men
of his army made a march of two days and came to
Dodona, in order to consult the oracle ; and there
they found the Trojans who had come thither with
Helenus. Then, after receiving responses concerning
their colony and after dedicating to the god various
Trojan offerings, including bronze mixing bowls,—
some of which are still in existence and by their
inscriptions, which are very ancient, show by whom
they were given,—they rejoined the fleet after a
march of about four days. The presence of the
Trojans at Buthrotum is proved by a hill called
Troy, where they encamped at that time. From
Buthrotum they sailed along the coast and came
to a place which was then called the Harbour of
Anchises but now has a less significant name ;[1]
there also they built a temple to Aphroditê, and
then crossed the Ionian Gulf, having for guides on
the voyage Patron the Thyrian[2] and his men, who

[1] Onchesmus, opposite the northern point of Corcyra.

[2] Θούριος generally means a man from Thurii in Italy.
But Androtion is cited by Stephanus of Byzantium as
using it for Θυριεύς, a man of Thyrium (or Thyreum)
in Acarnania. Virgil (*Aen.* v. 298) names Patron, an
Acarnanian, as one of the contestants in the funeral
games in honour of Anchises.

167

αὐτῶν οἱ μὲν πλείους, ἐπειδὴ σῶος ὁ στρατὸς εἰς
Ἰταλίαν ἀφίκετο, ἐπ᾽ οἴκου αὖθις ἀνεκομίσθησαν,
Πάτρων δὲ πεισθεὶς ὑπ᾽ Αἰνείου κοινωνεῖν τῆς
ἀποικίας καὶ σὺν αὐτῷ τινες τῶν φίλων ὑπέμειναν
ἐν τῷ στόλῳ [1]· οὓς ἔνιοί φασιν ἐν Ἀλοντίῳ
κατοικῆσαι τῆς Σικελίας. ταύτης ὑπομνήσει τῆς
εὐεργεσίας Ἀκαρνᾶσι Ῥωμαῖοι Λευκάδα καὶ Ἀνα-
κτόριον ἀφελόμενοι Κορινθίους ἀνὰ χρόνον ἐχαρί-
σαντο Οἰνιάδας τε ἀποκαταστῆσαι βουλομένοις
ἐπέτρεψαν καὶ τὰς Ἐχινάδας νήσους καρποῦσθαι
3 κοινῇ μετ᾽ Αἰτωλῶν ἔδωκαν. οἱ δὲ σὺν Αἰνείᾳ
ποιησάμενοι τὴν ἀπόβασιν οὐ καθ᾽ ἓν χωρίον τῆς
Ἰταλίας, ἀλλὰ ταῖς μὲν πλείσταις ναυσὶ πρὸς
ἄκραν Ἰαπυγίας ὁρμισάμενοι, ᾗ τότε Σαλεντῖνος
ἐλέγετο, ταῖς δὲ λοιπαῖς κατὰ τὸ καλούμενον Ἀθή-
ναιον, ἔνθα καὶ αὐτὸς Αἰνείας ἐτύγχανεν ἐπιβὰς
Ἰταλίας (τοῦτο δὲ τὸ χωρίον ἐστὶν ἀκρωτήριον καὶ
ἐπ᾽ αὐτῷ θερινὸς ὅρμος, ὃς ἐξ ἐκείνου λιμὴν Ἀφροδίτης καλεῖται), παρέπλευσαν ἄχρι πορθμοῦ ἐκ δεξιᾶς

[1] ἐν τῷ στόλῳ Steph., ἐν τῷ πλῷ Madvig, ἐν τῇ Σικελίᾳ
Kiessling: ἐν τῷ σίλῳ AB.

---

[1] Kiessling, rejecting this interpretation, supplied the
word "Acarnanians" and retained the MS. reading
συνεπισπώμενοι, the meaning then being: "having for
guides . . . some Acarnanians who accompanied them of
their own accord, bringing along with them Patron the
Thyrian and his men."

[2] In 196 B.C. these two cities were apparently recognized
by Rome as belonging to the Acarnanian League. The
statement that the Romans had taken them from the
Corinthians is utterly erroneous; the cities had been
founded by the Corinthians, but had long been in the
hands of the Acarnanians.

accompanied them of their own accord.[1] The greater part of these, after the army had arrived safely in Italy, returned home; but Patron with some of his friends, being prevailed on by Aeneas to join the colony, stayed with the expedition. These, according to some, settled at Aluntium in Sicily. In memory of this service the Romans in the course of time bestowed Leucas and Anactorium, which they had taken from the Corinthians, upon the Acarnanians;[2] and when the latter desired to restore the Oeniadae to their old home,[3] they gave them leave to do so, and also to enjoy the produce of the Echinades jointly with the Aetolians.[4] As for Aeneas and his companions, they did not all go ashore at the same place in Italy, but most of the ships came to anchor at the Promontory of Iapygia, which was then called the Salentine Promontory, and the others at a place named after Minerva,[5] where Aeneas himself chanced to set foot first in Italy. This place is a promontory that offers a harbour in the summer, which from that time has been called the Harbour of Venus.[6] After this they sailed along

[3] Or, " restore Oeniadae to its old status." Oeniadae was the name of both town and people. Our only other sources for this incident (Livy xxxviii. 11, 9; Polybius xxi. 32, 14) merely state that in the peace terms between Rome and the Aetolians in 189 it was provided that the city and territory of Oeniadae should belong to the Acarnanians.

[4] We have no further information concerning this arrangement with regard to the Echinades. Oberhummer (op. cit., p. 186, n. 4) suggests that these islands must have been divided up between the Aetolians and Acarnanians.

[5] Castrum Minervae. The temple on this promontory was a well-known landmark.   [6] Portus Veneris.

DIONYSIUS OF HALICARNASSUS

χειρὸς [1] ἔχοντες Ἰταλίαν, ἴχνη τινὰ κἂν τούτοις ὑπο-
λειπόμενοι τοῖς τόποις τῆς ἀφίξεως ἄλλα τε καὶ
φιάλην χαλκῆν ἐν Ἥρας ἱερῷ ἐπιγραφῇ δηλοῦσαν
ἀρχαίᾳ [2] τοῦ δωρησαμένου τῇ θεῷ Αἰνείου τοὔνομα.
LII. Γενόμενοι δὲ κατὰ Σικελίαν, εἴτε γνώμῃ
χρησάμενοι τῇδε ὁρμίσασθαι εἴτε καὶ ὑπ' ἀνέμων
πονηρῶν βιασθέντες, ἃ δὴ φιλεῖ περὶ τὴν θάλατταν
τήνδε γίνεσθαι, κατάγονται τῆς νήσου περὶ τὰ
καλούμενα Δρέπανα· ἔνθα περιτυγχάνουσι τοῖς σὺν
Ἐλύμῳ καὶ Αἰγέστῳ προεξελθοῦσιν ἐκ τῆς Τροίας,
οἳ τύχης τε καὶ πνεύματος οὐρίου λαβόμενοι καὶ
ἅμα οὐ πολλῇ ἀποσκευῇ βαρυνόμενοι δι' ὀλίγου
κατήχθησαν εἰς Σικελίαν καὶ ᾤκησαν περὶ ποταμὸν
καλούμενον Κριμισὸν ἐν γῇ Σικανῶν, πρὸς φιλίαν
λαβόντες παρ' αὐτῶν τὸ χωρίον διὰ τὴν Αἰγέστου
συγγένειαν γενομένου τε καὶ τραφέντος ἐν Σικελίᾳ
2 κατὰ τοιόνδε τι πάθος. τῶν προγόνων αὐτοῦ τις
ἀνὴρ ἐπιφανὴς ἐκ τοῦ Τρωικοῦ γένους ὢν Λαομέ-
δοντι διάφορος γίνεται, καὶ αὐτὸν ὁ βασιλεὺς ἐπ'
αἰτίᾳ δή τινι λαβὼν κτείνει καὶ γένος αὐτοῦ τὸ
ἄρρεν ἅπαν, ὑπὸ δέους μή τι πρὸς αὐτῶν πάθῃ·
τὰς δὲ θυγατέρας παρθένους ἔτι οὔσας ἀποκτεῖναι
μὲν οὐκ εὐπρεπὲς ἐνόμισε, Τρωσὶ δὲ συνοικούσας
περιιδεῖν οὐκ ἀσφαλές, δίδωσι δ' αὐτὰς ἐμπόροις
3 ὡς προσωτάτω κελεύσας ἀπάγειν. ταύταις ἀπιού-
σαις συνεκπλεῖ μειράκιόν τι τῶν ἐπιφανῶν κρατού-
μενον ἔρωτι τῆς ἑτέρας καὶ γαμεῖ τὴν παιδίσκην

[1] ἐκ δεξιᾶς χειρὸς Hertlein : διὰ χειρὸς O, Jacoby.
[2] ἐπιγραφῇ δ. ἀρχαίᾳ Kiessling, γραφῇ δ. ἀρχαίᾳ Steph.:
γραφὴν δ. ἀρχαίαν AB.

170

the coast until they reached the strait, having Italy
on the right hand, and left in these places also some
traces of their arrival, among others a bronze patera
in the temple of Juno, on which there is an ancient
inscription showing the name of Aeneas as the one
who dedicated it to the goddess.

LII. When they were off Sicily, whether they had
any design of landing there or were forced from their
course by tempests, which are common around this
sea, they landed in that part of the island which is
called Drepana. Here they found the Trojans who
with Elymus and Aegestus had left Troy before
them and who, being favoured by both fortune and
the wind, and at the same time being not over-
burdened with baggage, had made a quick passage
to Sicily and were settled near the river Crimisus
in the country of the Sicanians. For the latter had
bestowed the land upon them out of friendship
because of their kinship to Aegestus, who had been
born and reared in Sicily owing to the following
circumstance. One of his ancestors, a distinguished
man of Trojan birth, became at odds with Laomedon
and the king seized him on some charge or other and
put him to death, together with all his male children,
lest he should suffer some mischief at their hands.
But thinking it unseemly to put the man's daughters
to death, as they were still maidens, and at the same
time unsafe to permit them to live among the
Trojans, he delivered them to some merchants, with
orders to carry them as far away as possible. They
were accompanied on the voyage by a youth of
distinguished family, who was in love with one of
them ; and he married the girl when she arrived in

171

DIONYSIUS OF HALICARNASSUS

ἀχθεῖσαν εἰς Σικελίαν, καὶ γίνεται αὐτοῖς παῖς ἐν
Σικελοῖς διατρίβουσιν Αἴγεστος ὄνομα· ὃς ἤθη καὶ
γλῶσσαν τῶν ἐπιχωρίων ἐκμαθών, ἐπειδὴ τοὺς
γονεῖς αὐτῷ τελευτῆσαι συνέβη, βασιλεύοντος ἐν
Τροίᾳ Πριάμου κάθοδον αὐτῷ δοθῆναι διαπράτ-
τεται, καὶ συνδιενέγκας τὸν πρὸς τοὺς Ἀχαιοὺς
πόλεμον ἁλισκομένης τῆς πόλεως ἀπέπλει πάλιν εἰς
Σικελίαν σὺν Ἐλύμῳ ποιησάμενος τὴν φυγὴν ἐν
τρισὶ ναυσίν, ἃς Ἀχιλλεὺς ἔχων ὅτε τὰς Τρωάδας
ἐληΐζετο πόλεις ἕρμασιν ὑφάλοις περιπεσούσας
4 ἀπέβαλεν. ἐντυχὼν δὴ τοῖς εἰρημένοις Αἰνείας
ἀνδράσι φιλοφρονεῖταί τε αὐτοὺς καὶ κατασκευά-
ζεται αὐτοῖς πόλεις Αἴγεσταν καὶ Ἔλυμα[1] καί
τινα καὶ μοῖραν τῆς ἑαυτοῦ στρατιᾶς ἐν τοῖς
πολίσμασιν ὑπολείπεται, ὡς μὲν ἐγὼ εἰκάζω, γνώμῃ
ἑκουσίῳ χρησάμενος, ἵνα τοῖς ὑπὸ καμάτων βαρυνο-
μένοις ἢ καὶ ἄλλως θαλάττῃ ἀχθομένοις ἀναπαύσεις
γίνοιντο ἀσφαλεῖς καὶ καταγωγαί, ὡς δέ τινες
γράφουσι, τοῦ ναυτικοῦ μειωθέντος αὐτῷ διὰ τὴν
ἔμπρησιν, ἣν ἐποιήσαντο τῶν γυναικῶν τινες ἀχθόμεναι τῇ πλάνῃ, τὸν οὐκέτι δυνάμενον συμπλεῖν
ὄχλον ἐκ τῶν κατακεκαυμένων νεῶν ἀνάγκῃ καταλιπών.

[1] ἔλυμα R, ἐλύμαν Bb: Ἔρυκα Sylburg, Portus.

---

[1] The incident here mentioned does not seem to be
recorded by any other extant writer. The sacking of the
Trojan cities was described in the lost *Cypria*.

[2] Called Segesta by the Romans.

[3] Some of the early editors proposed to read Eryx for
Elyma here and for Elymus in the next chapter, but later
editors have retained the readings of the MSS. Neither

172

Sicily. And during their stay among the Sicels they had a son, named Aegestus, who learned the manners and language of the inhabitants; but after the death of his parents, Priam being then king of Troy, he obtained leave to return home. And having assisted Priam in the war against the Achaeans, he then, when the city was about to be taken, sailed back again to Sicily, being accompanied in his flight by Elymus with the three ships which Achilles had had with him when he plundered the Trojan cities and had lost when they struck on some hidden rocks.[1] Aeneas, meeting with the men just named, showed them great kindness and built cities for them, Aegesta[2] and Elyma,[3] and even left some part of his army in these towns. It is my own surmise that he did this by deliberate choice, to the end that those who were worn out by hardships or otherwise irked by the sea might enjoy rest and a safe retreat. But some writers say that the loss of part of his fleet, which was set on fire by some of the women, who were dissatisfied with their wandering, obliged him to leave behind the people who belonged to the burned ships and for that reason could sail no longer with their companions.

Elyma nor Elymus is found anywhere else as the name of a city or mountain in Sicily, though Silius Italicus (*Pun.* xiv. 46 ff.) seems to state that both Acestes and Halymus (his names for the two Trojans) built cities named after themselves. There can be little doubt that Eryx, with the neighbouring mountain famous for its altar or temple of Aphroditê, was the place really meant; and it seems strange that Dionysius should have failed to make the identification, especially as he often gives both the earlier and later names of a place.

DIONYSIUS OF HALICARNASSUS

LIII. Τεκμήρια δὲ τῆς εἰς Σικελοὺς Αἰνείου τε καὶ Τρώων ἀφίξεως πολλὰ μὲν καὶ ἄλλα, περιφανέστατα δὲ τῆς Αἰνειάδος Ἀφροδίτης ὁ βωμὸς ἐπὶ τῇ κορυφῇ τοῦ Ἐλύμου¹ ἱδρυμένος καὶ ἱερὸν Αἰνείου ἱδρυμένον ἐν Αἰγέστῃ, τὸν μὲν αὐτοῦ κατασκευάσαντος Αἰνείου τῇ μητρί, τὸ δὲ ἱερὸν τῶν ὑπολειφθέντων ἀπὸ τοῦ στόλου τῇ μνήμῃ τοῦ σώσαντος σφᾶς ἀνάθημα ποιησαμένων. τὸ μὲν δὴ σὺν Ἐλύμῳ καὶ Αἰγέστῳ Τρωικὸν ἐν τούτοις κατέμεινε τοῖς χωρίοις, καὶ διετέλεσαν Ἔλυμοι καλούμενοι· προεῖχε² γὰρ κατὰ τὴν ἀξίωσιν Ἔλυμος ἀπὸ τοῦ βασιλικοῦ γένους ὤν, ἀφ᾽ οὗ τὴν κλῆσιν οἱ σύμπαντες ἔλαβον. οἱ δὲ σὺν τῷ Αἰνείᾳ πλέοντες ἀπὸ Σικελίας διὰ τοῦ Τυρρηνικοῦ πελάγους πρῶτον μὲν ὡρμίσαντο τῆς Ἰταλίας κατὰ λιμένα τὸν Παλίνουρον, ὃς ἀφ᾽ ἑνὸς τῶν Αἰνείου κυβερνητῶν τελευτήσαντος αὐτόθι ταύτης τυχεῖν λέγεται τῆς ὀνομασίας. ἔπειτα νήσῳ προσέσχον, ᾗ τοὔνομα ἔθεντο Λευκωσίαν³ ἀπὸ γυναικὸς ἀνεψιᾶς Αἰνείου περὶ τόνδε τὸν τόπον ἀποθανούσης. ἐκεῖθεν δὲ κατάραντες εἰς λιμένα βαθὺν καὶ καλὸν ἐν Ὀπικοῖς, τελευτήσαντος καὶ αὐτόθι Μισηνοῦ τῶν ἐπιφανῶν τινος, ἀπ᾽ ἐκείνου τὸν λιμένα ὠνόμασαν, νήσῳ τε Προχύτῃ καὶ ἀκρωτηρίῳ Καιήτῃ τύχῃ⁴ προσορμισάμενοι κατὰ ταὐτὰ τίθενται τὰς ἐπικλήσεις τοῖς τόποις, γυναικῶν ἀποθανουσῶν βουλόμενοι μνημεῖα ποιῆσαι τὰ χωρία. τούτων δὲ ἡ μὲν συγγενὴς Αἰνείου λέγεται γενέσθαι, ἡ δὲ τροφός. τελευτῶν-

---

¹ ἐλύμου O : Ἔρυκος Sylburg, Portus.
² προεῖχεν Sylburg : πρόσθεν R, πρόσθε B.

LIII. There are many proofs of the coming of Aeneas and the Trojans to Sicily, but the most notable are the altar of Aphroditê Aeneias erected on the summit of Elymus and a temple erected to Aeneas in Aegesta ; the former was built by Aeneas himself in his mother's honour, but the temple was an offering made by those of the expedition who remained behind to the memory of their deliverer. The Trojans with Elymus and Aegestus, then, remained in these parts and continued to be called Elymians ; for Elymus was the first in dignity, as being of the royal family, and from him they all took their name. But Aeneas and his companions, leaving Sicily, crossed the Tyrrhenian sea and first came to anchor in Italy in the harbour of Palinurus, which is said to have got this name from one of the pilots of Aeneas who died there. After that they put in at an island which they called Leucosia, from a woman cousin of Aeneas who died at that place. From there they came into a deep and excellent harbour of the Opicans, and when here also one of their number died, a prominent man named Misenus, they called the harbour after him. Then, putting in by chance at the island of Prochyta and at the promontory of Caieta, they named these places in the same manner, desiring that they should serve as memorials of women who died there, one of whom is said to have been a cousin of Aeneas and the other his nurse. At last they arrived at

---

³ Salmasius : λευκασίαν O.

⁴ Καιήτῃ τύχῃ Casaubon, Steph.² : καὶ ἐπὶ τύχῃ B, καὶ ἐπιτυχεῖ A.

τες δὲ ἀφικνοῦνται τῆς Ἰταλίας εἰς Λαύρεντον,
ἔνθα τῆς πλάνης παυσάμενοι χάρακα ἔθεντο, καὶ
τὸ χωρίον ἐν ᾧ κατεστρατοπεδεύσαντο ἐξ ἐκείνου
Τροία καλεῖται, ἀπέχει δὲ τῆς θαλάττης ἀμφὶ
τοὺς τέτταρας σταδίους.

4 Ἔγραψα δὲ ταῦτα καὶ τὴν παρέκβασιν ἐποιησάμην τοῦ ἀναγκαίου χάριν, ἐπειδὴ τῶν[1] συγγραφέων
οἱ μὲν οὐδ᾽ ἐλθεῖν Αἰνείαν φασὶν εἰς Ἰταλίαν ἅμα
Τρωσίν, οἱ δ᾽ ἕτερον Αἰνείαν, οὐ τὸν ἐξ Ἀφροδίτης
καὶ Ἀγχίσου γενόμενον, οἱ δ᾽ Ἀσκάνιον τὸν
Αἰνείου, οἱ δ᾽ ἄλλους τινάς εἰσὶ δ᾽ οἳ τὸν ἐξ
Ἀφροδίτης Αἰνείαν λέγουσι καταστήσαντα τὸν
λόχον[2] εἰς Ἰταλίαν ἀνακομισθῆναι πάλιν οἴκαδε
καὶ βασιλεῦσαι τῆς Τροίας, τελευτῶντα δὲ καταλιπεῖν Ἀσκανίῳ τῷ παιδὶ τὴν βασιλείαν, καὶ τὸ
ἀπ᾽ ἐκείνου γένος ἐπὶ πλεῖστον κατασχεῖν τὴν
ἀρχήν· ὡς μὲν ἐγὼ εἰκάζω τοῖς Ὁμήρου ἔπεσιν οὐκ
5 ὀρθῶς λαμβανομένοις παρακρουσθέντες. πεποίηται
γὰρ αὐτῷ ἐν Ἰλιάδι Ποσειδῶν προλέγων τὴν
μέλλουσαν ἔσεσθαι περὶ τὸν Αἰνείαν καὶ τοὺς ἐξ
ἐκείνου γενησομένους ἐπιφάνειαν ὧδέ πως·

νῦν δὲ δὴ Αἰνείαο βίη Τρώεσσιν ἀνάξει
καὶ παῖδες παίδων, τοί κεν μετόπισθε γένωνται.

ὑπολαβόντες οὖν τὸν Ὅμηρον ἐν Φρυγίᾳ δυναστεύ-
οντας εἰδέναι τοὺς ἄνδρας, ὡς δὴ οὐ δυνατὸν ὂν[3] ἐν
Ἰταλίᾳ οἰκοῦντας βασιλεύειν Τρώων, τὴν ἀνακομι-
δὴν τοῦ Αἰνείου ἀνέπλασαν. ἄρχειν δὲ δὴ τῶν
Τρώων οὓς ἐπήγετο καὶ ἄλλοθι πολιτευομένων οὐκ

[1] τῶν added by Pflugk.

176

Laurentum in Italy, where, coming to the end of their wandering, they made an entrenched camp, and the place where they encamped has from that time been called Troy. It is distant from the sea about four stades.

It was necessary for me to relate these things and to make this digression, since some historians affirm that Aeneas did not even come into Italy with the Trojans, and some that it was another Aeneas, not the son of Anchises and Aphroditê, while yet others say that it was Ascanius, Aeneas' son, and others name still other persons. And there are those who claim that Aeneas, the son of Aphroditê, after he had settled his company in Italy, returned home, reigned over Troy, and dying, left his kingdom to Ascanius, his son, whose posterity possessed it for a long time. According to my conjecture these writers are deceived by mistaking the sense of Homer's verses. For in the *Iliad* he represents Poseidon as foretelling the future splendour of Aeneas and his posterity on this wise :

" On great Aeneas shall devolve the reign,
  And sons succeeding sons the lasting line sustain." [1]

Thus, as they supposed that Homer knew these men reigned in Phrygia, they invented the return of Aeneas, as if it were not possible for them to reign over Trojans while living in Italy. But it was not impossible for Aeneas to reign over the Trojans he had taken with him, even though they were settled

[1] *Iliad* xx. 307 f. (Pope's translation).

---

[2] λόχον O : ὄχλον Pflugk, στόλον Naber.
[3] ὃν added by Steph.².

ἀδύνατον ἦν· ἔχοι δ᾽ ἄν τις τῆς ἀπάτης καὶ ἑτέρας
αἰτίας λαβεῖν.

LIV. Εἰ δέ τινας ταράττει τὸ πολλαχῇ λέγεσθαί
τε καὶ δείκνυσθαι τάφους Αἰνείου, ἀμηχάνου ὄντος
ἐν πλείοσι τὸν αὐτὸν τεθάφθαι χωρίοις, ἐνθυμηθέντες
ὅτι κοινόν ἐστιν ἐπὶ πολλῶν τοῦτό γε τὸ ἄπορον
καὶ μάλιστα τῶν ἐπιφανεῖς μὲν[1] τὰς τύχας, πλάνητας
δὲ τοὺς βίους ἐσχηκότων, μαθέτωσαν ὅτι χωρίον μὲν
ἓν τὸ δεξάμενον τὰ σώματα αὐτῶν ἦν, μνημεῖα δὲ
παρὰ πολλοῖς κατεσκεύαστο δι᾽ εὔνοιαν τῶν ἐν ὠφε-
λείαις τισὶ δι᾽ αὐτοὺς γενομένων, μάλιστα εἰ τοῦ
γένους αὐτῶν τι περιῆν ἢ πόλεώς τινος ἀπόκτισις ἢ
χρόνιοί τινες καὶ φιλάνθρωποι μοναί· οἷα δὴ καὶ
2 περὶ τόνδε τὸν ἥρωα μυθολογούμενα ἴσμεν. Ἰλίῳ
μὲν γὰρ τὸ μὴ πασσυδὶ διαφθαρῆναι κατὰ τὴν
ἅλωσιν παρασχών, τῇ δὲ καλουμένῃ Βεβρυκίᾳ τὸ
ἐπικουρικὸν διασωθῆναι παρασκευάσας, ἐν Φρυγίᾳ
δὲ τὸν υἱὸν Ἀσκάνιον βασιλέα καταλιπών, ἐν Παλ-
λήνῃ δὲ πόλιν ἐπώνυμον κτίσας, ἐν Ἀρκαδίᾳ δὲ
θυγατέρας κηδεύσας, ἐν Σικελίᾳ δὲ μέρος τῆς
στρατιᾶς ὑπολιπόμενος, πολλοῖς[2] δὲ ἄλλοις χωρίοις
φιλανθρώπους τὰς διατριβὰς δωρήσασθαι δοκῶν,
ἑκούσιον εἶχε παρ᾽ αὐτῶν τὴν εὔνοιαν, δι᾽ ἣν τὸν
μετ᾽ ἀνθρώπων βίον ἐκλιπὼν ἡρῴοις ἐκοσμεῖτο καὶ
3 μνημάτων κατασκευαῖς πολλαχῇ. ἐπεὶ φέρε τίνας
ἂν αἰτίας ἔχοι τις ὑποθέσθαι τῶν ἐν Ἰταλίᾳ αὐτοῦ

[1] ἐπιφανεῖς μὲν Sylburg : μὲν ἐπιφανεῖς O, Jacoby.
[2] πολλοῖς Kiessling : ἐν πολλοῖς O, Jacoby.

in another country. However, other reasons also might be given for this error.

LIV. But if it creates a difficulty for any that tombs of Aeneas are both said to exist, and are actually shown, in many places, whereas it is impossible for the same person to be buried in more than one place, let them consider that this difficulty arises in the case of many other men, too, particularly men who have had remarkable fortunes and led wandering lives; and let them know that, though only one place received their bodies, yet their monuments were erected among many peoples through the gratitude of those who had received some benefits from them, particularly if any of their race still survived or if any city had been built by them or if their residence among any people had been long and distinguished by great humanity—just such things, in fact, as we know are related of this hero. For he preserved Ilium from utter destruction at the time of its capture and sent away the Trojan allies safe to Bebrycia,[1] he left his son Ascanius as king in Phrygia, built a city named after himself in Pallenê, married off his daughters in Arcadia, left part of his army in Sicily, and during his residence in many other places had the reputation of conducting himself with great humanity; thus he gained the voluntary affection of those people and accordingly after he left this mortal life he was honoured with hero-shrines and monuments erected to him in many places. What reasons, pray, could anyone assign for

---

[1] Bebrycia was an early name for the district about Lampsacus on the Hellespont. The incident here mentioned is otherwise unknown.

μνημάτων, εἰ μήτε ἦρξε τούτων τῶν χωρίων μήτε
καταγωγὰς ἐν αὐτοῖς ἐποιήσατο μήθ' ὅλως ἐγνώσθη
πρὸς αὐτῶν¹ ; ἀλλ' ὑπὲρ μὲν τούτων καὶ αὖθις
λεχθήσεται, καθότι ἂν ὁ λόγος ἐφ' ἑκάστου καιροῦ
δηλωθῆναι ἀπαιτῇ.

LV. Τοῦ δὲ μηκέτι προσωτέρω τῆς Εὐρώπης
πλεῦσαι τὸν Τρωικὸν στόλον οἵ τε χρησμοὶ αἴτιοι
ἐγένοντο τέλος λαβόντες ἐν τούτοις τοῖς χωρίοις
καὶ τὸ δαιμόνιον πολλαχῶς τὴν ἑαυτοῦ βούλησιν
ἐνδεικνύμενον· ἐπειδὴ γὰρ ὅρμῳ χρησάμενοι τῷ
Λαυρέντῳ σκηνὰς ἐπήξαντο περὶ τὸν αἰγιαλόν,
πρῶτον μὲν πιεζομένοις τοῖς ἀνθρώποις ὑπὸ δίψης
οὐκ ἔχοντος ὕδωρ τοῦ τόπου (λέγω δὲ ἃ παρὰ τῶν
ἐγχωρίων παρέλαβον) λιβάδες αὐτόματοι νάματος
ἡδίστου ἐκ γῆς ἀνελθοῦσαι ὤφθησαν, ἐξ ὧν ἥ τε
στρατιὰ πᾶσα ὑδρεύσατο καὶ ὁ τόπος περίρρυτος
ἐγένετο² μέχρι θαλάττης καταβάντος ἀπὸ τῶν
2 πηγῶν τοῦ ῥεύματος.   νῦν μέντοι οὐκέτι πλήθουσιν
ὥστε καὶ ἀπορρεῖν αἱ λιβάδες, ἀλλ' ἔστιν ὀλίγον
ὕδωρ ἐν κοίλῳ χωρίῳ συνεστηκός, λεγόμενον ὑπὸ
τῶν ἐγχωρίων ἱερὸν ἡλίου· καὶ βωμοὶ δύο παρ'
αὐτῷ δείκνυνται, ὁ μὲν πρὸς ἀνατολὰς τετραμμένος,
ὁ δὲ πρὸς δύσεις, Τρωικὰ ἱδρύματα, ἐφ' ὧν τὸν
Αἰνείαν μυθολογοῦσι πρώτην θυσίαν ποιήσασθαι
3 τῷ θεῷ χαριστήριον τῶν ὑδάτων.   ἔπειτα ἄριστον
αὐτοῖς αἱρουμένοις ἐπὶ τοῦ δαπέδου σέλινα μὲν
πολλοῖς ὑπέστρωτο καὶ ἦν ταῦτα ὥσπερ τράπεζα
τῶν ἐδεσμάτων· ὡς δέ φασί τινες, ἴτρια καρποῦ
πεποιημένα πυρίνου, καθαριότητος ταῖς τροφαῖς

his monuments in Italy if he never reigned in these parts or resided in them or if he was entirely unknown to the inhabitants ? But this point shall be again discussed, according as my narrative shall from time to time require it to be made clear.

LV. The failure of the Trojan fleet to sail any farther into Europe was due both to the oracles which reached their fulfilment in those parts and to the divine power which revealed its will in many ways. For while their fleet lay at anchor off Laurentum and they had set up their tents near the shore, in the first place, when the men were oppressed with thirst and there was no water in the place (what I say I had from the inhabitants), springs of the sweetest water were seen rising out of the earth spontaneously, of which all the army drank and the place was flooded as the stream ran down to the sea from the springs. To-day, however, the springs are no longer so full as to overflow, but there is just a little water collected in a hollow place, and the inhabitants say it is sacred to the Sun ; and near it two altars are pointed out, one facing to the east, the other to the west, both of them Trojan structures, upon which, the story goes, Aeneas offered up his first sacrifice to the god as a thank-offering for the water. After that, while they were taking their repast upon the ground, many of them strewed parsley under their food to serve as a table ; but others say that they thus used wheaten cakes, in order to keep their victuals clean. When all the

---

[1] εἰ μήτε ἦρξε . . . αὐτῶν BC (?): om. R.
[2] ἐγένετο B : γέγονε A, Jacoby.

ἕνεκα. ἐπεὶ δὲ αἱ παρατεθεῖσαι τροφαὶ κατανά-
λωντο, τῶν ὑπεστρωμένων αὐτοῖς σελίνων εἴτε
ἰτρίων ἔφαγέ τις καὶ αὖθις ἕτερος· ἐν τούτῳ[1] τυγχάνει τις εἰπών, εἴτε τῶν Αἰνείου παίδων, ὡς λόγος ἔχει, εἴτε τῶν ὁμοσκήνων, "᾿Αλλ᾿ ἡμῖν γε ἤδη
καὶ ἡ τράπεζα κατεδήδεσται." ὡς δὲ τοῦτο ἤκουσαν,
ἅπαντες ἀνεθορύβησαν, ὡς τὰ πρῶτα τοῦ μαντεύ-
4 ματος ἤδη σφίσι τέλος ἔχοι. ἦν γάρ τι θέσφατον
αὐτοῖς, ὡς μέν τινες λέγουσιν ἐν Δωδώνῃ γενόμενον, ὡς δ᾿ ἕτεροι γράφουσιν ἐν ᾿Ερυθραῖς,[2]
χωρίῳ[3] τῆς ῎Ιδης, ἔνθα ᾤκει Σίβυλλα ἐπιχωρία
νύμφη χρησμῳδός, ἣ αὐτοῖς ἔφρασε πλεῖν ἐπὶ
δυσμῶν ἡλίου, ἕως[4] ἂν εἰς τοῦτο τὸ χωρίον ἔλθω-
σιν ἐν ᾧ κατέδονται τὰς τραπέζας· ὅταν δὲ τοῦτο
μάθωσι γενόμενον, ἡγεμόνα τετράποδα ποιησαμένους, ὅπου ἂν κάμῃ τὸ ζῷον, ἐνταῦθα δείμασθαι
5 πόλιν. τοῦτο δὴ τὸ θεοπρόπιον ἀναμνησθέντες,
οἱ μὲν τὰ ἔδη τῶν θεῶν Αἰνείου κελεύσαντος εἰς τὸ
ἀποδειχθὲν χωρίον ἐκ τῆς νεὼς ἐξέφερον, οἱ δὲ

---

[1] ἐν τούτῳ Reiske : τούτω B, τοῦτο R.
[2] ἐρυθραῖς A : ἐρυθρᾶ B, Jacoby.
[3] χωρίῳ Portus : σχεσίω A B; σχεδὸν Sylburg, σχεδίω
Steph., σπηλαίῳ Reiske, χρηστηρίῳ Sintenis, πεδίῳ Schaller,
ἐχυρῷ Meutzner, χέρσῳ Jacoby.
[4] ἕως O : τέως Jacoby.

---

[1] Varro, according to Servius' comment on the *Aeneid*,
iii. 256, named Dodona as the place where Aeneas received
the oracle about the "tables." Virgil (*Aen.* iii. 253-7),
with a poet's licence, put the prophecy into the mouth of
Celaeno, the harpy. *Cf.* p. 187, n. 1.
[2] The text is uncertain here ; see critical note. Most
editors agree on Erythrae, though we do not hear elsewhere

victuals that were laid before them were consumed,
first one of them ate of the parsley, or cakes, that were
placed underneath, and then another. Thereupon
one of Aeneas' sons, as the story goes, or some other
of his messmates, happened to exclaim, " Look you,
at last we have eaten even the table." As soon as
they heard this, they all cried out with joy that the
first part of the oracle was now fulfilled. For a
certain oracle had been delivered to them, as some
say, in Dodona,[1] but, according to others, in Erythrae, a place [2] on Mount Ida, where lived a Sibyl of
that country, a prophetic nymph, who ordered them
to sail westward till they came to a place where they
should eat their tables ; and that, when they found
this had happened, they should follow a four-footed
beast as their guide, and wherever the animal grew
wearied, there they should build a city. Calling to
mind, then, this prophecy, some at the command of
Aeneas brought the images of the gods out of the
ship to the place appointed by him, others prepared

of any Erythrae near Ida ; conjectures as to the meaning
of the following word vary from " near " to " oracle " and
" cave." For the two words together Jacoby reads " red
land." If Erythrae is the correct reading here, it would
seem that Dionysius confused the Sibyl of Marpessus in
the Troad with the famous Sibyl of Erythrae in Ionia.
With this exception, the story here related may be assumed
to be approximately the original form of the legend, which
would naturally represent Aeneas as receiving the oracle
from the local Sibyl before setting out on his voyage ;
later, when her fame became eclipsed by that of the
Erythraean Sibyl, her rôle in the legend may have been
transferred to the latter. For a recent discussion of the
Sibyls see Buchholz in Roscher's *Lexikon der griech. und
röm. Mythologie, s.v.* Sibylla.

βάθρα καὶ βωμοὺς κατεσκεύαζον αὐτοῖς, αἱ δὲ
γυναῖκες ὀλολυγῇ καὶ χορείαις χρώμεναι παρεκό-
μιζον τὰ ἱερά, οἱ δὲ ἀμφὶ τὸν Αἰνείαν παρα-
σκευασθείσης θυσίας ἔχοντες τοὺς στεφάνους περὶ
τὸν βωμὸν ἔστησαν.

LVI. Ἐν ᾧ δὲ οὗτοι τὰς εὐχὰς ἐποιήσαντο, ἡ
μέλλουσα καθιεροῦσθαι ὗς ἐγκύμων οὖσα καὶ οὐ
πρόσω τόκου καταρχομένων αὐτῆς τῶν θυτήρων
διασεισαμένη καὶ ἀποφυγοῦσα τοὺς κατέχοντας
ἄνω [1] ἔθει. Αἰνείας δὲ μαθὼν ὅτι ταύτην ἄρα τὴν
τετράποδα ἡγεμόνα τὸ θέσφατον αὐτοῖς ἐδήλου
παρηκολούθει σὺν ὀλίγοις μικρὸν ὑπολειπόμενος,
δεδοικὼς μὴ ὑπὸ θορύβου τῶν διωκόντων ἀποτρα-
2 πείη τῆς κατὰ δαίμονα ὁδοῦ. καὶ ἡ μὲν ἀμφὶ
τοὺς εἴκοσι καὶ τέτταρας σταδίους ἀπὸ θαλάττης
διελθοῦσα λόφον τινὰ προσανατρέχει, ἔνθα ὑπὸ
καμάτου μοχθήσασα καθέζεται. τῷ δὲ Αἰνείᾳ
(τέλος γὰρ τὰ μαντεύματα ἐφαίνετο ἔχειν) ὁρῶντι
τὸ χωρίον γῆς τε οὐκ ἐν καλῷ καὶ θαλάττης πρόσω
καὶ οὐδὲ ταύτης ἐνορμίσασθαι ἀγαθῆς, πολλὴ παρ-
ίσταται ἀμηχανία, πότερα χρὴ τῷ θεσφάτῳ πειθομένους αὐτοῦ κατοικεῖν, ἔνθα λυπηρὸν εἰσαεὶ βίον
τρίψουσιν οὐδενὸς χρηστοῦ ἀπολαύοντες, ἢ προσωτέρω χωρητέον ἐπὶ γῆς ἀμείνονος μάστευσιν.
3 ταῦτα δὲ αὐτῷ διανοουμένῳ καὶ τοὺς θεοὺς ἔχοντι
δι᾽ αἰτίας ἄφνω λέγεται φωνή τις ἐκ τῆς νάπης
ἀφανοῦς ὄντος τοῦ φθεγγομένου προσπεσεῖν κελεύ-
ουσα μένειν τε αὐτόθι καὶ πολίζεσθαι διὰ ταχέων
καὶ μὴ τῷ ἀπόρῳ τῆς παρούσης δόξης ἐπιτρέψαντα,

──────────

[1] ἄνω Jacoby : ἄνω θαλάττης O ; ἀπὸ θαλάττης Kiessling.

pedestals and altars for them, and the women with shouts and dancing accompanied the images. And Aeneas with his companions, when a sacrifice had been made ready, stood round the altar with the customary garlands on their heads.

LVI. While these were offering up their prayers, the sow which was the destined victim, being big with young and near her time, shook herself free as the priests were performing the initial rites, and fleeing from those who held her, ran back into the country. And Aeneas, understanding that this, then, was the four-footed beast the oracle indicated as their guide, followed the sow with a few of his people at a small distance, fearing lest, disturbed by her pursuers, she might be frightened from the course fate had appointed for her. And the sow, after going about twenty-four stades from the sea, ran up a hill and there, spent with weariness, she lay down. But Aeneas,—for the oracles seemed now to be fulfilled,—observing that the place was not only in a poor part of the land, but also at a distance from the sea, and that even the latter did not afford a safe anchorage, found himself in great perplexity whether they ought in obedience to the oracle to settle there, where they would lead a life of perpetual misery without enjoying any advantage, or ought to go farther in search of better land. While he was pondering thus and blaming the gods, on a sudden, they say, a voice came to him from the wood,—though the speaker was not to be seen,—commanding him to stay there and build a city immediately, and not, by giving way to the difficulty occasioned by his present opinion, just

εἰ μὴ ἐν εὐβότῳ γῇ τὸν βίον ἱδρύσεται, τὴν μέλλου-
σάν τε καὶ ὅσον οὔπω παροῦσαν εὐτυχίαν ἀπώσασθαι.
4 εἶναι γὰρ αὐτῷ πεπρωμένον ἐκ ταύτης ὁρμώμενον
τῆς λυπρᾶς καὶ ὀλίγης τὸ πρῶτον οἰκήσεως πολλὴν
καὶ ἀγαθὴν ἐπικτήσασθαι γῆν σὺν χρόνῳ· παισὶ δὲ
αὐτοῦ καὶ ἐγγόνοις ἀρχὴν[1] μεγίστην καὶ ἐπὶ πλεῖστον χρόνον ἐκμηκυνθησομένην ὑπάρξαι. ταύτην
μὲν οὖν ἐν τῷ παρόντι καταγωγὴν ἔσεσθαι τοῖς
Τρωσί· μετὰ δὲ τοσούτους ἐνιαυτοὺς ὅσους ἂν ἡ
ὗς τέκῃ χοίρους κτισθήσεσθαι πρὸς τῶν ἐξ ἐκείνου
γενησομένων πόλιν ἑτέραν εὐδαίμονα καὶ μεγάλην.
μαθόντα δὲ τὸν Αἰνείαν καὶ νομίσαντα δαιμόνιόν τι
τὸ[2] χρῆμα τῆς φωνῆς εἶναι ποιεῖν ὡς ὁ θεὸς ἐκέ-
5 λευεν. ἕτεροι δὲ λέγουσιν ἀδημονοῦντι τῷ ἀνδρὶ
καὶ παρεικότι τὸ σῶμα ὑπὸ λύπης καὶ οὔτε ἐπὶ
τὸ στρατόπεδον[3] καταβάντι οὔτε σῖτα προσενεγ-
καμένῳ, αὐτοῦ δὲ ὡς ἔτυχεν αὐλισθέντι τὴν νύκτα
ἐκείνην, ἐπιστῆναι μεγάλην τινὰ καὶ θαυμαστὴν
ἐνυπνίου τῶν θεῶν τινι τῶν πατρίων εἰκασθεῖσαν
ὄψιν τὰ λεχθέντα μικρῷ πρότερον ὑποτιθεμένην·
ὁποτέρως δὲ τἀληθὲς ἔχει θεοῖς ἂν εἴη γνώριμον.
τῇ δ' ἑξῆς ἡμέρᾳ τριάκοντα λέγεται χοίρους ἡ ὗς
ἐκτεκεῖν, καὶ τοσούτοις ἐνιαυτοῖς ὕστερον ὑπὸ τῶν
Τρώων ἑτέρα κτισθῆναι πόλις κατὰ τὸ θέσφατον,
ὑπὲρ ἧς ἐν τῷ[4] οἰκείῳ τόπῳ διαλέξομαι.

---

[1] ἀρχὴν Kiessling : ἔσεσθαι ἀρχὴν O, Jacoby.
[2] τὸ added by Bücheler.
[3] ἐπὶ τὸ στρατόπεδον Bücheler : ἐπὶ (ὑπὸ A) τοῦ στρατοπέδου AB.
[4] τῷ added by Grasberger.

because he would be establishing his abode in a
barren country, to reject his future good fortune,
that was indeed all but actually present. For
it was fated that, beginning with this sorry and, at
first, small habitation, he should in the course of
time acquire a spacious and fertile country, and that
his children and posterity should possess a vast
empire which should be prolonged for many ages.
For the present, therefore, this settlement should be
a refuge for the Trojans, but, after as many years
as the sow should bring forth young ones, another
city, large and flourishing, should be built by his posterity. It is said that Aeneas, hearing this and
looking upon the voice as something divine, did as
the god commanded. But others say that while
he was dismayed and had neglected himself in his
grief, to such a degree that he neither came into the
camp nor took any food, but spent that night just as
he was, a great and wonderful vision of a dream appeared to him in the likeness of one of his country's
gods and gave him the advice just before mentioned.
Which of these accounts is the true one the gods only
know.[1] The next day, it is said, the sow brought
forth thirty young ones, and just that many years
later, in accordance with the oracle, another city
was built by the Trojans, concerning which I shall
speak in the proper place.[2]

[1] Virgil (*Aen.* viii. 42-48) represents the river-god
Tiberinus as announcing the omen of the sow and her
young to Aeneas and this omen is seen the very next day
(vs. 81-85).
[2] Chap. 66.

DIONYSIUS OF HALICARNASSUS

LVII Αἰνείας δὲ τῆς μὲν ὑὸς τὸν τόκον ἅμα τῇ
γειναμένῃ τοῖς πατρῴοις ἁγίζει θεοῖς ἐν τῷ χωρίῳ
τῷδ᾽, οὗ νῦν ἐστιν ἡ καλιάς, καὶ αὐτὴν οἱ Λαουινιά-
ται τοῖς ἄλλοις ἄβατον φυλάττοντες ἱερὰν νομίζουσι·
τοῖς δὲ Τρωσὶ μεταστρατοπεδεῦσαι κελεύσας ἐπὶ τὸν
λόφον ἱδρύεται τὰ ἔδη τῶν θεῶν ἐν τῷ κρατίστῳ καὶ
αὐτίκα περὶ τὴν κατασκευὴν τοῦ πολίσματος ἁπάσῃ
προθυμίᾳ ὥρμητο ἐλάμβανέ τε καταθέων ἐκ τῶν
πέριξ χωρίων ὁπόσα εἰς τὸν πολισμὸν αὐτῷ ἦν χρήσιμα καὶ μάλιστα ἔμελλε λυπηρὰ τοῖς ἀφαιρεθεῖσι
φανήσεσθαι, σίδηρον καὶ ξύλα καὶ τὰς γεωργικὰς
2 παρασκευάς. Λατίνῳ δέ, ὃς ἦν τότε βασιλεύς,
πολεμοῦντι πρὸς ἔθνος ὅμορον τοὺς καλουμένους
Ῥοτόλους καὶ δυσημεροῦντι κατὰ τὰς μάχας ἀγγέλ-
λεται τὰ γινόμενα ἐπὶ τὸ φοβερώτατον, ὡς ἀνά-
στατος αὐτοῦ γίνεται πᾶσα ἡ παράλιος ὑπερορίῳ
στρατιᾷ, καὶ εἰ μὴ σὺν τάχει κωλύσει τὰ δρώμενα,
χρυσὸς [1] αὐτῷ φανήσεται ὁ πρὸς τοὺς ἀστυγείτονας
ἀγών. ἀκούσαντι δὲ τῷ ἀνδρὶ δέος εἰσέρχεται καὶ
αὐτίκα τοῦ παρόντος πολέμου μεθέμενος ἐπὶ τοὺς
3 Τρῶας ἐλαύνει πολλῇ στρατιᾷ. ὁρῶν δὲ αὐτοὺς

---

[1] χρυσός Cobet: ὀχυρὸς AB. Cobet, in his *Variae
Lectiones*, pp. 235 f., points out several passages in Greek
authors where χρυσός has been similarly corrupted (among
them Dionysius ix. 25, 1, where only Ba reads χρυσός,
the others χρηστός). The expression first appears in
Euripides, *Troades* 431 ff. :

> δύστηνος, οὐκ οἶδ᾽ οἷά νιν μένει παθεῖν·
> ὡς χρυσὸς αὐτῷ τἀμὰ καὶ Φρυγῶν κακὰ
> δόξει ποτ᾽ εἶναι.

LVII. Aeneas sacrificed the sow with her young to his household gods in the place where now stands the chapel, which the Lavinians look upon as sacred and preserve inaccessible to all but themselves. Then, having ordered the Trojans to remove their camp to the hill, he placed the images of the gods in the best part of it and immediately addressed himself to the building of the town with the greatest zeal. And making descents into the country round about, he took from there such things as were of use to him in building and the loss of which was likely to be the most grievous to the owners, such as iron, timber and agricultural implements. But Latinus, the king of the country at that time, who was at war with a neighbouring people called the Rutulians and had fought some battles with ill success, received an account of what had passed in the most alarming form, to the effect that all his coast was being laid waste by a foreign army and that, if he did not immediately put a stop to their depredations, the war with his neighbours would seem to him a joy [1] in comparison. Latinus was struck with fear at this news, and immediately abandoning the war in which he was then engaged, he marched against the Trojans with a great army. But

---

[1] Literally " gold." This expression seems to have become proverbial in comparisons between a lesser and a greater evil. See critical note.

" Wretch !—he knows not what sufferings wait for him,
    Such that my woes and Phrygia's yet shall seem
    As gold to them."
        (Way's translation in the Loeb Classical Library.)

ὡπλισμένους τε ὡς Ἕλληνας καὶ ἐν τάξει εὐκόσμῳ
ἀκαταπλήκτως τὸ δεινὸν ὑπομένοντας, τῆς μὲν
αὐτίκα παρακινδυνεύσεως, ὡς οὐκ ἂν ἐξ ἐφόδου
αὐτοὺς ἔτι χειρωσάμενος,[1] καθ᾽ ἣν [2] ἔσχε διάνοιαν [3]
οἴκοθεν ὁρμώμενος, ἀποτρέπεται· στρατοπεδευσά-
μενος δ᾽ ἐπὶ λόφου τινὸς τὸ πρῶτον ἀναλαβεῖν
ᾤετο δεῖν τὴν δύναμιν ἐκ τοῦ παρόντος κόπου, ὃς
πολὺς ἐκ μακρᾶς ὁδοῦ καὶ συντόνου διώξεως αὐτοῖς
4 ἐγένετο. αὐλισάμενος [4] δὲ διὰ νυκτὸς αὐτόθι γνώμην
ἐποιεῖτο ἀρχομένης ἕω συμφέρεσθαι τοῖς πολεμίοις.
ἐγνωκότι δὲ αὐτῷ ταῦτα λέγει τις ἐπιστὰς καθ᾽
ὕπνον ἐπιχώριος δαίμων δέχεσθαι τοὺς Ἕλληνας τῇ
χώρᾳ συνοίκους· ἥκειν γὰρ αὐτοὺς μέγα ὠφέλημα
Λατίνῳ καὶ κοινὸν Ἀβοριγίνων ἀγαθόν· Αἰνείᾳ τε
οἱ πατρῷοι θεοὶ τῆς αὐτῆς νυκτὸς φανέντες παρα-
κελεύονται πείθειν Λατῖνον ἑκόντα παρασχεῖν σφίσι
τὴν οἴκησιν ἐν ᾧ βούλονται χωρίῳ, καὶ χρήσασθαι
δυνάμει Ἑλληνικῇ συμμάχῳ μᾶλλον ἢ διαφόρῳ·
ἀμφοτέρους δὲ τὸ ὄναρ ἐκώλυεν ἄρχειν μάχης. ὡς
δὲ ἡμέρα τε ἐγένετο καὶ διεκοσμήθησαν εἰς μάχην
αἱ δυνάμεις, κήρυκες ἧκον ὡς τοὺς ἡγεμόνας ἑκατέρωθεν τὸ αὐτὸ ἀξιοῦντες, συνελθεῖν ἀλλήλοις εἰς
λόγους· καὶ ἐγένετο τοῦτο. LVIII. Πρῶτος δὲ ὁ Λατῖνος ἔγκλημα ποιούμενος τὸν αἰφνίδιόν τε καὶ ἀκατάγγελτον πόλεμον
ἠξίου τὸν Αἰνείαν λέγειν, ὅστις ὢν καὶ τί βουλόμενος ἄγει καὶ φέρει τὰ χωρία πεπονθώς τε οὐδὲν

---

[1] Madvig : χειρωσόμενος O.
[2] καθ᾽ ἣν O : ἣν Kiessling, Jacoby.
[3] διάνοιαν Reiske : λοαν ABa, δόξαν Bb.
[4] Steph. : αὐλισαμένοις AB.

seeing them armed like Greeks, drawn up in good order and resolutely awaiting the conflict, he gave up the idea of hazarding an immediate engagement, since he saw no probability now of defeating them at the first onset, as he had expected when he set out from home against them. And encamping on a hill, he thought he ought first to let his troops recover from their present fatigue, which from the length of the march and the eagerness of the pursuit was very great; and passing the night there, he was resolving to engage the enemy at break of day. But when he had reached this decision, a certain divinity of the place appeared to him in his sleep and bade him receive the Greeks into his land to dwell with his own subjects, adding that their coming was a great advantage to him and a benefit to all the Aborigines alike. And the same night Aeneas' household gods appeared to him and admonished him to persuade Latinus to grant them of his own accord a settlement in the part of the country they desired and to treat the Greek forces rather as allies than as enemies. Thus the dream hindered both of them from beginning an engagement. And as soon as it was day and the armies were drawn up in order of battle, heralds came to each of the commanders from the other with the same request, that they should meet for a parley; and so it came to pass.

LVIII. And first Latinus complained of the sudden war which they had made upon his subjects without any previous declaration and demanded that Aeneas tell him who he was and what he meant by plundering the country without any provocation, since he

δεινὸν πρότερος καὶ οὐκ ἀγνοῶν ὅτι τὸν ἄρχοντα
πολέμου πᾶς ὁ προπαθὼν ἀμύνεται· παρασχόν τε
ἂν αὐτῷ πᾶν, εἴ τινος ἐδεῖτο μετρίου, πρὸς φιλίαν
καὶ παρ' ἑκόντων εὑρίσκεσθαι τῶν ἐγχωρίων, παρελθὼν τὴν ἁπάντων ἀνθρώπων δικαίωσιν αἴσχιον ἢ
κάλλιον ἠξίωσε βίαν προσφέρων τὰ αὐτὰ λαμβάνειν.
2 τοιαῦτα δὲ αὐτοῦ διαλεχθέντος ἀπεκρίνατο Αἰνείας·
" Ἡμεῖς γένος μὲν Τρῶές ἐσμεν, πόλεως δὲ οὐ τῆς
ἀφανεστάτης ἐν Ἕλλησιν ἐγενόμεθα· ἣν ἀφαιρε-
θέντες ὑπ' Ἀχαιῶν δεκαετεῖ πολέμῳ χειρωθεῖσαν,
ἀλῆται περιερχόμενοι πόλεώς τε καὶ χώρας ἐν ᾗ τὸ
λοιπὸν οἰκήσομεν ἀπορίᾳ, θεοῖς δὲ κελεύουσι πειθόμενοι δεῦρ' ἀφίγμεθα καὶ ἡμῖν ὡς τὰ θέσφατα
λέγει λιμὴν τῆς πλάνης ἥδε ἡ γῆ μόνη λείπεται.
ποριζόμεθα δὲ ἐκ τῆς χώρας ὧν ἡμῖν δεῖ δυστυχέ-
στερον μᾶλλον ἢ εὐπρεπέστερον, ὡς ἥκιστα[1] τέως
3 γε[2] ἐβουλόμεθα. ἀμειψόμεθα δὲ αὐτὰ πολλαῖς καὶ
ἀγαθαῖς ἔργων ἀμοιβαῖς παρέχοντες ὑμῖν καὶ σώματα καὶ ψυχὰς εὖ πρὸς τὰ δεινὰ πεπαιδευμένας
χρῆσθαι ὁπόσα βούλεσθε, τὴν ὑμετέραν γῆν φυλάττοντες ἀδήωτον, τὴν δὲ τῶν πολεμίων προθύμως
συγκατακτώμενοι. ἱκέται δὲ ὑμῶν γινόμεθα μὴ
πρὸς ὀργὴν τὰ πεπραγμένα λαμβάνειν, ἐνθυμηθέντας
ὡς οὐ σὺν ὕβρει, ἀλλ' ὑπ' ἀνάγκης ταῦτα βιασθέντες

could not be ignorant that every one who is attacked
in war defends himself against the aggressor;
and he complained that when Aeneas might have
obtained amicably and with the consent of the
inhabitants whatever he could reasonably desire,
he had chosen to take it by force, contrary to the
universal sense of justice and with greater dishonour
than credit to himself. After he had spoken thus
Aeneas answered: " We are natives of Troy, not the
least famous city among the Greeks; but since this
has been captured and taken from us by the Achaeans
after a ten-years' war, we have been wanderers,
roving about for want both of a city and a country
where we may henceforth live, and are come hither in
obedience to the commands of the gods; and this
land alone, as the oracles tell us, is left for us as the
haven of our wandering. We are indeed taking
from the country the things we need, with greater
regard to our unfortunate situation than to propriety,—a course which until recently we by no
means wished to pursue. But we will make com-
pensation for them with many good services in
return, offering you our bodies and our minds, well
disciplined against dangers, to employ as you think
proper in keeping your country free from the ravages
of enemies and in heartily assisting you to conquer
their lands. We humbly entreat you not to resent
what we have done, realizing, as you must, that we
did it, not out of wantonness, but constrained by

---

[1] ἥκιστα O: ἥδιστα Jacoby.
[2] ἕως γε Schmitz: νεωστὶ O, Jacoby.

4 ἐποιοῦμεν· ἅπαν δὲ σύγγνωμον [1] τὸ ἀκούσιον. καὶ δεῖ ὑμᾶς μηδὲν ἐναντίον βουλεῦσαι περὶ ἡμῶν χεῖρας προεχομένων, εἰ δὲ μή, θεοὺς καὶ δαίμονας οἳ κατέχουσι τήνδε τὴν γῆν παραιτούμενοι συγγνώμονας ἡμῖν γενέσθαι καὶ ὧν ἠναγκασμένοι δρῶμεν πειρασόμεθα πολέμου ἄρχοντας ὑμᾶς ἀμύνεσθαι. οὐ γὰρ ἂν νῦν πρώτου [2] οὐδὲ μεγίστου πολέμου 5 τοῦδε ἀπολαύσαιμεν." ὡς δὲ ταῦτα ὁ Λατῖνος ἤκουσεν ἀπεκρίνατο πρὸς αὐτόν· "Ἀλλ' ἔγωγε εὔνοιάν τε πρὸς ἅπαν τὸ Ἑλληνικὸν γένος ἔχω καὶ συμφοραῖς ἀνθρώπων ἀναγκαίαις πάνυ ἄχθομαι, σώζεσθαί τε ὑμᾶς περὶ πολλοῦ ἂν ποιησαίμην, εἴ μοι δῆλοι γένοισθε οἰκήσεως δεόμενοι ἥκειν ἐν ἀποχρώσῃ τε γῆς μοίρᾳ καὶ πρὸς φιλίαν τῶν δοθησομένων μεθέξοντες, ἀλλ' οὐ τὴν ἐμὴν δυναστείαν ἀφαιρησόμενοι πρὸς βίαν. εἰ δ' ἐπαληθεύεται ὑμῖν ὅδ' ὁ λόγος πίστεις τούτων ἀξιῶ δοῦναι καὶ λαβεῖν, αἳ φυλάξουσιν ἡμῖν ἀδόλους τὰς ὁμολογίας."

LIX. Αἰνείου δὲ ἐπαινέσαντος τὰ λεγόμενα γίνονται συνθῆκαι τοῖς ἔθνεσιν ἐφ' [3] ὁρκίων τοιαίδε· Ἀβοριγῖνας μὲν Τρωσὶ δοῦναι χώραν ὅσην ἠξίουν ἀμφὶ τοὺς τετταράκοντα σταδίους πανταχοῦ πορευομένοις ἀπὸ τοῦ λόφου· Τρῶας δὲ Ἀβοριγῖσι τοῦ τ'

---

[1] Kiessling: συγγνώμη ABb, συγγνώμης Ba.
[2] Sylburg: πρῶτον O.   [3] ἐφ' Kiessling: ὑφ' O.

---

[1] In Thucydides iii. 40, 1, we find the expression ξύγγνωμόν δ' ἐστὶ τὸ ἀκούσιον. But Jacoby points out that the two passages are otherwise very different in their tenor, and hence concludes that Dionysius was not imitating the

necessity; and everything that is involuntary deserves forgiveness.[1]   And you ought not to take any hostile resolution concerning us as we stretch forth our hands to you ; but if you do so, we will first beg the gods and divinities who possess this land to forgive us even for what we do under the constraint of necessity and will then endeavour to defend ourselves against you who are the aggressors in the war ; for this will not be the first nor the greatest war that we have experienced." When Latinus heard this he answered him : " Nay, but I cherish a kindly feeling towards the whole Greek race and am greatly grieved by the inevitable calamities of mankind.   And I should be very solicitous for your safety if it were clear to me that you have come here in search of a habitation and that, contented with a suitable share of the land and enjoying in a spirit of friendship what shall be given you, you will not endeavour to deprive me of the sovereignty by force; and if the assurances you give me are real, I desire to give and receive pledges which will preserve our compact inviolate."

LIX. Aeneas having accepted this proposal, a treaty was made between the two nations and confirmed by oaths to this effect : the Aborigines were to grant to the Trojans as much land as they desired, that is, the space of about forty stades in every direction from the hill ; the Trojans, on their part,

older historian. He believes, rather, that the source of both was a verse of some poet, probably ξύγγνωμόν ἐστ' ◡ – ἅπαν τἀκούσιον. The same sentiment, though not expressed in exactly the same words, is met with in Thuc. iv. 98, 6, Plato, *Phaedrus* 233c, and Aristotle, *Eth. Nicom.* iii. 1, 1.

ἐν χερσὶ πολέμου συλλαβέσθαι καὶ ὅπου ἂν ἄλλῃ
παρακαλῶνται συστρατεύειν· κοινῇ δὲ ἀμφοτέρους
τὰ κράτιστα ὑπὲρ ἀλλήλων πράττειν καὶ χειρὶ καὶ
2 γνώμῃ. συνθέμενοι δὲ ταῦτα καὶ τέκνων ὁμηρείαις
τὰς πίστεις βεβαιώσαντες κοινῇ στρατεύουσιν ἐπὶ
τὰς πόλεις τῶν Ῥοτόλων· δι᾽ ὀλίγου δὲ τἀκεῖ
πάντα χειρωσάμενοι παρῆσαν ἐπὶ τὸ πόλισμα τὸ
Τρωικὸν ἡμιτελὲς ἔτ᾽ ὂν¹ καὶ μιᾷ προθυμίᾳ πάντες
3 χρώμενοι τειχίζουσιν αὐτό. ὄνομα δὲ τῷ κτίσματι
Αἰνείας τίθεται Λαουΐνιον, ὡς μὲν αὐτοὶ Ῥωμαῖοι
λέγουσιν, ἀπὸ τῆς Λατίνου θυγατρός, ᾗ Λαουϊνίαν²
εἶναί φασι τοὔνομα· ὡς δ᾽ ἄλλοι τινὲς τῶν Ἑλληνικῶν μυθογράφων ἔλεξαν, ἀπὸ τῆς Ἀνίου³ τοῦ
Δηλίων⁴ βασιλέως θυγατρός, Λαουϊνίας καὶ τῆσδε
ὀνομαζομένης, ἧς⁵ ἀποθανούσης νόσῳ περὶ τὸν
οἰκισμὸν τῆς πόλεως πρώτης καὶ ἐν ᾧ ἔκαμε
χωρίῳ ταφείσης μνῆμα γενέσθαι τὴν πόλιν. συμ-
πλεῦσαι δ᾽ αὐτὴν τοῖς Τρωσὶ λέγεται δοθεῖσαν ὑπὸ
τοῦ πατρὸς Αἰνείᾳ δεηθέντι μαντικὴν οὖσαν καὶ
4 σοφήν. λέγεται δὲ κατὰ τὸν πολισμὸν τοῦ Λαουϊνίου σημεῖα τοῖς Τρωσὶ γενέσθαι τοιάδε· πυρὸς
αὐτομάτως ἀναφθέντος ἐκ τῆς νάπης λύκον μὲν
κομίζοντα τῷ στόματι τῆς ξηρᾶς ὕλης ἐπιβάλλειν
ἐπὶ τὸ πῦρ, ἀετὸν δὲ προσπετόμενον ἀναρριπίζειν

---

¹ ἡμιτελὲς ἔτ᾽ ὂν Sintenis: ἡμιτέλεστον ABa, ἡμιτέλεστον ὂν Bb.
² Cary (after Sylburg): λαῦναν Ba, λάνναν A, λανινίαν Bb.
Three lines below, and in 64, 1 B has λαουινίας, in 60, 1 Bb
has λαουινίαν; elsewhere B agrees with the other MSS.
in reading λαῦνα or λαύνα (δύνας in 32, 1). Λαῦνα is not a
Greek name, and Dionysius can hardly have written such
an inaccurate form.

were to assist the Aborigines in the war they were then engaged in and also to join them with their forces upon every other occasion when summoned ; and, mutually, both nations were to aid each other to the utmost of their power, both with their arms and with their counsel. After they had concluded this treaty and had given pledges by handing over children as hostages, they marched with joint forces against the cities of the Rutulians ; and having soon subdued all opposition there, they came to the town of the Trojans, which was still but half-finished, and all working with a common zeal, they fortified the town with a wall. This town Aeneas called Lavinium, after the daughter of Latinus, according to the Romans' own account ; for her name, they say, was Lavinia. But according to some of the Greek mythographers he named it after the daughter of Anius, the king of the Delians, who was also called Lavinia ; for as she was the first to die of illness at the time of the building of the city and was buried in the place where she died, the city was made her memorial. She is said to have embarked with the Trojans after having been given by her father to Aeneas at his desire as a prophetess and a wise woman. While Lavinium was building, the following omens are said to have appeared to the Trojans. When a fire broke out spontaneously in the forest, a wolf, they say, brought some dry wood in his mouth and threw it upon the fire, and an eagle, flying thither, fanned the flame with the

---

³ τῆς 'Ανίου Steph. : σαινίου ABa, σελινίου Bb.
⁴ δηλίων B : δήλου A.   ⁵ ἧς added by Steph.

τῇ κινήσει τῶν πτερύγων τὴν φλόγα· τούτοις δὲ
τἀναντία μηχανωμένην ἀλώπεκα τὴν οὐρὰν διά-
βροχον ἐκ τοῦ ποταμοῦ φέρουσαν ἐπιρραπίζειν τὸ
καιόμενον πῦρ, καὶ τοτὲ μὲν τοὺς ἀνάπτοντας
ἐπικρατεῖν, τοτὲ δὲ τὴν ἀποσβέσαι βουλομένην·
τέλος δὲ νικῆσαι τοὺς δύο, καὶ τὴν ἑτέραν οἴχεσθαι
5 μηδὲν ἔτι ποιεῖν δυναμένην. ἰδόντα δὲ τὸν Αἰνείαν
εἰπεῖν ὡς ἐπιφανὴς μὲν ἔσται καὶ θαυμαστὴ καὶ
γνώσεως ἐπὶ πλεῖστον ἥξουσα ἡ ἀποικία, ἐπίφθονος
δὲ τοῖς πέλας αὐξομένη καὶ λυπηρά, κρατήσει δ᾽
ὅμως τῶν ἀντιπραττόντων κρείττονα τὴν ἐκ τοῦ
θείου τύχην λαβοῦσα τοῦ παρ᾽ ἀνθρώπων ἐναντιω-
σομένου φθόνου. ταῦτα μὲν δὴ οὕτω περιφανῆ
μηνύματα λέγεται γενέσθαι τῶν συμβησομένων τῇ
πόλει, καὶ ἔστιν αὐτῶν μνημεῖα ἐν τῇ Λαουϊνιατῶν
ἀγορᾷ χάλκεα εἴδωλα τῶν ζῴων ἐκ πολλοῦ πάνυ
χρόνου διατηρούμενα.

LX. Ἐπειδὴ δὲ κατεσκευάσθη τοῖς Τρωσὶν ἡ
πόλις, ἐπιθυμία πάντας ἴσχεν ἰσχυρὰ[1] τοῦ παρ᾽
ἀλλήλων ἀπολαῦσαι χρησίμου, καὶ οἱ βασιλεῖς αὐτῶν πρῶτοι ἄρχουσι μίξαντες τοῦ τε ἐπιχωρίου καὶ
τοῦ ἐπήλυδος γένους τὴν ἀξίωσιν ἐπὶ συναλλαγαῖς
γάμου, δόντος Λατίνου τὴν θυγατέρα Λαουϊνίαν Αἰ-
2 νείᾳ γυναῖκα. ἔπειτα καὶ οἱ ἄλλοι τὴν αὐτὴν τοῖς
βασιλεῦσιν ἐπιθυμίαν λαβόντες καὶ δι᾽ ὀλίγου πάνυ
χρόνου συνενεγκάμενοι ἔθη καὶ νόμους καὶ θεῶν ἱερά,
κηδείας τε[2] συνάψαντες ἀλλήλοις καὶ κοινωνίαις
πολέμων[3] ἀνακερασθέντες, οἱ[4] σύμπαντες κοινῇ[5]

---

[1] ἴσχεν ἰσχυρὰ Bb : ἰσχυρὰ Ba, ἴσχει A.
[2] τε added by Kiessling.
[3] πολέμων Bb : πόλεων Ba, πόλεως A.

198

motion of his wings. But working in opposition
to these, a fox, after wetting his tail in the river,
endeavoured to beat out the flames ; and now those
that were kindling it would prevail, and now the
fox that was trying to put it out. But at last the
two former got the upper hand, and the other went
away, unable to do anything further. Aeneas, on
observing this, said that the colony would become
illustrious and an object of wonder and would gain
the greatest renown, but that as it increased it
would be envied by its neighbours and prove grievous to them ; nevertheless, it would overcome its
adversaries, the good fortune that it had received
from Heaven being more powerful than the envy
of men that would oppose it. These very clear
indications are said to have been given of what was
to happen to the city ; of which there are monuments now standing in the forum of the Lavinians,
in the form of bronze images of the animals, which
have been preserved for a very long time.

LX. After the Trojans' city was built all were
extremely desirous of enjoying the mutual benefit
of their new alliance. And their kings setting the
example, united the excellence of the two races,
the native and the foreign, by ties of marriage,
Latinus giving his daughter Lavinia to Aeneas.
Thereupon the rest also conceived the same desire
as their kings ; and combining in a very brief
time their customs, laws and religious ceremonies,
forming ties through intermarriages and becoming
mingled together in the wars they jointly waged,

---

[4] οἱ Sintenis : τε οἱ O.   [5] κοινῇ Sintenis : καὶ R, om. B.

ὀνομασίᾳ προσαγορεύοντες ἑαυτοὺς ἀπὸ τοῦ βασιλέως τῶν Ἀβοριγίνων Λατίνους, οὕτω βεβαίως
ἔμειναν ἐπὶ τοῖς συγκειμένοις ὥστ' οὐδεὶς αὐτοὺς
ἔτι χρόνος ἀπ' ἀλλήλων διέστησε.

3   Τὰ μὲν δὴ συνελθόντα ἔθνη καὶ κοινωσάμενα
τοὺς βίους, ἐξ ὧν τὸ Ῥωμαίων γένος ὥρμηται,
πρὶν ἣν νῦν ἔχουσιν οἰκισθῆναι πόλιν, ταῦτά ἐστιν·
Ἀβοριγῖνες μὲν πρῶτον, οἳ Σικελοὺς ἐξανέστησαν
ἐκ τούτων τῶν χωρίων, Ἕλληνες ὄντες τὸ ἀρχαῖον
ἐκ Πελοποννήσου τῶν σὺν Οἰνώτρῳ μετενεγκαμένων τὴν οἴκησιν ἐκ τῆς καλουμένης νῦν
Ἀρκαδίας, ὡς ἐγὼ πείθομαι· ἔπειθ' οἱ μεταναστάντες ἐκ τῆς τότε μὲν Αἱμονίας, νῦν δὲ
Θετταλίας καλουμένης, Πελασγοί· τρίτοι δὲ οἱ
σὺν Εὐάνδρῳ παραγενηθέντες εἰς Ἰταλίαν ἐκ
Παλλαντίου πόλεως· μετὰ δὲ τούτους τῶν σὺν
Ἡρακλεῖ στρατευομένων Πελοποννησίων Ἐπειοί
τε καὶ Φενεᾶται, οἷς καὶ Τρωικόν τι ἐμμέμικται·
τελευταῖοι δὲ οἱ διασωθέντες σὺν Αἰνείᾳ Τρῶες ἐξ
Ἰλίου τε καὶ Δαρδάνου καὶ τῶν ἄλλων Τρωικῶν
πόλεων.

LXI. Ὅτι δὲ καὶ τὸ τῶν Τρώων ἔθνος Ἑλληνικὸν ἐν τοῖς μάλιστα ἦν ἐκ Πελοποννήσου ποτὲ
ὡρμημένον, εἴρηται μὲν καὶ ἄλλοις τισὶ πάλαι,
λεχθήσεται δὲ καὶ πρὸς ἐμοῦ δι' ὀλίγων. ἔχει δὲ
ὁ λόγος περὶ αὐτῶν ὧδε· Ἄτλας γίνεται βασιλεὺς
πρῶτος ἐν τῇ καλουμένῃ νῦν Ἀρκαδίᾳ, ᾤκει δὲ περὶ
τὸ λεγόμενον Θαυμάσιον[1] ὄρος. τούτῳ θυγατέρες
ἦσαν ἑπτὰ αἱ νῦν ἐν οὐρανῷ κατηστερίσθαι λεγό-

---

[1] Glareanus: καυκάσιον O; Καυκώνιον Jacoby.

and all calling themselves by the common name of
Latins, after the king of the Aborigines, they ad-
hered so firmly to their pact that no lapse of time
has yet severed them from one another.

The nations, therefore, which came together and
shared in a common life and from which the Roman
people derived their origin before the city they now
inhabit was built, are these : first, the Aborigines,
who drove the Sicels out of these parts and were
originally Greeks from the Peloponnesus, the same
who with Oenotrus removed from the country now
called Arcadia, according to my opinion ; then,
the Pelasgians, who came from Haemonia, as it
was then called, but now Thessaly ; third, those
who came into Italy with Evander from the city of
Pallantium ; after them the Epeans and Pheneats,
who were part of the Peloponnesian army commanded by Hercules, with whom a Trojan element
also was commingled ; and, last of all, the Trojans
who had escaped with Aeneas from Ilium, Dardanus
and the other Trojan cities.

LXI. That the Trojans, too, were a nation as
truly Greek as any and formerly came from the Peloponnesus has long since been asserted by some
authors and shall be briefly related by me also. The
account concerning them is as follows. Atlas was the
first king of the country now called Arcadia, and
he lived near the mountain called Thaumasius.[1] He
had seven daughters, who are said to be numbered

---

[1] This mountain is mentioned by Pausanias (viii. 36, 2)
and by Stephanus of Byzantium. Cauconius, suggested by
Jacoby, appears to be purely a conjectural name.

μεναι Πλειάδες ἐπίκλησιν, ὧν μίαν μὲν Ἠλέκτραν
Ζεὺς γαμεῖ καὶ γεννᾷ παῖδας ἐξ αὐτῆς Ἴασον καὶ
2 Δάρδανον. Ἴασος μὲν οὖν ἠίθεος μένει, Δάρδανος
δὲ ἄγεται γυναῖκα Χρύσην Πάλλαντος θυγατέρα,
ἐξ ἧς αὐτῷ γίνονται παῖδες Ἰδαῖος καὶ Δείμας.
οὗτοι¹ τέως μὲν ἐν Ἀρκαδίᾳ παραλαβόντες τὴν
Ἄτλαντος δυναστείαν ἐβασίλευον, ἔπειτα κατα-
κλυσμοῦ γενομένου μεγάλου περὶ τὴν Ἀρκαδίαν
τὰ μὲν πεδία ἐξελιμνώθη καὶ πολλοῦ χρόνου
γεωργεῖσθαι ἀδύνατα ἦν, οἱ δὲ ἄνθρωποι (ᾤκουν
γὰρ ἀνὰ τὰ ὄρη γλίσχρως ποριζόμενοι τὰς τροφάς)
συμφρονήσαντες ὡς οὐχ ἱκανὴ βόσκειν ἔσται πάντας
ἡ περιοῦσα γῆ νέμονται σφᾶς αὐτοὺς διχῇ· καὶ
αὐτῶν οἱ μὲν ἐν Ἀρκαδίᾳ ὑπομένουσι βασιλέα
καταστησάμενοι² Δείμαντα τὸν Δαρδάνου, οἱ δὲ
λοιποὶ ἀπανίστανται Πελοποννήσου στόλῳ μεγάλῳ.
3 ποιούμενοι δὲ τὸν πλοῦν παρὰ τὴν Εὐρώπην εἰς τὸν
Μέλανα καλούμενον ἀφικνοῦνται κόλπον καὶ τυγχάνουσιν ἐν νήσῳ τινὶ τῆς Θρᾴκης ὁρμισάμενοι, ἣν
οὐκ ἔχω εἰπεῖν εἴτε ἦν οἰκουμένη καὶ πρότερον εἴτ'
ἔρημος³· ᾗ τίθενται τοὔνομα σύνθετον ἐκ τε ἀνδρὸς
καὶ τόπου, Σαμοθράκην· τὸ μὲν γὰρ χωρίον τῆς
Θρᾴκης, ὁ δὲ οἰκιστὴς Σάμων, υἱὸς Ἑρμοῦ καὶ
4 νύμφης Κυλληνίδος Ῥήνης ὀνομαζομένης. ἐκεῖ δὲ
χρόνον οὐ πολὺν διατρίψαντες, ὡς οὐκ εὐμαρὴς ἦν
ὁ βίος αὐτοῖς γῇ τε λυπρᾷ καὶ θαλάττῃ ἀγρίᾳ
μαχομένοις, ὀλίγους τινὰς ἐν τῇ νήσῳ λειπόμενοι
ἀπανίστανται πάλιν οἱ πλείους εἰς τὴν Ἀσίαν

¹ οὗτοι Kiessling : οἱ (οἳ B) τὸ AB, οἳ τω Bb.
² Reiske : στησάμενοι O.

now among the constellations under the name of
the Pleiades ; Zeus married one of these, Electra,
and had by her two sons, Iasus and Dardanus. Iasus
remained unmarried, but Dardanus married Chrysê,
the daughter of Pallas, by whom he had two sons,
Idaeus and Deimas ; and these, succeeding Atlas in
the kingdom, reigned for some time in Arcadia.
Afterwards, a great deluge occurring throughout
Arcadia, the plains were overflowed and for a long
time could not be tilled ; and the inhabitants,
living upon the mountains and eking out a sorry
livelihood, decided that the land remaining would
not be sufficient for the support of them all, and so
divided themselves into two groups, one of which
remained in Arcadia, after making Deimas, the
son of Dardanus, their king, while the other left
the Peloponnesus on board a large fleet. And
sailing along the coast of Europe, they came to
a gulf called Melas and chanced to land on a certain
island of Thrace, as to which I am unable to say
whether it was previously inhabited or not. They
called the island Samothrace, a name compounded of
the name of a man and the name of a place. For
it belongs to Thrace and its first settler was Samon,
the son of Hermes and a nymph of Cyllenê, named
Rhenê. Here they remained but a short time,
since the life proved to be no easy one for them,
forced to contend, as they were, with both a poor
soil and a boisterous sea ; but leaving some few of
their people in the island, the greater part of them
removed once more and went to Asia under Dardanus

---

[3] ἔρημος Kiessling : ἐρήμη ἦν B, ἐρήμη R.

ἔχοντες ἡγεμόνα τῆς ἀποικίας Δάρδανον· "Ιασος
γὰρ ἐν τῇ νήσῳ κεραυνῷ πληγεὶς τελευτᾷ Δήμητρος
εὐνῆς[1] ὀριγνώμενος[2]· ποιησάμενοί τε τὴν ἀπόβασιν ἐν τῷ καλουμένῳ νῦν Ἑλλησπόντῳ περὶ τὴν
ὕστερον κληθεῖσαν οἰκίζονται Φρυγίαν, Ἰδαῖος μὲν
ὁ Δαρδάνου μέρος τῆς στρατιᾶς ἔχων ἐν τοῖς ὄρεσιν,
ἃ νῦν Ἰδαῖα ἀπ' ἐκείνου λέγεται, ἔνθα μητρὶ θεῶν
ἱερὸν ἱδρυσάμενος ὄργια καὶ τελετὰς κατεστήσατο,
αἳ καὶ εἰς τόδε χρόνου διαμένουσιν ἐν ἁπάσῃ
Φρυγίᾳ· Δάρδανος δ' ἐν τῇ καλουμένῃ νῦν Τρωάδι
πόλιν ὁμώνυμον αὑτῷ κατασκευάσας, δόντος αὐτῷ
τὰ χωρία Τεύκρου βασιλέως, ἀφ' οὗ Τευκρὶς τὸ
5 ἀρχαῖον ἡ γῆ ἐλέγετο· τοῦτον δὲ ἄλλοι τε πολλοὶ
καὶ Φανόδημος ὁ τὴν Ἀττικὴν γράψας ἀρχαιολογίαν
ἐκ τῆς Ἀττικῆς μετοικῆσαί φασιν εἰς τὴν Ἀσίαν
δήμου Ξυπεταιέως[3] ἄρχοντα καὶ πολλὰ παρέχονται
τοῦ λόγου τεκμήρια. κρατήσαντα δὲ χώρας συχνῆς
τε καὶ ἀγαθῆς καὶ οὐ πολὺ τὸ ἐπιχώριον ἐχούσης
γένος ἀσμένως τὸν Δάρδανον ἰδεῖν καὶ τὸ σὺν αὐτῷ
παραγενόμενον Ἑλληνικόν, τῶν τε πρὸς τοὺς βαρβάρους πολέμων συμμαχίας ἕνεκα καὶ ἵνα ἡ γῆ μὴ
ᾖ ἔρημος.

---

[1] εὐνῆς Bb : εὐνὴν ABa.

[2] After ὀριγνώμενος B has ὡς οἱ ἔχει, deleted by Bb, R have
ὡς οἱ ἔχειν. Kiessling read ὡς ὁ λόγος ἔχει, Grasberger εὐνὴν
ὀριγνώμενος αἰσχύνειν.

[3] Ξυπεταιέως Sylburg : ἐξυπεταιέως B, ἐξυπταιέως A. But
the form Ξυπεταιεύς is questionable, even as a noun; elsewhere the word for an inhabitant of the deme Ξυπέτη (also
spelled Ξυπετέα or Ξυπεταία) is Ξυπεταιών. The normal construction with δήμου would be Ξυπεταιόνων (cf. δήμου Τρώων

as leader of their colony (for Iasus had died in the
island, being struck with a thunderbolt for desiring
to have intercourse with Demeter), and disembark-
ing in the strait now called the Hellespont, they
settled in the region which was afterwards called
Phrygia. Idaeus, the son of Dardanus, with part
of the company occupied the mountains which are
now called after him the Idaean mountains, and there
built a temple to the Mother of the Gods and instituted mysteries and ceremonies which are observed to this day throughout all Phrygia. And
Dardanus built a city named after himself in the
region now called the Troad; the land was given
to him by Teucer, the king, after whom the country
was anciently called Teucris. Many authors, and
particularly Phanodemus, who wrote about the
ancient lore of Attica,[1] say that Teucer had come
into Asia from Attica, where he had been chief of
the deme called Xypetê, and of this tale they offer
many proofs. They add that, having possessed
himself of a large and fertile country with but a
small native population, he was glad to see Dardanus
and the Greeks who came with him, both because
he hoped for their assistance in his wars against the
barbarians and because he desired that the land
should not remain unoccupied.

[1] His work was an *Atthis* (*cf.* p. 27, n. 1). Müller, *Frag.
Hist. Graec.* i. 367, 8).

---

in the parallel passage in Strabo xiii. 1, 78); other possible
readings are Ξυπεταιόνος, if this form can be used as an
adjective, and Ξυπεταίας.

LXII. Ἀπαιτεῖ δὲ ὁ λόγος καὶ τὸν Αἰνείαν ἐξ ὧν ἔφυ διηγήσασθαι· βραχεία δὴ καὶ τοῦτο δηλώσει σημανῶ. Δάρδανος ἐπειδὴ Χρύσην τὴν Πάλλαντος θυγατέρα, ἐξ ἧς οἱ πρότεροι παῖδες ἐγένοντο αὐτῷ, τελευτῆσαι συνέπεσε, Βάτειαν γαμεῖ τὴν Τεύκρου θυγατέρα· καὶ γίνεται παῖς αὐτῷ Ἐριχθόνιος, ὃς ἁπάντων ἀνθρώπων εὐδαιμονέστατος λέγεται γενέσθαι τῆς τε πατρῴας καὶ τῆς ὑπὸ τῷ μητροπά-
2 τορι γενομένης κληρονομήσας ἀρχῆς. Ἐριχθονίου δὲ καὶ Καλλιρρόης [1] τῆς Σκαμάνδρου γίνεται Τρώς, ἀφ' οὗ τὴν ἐπωνυμίαν τὸ ἔθνος ἔχει· Τρωὸς δὲ καὶ Ἀκαλλαρίδος τῆς Εὐμήδους Ἀσσάρακος ἦν· τούτου δὲ καὶ Κλυτοδώρας τῆς Λαομέδοντος Κάπυς· Κάπυος δὲ καὶ νύμφης Ναϊάδος Ἱερομνήμης [2] Ἀγχίσης· Ἀγχίσου δὲ καὶ Ἀφροδίτης Αἰνείας. ὡς μὲν δὴ καὶ τὸ Τρωικὸν γένος Ἑλληνικὸν ἀρχῆθεν ἦν δεδήλωταί μοι.

LXIII. Περὶ δὲ τῶν χρόνων ἐν οἷς ἐκτίσθη τὸ Λαουΐνιον ἄλλοι μὲν ἄλλως λέγουσιν· ἐμοὶ μέντοι δοκοῦσιν οἱ δευτέρῳ μετὰ τὴν ἔξοδον τὴν ἐκ Τροίας ἔτει φέροντες αὐτὴν [3] εἰκότα μᾶλλον λέγειν. Ἴλιος μὲν γὰρ ἑάλω τελευτῶντος ἤδη τοῦ ἔαρος, [4] ἑπτακαίδεκα πρότερον ἡμέραις τῆς θερινῆς τροπῆς, ὀγδόῃ φθίνοντος μηνὸς Θαργηλιῶνος, ὡς Ἀθηναῖοι τοὺς

---

[1] Jacoby: καλλιρόης O.   [2] Kiessling: εἰρομένης AB.
[3] ἔτει φέροντες αὐτὴν O: ἐπιφέροντες ἐνιαυτῷ Madvig.
[4] ἔαρος Camerarius: θέρους O, Jacoby.

---

[1] This would be 1181 B.C. according to Dionysius, since Eratosthenes, whose chronology he follows (chap. 74, 2), placed the fall of Troy in 1183.

LXII. But the subject requires that I relate also how Aeneas was descended : this, too, I shall do briefly. Dardanus, after the death of Chrysê, the daughter of Pallas, by whom he had his first sons, married Bateia, the daughter of Teucer, and by her had Erichthonius, who is said to have been the most fortunate of all men, since he inherited both the kingdom of his father and that of his maternal grandfather. Of Erichthonius and Callirrhoê, the daughter of Scamander, was born Tros, from whom the nation has received its name ; of Tros and Acallaris, the daughter of Eumedes, Assaracus ; of Assaracus and Clytodora, the daughter of Laomedon, Capys ; of Capys and a Naiad nymph, Hieromnemê, Anchises ; of Anchises and Aphroditê, Aeneas. Thus I have shown that the Trojan race, too, was originally Greek.

LXIII. Concerning the time when Lavinium was built there are various reports, but to me the most probable seems to be that which places it in the second year after the departure of the Trojans from Troy.[1] For Ilium was taken at the end of the spring, seventeen days before the summer solstice, and the eighth from the end of the month Thargelion,[2] according to the calendar of the Athenians ; and

[2] The Athenians divided their months into three periods of ten days each (nine in the last period in the shorter months), in the first two of which they counted the days forwards, as we do, while in the third they reckoned backwards from the end of the month. The eighth from the end of the month, reckoning inclusively, would be the 23rd (or 22nd). Their year seems to have begun with the new moon immediately following the summer solstice.

χρόνους ἄγουσι, περιτταὶ δὲ ἦσαν αἱ τὸν ἐνιαυτὸν
ἐκεῖνον ἐκπληροῦσαι μετὰ τὴν τροπὴν εἴκοσιν ἡμέ-
ραι. ἐν δὴ ταῖς ἑπτὰ καὶ τριάκοντα ταῖς ἀπὸ τῆς
ἁλώσεως διαγενομέναις τά τε περὶ τὴν πόλιν οἴομαι
διοικήσασθαι τοὺς Ἀχαιοὺς καὶ τὰς πρεσβείας ἐπι-
δέξασθαι τὰς παρὰ τῶν ἀφεστηκότων καὶ τὰ ὅρκια
2 ποιήσασθαι πρὸς αὐτούς· τῷ δ' ἑξῆς ἔτει, πρώτῳ
δὲ μετὰ τὴν ἅλωσιν, ὑπὸ τὴν μετοπωρινὴν ἰσημερίαν
ἄραντες οἱ Τρῶες ἐκ τῆς γῆς περαιοῦνται τὸν
Ἑλλήσποντον καὶ καταχθέντες εἰς τὴν Θράκην
αὐτοῦ διατρίβουσι τὴν χειμερινὴν ὥραν δεχόμενοί
τε τοὺς ἐπισυνιόντας ἐκ τῆς φυγῆς καὶ παρα-
σκευαζόμενοι τὰ εἰς τὸν ἀπόπλουν. ἐκ δὲ τῆς
Θράκης ἀναστάντες ἔαρος ἀρχομένου τελοῦσι τὸν
μεταξὺ πλοῦν ἄχρι Σικελίας· ἐκεῖ δὲ ὁρμισαμένοις
αὐτοῖς τὸ ἔτος τοῦτο τελευτᾷ, καὶ διατρίβουσι τὸν
δεύτερον χειμῶνα τὰς πόλεις συνοικίζοντες τοῖς
3 Ἐλύμοις ἐν Σικελίᾳ. πλοΐμων δὲ γενομένων
ἄραντες ἀπὸ τῆς νήσου περῶσι τὸ Τυρρηνικὸν
πέλαγος καὶ τελευτῶντες εἰς Λαύρεντον ἀφικνοῦνται
τὸν Ἀβοριγίνων αἰγιαλὸν μεσούσης θερείας. λαβόντες δὲ τὸ χωρίον οἰκίζουσιν ἐν αὐτῷ Λαουΐνιον
τὸν δεύτερον ἀπὸ τῆς ἁλώσεως ἐκπληρώσαντες
ἐνιαυτόν. καὶ περὶ μὲν τούτων ὡς ἔχω δόξης
δεδήλωταί μοι.

LXIV. Αἰνείας δὲ κατασκευάσας ἱεροῖς τε καὶ
τοῖς ἄλλοις κόσμοις ἀποχρώντως τὴν πόλιν, ὧν τὰ
πλεῖστα ἔτι καὶ εἰς ἐμὲ ἦν, τῷ μὲν ἑξῆς ἐνιαυτῷ,

---

[1] *Cf.* Livy i. 2. From this point onward parallel passages in Livy will be thus indicated by a note attached

there still remained twenty days after the solstice to complete that year. During the thirty-seven days that followed the taking of the city I imagine the Achaeans were employed in regulating the affairs of the city, in receiving embassies from those who had withdrawn themselves, and in concluding a treaty with them. In the following year, which was the first after the taking of the city, the Trojans set sail about the autumnal equinox, crossed the Hellespont, and landing in Thrace, passed the winter season there, during which they received the fugitives who kept flocking to them and made the necessary preparations for their voyage. And leaving Thrace in the beginning of spring, they sailed as far as Sicily; when they had landed there that year came to an end, and they passed the second winter in assisting the Elymians to found their cities in Sicily. But as soon as conditions were favourable for navigation they set sail from the island, and crossing the Tyrrhenian sea, arrived at last at Laurentum on the coast of the Aborigines in the middle of the summer. And having received the ground from them, they founded Lavinium, thus bringing to an end the second year from the taking of Troy. With regard to these matters, then, I have thus shown my opinion.

LXIV. But [1] when Aeneas had sufficiently adorned the city with temples and other public buildings, of which the greatest part remained even to my day,

to the initial word of a chapter or series of chapters in Dionysius.

τρίτῳ δὲ ἀπὸ τῆς ἐξόδου, Τρώων ἐβασίλευσε
μόνων· τῷ δὲ τετάρτῳ τελευτήσαντος Λατίνου
καὶ τὴν ἐκείνου βασιλείαν παραλαμβάνει τῆς τε
κηδείας οἰκειότητι τῆς πρὸς αὐτόν, ἐπικλήρου τῆς
Λαουϊνίας γενομένης μετὰ τὸν Λατίνου θάνατον, καὶ
τοῦ πρὸς τοὺς ἀστυγείτονας πολέμου τῆς στρατη-
2 γίας ἕνεκα. ἀπέστησαν γὰρ αὖθις ἀπὸ τοῦ Λατίνου ῾Ρότολοι λαβόντες ἡγεμόνα τῶν αὐτομόλων
τινὰ τῆς Λατίνου γυναικὸς Ἀμάτας¹ ἀνεψιὸν ὄνομα
Τυρρηνόν.² ὁ δὲ ἀνὴρ οὗτος ἐπὶ τῷ γάμῳ τῆς
Λαουϊνίας τὸν κηδεστὴν μεμφόμενος, ὅτι παρελθὼν
τὸ συγγενὲς ὀθνείοις³ ἐκήδευσε, τῆς τε Ἀμάτας
παροξυνούσης καὶ ἄλλων τινῶν συλλαμβανόντων,
ἄγων τὴν δύναμιν ἧς αὐτὸς ἦρχε προστίθεται τοῖς
3 ῾Ροτόλοις. πολέμου δ' ἐκ τῶν ἐγκλημάτων τούτων
γενομένου καὶ μάχης ἰσχυρᾶς Λατῖνός τε ἀποθνήσκει καὶ Τυρρηνὸς καὶ τῶν ἄλλων συχνοί,
κρατοῦσι δ' ὅμως οἱ σὺν Αἰνείᾳ. ἐκ δὲ τούτου
τὴν ὑπὸ τῷ κηδεστῇ γενομένην ἀρχὴν Αἰνείας
παραλαμβάνει. τρία δὲ βασιλεύσας ἔτη μετὰ τὴν
Λατίνου τελευτὴν τῷ τετάρτῳ θνήσκει κατὰ πόλε-
4 μον. ῾Ρότολοί τε γὰρ ἐκ τῶν πόλεων στρατεύουσιν

¹ Ἀμάτας Cobet, Ἀμάτης Steph.: ἀμίτας O, Jacoby (and
so just below).
² τυρρηνόν O (and similarly below): Τυρνόν Sylburg, Cobet.
³ ὀθνείοις B: ὀθνείους R.

¹ It is perhaps wiser to follow the MSS. in the spelling of
this name than to emend to Turnus. Granted that Τύρνος
might easily have been changed to Τυρρηνός by a scribe,
yet it is just as conceivable that Greek writers, seeing in

the next year, which was the third after his departure from Troy, he reigned over the Trojans only. But in the fourth year, Latinus having died, he succeeded to his kingdom also, not only in consideration of his relationship to him by marriage, Lavinia being the heiress after the death of Latinus, but also because of his being commander in the war against the neighbouring tribes. For the Rutulians had again revolted from Latinus, choosing for their leader one of the deserters, named Tyrrhenus,[1] who was a nephew of Amata,[2] the wife of Latinus. This man, blaming Latinus in the matter of Lavinia's marriage, because he had ignored his kinsmen and allied his family with outsiders, and being goaded on by Amata and encouraged by others, had gone over to the Rutulians with the forces he commanded. War arose out of these complaints and in a sharp battle that ensued Latinus, Tyrrhenus and many others were slain; nevertheless, Aeneas and his people gained the victory. Thereupon Aeneas succeeded to the kingdom of his father-in-law ; but when he had reigned three years after the death of Latinus, in the fourth he lost his life in battle. For the Rutulians marched out in full force from their cities against

Turnus nothing but a modified form of Tyrrhenus, may have preferred to use the normal form ; we have already met with a Tyrrhenus as the eponymous founder of the Tyrrhenian race (chaps. 27 f.). Yet for Turnus Herdonius (iv. 45, 47 f.) Dionysius evidently used the spelling Τύρνος (corrupted to Τύρδος in the MSS.).

[2] In the case of this name we may emend to Amata with little hesitation, since the form Amita (" paternal aunt ") is not appropriate as a proper name and is unlike any Greek name.

ἅπαντες ἐπ᾽ αὐτόν, καὶ σὺν αὐτοῖς βασιλεὺς Τυρρηνῶν Μεσέντιος δείσας περὶ τῆς αὐτοῦ χώρας· ἤδη
γὰρ ἐπὶ μέγα χωροῦσαν τὴν Ἑλληνικὴν ὁρῶν
δύναμιν ἤχθετο. μάχης δὲ γενομένης καρτερᾶς οὐ
πρόσω τοῦ Λαουϊνίου καὶ πολλῶν ἑκατέρωθεν ἀπο-
λομένων τὰ μὲν στρατεύματα νυκτὸς ἐπελθούσης
διελύθη, τὸ δὲ Αἰνείου σῶμα φανερὸν οὐδαμῇ γενόμενον οἱ μὲν εἰς θεοὺς μεταστῆναι εἴκαζον, οἱ δ᾽ ἐν
τῷ ποταμῷ, παρ᾽ ὃν ἡ μάχη ἐγένετο, διαφθαρῆναι.
5 καὶ αὐτῷ κατασκευάζουσιν οἱ Λατῖνοι ἡρῷον ἐπιγραφῇ τοιᾷδε κοσμούμενον· "Πατρὸς θεοῦ
χθονίου, ὃς ποταμοῦ Νομικίου ῥεῦμα
διέπει." εἰσὶ δ᾽ οἳ λέγουσιν ἐπ᾽ Ἀγχίσῃ κατασκευασθῆναι αὐτὸ ὑπ᾽ Αἰνείου, ἐνιαυτῷ πρότερον
τοῦ πολέμου τούτου τελευτήσαντι. ἔστι δὲ χωμά-
τιον οὐ μέγα καὶ περὶ αὐτὸ δένδρα στοιχηδὸν
πεφυκότα θέας ἄξια.

LXV. Αἰνείου δ᾽ ἐξ ἀνθρώπων μεταστάντος
ἑβδόμῳ μάλιστα ἔτει μετὰ τὴν Ἰλίου ἅλωσιν
Εὐρυλέων παρέλαβε τὴν Λατίνων ἡγεμονίαν ὁ
μετονομασθεὶς Ἀσκάνιος ἐν τῇ φυγῇ. ἦσαν δὲ
τειχήρεις οἱ Τρῶες ἐν τῷ χρόνῳ τούτῳ, καὶ τοῖς
μὲν πολεμίοις ἀεὶ προσῄει δύναμις, αἱ δὲ τῶν
Λατίνων ἀδύνατοι ἦσαν τοῖς ἐν τῷ Λαουϊνίῳ πολι-
2 ορκουμένοις ἐπικουρεῖν. τὸ μὲν δὴ πρῶτον εἰς
φιλίαν τε καὶ συνθήκας μετρίας προυκαλοῦντο τοὺς
πολεμίους οἱ περὶ τὸν Ἀσκάνιον· ὡς δ᾽ οὐδὲν
προσεῖχον αὐτοῖς, ἐπιτρέπειν ἐκείνοις ἠναγκάζοντο
καταλύσασθαι τὸν πόλεμον ἐφ᾽ οἷς ἂν αὐτοὶ

him, and with them Mezentius, king of the Tyrrhenians, who thought his own country in danger; for he was troubled at seeing the Greek power already making rapid headway. A severe battle took place not far from Lavinium and many were slain on both sides, but when night came on the armies separated; and when the body of Aeneas was nowhere to be seen, some concluded that it had been translated to the gods and others that it had perished in the river beside which the battle was fought. And the Latins built a hero-shrine to him with this inscription : " To the father and god of this place,[1] who presides over the waters of the river Numicius." But there are some who say the shrine was erected by Aeneas in honour of Anchises, who died in the year before this war. It is a small mound, round which have been set out in regular rows trees that are well worth seeing.

LXV. Aeneas having departed this life about the seventh year after the taking of Troy, Euryleon, who in the flight had been renamed Ascanius, succeeded to the rule over the Latins. At this time the Trojans were undergoing a siege ; the forces of the enemy were increasing daily, and the Latins were unable to assist those who were shut up in Lavinium. Ascanius and his men, therefore, first invited the enemy to a friendly and reasonable accommodation, but when no heed was paid to them, they were forced to allow their enemies to put an end to the war upon their own terms. When,

---

[1] Dionysius evidently uses χθόνιος here to translate the Latin term *indiges*. Livy (i. 2, 6) does not specifically cite the inscription, but says *Iovem Indigitem appellant*.

δικαιῶσι. τοῦ δὲ βασιλέως τῶν Τυρρηνῶν τά τε ἄλλα ὡς δεδουλωμένοις ἀφόρητα ἐπιτάσσοντος καὶ τὸν οἶνον ὅσον ἂν ἡ Λατίνων γῆ φέρῃ Τυρρηνοῖς ἀπάγειν ἀνὰ πᾶν ἔτος, οὐκ ἀνασχετὸν ἡγησάμενοι τὸ πρᾶγμα τῆς μὲν ἀμπέλου τὸν καρπὸν ἱερὸν ἐψηφίσαντο τοῦ Διὸς εἶναι γνώμην ἀγορεύσαντος Ἀσκανίου, αὐτοὶ δὲ ἀλλήλοις παρακελευσάμενοι προθύμοις ἀγωνισταῖς γενέσθαι καὶ θεοὺς αἰτησάμενοι συλλαβέσθαι τοῦ κινδυνεύματος ἐξῆλθον ἐκ
3 τῆς πόλεως φυλάξαντες νύκτα ἀσέληνον. εὐθὺς δὲ προσβαλόντες τῷ χάρακι τῶν πολεμίων, ὃς ἐγγυτάτω τῆς πόλεως ἔκειτο καὶ ἦν προτείχισμα τῆς ἄλλης δυνάμεως ἐν ἐρυμνῷ τε κατεσκευασμένος χωρίῳ καὶ τὴν κρατίστην νεότητα Τυρρηνῶν ἔχων, ἧς ἡγεῖτο Μεσεντίου παῖς Λαῦσος ὄνομα, οὐδενὸς προϊδομένου τὴν ἔφοδον αἱροῦσιν εὐπετῶς τὸ ὀχύρωμα. ἐν ᾧ δὲ τὸ χωρίον τοῦτο ἡλίσκετο, φῶς τε ἄκαιρον ὁρῶντες οἱ ἐν τοῖς πεδίοις ἐστρατοπεδευκότες καὶ βοὴν τῶν ἀπολλυμένων ἀκούοντες ἔφευγον
4 ἐκλιπόντες τοὺς πεδινοὺς τόπους ἐπὶ τὰ ὄρη. ἐν δὲ τούτῳ πολλὴ ἐγένετο ταραχὴ καὶ θόρυβος, οἷα ἐν νυκτὶ κινουμένης στρατιᾶς, ὡς αὐτίκα μάλα τῶν πολεμίων σφίσιν ἐπιθησομένων οὐ σὺν κόσμῳ οὐδὲ κατὰ τέλη τὴν ἔλασιν ποιουμένοις[1] · οἱ δὲ Λατῖνοι, ἐπειδὴ τό τε φρούριον ἐξ ἐφόδου κατειλήφεσαν καὶ τὸ ἄλλο στράτευμα ἔμαθον τεταραγμένον, ἐπέκειντο αὐτοῖς κτείνοντες καὶ διώκοντες. τῶν δ' οὐχ ὅπως

---

[1] ⟨τὴν⟩ ἔλασι ⟨ποιουμένοις⟩ Meutzner, ἐλαύνουσιν Kayser: ἔλασιν A, ἔλωσιν Ba, ἐλάσειν Bb.

however, the king of the Tyrrhenians, among other
intolerable conditions that he imposed upon them,
as upon a people already become his slaves, commanded them to bring to the Tyrrhenians every
year all the wine the country of the Latins produced,
they looked upon this as a thing beyond all endurance,
and following the advice of Ascanius, voted that the
fruit of the vine should be sacred to Jupiter. Then,
exhorting one another to prove their zeal and valour
and praying the gods to assist them in their dangerous enterprise, they fixed upon a moonless night
and sallied out of the city. And they immediately
attacked that part of the enemy's rampart which
lay nearest to the city and which, being designed
as an advanced post to cover the rest of their forces,
had been constructed in a strong position and was
defended by the choicest youth of the Tyrrhenians,
under the command of Lausus, the son of Mezentius ;
and their attack being unforeseen, they easily made
themselves masters of the stronghold. While they
were employed in taking this post, those of the
enemy who were encamped on the plains, seeing an
unusual light and hearing the cries of the men who
were perishing, left the level country and were fleeing
to the mountains. During this time there was great
confusion and tumult, as was but natural with an
army moving at night ; for they expected the enemy
would every moment fall upon them while they were
withdrawing in disorder and with ranks broken.
The Latins, after they had taken the fort by storm
and learned that the rest of the army was in disorder,
pressed after them, killing and pursuing. And not

τις πρὸς ἀλκὴν τραπέσθαι ἐπεχείρησεν, ἀλλ᾽ οὐδὲ
μαθεῖν ἐν οἷς ἦσαν κακοῖς [1] ἠδύνατο· ὑπὸ δὲ θορύβου καὶ ἀμηχανίας οἱ μὲν κατὰ κρημνῶν φερόμενοι
διεφθείροντο, οἱ δ᾽ εἰς φάραγγας ἀνεξόδους ἐμπί-
πτοντες ἡλίσκοντο, οἱ δὲ πλεῖστοι ἀγνοήσαντες
ἀλλήλους ἀνὰ τὸ σκότος ὅσα πολεμίους διέθεσαν,
καὶ ὁ πλεῖστος αὐτῶν φθόρος ἀλληλοκτόνος ἐγίνετο.
5 Μεσέντιος δὲ σὺν ὀλίγοις λόφον τινὰ καταλαβών,
ἐπειδὴ τοῦ παιδὸς τὸν μόρον ἐπύθετο καὶ ὅσος
αὐτῷ στρατὸς διέφθαρτο ἐν οἵῳ τε χωρίῳ κατα-
κεκλεικὼς ἑαυτὸν ἦν, ὡς ὢν παντὸς [2] ἐν ἀπορίᾳ [3]
χρήματος, ἔπεμψε κήρυκας εἰς τὸ Λαουΐνιον περὶ
φιλίας διαλεξομένους, Ἀσκανίου δὲ τοῖς Λατίνοις
ταμιεύεσθαι τὴν τύχην συμβουλεύοντος ἄδειαν εὑρόμενος ἀπῆλθεν ὑπόσπονδος μεθ᾽ ὅσης εἶχε δυνάμεως
καὶ τὸν ἀπὸ τοῦδε χρόνον ἅπαντα διαλυσάμενος τὴν
ἔχθραν πρὸς τοὺς Λατίνους βέβαιος φίλος ἦν.

LXVI. Τριακοστῷ δὲ ὕστερον ἔτει μετὰ τὴν
κτίσιν τοῦ Λαουϊνίου πόλιν ἑτέραν οἰκίζει κατὰ τὸ
γενόμενον Αἰνείᾳ θέσφατον Ἀσκάνιος ὁ Αἰνείου καὶ
μετάγει τούς τ᾽ ἐκ Λαουϊνίου [4] καὶ τῶν ἄλλων Λατίνων ὅσοις ἦν βουλομένοις ἄμεινον οἰκεῖν εἰς τὴν
νεόκτιστον, ὄνομα τῇ πόλει θέμενος Ἄλβαν. ἔστι
δ᾽ ἡ Ἄλβα καθ᾽ Ἑλλάδα γλῶσσαν Λευκή, σαφη-
νισμοῦ δ᾽ ἕνεκα διορίζεται παρ᾽ ἑτέραν πόλιν
ὁμώνυμον ἐπικλήσει τὸ σχῆμα ἐπικατηγορούσῃ,[5]

[1] οἷς ἦσαν κακοῖς Bb : οἷς ἦν κακοῖς Ba, οἷς κακοῖς ἦν A.
[2] ὡς ὢν παντὸς Capps, παντὸς Kiessling, ὡς ὢν Jacoby : ὡς O.
[3] ἐν ἀπορίᾳ Steph. : ἐν ἀπόρῳ AB.
[4] πόλιν   Λαουϊνίου Bmg : om. ABa.
[5] ἐπικατηγορούσῃ L. Dindorf : ἐπικατηγορήσει AB.

only did none of the enemy attempt to turn and resist, but it was not even possible for them to know in what evil plight they were, and in their confusion and helplessness some were falling over precipices and perishing, while others were becoming entangled in blind ravines and were being taken prisoner ; but most of them, failing to recognize their comrades in the dark, treated them as enemies, and the greatest part of their loss was due to their slaying of one another. Mezentius with a few of his men seized a hill, but when he learned of the fate of his son and of the numbers he had lost and discovered the nature of the place in which he had shut himself up, realizing that he was lacking in everything needful, he sent heralds to Lavinium to treat for peace. And since Ascanius advised the Latins to husband their good fortune, Mezentius obtained permission to retire under a truce with the forces he had left ; and from that time, laying aside all his enmity with the Latins, he was their constant friend.

LXVI. In the thirtieth year[1] after the founding of Lavinium Ascanius, the son of Aeneas, in pursuance of the oracle given to his father, built another city and transferred both the inhabitants of Lavinium and the other Latins who were desirous of a better habitation to this newly-built city, which he called Alba. Alba means in the Greek tongue *Leukê* or " White " ; but for the sake of clearness it is distinguished from another city of the same name by the addition of an epithet descriptive of its shape,

---

[1] *Cf.* Livy i. 3, 3-4. According to Dionysius' reckoning (see p. 206, n. 1), Alba was founded in 1151 B.C.

καί ἐστιν ὥσπερ σύνθετον ἤδη τοὔνομα ἐξ ἀμφοῖν
2 Ἄλβα λόγγα, τοῦτο δ' ἔστι Λευκὴ μακρά. νῦν
μὲν οὖν ἔρημός ἐστιν· ἐπὶ γὰρ Ὁστιλίου Τύλλου
Ῥωμαίων βασιλέως στασιάζειν δόξασα πρὸς τὴν
ἀποικίαν περὶ τῆς ἀρχῆς ἀνῃρέθη· τὸ δ' ἐν αὐτῇ
πολιτευόμενον πλῆθος ἡ καθελοῦσα τὴν μητρόπολιν
ὑπεδέξατο Ῥώμη. ἀλλὰ ταῦτα μὲν ἐν τοῖς ἱκνου-
μένοις χρόνοις ἐγένετο, ἡνίκα δὲ ᾠκίζετο πρὸς ὄρει
καὶ λίμνῃ κατεσκευάσθη τὸ μέσον ἐπέχουσα ἀμφοῖν,
καὶ ἦν ὥσπερ τείχη τῆς πόλεως ταῦτα δυσάλωτον
αὐτὴν ποιοῦντα. τό τε γὰρ ὄρος ἐν τοῖς πάνυ
ὀχυρόν τε καὶ ὑψηλόν ἐστιν ἥ τε λίμνη βαθεῖα καὶ
μεγάλη, καὶ αὐτὴν διὰ κλισιάδων ἀνοιγομένων ὑποδέχεται τὸ πεδίον ταμιευομένων ὁπόσον βούλονται
3 τῶν ἀνθρώπων τὸ ὕδωρ. ὑπόκειται δὲ τῇ πόλει
πεδία θαυμαστὰ μὲν ἰδεῖν, πλούσια δὲ καὶ οἴνους
καὶ καρποὺς¹ ἐξενεγκεῖν παντοδαποὺς καὶ οὐδὲν
ἐνδεεστέρους τῆς ἄλλης Ἰταλίας, μάλιστα δὲ τὸν
καλούμενον Ἀλβανὸν οἶνον ἡδὺν καὶ καλόν, ἔξω
τοῦ Φαλερίνου λεγομένου τῶν γοῦν ἄλλων ἁπάντων
διαφορώτατον.

LXVII. Ἐν δὲ τῇ κτίσει τῆς πόλεως θαῦμα
μέγιστον λέγεται γενέσθαι. κατασκευασθέντος τοῖς
ἔδεσι τῶν θεῶν, οὓς Αἰνείας ἐκ τῆς Τρωάδος ἠνέγ-
κατο καὶ καθίδρυσεν ἐν τῷ Λαουϊνίῳ, ναοῦ χωρίον
ἔχοντος ἄβατον καὶ τῶν ἱδρυμάτων ἐκ τοῦ Λαουϊνίου
μετακομισθέντων² εἰς τοῦτον τὸν μυχόν, ὑπὸ τὴν

_____

¹ καὶ οἴνους καὶ καρποὺς Jacoby: καὶ οἴνους ΑΒα, καὶ καρποὺς Bmg.

and its name is now, as it were, a compound, made up of the two terms, Alba Longa, that is *Leuké Makra* or " Long White (town)." This city is now uninhabited, since in the time of Tullus Hostilius, king of the Romans, Alba seemed to be contending with her colony for the sovereignty and hence was destroyed ; but Rome, though she razed her mother-city to the ground, nevertheless welcomed its citizens into her midst. But these events belong to a later time. To return to its founding, Alba was built near a mountain and a lake, occupying the space between the two, which served the city in place of walls and rendered it difficult to be taken. For the mountain is extremely strong and high and the lake is deep and large ; and its waters are received by the plain when the sluices are opened, the inhabitants having it in their power to husband the supply as much as they wish. Lying below the city are plains marvellous to behold and rich in producing wines and fruits of all sorts in no degree inferior to the rest of Italy, and particularly what they call the Alban wine, which is sweet and excellent and, with the exception of the Falernian, certainly superior to all others.

LXVII. While the city was building, a most remarkable prodigy is said to have occurred. A temple with an inner sanctuary had been built for the images of the gods which Aeneas had brought with him from the Troad and set up in Lavinium, and the statues had been removed from Lavinium to this

---

² ἐκ τοῦ νεὼ (ναοῦ B) after μετακομισθέντων deleted by Schmitz.

ἐπιοῦσαν νύκτα κεκλεισμένων τε ὡς μάλιστα τῶν
θυρῶν καὶ οὐδὲν παθόντων οὔτε περιβόλων οὔτε
ὀροφῶν διαμείψαντα τὰ βρέτη τὴν στάσιν ἐπὶ τῶν
2 ἀρχαίων εὑρεθῆναι κείμενα βάθρων· μετακομι-
σθέντα δὲ αὖθις ἐκ τοῦ Λαουινίου σὺν ἱκετείαις καὶ
θυσίαις ἀρεστηρίοις εἰς τὸ αὐτὸ χωρίον ὁμοίως
ἀνελθεῖν. τοὺς δὲ ἀνθρώπους τέως μὲν ἀπορεῖν
ὅ τι χρήσονται τοῖς πράγμασιν οὔτε δίχα τῶν
πατρώων θεῶν οἰκεῖν ἀξιοῦντας οὔτε ἐπὶ τὴν
ἐκλειφθεῖσαν οἴκησιν αὖθις ἀναστρέφειν, τελευτῶντας δὲ γνώμην εὑρέσθαι, ἣ ἔμελλεν ἀποχρώντως
πρὸς ἀμφότερα ἕξειν· τὰ μὲν ἔδη κατὰ χώραν
ἐᾶσαι μένειν, ἄνδρας δὲ τοὺς ἐπιμελησομένους
αὐτῶν ἐκ τῆς Ἄλβας εἰς τὸ Λαουίνιον αὖθις
ἐποίκους μεταγαγεῖν. καὶ ἐγένοντο οἱ πεμφθέντες
ἑξακόσιοι μελεδωνοὶ τῶν ἱερῶν αὐτοῖς μεταναστάντες ἐφεστίοις· ἡγεμὼν δ' ἐπ' αὐτοῖς ἐτάχθη
3 Αἴγεστος. τοὺς δὲ θεοὺς τούτους Ῥωμαῖοι μὲν
Πενάτας καλοῦσιν· οἱ δ' ἐξερμηνεύοντες εἰς τὴν
Ἑλλάδα γλῶσσαν τοὔνομα οἱ μὲν Πατρῴους ἀποφαίνουσιν, οἱ δὲ Γενεθλίους, εἰσὶ δ' οἳ Κτησίους,
ἄλλοι δὲ Μυχίους, οἱ δὲ Ἑρκείους. ἔοικε δὲ
τούτων ἕκαστος ἀπό[1] τινος τῶν συμβεβηκότων
αὐτοῖς ποιεῖσθαι τὴν ἐπίκλησιν κινδυνεύουσί τε
4 πάντες ἀμωσγέπως τὸ αὐτὸ λέγειν.[2] σχήματος δὲ
καὶ μορφῆς αὐτῶν πέρι Τίμαιος μὲν ὁ συγγραφεὺς
ὧδε ἀποφαίνει·[3] κηρύκεια[4] σιδηρᾶ καὶ χαλκᾶ

---

[1] Schwartz: κατά O, Jacoby.
[2] κινδυνεύουσί . . . λέγειν B: κινδυνεύουσί τε οὐ τὸ αὐτὸ πάντες
ὁμωσγέπως τὸ αὐτὸ λέγειν R.
[3] Schwartz: ἀποφαίνεται O, Jacoby.
[4] κηρύκεια ABa: κηρύκια Bb, Jacoby.

sanctuary ; but during the following night, although
the doors were most carefully closed and the walls of
the enclosure and the roof of the temple suffered no
injury, the statues changed their station and were
found upon their old pedestals. And after being
brought back again from Lavinium with supplica-
tions and propitiatory sacrifices they returned in like
manner to the same place. Upon this the people
were for some time in doubt what they should do,
being unwilling either to live apart from their ancestral gods or to return again to their deserted
habitation. But at last they hit upon an expedient
which promised to meet satisfactorily both these
difficulties. This was to let the images remain where
they were and to conduct men back from Alba to
Lavinium to live there and take care of them. Those
who were sent to Lavinium to have charge of their
rites were six hundred in number ; they removed
thither with their entire households, and Aegestus
was appointed their chief. As for these gods, the
Romans call them Penates. Some who translate
the name into the Greek language render it *Patrôoi*,
others *Genethlioi*, some *Ktêsioi*, others *Mychioi*, and
still others *Herkeioi*.[1] Each of these seems to be
giving them their name from some one of their
attributes, and it is probable that they are all expressing more or less the same idea. Concerning
their figure and appearance, Timaeus, the historian,
makes the statement that the holy objects preserved

---

[1] These Greek terms, all adjectives in form, mean the
gods, respectively, (*a*) of the race. (*b*) of the family,
(*c*) of house and property, (*d*) of the inner house, (*e*) of
the front court.

καὶ κέραμον Τρωικὸν εἶναι τὰ ἐν τοῖς ἀδύτοις τοῖς ἐν Λαουϊνίῳ κείμενα ἱερά, πυθέσθαι δὲ αὐτὸς ταῦτα παρὰ τῶν ἐπιχωρίων. ἐγὼ δὲ ὅσα μὲν ὁρᾶν ἅπασιν οὐ θέμις οὔτε[1] παρὰ τῶν ὁρώντων ἀκούειν οὔτε ἀναγράφειν[2] οἴομαι δεῖν, νεμεσῶ δὲ καὶ τοῖς ἄλλοις, ὅσοι πλείω τῶν συγχωρουμένων ὑπὸ νόμου ζητεῖν ἢ γινώσκειν ἀξιοῦσιν.

LXVIII. Ἃ δὲ αὐτός τε ἰδὼν ἐπίσταμαι καὶ δέος οὐδὲν ἀποκωλύει με περὶ αὐτῶν γράφειν τοιάδε ἐστί· νεὼς ἐν Ῥώμῃ δείκνυται τῆς ἀγορᾶς οὐ πρόσω κατὰ τὴν ἐπὶ Καρίνας[3] φέρουσαν ἐπίτομον ὁδὸν ὑπεροχῇ σκοτεινὸς ἱδρυμένος οὐ μέγας. λέγεται δὲ κατὰ τὴν ἐπιχώριον γλῶτταν Οὐελία[4] τὸ χωρίον. ἐν δὲ τούτῳ κεῖνται τῶν Τρωικῶν θεῶν εἰκόνες, ἃς ἅπασιν ὁρᾶν θέμις,[5] ἐπιγραφὴν 2 ἔχουσαι δηλοῦσαν τοὺς Πενάτας.[6] εἰσὶ δὲ νεανίαι

[1] οὔτε O : οὐδὲ Sauppe.
[2] οὔτε ἀναγράφειν Reiske : οὐδ' ἂν ἐπιγράφειν O.
[3] Καρίνας Steph. : καιριάνας AB.
[4] Οὐελία Cary, Οὐέλιαι Casaubon, ὑπ' Οὐελίας Nibby, ὑπ' Ἐλαίας Jacoby : ὑπ' ἐλαίως A, ὑπελαίαις B.
[5] θέμις B : δέμας A.
[6] τοὺς Πενάτας O : δέους Πενάτας Sauppe. After Πενάτας the MSS. have the sentence δοκοῦσι γάρ μοι τοῦ θ μήπω γράμματος εὑρημένου τῷ δ δηλοῦν τὴν ἐκείνου δύναμιν οἱ παλαιοί (" for in my opinion, the letter θ being not yet discovered, the ancients expressed its force by the letter δ "), which Ambrosch deleted as the comment of an early scribe. He argues that the text of Dionysius originally read εἰκόνες ἅπασιν ὁρᾶν, ΔΙΣ ΜΑΓΝΙΣ (Dis Magnis) ἐπιγραφὴν ἔχουσαι, δηλοῦσαν τοὺς Πενάτας, that the Latin words became corrupted into ΔΕΜΑΣ (so in A) and ΔΕΜΙΣ, and that the second form, taken for a variant of θέμις, inspired the scribe's remark. Inserted later in the text, θέμις called for the addition of ἅς. But Ambrosch admits that this would

in the sanctuary at Lavinium are iron and bronze
caducei or " heralds' wands," and a Trojan earthen-
ware vessel ; this, he says, he himself learned from
the inhabitants.[1] For my part, I believe that in the
case of those things which it is not lawful for all to
see I ought neither to hear about them from those who
do see them nor to describe them ; and I am indignant with every one else, too, who presumes to inquire
into or to know more than what is permitted by law.

LXVIII. But the things which I myself know by
having seen them and concerning which no scruple
forbids me to write are as follows. They show you
in Rome a temple [2] built not far from the Forum in
the short street that leads to the Carinae ; it is a
small shrine, and is darkened by the height of the
adjacent buildings. The place is called in the native
speech Velia. In this temple there are images of
the Trojan gods which it is lawful for all to see,
with an inscription showing them to be the Penates.

[1] Müller, *Frag. Hist. Graec.* i. 197, 20. For Timaeus see
p. 19, n. 2.

[2] The *aedes deum Penatium in Velia* (Livy xlv. 16, 5 ;
Mon. Ancyr. iv. 7; Varro, *de Ling. Lat.* v. 54). The
statues really represented the Dioscuri, but had long been
identified with the Penates. Servius (on *Aen.* iii. 12),
citing Varro, says that on the base of the statues was the
inscription MAGNIS DIIS ; but there was probably more
to the inscription, including PENATIBVS.

---

be the only instance in Dionysius of the citing of the
Latin words of an inscription ; he usually gives merely the
purport. Sauppe's δέους Πενάτας (*i.e., Dis Penatibus* put
into the accusative, following δηλοῦσαν) might have been
taken by a scribe, ignorant of Latin, as early Greek for
θεοὺς Πενάτας. But δηλοῦσαν is hardly the verb to introduce
the exact words of an inscription.

δύο καθήμενοι δόρατα διειληφότες, τῆς παλαιᾶς
ἔργα τέχνης. πολλὰ δὲ καὶ ἄλλα ἐν ἱεροῖς ἀρχαίοις
εἴδωλα τῶν θεῶν τούτων ἐθεασάμεθα, καὶ ἐν ἅπασι
νεανίσκοι δύο στρατιωτικὰ σχήματα ἔχοντες φαί-
νονται. ὁρᾶν μὲν δὴ ταῦτα ἔξεστιν, ἀκούειν δὲ
καὶ γράφειν ὑπὲρ αὐτῶν, ἃ Καλλίστρατός τε ὁ
περὶ Σαμοθράκης συνταξάμενος ἱστορεῖ καὶ Σά-
τυρος ὁ τοὺς ἀρχαίους μύθους συναγαγὼν καὶ
ἄλλοι συχνοί, παλαιότατος δὲ ὧν ἡμεῖς ἴσμεν
3 ποιητὴς Ἀρκτῖνος. λέγουσι γοῦν ὧδε· Χρύσην
τὴν Πάλλαντος θυγατέρα γημαμένην Δαρδάνῳ
φερνὰς ἐπενέγκασθαι δωρεὰς Ἀθηνᾶς τά τε Παλλάδια καὶ τὰ ἱερὰ τῶν μεγάλων θεῶν διδαχθεῖσαν
αὐτῶν τὰς τελετάς. ἐπειδὴ δὲ τὴν ἐπομβρίαν
φεύγοντες Ἀρκάδες Πελοπόννησον μὲν ἐξέλιπον,
ἐν δὲ τῇ Θρᾳκίᾳ νήσῳ τοὺς βίους ἱδρύσαντο,
κατασκευάσαι τὸν Δάρδανον ἐνταῦθα τῶν θεῶν
τούτων ἱερὸν ἀρρήτους τοῖς ἄλλοις ποιοῦντα τὰς
ἰδίους αὐτῶν ὀνομασίας καὶ τὰς τελετὰς αὐτοῖς τὰς
καὶ εἰς τόδε χρόνου γινομένας ὑπὸ Σαμοθράκων
4 ἐπιτελεῖν. ὡς δὲ μετῆγε τοῦ λεὼ τὴν πλείω
μοῖραν εἰς τὴν Ἀσίαν τὰ μὲν ἱερὰ τῶν θεῶν καὶ
τὰς τελετὰς τοῖς ὑπομείνασιν ἐν τῇ νήσῳ καταλιπεῖν, τὰ δὲ Παλλάδια καὶ τὰς τῶν[1] θεῶν εἰκόνας
κατασκευασάμενον ἀγαγέσθαι μετ᾽ αὐτοῦ. διαμαν-

---

[1] τῶν added by Reiske.

---

[1] Müller, *Frag. Hist. Graec.* iv. 355 f., 10. Domitius
Callistratus seems to have been a Roman freedman.

They are two seated youths holding spears, and are pieces of ancient workmanship. We have seen many other statues also of these gods in ancient temples and in all of them are represented two youths in military garb. These it is permitted to see, and it is also permitted to hear and to write about them what Callistratus,[1] the author of the history of Samothrace, relates, and also Satyrus, who collected the ancient legends, and many others, too, among whom the poet Arctinus is the earliest we know of. At any rate, the following is the account they give. Chrysê, the daughter of Pallas, when she was married to Dardanus, brought for her dowry the gifts of Athena, that is, the Palladia and the sacred symbols of the Great Gods, in whose mysteries she had been instructed. When the Arcadians, fleeing from the deluge,[2] left the Peloponnesus and established their abode in the Thracian island,[3] Dardanus built there a temple to these gods, whose particular names he kept secret from all others, and performed the mysteries in their honour which are observed to this day by the Samothracians. Then, when he was conducting the greater part of the people into Asia, he left the sacred rites and mysteries of the gods with those who remained in the island, but packed up and carried with him the Palladia and the images of the gods. And upon consulting the oracle concerning the place

Satyrus is unknown, but was probably not the same as the biographer of that name. Arctinus was regarded in later times as the author of two of the poems in the Epic Cycle, the *Aethiopis* and the *Iliou Persis* ; but classical writers cited the poems anonymously.
[2] See chap. 61, 2.   [3] Samothrace.

τευόμενον δὲ περὶ τῆς οἰκήσεως τά τε ἄλλα μαθεῖν
καὶ περὶ τῶν ἱερῶν τῆς φυλακῆς τόνδε τὸν χρησμὸν
λαβεῖν·

Εἰς πόλιν ἦν κτίζησθα[1] θεοῖς σέβας ἄφθιτον αἰεὶ
θεῖναι, καὶ φυλακαῖς τε σέβειν θυσίαις τε χοροῖς τε.
ἔστ᾽[2] ἂν γὰρ τάδε σεμνὰ καθ᾽ ὑμετέρην[3] χθόνα μίμνῃ
δῶρα Διὸς κούρης ἀλόχῳ σέθεν, ἡ δὲ πόλις σοι
ἔσται ἀπόρθητος τὸν ἀεὶ χρόνον ἤματα πάντα.

LXIX. Δάρδανον μὲν ἐν τῇ κτισθείσῃ τε ὑφ᾽
ἑαυτοῦ καὶ ὀνομασίας ὁμοίας τυχούσῃ πόλει τὰ ἔδη
καταλιπεῖν, Ἰλίου δ᾽ ἐν ὑστέρῳ χρόνῳ συνοικισθέν-
τος ἐκεῖ[4] μετενεχθῆναι πρὸς τῶν ἐγγόνων αὐτοῦ
τὰ ἱερά. ποιήσασθαι δὲ τοὺς Ἰλιεῖς νεών τε καὶ
ἄδυτον αὐτοῖς ἐπὶ τῆς ἄκρας καὶ φυλάττειν δι᾽
ἐπιμελείας ὅσης[5] ἐδύναντο πλείστης θεόπεμπτά τε
ἡγουμένους εἶναι καὶ σωτηρίας κύρια τῇ πόλει.
2 ἁλισκομένης δὲ τῆς κάτω πόλεως τὸν Αἰνείαν
καρτερὸν τῆς ἄκρας γενόμενον, ἄραντα ἐκ τῶν
ἀδύτων τά τε ἱερὰ τῶν μεγάλων θεῶν καὶ ὅπερ
ἔτι περιῆν Παλλάδιον (θάτερον γὰρ Ὀδυσσέα καὶ
Διομήδην νυκτός φασιν εἰς Ἴλιον ἀφικομένους
κλοπῇ λαβεῖν) οἴχεσθαί τε κομίσαντα[6] ἐκ τῆς
3 πόλεως καὶ ἐλθεῖν ἄγοντα εἰς Ἰταλίαν. Ἀρκτῖνος
δέ φησιν ὑπὸ Διὸς δοθῆναι Δαρδάνῳ Παλλάδιον ἓν
καὶ εἶναι τοῦτο ἐν Ἰλίῳ τέως ἡ πόλις ἡλίσκετο
κεκρυμμένον ἐν ἀβάτῳ· εἰκόνα δ᾽ ἐκείνου κατε-

---

[1] Kiessling: κτίζει AB. [2] Reiske: εὖτ᾽ O.
[3] Cobet: ὑμετέραν O.
[4] ἐκεῖ O: ἐκεῖσε Reudler, Jacoby.

where he should settle, among other things that he
learned he received this answer relating to the custody
of the holy objects :

" In the town thou buildest worship undying found
 To gods ancestral ; guard them, sacrifice,
 Adore with choirs. For whilst these holy things
 In thy land remain, Zeus' daughter's gifts of old
 Bestowed upon thy spouse, secure from harm
 Thy city shall abide forevermore."

LXIX. Dardanus, accordingly, left the statues in
the city which he founded and named after himself,
but when Ilium was settled later, they were removed
thither by his descendants ; and the people of
Ilium built a temple and a sanctuary for them upon
the citadel and preserved them with all possible
care, looking upon them as sent from Heaven and
as pledges of the city's safety. And while the
lower town was being captured, Aeneas, possessing
himself of the citadel, took out of the sanctuary the
images of the Great Gods and the Palladium which
still remained (for Odysseus and Diomed, they say,
when they came into Ilium by night, had stolen
the other away), and carrying them with him out
of the city, brought them into Italy. Arctinus,
however, says that only one Palladium was given
by Zeus to Dardanus and that this remained in
Ilium, hidden in the sanctuary, till the city was being
taken ; but that from this a copy was made, differing

---

⁵ ὅσης Jacoby, ὡς Cobet : ἦ A, ἤ B.
⁶ τὸν Αἰνείαν after κομίσαντα deleted by Grimm .

DIONYSIUS OF HALICARNASSUS

σκευασμένην ὡς μηδὲν τῆς ἀρχετύπου διαφέρειν
ἀπάτης τῶν ἐπιβουλευσόντων [1] ἕνεκεν ἐν φανερῷ
τεθῆναι καὶ αὐτὴν Ἀχαιοὺς ἐπιβουλεύσαντας λαβεῖν.
4 τὰ μὲν οὖν εἰς Ἰταλίαν ὑπ᾽ Αἰνείου κομισθέντα
ἱερὰ τοῖς εἰρημένοις ἀνδράσι πειθόμενος γράφω τῶν
τε μεγάλων θεῶν εἰκόνας εἶναι, οὓς Σαμοθρᾷκες
Ἑλλήνων μάλιστα ὀργιάζουσι, καὶ τὸ μυθευόμενον [2]
Παλλάδιον, ὅ φασι τὰς ἱερὰς φυλάττειν παρθένους
ἐν ναῷ κείμενον Ἑστίας, ἔνθα καὶ τὸ ἀθάνατον
διασώζεται πῦρ· ὑπὲρ ὧν ἐν ὑστέρῳ λεχθήσεται
λόγῳ. εἴη δ᾽ ἂν καὶ παρὰ ταῦτα τοῖς βεβήλοις
ἡμῖν ἄδηλα ἕτερα. καὶ περὶ μὲν τῶν Τρωικῶν
ἱερῶν τοσαῦτα εἰρήσθω.

LXX. Ἀσκανίου δὲ ὀγδόῳ καὶ τριακοστῷ ἔτει
τῆς βασιλείας τελευτήσαντος παρέλαβε τὴν ἡγεμονίαν Σιλούιος ἀδελφὸς ὢν Ἀσκανίου, μετὰ τὸν
Αἰνείου θάνατον γενόμενος ἐκ Λαουϊνίας τῆς Λατίνου
θυγατρός, ὃν φασιν ἐν τοῖς ὄρεσιν ὑπὸ τῶν νομέων
2 ἐκτραφῆναι. τοῦ γὰρ Ἀσκανίου παραλαβόντος τὴν
βασιλείαν περιδεὴς ἡ Λαουϊνία γενομένη μή τι
δεινὸν ὑπ᾽ αὐτοῦ πάθῃ κατὰ τὸ τῆς μητρυιᾶς
ὄνομα, ἐγκύμων οὖσα δίδωσιν ἑαυτὴν Τυρρηνῷ [3] τινι
συοφορβίων ἐπιμελητῇ βασιλικῶν, ὃν ᾔδει Λατίνῳ
γενόμενον ἐν τοῖς μάλιστα προσήγορον. ὁ δ᾽ εἰς

---

[1] Schwartz: ἐπιβουλευόντων O, Jacoby.
[2] Kiessling: μεμυθευμένον O.
[3] Τυρρηνῷ Steph., Τύρρῳ Gelenius, Portus: τυράννωι ABa,
συρρηνὼ Bb.

228

in no respect from the original, and exposed to public view, on purpose to deceive those who might be planning to steal it, and that the Achaeans, having formed such a plan, took the copy away. I say, therefore, upon the authority of the men above-mentioned, that the holy objects brought into Italy by Aeneas were the images of the Great Gods, to whom the Samothracians, of all the Greeks, pay the greatest worship, and the Palladium, famous in legend, which they say is kept by the holy virgins in the temple of Vesta, where the perpetual fire is also preserved; but concerning these matters I shall speak hereafter.[1] And there may also be other objects besides these which are kept secret from us who are not initiated. But let this suffice concerning the holy objects of the Trojans.

LXX. Upon [2] the death of Ascanius in the thirty-eighth year of his reign, Silvius, his brother, succeeded to the rule. He was born of Lavinia, the daughter of Latinus, after the death of Aeneas, and they say that he was brought up on the mountains by the herdsmen. For when Ascanius took over the rule, Lavinia, becoming alarmed lest her relationship as step-mother might draw upon her some severity from him, and being then with child, entrusted herself to a certain Tyrrhenus,[3] who had charge of the royal herds of swine and whom she knew to have been on very intimate terms with Latinus. He, carrying

---

[1] ii. 66.   [2] For chaps. 70-71 cf. Livy i. 3, 6-10.
[3] The name appears as Tyrrheus or Tyrrhus in Virgil (*Aen.* vii. 485), the only other author who mentions such an individual. Tyrrh(e)us, like Turnus, is apparently a modified form of Tyrrhenus; cf. p. 211, n. 1.

ὕλας ἐρήμους ἀγαγὼν αὐτὴν ὡς τῶν ἐπιτυχουσῶν
τινα, φυλαττόμενος ὀφθῆναι τοῖς εἰδόσιν ἔτρεφεν
ἐν τῇ νάπῃ κατασκευάσας οἴκησιν οὐ πολλοῖς
γνώριμον, καὶ τὸ παιδίον γενόμενον [1] ἀναιρεῖταί τε
καὶ τρέφει Σιλούιον ὀνομάσας ἀπὸ τῆς ὕλης, ὥσπερ
3 ἂν εἴ τις Ἑλλάδι γλώσσῃ λέξειεν Ὑλαῖον. χρόνου
δὲ προϊόντος ὡς πολλὴν ζήτησιν ἔγνω τῆς γυναικὸς
ὑπὸ τῶν Λατίνων γινομένην καὶ δι' αἰτίας ὄντα
παρὰ τῷ πλήθει τὸν Ἀσκάνιον, ὡς ἀνῃρηκότα τὴν
παιδίσκην, φράζει τῷ δήμῳ τὸ πρᾶγμα καὶ τὴν
ἄνθρωπον ἄγει μετὰ τοῦ παιδὸς ἐκ τῆς νάπης.
τύχῃ μὲν δὴ τοιαύτῃ χρησάμενος ὁ Σιλούιος τὴν
εἰρημένην ἔσχεν ὀνομασίαν καὶ τὸ ἐξ ἐκείνου γένος
ἅπαν, τὴν δὲ [2] βασιλείαν παρέλαβεν, ἐπειδὴ τὸν
ἀδελφὸν αὐτοῦ τελευτῆσαι συνέπεσεν, ἀμφίλογον
γενομένην πρὸς ἕνα τὸν πρεσβεύσαντα τῶν Ἀσκανίου παίδων Ἴουλον ἀξιοῦντα τὴν πατρῴαν ἀρχὴν
4 διαδέξασθαι. τὴν δὲ δίκην ἐπεψήφισεν ὁ δῆμος
ἄλλοις τε ὑπαχθεὶς λόγοις καὶ οὐχ ἥκιστα ὅτι
μητρὸς ἦν ὁ Σιλούιος ἐπικλήρου τῆς ἀρχῆς.[3] Ἰούλῳ
δὲ ἀντὶ τῆς βασιλείας ἱερά τις ἐξουσία προσετέθη
καὶ τιμὴ τῷ τε ἀκινδύνῳ προὔχουσα τῆς μοναρχίας [4]
καὶ τῇ ῥᾳστώνῃ τοῦ βίου, ἣν ἔτι καὶ εἰς ἐμὲ τὸ ἐξ
αὐτοῦ γένος ἐκαρποῦτο, Ἰούλιοι [5] κληθέντες ἀπ'
ἐκείνου. ἐγένετο δὲ μέγιστος ἅμα καὶ λαμπρότατος
οἴκων οὗτος ὧν ἡμεῖς ἴσμεν, ἄνδρας τε διαφορωτά-

[1] οὐ πολλοῖς . . . γενόμενον BC : om. A, ἧς τὸ ἐγκυμονούμενον
ἀποκυησάσης CmgD.
[2] δὲ added by Gelenius.
[3] τῆς ἀρχῆς Reiske : τῇ ἀρχῇ O.

her into the lonely woods as if she were an ordinary woman, and taking care that she was not seen by anyone who knew her, supported her in a house he built in the forest, which was known to but few. And when the child was born, he took it up and reared it, naming it, from the wood, Silvius, or, as one might say in Greek, *Hylaios*. But in the course of time, finding that the Latins made great search for the woman and that the people accused Ascanius of having put her to death, he acquainted them with the whole matter and brought the woman and her son out of the forest. From this experience Silvius got his name, as I have related, and so did all his posterity. And he became king after the death of his brother, though not without a contest with one of the sons of Ascanius,—Iulus, the eldest,—who claimed the succession to his father's rule ; the issue was decided by vote of the people, who were influenced chiefly by this consideration, among others, that Silvius' mother was heiress to the kingdom. Upon Iulus was conferred, instead of the sovereignty, a certain sacred authority and honour preferable to the royal dignity both for security and ease of life, and this prerogative [1] was enjoyed even to my day by his posterity, who were called Julii after him. This house became the greatest and at the same time the most illustrious of any we know of, and

---

[1] The reference is probably to the office of *pontifex maximus*, held by both Julius Caesar and Augustus.

---

[4] μοναρχίας B : μοναρχικῆς R.
[5] Gelenius : ἴουλοι O.

τοὺς ἡγεμόνων ἤνεγκεν, οἷς τὸ εὐγενὲς αἱ ἀρεταὶ μὴ
ἀπιστεῖσθαι παρέσχον· ὑπὲρ ὧν ἐν ἄλλῳ δηλωθήσεται
λόγῳ τὰ προσήκοντα.

LXXI. Σιλουΐου δ' ἑνὸς δέοντα τριάκοντα ἔτη
κατασχόντος τὴν ἀρχὴν Αἰνείας υἱὸς αὐτοῦ διαδεξάμενος τὴν δυναστείαν ἑνὶ πλείω τριάκοντα ἐτῶν
ἐβασίλευσεν. μετὰ δὲ τοῦτον ἓν καὶ πεντήκοντα
Λατῖνος ἦρξεν ἔτη· Ἄλβας δὲ μετὰ τοῦτον ἑνὸς
δέοντα τετταράκοντα ἔτη· μετὰ δὲ Ἄλβαν Κάπετος
ἓξ ἐπὶ τοῖς εἴκοσιν· ἔπειτα Κάπυς δυεῖν δέοντα
τριάκοντα. μετὰ δὲ Κάπυν Κάλπετος ἄχρι τρισκαί-
2 δεκα ἐτῶν κατέσχε τὴν ἀρχήν. ἑξῆς δὲ Τιβερῖνος
ὀκταετῆ χρόνον ἐβασίλευσεν. τελευτῆσαι δ' οὗτος
ἐν μάχῃ παρὰ ποταμῷ γενομένῃ λέγεται· παρενε-
χθεὶς δὲ ὑπὸ τοῦ ῥεύματος ἐπώνυμον ἑαυτῷ κατέλιπε τὸν ποταμὸν Ἄλβουλαν[1] καλούμενον πρότερον.
Τιβερίνου δὲ διάδοχος Ἀγρίππας ἓν καὶ τετταρά-
3 κοντα ἐβασίλευσεν ἔτη. μετὰ δὲ Ἀγρίππαν Ἀλλώ-
διος τυραννικόν τι χρῆμα καὶ θεοῖς ἀπεχθόμενον
ἑνὸς δέοντα εἴκοσιν· ᾧ περιφρονοῦντι τὰ δαιμόνια
κατεσκεύαστο κεραυνῶν τε μιμήματα καὶ κτύποι
βρονταῖς ἐμφερεῖς, οἷς δεδίττεσθαι τοὺς ἀνθρώπους
ὡς θεὸς ἠξίου. ὄμβρων δὲ καὶ κεραυνῶν εἰς τὸν
οἶκον αὐτοῦ κατασκηψάντων τῆς τε λίμνης, παρ'
ἣν οἰκῶν ἐτύγχανε, πλημμύραν οὐκ εἰωθυῖαν λαβούσης κατακλυσθεὶς πανοίκιος ἀπόλλυται. καὶ νῦν
ἔτι διαλαμπούσης τῆς λίμνης ἐν μέρει τινί, ὅταν
ὑπονοστήσῃ τὸ νᾶμα καὶ σταθερὸς ὁ βυθὸς γένηται,

produced the most distinguished commanders, whose virtues were so many proofs of their nobility. But concerning them I shall say what is requisite in another place.[1]

LXXI. Silvius, after holding the sovereignty twenty-nine years, was succeeded by Aeneas, his son, who reigned thirty-one years. After him, Latinus reigned fifty-one, then Alba thirty-nine; after Alba, Capetus reigned twenty-six, then Capys twenty-eight, and after Capys, Calpetus held the rule for thirteen years. Then Tiberinus reigned for a period of eight years. This king, it is said, was slain in a battle that was fought near a river, and being carried away by the stream, gave his name to the river, which had previously been called the Albula. Tiberinus' successor, Agrippa, reigned forty-one years. After Agrippa, Allodius, a tyrannical creature and odious to the gods, reigned nineteen years. Contemptuous of the divine powers, he had contrived imitations of lightning and sounds resembling thunder-claps, with which he proposed to terrify people as if he were a god. But rain and lightning descended upon his house, and the lake beside which it stood rose to an unusual height, so that he was overwhelmed and destroyed with his whole household. And even now when the lake is clear in a certain part, which happens whenever the flow of water subsides and the depths

---

[1] This promise is not fulfilled in the extant portions of the history.

---

[1] Steph.: ἄλβυλαν Bb, ἄλβαν ABa.

παστάδων ἐρείπια καὶ ἄλλα οἰκήσεως ἴχνη φαίνεται.
4 Ἀουεντῖνος δὲ παρὰ τούτου τὴν δυναστείαν διαδεξάμενος, ἀφ' οὗ τῶν ἑπτὰ λόφων τις ἐπώνυμος ἐγένετο
τῶν συμπεπολισμένων τῇ Ῥώμῃ, τριάκοντα καὶ
ἑπτὰ ἔτη τὴν ἀρχὴν κατέσχεν. Πρόκας δὲ μετὰ
τοῦτον ἔτη εἴκοσι καὶ τρία. ἔπειτα Ἀμόλιος οὐ
σὺν δίκῃ τὴν βασιλείαν κατασχὼν Νεμέτορι προσήκουσαν, ὃς ἦν αὐτῷ πρεσβύτερος ἀδελφός, δύο
5 καὶ τετταράκοντα ἔτη δυναστεύει. Ἀμολίου δὲ
ἀναιρεθέντος ὑπὸ Ῥωμύλου καὶ Ῥώμου[1] τῶν ἐκ
τῆς ἱερᾶς κόρης γενομένων, ὡς αὐτίκα λεχθήσεται,
μετὰ τὸν ἐκείνου θάνατον ἀπολαμβάνει τὴν κατὰ
νόμον δυναστείαν Νεμέτωρ ὁ τῶν νεανίσκων μητροπάτωρ. τῷ δ' ἑξῆς ἔτει τῆς Νεμέτορος ἀρχῆς,
δευτέρῳ δὲ καὶ τριακοστῷ καὶ τετρακοσιοστῷ μετὰ
τὴν Ἰλίου ἅλωσιν, ἀποικίαν στείλαντες Ἀλβανοὶ
Ῥωμύλου καὶ Ῥώμου τὴν ἡγεμονίαν αὐτῆς ἐχόντων κτίζουσι Ῥώμην ἔτους ἐνεστῶτος πρώτου τῆς
ἑβδόμης ὀλυμπιάδος, ἣν ἐνίκα στάδιον Δαϊκλῆς
Μεσσήνιος, ἄρχοντος Ἀθήνησι Χάροπος ἔτος τῆς
δεκαετίας πρῶτον.

LXXII. Ἀμφισβητήσεως δὲ πολλῆς οὔσης καὶ
περὶ τοῦ χρόνου τῆς κτίσεως καὶ περὶ τῶν οἰκιστῶν
τῆς πόλεως οὐδὲ αὐτὸς ᾤμην δεῖν ὥσπερ ὁμολογού-

---

[1] ῥέμου A (a spelling found in several later passages, now in A, now in B).

---

[1] Kirby F. Smith has pointed out (*Am. Jour. Philol.* xvi., 1895, p. 205) that the Alban Lake is fed entirely from the bottom by gushing springs, so that νᾶμα here has its

are undisturbed,[1] the ruins of porticoes and other traces of a dwelling appear. Aventinus, after whom was named one of the seven hills that are joined to make the city of Rome, succeeded him in the sovereignty and reigned thirty-seven years, and after him Proca twenty-three years. Then Amulius, having unjustly possessed himself of the kingdom which belonged to Numitor, his elder brother, reigned forty-two years. But when Amulius had been slain by Romulus and Remus, the sons of the holy maiden, as shall presently be related, Numitor, the maternal grandfather of the youths, after his brother's death resumed the sovereignty which by law belonged to him. In the next year of Numitor's reign, which was the four hundred and thirty-second after the taking of Troy, the Albans sent out a colony, under the leadership of Romulus and Remus, and founded Rome, in the beginning of the first year of the seventh Olympiad, when Daïcles of Messenê was victor in the foot race, and at Athens Charops was in the first year of his ten-year term as archon.[2]

LXXII. But as there is great dispute concerning both the time of the building of the city and the founders of it, I have thought it incumbent on me also not to give merely a cursory account of these

ordinary meaning of "spring" or "running water," and σταθερός is used with particular appropriateness of the depths of this lake.

[2] 751 B.C. According to the common tradition the archonship, which was at first held for life, was in 752 limited to a ten-year term, and finally, ca. 683, to a single year. See Grote, *History of Greece*, Part ii., chap. x. (beginning); von Schoeffer in Pauly-Wissowa, *Real-Encyclopädie*, *s.v.* Archontes, cols. 569 f.

μενα πρὸς ἁπάντων ἐξ ἐπιδρομῆς ἐπελθεῖν. Κεφά
λων μὲν γὰρ ὁ Γεργίθιος συγγραφεὺς παλαιὸς πάνυ
δευτέρᾳ γενεᾷ μετὰ τὸν Ἰλιακὸν πόλεμον ἐκτίσθαι
λέγει τὴν πόλιν ὑπὸ τῶν ἐξ Ἰλίου διασωθέντων σὺν
Αἰνείᾳ, οἰκιστὴν δὲ αὐτῆς ἀποφαίνει τὸν ἡγησάμενον
τῆς ἀποικίας Ῥῶμον, τοῦτον δ' εἶναι τῶν Αἰνείου
παίδων ἕνα· τέτταρας δέ φησιν Αἰνείᾳ γενέσθαι
παῖδας, Ἀσκάνιον, Εὐρυλέοντα, Ῥωμύλον, Ῥῶμον.
εἴρηται δὲ καὶ Δημαγόρᾳ καὶ Ἀγαθύλλῳ καὶ ἄλλοις
συχνοῖς ὅ τε χρόνος καὶ ὁ τῆς ἀποικίας ἡγεμὼν ὁ
2 αὐτός. ὁ δὲ τὰς ἱερείας τὰς ἐν Ἄργει καὶ τὰ καθ'
ἑκάστην πραχθέντα συναγαγὼν Αἰνείαν φησὶν ἐκ
Μολοττῶν εἰς Ἰταλίαν ἐλθόντα μετ' Ὀδυσσέως[1]
οἰκιστὴν γενέσθαι τῆς πόλεως, ὀνομάσαι δ' αὐτὴν
ἀπὸ μιᾶς τῶν Ἰλιάδων Ῥώμης. ταύτην δὲ λέγει
ταῖς ἄλλαις Τρωάσι παρακελευσαμένην κοινῇ μετ'
αὐτῶν ἐμπρῆσαι τὰ σκάφη βαρυνομένην τῇ πλάνῃ.
ὁμολογεῖ δ' αὐτῷ καὶ Δαμάστης ὁ Σιγεὺς καὶ ἄλλοι
3 τινές Ἀριστοτέλης δὲ ὁ φιλόσοφος Ἀχαιῶν τινας

[1] ὀδυσσέως R : ὀδυσσέα B, Jacoby.

---

[1] See p. 157, n. 3.

[2] Ῥῶμος was the name invented by the Greeks for the
founder of Rome before they had heard of any Romulus or
Remus ; later they used it as the equivalent of Remus.   It
seems best to translate it as Romus (or Romos), except
where we are clearly dealing with the Roman legend of
the twin brothers.   See recent discussions of the growth of
the legend by Carter in Roscher's *Lexikon der griech. u. röm.
Mythologie, s.v.* Romulus, cols. 167-83 ; Rosenberg in Pauly-
Wissowa, *Real-Enc., s.v.* Romulus, cols. 1074-92 ; De Sanctis,
Storia dei Romani, i. pp. 206-17.

things, as if they were universally agreed on. For
Cephalon of Gergis,[1] a very ancient writer, says that
the city was built in the second generation after the
Trojan war by those who had escaped from Troy with
Aeneas, and he names as the founder of it Romus,[2]
who was the leader of the colony and one of Aeneas'
sons ; he adds that Aeneas had four sons, Ascanius,
Euryleon, Romulus and Romus. And Demagoras,[3]
Agathyllus and many others agree with him as regards
both the time and the leader of the colony. But the
author of the history of the priestesses at Argos [4]
and of what happened in the days of each of them
says that Aeneas came into Italy from the land of the
Molossians with Odysseus [5] and became the founder
of the city, which he named after Romê, one of the
Trojan women. He says that this woman, growing
weary with wandering, stirred up the other Trojan
women and together with them set fire to the ships.
And Damastes of Sigeum [6] and some others agree
with him. But Aristotle, the philosopher, relates [7]

[3] Demagoras of Samos apparently wrote a work on
Trojan or Samothracian antiquities. Agathyllus has
already been cited in chap. 49, 2.

[4] The author of this work was Hellanicus (see p. 71, n. 1).
The present quotation is frag. 53 (end) in Müller, *Frag.
Hist. Graec.* i. 52.

[5] A variant reading is "after Odysseus." See critical
note.

[6] Damastes (*ca.* 400) wrote the genealogies of the Greek
leaders before Troy ; also a description of the earth and its
peoples, to accompany his map of the world.

[7] Probably in his *Instituta Barbarica.* Müller, *Frag.
Hist. Graec.* ii. 178, 242.

ἱστορεῖ τῶν ἀπὸ Τροίας ἀνακομισαμένων περιπλέον-
τας Μαλέαν, ἔπειτα χειμῶνι βιαίῳ καταληφθέντας
τέως μὲν ὑπὸ τῶν πνευμάτων φερομένους πολλαχῇ
τοῦ πελάγους πλανᾶσθαι, τελευτῶντας δ᾽ ἐλθεῖν εἰς
τὸν τόπον τοῦτον τῆς Ὀπικῆς, ὃς καλεῖται Λατίνιον[1]
4 ἐπὶ τῷ Τυρρηνικῷ πελάγει κείμενος. ἀσμένους δὲ
τὴν γῆν ἰδόντας ἀνελκῦσαί τε τὰς ναῦς αὐτόθι καὶ
διατρῖψαι τὴν χειμερινὴν ὥραν παρασκευαζομένους
ἔαρος ἀρχομένου πλεῖν. ἐμπρησθεισῶν δὲ αὐτοῖς
ὑπὸ νύκτα τῶν νεῶν οὐκ ἔχοντας ὅπως ποιήσονται
τὴν ἄπαρσιν, ἀβουλήτῳ ἀνάγκῃ τοὺς βίους ἐν ᾧ
κατήχθησαν χωρίῳ ἱδρύσασθαι. συμβῆναι δὲ αὐτοῖς τοῦτο διὰ γυναῖκας αἰχμαλώτους, ἃς ἔτυχον
ἄγοντες ἐξ Ἰλίου. ταύτας δὲ κατακαῦσαι τὰ πλοῖα
φοβουμένας τὴν οἴκαδε τῶν Ἀχαιῶν ἄπαρσιν, ὡς
5 εἰς δουλείαν ἀφιξομένας. Καλλίας δὲ ὁ τὰς Ἀγα-
θοκλέους πράξεις ἀναγράψας Ῥώμην τινὰ Τρωάδα
τῶν ἀφικνουμένων ἅμα τοῖς ἄλλοις Τρωσὶν εἰς
Ἰταλίαν γήμασθαι Λατίνῳ τῷ βασιλεῖ τῶν Ἀβοριγίνων καὶ γεννῆσαι τρεῖς[2] παῖδας, Ῥῶμον καὶ
Ῥωμύλον καὶ[3] Τηλέγονον[4] . . . οἰκίσαντας δὲ
πόλιν, ἀπὸ τῆς μητρὸς αὐτῇ θέσθαι τοὔνομα.
Ξεναγόρας δὲ ὁ συγγραφεὺς Ὀδυσσέως καὶ Κίρκης

---

[1] Λατίνιον O : Λάτιον Steph., Λαουίνιον Kiessling.
[2] τρεῖς B : δύο R.
[3] καὶ B : om. R.
[4] Τηλέγονον added (from Syncellus) by Ritschl, who indicated the loss of other words following this.

that some of the Achaeans, while they were doubling
Cape Malea on their return from Troy, were overtaken
by a violent storm, and being for some time driven
out of their course by the winds, wandered over
many parts of the sea, till at last they came to this
place in the land of the Opicans which is called
Latinium,[1] lying on the Tyrrhenian sea. And being
pleased with the sight of land, they hauled up their
ships, stayed there the winter season, and were preparing to sail at the beginning of spring ; but when
their ships were set on fire in the night and they
were unable to sail away, they were compelled
against their will to fix their abode in the place
where they had landed. This fate, he says, was
brought upon them by the captive women they were
carrying with them from Troy, who burned the
ships, fearing that the Achaeans in returning home
would carry them into slavery. Callias,[2] who wrote
of the deeds of Agathocles, says that Romê, one
of the Trojan women who came into Italy with the
other Trojans, married Latinus, the king of the
Aborigines, by whom she had three sons, Romus,
Romulus and Telegonus, . . . and having built a
city, gave it the name of their mother. Xenagoras,
the historian,[3] writes that Odysseus and Circê had

---

[1] Probably originally an adjective (like the later Λατίνη),
"the Latin land." Some have wished to read Latium or
Lavinium.

[2] Callias wrote the history of Agathocles in 22 books.
His account was so biased in favour of that tyrant that
he was accused of having been heavily bribed by him.

[3] Xenagoras (date uncertain) wrote a historical work
called Χρόνοι and a book about islands. Müller, *Frag.
Hist. Graec.* iv. 527, 6.

υἱοὺς γενέσθαι τρεῖς, Ῥῶμον, Ἀντείαν,[1] Ἀρδείαν[2]·
οἰκίσαντας δὲ τρεῖς πόλεις ἀφ' ἑαυτῶν θέσθαι τοῖς
6 κτίσμασι τὰς ὀνομασίας. Διονύσιος δὲ ὁ Χαλκιδεὺς
οἰκιστὴν μὲν ἀποφαίνει τῆς πόλεως Ῥῶμον· τοῦτον
δὲ λέγει κατὰ μέν τινας Ἀσκανίου, κατὰ δέ τινας
Ἡμαθίωνος εἶναι παῖδα. εἰσὶ δέ τινες οἳ τὴν
Ῥώμην ἐκτίσθαι λέγουσιν ὑπὸ Ῥώμου τοῦ Ἰταλοῦ,
μητρὸς δὲ Λευκαρίας[3] τῆς Λατίνου θυγατρός

LXXIII. Ἔχων δὲ πολλοὺς καὶ ἄλλους τῶν
Ἑλληνικῶν παρέχεσθαι συγγραφέων, οἳ διαφόρους
ἀποφαίνουσι τοὺς οἰκιστὰς τῆς πόλεως, ἵνα μὴ
δόξω[4] μακρηγορεῖν ἐπὶ τοὺς Ῥωμαίων ἐλεύσομαι
συγγραφεῖς   παλαιὸς μὲν οὖν οὔτε συγγραφεὺς
οὔτε λογογράφος ἐστὶ Ῥωμαίων οὐδὲ εἷς· ἐκ
παλαιῶν μέντοι λόγων ἐν ἱεραῖς δέλτοις σωζομένων
2 ἕκαστός τι παραλαβὼν ἀνέγραψεν. τούτων δέ τινες
μὲν Αἰνείου γενέσθαι υἱοὺς λέγουσι Ῥωμύλον τε
καὶ Ῥῶμον τοὺς οἰκιστὰς τῆς Ῥώμης, ἕτεροι δὲ
θυγατρὸς Αἰνείου παῖδας, ὅτου δὲ πατρὸς οὐκέτι
διορίζοντες   δοθῆναι δ' αὐτοὺς ὑπ' Αἰνείου Λατίνῳ
τῷ βασιλεῖ τῶν Ἀβοριγίνων ὁμηρεύσοντας, ὅτε καὶ
αἱ πίστεις τοῖς ἐπιχωρίοις πρὸς τοὺς ἐπήλυδας
ἐγένοντο. ἀσπαζόμενον δὲ αὐτοὺς Λατῖνον τῇ τε
ἄλλῃ θεραπείᾳ περιέπειν εὖ καὶ ἐκγόνου ἄρρενος
ἄπαιδα τελευτῶντα διαδόχους μέρους τινὸς τῆς

---

[1] Ἀντείαν Steph. Byz.: ἀντίαν O.
[2] ἀρδείαν B: ἀρδίαν A.
[3] Kiessling: ἠλέκτρας A, λεύκτρας B.
[4] Bücheler: δόξαιμι AB.

240

three sons, Romus, Anteias and Ardeias, who built three cities and called them after their own names.[1] Dionysius of Chalcis [2] names Romus as the founder of the city, but says that according to some this man was the son of Ascanius, and according to others the son of Emathion. There are others who declare that Rome was built by Romus, the son of Italus and Leucaria, the daughter of Latinus.

LXXIII. I could cite many other Greek historians who assign different founders to the city, but, not to appear prolix, I shall come to the Roman historians. The Romans, to be sure, have not so much as one single historian or chronicler who is ancient ; however, each of their historians has taken something out of ancient accounts that are preserved on sacred tablets.[3] Some of these say that Romulus and Remus, the founders of Rome, were the sons of Aeneas, others say that they were the sons of a daughter of Aeneas, without going on to determine who was their father ; that they were delivered as hostages by Aeneas to Latinus, the king of the Aborigines, when the treaty was made between the inhabitants and the new-comers, and that Latinus, after giving them a kindly welcome, not only did them many other good offices, but, upon dying without male issue, left them his successors to some part

[1] Rome, Antium and Ardea.

[2] Dionysius of Chalcis (fourth century ?) wrote several books of Κτίσεις or " Foundings of Cities." Müller, *Frag. Hist. Graec:* iv. 395, 11.

[3] This probably refers to the *annales maximi*, the brief record of magistrates, prodigies and important public events of each year kept by the *pontifex maximus. Cf.* iv. 30, 3.

3 ἑαυτοῦ ἀρχῆς καταλιπεῖν. ἄλλοι δὲ λέγουσιν
Αἰνείου τελευτήσαντος Ἀσκάνιον ἅπασαν τὴν Λατίνων ἀρχὴν παραλαβόντα νείμασθαι πρὸς τοὺς
ἀδελφοὺς Ῥωμύλον τε καὶ Ῥῶμον τήν τε χώραν
καὶ τὴν δύναμιν τὴν Λατίνων τριχῇ· αὐτὸν μὲν
δὴ τήν τε Ἄλβαν κτίσαι καὶ ἄλλ' ἄττα πολίσματα·
Ῥῶμον δὲ Καπύην μὲν ἀπὸ τοῦ προπάππου Κάπυος,
Ἀγχίσην δὲ ἀπὸ τοῦ προπάτορος Ἀγχίσου, Αἰνείαν
δὲ τὴν ὕστερον κληθεῖσαν Ἰάνικλον ἀπὸ τοῦ πατρός,
Ῥώμην δὲ ἀφ' ἑαυτοῦ ὀνομασθείσας.¹ ταύτην δὲ
χρόνους τινὰς ἐρημωθεῖσαν ἑτέρας αὖθις ἐλθούσης
ἀποικίας, ἣν Ἀλβανοὶ ἔστειλαν ἡγουμένου Ῥωμύλου
καὶ Ῥώμου, τὴν ἀρχαίαν κλῆσιν ² ἀπολαβεῖν· ὥστε
διττὰς εἶναι τῆς Ῥώμης τὰς κτίσεις, τὴν μὲν ὀλίγον
ὕστερον τῶν Τρωικῶν γενομένην, τὴν δὲ πεντεκαί-
4 δεκα γενεαῖς ὑστεροῦσαν τῆς προτέρας. εἰ δέ τις
ἀπιδεῖν βουλήσεται τὰ προσωτέρω καὶ τρίτη τις
ἀρχαιοτέρα τούτων εὑρεθήσεται Ῥώμη γενομένη
πρὶν Αἰνείαν καὶ Τρῶας ἐλθεῖν εἰς Ἰταλίαν. ταῦτα
δὲ οὐ τῶν ἐπιτυχόντων τις οὐδὲ νέων συγγραφεὺς
ἱστόρηκεν, ἀλλ' Ἀντίοχος ὁ Συρακούσιος, οὗ καὶ
πρότερον ἐμνήσθην. φησὶ δὲ Μόργητος ἐν Ἰταλίᾳ
βασιλεύοντος (ἦν δὲ τότε Ἰταλία ἡ ἀπὸ Τάραντος

---

¹ ὀνομασθείσας added by Sauppe, who assumed the loss
of several lines here, in which mention was made of the
cities founded by Romulus. But it is quite probable that
in this earlier tradition, which would appear to be more
Greek than Roman, Romulus played somewhat the same
subordinate rôle that Remus did at a later stage ; he may
simply have aided his brother (who might better be called
Romus here) in founding the four cities named. Indeed,
the *Etymologicum Magnum* (*s.v.* Καπύη et Ῥώμη) states

of his kingdom. Others say that after the death of Aeneas Ascanius, having succeeded to the entire sovereignty of the Latins, divided both the country and the forces of the Latins into three parts, two of which he gave to his brothers, Romulus and Remus. He himself, they say, built Alba and some other towns ; Remus built cities which he named Capua, after Capys, his great-grandfather, Anchisa, after his grandfather Anchises, Aeneia (which was afterwards called Janiculum), after his father, and Rome, after himself.[1] This last city was for some time deserted, but upon the arrival of another colony, which the Albans sent out under the leadership of Romulus and Remus, it received again its ancient name. So that, according to this account, there were two settlements of Rome, one a little after the Trojan war, and the other fifteen generations after the first.[2] And if anyone desires to look into the remoter past, even a third Rome will be found, more ancient than these, one that was founded before Aeneas and the Trojans came into Italy. This is related by no ordinary or modern historian, but by Antiochus of Syracuse, whom I have mentioned before.[3] He says that when Morges reigned in Italy (which at that time comprehended all the seacoast

[1] Anchisa and Aeneia are otherwise unknown. See critical note.

[2] See chap. 45, 3.

[3] Chap. 12, 3 ; 22, 5 ; 35, 1. The present quotation is found in Müller, *Frag. Hist. Græc.* i. 182, 7.

---

on the authority of Greek writers that Capua and Rome were founded by Romus and Romulus, the sons of Aeneas.

[2] Schwartz : κτίσιν O, Jacoby.

ἄχρι Ποσειδωνίας παράλιος) ἐλθεῖν ὡς αὐτὸν ἄνδρα
φυγάδα ἐκ Ῥώμης. λέγει δὲ ὧδε· " ἐπεὶ δὲ Ἰταλὸς
κατεγήρα, Μόργης ἐβασίλευσεν. ἐπὶ τούτου δὲ ἀνὴρ
ἀφίκετο ἐκ Ῥώμης φυγάς· Σικελὸς ὄνομα αὐτῷ."
5 κατὰ μὲν δὴ τὸν Συρακούσιον συγγραφέα παλαιά τις
εὑρίσκεται καὶ προτεροῦσα τῶν Τρωικῶν[1] Ῥώμη.[2]
πότερον δὲ περὶ τοὺς αὐτοὺς ἦν τόπους, ἐν οἷς ἡ νῦν
οἰκουμένη πόλις ἐστίν, ἢ χωρίον ἕτερον ἐτύγχανεν
οὕτως ὀνομαζόμενον ἀσαφὲς ἐκείνου καταλιπόντος
οὐδ᾽ ἐγὼ δύναμαι συμβαλεῖν. περὶ μὲν οὖν τῶν
παλαιῶν κτίσεων ἱκανὰ ἡγοῦμαι τὰ προειρημένα.

LXXIV. Τὸν δὲ τελευταῖον γενόμενον τῆς Ῥώμης
οἰκισμὸν ἢ κτίσιν ἢ ὅ τι δήποτε χρὴ καλεῖν Τίμαιος
μὲν ὁ Σικελιώτης οὐκ οἶδ᾽ ὅτῳ κανόνι χρησάμενος
ἅμα Καρχηδόνι κτιζομένῃ γενέσθαι φησὶν ὀγδόῳ καὶ
τριακοστῷ πρότερον ἔτει τῆς πρώτης ὀλυμπιάδος·
Λεύκιος δὲ Κίγκιος, ἀνὴρ τῶν ἐκ τοῦ βουλευτικοῦ
συνεδρίου, περὶ τὸ τέταρτον ἔτος τῆς δωδεκάτης
ὀλυμπιάδος· Κόϊντος δὲ Φάβιος κατὰ τὸ πρῶτον
2 ἔτος τῆς ὀγδόης ὀλυμπιάδος. Κάτων δὲ Πόρκιος
Ἑλληνικὸν μὲν οὐχ ὁρίζει χρόνον, ἐπιμελὴς δὲ
γενόμενος εἰ καί τις ἄλλος περὶ[3] τὴν συναγωγὴν
τῆς ἀρχαιολογουμένης ἱστορίας ἔτεσιν ἀποφαίνει
δυσὶ καὶ τριάκοντα καὶ τετρακοσίοις ὑστεροῦσαν
τῶν Ἰλιακῶν. ὁ δὲ χρόνος οὗτος ἀναμετρηθεὶς

from Tarentum to Posidonia [1]), a man came to him
who had been banished from Rome. His words
are these : " When Italus was growing old, Morges
reigned. In his reign there came a man who had
been banished from Rome ; his name was Sicelus."
According to the Syracusan historian, therefore, an
ancient Rome is found even earlier than the Trojan
war. However, as he has left it doubtful whether it
was situated in the same region where the present city
stands or whether some other place happened to be
called by this name, I, too, can form no conjecture.
But as regards the ancient settlements of Rome, I
think what has already been said is sufficient.

LXXIV. As to the last settlement or founding of
the city, or whatever we ought to call it, Timaeus
of Sicily,[2] following what principle I do not know,
places it at the same time as the founding of Carthage,
that is, in the thirty-eighth year before the first
Olympiad [3] ; Lucius Cincius, a member of the senate,
places it about the fourth year of the twelfth Olympiad,[4] and Quintus Fabius in the first year of the
eighth Olympiad.[5] Porcius Cato does not give the
time according to Greek reckoning, but being as
careful as any writer in gathering the data of ancient
history, he places its founding four hundred and
thirty-two years after the Trojan war ; and this

[1] Later Paestum. [2] See p. 19, n. 2.
[3] 813 B.C. [4] 728 B.C. [5] 747 B.C.

---

[1] Τρωικῶν Reudler : τρωικῶν χρόνων O.
[2] 'Ρώμη Sylburg, om. Jacoby : ἡ ῥώμη O.
[3] περὶ B : εἰς R.

ταῖς Ἐρατοσθένους χρονογραφίαις κατὰ τὸ πρῶτον
ἔτος πίπτει τῆς ἑβδόμης ὀλυμπιάδος. ὅτι δέ εἰσιν
οἱ κανόνες ὑγιεῖς, οἷς Ἐρατοσθένης κέχρηται, καὶ
πῶς ἄν τις ἀπευθύνοι τοὺς Ῥωμαίων χρόνους πρὸς
τοὺς Ἑλληνικούς, ἐν ἑτέρῳ δεδήλωταί μοι λόγῳ.
3 οὐ γὰρ ἠξίουν ὡς Πολύβιος ὁ Μεγαλοπολίτης
τοσοῦτο μόνον εἰπεῖν, ὅτι κατὰ τὸ δεύτερον ἔτος
τῆς ἑβδόμης ὀλυμπιάδος τὴν Ῥώμην ἐκτίσθαι
πείθομαι, οὐδ' ἐπὶ τοῦ παρὰ τοῖς ἀρχιερεῦσι[1]
κειμένου πίνακος ἑνὸς καὶ μόνου τὴν πίστιν
ἀβασάνιστον καταλιπεῖν, ἀλλὰ τοὺς ἐπιλογισμούς,
οἷς αὐτὸς προσεθέμην, εἰς μέσον ὑπευθύνους τοῖς
4 βουληθεῖσιν ἐσομένους ἐξενεγκεῖν. ἡ μὲν οὖν
ἀκρίβεια ἐν ἐκείνῳ δηλοῦται τῷ λόγῳ, λεχθήσεται
δὲ καὶ διὰ τῆσδε τῆς πραγματείας αὐτὰ τἀναγκαιό-
τατα. ἔχει δὲ οὕτως· ἡ Κελτῶν ἔφοδος, καθ' ἣν
ἡ Ῥωμαίων πόλις ἑάλω, συμφωνεῖται σχεδὸν ὑπὸ
πάντων ἄρχοντος Ἀθήνησι Πυργίωνος γενέσθαι
κατὰ τὸ πρῶτον ἔτος τῆς ὀγδόης καὶ ἐνενηκοστῆς
ὀλυμπιάδος. ὁ δὲ πρὸ τῆς καταλήψεως χρόνος
ἀναγόμενος εἰς Λεύκιον Ἰούνιον Βροῦτον καὶ
Λεύκιον Ταρκύνιον Κολλατῖνον τοὺς πρώτους ὑπα-
τεύσαντας ἐν Ῥώμῃ μετὰ τὴν κατάλυσιν τῶν
βασιλέων ἔτη περιείληφεν εἴκοσι πρὸς τοῖς ἑκατόν.

[1] Niebuhr: ἀγχιστεῦσι AB.

---

[1] Eratosthenes was perhaps the most versatile scholar
of antiquity. Eminent not only as an astronomer,
mathematician and geographer, he also won distinction as
an historian, philosopher and grammarian. His *Chrono-
graphiae* was an annalistic history, both political and
literary, in which especial attention was devoted to the

time, being compared with the *Chronicles* of Eratosthenes,[1] corresponds to the first year of the seventh Olympiad.[2] That the canons of Eratosthenes are sound I have shown in another treatise,[3] where I have also shown how the Roman chronology is to be synchronized with that of the Greeks. For I did not think it sufficient, like Polybius of Megalopolis,[4] to say merely that I believe Rome was built in the second year of the seventh Olympiad.[5] nor to let my belief rest without further examination upon the single tablet preserved by the high priests. the only one of its kind, but I determined to set forth the reasons that had appealed to me, so that all might examine them who so desired. In that treatise, therefore, the detailed exposition is given ; but in the course of the present work also the most essential of the conclusions there reached will be mentioned. The matter stands thus : It is generally agreed that the invasion of the Gauls,[6] during which the city of Rome was taken, happened during the archonship of Pyrgion at Athens, in the first year of the ninety-eighth Olympiad.[7] Now if the time before the taking of the city is reckoned back to Lucius Junius Brutus and Lucius Tarquinius Collatinus, the first consuls at Rome after the overthrow of the kings, it comprehends one hundred

accurate determination of the chronology. The work began with the fall of Troy, which he placed in 1183 B.C.

[2] 751 B.C.

[3] This work, now lost, is cited by Clement of Alexandria (*Strom.* i. 102) as Χρόνοι.

[4] Probably in a lost portion of his Book VI.

[5] 750 B.C.

[6] Literally "Celts." See p. 123, n. 1.   [7] 387 B.C.

5 δηλοῦται δὲ ἐξ ἄλλων τε πολλῶν καὶ τῶν καλουμένων τιμητικῶν ὑπομνημάτων, ἃ διαδέχεται παῖς
παρὰ πατρὸς καὶ περὶ πολλοῦ ποιεῖται τοῖς μεθ᾽
ἑαυτὸν ἐσομένοις ὥσπερ ἱερὰ πατρῷα παραδιδόναι·
πολλοὶ δ᾽ εἰσὶν ἀπὸ τῶν τιμητικῶν οἴκων ἄνδρες
ἐπιφανεῖς οἱ διαφυλάττοντες αὐτά· ἐν οἷς εὑρίσκω
δευτέρῳ πρότερον ἔτει τῆς ἁλώσεως τίμησιν τοῦ¹
Ῥωμαίων δήμου γενομένην, ᾗ παραγέγραπται
καθάπερ καὶ ταῖς ἄλλαις χρόνος οὗτος· " Ὑπατεύον-
τος Λευκίου Οὐαλερίου Ποτίτου καὶ Τίτου Μαλλίου
6 Καπιτωλίνου μετὰ τὴν ἐκβολὴν τῶν βασιλέων ἑνὸς
δέοντι εἰκοστῷ καὶ ἑκατοστῷ² ἔτει." ὥστε τὴν
Κελτικὴν ἔφοδον, ἣν τῷ δευτέρῳ μετὰ τὴν τίμησιν
ἔτει γενομένην εὑρίσκομεν, ἐκπεπληρωμένων τῶν
εἴκοσι καὶ ἑκατὸν ἐτῶν γενέσθαι. εἰ δὲ τοῦτο τὸ
διάστημα τοῦ χρόνου τριάκοντα ὀλυμπιάδων εὑρίσκεται γενόμενον, ἀνάγκη τοὺς πρώτους ἀπο-
δειχθέντας ὑπάτους ὁμολογεῖν ἄρχοντος Ἀθήνησιν
Ἰσαγόρου³ παρειληφέναι τὴν ἀρχὴν κατὰ τὸ πρῶτον ἔτος τῆς ὀγδόης καὶ ἑξηκοστῆς ὀλυμπιάδος.

LXXV. Καὶ μὴν ἀπό γε τῆς ἐκβολῆς τῶν
βασιλέων ἐπὶ τὸν πρῶτον ἄρξαντα τῆς πόλεως
Ῥωμύλον ἀναβιβασθεὶς ὁ χρόνος ἔτη τέτταρα
πρὸς τοῖς⁴ τετταράκοντα καὶ διακοσίοις ἀποτελεῖ.
γνωρίζεται δὲ τοῦτο ταῖς διαδοχαῖς τῶν βασιλέων
καὶ τοῖς ἔτεσιν οἷς ἕκαστοι κατέσχον τὴν ἀρχήν.
Ῥωμύλος μὲν γὰρ ὁ κτίσας τὴν πόλιν ἑπτὰ καὶ

and twenty years. This is proved in many other
ways, but particularly by the records of the censors,
which the son receives in succession from the father
and takes great care to transmit to his posterity,
like family rites ; and there are many illustrious
men of censorian families who preserve these records.   In them I find that in the second year before
the taking of the city there was a census of the Roman
people, to which, as to the rest of them, there is
affixed the date, as follows : " In the consulship of
Lucius Valerius Potitus and Titus Manlius Capi-
tolinus, in the one hundred and nineteenth year
after the expulsion of the kings."   So that the
Gallic invasion, which we find to have occurred in the
second year after the census, happened when the
hundred and twenty years were completed.   If, now,
this interval of time is found to consist of thirty
Olympiads, it must be allowed that the first consuls
to be chosen entered upon their magistracy in the
first year of the sixty-eighth Olympiad, the same
year that Isagoras was archon at Athens.[1]

LXXV. And, again, if from the expulsion of the
kings the time is reckoned back to Romulus, the first
ruler of the city, it amounts to two hundred and forty-
four years.   This is known from the order in which
the kings succeeded one another and the number of
years each of them ruled.   For Romulus, the founder

[1] 507 B.C.

---

[1] τοῦ Madvig : ὑπὸ τοῦ B, ὑπὸ τῶν A.
[2] καὶ ἑκατοστῷ Bb : om. ABa.
[3] Ἰσαγόρου Sylburg : ἰσάγρου B, εἰς ἀγροῦ A.
[4] τοῖς added by Kiessling.

τριάκοντα ἔτη λέγεται κατασχεῖν τὴν δυναστείαν·
μετὰ δὲ τὸν Ῥωμύλου θάνατον ἀβασίλευτος ἡ
2 πόλις γενέσθαι χρόνον ἐνιαύσιον. ἔπειτα Νόμας
Πομπίλιος αἱρεθεὶς ὑπὸ τοῦ δήμου τρία καὶ τετταράκοντα ἔτη βασιλεῦσαι. Τύλλος δὲ Ὁστίλιος
μετὰ Νόμαν δύο καὶ τριάκοντα. ὁ δ' ἐπὶ τούτῳ
βασιλεύσας Ἄγκος Μάρκιος τέτταρα πρὸς τοῖς
εἴκοσι. μετὰ δὲ Μάρκιον Λεύκιος Ταρκύνιος ὁ
κληθεὶς Πρίσκος ὀκτὼ καὶ τριάκοντα. τοῦτον δὲ
διαδεξάμενος Σερούϊος Τύλλιος τετταράκοντα καὶ
τέτταρα. ὁ Σερούϊον δὲ ἀνελὼν Λεύκιος Ταρκύνιος
ὁ τυραννικὸς καὶ διὰ τὴν τοῦ δικαίου ὑπεροψίαν
κληθεὶς Σούπερβος ἕως εἰκοστοῦ καὶ πέμπτου
3 προαγαγεῖν τὴν ἀρχήν. τεττάρων δὲ καὶ τετταράκοντα καὶ διακοσίων ἀναπληρουμένων ἐτῶν, ἃ
κατέσχον οἱ βασιλεῖς, ὀλυμπιάδων δὲ μιᾶς καὶ
ἑξήκοντα, πᾶσα ἀνάγκη τὸν πρῶτον ἄρξαντα τῆς
πόλεως Ῥωμύλον ἔτει πρώτῳ τῆς ἑβδόμης ὀλυμπιάδος παρειληφέναι τὴν βασιλείαν ἄρχοντος Ἀθήνησι
τῆς δεκαετίας Χάροπος ἔτος πρῶτον. τοῦτο γὰρ
ὁ λογισμὸς τῶν ἐτῶν ἀπαιτεῖ. ὅτι δὲ τοσαῦτα
ἕκαστος τῶν βασιλέων ἦρξεν ἔτη δι' ἐκείνου δη-
λοῦταί μοι τοῦ λόγου.

4 Τὰ μὲν δὴ περὶ τοῦ χρόνου καθ' ὃν ἡ νῦν
δυναστεύουσα πόλις ᾠκίσθη τοῖς τε πρὸ ἐμοῦ
γενομένοις εἰρημένα κἀμοὶ δοκοῦντα τοιάδ' ἐστίν.
οἰκισταὶ δ' αὐτῆς οἵτινες ἦσαν καὶ¹ τίσι τύχαις
χρησάμενοι τὴν ἀποικίαν ἔστειλαν ὅσα τε ἄλλα
περὶ τὴν κτίσιν ταύτην ἱστόρηται πολλοῖς μὲν
εἴρηται καὶ διαφόρως τὰ πλεῖστα ἐνίοις, λεχθήσεται

of Rome, reigned thirty-seven years, it is said, and
after his death the city was a year without a king.
Then Numa Pompilius, who was chosen by the
people, reigned forty-three years ; after Numa,
Tullus Hostilius thirty-two ; and his successor, Ancus Marcius, twenty-four ; after Marcius, Lucius
Tarquinius, called Priscus, thirty-eight ; Servius
Tullius, who succeeded him, forty-four. And the
slayer of Servius, Lucius Tarquinius, the tyrannical
prince who, from his contempt of justice, was called
Superbus, extended his reign to the twenty-fifth
year. As the reigns, therefore, of the kings amount
to two hundred and forty-four years or sixty-one
Olympiads, it follows necessarily that Romulus,
the first ruler of the city, began his reign in the first
year of the seventh Olympiad, when Charops at
Athens was in the first year of his ten-year term as
archon.[1] For the count of the years requires this ;
and that each king reigned the number of years
stated is shown in that treatise of mine to which I
have referred.

This, therefore, is the account given by those who
lived before me and adopted by me concerning the
time of the settlement of the city which now rules
supreme. As to its founders, who they were and
by what turns of fortune they were induced to lead
out the colony, and any other details told concerning
its settlement, all this has been related by many,
and the greatest part of it in a different manner by

[1] 751 B.C.

---

[1] καὶ Kiessling : ἤ O.

δὲ κἀμοὶ τὰ πιθανώτατα τῶν μνημονευομένων.
ἔχει δὲ ὧδε·

LXXVI. Ἀμόλιος ἐπειδὴ παρέλαβε τὴν Ἀλβανῶν
βασιλείαν τὸν πρεσβύτερον ἀδελφὸν Νεμέτορα τῷ
κατισχῦσαι τῆς πατρίου τιμῆς ἀπείρξας, τά τε
ἄλλα κατὰ πολλὴν ὑπεροψίαν τῶν δικαίων ἔδρα καὶ
τελευτῶν ἔρημον γένους τὸν οἶκον τοῦ Νεμέτορος
ἐπεβούλευσε ποιῆσαι, τοῦ τε δίκην ὑποσχεῖν φόβῳ
καὶ ἔρωτι τοῦ¹ μὴ παυθῆναί ποτε τῆς ἀρχῆς.
2 βουλευσάμενος δὲ ταῦτα ἐκ πολλοῦ πρῶτον μὲν τὸν
υἱὸν τοῦ Νεμέτορος Αἴγεστον ἄρτι γενειάζοντα
φυλάξας ἔνθα ἐκυνηγέτει, προλοχίσας τοῦ χωρίου τὸ
ἀφανέστατον, ἐξελθόντα ἐπὶ θήραν ἀποκτείνει καὶ
παρεσκεύασε λέγεσθαι μετὰ τὸ ἔργον ὡς ὑπὸ λῃ-
στῶν ἀναιρεθείη τὸ μειράκιον. οὐ μέντοι κρείττων
ἡ κατασκευαστὴ δόξα τῆς σιωπωμένης ἀληθείας
ἐγένετο, ἀλλὰ πολλοῖς καὶ παρὰ τὸ ἀσφαλὲς ἐτολ-
3 μᾶτο λέγεσθαι τὸ πραχθέν. Νεμέτωρ δὲ ᾔδει μὲν
τὸ ἔργον, λογισμῷ δὲ κρείττονι τοῦ πάθους χρώμενος
ἄγνοιαν ἐσκήπτετο εἰς ἀκινδυνότερον ἀναβαλέσθαι
χρόνον τὴν ὀργὴν βουλευσάμενος. Ἀμόλιος δὲ τὰ
τοῦ μειρακίου ὑπολαβὼν λεληθέναι δεύτερα τάδε
ἐποίει· τὴν θυγατέρα τοῦ Νεμέτορος Ἰλίαν, ὡς
δὲ τινες γράφουσι Ῥέαν ὄνομα, Σιλουΐαν² δ᾽ ἐπίκλησιν, ἐν ἀκμῇ γάμου γενομένην ἱέρειαν ἀπο-
δείκνυσιν Ἑστίας, ὡς μὴ τάχιον εἰς ἀνδρὸς ἐλθοῦσα

¹ τοῦ added by Steph.²; om. Jacoby.
² Σιλουΐαν Glareanus: ἰουλίαν A, ἰλουίαν B.

some ; and I, also, shall relate the most probable
of these stories. They are as follows :

LXXVI. When [1] Amulius succeeded to the kingdom of the Albans, after forcibly excluding his elder
brother Numitor from the dignity that was his by
inheritance, he not only showed great contempt
for justice in everything else that he did, but he
finally plotted to deprive Numitor's family of issue,
both from fear of suffering punishment for his
usurpation and also because of his desire never to
be dispossessed of the sovereignty. Having long
resolved upon this course, he first observed the
neighbourhood where Aegestus, Numitor's son, who
was just coming to man's estate, was wont to follow
the chase, and having placed an ambush in the most
hidden part of it, he caused him to be slain when he
had come out to hunt ; and after the deed was committed he contrived to have it reported that the
youth had been killed by robbers. Nevertheless, the
rumour thus concocted could not prevail over the
truth which he was trying to keep concealed, but
many, though it was unsafe to do so, ventured to
tell what had been done. Numitor was aware of
the crime, but his judgment being superior to his
grief, he affected ignorance, resolving to defer his
resentment to a less dangerous time. And Amulius,
supposing that the truth about the youth had been
kept secret, set a second plan on foot, as follows : he
appointed Numitor's daughter, Ilia,—or, as some
state, Rhea, surnamed Silvia,—who was then ripe
for marriage, to be a priestess of Vesta, lest, if she
first entered a husband's house, she might bring

[1] *Cf.* Livy i. 3, 11.

τέκῃ τιμωροὺς τῷ γένει. πενταετοῦς[1] δὲ οὐκ
ἐλάττω χρόνου ἔδει τὰς ἱερὰς κόρας ἁγνὰς διαμεῖναι
γάμων, αἷς ἀνατέθειται τοῦ τε ἀσβέστου πυρὸς ἡ
φυλακὴ καὶ εἴ τι ἄλλο θρησκεύεσθαι τῷ κοινῷ διὰ
4 παρθένων νόμιμον ἦν. ἔπραττε δὲ Ἀμόλιος τοῦτο
μετ᾽ ὀνομάτων καλῶν, ὡς τιμὴν τῷ γένει καὶ
κόσμον περιτιθείς, οὔτε αὐτὸς εἰσηγησάμενος τὸν
νόμον τόνδε οὔτε κοινῷ ὄντι πρῶτον ἀναγκάσας
τῶν ἐν ἀξιώματι χρῆσθαι τὸν ἀδελφόν, ἐν ἔθει δὲ
τοῖς Ἀλβανοῖς καὶ ἐν καλῷ ὂν τὰς εὐγενεστάτας
ἀποδείκνυσθαι κόρας τῆς Ἑστίας προπόλους. ὁ
δὲ Νεμέτωρ αἰσθόμενος οὐκ ἀπὸ τοῦ βελτίστου
ταῦτα πράττοντα τὸν ἀδελφὸν ὀργὴν φανερὰν οὐκ
ἐποιεῖτο, ἵνα μὴ τῷ δήμῳ ἀπέχθοιτο, ἀπόρρητον δὲ
καὶ τοῦτο ἐφύλαττε τὸ ἔγκλημα.

LXXVII. Τετάρτῳ δ᾽ ὕστερον ἔτει τὴν Ἰλίαν
ἐλθοῦσαν εἰς ἱερὸν ἄλσος Ἄρεος ὕδατος ἁγνοῦ κομιδῆς ἕνεκα, ᾧ πρὸς τὰς θυσίας ἔμελλε χρήσασθαι,
βιάζεταί τις ἐν τῷ τεμένει. τοῦτον δέ τινες μὲν
ἀποφαίνουσι τῶν μνηστήρων ἕνα γενέσθαι τῆς
κόρης ἐρῶντα τῆς παιδίσκης,[2] οἱ δὲ αὐτὸν Ἀμόλιον
οὐκ ἐπιθυμίας μᾶλλον ἢ ἐπιβουλῆς ἕνεκα φραξά-
μενόν τε ὅπλοις ὡς ἐκπληκτικώτατος ὀφθήσεσθαι

---

[1] πενταετοῦς O : τριακονταετοῦς Glareanus, Sylburg.
[2] ἐρῶντα τῆς παιδίσκης rejected by Urlichs as a gloss;
Sauppe rejected τῆς παιδίσκης, Bücheler τῆς κόρης.

---

[1] Thirty years was the period required at Rome from the
time of Numa; cf. ii. 67, 2. Some early editors wished
to emend the present passage to agree with the later
practice.

forth avengers for her family. These holy maidens
who were intrusted with the custody of the perpetual
fire and with the carrying out of any other rites
that it was customary for virgins to perform in behalf
of the commonwealth, were required to remain undefiled by marriage for a period of not less than five [1]
years. Amulius was carrying out his plan under
specious pretences, as if he were conferring honour
and dignity on his brother's family ; for he was not
the author of this law, which was a general one, nor,
again, was his brother the first person of consideration whom he had obliged to yield obedience to it,
but it was both customary and honourable among
the Albans for maidens of the highest birth to be
appointed to the service of Vesta. But Numitor,
perceiving that these measures of his brother proceeded from no good intention, dissembled his resentment, lest he should incur the ill-will of the people,
and stifled his complaints upon this occasion also.

LXXVII. The [2] fourth year after this, Ilia, upon
going to a grove consecrated to Mars to fetch pure
water for use in the sacrifices, was ravished by somebody or other in the sacred precinct. Some say
that the author of the deed was one of the maiden's
suitors, who was carried away by his passion for
the girl [3] ; others say that it was Amulius himself,
and that, since his purpose was to destroy her quite
as much as to satisfy his passion, he had arrayed himself in such armour as would render him most terrible

[2] *Cf.* Livy i. 4, 1-3.
[3] The last clause (literally, " loving the girl ") may
well be a gloss to explain the preceding words " one of
the maiden's suitors." See critical note.

ἔμελλε καὶ τὸ τῆς ὄψεως γνώριμον εἰς ἀσαφὲς ὡς
2 μάλιστα ἐδύνατο καθιστάντα· οἱ δὲ πλεῖστοι μυθολογοῦσι τοῦ δαίμονος εἴδωλον, οὗ τὸ χωρίον ἦν,
πολλὰ καὶ ἄλλα τῷ πάθει δαιμόνια ἔργα προσάπτοντες [1] ἡλίου τε ἀφανισμὸν αἰφνίδιον καὶ ζόφον ἐν
οὐρανῷ κατασχόντα· καὶ[2] ὄψιν δέ, ἣν τὸ εἴδωλον
εἶχε, θαυμασιωτέραν μακρῷ δή τινι [3] κατὰ μέγεθος
καὶ κάλλος ἀνθρώπων. φασί τε εἰπεῖν τῇ κόρῃ
παρηγοροῦντα τὴν λύπην τὸν βιασάμενον, ἐξ οὗ
γενέσθαι δῆλον ὅτι θεὸς ἦν, μηδὲν ἄχθεσθαι τῷ
πάθει· τὸ γὰρ κοινώνημα τῶν γάμων αὐτῇ γεγονέναι πρὸς τὸν ἐμβατεύοντα τῷ χωρίῳ δαίμονα,
τέξεσθαι δ' αὐτὴν ἐκ τοῦ βιασμοῦ δύο παῖδας
ἀνθρώπων μακρῷ κρατίστους ἀρετὴν καὶ τὰ πολέμια. ταῦτα δὲ εἰπόντα νέφει περικαλυφθῆναι καὶ
3 ἀπὸ γῆς ἀρθέντα φέρεσθαι δι' ἀέρος ἄνω. ὅπως
μὲν οὖν χρὴ περὶ τῶν τοιῶνδε δόξης ἔχειν, πότερον
καταφρονεῖν ὡς ἀνθρωπίνων ῥᾳδιουργημάτων εἰς
θεοὺς ἀναφερομένων, μηδὲν ἂν τοῦ θεοῦ λειτούργημα
τῆς ἀφθάρτου καὶ μακαρίας φύσεως ἀνάξιον ὑπο-
μένοντος, ἢ καὶ ταύτας παραδέχεσθαι τὰς ἱστορίας,
ὡς ἀνακεκραμένης τῆς ἁπάσης οὐσίας τοῦ κόσμου
καὶ μεταξὺ τοῦ θείου καὶ θνητοῦ γένους τρίτης
τινὸς ὑπαρχούσης φύσεως, ἣν τὸ δαιμόνων φῦλον
ἐπέχει, τοτὲ μὲν ἀνθρώποις, τοτὲ δὲ θεοῖς ἐπι-
μιγνύμενον, ἐξ οὗ ὁ λόγος ἔχει τὸ μυθευόμενον
ἡρώων φῦναι γένος, οὔτε καιρὸς ἐν τῷ παρόντι
διασκοπεῖν ἀρκεῖ τε ὅσα [4] φιλοσόφοις περὶ αὐτῶν

---

[1] προσάπτοντες added by Casaubon.
[2] καὶ placed here by Urlichs: after ἦν by O, Jacoby.
[3] Schwartz: τι O, Jacoby.   [4] Steph.[2]: ὡς O.

to behold and that he also kept his features disguised
as effectively as possible. But most writers relate a
fabulous story to the effect that it was a spectre of
the divinity to whom the place was consecrated;
and they add that the adventure was attended by
many supernatural signs, including a sudden disappearance of the sun and a darkness that spread over
the sky, and that the appearance of the spectre was
far more marvellous than that of a man both in
stature and in beauty. And they say that the
ravisher, to comfort the maiden (by which it became
clear that he was a god), commanded her not to
grieve at all at what had happened, since she had
been united in marriage to the divinity of the place
and as a result of her violation should bear two sons
who would far excel all men in valour and warlike
achievements. And having said this, he was
wrapped in a cloud and, being lifted from the
earth, was borne upwards through the air. This
is not a proper place to consider what opinion we
ought to entertain of such tales, whether we should
scorn them as instances of human frailty attributed
to the gods,—since God is incapable of any action
that is unworthy of his incorruptible and blessed
nature,—or whether we should admit even these
stories, upon the supposition that all the substance
of the universe is mixed, and that between the race
of gods and that of men some third order of being
exists which is that of the daemons, who, uniting
sometimes with human beings and sometimes with
gods, beget, it is said, the fabled race of heroes. This,
I say, is not a proper place to consider these things,
and, moreover, what the philosophers have said

4 ἐλέχθη. ἡ δ' οὖν κόρη μετὰ τὸν βιασμὸν ἀρρωστεῖν σκηψαμένη (τοῦτο γὰρ αὐτῇ παρήνεσεν ἡ μήτηρ ἀσφαλείας τε καὶ τῶν πρὸς τοὺς θεοὺς ὁσίων ἕνεκα) οὐκέτι προσῄει τοῖς ἱεροῖς, ἀλλὰ διὰ τῶν ἄλλων ἐγίνετο παρθένων, αἷς τὸ αὐτὸ προσέκειτο ἔργον, ὅσα λειτουργεῖν ἐκείνην ἔδει.

LXXVIII. Ἀμόλιος δὲ εἴτε κατὰ τὴν συνείδησιν τῶν πραχθέντων εἴτε ὑπονοίᾳ τῶν εἰκότων προαχθεὶς ἔρευναν ἐποιεῖτο τῆς χρονίου τῶν ἱερῶν ἀποστάσεως, κατὰ τίνα γίνεται μάλιστ' αἰτίαν, ἰατρούς τε οἷς μάλιστα ἐπίστευεν εἰσπέμπων καί, ἐπειδὴ τὴν νόσον αἱ γυναῖκες ἀπόρρητον ἄλλοις[1] ᾐτιῶντο εἶναι, τὴν ἑαυτοῦ γυναῖκα φύλακα τῆς κόρης κατα-
2 λιπών.[2] ὡς δὲ κατήγορος αὐτὴ τοῦ πάθους ἐγένετο γυναικείᾳ τεκμάρσει τὸ ἀφανὲς τοῖς ἄλλοις ἀνευροῦσα, τῆς μὲν παιδός, ὡς μὴ λάθῃ τεκοῦσα (ἦν δὲ οὐ πρόσω τοῦ τόκου), φυλακὴν ἐποιεῖτο δι' ὅπλων· αὐτὸς δὲ καλέσας τὸν ἀδελφὸν εἰς τὸ συνέδριον τῆς τε λανθανούσης τοὺς ἄλλους φθορᾶς μηνυτὴς γίνεται καὶ ᾐτιᾶτο συγκακουργεῖν τῇ κόρῃ τοὺς γονεῖς ἐκέλευέ τε μὴ κρύπτειν τὸν[3]
3 εἰργασμένον, ἀλλ' εἰς μέσον ἄγειν. Νεμέτωρ δὲ παραδόξων τε λόγων ἀκούειν ἔφη καὶ παντὸς ἀναίτιος εἶναι τοῦ λεγομένου χρόνον τε ἠξίου βασάνου τῆς ἀληθείας ἕνεκα λαβεῖν· τυχὸν δὲ ἀναβολῆς μόλις, ἐπειδὴ τὸ πρᾶγμα παρὰ τῆς γυναικὸς ἔμαθεν ὡς ἡ παῖς ἐν ἀρχαῖς ἀφηγήσατο,

---

[1] ἄλλοις (or τοῖς ἄλλοις) Naber, ἀνδράσιν Kayser: ἀνθρώποις O, Jacoby.

concerning them is sufficient. But, be that as it may, the maid after her violation feigned illness (for this her mother advised out of regard both for her own safety and for the sacred services of the gods) and no longer attended the sacrifices, but her duties were performed by the other virgins who were joined with her in the same ministry.

LXXVIII. But Amulius, moved either by his own knowledge of what had happened or by a natural suspicion of the truth, began to inquire into her long absence from the sacrifices, in order to discover the real reason. To this end he kept sending in to her some physicians in whom he had the greatest confidence; and then, since the women alleged that her ailment was one that must be kept secret from others, he left his wife to watch her. She, having by a woman's marking of the signs discovered what was a secret to the others, informed him of it, and he, lest the girl should be delivered in secret, for she was now near her time, caused her to be guarded by armed men. And summoning his brother to the council, he not only announced the deflowering of the girl, of which the rest knew naught, but even accused her parents of being her accomplices; and he ordered Numitor not to hide the guilty man, but to expose him. Numitor said he was amazed at what he heard, and protesting his innocence of everything that was alleged, desired time to test the truth of it. Having with difficulty obtained this delay, and being informed by his wife of the affair as his daughter had related it in the

---

² Kiessling: κατέλιπεν O. ³ τὸν B: τὸ R.

τόν τε βιασμὸν τὸν ὑπὸ τοῦ θεοῦ γενόμενον ἀπέφαινε καὶ τοὺς λεχθέντας ὑπ' αὐτοῦ περὶ τῶν
διδύμων παίδων λόγους διεξῆλθεν ἠξίου τε πίστιν
ποιήσασθαι ταύτην τῶν λεγομένων, εἰ τοιοῦτος ὁ
τῆς ὠδῖνος ἔσται γόνος, οἷον ὁ θεὸς ὑφηγήσατο.
καὶ γὰρ ὁμοῦ τι τῷ τίκτειν εἶναι τὴν κόρην, ὥστε
οὐκ εἰς[1] μακρὰν εἰ ῥᾳδιουργεῖ[2] φανήσεται. παρεδίδου δὲ καὶ τὰς φυλαττούσας τὴν κόρην καὶ ἐλέγχων
4 οὐδενὸς ἀφίστατο. ταῦτα λέγοντος αὐτοῦ τὸ μὲν
τῶν συνέδρων πλῆθος ἐπείθετο, Ἀμόλιος δὲ οὐδὲν
ὑγιὲς ἀπέφαινε τῶν ἀξιουμένων,[3] ἀλλ' ἐκ παντὸς
ὥρμητο τρόπου τὴν ἄνθρωπον ἀπολέσαι. ἐν ὅσῳ
δὲ ταῦτ' ἐγένετο παρῆσαν οἱ τὴν ὠδῖνα φρουρεῖν
ταχθέντες ἀποφαίνοντες ἄρρενα βρέφη δίδυμα τεκεῖν
τὴν κόρην, καὶ αὐτίκα Νεμέτωρ μὲν ἐν τῷ αὐτῷ
πολὺς ἦν λόγῳ τοῦ θεοῦ τε ἀποδεικνὺς τὸ ἔργον
καὶ μηδὲν εἰς τὴν κόρην ἀναίτιον οὖσαν τοῦ πάθους
παρανομεῖν ἀξιῶν· Ἀμολίῳ δὲ τῶν ἀνθρωπείων τι
μηχανημάτων καὶ τὸ περὶ τὸν τόκον ἐδόκει γενέσθαι
παρασκευασθέντος ἑτέρου ταῖς γυναιξὶ βρέφους ἢ
κρύφα τῶν φυλάκων ἢ συγκακουργούντων, καὶ
5 πολλὰ εἰς τοῦτο ἐλέχθη. ὡς δὲ τὴν γνώμην τοῦ
βασιλέως ἔμαθον οἱ σύνεδροι ἀπαραιτήτῳ τῇ[4] ὀργῇ
χρωμένην ἐδικαίωσαν καὶ αὐτοὶ καθάπερ ἐκεῖνος
ἠξίου χρήσασθαι τῷ νόμῳ κελεύοντι τὴν μὲν αἰσχύ-
νασαν τὸ σῶμα ῥάβδοις αἰκισθεῖσαν ἀποθανεῖν, τὸ

---

[1] οὐκ εἰς added by Steph.
[2] εἰ ῥᾳδιουργεῖ Reiske : ῥᾳδιουργεῖν O, Jacoby.
[3] ἀξιουμένων Steph. : ἀξιολογουμένων O.
[4] τῇ added by Grasberger.

beginning, he acquainted the council with the rape committed by the god and also related what the god had said concerning the twins, and asked that his story should be believed only if the fruit of her travail should prove to be such as the god had foretold; for the time of her delivery was near at hand, so that it would not be long, if he were playing the rogue, before the fact would come to light. Moreover, he offered to put at their disposal for examination the women who were watching his daughter, and he was ready to submit to any and every test. As he spoke thus the majority of the councillors were persuaded, but Amulius declared that his demands were altogether insincere, and was bent on destroying the girl by every means. While this was taking place, those who had been appointed to keep guard over Ilia at the time of her delivery came to announce that she had given birth to male twins. And at once Numitor began to urge at length the same arguments, showing the deed to be the work of the god and demanding that they take no unlawful action against his daughter, who was innocent of her condition. On the other hand, Amulius thought that even in connexion with her delivery there had been some human trickery and that the women had provided another child, either unknown to the guards or with their connivance, and he said much more to the same purport. When the councillors found that the king's decision was inspired by implacable anger, they, too, voted, as he demanded, that the law should be carried out which provided that a Vestal who suffered herself to be defiled should be scourged with rods and put to death and her offspring thrown

δὲ γεννηθὲν εἰς τὸ τοῦ ποταμοῦ βάλλεσθαι ῥεῖθρον·
νῦν μέντοι ζώσας κατορύττεσθαι τὰς τοιαύτας ὁ
τῶν ἱερῶν ἀγορεύει[1] νόμος.

LXXIX. Μέχρι μὲν δὴ τούτων οἱ πλεῖστοι τῶν
συγγραφέων τὰ αὐτὰ ἢ μικρὸν παραλλάττοντες, οἱ
μὲν ἐπὶ τὸ μυθωδέστερον, οἱ δ' ἐπὶ τὸ τῇ ἀληθείᾳ
ἐοικὸς μᾶλλον, ἀποφαίνουσι, περὶ δὲ τῶν ἑξῆς δια-
2 φέρονται. οἱ μὲν γὰρ εὐθὺς ἀναιρεθῆναι λέγουσι
τὴν κόρην, οἱ δ' ἐν εἱρκτῇ φυλαττομένην ἀδήλῳ
διατελέσαι δόξαν τῷ δήμῳ παρασχοῦσαν ἀφανοῦς
θανάτου. ἐπικλασθῆναι δὲ τὸν[2] Ἀμόλιον εἰς τοῦτο
ἱκετευούσης τῆς θυγατρὸς χαρίσασθαι τὴν ἀνεψιὰν
αὐτῇ· ἦσαν δὲ σύντροφοί τε καὶ ἡλικίαν ἔχουσαι
τὴν αὐτὴν ἀσπαζόμεναί τε ἀλλήλας ὡς ἀδελφάς.
χαριζόμενον οὖν ταύτῃ τὸν[2] Ἀμόλιον, μόνη δ' ἦν
αὐτῷ θυγάτηρ, θανάτου μὲν ἀπολῦσαι τὴν Ἰλίαν,
φυλάττειν δὲ καθείρξαντα ἐν ἀφανεῖ· λυθῆναι δὲ
3 αὐτὴν ἀνὰ χρόνῳ Ἀμολίου τελευτήσαντος. περὶ
μὲν οὖν τῆς Ἰλίας οὕτω διαλλάττουσιν αἱ τῶν
παλαιῶν γραφαί, λόγον δ' ἔχουσιν ὡς ἀληθεῖς
ἑκάτεραι. διὰ τοῦτο κἀγὼ μνήμην ἀμφοτέρων
ἐποιησάμην, ὁποτέρᾳ δὲ χρὴ πιστεύειν αὐτός τις
εἴσεται τῶν ἀναγνωσομένων.

4 περὶ δὲ τῶν ἐκ τῆς Ἰλίας γενομένων Κόιντος
μὲν Φάβιος ὁ Πίκτωρ λεγόμενος, ᾧ Λεύκιός τε
Κίγκιος καὶ Κάτων Πόρκιος καὶ Πείσων Καλ-
πούρνιος καὶ τῶν ἄλλων συγγραφέων οἱ πλείους
ἠκολούθησαν, γέγραφε[3]· ὡς κελεύσαντος Ἀμολίου

---

[1] ἀγορεύει Β : διαγορεύει R.
[2] τὸν Ο : om. Sintenis, Jacoby.

into the current of the river. To-day, however, the sacred law ordains that such offenders shall be buried alive.

LXXIX. Up [1] to this point the greater part of the historians give the same account or differ but slightly, some in the direction of what is legendary, others of what is more probable ; but they disagree in what follows. Some say that the girl was put to death immediately ; others that she remained in a secret prison under a guard, which caused the people to believe that she had been put to death secretly. The latter authors say that Amulius was moved to do this when his daughter begged him to grant her the life of her cousin ; for, having been brought up together and being of the same age, they loved each other like sisters. Amulius, accordingly, to please her,—for she was his only daughter,—saved Ilia from death, but kept her confined in a secret prison ; and she was at length set at liberty after the death of Amulius. Thus do the accounts of the ancient authors vary concerning Ilia, and yet both opinions carry with them an appearance of truth ; for this reason I, also, have mentioned them both, but each of my readers will decide for himself which to believe.

But concerning the babes born of Ilia, Quintus Fabius, called Pictor, whom Lucius Cincius, Porcius Cato, Calpurnius Piso and most of the other historians have followed, writes thus : By the order

[1] *Cf.* Livy i. 4, 3-9.

---

[3] γέγραφε Plüss : τῆι γραφῆι O.

τὰ βρέφη λαβόντες ἐν σκάφῃ κείμενα τῶν ὑπηρετῶν
τινες ἔφερον ἐμβαλοῦντες εἰς τὸν ποταμὸν ἀπέχοντα
5 τῆς πόλεως ἀμφὶ τοὺς ἑκατὸν εἴκοσι σταδίους. ἐπεὶ
δὲ ἐγγὺς ἐγένοντο καὶ εἶδον ἔξω τοῦ γνησίου ῥείθρου
τὸν Τέβεριν ὑπὸ χειμώνων συνεχῶν ἐκτετραμμένον
εἰς τὰ πεδία, καταβάντες ἀπὸ τοῦ Παλλαντίου τῆς
κορυφῆς ἐπὶ τὸ προσεχέστατον ὕδωρ (οὐ γὰρ ἔτι
προσωτέρω χωρεῖν οἷοί τε ἦσαν), ἔνθα πρῶτον ἡ
τοῦ ποταμοῦ πλήμη τῆς ὑπωρείας ἥπτετο, τίθενται
τὴν σκάφην ἐπὶ τοῦ ὕδατος. ἡ δὲ μέχρι μέν τινος
ἐνήχετο, ἔπειτα τοῦ ῥείθρου κατὰ μικρὸν ὑπο-
χωροῦντος ἐκ τῶν περιεσχάτων[1] λίθου προσπταίσει
6 περιτραπεῖσα ἐκβάλλει τὰ βρέφη. τὰ μὲν δὴ
κνυζούμενα κατὰ τοῦ τέλματος ἐκυλινδεῖτο, λύκαινα
δέ τις ἐπιφανεῖσα νεοτόκος σπαργῶσα τοὺς μαστοὺς
ὑπὸ γάλακτος ἀνεδίδου τὰς θηλὰς τοῖς στόμασιν
αὐτῶν καὶ τῇ γλώττῃ τὸν πηλόν, ᾧ κατάπλεοι
ἦσαν, ἀπελίχμα. ἐν δὲ τούτῳ τυγχάνουσιν οἱ
νομεῖς ἐξελαύνοντες τὰς ἀγέλας ἐπὶ νομήν (ἤδη
γὰρ ἐμβατὸν ἦν τὸ χωρίον) καί τις αὐτῶν ἰδὼν
τὴν λύκαιναν ὡς ἠσπάζετο τὰ βρέφη τέως μὲν
ἀχανὴς ἦν ὑπό τε θάμβους καὶ ἀπιστίας τῶν
θεωρουμένων· ἔπειτ' ἀπελθὼν[2] καὶ συλλέξας ὅσους
ἐδύνατο πλείστους τῶν ἀγχοῦ νεμόντων (οὐ γὰρ
ἐπιστεύετο λέγων) ἄγει τοὔργον αὐτὸ θεασομένους.
7 ὡς δὲ κἀκεῖνοι πλησίον ἐλθόντες ἔμαθον τὴν μὲν
ὥσπερ τέκνα περιέπουσαν,[3] τὰ δ' ὡς μητρὸς

---

[1] περιεσχάτων Naber, περὶξ ἐσχάτων Sylburg, περὶ τὰ ἔσχατα
Meutzner: περιέσχατα A, περὶ ἔσχατα B, Jacoby.
[2] ἔπειτ' ἀπελθὼν Kiessling: ἔπειτα ἐλθὼν O.
[3] Sylburg: περισπῶσαν O.

of Amulius some of his servants took the babes
in an ark and carried them to the river, distant about
a hundred and twenty stades from the city, with the
intention of throwing them into it.   But when they
drew near and perceived that the Tiber, swollen by
continual rains, had left its natural bed and overflowed the plains, they came down from the top of
the Palatine hill [1] to that part of the water that lay
nearest (for they could no longer advance any farther) and set down the ark upon the flood where it
washed the foot of the hill.   The ark floated for
some time, and then, as the waters retired by degrees
from their extreme limits, it struck against a stone
and, overturning, threw out the babes, who lay
whimpering and wallowing in the mud.   Upon this,
a she-wolf that had just whelped appeared and, her
udder being distended with milk, gave them her
paps to suck and with her tongue licked off the mud
with which they were besmeared.   In the meantime the herdsmen happened to be driving their
flocks forth to pasture (for the place was now become passable) and one of them, seeing the wolf
thus fondling the babes, was for some time struck
dumb with astonishment and disbelief of what he
saw.   Then going away and getting together as
many as he could of his fellows who kept their
herds near at hand (for they would not believe what
he said), he led them to see the sight themselves.
When these also drew near and saw the wolf caring
for the babes as if they had been her young and the

[1] From this point the word Παλλάντιον will be rendered
" Palatine hill " instead of " Pallantium," unless the context shows clearly that the village itself is meant.

ἐξεχόμενα, δαιμόνιόν τι χρῆμα ὁρᾶν ὑπολαβόντες
ἐγγυτέρω προσῄεσαν ἀθρόοι δεδιττόμενοι βοῇ τὸ
θηρίον. ἡ δὲ λύκαινα οὐ μάλα ἀγριαίνουσα τῶν
ἀνθρώπων τῇ προσόδῳ, ἀλλ' ὡσπερὰν χειροήθης
ἀποστᾶσα τῶν βρεφῶν ἠρέμα καὶ κατὰ πολλὴν
8 ἀλογίαν τοῦ ποιμενικοῦ ὁμίλου ἀπῄει.   καὶ ἦν γάρ
τις οὐ πολὺ ἀπέχων ἐκεῖθεν ἱερὸς χῶρος ὕλῃ βαθείᾳ
συνηρεφὴς καὶ πέτρα κοίλη πηγὰς ἐνιεῖσα, ἐλέγετο
δὲ Πανὸς εἶναι τὸ νάπος, καὶ βωμὸς ἦν αὐτόθι τοῦ
θεοῦ· εἰς τοῦτο τὸ χωρίον ἐλθοῦσα ἀποκρύπτεται.
τὸ μὲν οὖν ἄλσος οὐκέτι διαμένει, τὸ δὲ ἄντρον, ἐξ
οὗ ἡ λιβὰς ἐκδίδοται, τῷ Παλλαντίῳ προσῳκοδο-
μημένον δείκνυται κατὰ τὴν ἐπὶ τὸν ἱππόδρομον
φέρουσαν ὁδόν, καὶ τέμενός ἐστιν αὐτοῦ πλησίον,
ἔνθα εἰκὼν κεῖται τοῦ πάθους λύκαινα παιδίοις δυσὶ
τοὺς μαστοὺς ἐπίσχουσα, χαλκᾶ ποιήματα παλαιᾶς
ἐργασίας. ἦν δὲ τὸ χωρίον τῶν σὺν Εὐάνδρῳ ποτὲ
οἰκισάντων αὐτὸ Ἀρκάδων ἱερὸν ὡς λέγεται.
9 ὡς δὲ ἀπέστη τὸ θηρίον αἴρουσιν οἱ νομεῖς τὰ
βρέφη σπουδὴν ποιούμενοι τρέφειν ὡς θεῶν αὐτὰ
σώζεσθαι βουλομένων. ἦν δέ τις ἐν αὐτοῖς συοφορβίων βασιλικῶν ἐπιμελούμενος ἐπιεικὴς ἀνὴρ

---

[1] Compare the description of the Lupercal already given
in chap. 32.

[2] The cave became a shrine and received some sort of
architectural adornment, which must have included at
least a dignified entrance. The Lupercal is named in
the *Monumentum Ancyranum* (4, 2) in a list of public
buildings repaired by Augustus.

[3] The statue here mentioned is doubtless the one erected
by Cn. and Q. Ogulnius near the *Ficus Ruminalis* in

babes clinging to her as to their mother, they thought
they were beholding a supernatural sight and advanced in a body, shouting to terrify the creature.
The wolf, however, far from being provoked at the
approach of the men, but as if she had been tame,
withdrew gently from the babes and went away,
paying little heed to the rabble of shepherds. Now
there was not far off a holy place, arched over by a
dense wood, and a hollow rock from which springs
issued; the wood was said to be consecrated to Pan,
and there was an altar there to that god.[1] To this
place, then, the wolf came and hid herself. The
grove, to be sure, no longer remains, but the cave
from which the spring flows is still pointed out, built
up [2] against the side of the Palatine hill on the road
which leads to the Circus, and near it is a sacred
precinct in which there is a statue commemorating
the incident; it represents a she-wolf suckling two
infants, the figures being in bronze and of ancient
workmanship.[3] This spot is said to have been a
holy place of the Arcadians who formerly settled
there with Evander.

As soon as the beast was gone the herdsmen took
up the babes, and believing that the gods desired their
preservation, were eager to bring them up. There
was among them the keeper of the royal herds of

295 B.C. (Livy x. 23). Another similar group stood on
the summit of the Capitol, and was struck by lightning in
65 B.C. The wolf of this second group is almost certainly the
famous one still preserved in the Palazzo dei Conservatori,
since the animal's hind legs show the effects of lightning;
the wolf is dated about 600 B.C., but the infants are a modern
restoration.

Φαυστύλος[1] ὄνομα, ὃς ἐν τῇ πόλει κατὰ δή τι ἀναγκαῖον ἐγεγόνει καθ᾽ ὃν χρόνον ἡ φθορὰ τῆς Ἰλίας
καὶ ὁ τόκος ἠλέγχετο, καὶ μετὰ ταῦτα κομιζομένων
ἐπὶ τὸν ποταμὸν τῶν βρεφῶν τοῖς φέρουσιν αὐτὰ
κατὰ θείαν τύχην ἅμα διεληλύθει τὴν αὐτὴν ὁδὸν
εἰς τὸ Παλλάντιον ἰών· ὃς ἥκιστα τοῖς ἄλλοις
καταφανὴς γενόμενος ὡς ἐπίσταταί τι τοῦ πράγματος ἀξιώσας αὑτῷ συγχωρηθῆναι τὰ βρέφη λαμ-
βάνει τε αὐτὰ παρὰ τοῦ κοινοῦ καὶ φέρων ὡς τὴν
10 γυναῖκα ἔρχεται. τετοκυῖαν δὲ καταλαβὼν καὶ
ἀχθομένην ὅτι νεκρὸν αὐτῇ τὸ βρέφος ἦν παρα-
μυθεῖταί τε καὶ δίδωσιν ὑποβαλέσθαι τὰ παιδία
πᾶσαν ἐξ ἀρχῆς διηγησάμενος τὴν κατασχοῦσαν
αὐτὰ τύχην. αὐξομένοις δὲ αὐτοῖς ὄνομα τίθεται
τῷ μὲν Ῥωμύλον, τῷ δὲ Ῥῶμον. οἱ δὲ ἀνδρω-
θέντες γίνονται κατά τε ἀξίωσιν μορφῆς καὶ φρονήματος ὄγκον οὐ συοφορβοῖς καὶ βουκόλοις ἐοικότες,
ἀλλ᾽ οἵους ἄν τις ἀξιώσειε τοὺς ἐκ βασιλείου τε
φύντας γένους καὶ ἀπὸ δαιμόνων σπορᾶς γενέσθαι
νομιζομένους, ὡς ἐν τοῖς πατρίοις ὕμνοις ὑπὸ
11 Ῥωμαίων ἔτι καὶ νῦν ᾄδεται. βίος δ᾽ αὐτοῖς ἦν
βουκολικὸς καὶ δίαιτα αὐτουργὸς ἐν ὄρεσι τὰ πολλὰ
πηξαμένοις διὰ ξύλων καὶ καλάμων σκηνὰς αὐτορό-

---

[1] Steph. (cf. Φαυστῖνος, 84, 3): φαιστύλος O (and similarly
elsewhere), Jacoby.

---

[1] This meaning (on the analogy of such words as αὔτανδρος,
αὐτόκλαδος, αὐτόρριζος) seems to be the one required here.
The only meaning given in the lexicons, "self-covered"
or "roofed by nature," would imply huts depending for
their roofs on natural shelters, such as overhanging rocks
or overarching trees,—in other words, huts technically

swine, whose name was Faustulus, an upright man, who had been in town upon some necessary business at the time when the deflowering of Ilia and her delivery were made public. And afterwards, when the babes were being carried to the river, he had by some providential chance taken the same road to the Palatine hill and gone along with those who were carrying them. This man, without giving the least intimation to the others that he knew anything of the affair, asked that the babes might be delivered to him, and having received them by general consent, he carried them home to his wife. And finding that she had just given birth to a child and was grieving because it was still-born, he comforted her and gave her these children to substitute in its place, informing her of every circumstance of their fortune from the beginning. And as they grew older he gave to one the name of Romulus and to the other that of Remus. When they came to be men, they showed themselves both in dignity of aspect and elevation of mind not like swineherds and neatherds, but such as we might expect those to be who are born of royal race and are looked upon as the offspring of the gods ; and as such they are still celebrated by the Romans in the hymns of their country. But their life was that of herdsmen, and they lived by their own labour, generally upon the mountains in huts which they built, roofs and all,[1]

roofless. But the thatched roof of the " hut of Romulus " was to the Romans one of its most striking features ; see next note. καλάμων, here rendered "reeds," in accordance with its usual meaning, is also used sometimes for " straw," which may be what Dionysius intended.

φους· ὧν ἔτι καὶ εἰς ἐμὲ ἦν τις τοῦ[1] Παλλαντίου
ἐπὶ τῆς πρὸς τὸν ἱππόδρομον στρεφούσης[2] λαγόνος
'Ρωμύλου λεγομένη, ἣν φυλάττουσιν ἱερὰν οἷς τούτων ἐπιμελὲς οὐδὲν ἐπὶ τὸ σεμνότερον ἐξάγοντες,
εἰ δέ τι πονήσειεν ὑπὸ χειμῶνος ἢ χρόνου τὸ
λεῖπον ἐξακούμενοι καὶ τῷ πρόσθεν ἐξομοιοῦντες
εἰς δύναμιν.

12   ἐπεὶ δὲ ἀμφὶ τὰ ὀκτωκαίδεκα ἔτη γεγονότες ἦσαν
ἀμφίλογόν τι περὶ τῆς νομῆς αὐτοῖς γίνεται πρὸς
τοὺς Νεμέτορος βουκόλους, οἳ περὶ τὸ Αὐεντῖνον
ὄρος ἀντικρὺ τοῦ Παλλαντίου κείμενον εἶχον τὰς
βουστάσεις. ᾐτιῶντο δὲ ἀλλήλους ἑκάτεροι θαμινὰ
ἢ τὴν μὴ προσήκουσαν ὀργάδα κατανέμειν ἢ τὴν
κοινὴν μόνους διακρατεῖν ἢ ὅ τι δήποτε τύχοι. ἐκ
δὲ τῆς ἀψιμαχίας ταύτης ἐγένοντο πληγαί ποτε διὰ
13 χειρῶν, εἶτα δι' ὅπλων. τραύματα δὲ πολλὰ πρὸς
τῶν μειρακίων λαβόντες οἱ τοῦ Νεμέτορος καί
τινας καὶ ἀπολέσαντες τῶν σφετέρων καὶ τῶν
χωρίων ἤδη κατὰ κράτος ἐξειργόμενοι παρεσκευάζοντο δόλον τινὰ ἐπ' αὐτούς. προλοχίσαντες δὴ
τῆς φάραγγος τὸ ἀφανὲς καὶ συνθέμενοι τοῖς
λοχῶσι τὰ μειράκια τὸν τῆς ἐπιθέσεως καιρὸν οἱ

---

[1] τοῦ Kiessling : ἐκ τοῦ O.
[2] ἐπὶ τῆς . . στρεφούσης Steph. : τῆς . . . ἐπιστρεφούσης O.

---

[1] The present passage gives us our most detailed account
of the *casa Romuli*. Plutarch (*Rom.* 20) adds the detail
that it stood near the *scalae Caci*, a landmark on the south-

out of sticks and reeds. One of these, called the hut of Romulus,[1] remained even to my day on the flank of the Palatine hill which faces towards the Circus, and it is preserved holy by those who have charge of these matters ; they add nothing to it to render it more stately, but if any part of it is injured, either by storms or by the lapse of time, they repair the damage and restore the hut as nearly as possible to its former condition.

When Romulus and Remus were about eighteen years of age, they had some dispute about the pasture with Numitor's herdsmen, whose herds were quartered on the Aventine hill, which is over against the Palatine. They frequently accused one another either of grazing the meadow-land that did not belong to them or of monopolizing that which belonged to both in common, or of whatever the matter chanced to be. From this wrangling they had recourse sometimes to blows and then to arms. Finally Numitor's men, having received many wounds at the hands of the youths and lost some of their number and being at last driven by force from the places in dispute, devised a stratagem against them. They placed an ambuscade in the hidden part of the ravine and having concerted the time of the attack with those who lay in wait for the youths, the rest in a body

west corner of the Palatine hill. There was also another *casa Romuli* on the Capitoline, probably a replica of the first. Vitruvius (ii. 1, 5), after mentioning the primitive custom of constructing roofs out of reeds, brushwood or straw, cites the hut of Romulus on the Capitoline as a good example of the ancient practice. *Cf.* Virgil (*Aen.* viii. 654), *Romuleoque recens horrebat regia culmo ;* and Ovid's similar description of the original temple of Vesta (*Fasti* vi. 261 f.).

DIONYSIUS OF HALICARNASSUS

λοιποὶ κατὰ πλῆθος ἐπὶ τὰ μανδρεύματα αὐτῶν
νύκτωρ ἐπέβαλον. Ῥωμύλος μὲν οὖν τὸν χρόνον
τοῦτον ἐτύγχανεν ἅμα τοῖς ἐπιφανεστάτοις τῶν
κωμητῶν πεπορευμένος εἴς τι χωρίον Καινίνην[1]
ὀνομαζόμενον ἱερὰ ποιήσων ὑπὲρ τοῦ κοινοῦ πάτρια·
14 Ῥῶμος δὲ τὴν ἔφοδον αὐτῶν αἰσθόμενος ἐξεβοήθει
λαβὼν τὰ ὅπλα διὰ ταχέων ὀλίγους τῶν ἐκ τῆς
κώμης φθάσαντας καθ᾽ ἓν γενέσθαι παραλαβών.
κἀκεῖνοι οὐ δέχονται αὐτόν, ἀλλὰ φεύγουσιν ὑπαγό-
μενοι ἔνθα ἔμελλον ἐν καλῷ ὑποστρέψαντες ἐπι-
θήσεσθαι· ὁ δὲ Ῥῶμος κατ᾽ ἄγνοιαν τοῦ μηχανή-
ματος ἄχρι πολλοῦ διώκων αὐτοὺς παραλλάττει
τὸ λελοχισμένον χωρίον, κἂν τούτῳ ὅ τε λόχος
ἀνίσταται καὶ οἱ φεύγοντες ὑποστρέφουσι. κυκλω-
σάμενοι δὲ αὐτοὺς καὶ πολλοῖς ἀράττοντες λίθοις
λαμβάνουσιν ὑποχειρίους. ταύτην γὰρ εἶχον ἐκ
τῶν δεσποτῶν τὴν παρακέλευσιν, ζῶντας αὐτοῖς
τοὺς νεανίσκους κομίσαι. οὕτω μὲν δὴ χειρωθεὶς
ὁ Ῥῶμος ἀπήγετο.

LXXX. Ὡς δὲ Τουβέρων Αἴλιος δεινὸς ἀνὴρ
καὶ περὶ τὴν συναγωγὴν τῆς ἱστορίας ἐπιμελὴς
γράφει, προειδότες οἱ τοῦ Νεμέτορος θύσοντες τὰ
Λύκαια τοὺς νεανίσκους τῷ Πανὶ τὴν Ἀρκαδικὴν
ὡς Εὔανδρος κατεστήσατο θυσίαν ἐνήδρευσαν τὸν
καιρὸν ἐκεῖνον τῆς ἱερουργίας, ἡνίκα χρῆν τοὺς περὶ
τὸ Παλλάντιον οἰκοῦντας τῶν νέων ἐκ τοῦ Λυκαίου

---

[1] Καινίνην (as in ii. 32, 35, and Steph. Byz.) Cary, Καίνιναν
Cobet, Jacoby: καινιμᾶν A, καινιμὰν B.

---

[1] Cf. Livy i. 5, 1-3.   [2] See p. 25, n. 2.

attacked the others' folds by night. No wit happened that Romulus, together with the chief men of
the village, had gone at the time to a place called
Caenina to offer sacrifices for the community according to the custom of the country; but Remus,
being informed of the foe's attack, hastily armed
himself and with a few of the villagers who had
already got together went out to oppose them. And
they, instead of awaiting him, retired, in order to
draw him to the place where they intended to face
about and attack him to advantage. Remus, being
unaware of their stratagem, pursued them for a long
distance, till he passed the place where the rest
lay in ambush; thereupon these men rose up and
at the same time the others who had been fleeing
faced about. And having surrounded Remus and
his men, they overwhelmed them with a shower of
stones and took them prisoners; for they had received orders from their masters to bring the youths
to them alive. Thus Remus was captured and led
away.

LXXX. But[1] Aelius Tubero,[2] a shrewd man and
careful in collecting his historical data, writes that
Numitor's people, knowing beforehand that the
youths were going to celebrate in honour of Pan the
Lupercalia,[3] the Arcadian festival as instituted by
Evander, set an ambush for that moment in the
celebration when the youths living near the Palatine
were, after offering sacrifice, to proceed from the

[3] For a detailed discussion of the Lupercalia the reader
is referred to Sir James Frazer's note on Ovid's *Fasti* ii. 267
(Vol. ii. pp. 327 ff.; condensed in his Loeb Classical
Library edition, pp. 389 ff.).

τεθυκότας περιελθεῖν δρόμῳ τὴν κώμην γυμνοὺς
ὑπεζωσμένους τὴν αἰδῶ ταῖς δοραῖς τῶν νεοθύτων.
τοῦτο δὲ καθαρμόν τινα τῶν κωμητῶν πάτριον
2 ἐδύνατο, ὡς καὶ νῦν ἔτι δρᾶται. ἐν δὴ τούτῳ τῷ
χρόνῳ τοὺς ἱεροποιοὺς νεανίσκους οἱ βουκόλοι
λοχήσαντες κατὰ τὸ στενόπορον τῆς ὁδοῦ, ἐπειδὴ
τὸ πρῶτον τάγμα τὸ σὺν τῷ Ῥώμῳ κατ' αὐτοὺς
ἐγένετο, τῶν ἀμφὶ Ῥωμύλον τε καὶ τῶν[1] ἄλλων
ὑστεριζόντων (τριχῇ γὰρ ἐνενέμηντο καὶ ἐκ διαστή-
ματος ἔθεον) οὐ περιμείναντες τοὺς λοιποὺς ὁρμῶσιν
ἐπὶ τοὺς πρώτους ἐμβοήσαντες ἀθρόοι καὶ περι-
στάντες ἔβαλλον οἱ μὲν ἀκοντίοις, οἱ δὲ λίθοις, οἱ δ'
ὡς ἕκαστοί τι διὰ χειρὸς εἶχον. οἱ δ' ἐκπλαγέντες
τῷ παραδόξῳ τοῦ πάθους καὶ ἀμηχανοῦντες ὅ τι
δράσειαν πρὸς ὡπλισμένους ἄνοπλοι μαχόμενοι κατὰ
3 πολλὴν εὐπέτειαν ἐχειρώθησαν. ὁ μὲν οὖν Ῥῶμος
ἐπὶ τοῖς πολεμίοις γενόμενος οὕτως, εἶθ' ὡς ὁ
Φάβιος παραδέδωκε, δέσμιος εἰς τὴν Ἄλβαν ἀπήγετο. Ῥωμύλος δ' ἐπειδὴ τὸ περὶ τὸν ἀδελφὸν
ἔγνω πάθος, διώκειν εὐθὺς ᾤετο δεῖν τοὺς ἀκ-
μαιοτάτους ἔχων τῶν νομέων, ὡς ἔτι κατὰ τὴν
ὁδὸν ὄντα καταληψόμενος τὸν Ῥῶμον· ἀποτρέπεται
δ' ὑπὸ τοῦ Φαυστύλου. ὁρῶν γὰρ αὐτοῦ τὴν σπουδὴν μανικωτέραν οὖσαν οὗτος[2] νομισθεὶς ὁ πατήρ,
ἃ[3] τὸν ἔμπροσθεν χρόνον ἀπόρρητα ποιούμενος
τοῖς μειρακίοις διετέλεσεν, ὡς μὴ θᾶττον ὁρμήσωσι
παρακινδυνεῦσαί τι πρὶν ἐν τῷ κρατίστῳ τῆς ἀκμῆς
γενέσθαι, τότε δὴ[4] πρὸς τῆς ἀνάγκης βιασθεὶς

---

[1] τῶν added by Kiessling.
[2] οὗτος added here by Jacoby, after ὁρῶν γὰρ by Schnelle.

Lupercal and run round the village naked, their loins
girt with the skins of the victims just sacrificed.
This ceremony signified a sort of traditional purification of the villagers, and is still performed even to
this day. On this occasion, then, the herdsmen lay
in wait in the narrow part of the road for the youths
who were taking part in the ceremony, and when the
first band with Remus came abreast of them, that
with Romulus and the rest being behind (for they
were divided into three bands and ran at a distance
from one another), without waiting for the others
they set up a shout and all rushed upon the first
group, and, surrounding them, some threw darts at
them, others stones, and others whatever they could
lay their hands on. And the youths, startled by the
unexpected attack and at a loss how to act, fighting
unarmed as they were against armed men, were easily
overpowered. Remus, therefore, having fallen into
the hands of the enemy in this manner or in the way
Fabius relates, was being led away, bound, to Alba.
When Romulus heard of his brother's fate, he
thought he ought to follow immediately with the
stoutest of the herdsmen in the hope of overtaking
Remus while he was still on the road, but he was
dissuaded by Faustulus. For seeing that his haste
was too frenzied, this man, who was looked upon as
the father of the youths and who had hitherto kept
everything a secret from them, lest they should ven-
ture upon some hazardous enterprise before they were
in their prime, now at last, compelled by necessity,

---

³ ἂ added by Kiessling.
⁴ δὴ Schnelle: δὲ O.

DIONYSIUS OF HALICARNASSUS

4 μονωθέντι τῷ Ῥωμύλῳ λέγει. μαθόντι δὲ τῷ
νεανίσκῳ πᾶσαν ἐξ ἀρχῆς τὴν κατασχοῦσαν αὐτοὺς
τύχην τῆς τε μητρὸς οἶκτος εἰσέρχεται καὶ Νεμέτορος φροντίς, καὶ πολλὰ βουλευσαμένῳ μετὰ τοῦ
Φαυστύλου τῆς μὲν αὐτίκα ὁρμῆς ἐπισχεῖν ἐδόκει,
πλείονι δὲ παρασκευῇ δυνάμεως χρησάμενον ὅλον
ἀπαλλάξαι τὸν οἶκον τῆς Ἀμολίου παρανομίας
κίνδυνόν τε τὸν ἔσχατον ὑπὲρ τῶν μεγίστων ἄθλων
ἀναρρῖψαι, πράττειν δὲ μετὰ τοῦ μητροπάτορος ὅ
τι ἂν ἐκείνῳ δοκῇ.

LXXXI. Ὡς δὲ ταῦτα κράτιστα εἶναι ἔδοξε
συγκαλέσας τοὺς κωμήτας ἅπαντας ὁ Ῥωμύλος
καὶ δεηθεὶς εἰς τὴν Ἄλβαν ἐπείγεσθαι διὰ ταχέων
μὴ κατὰ τὰς αὐτὰς πύλας ἅπαντας μηδ' ἀθρόους
εἰσιόντας, μή τις ὑπόνοια πρὸς τοὺς ἐν τῇ πόλει
γένηται, καὶ περὶ τὴν ἀγορὰν ὑπομένοντας ἑτοίμους
εἶναι δρᾶν τὸ κελευόμενον, ἀπῄει πρῶτος εἰς τὴν
2 πόλιν. οἱ δὲ τὸν Ῥῶμον ἄγοντες, ἐπειδὴ κατέστησαν ἐπὶ τὸν βασιλέα, τάς τε ὕβρεις ἁπάσας,
ὅσας ἦσαν ὑβρισμένοι πρὸς τῶν μειρακίων, κατηγόρουν καὶ τοὺς τραυματίας σφῶν ἐπεδείκνυσαν,
τιμωρίας εἰ μὴ τεύξονται καταλείψειν προλέγοντες
τὰ βουφόρβια. Ἀμόλιος δὲ τοῖς χωρίταις κατὰ
πλῆθος ἐληλυθόσι χαρίζεσθαι βουλόμενος καὶ τῷ
Νεμέτορι (παρὼν γὰρ ἐτύγχανε συναγανακτῶν τοῖς
πελάταις) εἰρήνην τε ἀνὰ τὴν χώραν σπεύδων εἶναι
καὶ ἅμα καὶ τὸ αὔθαδες τοῦ μειρακίου, ὡς ἀκατά-
πληκτον ἦν ἐν τοῖς λόγοις, δι' ὑποψίας λαμβάνων
καταψηφίζεται τὴν δίκην· τῆς δὲ τιμωρίας τὸν

276

took Romulus aside and told him everything. When the youth heard every circumstance of their fortune from the beginning, he was touched both with compassion for his mother and with solicitude for Numitor. And after taking much counsel with Faustulus, he decided to give up his plan for an immediate attack, but to get ready a larger force, in order to free his whole family from the lawlessness of Amulius, and he resolved to risk the direst peril for the sake of the greatest rewards, but to act in concert with his grandfather in whatever the other should see fit to do.

LXXXI. This[1] plan having been decided upon as the best, Romulus called together all the inhabitants of the village and after asking them to hasten into Alba immediately, but not all by the same gates nor in a body, lest the suspicions of the citizens should be aroused, and then to stay in the market-place and be ready to do whatever should be ordered, he himself set out first for the city. In the meantime those who had carried off Remus brought him before the king and complained of all the outrageous treatment they had received from the youths, producing their wounded, and threatening, if they found no redress, to desert their herds. And Amulius, desiring to please both the countrymen, who had come in great numbers, and Numitor (for he happened to be present and shared the exasperation of his retainers), and longing to see peace throughout the country, and at the same time suspecting the boldness of the youth, so fearless was he in his answers, gave judgment against him; but he left his

[1] For chaps. 81-83 *cf.* Livy i. 5, 4–6, 2.

277

Νεμέτορα ποιεῖ κύριον, εἰπών ὡς τῷ δράσαντι δεινὰ τὸ ἀντιπαθεῖν οὐ πρὸς ἄλλου τινὸς μᾶλλον ἢ τοῦ 3 πεπονθότος ὀφείλεται. ἐν ὅσῳ δ' ὁ Ῥῶμος ὑπὸ τῶν τοῦ Νεμέτορος βουκόλων ἤγετο δεδεμένος τε ὀπίσω τὼ χεῖρε καὶ πρὸς τῶν ἀγόντων ἐπικερτο- μούμενος, ἀκολουθῶν ὁ Νεμέτωρ τοῦ τε σώματος τὴν εὐπρέπειαν ἀπεθαύμαζεν, ὡς πολὺ τὸ βασιλικὸν εἶχε, καὶ τοῦ φρονήματος τὴν εὐγένειαν ἐνεθυμεῖτο, ἣν καὶ παρὰ τὰ δεινὰ διέσωσεν οὐ πρὸς οἶκτον οὐδὲ λιπαρήσεις, ὡς ἅπαντες ἐν ταῖς τοιαῖσδε ποιοῦσι τύ- χαις, τραπόμενος, ἀλλὰ σὺν εὐκόσμῳ σιωπῇ πρὸς[1] 4 τὸν μόρον ἀπιών. ὡς δ' εἰς τὴν οἰκίαν ἀφίκοντο μεταστῆναι τοὺς ἄλλους κελεύσας μονωθέντα τὸν Ῥῶμον ἤρετο τίς εἴη καὶ τίνων, ὡς οὐκ ἂν ἐκ τῶν τυχόντων γε ἄνδρα τοιοῦτον γενόμενον. εἰπόντος δὲ τοῦ Ῥώμου τοσοῦτον εἰδέναι μόνον κατὰ πύστιν τοῦ τρέφοντος, ὅτι σὺν ἀδελφῷ διδύμῳ ἐκτεθείη βρέφος εἰς νάπην εὐθὺς ἀπὸ γονῆς καὶ πρὸς τῶν νομέων ἀναιρεθεὶς ἐκτραφείη, βραχὺν ἐπισχὼν χρόνον εἴτε ὑποτοπηθείς τι τῶν ἀληθῶν εἴτε τοῦ δαίμονος ἄγοντος εἰς τοὐμφανὲς τὸ πρᾶγμα λέγει 5 πρὸς αὐτόν· " "Ὅτι μὲν ἐπ' ἐμοὶ γέγονας, ὦ Ῥῶμε, παθεῖν ὅ τι ἂν δικαιώσω, καὶ ὡς περὶ πολλοῦ ποιήσαιντ' ἂν οἱ κομίσαντές σε δεῦρο πολλὰ καὶ δεινὰ παθόντες ἀποθανεῖν, οὐδὲν δεῖ πρὸς εἰδότα λέγειν. εἰ δέ σε θανάτου τε καὶ ἄλλου παντὸς ἐκλυσαίμην κακοῦ, ἆρ' ἂν εἰδείης μοι χάριν καὶ δεο- μένῳ ὑπουργήσειας ὃ κοινὸν ἀμφοῖν ἔσται ἀγαθόν; "

[1] πρὸς B: ἐπι R.

punishment to Numitor, saying that the one who had
done an injury could be punished by none so justly
as by the one who had suffered it. While Numitor's
herdsmen were leading Remus away with his hands
bound behind him and mocking him, Numitor followed and not only admired his grace of body, so
much was there that was kingly in his bearing,
but also observed his nobility of spirit, which he
preserved even in distress, not turning to lamentations and entreaties, as all do under such afflictions,
but with a becoming silence going away to his fate.
As soon as they were arrived at his house he ordered
all the rest to withdraw, and Remus being left alone,
he asked him who he was and of what parents;
for he did not believe such a man could be meanly
born. Remus answered that he knew this much
only from the account he had received from the
man who brought him up, that he with his twin
brother had been exposed in a wood as soon as they
were born and had then been taken up by the
herdsmen and reared by them. Upon which
Numitor, after a short pause, either because he suspected something of the truth or because Heaven
was bringing the matter to light, said to him:
" I need not inform you, Remus, that you are in
my power to be punished in whatever way I may see
fit, and that those who brought you here, having
suffered many grievous wrongs at your hands,
would give much to have you put to death. All
this you know. But if I should free you from death
and every other punishment, would you show your
gratitude and serve me when I desire your assistance
in an affair that will conduce to the advantage of us

279

6 ἀποκριναμένου δὲ τοῦ μειρακίου ὁπόσα τοὺς ἐν
ἀπογνώσει βίου κειμένους ἢ τοῦ σωθήσεσθαι
ἐλπὶς τοῖς κυρίοις τούτου λέγειν καὶ ὑπισχνεῖσθαι
ἐπαίρει, λῦσαι κελεύσας αὐτὸν ὁ Νεμέτωρ καὶ
πάντας ἀπελθεῖν ἐκποδὼν φράζει τὰς αὐτοῦ τύχας,
ὡς Ἀμόλιος αὐτὸν ἀδελφὸς ὢν ἀπεστέρησε τῆς
βασιλείας ὀρφανόν τε[1] τέκνων ἔθηκε, τὸν μὲν ἐπὶ
θήρᾳ κρύφα διαχειρισάμενος, τὴν δ' ἐν εἰρκτῇ δε-
δεμένην φυλάττων, τά τε ἄλλα ὁπόσα δεσπότης
χρώμενος δούλῳ διατελεῖ.[2]

LXXXII. Ταῦτ' εἰπὼν καὶ πολὺν θρῆνον ἅμα
τοῖς λόγοις καταχεάμενος ἠξίου τιμωρὸν τοῖς κατ'
οἶκον[3] αὐτοῦ[4] κακοῖς[5] τὸν Ῥῶμον γενέσθαι.
ἀσμένως δὲ ὑποδεξαμένου τὸν λόγον τοῦ μειρακίου
καὶ παραυτίκα[6] τάττειν αὐτὸν ἐπὶ τὸ ἔργον ἀξιοῦντος
ἐπαινέσας ὁ Νεμέτωρ τὴν προθυμίαν, " Τῆς μὲν πράξεως," ἔφη, " τὸν καιρὸν ἐγὼ ταμιεύσομαι, σὺ δὲ
τέως πρὸς τὸν ἀδελφὸν ἀπόρρητον ἅπασι τοῖς ἄλλοις
ἀγγελίαν πέμψον, ὅτι σώζῃ τε δηλῶν καὶ διὰ ταχέων
2 αὐτὸν ἥκειν ἀξιῶν." ἐκ δὲ τούτου πέμπεταί τις
ἐξευρεθείς, ὃς ἐδόκει[7] ὑπηρετήσειν, καὶ περιτυχὼν
οὐ πρόσω τῆς πόλεως ὄντι Ῥωμύλῳ διασαφεῖ τὰς
ἀγγελίας· ὁ δὲ περιχαρὴς γενόμενος ἔρχεται σπουδῇ
πρὸς Νεμέτορα καὶ περιπλακεὶς ἀμφοῖν ἀσπάζεται
μὲν πρῶτον, ἔπειτα φράζει τὴν ἔκθεσιν σφῶν καὶ
τροφὴν καὶ τἆλλα ὅσα παρὰ τοῦ Φαυστύλου ἐπύθετο.

[1] τε Meutzner : δὲ O.
[2] διατελεῖ added by Sintenis, λωβᾶται by Meutzner, Jacoby.
[3] κατ' οἶκον Kiessling : κατοίκοις ABa, κατ' οἴκους Bb.
[4] αὐτοῦ Kiessling : αὐτοῦ AB.
[5] κακοῖς added by Kiessling ; Reiske had suggested κακοῖς
for κατοίκοις of the MSS.

both ? " The youth, having in answer said everything which the hope of life prompts those who are in
despair of it to say and promise to those on whom
their fate depends, Numitor ordered him to be
unbound. And commanding everybody to leave the
place, he acquainted him with his own misfortunes—
how Amulius, though his brother, had deprived him
of his kingdom and bereft him of his children, having
secretly slain his son while he was hunting and keeping his daughter bound in prison, and in all other
respects continued to treat him as a master would
treat his slave.

LXXXII. Having spoken thus and accompanied
his words with many lamentations, he entreated
Remus to avenge the wrongs of his house. And
when the youth gladly embraced the proposal and
begged him to set him at the task immediately,
Numitor commended his eagerness and said : " I myself will determine the proper time for the enterprise ;
but do you meanwhile send a message privately to
your brother, informing him that you are safe and
asking him to come here in all haste." Thereupon
a man who seemed likely to serve their purpose
was found and sent ; and he, meeting Romulus not
far from the city, delivered his message. Romulus
was greatly rejoiced at this and went in haste to
Numitor ; and having embraced them both, he first
spoke words of greeting and then related how he and
his brother had been exposed and brought up and

---

⁶ παραυτίκα Jacoby : πάλαι O.
⁷ After ἐδόκει Meineke supplied εὖ ; Reiske proposed to
read ὃς προθύμως καὶ πιστῶς ἐδόκει ὑπηρετήσειν.

DIONYSIUS OF HALICARNASSUS

τοῖς δὲ βουλομένοις τε καὶ οὐ πολλῶν ἵνα πιστεύσειαν
τεκμηρίων δεομένοις καθ' ἡδονὰς τὸ λεγόμενον ἦν.[1]
ἐπεὶ δὲ ἀνέγνωσαν ἀλλήλους αὐτίκα συνετάττοντο
καὶ διεσκόπουν ὅστις ἔσται τρόπος ἢ καιρὸς εἰς τὴν
3 ἐπίθεσιν ἐπιτήδειος. ἐν ᾧ δὲ οὗτοι περὶ ταῦτ' ἦσαν
ὁ Φαυστύλος ἀπάγεται πρὸς Ἀμόλιον. δεδοικὼς γὰρ
μὴ οὐ πιστὰ δόξῃ τῷ Νεμέτορι λέγειν ὁ Ῥωμύλος[2]
ἄνευ σημείων ἐμφανῶν μεγάλου πράγματος μηνυτὴς
γενόμενος, τὸ γνώρισμα τῆς ἐκθέσεως τῶν βρεφῶν
τὴν σκάφην ἀναλαβὼν ὀλίγον ὕστερον ἐδίωκεν εἰς
4 τὴν πόλιν. διερχόμενον δ' αὐτὸν τὰς πύλας ταρα-
χωδῶς πάνυ καὶ περὶ πολλοῦ ποιούμενον μηδενὶ
ποιῆσαι καταφανὲς τὸ φερόμενον[3] τῶν φυλάκων τις
καταμαθών (ἦν δὲ πολεμίων ἐφόδου δέος καὶ τὰς
πύλας οἱ μάλιστα πιστευόμενοι πρὸς τοῦ βασιλέως
ἐφρούρουν) συλλαμβάνει τε καὶ τὸ κρυπτὸν ὅ τι
δήποτ' ἦν καταμαθεῖν ἀξιῶν ἀποκαλύπτει βίᾳ τὴν
περιβολήν. ὡς δὲ τὴν σκάφην ἐθεάσατο καὶ τὸν
ἄνθρωπον ἔμαθεν ἀπορούμενον, ἠξίου λέγειν τίς ἡ
ταραχὴ καὶ τί τὸ βούλημα τοῦ μὴ φανερῶς εἰσφέρειν[4]
5 σκεῦος οὐδὲν δεόμενον ἀπορρήτου φορᾶς. ἐν δὲ
τούτῳ πλείους τῶν φυλάκων συνέρρεον καί τις
αὐτῶν γνωρίζει τὴν σκάφην αὐτὸς ἐν ἐκείνῃ τὰ
παιδία κομίσας ἐπὶ τὸν ποταμὸν καὶ φράζει πρὸς
τοὺς παρόντας. οἱ δὲ συλλαβόντες τὸν Φαυστύλον
ἄγουσιν ἐπ' αὐτὸν τὸν βασιλέα καὶ διηγοῦνται τὰ

---

[1] ἦν added by Steph.
[2] Sylburg: φαιστύλος AB.

282

all the other circumstances he had learned from
Faustulus. The others, who wished his story might
be true and needed few proofs in order to believe
it, heard what he said with pleasure. And as soon
as they knew one another they proceeded to consult
together and consider the proper method and occasion for making their attack. While they were thus
employed, Faustulus was brought before Amulius.
For, fearing lest the information given by Romulus
might not be credited by Numitor, in an affair of
so great moment, without manifest proofs, he soon
afterwards followed him to town, taking the ark
with him as evidence of the exposing of the babes.
But as he was entering the gates in great confusion,
taking all possible pains to conceal what he carried,
one of the guards observed him (for there was fear
of an incursion of the enemy and the gates were being
guarded by those who were most fully trusted by
the king) and laid hold of him ; and insisting upon
knowing what the concealed object was, he forcibly
threw back his garment. As soon as he saw the ark
and found the man embarrassed, he demanded to
know the cause of his confusion and what he meant
by not carrying in openly an article that required
no secrecy. In the meantime more of the guards
flocked to them and one of them recognized the ark,
having himself carried the children in it to the river ;
and he so informed those who were present. Upon
this they seized Faustulus, and carrying him to the
king himself, acquainted him with all that had

---

³ φερόμενον Gelenius, στεγόμενον Reiske : λεγόμενον O.
⁴ εἰσφέρειν B : ἐκφέρειν A.

6 γενόμενα. Ἀμόλιος δὲ ἀπειλῇ βασάνων καταπληξά-
μενος τὸν ἄνθρωπον, εἰ μὴ λέξοι τὰς ἀληθείας ἑκών,
πρῶτον μὲν εἰ ζῶσιν οἱ παῖδες ἤρετο· ὡς δὲ τοῦτ᾽
ἔμαθε, τῆς σωτηρίας αὐτοῖς ὅστις ὁ τρόπος ἐγένετο·
διηγησαμένου δὲ αὐτοῦ πάντα ὡς ἐπράχθη, " Ἄγε
δή, φησὶν ὁ βασιλεύς, ἐπειδὴ ταῦτ᾽ ἀληθεύσας ἔχεις,
φράσον ὅπου νῦν ἂν εὑρεθεῖεν. οὐ γὰρ ἔτι δίκαιοί
εἰσιν ἐν βουκόλοις καὶ ἄδοξον βίον[1] ζῆν ἔμοιγε ὄντες
συγγενεῖς, ἄλλως τε καὶ θεῶν προνοίᾳ σωζόμενοι."

LXXXIII. Φαυστύλος δὲ τῆς ἀλόγου πραότητος
ὑποψίᾳ κινηθεὶς μὴ φρονεῖν αὐτὸν ὅμοια τοῖς λόγοις
ἀποκρίνεται ὧδε· " Οἱ μὲν παῖδές εἰσιν ἐν τοῖς ὄρεσι
βουκολοῦντες, ὥσπερ ἐκείνων βίος, ἐγὼ δ᾽ ἐπέμφθην
παρ᾽ αὐτῶν τῇ μητρὶ δηλώσων ἐν αἷς εἰσι τύχαις·
ταύτην δὲ παρά σοι φυλάττεσθαι ἀκούων δεήσεσθαι
τῆς σῆς θυγατρὸς ἔμελλον, ἵνα με πρὸς αὐτὴν ἀγάγοι.
τὴν δὲ σκάφην ἔφερον ἵν᾽ ἔχω δεικνύναι τεκμήριον
ἐμφανὲς ἅμα τοῖς λόγοις. νῦν οὖν, ἐπεὶ δέδοκταί
σοι τοὺς νεανίσκους δεῦρο κομίσαι, χαίρω τε καὶ
πέμψον οὕστινας βούλει σὺν ἐμοί. δείξω μὲν οὖν
τοῖς ἐλθοῦσι τοὺς παῖδας, φράσουσι δ᾽ αὐτοῖς ἐκεῖνοι
2 τὰ παρά σου." ὁ μὲν δὴ ταῦτ᾽ ἔλεγεν ἀναβολὴν
εὑρέσθαι βουλόμενος τοῖς παισὶ τοῦ θανάτου καὶ
ἅμα αὐτὸς ἀποδράσεσθαι τοὺς ἄγοντας, ἐπειδὰν ἐν
τοῖς ὄρεσι γένηται, ἐλπίσας. Ἀμόλιος δὲ τοῖς

[1] ἄδοξον βίον Usener : ἀδόξῳ βίῳ O.

284

passed. Amulius, having terrified the man by the threat of torture if he did not willingly tell the truth, first asked him if the children were alive; and learning that they were, he desired to know in what manner they had been preserved. And when the other had given him a full account of everything as it had happened, the king said : " Well then, since you have spoken the truth about these matters, say where they may now be found ; for it is not right that they who are my relations should any longer live ingloriously among herdsmen, particularly since it is due to the providence of the gods that they have been preserved."

LXXXIII. But Faustulus, suspecting from the king's unaccountable mildness that his intentions were not in harmony with his professions, answered him in this manner : " The youths are upon the mountains tending their herds, which is their way of life, and I was sent by them to their mother to give her an account of their fortunes ; but, hearing that she was in your custody, I was intending to ask your daughter to have me brought to her. And I was bringing the ark with me that I might support my words with a manifest proof. Now, therefore, since you have decided to have the youths brought here, not only am I glad, but I ask you to send such persons with me as you wish. I will point out to them the youths and they shall acquaint them with your commands." This he said in the desire to discover some means of delaying the death of the youths and at the same time in the hope of making his own escape from the hands of those who were conducting him, as soon as he should arrive upon the mountains. And Amulius speedily sent the most

πιστοτάτοις τῶν ὁπλοφόρων ἐπιστείλας κρύφα, οὓς
ἂν ὁ συοφορβὸς αὐτοῖς δείξῃ συλλαβόντας ὡς αὐτὸν
ἄγειν, ἀποστέλλει διὰ ταχέων. ταῦτα δὲ διαπραξάμενος αὐτίκα γνώμην ἐποιεῖτο καλέσας τὸν ἀδελφὸν ἐν φυλακῇ ἀδέσμῳ¹ ἔχειν, ἕως ἂν εὖ θῆται τὰ
3 παρόντα, καὶ αὐτὸν ὡς ἐπ' ἄλλο δή τι ἐκάλει. ὁ δὲ
ἀποσταλεὶς ἄγγελος εὐνοίᾳ τε τοῦ κινδυνεύοντος καὶ
ἐλέῳ τῆς τύχης ἐπιτρέψας κατήγορος γίνεται Νεμέτορι τῆς Ἀμολίου γνώμης. ὁ δὲ τοῖς παισὶ δηλώσας
τὸν κατειληφότα κίνδυνον αὐτοὺς καὶ παρακελευσάμενος ἄνδρας ἀγαθοὺς γενέσθαι παρῆν ἄγων ὡπλισμένους ἐπὶ τὰ βασίλεια τῶν τε ἄλλων πελατῶν καὶ
ἑταίρων καὶ θεραπείας πιστῆς χεῖρα οὐκ ὀλίγην.
ἧκον δὲ καὶ οἱ ἐκ τῶν ἀγρῶν συνελθόντες εἰς τὴν
πόλιν ἐκλιπόντες τὴν ἀγορὰν ἔχοντες ὑπὸ ταῖς περιβολαῖς ξίφη κεκρυμμένα, στῖφος καρτερόν. βιασά-
μενοι δὲ τὴν εἴσοδον ἀθρόᾳ ὁρμῇ πάντες οὐ πολλοῖς
ὁπλίταις φρουρουμένην ἀποσφάττουσιν εὐπετῶς
Ἀμόλιον καὶ μετὰ τοῦτο τὴν ἄκραν καταλαμβάνονται. ταῦτα μὲν οὖν τοῖς περὶ Φάβιον εἴρηται.

LXXXIV. Ἕτεροι δὲ οὐδὲν τῶν μυθωδεστέρων
ἀξιοῦντες ἱστορικῇ γραφῇ προσήκειν τήν τε ἀπό-
θεσιν τὴν τῶν βρεφῶν οὐχ ὡς ἐκελεύσθη τοῖς
ὑπηρέταις γενομένην ἀπίθανον εἶναί φασι, καὶ
τῆς λυκαίνης τὸ τιθασόν, ἣ τοὺς μαστοὺς ἐ πεῖχε
τοῖς παιδίοις, ὡς δραματικῆς¹ μεστὸν ἀτοπίας

---

¹ δραματικῆς B : δραστικῆς R.

---

¹ Literally " under guard without chains," probably a
translation of the Latin *libera custodia.* In later times

286

trustworthy of his guards with secret orders to seize
and bring before him the persons whom the swine-
herd should point out to them.   Having done this,
he at once determined to summon his brother and
keep him under mild guard [1] till he had ordered the
present business to his satisfaction, and he sent for
him as if for some other purpose ; but the messenger
who was sent, yielding both to his good-will toward
the man in danger and to compassion for his fate,
informed Numitor of the design of Amulius.   And
Numitor, having revealed to the youths the danger
that threatened them and exhorted them to show
themselves brave men, came to the palace with
a considerable band of his retainers and friends and
loyal servants.   These were joined by the countrymen who had entered the city earlier and now came
from the market-place with swords concealed under
their clothes, a sturdy company.   And having by
a concerted attack forced the entrance, which was
defended by only a few heavy-armed troops, they
easily slew Amulius and afterwards made themselves
masters of the citadel.   Such is the account given
by Fabius.

LXXXIV. But others, who hold that nothing
bordering on the fabulous has any place in historical
writing, declare that the exposing of the babes by
the servants in a manner not in accordance with their
instructions is improbable, and they ridicule the
tameness of the she-wolf that suckled the children as
a story full of melodramatic absurdity.   In place of

persons of rank were often thus kept under surveillance in
their own houses or in the house of a magistrate.

2 διασύρουσιν· ἀντιδιαλλαττόμενοι δὲ πρὸς ταῦτα
λέγουσιν ὡς ὁ Νεμέτωρ, ἐπειδὴ τὴν Ἰλίαν ἔγνω
κύουσαν, ἕτερα παρασκευασάμενος παιδία νεογνὰ
διηλλάξατο τεκούσης αὐτῆς τὰ βρέφη καὶ τὰ μὲν
ὀθνεῖα δέδωκε τοῖς φυλάττουσι τὰς ὠδῖνας ἀποφέρειν,
εἴτε χρημάτων τὸ πιστὸν τῆς χρείας αὐτῶν πριά-
μενος εἴτε διὰ γυναικῶν τὴν ὑπαλλαγὴν μηχανησά-
μενος, καὶ αὐτὰ λαβὼν Ἀμόλιος ὅτῳ δή τινι τρόπῳ
ἀναιρεῖ· τὰ δ' ἐκ τῆς Ἰλίας γενόμενα περὶ παντὸς
ποιούμενος ὁ μητροπάτωρ διασώζεσθαι δίδωσι τῷ
3 Φαυστύλῳ. τὸν δὲ Φαυστύλον τοῦτον Ἀρκάδα μὲν
εἶναί φασι τὸ γένος ἀπὸ τῶν σὺν Εὐάνδρῳ, κατοικεῖν δὲ περὶ τὸ Παλλάντιον ἐπιμέλειαν ἔχοντα τῶν
Ἀμολίου κτημάτων. χαρίσασθαι δὲ Νεμέτορι τὴν
ἐκτροφὴν τῶν παίδων τἀδελφῷ[1] πειθόμενον ὄνομα
Φαυστίνῳ τὰς περὶ τὸν Αὐεντῖνον τρεφομένας τοῦ
4 Νεμέτορος ἀγέλας ἐπιτροπεύοντι· τήν τε τιθηνησα-
μένην τὰ παιδία καὶ μαστοὺς ἐπισχοῦσαν οὐ λύκαιναν εἶναί φασιν, ἀλλ' ὥσπερ εἰκὸς γυναῖκα τῷ
Φαυστύλῳ συνοικοῦσαν Λαυρεντίαν ὄνομα, ᾗ δη-
μοσιευούσῃ ποτὲ τὴν τοῦ σώματος ὥραν οἱ περὶ
τὸ Παλλάντιον διατρίβοντες ἐπίκλησιν ἔθεντο τὴν
Λούπαν·[2] ἔστι δὲ τοῦτο Ἑλληνικόν τε καὶ ἀρχαῖον

[1] Hertlein: ἀδελφῷ O.
[2] λούππαν AB (and similarly just below).

---

[1] Cf. Livy i. 4, 7. lupa is found in various Latin
authors in the sense of " prostitute," and lupanar meant
" brothel."

this they give the following account of the matter :
Numitor, upon learning that Ilia was with child,
procured other new-born infants and when she had
given birth to her babes, he substituted the former
in place of the latter. Then he gave the supposititious children to those who were guarding her at the
time of her delivery to be carried away, having either
secured the loyalty of the guards by money or contrived this exchange by the help of women ; and
when Amulius had received them, he made away
with them by some means or other. As for the
babes that were born of Ilia, their grandfather, who
was above all things solicitous for their preservation,
handed them over to Faustulus. This Faustulus,
they say, was of Arcadian extraction, being descended
from those Arcadians who came over with Evander ;
he lived near the Palatine hill and had the care oι
Amulius' possessions, and he was prevailed on by
his brother, named Faustinus, who had the oversight of Numitor's herds that fed near the Aventine
hill, to do Numitor the favour of bringing up the
children. They say, moreover, that the one who
nursed and suckled them was not a she-wolf, but,
as may well be supposed, a woman, the wife of
Faustulus, named Laurentia, who, having formerly
prostituted her beauty, had received from the
people living round the Palatine hill the nickname
of Lupa.[1] This is an ancient Greek [2] term applied

---

[2] It would seem as if " Greek " must be an error here for
"Latin." Not even the Greek equivalent of *lupa* (λύκαινα)
is found used in this sense. Hesychius' gloss, λύπτα (for
λύππα ?)· ἑταίρα, πόρνη, may well have been taken from some
Roman history.

ἐπὶ ταῖς μισθαρνούσαις τἀφροδίσια τιθέμενον, αἳ
νῦν εὐπρεπεστέρᾳ κλήσει ἑταῖραι προσαγορεύονται.
ἀγνοοῦντας δέ τινας αὐτὸ πλάσαι τὸν περὶ τῆς
λυκαίνης μῦθον, ἐπειδὴ κατὰ τὴν γλῶτταν, ἣν τὸ
Λατίνων ἔθνος φθέγγεται, λούπα καλεῖται τοῦτο τὸ
5 θηρίον. ἡνίκα δὲ τῆς ἐν τῷ γάλακτι τροφῆς ἀπηλ-
λάγη τὰ παιδία, δοθῆναι πρὸς τῶν τρεφόντων εἰς
Γαβίους πόλιν οὐ μακρὰν ἀπὸ τοῦ Παλλαντίου
κειμένην, ὡς Ἑλλάδα παιδείαν ἐκμάθοιεν, κἀκεῖ
παρ' ἀνδράσιν ἰδιοξένοις τοῦ Φαυστύλου τραφῆναι
γράμματα καὶ μουσικὴν καὶ χρῆσιν ὅπλων Ἑλληνι-
6 κῶν[1] ἐκδιδασκομένους μέχρις ἥβης. ἐπεὶ δὲ ἀφίκοντο πρὸς τοὺς νομιζομένους γονεῖς συμβῆναι τὴν
διαφορὰν αὐτοῖς πρὸς τοὺς Νεμέτορος βουκόλους
περὶ τῶν συννόμων χωρίων· ἐκ δὲ τούτου πληγὰς
αὐτοῖς δόντας ὡς αὐτοὺς ἀπελάσαι τὰς ἀγέλας,
ποιῆσαι δὲ ταῦτα τῇ γνώμῃ τοῦ Νεμέτορος, ἵν'
ἀρχὴ γένοιτο ἐγκλημάτων καὶ ἅμα παρουσίας εἰς
7 τὴν πόλιν τῷ νομευτικῷ πλήθει πρόφασις. ὡς δὲ
ταῦτ' ἐγένετο Νεμέτορα μὲν Ἀμολίου καταβοᾶν,
ὡς δεινὰ πάσχοι διαρπαζόμενος ὑπὸ τῶν ἐκείνου
βουκόλων, καὶ ἀξιοῦν εἰ μηδενὸς αἴτιός[2] ἐστι παραδοῦναι τὸν βουφορβὸν[3] αὐτῷ καὶ τοὺς υἱοὺς ἐπὶ
δίκῃ· Ἀμόλιον δὲ ἀπολύσασθαι βουλόμενον τὴν
αἰτίαν τούς τε αἰτηθέντας καὶ τοὺς ἄλλους ἅπαντας,
ὅσοι παρεῖναι τοῖς γενομένοις εἶχον αἰτίαν, ἥκειν
8 κελεύειν δίκας ὑφέξοντας τῷ Νεμέτορι. πολλῶν δὲ

---

[1] ἑλληνικῶν B : ἑλληνικὴν R.
[2] αἴτιός Kiessling : αἴτιος ἐκείνου A, αἴτιος τῶν ἐκείνου B.

to women who prostitute themselves for gain ; but
they are now called by a more respectable name,
hetaerae or " companions." But some who were
ignorant of this invented the myth of the she-wolf,
this animal being called in the Latin tongue *lupa*.
The story continues that after the children were
weaned they were sent by those who were rearing
them to Gabii, a town not far from the Palatine
hill, to be instructed in Greek learning ; and there
they were brought up by some personal friends of
Faustulus, being taught letters, music, and the
use of Greek arms until they grew to manhood.
After their return to their supposed parents the
quarrel arose between them and Numitor's herdsmen concerning their common pastures ; thereupon
they beat Numitor's men so that these drove away
their cattle, doing this by Numitor's direction, to
the intent that it might serve as a basis for his complaints and at the same time as an excuse for the
crowd of herdsmen to come to town.   When this had
been brought about, Numitor raised a clamour
against Amulius, declaring that he was treated
outrageously, being plundered by the herdsmen of
Amulius, and demanding that Amulius, if he was
not responsible for any of this, should deliver up to
him the herdsman and his sons for trial ; and Amulius,
wishing to clear himself of the charge, ordered not
only those who were complained of, but all the rest
who were accused of having been present at the conflict, to come and stand trial before Numitor.   Then,

---

³ Kiessling : συοφορβὸν O.

συνελθόντων ἅμα τοῖς ἐπαιτίοις ἐπὶ τῇ προφάσει τῆς
δίκης φράσαντα τοῖς νεανίσκοις τὸν μητροπάτορα
πᾶσαν τὴν καταλαβοῦσαν αὐτοὺς τύχην καὶ φήσαντα
τιμωρίαν νῦν εἴ ποτε καιρὸν εἶναι λαβεῖν, αὐτίκα
ποιήσασθαι σὺν τῷ νομευτικῷ πλήθει τὴν ἐπίθεσιν.
περὶ μὲν οὖν γενέσεως καὶ τροφῆς τῶν οἰκιστῶν
τῆς Ῥώμης ταῦτα λέγεται.

LXXXV. Τὰ δὲ κατὰ τὴν κτίσιν αὐτὴν γενόμενα
(τοῦτο δρλ ἔτι μοι τὸ μέρος τῆς γραφῆς λείπεται)
νῦν ἔρχομαι διηγησόμενος. ἐπειδὴ γὰρ Ἀμολίου
τελευτήσαντος ἀνενεώσατο τὴν ἀρχὴν ὁ Νεμέτωρ
ὀλίγον ἐπισχὼν χρόνον, ἐν ᾧ τὴν πόλιν ἐκ τῆς πρότερον ἐπεχούσης ἀκοσμίας[1] εἰς τὸν ἀρχαῖον ἐκόσμει
τρόπον, εὐθὺς ἐπενόει τοῖς μειρακίοις ἰδίαν ἀρχὴν
2 κατασκευάσαι ἑτέραν πόλιν οἰκίσας. ἅμα δὲ καὶ τοῦ
πολιτικοῦ πλήθους ἐπίδοσιν εἰς εὐανδρίαν ἐσχηκότος
ἀπαναλῶσαί τι καλῶς ἔχειν ᾤετο, καὶ μάλιστα τὸ
διάφορον αὐτῷ ποτε γενόμενον, ὡς μὴ δι' ὑποψίας
αὐτοὺς ἔχοι. κοινωσάμενος δὲ τοῖς μειρακίοις,
ἐπειδὴ κἀκείνοις ἐδόκει, δίδωσιν αὐτοῖς χωρία μὲν
ὧν ἄρξουσιν, ἔνθα παῖδες ὄντες ἐτράφησαν, ἐκ δὲ
τοῦ λεὼ τόν[2] τε δι' ὑποψίας αὐτῷ γενόμενον, ὃς
ἔμελλε νεωτερισμοῦ εἰσαῦθις ἄρχειν, καὶ εἴ τι
3 ἑκούσιον ἀπαναστῆναι ἐβούλετο. ἦν δὲ ἐν τούτοις
πολὺ μὲν ὥσπερ εἰκὸς ἐν πόλει κινουμένῃ τὸ δημοτικὸν γένος, ἱκανὸν δὲ καὶ τὸ ἀπὸ τοῦ κρατίστου

---

[1] ἀκοσμίας B : ἀνομίας R.   [2] τὸν Kiessling : τὸ O.

when great numbers came to town together with the accused, ostensibly to attend the trial, the grandfather of the youths acquainted them with all the circumstances of their fortune, and telling them that now, if ever, was the time to avenge themselves, he straightway made his attack upon Amulius with the crowd of herdsmen. These, then, are the accounts that are given of the birth and rearing of the founders of Rome.

LXXXV. I[1] am now going to relate the events that happened at the very time of its founding; for this part of my account still remains. When Numitor, upon the death of Amulius, had resumed his rule and had spent a little time in restoring the city from its late disorder to its former orderly state, he presently thought of providing an independent rule for the youths by founding another city. At the same time, the inhabitants being much increased in number, he thought it good policy to get rid of some part of them, particularly of those who had once been his enemies, lest he might have cause to suspect any of his subjects. And having communicated this plan to the youths and gained their approval, he gave them, as a district to rule, the region where they had been brought up in their infancy, and, for subjects, not only that part of the people which he suspected of a design to begin rebellion anew, but also any who were willing to migrate voluntarily. Among these, as is likely to happen when a city sends out a colony, there were great numbers of the common people, but there were also a sufficient number of the prominent men of

[1] For chaps. 85-88 *cf.* Livy i. 6, 3–7, 3.

γνώριμον, ἐκ δὲ τοῦ Τρωικοῦ τὸ εὐγενέστατον δὴ
νομιζόμενον, ἐξ οὗ καὶ γενεαί τινες ἔτι περιῆσαν
εἰς ἐμέ, πεντήκοντα μάλιστ' οἶκοι. ἐχορηγεῖτο δὲ
τοῖς νεανίσκοις καὶ χρήματα καὶ ὅπλα καὶ σῖτος καὶ
ἀνδράποδα καὶ ὑποζύγια ἀχθοφόρα καὶ εἴ τι ἄλλο
4 πόλεως ἦν κατασκευῇ πρόσφορον. ὡς δὲ ἀνέστησαν
ἐκ τῆς Ἄλβας οἱ νεανίσκοι τὸν λεὼν μίξαντες αὐτῷ
τὸν αὐτόθεν, ὅσος ἦν ἐν τῷ Παλλαντίῳ καὶ περὶ τὴν
Σατορνίαν ὑπολιπής, μερίζονται τὸ πλῆθος ἅπαν
διχῇ. τοῦτο δὲ αὐτοῖς δόξαν παρέσχε φιλοτιμίας,
ἵνα θᾶττον ἀνύηται τῇ πρὸς ἀλλήλους ἁμίλλῃ τὰ
ἔργα, αἴτιον δὲ τοῦ μεγίστου κακοῦ, στάσεως,
5 ἐγένετο. οἵ τε γὰρ προσνεμηθέντες αὐτοῖς τὸν
ἑαυτῶν ἡγεμόνα ἑκάτεροι[1] κυδαίνοντες ὡς ἐπιτήδειον
ἁπάντων ἄρχειν ἐπῆρον, αὐτοί τε οὐκέτι μίαν γνώμην ἔχοντες οὐδὲ ἀδελφὰ διανοεῖσθαι ἀξιοῦντες, ὡς
αὐτὸς ἄρξων ἑκάτερος θατέρου, παρώσαντες τὸ
ἴσον τοῦ πλείονος ὠρέγοντο. τέως μὲν οὖν ἀφανῆ
τὰ πλεονεκτήματα αὐτῶν ἦν, ἔπειτα δὲ ἐξερράγη
6 σὺν τοιᾷδε προφάσει. τὸ χωρίον ἔνθα ἔμελλον
ἰδρύσειν τὴν πόλιν οὐ τὸ αὐτὸ ᾑρεῖτο ἑκάτερος.
Ῥωμύλου μὲν γὰρ ἦν γνώμη τὸ Παλλάντιον οἰκίζειν τῶν τε ἄλλων ἕνεκα καὶ τῆς τύχης τοῦ τόπου,
ᾗ τὸ σωθῆναί τε αὐτοῖς καὶ τραφῆναι παρέσχε·
Ῥώμῳ δὲ ἐδόκει τὴν καλουμένην νῦν ἀπ' ἐκείνου
Ῥεμορίαν οἰκίζειν. ἔστι δὲ τὸ χωρίον ἐπιτήδειον

---

[1] Schwartz: ἕκαστοι O, Jacoby.

---

[1] This hill cannot be identified. The name was also

the best class, and of the Trojan element all those
who were esteemed the noblest in birth, some of
whose posterity remained even to my day, consisting
of about fifty families. The youths were supplied
with money, arms and corn, with slaves and beasts
of burden and everything else that was of use in the
building of a city. After they had led their people
out of Alba and intermingled with them the local
population that still remained in Pallantium and
Saturnia, they divided the whole multitude into two
parts. This they did in the hope of arousing a spirit
of emulation, so that through their rivalry with each
other their tasks might be the sooner finished ;
however, it produced the greatest of evils, discord.
For each group, exalting its own leader, extolled
him as the proper person to command them all ;
and the youths themselves, being now no longer
one in mind or feeling it necessary to entertain
brotherly sentiments toward each other, since each
expected to command the other, scorned equality and
craved superiority. For some time their ambitions
were concealed, but later they burst forth on the
occasion which I shall now describe. They did
not both favour the same site for the building of the
city ; for Romulus proposed to settle the Palatine
hill, among other reasons, because of the good fortune
of the place where they had been preserved and
brought up, whereas Remus favoured the place that
is now named after him Remoria.[1] And indeed this
place is very suitable for a city, being a hill not far

given (according to Paulus in his epitome of Festus,
p. 276) to a site on the summit of the Aventine where
Remus was said to have taken the auspices (chap. 86).

ὑποδέξασθαι πόλιν λόφος οὐ πρόσω τοῦ Τεβέριος
κείμενος, ἀπέχων τῆς Ῥώμης ἀμφὶ τοὺς τριάκοντα
σταδίους. ἐκ δὲ τῆς φιλονεικίας ταύτης ἀκοινώνη-
τος εὐθὺς ὑπεδηλοῦτο φιλαρχία. τῷ γὰρ εἴξαντι τὸ
κρατῆσαν ἅπαντα[1] ὁμοίως ἐπιθήσεσθαι ἔμελλεν.

LXXXVI. Χρόνου δέ τινος ἐν τούτῳ διαγενομέ-
νου, ἐπειδὴ οὐδὲν ἐμειοῦτο τῆς[2] στάσεως, δόξαν
ἀμφοῖν τῷ μητροπάτορι ἐπιτρέψαι παρῆσαν εἰς τὴν
Ἄλβαν. ὁ δὲ αὐτοῖς ταῦτα ὑποτίθεται· θεοὺς
ποιήσασθαι δικαστάς, ὁποτέρου χρὴ τὴν ἀποικίαν
λέγεσθαι καὶ τὴν ἡγεμονίαν εἶναι. ταξάμενος δὲ
αὐτοῖς ἡμέραν ἐκέλευσεν ἐξ ἑωθινοῦ καθέζεσθαι
χωρὶς ἀλλήλων, ἐν αἷς ἑκάτεροι ἀξιοῦσιν ἕδραις·
προθύσαντας δὲ τοῖς θεοῖς ἱερὰ τὰ νομιζόμενα
φυλάττειν οἰωνοὺς αἰσίους· ὁποτέρῳ δ᾽ ἂν οἱ
ὄρνιθες προτέρῳ κρείττους γένωνται, τοῦτον ἄρχειν
2 τῆς ἀποικίας. ἀπῇεσαν οἱ νεανίσκοι ταῦτ᾽ ἐπαινέ-
σαντες καὶ κατὰ τὰ συγκείμενα παρῆσαν ἐν τῇ
κυρίᾳ τῆς πράξεως ἡμέρᾳ. ἦν δὲ Ῥωμύλῳ μὲν
οἰωνιστήριον, ἔνθα ἠξίου τὴν ἀποικίαν ἱδρῦσαι, τὸ
Παλλάντιον, Ῥώμῳ δ᾽ ὁ προσεχὴς ἐκείνῳ λόφος
Αὐεντῖνος καλούμενος, ὡς δέ τινες ἱστοροῦσιν ἡ
Ῥεμορία· φυλακή τε ἀμφοῖν παρῆν οὐκ ἐπιτρέ-
3 ψουσα[3] ὅ τι μὴ φανείη λέγειν.[4] ὡς δὲ τὰς προση-
κούσας ἕδρας ἔλαβον ὀλίγον ἐπισχὼν χρόνον ὁ
Ῥωμύλος ὑπὸ σπουδῆς τε καὶ τοῦ πρὸς τὸν ἀδελφὸν φθόνου,[5] ἴσως δὲ καὶ ὁ θεὸς οὕτως ἐνῆγε, πρὶν

---

[1] ἅπαντα Kiessling, εἰς ἅπαντα Jacoby : εἰς πάντα O.
[2] τῆς O : τὸ τῆς Hertlein, Jacoby.

from the Tiber and about thirty stades from Rome. From this rivalry their unsociable love of rule immediately began to disclose itself; for on the one who now yielded the victor would inevitably impose his will on all occasions alike.

LXXXVI. Meanwhile, some time having elapsed and their discord in no degree abating, the two agreed to refer the matter to their grandfather and for that purpose went to Alba. He advised them to leave it to the decision of the gods which of them should give his name to the colony and be its leader. And having appointed for them a day, he ordered them to place themselves early in the morning at a distance from one another, in such stations as each of them should think proper, and after first offering to the gods the customary sacrifices, to watch for auspicious birds; and he ordered that he to whom the more favourable birds first appeared should rule the colony. The youths, approving of this, went away and according to their agreement appeared on the day appointed for the test. Romulus chose for his station the Palatine hill, where he proposed settling the colony, and Remus the Aventine hill adjoining it, or, according to others, Remoria; and a guard attended them both, to prevent their reporting things otherwise than as they appeared. When they had taken their respective stations, Romulus, after a short pause, from eagerness and jealousy of his brother,—though possibly Heaven was thus directing

---

³ οὐκ ἐπιτρέψουσα Kiessling: οὐκ ἔτι ἐπιτρέφουσα (ἐπιστρέφουσα B) O.

⁴ Hertlein, Kayser: λέξειν O, Jacoby.

⁵ ὡς δὲ καὶ ὁ φθόνος after φθόνου deleted by Reiske.

ἢ¹ καὶ ὁτιοῦν σημεῖον θεάσασθαι πέμψας ὡς τὸν
ἀδελφὸν ἀγγέλους ἥκειν ἠξίου διὰ ταχέων, ὡς πρότερος ἰδὼν οἰωνοὺς αἰσίους. ἐν ᾧ δὲ οἱ πεμφθέντες
ὑπ᾽ αὐτοῦ δι᾽ αἰσχύνης ἔχοντες τὴν ἀπάτην οὐ
σπουδῇ ἐχώρουν, τῷ Ῥώμῳ γῦπες ἐπισημαίνουσιν
ἓξ ἀπὸ τῶν δεξιῶν πετόμενοι. καὶ ὁ μὲν ἰδὼν
τοὺς ὄρνιθας περιχαρὴς ἐγένετο, μετ᾽ οὐ πολὺ δὲ
οἱ παρὰ τοῦ Ῥωμύλου πεμφθέντες ἀναστήσαντες
4 αὐτὸν ἄγουσιν ἐπὶ τὸ Παλλάντιον. ἐπεὶ δὲ ἐν τῷ
αὐτῷ ἐγένοντο ἤρετο μὲν τὸν Ῥωμύλον ὁ Ῥῶμος
οὔστινας οἰωνοὺς ἴδοι πρότερος, ὁ δὲ ἐν ἀπόρῳ
γίνεται ὅ τι ἀποκρίναιτο. ἐν δὲ τούτῳ δώδεκα
γῦπες αἴσιοι πετόμενοι ὤφθησαν, οὓς ἰδὼν θαρρεῖ
τε καὶ τῷ Ῥώμῳ δείξας λέγει, " Τί γὰρ ἀξιοῖς τὰ
πάλαι γενόμενα μαθεῖν ; τούσδε γὰρ δή που τοὺς
οἰωνοὺς αὐτὸς ὁρᾷς." ὁ δὲ ἀγανακτεῖ τε καὶ δεινὰ
ποιεῖται, ὡς διηρτημένος ὑπ᾽ αὐτοῦ, τῆς τε ἀποικίας
οὐ μεθήσεσθαι αὐτῷ φησιν.

LXXXVII. Ἀνίσταται δὴ ἐκ τούτου μείζων τῆς
προτέρας ἔρις, ἑκατέρου τὸ πλέον ἔχειν ἀφανῶς
διωκομένου,² τὸ δὲ³ μὴ μεῖον⁴ ἀναφανδὸν ἀπὸ δι-
καιώσεως τοιᾶσδε ἐπισυνάπτοντος. εἰρημένον γὰρ
ἦν αὐτοῖς ὑπὸ τοῦ μητροπάτορος, ὅτῳ ἂν προτέρῳ
κρείττους ὄρνιθες ἐπισημήνωσι, τοῦτον ἄρχειν τῆς
ἀποικίας· γένους δὲ ὀρνίθων ἑνὸς ἀμφοῖν ὀφθέν-
τος ὁ μὲν τῷ πρότερος,⁵ ὁ δὲ τῷ πλείους ἰδεῖν

---

¹ ἢ added by Jacoby.
² διωκομένου Ο: διοικουμένου Schmitz, δικαιουμένου Jacoby,
διανοουμένου Hertlein. Madvig proposed τῷ πλέον ἔχειν ἀφανῶς
διωκομένῳ τὸ μὴ μεῖον . . . ἐπισυνάπτοντος.

him,—even before he saw any omen at all, sent
messengers to his brother desiring him to come
immediately, as if he had been the first to see some
auspicious birds. But while the persons he sent
were proceeding with no great haste, feeling ashamed
of the fraud, six vultures appeared to Remus, flying
from the right; and he, seeing the birds, rejoiced
greatly. And not long afterwards the men sent by
Romulus took him thence and brought him to the
Palatine hill. When they were together, Remus
asked Romulus what birds he had been the first to
see, and Romulus knew not what to answer. But
thereupon twelve auspicious vultures were seen
flying; and upon seeing these he took courage, and
pointing them out to Remus, said: " Why do you
demand to know what happened a long time ago?
For surely you see these birds yourself." But
Remus was indignant and complained bitterly
because he had been deceived by him; and he refused to yield to him his right to the colony.

LXXXVII. Thereupon greater strife arose between
them than before, as each, while secretly striving
for the advantage, was ostensibly willing to accept
equality, for the following reason. Their grandfather,
as I have stated, had ordered that he to whom the
more favourable birds first appeared should rule the
colony; but, as the same kind of birds had been
seen by both, one had the advantage of seeing them
first and the other that of seeing the greater number.

---

³ δὲ D (according to Kiessling), Steph.: om. AB.
⁴ μὴ μεῖον Steph., σημεῖον Schmitz, Sauppe: μνημεῖον A,
μεῖζον B.
⁵ Reiske: προτέρῳ O.

ἐκρατύνετο. συνελάμβανε δὲ αὐτοῖς τῆς φιλονεικίας
καὶ τὸ ἄλλο πλῆθος ἦρξέ τε πολέμου δίχα τῶν
ἡγεμόνων ὁπλισθέν, καὶ γίνεται μάχη καρτερὰ καὶ
2 φόνος ἐξ ἀμφοῖν πολύς. ἐν ταύτῃ φασί τινες τῇ
μάχῃ τὸν Φαυστύλον, ὃς ἐξεθρέψατο τοὺς νεανίσκους,
διαλῦσαι τὴν ἔριν τῶν ἀδελφῶν βουλόμενον, ὡς οὐδὲν
οἷός τ᾽ ἦν ἀνύσαι, εἰς μέσους ὤσασθαι τοὺς μαχο-
μένους ἄνοπλον θανάτου τοῦ ταχίστου τυχεῖν προ-
θυμούμενον, ὅπερ [1] ἐγένετο. τινὲς δὲ καὶ τὸν λέοντα
τὸν λίθινον, ὃς ἔκειτο τῆς ἀγορᾶς τῆς τῶν Ῥωμαίων
ἐν τῷ κρατίστῳ χωρίῳ παρὰ τοῖς ἐμβόλοις, ἐπὶ τῷ
σώματι τοῦ Φαυστύλου τεθῆναί φασιν, ἔνθα ἔπεσεν
3 ὑπὸ τῶν εὑρόντων ταφέντος. ἀποθανόντος δ᾽ ἐν τῇ
μάχῃ Ῥώμου νίκην οἰκτίστην ὁ Ῥωμύλος ἀπό τε
τοῦ ἀδελφοῦ καὶ πολιτικῆς ἀλληλοκτονίας ἀνελό-
μενος τὸν μὲν Ῥῶμον ἐν τῇ Ῥεμορίᾳ θάπτει, ἐπειδὴ
καὶ ζῶν τοῦ χωρίου τῆς κτίσεως περιείχετο, αὐτὸς
δὲ ὑπὸ [2] λύπης τε καὶ μετανοίας τῶν πεπραγμένων
παρεὶς ἑαυτὸν εἰς ἀπόγνωσιν τοῦ βίου τρέπεται. τῆς
δὲ Λαυρεντίας, ἣ νεογνοὺς παραλαβοῦσα ἐξεθρέψατο
καὶ μητρὸς οὐχ ἧττον ἠσπάζετο, δεομένης καὶ παρη-
γορούσης, ταύτῃ πειθόμενος ἀνίσταται · συναγαγὼν
δὲ τοὺς Λατίνους, ὅσοι μὴ κατὰ τὴν μάχην διεφθάρησαν,[3] ὀλίγῳ πλείους ὄντας τρισχιλίων ἐκ πάνυ
πολλοῦ κατ᾽ ἀρχὰς γενομένου πλήθους, ὅτε τὴν
ἀποικίαν ἔστελλε, πολίζει τὸ Παλλάντιον.
4 Ὁ μὲν οὖν πιθανώτατος τῶν λόγων περὶ τῆς Ῥώμου
τελευτῆς οὗτος εἶναί μοι δοκεῖ. λεγέσθω δ᾽ ὅμως

[1] ὅπερ O: ὅπερ καὶ Cobet, Jacoby.

The rest of the people also espoused their quarrel, and arming themselves without orders from their leaders, began war ; and a sharp battle ensued in which many were slain on both sides. In the course of this battle, as some say, Faustulus, who had brought up the youths, wishing to put an end to the strife of the brothers and being unable to do so, threw himself unarmed into the midst of the combatants, seeking the speediest death, which fell out accordingly. Some say also that the stone lion which stood in the principal part of the Forum near the rostra was placed over the body of Faustulus, who was buried by those who found him in the place where he fell. Remus having been slain in this action, Romulus, who had gained a most melancholy victory through the death of his brother and the mutual slaughter of citizens, buried Remus at Remoria, since when alive he had clung to it as the site for the new city. As for himself, in his grief and repentance for what had happened, he became dejected and lost all desire for life. But when Laurentia, who had received the babes when newly born and brought them up and loved them no less than a mother, entreated and comforted him, he listened to her and rose up, and gathering together the Latins who had not been slain in the battle (they were now little more than three thousand out of a very great multitude at first, when he led out the colony), he built a city on the Palatine hill.

The account I have given seems to me the most probable of the stories about the death of Remus.

καὶ εἴ τις ἑτέρως ἔχων παραδέδοται.[1] φασὶ δή
τινες συγχωρήσαντ' αὐτὸν τῷ Ῥωμύλῳ τὴν ἡγεμονίαν, ἀχθόμενον δὲ καὶ δι' ὀργῆς ἔχοντα τὴν
ἀπάτην, ἐπειδὴ κατεσκευάσθη τὸ τεῖχος φλαῦρον
ἀποδεῖξαι τὸ ἔρυμα βουλόμενον, " Ἀλλὰ τοῦτό γ',"
εἰπεῖν, " οὐ χαλεπῶς ἄν τις ὑμῖν ὑπερβαίη πολέμιος,
ὥσπερ ἐγώ·" καὶ αὐτίκα ὑπεραλέσθαι· Κελέριον δέ
τινα τῶν ἐπιβεβηκότων τοῦ τείχους, ὃς ἦν ἐπιστάτης
τῶν ἔργων, " Ἀλλὰ τοῦτόν γε τὸν πολέμιον οὐ
χαλεπῶς ἄν τις ἡμῶν ἀμύναιτο," εἰπόντα, πλῆξαι τῷ
σκαφείῳ κατὰ τῆς κεφαλῆς καὶ αὐτίκα ἀποκτεῖναι·
τὸ μὲν δὴ τέλος τῆς στάσεως τῶν ἀδελφῶν τοιοῦτο
λέγεται γενέσθαι.

LXXXVIII. Ἐπεὶ δὲ οὐδὲν ἔτι ἦν ἐμποδὼν τῷ
κτίσματι προειπὼν ὁ Ῥωμύλος ἡμέραν,[2] ἐν ᾗ τοὺς
θεοὺς ἀρεσάμενος ἔμελλε τὴν ἀρχὴν τῶν ἔργων
ποιήσασθαι, παρασκευασάμενός τε ὅσα εἰς θυσίας
καὶ ὑποδοχὰς τοῦ λεὼ χρησίμως ἕξειν ἔμελλεν, ὡς
ἧκεν ὁ συγκείμενος χρόνος αὐτός τε προθύσας τοῖς
θεοῖς καὶ τοὺς ἄλλους κελεύσας κατὰ δύναμιν τὸ
αὐτὸ δρᾶν ὄρνιθας μὲν πρῶτον αἰσίους[3] λαμβάνει·
μετὰ δὲ τοῦτο πυρκαϊὰς πρὸ τῶν σκηνῶν γενέσθαι
κελεύσας ἐξάγει τὸν λεὼν τὰς φλόγας ὑπερθρώσκοντα
2 τῆς ὁσιώσεως τῶν μιασμάτων ἕνεκα. ἐπεὶ δὲ πᾶν,
ὅσον ἦν ἐκ λογισμοῦ θεοῖς φίλον, ᾤετο πεπρᾶχθαι,
καλέσας ἅπαντας εἰς τὸν ἀποδειχθέντα τόπον περι-
γράφει τετράγωνον σχῆμα τῷ λόφῳ, βοὸς ἄρρενος

---

[1] Kiessling: παραδίδοται O.
[2] ἡμέραν added by Reiske.
[3] αἰσίους Kiessling: ἀετοὺς O.

However, if any has been handed down that differs from this, let that also be related. Some, indeed, say that Remus yielded the leadership to Romulus, though not without resentment and anger at the fraud, but that after the wall was built, wishing to demonstrate the weakness of the fortification, he cried, " Well, as for this wall, one of your enemies could as easily cross it as I do," and immediately leaped over it. Thereupon Celer, one of the men standing on the wall, who was overseer of the work, said, " Well, as for this enemy, one of us could easily punish him," and striking him on the head with a mattock, he killed him then and there. Such is said to have been the outcome of the quarrel between the brothers.

LXXXVIII. When no obstacle now remained to the building of the city, Romulus appointed a day on which he planned to begin the work, after first propitiating the gods. And having prepared everything that would be required for the sacrifices and for the entertainment of the people, when the appointed time came, he himself first offered sacrifice to the gods and ordered all the rest to do the same according to their abilities. He then in the first place took the omens, which were favourable. After that, having commanded fires to be lighted before the tents, he caused the people to come out and leap over the flames in order to expiate their guilt. When he thought everything had been done which he conceived to be acceptable to the gods, he called all the people to the appointed place and described a quadrangular figure about the hill, tracing with a plough drawn by a bull and a cow yoked

ἅμα θηλείᾳ ζευχθέντος ὑπ' ἄροτρον ἑλκύσας αὔλακα
διηνεκῆ τὴν μέλλουσαν ὑποδέξεσθαι τὸ τεῖχος· ἐξ
οὗ Ῥωμαίοις τὸ ἔθος τοῦτο τῆς περιαρόσεως τῶν
χωρίων ἐν οἰκισμοῖς πόλεων παραμένει. ἐργασά-
μενος δὲ ταῦτα καὶ τῶν βοῶν ἑκατέρους ἱερεύσας
ἄλλων τε πολλῶν θυμάτων καταρξάμενος ἐφίστησι
3 τοῖς ἔργοις τὸν λεών. ταύτην ἔτι καὶ εἰς ἐμὲ τὴν
ἡμέραν Ῥωμαίων ἡ πόλις ἑορτῶν οὐδεμιᾶς ἥττονα
τιθεμένη καθ' ἕκαστον ἔτος ἄγει, καλοῦσι δὲ[1]
Παρίλια.[2] θύουσι δ' ἐν αὐτῇ περὶ γονῆς τετρα-
πόδων οἱ γεωργοὶ καὶ νομεῖς θυσίαν χαριστήριον
ἔαρος ἀρχομένου. πότερον δὲ παλαίτερον ἔτι τὴν
ἡμέραν ταύτην ἐν εὐπαθείαις διάγοντες[3] ἐπιτηδειο-
τάτην οἰκισμῷ πόλεως ἐνόμισαν, ἢ τοῦ κτίσματος
ἄρξασαν ἱερὰν ἐποιήσαντο καὶ θεοὺς ἐν αὐτῇ τοὺς
ποιμέσι φίλους γεραίρειν ᾤοντο δεῖν, οὐκ ἔχω βεβαίως εἰπεῖν.

LXXXIX. Ἃ μὲν οὖν ἐμοὶ δύναμις ἐγένετο σὺν
πολλῇ φροντίδι ἀνευρεῖν Ἑλλήνων τε καὶ Ῥωμαίων
συχνὰς ἀναλεξαμένῳ γραφὰς ὑπὲρ τοῦ τῶν Ῥωμαίων
γένους, τοιάδ' ἐστίν. ὥστε θαρρῶν ἤδη τις ἀπο-
φαινέσθω, πολλὰ χαίρειν φράσας τοῖς βαρβάρων καὶ
δραπετῶν καὶ ἀνεστίων ἀνθρώπων καταφυγὴν τὴν
Ῥώμην ποιοῦσιν, Ἑλλάδα πόλιν αὐτήν, ἀποδεικνύ-

---

[1] καλοῦσι δὲ Bb, κάλους ABa ; καλοῦσα Steph.
[2] Sylburg : παρεντάλια O.
[3] διάγοντες added by Sintenis.

together a continuous furrow designed to receive the foundation of the wall ; and from that time this custom has continued among the Romans of plough-ing a furrow round the site where they plan to build a city. After he had done this and sacrificed the bull and the cow and also performed the initial rites over many other victims, he set the people to work. This day the Romans celebrate every year even down to my time as one of their greatest festivals and call it the Parilia.[1] On this day, which comes in the beginning of spring, the husbandmen and herdsmen offer up a sacrifice of thanksgiving for the increase of their cattle. But whether they had celebrated this day in even earlier times as a day of rejoicing and for that reason looked upon it as the most suitable for the founding of the city, or whether, because it marked the beginning of the building of the city, they consecrated it and thought they should honour on it the gods who are propitious to shepherds, I cannot say for certain.

LXXXIX. Such, then, are the facts concerning the origin of the Romans which I have been able to discover after reading very diligently many works written by both Greek and Roman authors. Hence, from now on let the reader forever renounce the views of those who make Rome a retreat of barbarians, fugitives and vagabonds, and let him confidently affirm it to be a Greek city,—which will be easy when

---

[1] The Parilia, or more properly Palilia, was an ancient festival celebrated by the shepherds and herdsmen on the 21st of April in honour of the divinity Pales. See the de-tailed description of its observance in Ovid, *Fasti* iv. 721 ff., with Sir James Frazer's note on that passage (vol. iii. pp. 336-42; condensed in his *L.C.L.* edition, pp. 411-13).

μένος μὲν[1] κοινοτάτην τε πόλεων καὶ φιλανθρωπο-
τάτην, ἐνθυμούμενος δὲ[2] ὅτι τὸ μὲν τῶν Ἀβοριγίνων
2 φῦλον Οἰνωτρικὸν ἦν, τοῦτο δὲ Ἀρκαδικόν · μεμνημένος δὲ τῶν συνοικησάντων αὐτοῖς Πελασγῶν, οἳ
Θετταλίαν καταλιπόντες Ἀργεῖοι τὸ γένος ὄντες εἰς
Ἰταλίαν ἀφίκοντο · Εὐάνδρου τε αὖ καὶ Ἀρκάδων
ἀφίξεως, οἳ περὶ τὸ Παλλάντιον ᾤκησαν, Ἀβοριγίνων
αὐτοῖς παρασχόντων τὸ χωρίον · ἔτι δὲ Πελοποννησίων τῶν σὺν Ἡρακλεῖ παραγενομένων, οἳ
κατῴκησαν ἐπὶ τοῦ Σατορνίου · τελευταῖον δὲ τῶν
ἀπαναστάντων ἐκ τῆς Τρωάδος καὶ συγκερασθέντων
τοῖς προτέροις. τούτων γὰρ ἂν οὐδὲν εὕροι τῶν
3 ἐθνῶν οὔτε ἀρχαιότερον οὔτε Ἑλληνικώτερον. αἱ
δὲ τῶν βαρβάρων ἐπιμιξίαι, δι' ἃς ἡ πόλις πολλὰ
τῶν ἀρχαίων ἐπιτηδευμάτων ἀπέμαθε, σὺν χρόνῳ
ἐγένοντο. καὶ θαῦμα μὲν τοῦτο πολλοῖς ἂν εἶναι
δόξειε τὰ εἰκότα λογισαμένοις, πῶς οὐχ ἅπασα
ἐξεβαρβαρώθη Ὀπικούς τε ὑποδεξαμένη καὶ Μαρ-
σοὺς καὶ Σαυνίτας καὶ Τυρρηνοὺς καὶ Βρεττίους
Ὀμβρικῶν τε καὶ Λιγύων καὶ Ἰβήρων καὶ Κελτῶν
συχνὰς μυριάδας ἄλλα τε πρὸς τοῖς εἰρημένοις ἔθνη,
τὰ μὲν ἐξ αὐτῆς Ἰταλίας, τὰ δ' ἐξ ἑτέρων ἀφιγμένα
τόπων, μυρία ὅσα οὔτε ὁμόγλωττα οὔτε ὁμοδί-
αιτα, ὧν[3] καὶ βίους σύγκλυδας ἀναταραχθέντας ἐκ
τοσαύτης διαφωνίας πολλὰ τοῦ παλαιοῦ κόσμου
4 τῆς πόλεως νεοχμῶσαι εἰκὸς ἦν · ἐπεὶ ἄλλοι γε
συχνοὶ ἐν βαρβάροις οἰκοῦντες ὀλίγου χρόνου

---

[1] μὲν added by Reiske. [2] δὲ added by Reiske.
[3] After ὧν the MSS. have οὔτε φωνὰς οὔτε δίαιταν, deleted
by Ritschl.

he shows that it is at once the most hospitable and friendly of all cities, and when he bears in mind that the Aborigines were Oenotrians, and these in turn Arcadians, and remembers those who joined with them in their settlement, the Pelasgians who were Argives by descent and came into Italy from Thessaly; and recalls, moreover, the arrival of Evander and of the Arcadians, who settled round the Palatine hill, after the Aborigines had granted the place to them; and also the Peloponnesians, who, coming along with Hercules, settled upon the Saturnian hill; and, last of all, those who left the Troad and were intermixed with the earlier settlers. For one will find no nation that is more ancient or more Greek than these. But the admixtures of the barbarians with the Romans, by which the city forgot many of its ancient institutions, happened at a later time. And it may well seem a cause of wonder to many who reflect on the natural course of events that Rome did not become entirely barbarized after receiving the Opicans, the Marsians, the Samnites, the Tyrrhenians, the Bruttians and many thousands of Umbrians, Ligurians, Iberians and Gauls, besides innumerable other nations, some of whom came from Italy itself and some from other regions and differed from one another both in their language and habits; for their very ways of life, diverse as they were and thrown into turmoil by such dissonance, might have been expected to cause many innovations in the ancient order of the city. For many others by living among barbarians have in a short time forgotten all their

διελθόντος ἅπαν τὸ Ἑλληνικὸν ἀπέμαθον, ὡς μήτε
φωνὴν Ἑλλάδα φθέγγεσθαι μήτε ἐπιτηδεύμασιν
Ἑλλήνων [1] χρῆσθαι, μήτε θεοὺς τοὺς αὐτοὺς νομίζειν, μήτε νόμους τοὺς ἐπιεικεῖς, ᾧ μάλιστα διαλ-
λάσσει φύσις Ἑλλὰς βαρβάρου, μήτε τῶν ἄλλων
συμβολαίων μηδ᾽ ὁτιοῦν.[2] ἀποχρῶσι δὲ τὸν λόγον
τόνδε[3] Ἀχαιῶν οἱ περὶ τὸν Πόντον ᾠκημένοι τεκμη-
ριῶσαι, Ἠλεῖοι [4] μὲν ἐκ τοῦ Ἑλληνικωτάτου γενόμενοι, βαρβάρων δὲ συμπάντων νῦν [5] ὄντες [6] ἀγριώ-
τατοι.

XC. Ῥωμαῖοι δὲ φωνὴν μὲν οὔτ᾽ ἄκρως [7] βάρβαρον
οὔτ᾽ ἀπηρτισμένως Ἑλλάδα φθέγγονται, μικτὴν δέ
τινα ἐξ ἀμφοῖν, ἧς ἐστιν ἡ πλείων Αἰολίς, τοῦτο
μόνον ἀπολαύσαντες ἐκ τῶν πολλῶν ἐπιμιξιῶν, τὸ
μὴ πᾶσι τοῖς φθόγγοις ὀρθοεπεῖν, τὰ δὲ ἄλλα ὁπόσα
γένους Ἑλληνικοῦ μηνύματ᾽ ἐστὶν [8] ὡς οὐχ ἕτεροί
τινες τῶν ἀποικησάντων διασῴζοντες, οὐ νῦν πρῶτον
ἀρξάμενοι πρὸς φιλίαν ζῆν, ἡνίκα τὴν τύχην πολλὴν
καὶ ἀγαθὴν ῥέουσαν διδάσκαλον ἔχουσι τῶν καλῶν

---

[1] ἑλλήνων B: ἑλλήνων ἔτι R.
[2] ὁτιοῦν Steph.[2]: ὅτι εἰσὶν O.
[3] ὡς ἀληθῆ εἶναι after τόνδε deleted by Cobet.
[4] Kiessling: ἠλείων Bb, Jacoby, ἤλων Ba (Kiessling reports ἠλοῖ for B), ὅλων A; φύλων Sintenis, πάλαι Urlichs.
[5] νῦν O: τῶν νῦν Meutzner, Jacoby.
[6] Sylburg: ὄντων O.
[7] Reiske: ἄκραν O.
[8] μηνύματ᾽ ἐστὶν Jacoby: μήνυμά ἐστιν A, ἐστὶν μήνυμα Ba.

---

[1] These Asiatic Achaeans were a barbarian people of the
Caucasus, whose name was made to coincide with that of
the Greek Achaeans; hence the belief arose that they were

Greek heritage, so that they neither speak the Greek
language nor observe the customs of the Greeks nor
acknowledge the same gods nor have the same equi-
table laws (by which most of all the spirit of the
Greeks differs from that of the barbarians) nor agree
with them in anything else whatever that relates
to the ordinary intercourse of life. Those Achaeans
who are settled near the Euxine sea are a sufficient
proof of my contention; for, though originally Eleans,
of a nation the most Greek of any, they are now the
most savage of all barbarians.[1]

XC. The language spoken by the Romans is
neither utterly barbarous nor absolutely Greek, but
a mixture, as it were, of both, the greater part of
which is Aeolic[2]; and the only disadvantage they
have experienced from their intermingling with
these various nations is that they do not pronounce
all their sounds properly. But all other indications
of a Greek origin they preserve beyond any other
colonists. For it is not merely recently, since they
have enjoyed the full tide of good fortune to instruct
them in the amenities of life, that they have begun
to live humanely; nor is it merely since they first

an offshoot of the latter. Strabo connected them either
with the Boeotian Orchomenus (ix. 2, 42) or with Phthiotis
(xi. 2, 12); other writers do not go into the same detail.
The name " Eleans " in the text must be regarded as very
uncertain; see the critical note.

[2] Dionysius is probably thinking particularly of the
letter digamma (*cf.* p. 65, n. 1) which Quintilian (i. 4, 8;
i. 7, 26) calls the Aeolic letter, and the preservation in
Aeolic, as well as Doric, of the original $\bar{a}$, as in $\phi\acute{a}\mu a$ (Lat.
$f\bar{a}ma$), $\mu\acute{a}\tau\eta\rho$ (*māter*), as contrasted with the Ionic $\phi\acute{\eta}\mu\eta$, $\mu\acute{\eta}\tau\eta\rho$.
Quintilian, too, regards the Aeolic dialect as being closest
to Latin (i. 6, 31).

οὐδ' ἀφ' οὗ πρῶτον ὠρέχθησαν τῆς διαποντίου τὴν
Καρχηδονίων καὶ Μακεδόνων ἀρχὴν καταλύσαντες,
ἀλλ' ἐκ παντὸς οὗ συνῳκίσθησαν χρόνου βίον ῞Ελ-
ληνα ζῶντες καὶ οὐδὲν ἐκπρεπέστερον ἐπιτηδεύοντες
2 πρὸς ἀρετὴν νῦν ἢ πρότερον. μυρία δ' εἰς τοῦτο
λέγειν ἔχων καὶ πολλοῖς τεκμηρίοις χρῆσθαι δυνά-
μενος ἀνδρῶν τε μαρτυρίας φέρειν οὐκ ἀξίων
ἀπιστεῖσθαι, πάντα ἀναβάλλομαι ταῦτα εἰς τὸν
περὶ τῆς πολιτείας αὐτῶν συγγραφησόμενον λόγον.
νυνὶ δὲ ἐπὶ τὴν ἑξῆς διήγησιν τρέψομαι τὴν ἀνα-
κεφαλαίωσιν τῶν ἐν ταύτῃ δεδηλωμένων τῇ βίβλῳ
τῆς ἐχομένης γραφῆς ποιησάμενος ἀρχήν.

aimed at the conquest of countries lying beyond
the sea, after overthrowing the Carthaginian and
Macedonian empires, but rather from the time
when they first joined in founding the city, that
they have lived like Greeks ; and they do not
attempt anything more illustrious in the pursuit
of virtue now than formerly. I have innumerable
things to say upon this subject and can adduce many
arguments and present the testimony of credible
authors ; but I reserve all this for the account I
propose to write of their government.[1] I shall now
resume the thread of my narrative, after prefacing
to the following Book a recapitulation of what is
contained in this.

[1] See especially vii. 70 ff., where Dionysius reminds the
reader of the promise made here. As contrasted with
Book I, which deals with the origin of the Romans. all
the rest of the work could be thought of as an account of
their government.

ΔΙΟΝΥΣΙΟΥ

ΑΛΙΚΑΡΝΑΣΕΩΣ

ΡΩΜΑΙΚΗΣ ΑΡΧΑΙΟΛΟΓΙΑΣ

ΛΟΓΟΣ ΔΕΥΤΕΡΟΣ

Ἡ Ῥωμαίων πόλις ἵδρυται μὲν ἐν τοῖς ἑσπερίοις μέρεσι τῆς Ἰταλίας περὶ ποταμὸν Τέβεριν, ὃς κατὰ μέσην μάλιστα τὴν ἀκτὴν ἐκδίδωσιν, ἀπέχουσα τῆς Τυρρηνικῆς θαλάττης ἑκατὸν εἴκοσι σταδίους. οἱ δὲ κατασχόντες αὐτὴν πρῶτοι τῶν μνημονευομένων βάρβαροί τινες ἦσαν αὐτόχθονες Σικελοὶ λεγόμενοι πολλὰ καὶ ἄλλα τῆς Ἰταλίας χωρία κατασχόντες, ὧν οὐκ ὀλίγα διέμεινεν οὐδ' ἀφανῆ μνημεῖα μέχρι τῶν καθ' ἡμᾶς χρόνων, ἐν οἷς καὶ τόπων τινῶν ὀνόματα Σικελικὰ λεγόμενα, μηνύοντα τὴν πάλαι ποτὲ αὐτῶν
2 ἐνοίκησιν. τούτους ἐκβαλόντες Ἀβοριγῖνες αὐτοὶ κατέσχον τὸν τόπον Οἰνώτρων ὄντες ἀπόγονοι τῶν κατοικούντων τὴν ἀπὸ Τάραντος ἄχρι Ποσειδωνίας παράλιον. ἱερά τις αὕτη νεότης καθοσιωθεῖσα θεοῖς κατὰ τὸν ἐπιχώριον νόμον ὑπὸ τῶν πατέρων ἀποσταλῆναι λέγεται χώραν οἰκήσουσα τὴν ὑπὸ τοῦ δαιμονίου σφίσι δοθησομένην. τὸ δὲ τῶν Οἰνώτρων γένος Ἀρκαδικὸν ἦν ἐκ τῆς τότε μὲν καλουμένης

312

THE ROMAN ANTIQUITIES

OF

DIONYSIUS OF HALICARNASSUS

BOOK II

The city of Rome is situated in the western part
of Italy near the river Tiber, which empties into
the Tyrrhenian sea about midway along the coast ;
from the sea the city is distant one hundred and
twenty stades. Its first known occupants were
certain barbarians, natives of the country, called
Sicels, who also occupied many other parts of Italy
and of whom not a few distinct memorials are left
even to our times ; among other things there are
even some names of places said to be Sicel names,
which show that this people formerly dwelt in the
land. They were driven out by the Aborigines,
who occupied the place in their turn ; these were
descendants of the Oenotrians who inhabited the
seacoast from Tarentum to Posidonia. They were
a band of holy youths consecrated to the gods
according to their local custom and sent out by
their parents, it is said, to inhabit the country which
Heaven should give them. The Oenotrians were an
Arcadian tribe who had of their own accord left

Λυκαονίας, νῦν δὲ Ἀρκαδίας, ἑκουσίως ἐξελθὸν
ἐπὶ γῆς κτῆσιν ἀμείνονος ἡγουμένου τῆς ἀποικίας
Οἰνώτρου τοῦ Λυκάονος, ἐφ᾽ οὗ τὴν ἐπίκλησιν τὸ
3 ἔθνος ἔλαβεν. Ἀβοριγίνων δὲ κατεχόντων τὰ χωρία
πρῶτοι μὲν αὐτοῖς γίνονται σύνοικοι Πελασγοὶ
πλάνητες ἐκ τῆς τότε μὲν καλουμένης Αἱμονίας,
νῦν δὲ Θετταλίας, ἐν ᾗ χρόνον τινὰ ᾤκησαν· μετὰ
δὲ τοὺς Πελασγοὺς Ἀρκάδες ἐκ Παλλαντίου πόλεως
ἐξελθόντες Εὔανδρον ἡγεμόνα ποιησάμενοι τῆς
ἀποικίας Ἑρμοῦ καὶ νύμφης Θέμιδος υἱόν, οἳ πρὸς
ἑνὶ τῶν ἑπτὰ λόφων πολίζονται ὃς ἐν μέσῳ μάλιστα
κεῖται τῆς Ῥώμης, Παλλάντιον ὀνομάσαντες τὸ
4 χωρίον ἐπὶ τῆς ἐν Ἀρκαδίᾳ πατρίδος. χρόνοις δ᾽
οὐ πολλοῖς ὕστερον Ἡρακλέους καταχθέντος εἰς
Ἰταλίαν, ὅτε τὴν στρατιὰν ἐξ Ἐρυθείας οἴκαδε
ἀπήγαγε, μοῖρά τις ὑπολειφθεῖσα τῆς σὺν αὐτῷ
δυνάμεως Ἑλληνικὴ πλησίον ἱδρύεται τοῦ Παλλαντίου, πρὸς ἑτέρῳ τῶν ἐμπεπολισμένων τῇ πόλει [1]
λόφων, ὃς τότε μὲν ὑπὸ τῶν ἐπιχωρίων Σατόρνιος
ἐλέγετο, νῦν δὲ Καπιτωλῖνος ὑπὸ Ῥωμαίων· Ἐπειοὶ
οἱ πλείους τούτων [2] ἦσαν ἐκ πόλεως Ἤλιδος ἐξανα-
στάντες διαπεπορθημένης αὐτοῖς τῆς πατρίδος ὑφ᾽
Ἡρακλέους.

II. Γενεᾷ δ᾽ ἑκκαιδεκάτῃ μετὰ τὸν Τρωικὸν
πόλεμον Ἀλβανοὶ συνοικίζουσιν ἄμφω τὰ χωρία
ταῦτα τείχει περιλαβόντες καὶ τάφρῳ. τέως δὲ ἦν
αὔλια βουφορβίων τε καὶ ποιμνίων [3] καὶ τῶν ἄλλων
καταγωγαὶ βοτήρων ἄφθονον ἀναδιδούσης πόαν τῆς

---

[1] πόλει B : ῥώμῃ R.

the country then called Lycaonia and now Arcadia,
in search of a better land, under the leadership of
Oenotrus, the son of Lycaon, from whom the nation
received its name. While the Aborigines occupied
this region the first who joined with them in their
settlement were the Pelasgians, a wandering people
who came from the country then called Haemonia
and now Thessaly, where they had lived for some
time. After the Pelasgians came the Arcadians
from the city of Pallantium, who had chosen as
leader of their colony Evander, the son of Hermes
and the nymph Themis. These built a town beside
one of the seven hills that stands near the middle
of Rome, calling the place Pallantium, from their
mother-city in Arcadia. Not long afterwards,
when Hercules came into Italy on his return home
with his army from Erytheia, a certain part of his
force, consisting of Greeks, remained behind and
settled near Pallantium, beside another of the hills
that are now inclosed within the city. This was
then called by the inhabitants the Saturnian hill,
but is now called the Capitoline hill by the Romans.
The greater part of these men were Epeans who had
abandoned their city in Elis after their country had
been laid waste by Hercules.

II. In the sixteenth generation after the Trojan
war the Albans united both these places into one
settlement, surrounding them with a wall and a
ditch. For until then there were only folds for
cattle and sheep and quarters of the other herdsmen,

---

² οἱ πλείους τούτων Kiessling, τούτων οἱ πλείους Reiske:
πλείους τούτων B, τούτων πλείους R.

³ ποιμνίων B: ποιμένων A.

αὐτόθι γῆς οὐ μόνον τὴν χειμερινήν ἀλλὰ καὶ τὴν
θερεινόμον διὰ τοὺς ἀναψύχοντάς τε καὶ κατάρδον-
2 τας αὐτὴν ποταμούς. γένος δὲ τὸ τῶν¹ Ἀλβανῶν²
μικτὸν ἦν ἔκ τε Πελασγῶν καὶ Ἀρκάδων καὶ
Ἐπειῶν τῶν ἐξ Ἤλιδος ἐλθόντων,³ τελευταίων δὲ
τῶν μετ᾽ Ἰλίου⁴ ἅλωσιν ἀφικομένων εἰς Ἰταλίαν
Τρώων, οὓς ἦγεν⁵ Αἰνείας ὁ Ἀγχίσου καὶ Ἀφροδίτης.
εἰκὸς δέ τι καὶ βαρβαρικὸν ἐκ τῶν προσοίκων ἢ
παλαιῶν οἰκητόρων ὑπολιπὲς τῷ Ἑλληνικῷ συγ-
καταμιγῆναι.⁶ ὄνομα δὲ κοινὸν οἱ σύμπαντες οὗτοι
Λατῖνοι ἐκλήθησαν ἐπ᾽ ἀνδρὸς δυναστεύσαντος τῶν
τόπων Λατίνου τὰς κατ᾽ ἔθνος⁷ ὀνομασίας ἀφαι-
3 ρεθέντες. ἐτειχίσθη μὲν οὖν ἡ πόλις ὑπὸ τούτων
τῶν ἐθνῶν ἐνιαυτῷ δευτέρῳ καὶ τριακοστῷ⁸ καὶ
τετρακοσιοστῷ μετ᾽ Ἰλίου⁴ ἅλωσιν ἐπὶ τῆς ἑβδόμης
ὀλυμπιάδος. οἱ δὲ ἀγαγόντες τὴν ἀποικίαν ἀδελφοὶ
δίδυμοι τοῦ βασιλείου γένους ἦσαν· Ῥωμύλος αὐτῶν
ὄνομα θατέρῳ, τῷ δ᾽ ἑτέρῳ Ῥῶμος· τὰ μητρόθεν
μὲν ἀπ᾽ Αἰνείου τε καὶ Δαρδανίδαι, πατρὸς δὲ
ἀκρίβειαν μὲν οὐ ῥάδιον εἰπεῖν ἐξ ὅτου φύντες,
πεπίστευνται δὲ ὑπὸ Ῥωμαίων Ἄρεος υἱοὶ γενέσθαι.
4 οὐ μέντοι διέμεινάν γε ἀμφότεροι τῆς ἀποικίας
ἡγεμόνες ὑπὲρ τῆς ἀρχῆς στασιάσαντες. ἀλλ᾽ ὁ
περιλειφθεὶς αὐτῶν Ῥωμύλος ἀπολομένου θατέρου

¹ τῶν added by Grasberger.
² ἀλβανῶν B : ἀλβανὸν R.
³ ἔκ τε Πελασγῶν καὶ Ἀρκάδων καὶ Ἐπειῶν τῶν ἐξ Ἤλιδος
ἐλθόντων Ambrosch: ἔκ τε ἀρκαδίων . . . ἐλθόντων καὶ πελασγῶν
B, ἔκ τε ἀρκάδων καὶ πελασγῶν καὶ τῶν ἐξ ἤλιδος ἐλθόντων
ἐπειῶν R.
⁴ μετὰ ἰλίου O : μετὰ τὴν Ἰλίου Jacoby.

as the land round about yielded plenty of grass, not
only for winter but also for summer pasture, by reason
of the rivers that refresh and water it. The Albans
were a mixed nation composed of Pelasgians, of
Arcadians, of the Epeans who came from Elis, and,
last of all, of the Trojans who came into Italy with
Aeneas, the son of Anchises and Aphroditê, after the
taking of Troy. It is probable that a barbarian
element also from among the neighbouring peoples
or a remnant of the ancient inhabitants of the place
was mixed with the Greek. But all these people,
having lost their tribal designations, came to be
called by one common name, Latins, after Latinus,
who had been king of this country. The walled
city, then, was built by these tribes in the four
hundred and thirty-second year after the taking of
Troy, and in the seventh Olympiad.[1] The leaders
of the colony were twin brothers of the royal family,
Romulus being the name of one and Remus of the
other. On the mother's side they were descended
from Aeneas and were Dardanidae; it is hard
to say with certainty who their father was, but the
Romans believe them to have been the sons of
Mars. However, they did not both continue to be
leaders of the colony, since they quarrelled over the
command; but after one of them had been slain
in the battle that ensued, Romulus, who survived,

[1] 751 B.C.

---

5 οὓς ἦγεν Reiske : ὃς ἦν O.
6 Bücheler : συγκαταλεγῆναι O.
7 κατὰ ἔθνος O : κατὰ τὸ ἔθνος Jacoby, κατὰ ἔθνη Reiske.
8 καὶ τριακοστῷ added by Gelenius.

κατὰ τὴν μάχην οἰκιστὴς γίνεται τῆς πόλεως καὶ τοὔνομα αὐτῇ τῆς ἰδίας κλήσεως ἐπώνυμον τίθεται. ἀριθμὸς δὲ τῶν μετασχόντων αὐτῷ[1] τῆς ἀποικίας ἀπὸ πολλοῦ τοῦ κατ' ἀρχὰς ἐξαποσταλέντος ὀλίγος ἦν ὁ καταλειφθείς, τρισχίλιοι πεζοὶ καὶ ἱππεῖς τριακόσιοι.

III. Ἐπεὶ οὖν ἥ τε τάφρος αὐτοῖς ἐξείργαστο καὶ τὸ ἔρυμα τέλος εἶχεν αἵ τε οἰκήσεις τὰς ἀναγκαίους κατασκευὰς ἀπειλήφεσαν, ἀπῄτει δ' ὁ καιρὸς καὶ περὶ κόσμου πολιτείας ᾧ χρήσονται σκοπεῖν, ἀγορὰν ποιησάμενος αὐτῶν ὁ Ῥωμύλος ὑποθεμένου τοῦ μητροπάτορος καὶ διδάξαντος ἃ χρὴ λέγειν, τὴν μὲν πόλιν ἔφη ταῖς τε δημοσίαις καὶ ταῖς ἰδίαις κατασκευαῖς ὡς νεόκτιστον ἀποχρώντως κεκοσμῆσθαι· ἠξίου δ' ἐνθυμεῖσθαι πάντας ὡς οὐ ταῦτ' ἐστὶ τὰ πλείστου ἄξια ἐν ταῖς πόλεσιν.

2 οὔτε γὰρ ἐν τοῖς ὀθνείοις πολέμοις τὰς βαθείας τάφρους καὶ τὰ[2] ὑψηλὰ ἐρύματα ἱκανὰ εἶναι τοῖς ἔνδον ἀπράγμονα σωτηρίας ὑπόληψιν παρασχεῖν, ἀλλ' ἕν τι μόνον ἐγγυᾶσθαι, τὸ μηθὲν ἐξ ἐπιδρομῆς κακὸν ὑπ' ἐχθρῶν παθεῖν προκαταληφθέντας, οὔθ' ὅταν ἐμφύλιοι ταραχαὶ τὸ κοινὸν κατάσχωσι, τῶν ἰδίων οἴκων καὶ ἐνδιαιτημάτων τὰς καταφυγὰς 3 ὑπάρχειν τινὶ ἀκινδύνους. σχολῆς γὰρ ἀνθρώποις ταῦτα καὶ ῥᾳστώνης βίων[3] εὑρῆσθαι παραμύθια, μεθ' ὧν οὔτε τὸ ἐπιβουλεῦον τῶν[4] πέλας κωλύεσθαι μὴ οὐ πονηρὸν εἶναι οὔτ' ἐν τῷ ἀκινδύνῳ βεβηκέναι θαρρεῖν τὸ ἐπιβουλευόμενον, πόλιν τε οὐδεμίαν πω

became the founder of the city and called it after his own name. The great numbers of which the colony had originally consisted when sent out with him were now reduced to a few, the survivors amounting to three thousand foot and three hundred horse.

III. When, therefore, the ditch was finished, the rampart completed and the necessary work on the houses done, and the situation required that they should consider also what form of government they were going to have, Romulus called an assembly of the people by the advice of his grandfather, who had instructed him what to say, and told them that the city, considering that it was newly built, was sufficiently adorned both with public and private buildings; but he asked them all to bear in mind that these were not the most valuable things in cities. For neither in foreign wars, he said, are deep ditches and high ramparts sufficient to give the inhabitants an undisturbed assurance of their safety, but guarantee one thing only, namely, that they shall suffer no harm through being surprised by an incursion of the enemy ; nor, again, when civil commotions afflict the State, do private houses and dwellings afford anyone a safe retreat. For these have been contrived by men for the enjoyment of leisure and tranquillity in their lives, and with them neither those of their neighbours who plot against them are prevented from doing mischief nor do those who are plotted against feel any confidence that they are free from danger ; and no

---

τούτοις ἐκλαμπρυνθεῖσαν ἐπὶ μήκιστον εὐδαίμονα
γενέσθαι καὶ μεγάλην, οὐδ᾽ αὖ παρὰ τὸ μὴ τυχεῖν
τινὰ κατασκευῆς ἰδίας τε καὶ δημοσίας πολυτελοῦς
κεκωλῦσθαι μεγάλην γενέσθαι καὶ εὐδαίμονα· ἀλλ᾽
ἕτερα εἶναι τὰ σώζοντα καὶ ποιοῦντα μεγάλας ἐκ
4 μικρῶν τὰς πόλεις· ἐν μὲν τοῖς ὀθνείοις πολέμοις
τὸ διὰ τῶν ὅπλων κράτος, τοῦτο δὲ τόλμῃ παραγίνεσθαι καὶ μελέτῃ, ἐν δὲ ταῖς ἐμφυλίοις ταραχαῖς
τὴν τῶν πολιτευομένων ὁμοφροσύνην, ταύτην δὲ
τὸν σώφρονα καὶ δίκαιον ἑκάστου βίον ἀπέφηνεν
5 ἱκανώτατον ὄντα τῷ κοινῷ παρασχεῖν. τοὺς δὴ τὰ
πολέμιά τε ἀσκοῦντας καὶ τῶν¹ ἐπιθυμιῶν κρατοῦν-
τας ἄριστα κοσμεῖν τὰς ἑαυτῶν πατρίδας τείχη τε
ἀνάλωτα τῷ κοινῷ καὶ καταγωγὰς τοῖς ἑαυτῶν
βίοις ἀσφαλεῖς τούτους εἶναι τοὺς παρασκευαζο-
μένους· μαχητὰς δέ γε καὶ δικαίους ἄνδρας καὶ
τὰς ἄλλας ἀρετὰς ἐπιτηδεύοντας τὸ τῆς πολιτείας
σχῆμα ποιεῖν τοῖς φρονίμως αὐτὸ καταστησαμένοις,
μαλθακούς τε αὖ καὶ πλεονέκτας καὶ δούλους αἰσχρῶν ἐπιθυμιῶν τὰ πονηρὰ ἐπιτηδεύματα ἐπιτελεῖν.
6 ἔφη τε παρὰ τῶν πρεσβυτέρων καὶ διὰ πολλῆς
ἱστορίας ἐληλυθότων ἀκούειν, ὅτι πολλαὶ μὲν ἀποικίαι
μεγάλαι καὶ εἰς εὐδαίμονας ἀφικόμεναι τόπους, αἱ
μὲν αὐτίκα διεφθάρησαν εἰς στάσεις ἐμπεσοῦσαι, αἱ
δ᾽ ὀλίγον ἀντισχοῦσαι χρόνον ὑπήκοοι τοῖς πλησιοχώροις ἠναγκάσθησαν γενέσθαι καὶ ἀντὶ κρείττονος
χώρας, ἣν κατέσχον, τὴν χείρονα τύχην διαλλάξασθαι
δοῦλαι ἐξ ἐλευθέρων γενόμεναι· ἕτεραι δ᾽ ὀλιγάν-

¹ τῶν Reiske: τὰ τῶν O.

city that has gained splendour from these adorn-
ments only has ever yet become prosperous and
great for a long period, nor, again, has any city from
a want of magnificence either in public or in private
buildings ever been hindered from becoming great
and prosperous. But it is other things that preserve cities and make them great from small beginnings : in foreign wars, strength in arms, which
is acquired by courage and exercise; and in civil
commotions, unanimity among the citizens, and
this, he showed, could be most effectually achieved
for the commonwealth by the prudent and just
life of each citizen. Those who practise warlike
exercises and at the same time are masters of
their passions are the greatest ornaments to their
country, and these are the men who provide
both the commonwealth with impregnable walls
and themselves in their private lives with safe
refuges ; but men of bravery, justice and the other
virtues are the result of the form of government
when this has been established wisely, and, on the
other hand, men who are cowardly, rapacious and
the slaves of base passions are the product of evil
institutions. He added that he was informed by
men who were older and had wide acquaintance with
history that of many large colonies planted in fruitful
regions some had been immediately destroyed by falling into seditions, and others, after holding out for
a short time, had been forced to become subject to
their neighbours and to exchange their more fruitful
country for a worse fortune, becoming slaves instead
of free men ; while others, few in numbers and

321

θρωποι καὶ εἰς χωρία οὐ πάνυ σπουδαῖα παραγενό-
μεναι ἐλεύθεραι μὲν πρῶτον, ἔπειτα δ' ἑτέρων
ἄρχουσαι διετέλεσαν· καὶ οὔτε ταῖς εὐπραγίαις τῶν
ὀλίγων οὔτε ταῖς δυστυχίαις τῶν πολλῶν ἕτερόν τι
7 ἢ τὸ τῆς πολιτείας σχῆμα ὑπάρχειν αἴτιον. εἰ μὲν
οὖν μία τις ἦν παρὰ πᾶσιν ἀνθρώποις βίου τάξις ἡ
ποιοῦσα εὐδαίμονας τὰς πόλεις, οὐ χαλεπὴν ἂν
γενέσθαι σφίσι τὴν αἵρεσιν αὐτῆς· νῦν δ' ἔφη
πολλὰς πυνθάνεσθαι τὰς κατασκευὰς παρ' Ἕλλησί
τε καὶ βαρβάροις ὑπαρχούσας, τρεῖς δ' ἐξ ἁπασῶν
ἐπαινουμένας μάλιστα ὑπὸ τῶν χρωμένων ἀκούειν,
καὶ τούτων οὐδεμίαν εἶναι τῶν πολιτειῶν εἰλικρινῆ,
προσεῖναι δέ τινας ἑκάστῃ κῆρας συμφύτους, ὥστε
χαλεπὴν αὐτῶν εἶναι τὴν αἵρεσιν. ἠξίου τε αὐτοὺς
βουλευσαμένους ἐπὶ σχολῆς εἰπεῖν εἴτε ὑφ' ἑνὸς ἄρχεσθαι θέλουσιν ἀνδρὸς εἴτε ὑπ' ὀλίγων εἴτε νόμους
καταστησάμενοι πᾶσιν ἀποδοῦναι τὴν τῶν κοινῶν
8 προστασίαν. " Ἐγὼ δ' ὑμῖν," ἔφη, " πρὸς ἣν ἂν [1]
καταστήσησθε πολιτείαν εὐτρεπής, καὶ οὔτε ἄρχειν
ἀπαξιῶ οὔτε ἄρχεσθαι ἀναίνομαι. τιμῶν δέ, ἅς
μοι προσεθήκατε ἡγεμόνα με πρῶτον ἀποδείξαντες
τῆς ἀποικίας, ἔπειτα καὶ τῇ πόλει τὴν ἐπωνυμίαν
ἐπ' ἐμοῦ θέντες, ἅλις ἔχω. ταύτας γὰρ οὔτε
πόλεμος ὑπερόριος οὔτε στάσις ἐμφύλιος οὔτε ὁ
πάντα μαραίνων τὰ καλὰ χρόνος ἀφαιρήσεταί με
οὔτε ἄλλη τύχη παλίγκοτος οὐδεμία· ἀλλὰ καὶ
ζῶντι καὶ τὸν βίον ἐκλιπόντι τούτων ὑπάρξει μοι
τῶν τιμῶν παρὰ πάντα τὸν λοιπὸν αἰῶνα τυγχάνειν."

[1] πρὸς ἣν ἂν Portus : προσῆν ἐὰν A, πρὸς τὸ νέαν B.

settling in places that were by no means desirable,
had continued, in the first place, to be free themselves, and, in the second place, to command others ;
and neither the successes of the smaller colonies nor
the misfortunes of those that were large were due to
any other cause than their form of government. If,
therefore, there had been but one mode of life among
all mankind which made cities prosperous, the choosing of it would not have been difficult for them ; but,
as it was, he understood there were many types of
government among both the Greeks and barbarians,
and out of all of them he heard three especially
commended by those who had lived under them,
and of these systems none was perfect, but each
had some fatal defects inherent in it, so that the
choice among them was difficult. He therefore asked
them to deliberate at leisure and say whether they
would be governed by one man or by a few, or whether
they would establish laws and entrust the protection
of the public interests to the whole body of the people.
" And whichever form of government you establish,"
he said, " I am ready to comply with your desire,
for I neither consider myself unworthy to command
nor refuse to obey. So far as honours are concerned,
I am satisfied with those you have conferred on
me, first, by appointing me leader of the colony, and,
again, by giving my name to the city. For of these
neither a foreign war nor civil dissension nor time,
that destroyer of all that is excellent, nor any other
stroke of hostile fortune can deprive me ; but both
in life and in death these honours will be mine to
enjoy for all time to come."

IV Τοιαῦτα μὲν ὁ Ῥωμύλος ἐκ διδαχῆς τοῦ μητροπάτορος, ὥσπερ ἔφην, ἀπομνημονεύσας ἐν τοῖς πλήθεσιν ἔλεξεν. οἱ δὲ βουλευσάμενοι κατὰ σφᾶς αὐτοὺς ἀποκρίνονται τοιάδε· "Ἡμεῖς πολιτείας μὲν καινῆς οὐδὲν δεόμεθα, τὴν δ᾽ ὑπὸ τῶν πατέρων δοκιμασθεῖσαν εἶναι κρατίστην παραλαβόντες οὐ μετατιθέμεθα, γνώμῃ τε ἑπόμενοι τῶν παλαιοτέρων, οὓς [1] ἀπὸ μείζονος οἰόμεθα φρονήσεως αὐτὴν κατα-στήσασθαι, καὶ τύχῃ ἀρεσκόμενοι οὐ γὰρ τήνδε μεμψαίμεθ᾽ ἂν εἰκότως, ἣ παρέσχεν ἡμῖν βασιλευο-μένοις τὰ μέγιστα τῶν ἐν ἀνθρώποις ἀγαθῶν,
2 ἐλευθερίαν τε καὶ ἄλλων ἀρχήν. περὶ μὲν δὴ πολιτείας ταῦτα ἐγνώκαμεν· τὴν δὲ τιμὴν ταύτην οὐχ ἑτέρῳ τινὶ μᾶλλον ἢ σοὶ προσήκειν ὑπολαμ-βάνομεν τοῦ τε βασιλείου γένους ἕνεκα καὶ ἀρετῆς, μάλιστα δ᾽ ὅτι τῆς ἀποικίας ἡγεμόνι κεχρήμεθά σοι καὶ πολλὴν σύνισμεν δεινότητα, πολλὴν δὲ σοφίαν, οὐ λόγῳ μᾶλλον ἢ ἔργῳ μαθόντες." ταῦτα ὁ Ῥωμύλος ἀκούσας ἀγαπᾶν μὲν ἔφη βασιλείας ἄξιος ὑπ᾽ ἀνθρώπων κριθείς· οὐ μέντοι γε λήψεσθαι τὴν τιμὴν πρότερον, ἐὰν μὴ καὶ τὸ δαιμόνιον ἐπι-θεσπίσῃ δι᾽ οἰωνῶν αἰσίων.

V. Ὡς δὲ κἀκείνοις ἦν βουλομένοις προειπὼν ἡμέραν, ἐν ᾗ διαμαντεύσασθαι περὶ τῆς ἀρχῆς ἔμελλεν, ἐπειδὴ καθῆκεν ὁ χρόνος ἀναστὰς περὶ τὸν ὄρθρον ἐκ τῆς σκηνῆς προῆλθεν· στὰς δὲ ὑπαίθριος ἐν καθαρῷ χωρίῳ καὶ προθύσας ἃ νόμος ἦν εὔχετο Διί τε βασιλεῖ καὶ τοῖς ἄλλοις θεοῖς, οὓς

---

[1] οὓς Steph. : ὡς O.

IV. Such was the speech that Romulus, following the instructions of his grandfather, as I have said, made to the people. And they, having consulted together by themselves, returned this answer: "We have no need of a new form of government and we are not going to change the one which our ancestors approved of as the best and handed down to us. In this we show both a deference for the judgment of our elders, whose superior wisdom we recognize in establishing it, and our own satisfaction with our present condition. For we could not reasonably complain of this form of government, which has afforded us under our kings the greatest of human blessings—liberty and the rule over others. Concerning the form of government, then, this is our decision; and to this honour we conceive none has so good a title as you yourself by reason both of your royal birth and of your merit, but above all because we have had you as the leader of our colony and recognize in you great ability and great wisdom, which we have seen displayed quite as much in your actions as in your words." Romulus, hearing this, said it was a great satisfaction to him to be judged worthy of the kingly office by his fellow men, but that he would not accept the honour until Heaven, too, had given its sanction by favourable omens.

V. And when the people approved, he appointed a day on which he proposed to consult the auspices concerning the sovereignty; and when the time was come, he rose at break of day and went forth from his tent. Then, taking his stand under the open sky in a clear space and first offering the customary sacrifice, he prayed to King Jupiter and to the

ἐποιήσατο τῆς ἀποικίας ἡγεμόνας, εἰ βουλομένοις αὐτοῖς ἐστι βασιλεύεσθαι τὴν πόλιν ὑφ' ἑαυτοῦ, 2 σημεῖα οὐράνια φανῆναι καλά. μετὰ δὲ τὴν εὐχὴν ἀστραπὴ διῆλθεν ἐκ τῶν ἀριστερῶν ἐπὶ τὰ δεξιά. τίθενται δὲ Ῥωμαῖοι τὰς ἐκ τῶν ἀριστερῶν ἐπὶ τὰ δεξιὰ ἀστραπὰς αἰσίους, εἴτε παρὰ Τυρρηνῶν διδαχθέντες, εἴτε πατέρων καθηγησαμένων, κατὰ τοιόνδε τινά, ὡς ἐγὼ πείθομαι, λογισμόν, ὅτι καθέδρα μέν ἐστι καὶ στάσις ἀρίστη τῶν οἰωνοῖς μαντευομένων ἡ βλέπουσα πρὸς ἀνατολάς, ὅθεν ἡλίου τε ἀναφοραὶ γίνονται καὶ σελήνης καὶ ἀστέρων πλανήτων τε καὶ ἀπλανῶν, ἥ τε τοῦ κόσμου περιφορά, δι' ἣν τοτὲ μὲν ὑπὲρ γῆς ἅπαντα τὰ ἐν αὐτῷ γίνεται, τοτὲ δὲ ὑπὸ γῆς, ἐκεῖθεν ἀρξαμένη 3 τὴν ἐγκύκλιον ἀποδίδωσι κίνησιν. τοῖς δὲ πρὸς ἀνατολὰς βλέπουσιν ἀριστερὰ μὲν γίνεται τὰ[1] πρὸς τὴν ἄρκτον ἐπιστρέφοντα μέρη, δεξιὰ δὲ τὰ[1] πρὸς μεσημβρίαν φέροντα· τιμιώτερα δὲ τὰ πρότερα πέφυκεν εἶναι τῶν ὑστέρων. μετεωρίζεται γὰρ ἀπὸ τῶν βορείων μερῶν ὁ τοῦ ἄξονος πόλος, περὶ ὃν ἡ τοῦ κόσμου στροφὴ γίνεται, καὶ τῶν πέντε κύκλων τῶν διεζωκότων τὴν σφαῖραν ὁ καλούμενος ἀρκτικὸς ἀεὶ τῇδε φανερός· ταπεινοῦται δ' ἀπὸ τῶν νοτίων ὁ καλούμενος ἀνταρκτικὸς κύκλος 4 ἀφανὴς κατὰ τοῦτο τὸ μέρος. εἰκὸς δὴ κράτιστα τῶν οὐρανίων καὶ μεταρσίων σημείων ὑπάρχειν, ὅσα ἐκ τοῦ κρατίστου γίνεται μέρους, ἐπειδὴ δὲ τὰ μὲν ἐστραμμένα πρὸς τὰς ἀνατολὰς ἡγεμονικωτέραν μοῖραν ἔχει τῶν προσεσπερίων, αὐτῶν δέ γε τῶν ἀνατολικῶν ὑψηλότερα τὰ βόρεια τῶν νοτίων, ταῦτα

[1] τὰ added by Sylburg.

other gods whom he had chosen for the patrons of
the colony, that, if it was their pleasure he should
be king of the city, some favourable signs might
appear in the sky. After this prayer a flash of
lightning darted across the sky from the left to the
right. Now the Romans look upon the lightning
that passes from the left to the right as a favourable
omen, having been thus instructed either by the
Tyrrhenians or by their own ancestors. Their
reason is, in my opinion, that the best seat and
station for those who take the auspices is that which
looks toward the east, from whence both the sun
and the moon rise as well as the planets and fixed
stars ; and the revolution of the firmament, by which
all things contained in it are sometimes above the
earth and sometimes beneath it, begins its circular
motion thence. Now to those who look toward
the east the parts [1] facing toward the north are on
the left and those extending toward the south are
on the right, and the former are by nature more
honourable than the latter. For in the northern
parts the pole of the axis upon which the firmament
turns is elevated, and of the five zones which girdle
the sphere the one called the arctic zone is always
visible on this side ; whereas in the southern parts
the other zone, called the antarctic, is depressed and
invisible on that side. So it is reasonable to assume
that those signs in the heavens and in mid-air are
the best which appear on the best side ; and since
the parts that are turned toward the east have
preëminence over the western parts, and, of the
eastern parts themselves, the northern are higher than

[1] " Parts " in this chapter means regions of the sky.

5 ἂν εἴη κράτιστα ὡς δέ τινες ἱστοροῦσιν ἐκ παλαιοῦ
τε καὶ πρὶν ἢ παρὰ Τυρρηνῶν μαθεῖν τοῖς Ῥωμαίων
προγόνοις αἴσιοι ἐνομίζοντο αἱ ἐκ τῶν ἀριστερῶν
ἀστραπαί. Ἀσκανίῳ γὰρ τῷ ἐξ Αἰνείου γεγονότι,
καθ᾽ ὃν χρόνον ὑπὸ Τυρρηνῶν, οὓς ἦγε βασιλεὺς
Μεσέντιος, ἐπολεμεῖτο καὶ τειχήρης ἦν, περὶ τὴν
τελευταίαν ἔξοδον, ἣν ἀπεγνωκὼς ἤδη τῶν πραγμάτων ἔμελλε ποιεῖσθαι, μετ᾽ ὀλοφυρμοῦ τόν τε
Δία καὶ τοὺς ἄλλους αἰτουμένῳ θεοὺς αἴσια σημεῖα
δοῦναι τῆς ἐξόδου φασὶν αἰθρίας οὔσης ἐκ τῶν
ἀριστερῶν ἀστράψαι τὸν οὐρανόν. τοῦ δ᾽ ἀγῶνος
ἐκείνου λαβόντος τὸ κράτιστον τέλος διαμεῖναι παρὰ
τοῖς ἐκγόνοις αὐτοῦ νομιζόμενον αἴσιον τόδε τὸ
σημεῖον.

VI. Τότε δ᾽ οὖν ὁ Ῥωμύλος ἐπειδὴ τὰ παρὰ τοῦ
δαιμονίου βέβαια προσέλαβε, συγκαλέσας τὸν δῆμον
εἰς ἐκκλησίαν καὶ τὰ μαντεῖα δηλώσας βασιλεὺς
ἀποδείκνυται πρὸς αὐτῶν καὶ κατεστήσατο ἐν ἔθει
τοῖς μετ᾽ αὐτὸν ἅπασι μήτε βασιλείας μήτε ἀρχὰς
λαμβάνειν, ἐὰν μὴ καὶ τὸ δαιμόνιον αὐτοῖς ἐπι-
θεσπίσῃ, διέμεινέ τε μέχρι πολλοῦ φυλαττόμενον
ὑπὸ Ῥωμαίων τὸ περὶ τοὺς οἰωνισμοὺς νόμιμον, οὐ
μόνον βασιλευομένης τῆς πόλεως, ἀλλὰ καὶ μετὰ
κατάλυσιν τῶν μονάρχων ἐν ὑπάτων καὶ στρατηγῶν
καὶ τῶν ἄλλων τῶν κατὰ νόμους ἀρχόντων αἱρέσει.

2 πέπαυται δ᾽ ἐν τοῖς καθ᾽ ἡμᾶς χρόνοις, πλὴν οἷον
εἰκών τις αὐτοῦ λείπεται τῆς ὁσίας αὐτῆς [1] ἕνεκα
γινομένη ἐπαυλίζονται μὲν γὰρ οἱ τὰς ἀρχὰς
μέλλοντες λαμβάνειν καὶ περὶ τὸν ὄρθρον ἀνιστά-

---

[1] Steph.[2]: ταύτης O.

the southern, the former would seem to be the best.
But some relate that the ancestors of the Romans
from very early times, even before they had learned
it from the Tyrrhenians, looked upon the lightning
that came from the left as a favourable omen. For
they say that when Ascanius, the son of Aeneas, was
warred upon and besieged by the Tyrrhenians led
by their king Mezentius, and was upon the point
of making a final sally out of the town, his situation
being now desperate, he prayed with lamentations
to Jupiter and to the rest of the gods to encourage
this sally with favourable omens, and thereupon
out of a clear sky there appeared a flash of lightning
coming from the left ; and as this battle had the
happiest outcome, this sign continued to be regarded
as favourable by his posterity.

VI. When Romulus, therefore, upon the occasion
mentioned had received the sanction of Heaven also,
he called the people together in assembly; and having
given them an account of the omens, he was chosen
king by them and established it as a custom, to
be observed by all his successors, that none of them
should accept the office of king or any other magistracy until Heaven, too, had given its sanction.
And this custom relating to the auspices long
continued to be observed by the Romans, not only
while the city was ruled by kings, but also, after the
overthrow of the monarchy, in the elections of their
consuls, praetors and other legal magistrates ; but it
has fallen into disuse in our days except as a certain
semblance of it remains merely for form's sake.
For those who are about to assume the magistracies
pass the night out of doors, and rising at break of

μενοι ποιοῦνταί τινας εὐχὰς ὑπαίθριοι, τῶν δὲ
παρόντων τινὲς ὀρνιθοσκόπων μισθὸν ἐκ τοῦ δημοσίου φερόμενοι ἀστραπὴν αὐτοῖς σημαίνειν[1] ἐκ
3 τῶν ἀριστερῶν φασιν τὴν οὐ γενομένην. οἱ δὲ τὸν
ἐκ τῆς φωνῆς οἰωνὸν λαβόντες ἀπέρχονται τὰς
ἀρχὰς παραληψόμενοι οἱ μὲν αὐτὸ τοῦθ' ἱκανὸν
ὑπολαμβάνοντες εἶναι τὸ μηδένα γενέσθαι τῶν
ἐναντιουμένων τε καὶ κωλυόντων οἰωνῶν, οἱ δὲ
καὶ παρὰ τὸ βούλημα τοῦ θεοῦ,[2] ἔστι γὰρ ὅτε
βιαζόμενοι καὶ τὰς ἀρχὰς ἁρπάζοντες μᾶλλον ἢ
4 λαμβάνοντες. δι' οὓς πολλαὶ μὲν ἐν γῇ στρατιαὶ
Ῥωμαίων ἀπώλοντο πανώλεθροι, πολλοὶ δ' ἐν θαλάττῃ στόλοι διεφθάρησαν αὔτανδροι, ἄλλαι τε μεγάλαι καὶ δειναὶ περιπέτειαι[3] τῇ πόλει συνέπεσον αἱ
μὲν ἐν ὀθνείοις πολέμοις, αἱ δὲ κατὰ τὰς ἐμφυλίους
διχοστασίας, ἐμφανεστάτη δὲ καὶ μεγίστη[4] κατὰ[5] τὴν
ἐμὴν ἡλικίαν, ὅτε Λικίννιος Κρᾶσσος ἀνὴρ οὐδενὸς
δεύτερος τῶν καθ' ἑαυτὸν ἡγεμόνων στρατιὰν ἦγεν
ἐπὶ τὸ Πάρθων ἔθνος, ἐναντιουμένου τοῦ δαιμονίου
πολλὰ χαίρειν φράσας τοῖς ἀποτρέπουσι τὴν ἔξοδον
οἰωνοῖς μυρίοις ὅσοις γενομένοις. ἀλλ' ὑπὲρ μὲν
τῆς εἰς τὸ δαιμόνιον ὀλιγωρίας, ᾗ χρῶνταί τινες ἐν
τοῖς καθ' ἡμᾶς χρόνοις, πολὺ ἔργον ἂν εἴη λέγειν.

VII. Ὁ δὲ Ῥωμύλος ἀποδειχθεὶς τοῦτον τὸν
τρόπον ὑπό τε ἀνθρώπων καὶ θεῶν βασιλεὺς τά
τε πολέμια δεινὸς καὶ φιλοκίνδυνος ὁμολογεῖται[6]

[1] Cobet: μηνύειν O, Jacoby. Perhaps σημῆναι is the true
form.
[2] Schwartz: τοῦ θεοῦ κωλύοντος O, Jacoby.
[3] περιπέτειαι Bb: om. ABa. Steph. added συμφοραὶ before
μεγάλαι.

330

day, offer certain prayers under the open sky ; whereupon some of the augurs present, who are paid by
the State, declare that a flash of lightning coming
from the left has given them a sign, although there
really has not been any. And the others, taking
their omen from this report, depart in order to take
over their magistracies, some of them assuming
this alone to be sufficient, that no omens have
appeared opposing or forbidding their intended
action, others acting even in opposition to the will
of the god ; indeed, there are times when they
resort to violence and rather seize than receive the
magistracies. Because of such men many armies
of the Romans have been utterly destroyed on land,
many fleets have been lost with all their people at
sea, and other great and dreadful reverses have
befallen the commonwealth, some in foreign wars
and others in civil dissensions. But the most remarkable and the greatest instance happened in
my time when Licinius Crassus, a man inferior to
no commander of his age, led his army against the
Parthian nation contrary to the will of Heaven and
in contempt of the innumerable omens that opposed
his expedition. But to tell about the contempt of
the divine power that prevails among some people
in these days would be a long story.

VII. Romulus, who was thus chosen king by
both men and gods, is allowed to have been a man
of great military ability and personal bravery and

---

⁴ Reiske : ἐμφανέστατα δὲ καὶ μέγισται O.
⁵ κατὰ Ambrosch : καὶ κατὰ O, Jacoby.
⁶ ὁμολογεῖται R : ὡμολόγηται B.

γενέσθαι καὶ πολιτείαν ἐξηγήσασθαι τὴν κρατίστην
φρονιμώτατος. διέξειμι δ' αὐτοῦ τὰς πράξεις τάς
τε πολιτικὰς καὶ τὰς¹ κατὰ πολέμους, ὧν καὶ
2 λόγον ἄν τις ἐν ἱστορίας ἀφηγήσει ποιήσαιτο. ἐρῶ
δὲ πρῶτον ὑπὲρ τοῦ κόσμου τῆς πολιτείας, ὃν ἐγὼ
πάντων ἡγοῦμαι πολιτικῶν κόσμων αὐταρκέστατον
ἐν εἰρήνῃ τε καὶ κατὰ πολέμους. ἦν δὲ τοιόσδε·
τριχῇ νείμας τὴν πληθὺν ἅπασαν ἑκάστῃ τῶν μοιρῶν
τὸν ἐπιφανέστατον ἐπέστησεν ἡγεμόνα ἔπειτα τῶν
τριῶν πάλιν μοιρῶν ἑκάστην εἰς δέκα μοίρας διελών,
ἴσους ἡγεμόνας καὶ τούτων ἀπέδειξε τοὺς ἀνδρειοτά-
τους· ἐκάλει δὲ τὰς μὲν μείζους μοίρας τρίβους,
τὰς δ' ἐλάττους κουρίας, ὡς καὶ κατὰ τὸν ἡμέτερον
3 βίον ἔτι προσαγορεύονται. εἴη δ' ἂν Ἑλλάδι γλώττῃ
τὰ ὀνόματα ταῦτα μεθερμηνευόμενα φυλὴ μὲν καὶ
τριττὺς ἡ τρίβος,² φράτρα δὲ καὶ λόχος ἡ κουρία,
καὶ τῶν ἀνδρῶν οἱ μὲν τὰς τῶν τρίβων ἡγεμονίας
ἔχοντες φύλαρχοί τε καὶ τριττύαρχοι, οὓς καλοῦσι
Ῥωμαῖοι τριβούνους· οἱ δὲ ταῖς κουρίαις ἐφεστη-
κότες καὶ φρατρίαρχοι καὶ λοχαγοί, οὓς ἐκεῖνοι
4 κουρίωνας ὀνομάζουσι. διῄρηντο δὲ καὶ εἰς δεκάδας
αἱ φράτραι πρὸς αὐτοῦ, καὶ ἡγεμὼν ἑκάστην ἐκόσμει
δεκάδα, δεκουρίων κατὰ τὴν ἐπιχώριον γλῶτταν
προσαγορευόμενος. ὡς δὲ διεκρίθησαν ἅπαντες καὶ
συνετάχθησαν εἰς φυλὰς καὶ φράτρας, διελὼν τὴν

¹ τὰς added by Sylburg.   ² τρίβος R: τριβους B, Jacoby.

¹ Dionysius is here thinking of these divisions of the
people both as political and military units.   The ordinary
Greek equivalent of " tribe " is *phylé*, but etymologically
trittys is probably the same word as *tribus*, both originally

332

of the greatest sagacity in instituting the best kind
of government. I shall relate such of his political
and military achievements as may be thought worthy
of mention in a history ; and first I shall speak of
the form of government that he instituted, which
I regard as the most self-sufficient of all political
systems both for peace and for war. This was the
plan of it : He divided all the people into three
groups, and set over each as leader its most distinguished man. Then he subdivided each of these
three groups into ten others, and appointed as many
of the bravest men to be the leaders of these also.
The larger divisions he called tribes and the smaller
curiae, as they are still termed even in our day.
These names may be translated into Greek as follows :
a tribe by *phylê* and *trittys*, and a *curia* by *phratra*
and *lochos* [1] ; the commanders of the tribes, whom
the Romans call tribunes, by *phylarchoi* and *trittyarchoi ;* and the commanders of the *curiae*, whom
they call *curiones*, by *phratriarchoi* and *lochagoi*.
These *curiae* were again divided by him into ten
parts, each commanded by its own leader, who was
called *decurio* in the native language. The people
being thus divided and assigned to tribes and *curiae*,

meaning a " third " ; in actual practice, however, *trittys*
was used of the third of a tribe. *Phratra* or *phratria*,
" brotherhood " or " clan," was also the third of a tribe,
and the phratries in their organization and rites offer a
number of parallels to the *curiae* (*cf.* chap. 23). *Lochos*
is a military term, " company " of indefinite size. The
phylarchoi were the commanders of the cavalry contingents
furnished by each tribe, and the *lochagoi* were infantry
captains. The *trittyarchoi* and *phratriarchoi* were simply
the heads of their respective political divisions.

γῆν εἰς τριάκοντα κλήρους ἴσους ἑκάστῃ φράτρᾳ
κλῆρον ἀπέδωκεν ἕνα, ἐξελὼν τὴν ἀρκοῦσαν εἰς ἱερὰ
καὶ τεμένη καί τινα καὶ τῷ κοινῷ γῆν καταλιπών.
μία μὲν αὕτη διαίρεσις ὑπὸ Ῥωμύλου τῶν τε
ἀνδρῶν καὶ τῆς χώρας ἡ [1] περιέχουσα τὴν κοινὴν
καὶ μεγίστην ἰσότητα, τοιάδε τις ἦν.

VIII. Ἑτέρα δὲ αὐτῶν πάλιν τῶν ἀνδρῶν ἡ τὰ
φιλάνθρωπα καὶ τὰς τιμὰς διανέμουσα κατὰ τὴν
ἀξίαν, ἣν μέλλω διηγεῖσθαι. τοὺς ἐπιφανεῖς κατὰ
γένος καὶ δι' ἀρετὴν ἐπαινουμένους καὶ χρήμασιν ὡς
ἐν τοῖς τότε καιροῖς εὐπόρους, οἷς ἤδη παῖδες ἦσαν,
διώριζεν ἀπὸ τῶν ἀσήμων καὶ ταπεινῶν καὶ ἀπόρων.
ἐκάλει δὲ τοὺς μὲν ἐν τῇ καταδεεστέρᾳ τύχῃ πληβεί-
ους, ὡς δ' ἂν Ἕλληνες εἴποιεν δημοτικούς· τοὺς δ'
ἐν τῇ κρείττονι πατέρας εἴτε διὰ τὸ πρεσβεύειν
ἡλικίᾳ τῶν ἄλλων, εἶθ' ὅτι παῖδες αὐτοῖς ἦσαν,
εἴτε διὰ τὴν ἐπιφάνειαν τοῦ γένους, εἴτε διὰ πάντα
ταῦτα· ἐκ τῆς Ἀθηναίων πολιτείας, ὡς ἄν τις
εἰκάσειε, τῆς κατ' ἐκεῖνον τὸν χρόνον ἔτι διαμενούσης
2 τὸ παράδειγμα λαβών. ἐκεῖνοι μὲν γὰρ εἰς δύο μέρη
νείμαντες τὸ πλῆθος εὐπατρίδας μὲν ἐκάλουν τοὺς ἐκ
τῶν ἐπιφανῶν οἴκων καὶ χρήμασι δυνατούς, οἷς ἡ
τῆς πόλεως ἀνέκειτο προστασία, ἀγροίκους δὲ τοὺς
ἄλλους πολίτας, οἳ τῶν κοινῶν οὐδενὸς ἦσαν κύριοι·

[1] ἡ added by Ambrosch.

---

[1] Both the Latin *plebeius* and the Greek *dēmotikos* are
adjectives, " belonging to the *plebs* or *dēmos*."

he divided the land into thirty equal portions and assigned one of them to each *curia*, having first set apart as much of it as was sufficient for the support of the temples and shrines and also reserved some part of the land for the use of the public. This was one division made by Romulus, both of the men and of the land, which involved the greatest equality for all alike.

VIII. But there was another division again of the men only, which assigned kindly services and honours in accordance with merit, of which I am now going to give an account. He distinguished those who were eminent for their birth, approved for their virtue and wealthy for those times, provided they already had children, from the obscure, the lowly and the poor. Those of the lower rank he called " plebeians " (the Greeks would call them *dēmotikoi* [1] or " men of the people "), and those of the higher rank " fathers," either because they were older than the others or because they had children or from their distinguished birth or for all these reasons. One may suspect that he found his model in the system of government which at that time still prevailed at Athens. For the Athenians had divided their population into two parts, the *eupatridai* or " wellborn," as they called those who were of the noble families and powerful by reason of their wealth, to whom the government of the city was committed, and the *agroikoi* [2] or " husbandmen," consisting of the rest of the citizens, who had no voice in public

---

[2] Called also *geōmoroi* or *geōrgoi*.

σὺν χρόνῳ δὲ καὶ οὗτοι προσελήφθησαν ἐπὶ τὰς
3 ἀρχάς. οἱ μὲν δὴ τὰ πιθανώτατα περὶ τῆς Ῥωμαίων
πολιτείας ἱστοροῦντες διὰ ταύτας τὰς αἰτίας κληθῆναί φασι τοὺς ἄνδρας ἐκείνους πατέρας καὶ τοὺς
ἐκγόνους αὐτῶν πατρικίους, οἱ δὲ πρὸς τὸν ἴδιον
φθόνον ἀναφέροντες τὸ πρᾶγμα καὶ διαβάλλοντες
εἰς δυσγένειαν τὴν πόλιν οὐ διὰ ταῦτα πατρικίους
ἐκείνους κληθῆναί φασιν, ἀλλ' ὅτι πατέρας εἶχον
ἀποδεῖξαι μόνοι, ὡς τῶν γε ἄλλων δραπετῶν ὄντων
καὶ οὐκ ἐχόντων ὀνομάσαι πατέρας ἐλευθέρους.
4 τεκμήριον δὲ τούτου παρέχονται,[1] ὅτι τοὺς μὲν
πατρικίους, ὁπότε δόξειε τοῖς βασιλεῦσι συγκαλεῖν,
οἱ κήρυκες ἐξ ὀνόματός τε καὶ πατρόθεν ἀνηγόρευον,
τοὺς δὲ δημοτικοὺς ὑπηρέται τινὲς ἀθρόους[2] κέρασι
βοείοις ἐμβυκανῶντες ἐπὶ τὰς ἐκκλησίας συνῆγον.
ἔστι δὲ οὔτε ἡ τῶν κηρύκων ἀνάκλησις τῆς εὐγενείας
τῶν πατρικίων τεκμήριον, οὔτε ἡ τῆς βυκάνης φωνὴ
τῆς ἀγνωσίας τῶν δημοτικῶν σύμβολον, ἀλλ' ἐκείνη
μὲν τιμῆς, αὕτη δὲ τάχους. οὐ γὰρ οἷόντε ἦν ἐν
ὀλίγῳ χρόνῳ τὴν πληθὺν καλεῖν ἐξ ὀνόματος.
IX. Ὁ δὲ Ῥωμύλος ἐπειδὴ διέκρινε τοὺς κρείττους ἀπὸ τῶν ἡττόνων, ἐνομοθέτει μετὰ τοῦτο καὶ
διέταττεν, ἃ χρὴ πράττειν ἑκατέρους· τοὺς μὲν
εὐπατρίδας ἱερᾶσθαί τε καὶ ἄρχειν καὶ δικάζειν καὶ

---

[1] Schwartz : παρέχουσιν O, Jacoby.
[2] Reiske : ἀθρόοι AB.

---

[1] Dionysius ignores the *dêmiourgoi* (artisans), the third
class of the three into which Theseus, according to tradition,
divided the population.

affairs, though in the course of time these, also, were admitted to the offices.[1] Those who give the most probable account of the Roman government say it was for the reasons I have given that those men were called " fathers " and their posterity " patricians " [2] ; but others, considering the matter in the light of their own envy and desirous of casting reproach on the city for the ignoble birth of its founders, say they were not called patricians for the reasons just cited, but because these men only could point out their fathers,[3]—as if all the rest were fugitives and unable to name free men as their fathers. As proof of this they cite the fact that, whenever the kings thought proper to assemble the patricians, the heralds called them both by their own names and by the names of their fathers, whereas public servants summoned the plebeians *en masse* to the assemblies by the sound of ox horns. But in reality neither the calling of the patricians by the heralds is any proof of their nobility nor is the sound of the horn any mark of the obscurity of the plebeians ; but the former was an indication of honour and the latter of expedition, since it was not possible in a short time to call every one of the multitude by name.

IX. After Romulus had distinguished those of superior rank from their inferiors, he next established laws by which the duties of each were prescribed. The patricians were to be priests, magistrates and

---

[2] This is the explanation given by Livy (i. 8, 7).

[3] *Cf.* Livy x. 8, 10 (part of a speech) : *patricios . . . qui patrem ciere possent, id est nihil ultra quam ingenuos.* This derivation of *patricius* from *pater* and *cieo* is a good instance of Roman etymologizing at its worst.

μεθ' ἑαυτοῦ τὰ κοινὰ πράττειν ἐπὶ τῶν κατὰ πόλιν [1]
ἔργων μένοντας, τοὺς δὲ δημοτικοὺς τούτων μὲν
ἀπολελύσθαι τῶν πραγματειῶν ἀπείρους τε αὐτῶν
ὄντας καὶ δι' ἀπορίαν χρημάτων ἀσχόλους, γεωργεῖν
δὲ καὶ κτηνοτροφεῖν καὶ τὰς χρηματοποιοὺς ἐργάζεσθαι τέχνας, ἵνα μὴ στασιάζωσιν, ὥσπερ ἐν ταῖς
ἄλλαις πόλεσιν, ἢ τῶν ἐν τέλει προπηλακιζόντων
τοὺς ταπεινοὺς ἢ τῶν φαύλων καὶ ἀπόρων τοῖς ἐν
2 ταῖς ὑπεροχαῖς φθονούντων. παρακαταθήκας δὲ
ἔδωκε τοῖς πατρικίοις τοὺς δημοτικοὺς ἐπιτρέψας
ἑκάστῳ τῶν ἐκ τοῦ πλήθους, ὃν αὐτὸς ἐβούλετο,
νέμειν προστάτην, ἔθος Ἑλληνικὸν καὶ ἀρχαῖον, ᾧ
Θετταλοί τε μέχρι πολλοῦ χρώμενοι διετέλεσαν
καὶ Ἀθηναῖοι κατ' ἀρχάς, ἐπὶ τὰ κρείττω λαβών.
ἐκεῖνοι μὲν γὰρ ὑπεροπτικῶς ἐχρῶντο τοῖς πελάταις
ἔργα τε ἐπιτάττοντες οὐ προσήκοντα ἐλευθέροις, καὶ
ὁπότε μὴ πράξειάν τι τῶν κελευομένων, πληγὰς
ἐντείνοντες καὶ τἆλλα ὥσπερ ἀργυρωνήτοις παρα-
χρώμενοι. ἐκάλουν δὲ Ἀθηναῖοι μὲν θῆτας τοὺς
πελάτας ἐπὶ τῆς λατρείας, Θετταλοὶ δὲ πενέστας
ὀνειδίζοντες αὐτοῖς εὐθὺς ἐν τῇ κλήσει τὴν τύχην.
3 ὁ δὲ Ῥωμύλος ἐπικλήσει τε εὐπρεπεῖ τὸ πρᾶγμα
ἐκόσμησε πατρωνείαν ὀνομάσας τὴν τῶν πενήτων
καὶ ταπεινῶν προστασίαν, καὶ τὰ ἔργα χρηστὰ
προσέθηκεν ἑκατέροις, καὶ φιλανθρώπους καὶ πολιτικὰς ἀπεργαζόμενος [2] αὐτῶν τὰς συζυγίας.

---

[1] πόλιν O : τὴν πόλιν Reiske, Jacoby.
[2] Kiessling : ἐργαζόμενος B, κατασκευαζόμενος A, Jacoby.

judges, and were to assist him in the management
of public affairs, devoting themselves to the business
of the city. The plebeians were excused from these
duties, as being unacquainted with them and because
of their small means wanting leisure to attend to
them, but were to apply themselves to agriculture,
the breeding of cattle and the exercise of gainful
trades. This was to prevent them from engaging
in seditions, as happens in other cities when either
the magistrates mistreat the lowly, or the common
people and the needy envy those in authority. He
placed the plebeians as a trust in the hands of the
patricians, by allowing every plebeian to choose
for his patron any patrician whom he himself
wished. In this he improved upon an ancient
Greek custom that was in use among the Thessalians
for a long time and among the Athenians in the
beginning. For the former treated their clients
with haughtiness, imposing on them duties un-
becoming to free men ; and whenever they disobeyed any of their commands, they beat them
and misused them in all other respects as if they
had been slaves they had purchased. The Athenians
called their clients *thêtes* or " hirelings," because
they served for hire, and the Thessalians called
theirs *penestai* or " toilers," by the very name
reproaching them with their condition. But
Romulus not only recommended the relationship
by a handsome designation, calling this protection
of the poor and lowly a " patronage," but he also
assigned friendly offices to both parties, thus making
the connexion between them a bond of kindness
befitting fellow citizens.

X. Ἦν δὲ τὰ ὑπ' ἐκείνου τότε ὁρισθέντα καὶ μέχρι πολλοῦ παραμείναντα χρόνου Ῥωμαίοις ἔθη περὶ τὰς πατρωνείας τοιάδε· τοὺς μὲν πατρικίους ἔδει τοῖς ἑαυτῶν πελάταις ἐξηγεῖσθαι τὰ δίκαια, ὧν οὐκ εἶχον ἐκεῖνοι τὴν ἐπιστήμην, παρόντων τε αὐτῶν καὶ μὴ παρόντων τὸν αὐτὸν ἐπιμελεῖσθαι τρόπον ἅπαντα πράττοντας, ὅσα περὶ παίδων πράττουσι πατέρες, εἰς χρημάτων τε καὶ τῶν περὶ χρήματα συμβολαίων λόγον· δίκας τε ὑπὲρ τῶν πελατῶν ἀδικουμένων λαγχάνειν, εἴ τις βλάπτοιτο περὶ τὰ συμβόλαια, καὶ τοῖς ἐγκαλοῦσιν ὑπέχειν· ὡς δὲ ὀλίγα περὶ πολλῶν ἄν τις εἴποι, πᾶσαν αὐτοῖς εἰρήνην τῶν τε ἰδίων καὶ τῶν κοινῶν πραγμάτων, 2 ἧς μάλιστα ἐδέοντο, παρέχειν. τοὺς δὲ πελάτας ἔδει τοῖς ἑαυτῶν προστάταις θυγατέρας τε συνεκδίδοσθαι γαμουμένας, εἰ σπανίζοιεν οἱ πατέρες χρημάτων, καὶ λύτρα καταβάλλειν πολεμίοις, εἴ τις αὐτῶν ἢ παίδων αἰχμάλωτος γένοιτο· δίκας τε ἁλόντων ἰδίας ἢ ζημίας ὀφλόντων δημοσίας ἀργυρικὸν ἐχούσας τίμημα ἐκ τῶν ἰδίων λύεσθαι χρημάτων, οὐ δανείσματα ποιοῦντας, ἀλλὰ χάριτας· ἔν τε ἀρχαῖς καὶ γερηφορίαις[1] καὶ ταῖς ἄλλαις ταῖς εἰς τὰ κοινὰ δαπάναις τῶν ἀναλωμάτων 3 ὡς τοὺς γένει προσήκοντας μετέχειν. κοινῇ δ' ἀμφοτέροις οὔτε ὅσιον οὔτε θέμις ἦν κατηγορεῖν ἀλλήλων ἐπὶ δίκαις ἢ καταμαρτυρεῖν ἢ ψῆφον

---

[1] This word does not occur elsewhere, but two inscriptions have yielded the adjectival forms γερηφόρος and γερεαφόρος; see the latest revision of Liddell and Scott's *Lexicon*. Kiessling proposed to read ἱεραφορίαις, and Jacoby (in a note) τελεσφορίαις.

X. The regulations which he then instituted
concerning patronage and which long continued in
use among the Romans were as follows : It was the
duty of the patricians to explain to their clients the
laws, of which they were ignorant ; to take the same
care of them when absent as present, doing everything for them that fathers do for their sons with
regard both to money and to the contracts that
related to money ; to bring suit on behalf of their
clients when they were wronged in connexion with contracts, and to defend them against any who brought
charges against them ; and, to put the matter
briefly, to secure for them both in private and in
public affairs all that tranquillity of which they
particularly stood in need. It was the duty of the
clients to assist their patrons in providing dowries
for their daughters upon their marriage if the fathers
had not sufficient means ; to pay their ransom to the
enemy if any of them or of their children were taken
prisoner ; to discharge out of their own purses their
patrons' losses in private suits and the pecuniary
fines which they were condemned to pay to the
State, making these contributions to them not as
loans but as thank-offerings ; and to share with
their patrons the costs incurred in their magistracies
and dignities [1] and other public expenditures, in the
same manner as if they were their relations. For
both patrons and clients alike it was impious and
unlawful to accuse each other in law-suits or to bear

---

[1] The word γερηφορία should mean literally the " bearing,
or enjoyment, of privileges," hence a " position of honour "
or a " dignity." Presumably the reference is to priesthoods.

ἐναντίαν ἐπιφέρειν ἢ μετὰ τῶν ἐχθρῶν ἐξετάζεσθαι.
εἰ δέ τις ἐξελεγχθείη τούτων τι διαπροττόμενος
ἔνοχος ἦν τῷ νόμῳ τῆς προδοσίας, ὃν ἐκύρωσεν
ὁ Ῥωμύλος, τὸν δὲ ἁλόντα τῷ βουλομένῳ κτείνειν
ὅσιον ἦν ὡς θῦμα τοῦ καταχθονίου Διός. ἐν ἔθει[1]
γὰρ Ῥωμαίοις, ὅσους ἐβούλοντο νηποινὶ τεθνάναι,
τὰ τούτων σώματα θεῶν ὀτῳδήτινι, μάλιστα δὲ τοῖς
καταχθονίοις κατονομάζειν· ὃ καὶ τότε ὁ Ῥωμύλος
4 ἐποίησε. τοιγάρτοι διέμειναν ἐν πολλαῖς γενεαῖς
οὐδὲν διαφέρουσαι συγγενικῶν ἀναγκαιοτήτων αἱ
τῶν πελατῶν τε καὶ προστατῶν συζυγίαι παισὶ
παίδων συνιστάμεναι, καὶ μέγας ἔπαινος ἦν τοῖς ἐκ
τῶν ἐπιφανῶν οἴκων ὡς πλείστους πελάτας ἔχειν
τάς τε προγονικὰς φυλάττουσι διαδοχὰς τῶν πα-
τρωνειῶν καὶ διὰ τῆς ἑαυτῶν ἀρετῆς ἄλλας ἐπικτω-
μένοις, ὅ τε ἀγὼν τῆς εὐνοίας[2] ὑπὲρ τοῦ μὴ
λειφθῆναι τῆς ἀλλήλων χάριτος ἔκτοπος ἡλίκος
ἀμφοτέροις ἦν, τῶν μὲν πελατῶν ἅπαντα τοῖς
προστάταις ἀξιούντων ὡς δυνάμεως εἶχον ὑπηρετεῖν, τῶν δὲ πατρικίων ἥκιστα βουλομένων τοῖς
πελάταις ἐνοχλεῖν χρηματικήν τε οὐδεμίαν δωρεὰν
προσιεμένων· οὕτως ἐγκρατὴς ὁ βίος ἦν αὐτοῖς
ἁπάσης ἡδονῆς καὶ τὸ μακάριον ἀρετῇ μετρῶν, οὐ
τύχῃ.

XI. Οὐ μόνον δ' ἐν αὐτῇ τῇ πόλει τὸ δημοτικὸν
ὑπὸ τὴν προστασίαν τῶν πατρικίων ἦν, ἀλλὰ καὶ

---

[1] ἐν ἔθει Kiessling : ἔνθεν O.
[2] τῆς εὐνοίας Kiessling : ὑπὲρ τῆς εὐνοίας O ; om. Cobet.

witness or to give their votes against each other or
to be found in the number of each other's enemies ;
and whoever was convicted of doing any of these
things was guilty of treason by virtue of the law
sanctioned by Romulus, and might lawfully be put
to death by any man who so wished as a victim
devoted to the Jupiter of the infernal regions.[1]
For it was customary among the Romans, whenever
they wished to put people to death without incurring
any penalty, to devote their persons to some god
or other, and particularly to the gods of the lower
world ; and this was the course which Romulus then
adopted. Accordingly, the connexions between the
clients and patrons continued for many generations,
differing in no wise from the ties of blood-relation-
ship and being handed down to their children's
children. And it was a matter of great praise to
men of illustrious families to have as many clients
as possible and not only to preserve the succession
of hereditary patronages but also by their own merit
to acquire others. And it is incredible how great
the contest of goodwill was between the patrons and
clients, as each side strove not to be outdone by the
other in kindness, the clients feeling that they should
render all possible services to their patrons and the
patrons wishing by all means not to occásion any
trouble to their clients and accepting no gifts of
money. So superior was their manner of life to
all pleasure ; for they measured their happiness by
virtue, not by fortune.

XI. It was not only in the city itself that the
plebeians were under the protection of the patricians,

---

[1] *i.e.* Dis or Pluto.

τῶν ἀποίκων αὐτῆς πόλεων καὶ τῶν ἐπὶ συμμαχίᾳ
καὶ φιλίᾳ προσελθουσῶν καὶ τῶν ἐκ πολέμου κεκρατημένων ἑκάστῃ φύλακας εἶχε καὶ προστάτας
οὓς ἐβούλετο Ῥωμαίων. καὶ πολλάκις ἡ βουλὴ τὰ
ἐκ τούτων ἀμφισβητήματα τῶν πόλεων καὶ ἐθνῶν
ἐπὶ τοὺς προϊσταμένους αὐτῶν ἀποστέλλουσα, τὰ
2 ὑπ᾽ ἐκείνων δικασθέντα κύρια ἡγεῖτο. οὕτω δὲ
ἄρα βέβαιος ἦν ἡ Ῥωμαίων ὁμόνοια τὴν ἀρχὴν
ἐκ τῶν ὑπὸ Ῥωμύλου κατασκευασθέντων λαβοῦσα
ἐθῶν, ὥστε οὐδέποτε δι᾽ αἵματος καὶ φόνου τοῦ
κατ᾽ ἀλλήλων ἐχώρησαν ἐντὸς ἑξακοσίων καὶ τριάκοντα ἐτῶν, πολλῶν καὶ μεγάλων ἀμφισβητημάτων
γενομένων τῷ δήμῳ πρὸς τοὺς ἐν τέλει περὶ τῶν
κοινῶν, ὡς ἐν ἁπάσαις φιλεῖ γίγνεσθαι μικραῖς τε
3 καὶ μεγάλαις πόλεσιν· ἀλλὰ πείθοντες καὶ διδάσκον-
τες ἀλλήλους καὶ τὰ μὲν εἴκοντες,[1] τὰ δὲ παρ᾽
εἰκόντων[2] λαμβάνοντες, πολιτικὰς ἐποιοῦντο τὰς
τῶν ἐγκλημάτων διαλύσεις. ἐξ οὗ δὲ Γάιος Γράκχος
ἐπὶ τῆς δημαρχικῆς ἐξουσίας γενόμενος διέφθειρε
τὴν τοῦ πολιτεύματος ἁρμονίαν, οὐκέτι πέπαυνται
σφάττοντες ἀλλήλους καὶ φυγάδας ἐλαύνοντες ἐκ
τῆς πόλεως καὶ οὐδενὸς τῶν ἀνηκέστων ἀπεχόμενοι
παρὰ τὸ νικᾶν. ἀλλὰ περὶ μὲν τούτων ἕτερος ἔσται
τοῖς λόγοις καιρὸς ἐπιτηδειότερος.

XII. Ὁ δὲ Ῥωμύλος ἐπειδὴ ταῦτα διεκόσμησε
βουλευτὰς εὐθὺς ἔγνω καταστήσασθαι, μεθ᾽ ὧν

----

[1] εἴκοντες R : ἑκόντες Bb.
[2] εἰκόντων Reiske : ἑκόντων O.

----

[1] Dionysius ignores the bloodshed in connexion with
the slaying of Tiberius Gracchus in 133 and the execution

but every colony of Rome and every city that had
joined in alliance and friendship with her and also
every city conquered in war had such protectors
and patrons among the Romans as they wished.
And the senate has often referred the controversies
of these cities and nations to their Roman patrons
and regarded their decisions as binding. And indeed, so secure was the Romans' harmony, which
owed its birth to the regulations of Romulus, that
they never in the course of six hundred and thirty
years [1] proceeded to bloodshed and mutual slaughter,
though many great controversies arose between the
populace and their magistrates concerning public
policy, as is apt to happen in all cities, whether large
or small; but by persuading and informing one
another, by yielding in some things and gaining
other things from their opponents, who yielded in
turn, they settled their disputes in a manner befitting fellow citizens. But from the time that
Gaius Gracchus, while holding the tribunician
power, destroyed the harmony of the government
they have been perpetually slaying and banishing
one another from the city and refraining from no
irreparable acts in order to gain the upper hand.
However, for the narration of these events another
occasion will be more suitable.

XII. As [2] soon as Romulus had regulated these
matters he determined to appoint senators to assist

of many Gracchans that followed. The overthrow of
Gaius Gracchus occurred at the very beginning of the
year 121, which was the year 631 of the City according to
Dionysius' reckoning.
[2] *Cf.* Livy i. 8, 7.

πράττειν τὰ κοινὰ ἔμελλεν, ἐκ τῶν πατρικίων ἄνδρας ἑκατὸν ἐπιλεξάμενος. ἐποιεῖτο δὲ αὐτῶν
τοιάνδε τὴν διαίρεσιν· αὐτὸς μὲν ἐξ ἁπάντων ἕνα
τὸν ἄριστον ἀπέδειξεν, ᾧ τὰς κατὰ πόλιν ᾤετο δεῖν
ἐπιτρέπειν οἰκονομίας, ὅτε αὐτὸς ἐξάγοι στρατιὰν
2 ὑπερόριον· τῶν δὲ φυλῶν ἑκάστη προσέταξε τρεῖς
ἄνδρας ἑλέσθαι τοὺς ἐν τῇ φρονιμωτάτῃ τότε ὄντας
ἡλικίᾳ καὶ δι᾽ εὐγένειαν ἐπιφανεῖς. μετὰ δὲ τοὺς
ἐννέα τούτους ἑκάστην φράτραν[1] πάλιν ἐκέλευσε
τρεῖς ἐκ τῶν πατρικίων ἀποδεῖξαι[2] τοὺς ἐπι-
τηδειοτάτους|· ἔπειτα τοῖς πρώτοις ἐννέα τοῖς ὑπὸ
τῶν φυλῶν ἀποδειχθεῖσι τοὺς ἐνενήκοντα προσθείς,
οὓς αἱ φρᾶτραι προεχειρίσαντο, καὶ τούτων, ὃν
αὐτὸς προέκρινεν, ἡγεμόνα ποιήσας τὸν τῶν ἑκατὸν
3 ἐξεπλήρωσε βουλευτῶν ἀριθμόν. τοῦτο τὸ συνέδριον[3] Ἑλληνιστὶ ἑρμηνευόμενον γερουσίαν δύναται
δηλοῦν καὶ μέχρι τοῦ παρόντος ὑπὸ Ῥωμαίων
οὕτως καλεῖται. πότερον δὲ διὰ γῆρας τῶν κατα-
λεγέντων εἰς αὐτὸ ἀνδρῶν ἢ δι᾽ ἀρετὴν ταύτης
ἔτυχε τῆς ἐπικλήσεως οὐκ ἔχω τὸ σαφὲς εἰπεῖν.
καὶ γὰρ τοὺς πρεσβυτέρους καὶ τοὺς ἀρίστους
γέροντας εἰώθεσαν οἱ παλαιοὶ καλεῖν. οἱ δὲ μετέ-
χοντες τοῦ βουλευτηρίου πατέρες ἔγγραφοι προση-
γορεύθησαν καὶ μέχρις ἐμοῦ ταύτης ἐτύγχανον τῆς
προσηγορίας. Ἑλληνικὸν δὲ ἄρα καὶ τοῦτο τὸ[4]
4 ἔθος ἦν. τοῖς γοῦν βασιλεῦσιν, ὅσοι τε πατρίους

---

[1] Jacoby: ἑκάστῃ φράτρᾳ O.
[2] Kiessling: ἐπιλέξαι O.
[3] After συνέδριον Reiske supplied ἐκάλει σενᾶτον ὅ.
[4] τὸ added by Kiessling.

him in administering the public business, and to this
end he chose a hundred men from among the patricians, selecting them in the following manner.
He himself appointed one, the best out of their
whole number, to whom he thought fit to entrust
the government of the city [1] whenever he himself
should lead the army beyond the borders. He
next ordered each of the tribes to choose three men
who were then at the age of greatest prudence and
were distinguished by their birth. After these nine
were chosen he ordered each *curia* likewise to name
three patricians who were the most worthy. Then
adding to the first nine, who had been named by
the tribes, the ninety who were chosen by the *curiae*,
and appointing as their head the man he himself
had first selected, he completed the number of a
hundred senators. The name of this council may
be expressed in Greek by *gerousia* or " council of
elders," and it is called by the Romans to this
day [2]; but whether it received its name from the advanced age of the men who were appointed to it or
from their merit, I cannot say for certain. For the
ancients used to call the older men and those of
greatest merit *gerontes* or " elders." The members
of the senate were called Conscript [3] Fathers, and
they retained that name down to my time. This
council, also, was a Greek institution. At any rate,
the Greek kings, both those who inherited the realms

---

[1] The reference is to the *praefectus urbi.*   [2] *i.e. senatus.*
[3] Literally, " enrolled." For the usual explanation of
Patres Conscripti see Livy ii. 1, 11.

ἀρχὰς παραλάβοιεν καὶ ὅσους ἡ πληθὺς αὐτὴ
καταστήσαιτο ἡγεμόνας, βουλευτήριον ἦν ἐκ τῶν
κρατίστων, ὡς Ὅμηρός τε καὶ οἱ παλαιότατοι τῶν
ποιητῶν μαρτυροῦσι· καὶ οὐχ ὥσπερ ἐν τοῖς καθ᾽
ἡμᾶς χρόνοις αὐθάδεις καὶ μονογνώμονες ἦσαν αἱ
τῶν ἀρχαίων βασιλέων δυναστεῖαι.

XIII. Ὡς δὲ κατεσκευάσατο καὶ τὸ βουλευτικὸν
τῶν γερόντων συνέδριον ἐκ τῶν ἑκατὸν ἀνδρῶν,
ὁρῶν ὅπερ εἰκὸς ὅτι καὶ νεότητος αὐτῷ δεήσει
τινὸς συντεταγμένης, ᾗ χρήσεται φυλακῆς ἕνεκα
τοῦ σώματος καὶ πρὸς τὰ κατεπείγοντα τῶν ἔργων
ὑπηρεσίᾳ, τριακοσίους ἄνδρας ἐκ τῶν ἐπιφανεστάτων
οἴκων τοὺς ἐρρωμενεστάτους τοῖς σώμασιν ἐπιλεξάμενος, οὓς ἀπέδειξαν αἱ φράτραι τὸν αὐτὸν τρόπον
ὅνπερ τοὺς βουλευτάς, ἑκάστη φράτρα δέκα νέους,[1]
2 τούτους τοὺς ἄνδρας ἀεὶ περὶ αὐτὸν εἶχεν· ὄνομα δὲ
κοινὸν ἅπαντες οὗτοι ἔσχον[2] κελέριοι, ὡς μὲν οἱ
πλείους γράφουσιν ἐπὶ τῆς ὀξύτητος τῶν ὑπηρεσιῶν
(τοὺς γὰρ ἑτοίμους καὶ ταχεῖς περὶ τὰ ἔργα κέλερας
οἱ Ῥωμαῖοι καλοῦσιν), ὡς δὲ Οὐαλέριος ὁ Ἀντιεύς
φησιν ἐπὶ τοῦ ἡγεμόνος αὐτῶν τοῦτ᾽ ἔχοντος τοῦ-
3 νομα. ἦν γὰρ καὶ τούτων ἡγεμὼν ὁ διαφανέστατος,
ᾧ τρεῖς ὑπετάγησαν ἑκατόνταρχοι[3] καὶ αὖθις ὑπ᾽
ἐκείνοις ἕτεροι τὰς ὑποδεεστέρας ἔχοντες ἀρχάς, οἳ
κατὰ πόλιν μὲν αἰχμοφόροι τε αὐτῷ παρηκολούθουν
καὶ τῶν κελευομένων ὑπηρέται, κατὰ δὲ τὰς στρατείας πρόμαχοί τε ἦσαν καὶ παρασπισταί· καὶ τὰ

---

[1] ἑκάστη . . . νέους deleted by Kiessling.
[2] ἅπαντες οὗτοι ἔσχον B: ἅπαντες ὃ καὶ νῦν κατέστησεν ἔσχον
A; ἅπαντες ὅσοι συγκατέστησαν Reiske.
[3] Kiessling: ἑκατοντάρχαι O.

of their ancestors and those who were elected by the people themselves to be their rulers, had a council composed of the best men, as both Homer and the most ancient of the poets testify ; and the authority of the ancient kings was not arbitrary and absolute as it is in our days.

XIII. After [1] Romulus had also instituted the senatorial body, consisting of the hundred men, he perceived, we may suppose, that he would also require a body of young men whose services he could use both for the guarding of his person and for urgent business, and accordingly he chose three hundred men, the most robust of body and from the most illustrious families, whom the *curiae* named in the same manner that they had named the senators, each *curia* choosing ten young men ; and these he kept always about his person. They were all called by one common name, *celeres* ; according to most writers this was because of the " celerity " required in the services they were to perform (for those who are ready and quick at their tasks the Romans call *celeres*), but Valerius Antias says that they were thus named after their commander. For among them, also, the most distinguished man was their commander ; under him were three centurions, and under these in turn were others who held the inferior commands. In the city these *celeres* constantly attended Romulus, armed with spears, and executed his orders ; and on campaigns they charged before him and defended his person. And as a

[1] *Cf.* Livy i. 15, 8.

πολλὰ οὗτοι κατώρθουν ἐν τοῖς ἀγῶσι πρῶτοί τε
ἄρχοντες μάχης καὶ τελευταῖοι τῶν ἄλλων ἀφιστά-
μενοι, ἱππεῖς μὲν ἔνθα ἐπιτήδειον εἴη πεδίον ἐνιπ-
πομαχῆσαι, πεζοὶ δὲ ὅπου τραχὺς εἴη καὶ ἄνιππος
4 τόπος. τοῦτό μοι δοκεῖ παρὰ Λακεδαιμονίων
μετενέγκασθαι τὸ ἔθος μαθὼν ὅτι καὶ παρ' ἐκείνοις
οἱ γενναιότατοι τῶν νέων τριακόσιοι φύλακες ἦσαν
τῶν βασιλέων, οἷς ἐχρῶντο κατὰ τοὺς πολέμους
παρασπισταῖς, ἱππεῦσί τε οὖσι καὶ πεζοῖς.

XIV. Καταστησάμενος δὴ ταῦτα διέκρινε τὰς
τιμὰς καὶ τὰς ἐξουσίας, ἃς ἑκάστους ἐβούλετο ἔχειν.
βασιλεῖ μὲν οὖν ἐξῄρητο τάδε τὰ γέρα· πρῶτον μὲν
ἱερῶν καὶ θυσιῶν ἡγεμονίαν ἔχειν καὶ πάντα δι'
ἐκείνου πράττεσθαι τὰ πρὸς τοὺς θεοὺς ὅσια, ἔπειτα
νόμων τε καὶ πατρίων ἐθισμῶν φυλακὴν ποιεῖσθαι
καὶ παντὸς τοῦ κατὰ φύσιν ἢ κατὰ συνθήκας δικαίου
προνοεῖν τῶν τε ἀδικημάτων τὰ μέγιστα μὲν αὐτὸν
δικάζειν, τὰ δ' ἐλάττονα τοῖς βουλευταῖς ἐπιτρέπειν
προνοούμενον ἵνα μηδὲν γίγνηται περὶ τὰς δίκας
πλημμελές, βουλήν τε συνάγειν καὶ δῆμον συγκαλεῖν
καὶ γνώμης ἄρχειν καὶ τὰ δόξαντα τοῖς πλείοσιν
ἐπιτελεῖν. ταῦτα μὲν ἀπέδωκε βασιλεῖ τὰ γέρα καὶ
ἔτι πρὸς τούτοις ἡγεμονίαν ἔχειν αὐτοκράτορα ἐν
2 πολέμῳ. τῷ δὲ συνεδρίῳ τῆς βουλῆς τιμὴν καὶ
δυναστείαν ἀνέθηκε τοιάνδε· περὶ παντὸς ὅτου ἂν
εἰσηγῆται βασιλεὺς διαγινώσκειν τε καὶ ψῆφον ἐπιφέρειν, καὶ ὅ τι ἂν δόξῃ τοῖς πλείοσι τοῦτο νικᾶν· ἐκ
τῆς Λακωνικῆς πολιτείας καὶ τοῦτο μετενεγκάμενος.
οὐδὲ γὰρ οἱ Λακεδαιμονίων βασιλεῖς αὐτοκράτορες

rule it was they who gave a favourable issue to the contest, as they were the first to engage in battle and the last of all to desist. They fought on horseback where there was level ground favourable for cavalry manœuvres, and on foot where it was rough and inconvenient for horses. This custom Romulus borrowed, I believe, from the Lacedaemonians, having learned that among them, also, three hundred of the noblest youths attended the kings as their guards and also as their defenders in war, fighting both on horseback and on foot.

XIV. Having made these regulations, he distinguished the honours and powers which he wished each class to have. For the king he had reserved these prerogatives : in the first place, the supremacy in religious ceremonies and sacrifices and the conduct of everything relating to the worship of the gods ; secondly, the guardianship of the laws and customs of the country and the general oversight of justice in all cases, whether founded on the law of nature or the civil law ; he was also to judge in person the greatest crimes, leaving the lesser to the senators, but seeing to it that no error was made in their decisions ; he was to summon the senate and call together the popular assembly, to deliver his opinion first and carry out the decision of the majority. These prerogatives he granted to the king and, in addition, the absolute command in war. To the senate he assigned honour and authority as follows : to deliberate and give their votes concerning everything the king should refer to them, the decision of the majority to prevail. This also Romulus took over from the constitution of the Lacedaemonians ; for their kings, too, did not have

ἦσαν ὅ τι βούλοιντο πράττειν, ἀλλ' ἡ γερουσία πᾶν
3 εἶχε τῶν κοινῶν τὸ κράτος. τῷ δὲ δημοτικῷ πλήθει
τρία ταῦτα ἐπέτρεψεν· ἀρχαιρεσιάζειν τε καὶ νόμους
ἐπικυροῦν καὶ περὶ πολέμου διαγινώσκειν, ὅταν ὁ
βασιλεὺς ἐφῇ, οὐδὲ τούτων ἔχοντι τὴν ἐξουσίαν
ἀνεπίληπτον, ἂν μὴ καὶ τῇ βουλῇ ταὐτὰ δοκῇ.
ἔφερε δὲ τὴν ψῆφον οὐχ ἅμα πᾶς ὁ δῆμος, ἀλλὰ
κατὰ τὰς φράτρας συγκαλούμενος· ὅ τι δὲ ταῖς
πλείοσι δόξειε φράτραις τοῦτο ἐπὶ τὴν βουλὴν
ἀνεφέρετο. ἐφ' ἡμῶν δὲ μετάκειται τὸ ἔθος· οὐ
γὰρ ἡ βουλὴ διαγινώσκει τὰ ψηφισθέντα ὑπὸ τοῦ
δήμου, τῶν δ' ὑπὸ τῆς βουλῆς γνωσθέντων ὁ δῆμός
ἐστι κύριος· πότερον δὲ τῶν ἐθῶν κρεῖττον, ἐν
4 κοινῷ τίθημι τοῖς βουλομένοις σκοπεῖν. ἐκ δὲ τῆς
διαιρέσεως ταύτης οὐ μόνον τὰ πολιτικὰ πράγματα
σώφρονας ἐλάμβανε καὶ τεταγμένας τὰς διοικήσεις,
ἀλλὰ καὶ τὰ πολεμικὰ ταχείας καὶ εὐπειθεῖς. ὁπότε
γὰρ αὐτῷ φανείη στρατιὰν ἐξάγειν, οὔτε χιλιάρχους
τότε ἔδει ἀποδείκνυσθαι κατὰ φυλὰς οὔτε ἑκατον-
τάρχους¹ κατὰ λόχους οὔτε ἱππέων ἡγεμόνας οὔτε
ἐξαριθμεῖσθαί τε καὶ λοχίζεσθαι καὶ τάξιν ἑκάστους
τὴν προσήκουσαν λαμβάνειν· ἀλλὰ βασιλεὺς μὲν τοῖς
χιλιάρχοις παρήγγελλεν, ἐκεῖνοι δὲ τοῖς λοχαγοῖς·
παρὰ δὲ τούτων οἱ δεκάδαρχοι² μαθόντες ἐξῆγον
τοὺς ὑποτεταγμένους ἑαυτοῖς ἕκαστοι, ἀφ' ἑνός τε
κελεύσματος εἴτε πᾶσα ἡ δύναμις εἴτε μοῖρά τις ἐξ

¹ ἑκατοντάρχους B : ἑκατοντάρχας R.
² Sylburg : δεκάρχαι A, δεκαδάρχαι B.

arbitrary power to do everything they wished, but the *gerousia* exercised complete control of public affairs. To the populace he granted these three privileges : to choose magistrates, to ratify laws, and to decide concerning war whenever the king left the decision to them ; yet even in these matters their authority was not unrestricted, since the concurrence of the senate was necessary to give effect to their decisions. The people did not give their votes all at the same time, but were summoned to meet by *curiae*, and whatever was resolved upon by the majority of the *curiae* was reported to the senate. But in our day this practice is reversed, since the senate does not deliberate upon the resolutions passed by the people, but the people have full power over the decrees of the senate ; and which of the two customs is the better I leave it open to others to determine. By this division of authority not only were the civil affairs administered in a prudent and orderly manner, but the business of war also was carried on with dispatch and strict obedience. For whenever the king thought proper to lead out his army there was then no necessity for tribunes to be chosen by tribes, or centurions by centuries, or commanders of the horse appointed, nor was it necessary for the army to be numbered or to be divided into centuries or for every man to be assigned to his appropriate post. But the king gave his orders to the tribunes and these to the centurions and they in turn to the decurions, each of whom led out those who were under his command ; and whether the whole army or part of it was called, at a single

αὐτῆς κληθείη τὰ ὅπλα ἔχουσα παρῆν εἰς τὸν
ἀποδειχθέντα τόπον εὐτρεπής.

XV. Τεταγμένην μὲν οὖν καὶ κεκοσμημένην πρὸς
εἰρήνην τε ἀποχρώντως καὶ πρὸς τὰ πολέμια ἐπιτη-
δείως ἐκ τούτων τῶν πολιτευμάτων τὴν πόλιν ὁ
Ῥωμύλος ἀπειργάσατο, μεγάλην δὲ καὶ πολυάνθρω-
2 πον ἐκ τῶνδε· πρῶτον μὲν εἰς ἀνάγκην κατέστησε
τοὺς οἰκήτορας αὐτῆς ἅπασαν ἄρρενα γενεὰν ἐκτρέ-
φειν καὶ θυγατέρων τὰς πρωτογόνους, ἀποκτιννύναι
δὲ μηδὲν τῶν γεννωμένων νεώτερον τριετοῦς, πλὴν
εἴ τι γένοιτο παιδίον ἀνάπηρον ἢ τέρας εὐθὺς ἀπὸ
γονῆς. ταῦτα δ᾽ οὐκ ἐκώλυσεν ἐκτιθέναι τοὺς γεινα-
μένους ἐπιδείξαντας πρότερον πέντε ἀνδράσι τοῖς
ἔγγιστα οἰκοῦσιν, ἐὰν κἀκείνοις συνδοκῇ. κατὰ δὲ
τῶν μὴ πειθομένων τῷ νόμῳ ζημίας ὥρισεν ἄλλας
τε καὶ τῆς οὐσίας αὐτῶν τὴν ἡμίσειαν εἶναι δη-
3 μοσίαν. ἔπειτα καταμαθὼν πολλὰς τῶν κατὰ τὴν
Ἰταλίαν πόλεων πονηρῶς ἐπιτροπευομένας ὑπὸ
τυραννίδων τε καὶ ὀλιγαρχιῶν, τοὺς ἐκ τούτων
ἐκπίπτοντας τῶν πόλεων συχνοὺς ὄντας, εἰ μόνον
εἶεν ἐλεύθεροι, διακρίνων οὔτε συμφορὰς οὔτε τύχας
αὐτῶν ὑποδέχεσθαι καὶ μετάγειν ὡς ἑαυτὸν ἐπε-
χείρει, τήν τε Ῥωμαίων δύναμιν αὐξῆσαι βουληθεὶς
καὶ τὰς τῶν περιοίκων ἐλαττῶσαι· ἐποίει δὲ ταῦτα
πρόφασιν ἐξευρὼν εὐπρεπῆ καὶ εἰς θεοῦ τιμὴν τὸ
4 ἔργον ἀναφέρων. τὸ γὰρ μεταξὺ χωρίον τοῦ τε
Καπιτωλίου καὶ τῆς ἄκρας, ὃ καλεῖται νῦν κατὰ
τὴν Ῥωμαίων διάλεκτον μεθόριον δυεῖν δρυμῶν
καὶ ἦν τότε τοῦ συμβεβηκότος ἐπώνυμον, ὕλαις
ἀμφιλαφέσι κατ᾽ ἀμφοτέρας τὰς συναπτούσας τοῖς

summons they presented themselves ready with arms
in hand at the designated post.

XV. By these institutions Romulus sufficiently
regulated and suitably disposed the city both for
peace and for war : and he made it large and populous
by the following means. In the first place, he obliged
the inhabitants to bring up all their male children
and the first-born of the females, and forbade them
to destroy any children under three years of age
unless they were maimed or monstrous from their
very birth. These he did not forbid their parents
to expose, provided they first showed them to their
five nearest neighbours and these also approved.
Against those who disobeyed this law he fixed various
penalties, including the confiscation of half their
property. Secondly, finding that many of the cities
in Italy were very badly governed, both by tyrannies
and by oligarchies, he undertook to welcome and
attract to himself the fugitives from these cities, who
were very numerous, paying no regard either to
their calamities or to their fortunes, provided only
they were free men. His purpose was to increase
the power of the Romans and to lessen that of their
neighbours ; but he invented a specious pretext for
his course, making it appear that he was showing
honour to a god. For he consecrated the place between the Capitol and the citadel which is now
called in the language of the Romans " the space
between the two groves," [1]—a term that was really
descriptive at that time of the actual conditions, as
the place was shaded by thick woods on both sides

---

[1] *inter duos lucos* ; *cf.* Livy i. 8, 5-6.

λόφοις λαγόνας ἐπίσκιον, ἱερὸν ἀνεὶς ἄσυλον ἱκέταις
καὶ ναὸν ἐπὶ τούτῳ κατασκευασάμενος (ὅτῳ δὲ ἄρα
θεῶν ἢ δαιμόνων οὐκ ἔχω τὸ σαφὲς εἰπεῖν) τοῖς
καταφεύγουσιν εἰς τοῦτο τὸ ἱερὸν ἱκέταις τοῦ τε
μηδὲν κακὸν ὑπ᾽ ἐχθρῶν παθεῖν ἐγγυητὴς ἐγίνετο
τῆς εἰς τὸ θεῖον εὐσεβείας προφάσει καὶ εἰ βούλοιντο
παρ᾽ αὐτῷ μένειν πολιτείας μετεδίδου καὶ γῆς
μοῖραν,¹ ἣν κτήσαιτο πολεμίους ἀφελόμενος. οἱ δὲ
συνέρρεον ἐκ παντὸς τόπου τὰ οἰκεῖα φεύγοντες
κακὰ καὶ οὐκέτι ἑτέρωσε ἀπανίσταντο ταῖς καθ᾽
ἡμέραν ὁμιλίαις καὶ χάρισιν ὑπ᾽ αὐτοῦ κατεχόμενοι.

XVI. Τρίτον ἦν ἔτι Ῥωμύλου πολίτευμα, ὃ πάντων μάλιστα τοὺς Ἕλληνας ἀσκεῖν ἔδει, κράτιστον
ἁπάντων πολιτευμάτων ὑπάρχον, ὡς ἐμὴ δόξα
φέρει, ὃ καὶ τῆς βεβαίου Ῥωμαίοις ἐλευθερίας ἦρχε
καὶ τῶν ἐπὶ τὴν ἡγεμονίαν ἀγόντων οὐκ ἐλαχίστην
μοῖραν παρέσχε, τὸ μήτε κατασφάττειν ἡβηδὸν τὰς
ἁλούσας πολέμῳ πόλεις μήτε ἀνδραποδίζεσθαι μηδὲ
γῆν αὐτῶν ἀνιέναι μηλόβοτον, ἀλλὰ κληρούχους εἰς
αὐτὰς ἀποστέλλειν ἐπὶ μέρει τινὶ τῆς χώρας καὶ
ποιεῖν ἀποικίας τῆς Ῥώμης τὰς κρατηθείσας, ἐνίαις
2 δὲ καὶ πολιτείας μεταδιδόναι. ταῦτά τε δὴ καὶ
τἆλλα τούτοις ὅμοια καταστησάμενος πολιτεύματα
μεγάλην ἐκ μικρᾶς ἐποίησε τὴν ἀποικίαν, ὡς αὐτὰ
τὰ ἔργα ἐδήλωσεν. οἱ μὲν γὰρ συνοικίσαντες μετ᾽
αὐτοῦ τὴν Ῥώμην οὐ πλείους ἦσαν ἀνδρῶν τρισχιλίων πεζοὶ καὶ τριακοσίων ἐλάττους ἱππεῖς· οἱ
δὲ καταλειφθέντες ὑπ᾽ ἐκείνου, ὅτ᾽ ἐξ ἀνθρώπων
ἠφανίσθη, πεζοὶ μὲν ἑξακισχίλιοι πρὸς τέτταρσι

¹ μοῖραν Kiessling: μοίρας O (?); om. Reudler.

where it joined the hills,—and made it an asylum
for suppliants. And building a temple there,—
but to what god or divinity he dedicated it I cannot
say for certain,—he engaged, under the colour of
religion, to protect those who fled to it from suffering any harm at the hands of their enemies ; and
if they chose to remain with him, he promised them
citizenship and a share of the land he should take
from the enemy. And people came flocking thither
from all parts, fleeing from their calamities at home ;
nor had they afterwards any thought of removing
to any other place, but were held there by daily
instances of his sociability and kindness.

XVI. There was yet a third policy of Romulus,
which the Greeks ought to have practised above all
others, it being, in my opinion, the best of all
political measures, as it laid the most solid foundation
for the liberty of the Romans and was no slight
factor in raising them to their position of supremacy.
It was this : not to slay all the men of military age or
to enslave the rest of the population of the cities
captured in war or to allow their land to go back
to pasturage for sheep, but rather to send settlers
thither to possess some part of the country by lot
and to make the conquered cities Roman colonies,
and even to grant citizenship to some of them. By
these and other like measures he made the colony
great from a small beginning, as the actual results
showed ; for the number of those who joined with
him in founding Rome did not amount to more
than three thousand foot nor quite to three hundred
horse, whereas he left behind him when he disappeared
from among men forty-six thousand foot and about

μυριάσιν, ἱππεῖς δ' οὐ πολὺ ἀπέχοντες χιλίων.
3 ἐκείνου δὲ ἄρξαντος τῶν πολιτευμάτων τούτων οἵ
τε βασιλεῖς οἱ μετ' αὐτὸν ἡγησάμενοι τῆς πόλεως
τὴν αὐτὴν ἐφύλαξαν προαίρεσιν καὶ οἱ μετ'
ἐκείνους τὰς ἐνιαυσίους λαμβάνοντες ἀρχάς, ἔστιν
ἃ καὶ προστιθέντες, οὕτως ὥστε μηδενὸς ἔθνους τοῦ
δοκοῦντος εἶναι πολυανθρωποτάτου τὸν Ῥωμαίων
γενέσθαι δῆμον ἐλάττονα.

XVII. Τὰ δὲ Ἑλλήνων ἔθη παρὰ ταῦτα ἐξετάζων
οὐκ ἔχω πῶς ἐπαινέσω τά τε Λακεδαιμονίων καὶ
τὰ τῶν Θηβαίων καὶ τῶν μέγιστον ἐπὶ σοφίᾳ
φρονούντων Ἀθηναίων, οἳ φυλάττοντες τὸ εὐγενὲς
καὶ μηδενὶ μεταδιδόντες εἰ μὴ σπανίοις τῆς παρ'
ἑαυτοῖς πολιτείας (ἐῶ γὰρ λέγειν ὅτι καὶ ξενηλα-
τοῦντες ἔνιοι) πρὸς τῷ μηδὲν ἀπολαῦσαι ταύτης
τῆς μεγαληγορίας ἀγαθὸν καὶ τὰ μέγιστα δι' αὐτὴν
2 ἐβλάβησαν. Σπαρτιᾶται μέν γε πταίσαντες μάχῃ
τῇ περὶ Λεῦκτρα, ἐν ᾗ χιλίους καὶ ἑπτακοσίους
ἄνδρας ἀπέβαλον, οὐκέτι τὴν πόλιν ἠδυνήθησαν ἐκ
τῆς συμφορᾶς ταύτης ἀναλαβεῖν, ἀλλ' ἀπέστησαν
τῆς ἡγεμονίας σὺν αἰσχύνῃ. Θηβαῖοι δὲ καὶ
Ἀθηναῖοι ἐξ ἑνὸς τοῦ περὶ Χαιρώνειαν ἀτυχήματος
ἅμα τήν τε προστασίαν τῆς Ἑλλάδος καὶ τὴν
ἐλευθερίαν τὴν πάτριον ὑπὸ Μακεδόνων ἀφηρέ-
3 θησαν. ἡ δὲ Ῥωμαίων πόλις ἐν Ἰβηρίᾳ τε καὶ
Ἰταλίᾳ πολέμους ἔχουσα μεγάλους Σικελίαν τε
ἀφεστῶσαν ἀνακτωμένη καὶ Σαρδόνα καὶ τῶν ἐν
Μακεδονίᾳ καὶ κατὰ τὴν Ἑλλάδα πραγμάτων ἐκ-
πεπολεμωμένων πρὸς αὐτὴν καὶ Καρχηδόνος ἐπὶ
τὴν ἡγεμονίαν πάλιν ἀνισταμένης καὶ τῆς Ἰταλίας
οὐ μόνον ἀφεστώσης ὀλίγου δεῖν πάσης, ἀλλὰ καὶ

a thousand horse. Romulus having instituted these measures, not alone the kings who ruled the city after him but also the annual magistrates after them pursued the same policy, with occasional additions, so successfully that the Roman people became inferior in numbers to none of the nations that were accounted the most populous.

XVII. When I compare the customs of the Greeks with these, I can find no reason to extol either those of the Lacedaemonians or of the Thebans or of the Athenians, who pride themselves most on their wisdom ; all of whom, jealous of their noble birth and granting citizenship to none or to very few (I say nothing of the fact that some even expelled foreigners), not only received no advantage from this haughty attitude, but actually suffered the greatest harm because of it. Thus, the Spartans after their defeat at Leuctra,[1] where they lost seventeen hundred men, were no longer able to restore their city to its former position after that calamity, but shamefully abandoned their supremacy. And the Thebans and Athenians through the single disaster at Chaeronea [2] were deprived by the Macedonians not only of the leadership of Greece but at the same time of the liberty they had inherited from their ancestors. But Rome, while engaged in great wars both in Spain and Italy and employed in recovering Sicily and Sardinia, which had revolted, at a time when the situation in Macedonia and Greece had become hostile to her and Carthage was again contending for the supremacy, and when all but a small portion of Italy was not only in open

[1] 371 B.C.   [2] 338 B.C.

συνεπαγούσης τὸν Ἀννιβιακὸν κληθέντα πόλεμον,
τοσούτοις περιπετὴς γενομένη κινδύνοις κατὰ τὸν
αὐτὸν χρόνον οὐχ ὅπως ἐκακώθη διὰ τὰς τότε
τύχας, ἀλλὰ καὶ προσέλαβεν ἰσχὺν ἐξ αὐτῶν ἔτι
μείζονα τῆς προτέρας, τῷ πλήθει τοῦ στρατιωτικοῦ
πρὸς ἅπαντα διαρκὴς γενομένη τὰ δεινά, ἀλλ' οὐχ
ὥσπερ ὑπολαμβάνουσί τινες εὐνοίᾳ τύχης χρησα-
4 μένη· ἐπεὶ ταύτης γε χάριν ᾤχετ' ἂν ὑποβρύχιος ἐξ
ἑνὸς τοῦ περὶ Κάννας πτώματος, ὅτε αὐτῇ ἀπὸ μὲν
ἑξακισχιλίων ἱππέων ἑβδομήκοντα καὶ τριακόσιοι
περιελείφθησαν, ἀπὸ δὲ μυριάδων ὀκτὼ τῶν εἰς τὸ
κοινὸν στράτευμα καταγραφεισῶν ὀλίγῳ πλείους
τρισχιλίων ἐσώθησαν.

XVIII. Ταῦτά τε δὴ τοῦ ἀνδρὸς ἄγαμαι καὶ ἔτι
πρὸς τούτοις ἃ μέλλω λέγειν, ὅτι τοῦ καλῶς οἰκεῖ-
σθαι τὰς πόλεις αἰτίας ὑπολαβών, ἃς θρυλοῦσι μὲν
ἅπαντες οἱ πολιτικοί, κατασκευάζουσι δ' ὀλίγοι,
πρῶτον μὲν τὴν παρὰ τῶν θεῶν εὔνοιαν, ἧς παρούσης
ἅπαντα τοῖς ἀνθρώποις ἐπὶ τὰ κρείττω συμφέρεται,
ἔπειτα τὴν [1] σωφροσύνην τε καὶ δικαιοσύνην, δι' ἃς
ἧττον ἀλλήλους βλάπτοντες μᾶλλον ὁμονοοῦσι καὶ
τὴν εὐδαιμονίαν οὐ ταῖς αἰσχίσταις μετροῦσιν ἡδοναῖς
ἀλλὰ τῷ καλῷ, τελευταίαν δὲ τὴν ἐν τοῖς πολέμοις
γενναιότητα τὴν παρασκευάζουσαν εἶναι καὶ τὰς
ἄλλας ἀρετὰς τοῖς ἔχουσιν ὠφελίμους, οὐκ ἀπὸ
ταὐτομάτου παραγίνεσθαι τούτων ἕκαστον τῶν
2 ἀγαθῶν ἐνόμισεν, ἀλλ' ἔγνω διότι [2] νόμοι σπουδαῖοι
καὶ καλῶν ζῆλος ἐπιτηδευμάτων εὐσεβῆ καὶ σώφρονα καὶ τὰ δίκαια ἀσκοῦσαν καὶ τὰ πολέμια

rebellion but was also drawing upon her the Hannibalic war, as it was called,—though surrounded, I say, by so many dangers at one and the same time, Rome was so far from being overcome by these misfortunes that she derived from them a strength even greater than she had had before, being enabled to meet every danger, thanks to the number of her soldiers, and not, as some imagine, to the favour of Fortune ; since for all of Fortune's assistance the city might have been utterly submerged by the single disaster at Cannae, where of six thousand horse only three hundred and seventy survived, and of eighty thousand foot enrolled in the army of the commonwealth little more than three thousand escaped.

XVIII. It is not only these institutions of Romulus that I admire, but also those which I am going to relate. He understood that the good government of cities was due to certain causes which all statesmen prate of but few succeed in making effective : first, the favour of the gods, the enjoyment of which gives success to men's every enterprise ; next, moderation and justice, as a result of which the citizens, being less disposed to injure one another, are more harmonious, and make honour, rather than the most shameful pleasures, the measure of their happiness ; and, lastly, bravery in war, which renders the other virtues also useful to their possessors. And he thought that none of these advantages is the effect of chance, but recognized that good laws and the emulation of worthy pursuits render a State pious, temperate, devoted to justice, and brave

---

¹ τὴν Naber : om. O, Jacoby.　　　² διότι B : ὅτι R.

ἀγαθὴν ἐξεργάζονται πόλιν· ὧν πολλὴν ἔσχε πρόνοιαν τὴν ἀρχὴν ποιησάμενος ἀπὸ τῶν περὶ τὰ
θεῖα καὶ δαιμόνια σεβασμῶν. ἱερὰ μὲν οὖν καὶ
τεμένη καὶ βωμοὺς καὶ ξοάνων ἱδρύσεις μορφάς τε
αὐτῶν καὶ σύμβολα καὶ δυνάμεις καὶ δωρεάς, αἷς τὸ
γένος ἡμῶν εὐηργέτησαν, ἑορτάς τε ὁποίας τινὰς
ἑκάστῳ θεῶν ἢ δαιμόνων ἄγεσθαι προσήκει καὶ
θυσίας, αἷς χαίρουσι γεραιρόμενοι πρὸς ἀνθρώπων,
ἐκεχειρίας τε αὖ καὶ πανηγύρεις καὶ πόνων ἀνα-
παύλας καὶ πάντα τὰ τοιαῦτα ὁμοίως κατεστήσατο
3 τοῖς κρατίστοις τῶν παρ' Ἕλλησι νομίμων· τοὺς
δὲ παραδεδομένους περὶ αὐτῶν μύθους, ἐν οἷς
βλασφημίαι τινὲς ἔνεισι κατ' αὐτῶν ἢ κακηγορίαι,[1]
πονηροὺς καὶ ἀνωφελεῖς καὶ ἀσχήμονας ὑπολαβὼν
εἶναι καὶ οὐχ ὅτι θεῶν ἀλλ' οὐδ' ἀνθρώπων ἀγαθῶν
ἀξίους, ἅπαντας ἐξέβαλε καὶ παρεσκεύασε τοὺς
ἀνθρώπους τὰ[2] κράτιστα περὶ θεῶν λέγειν τε καὶ
φρονεῖν μηδὲν αὐτοῖς προσάπτοντας ἀνάξιον ἐπιτή-
δευμα τῆς μακαρίας φύσεως.

XIX. Οὔτε γὰρ Οὐρανὸς ἐκτεμνόμενος ὑπὸ τῶν
ἑαυτοῦ παίδων παρὰ Ῥωμαίοις λέγεται οὔτε Κρόνος
ἀφανίζων τὰς ἑαυτοῦ γονὰς φόβῳ τῆς ἐξ αὐτῶν ἐπιθέσεως οὔτε Ζεὺς καταλύων τὴν Κρόνου δυναστείαν
καὶ κατακλείων ἐν τῷ δεσμωτηρίῳ τοῦ Ταρτάρου
τὸν ἑαυτοῦ πατέρα οὐδέ γε πόλεμοι καὶ τραύματα
2 καὶ δεσμοὶ καὶ θητεῖαι θεῶν παρ' ἀνθρώποις· ἑορτή
τε οὐδεμία παρ' αὐτοῖς μελανείμων ἢ πένθιμος
ἄγεται τυπετοὺς ἔχουσα καὶ θρήνους γυναικῶν ἐπὶ
θεοῖς ἀφανιζομένοις, ὡς παρ' Ἕλλησιν ἐπιτελεῖται
περί τε Φερσεφόνης ἁρπαγὴν καὶ τὰ Διονύσου πάθη

---

[1] Meineke : κατηγοριαι O.   [2] τὰ added by Kiessling.

in war. He took great care, therefore, to encourage these, beginning with the worship of the gods and genii. He established temples, sacred precincts and altars, arranged for the setting up of statues, determined the representations and symbols of the gods, and declared their powers, the beneficent gifts which they have made to mankind, the particular festivals that should be celebrated in honour of each god or genius, the sacrifices with which they delight to be honoured by men, as well as the holidays, festal assemblies, days of rest, and everything alike of that nature, in all of which he followed the best customs in use among the Greeks. But he rejected all the traditional myths concerning the gods that contain blasphemies or calumnies against them, looking upon these as wicked, useless and indecent, and unworthy, not only of the gods, but even of good men ; and he accustomed people both to think and to speak the best of the gods and to attribute to them no conduct unworthy of their blessed nature.

XIX. Indeed, there is no tradition among the Romans either of Caelus being castrated by his own sons or of Saturn destroying his own offspring to secure himself from their attempts or of Jupiter dethroning Saturn and confining his own father in the dungeon of Tartarus, or, indeed, of wars, wounds, or bonds of the gods, or of their servitude among men. And no festival is observed among them as a day of mourning or by the wearing of black garments and the beating of breasts and the lamentations of women because of the disappearance of deities, such as the Greeks perform in commemorating the rape of Persephonê and the adventures of

363

καὶ ὅσα ἄλλα τοιαῦτα· οὐδ' ἂν ἴδοι τις παρ' αὐτοῖς,
καίτοι διεφθαρμένων ἤδη τῶν ἐθῶν, οὐ θεοφορήσεις,
οὐ κορυβαντιασμούς, οὐκ ἀγυρμούς, οὐ βακχείας καὶ
τελετὰς ἀπορρήτους, οὐ διαπαννυχισμοὺς ἐν ἱεροῖς
ἀνδρῶν σὺν γυναιξίν, οὐκ ἄλλο τῶν παραπλησίων
τούτοις τερατευμάτων οὐδέν, ἀλλ' εὐλαβῶς ἅπαντα
πραττόμενά τε καὶ λεγόμενα τὰ περὶ τοὺς θεούς, ὡς
3 οὔτε παρ' Ἕλλησιν οὔτε παρὰ βαρβάροις· καὶ ὃ
πάντων μάλιστα ἔγωγε τεθαύμακα, καίπερ μυρίων
ὅσων εἰς τὴν πόλιν ἐληλυθότων ἐθνῶν, οἷς πολλὴ
ἀνάγκη σέβειν τοὺς πατρίους θεοὺς τοῖς οἴκοθεν
νομίμοις, οὐδενὸς εἰς ζῆλον ἐλήλυθε τῶν ξενικῶν
ἐπιτηδευμάτων ἡ πόλις δημοσίᾳ, ὃ πολλαῖς ἤδη
συνέβη παθεῖν, ἀλλὰ καὶ εἴ τινα κατὰ χρησμοὺς
ἐπεισηγάγετο ἱερά, τοῖς ἑαυτῆς αὐτὰ τιμᾷ νομίμοις
ἅπασαν ἐκβαλοῦσα τερθρείαν μυθικήν, ὥσπερ τὰ
4 τῆς Ἰδαίας θεᾶς ἱερά. θυσίας μὲν γὰρ αὐτῇ καὶ
ἀγῶνας ἄγουσιν ἀνὰ πᾶν ἔτος οἱ στρατηγοὶ κατὰ
τοὺς Ῥωμαίων νόμους, ἱερᾶται δὲ αὐτῆς ἀνὴρ Φρὺξ
καὶ γυνὴ Φρυγία καὶ περιάγουσιν ἀνὰ τὴν πόλιν

---

[1] The Bacchic rites, introduced into Rome shortly after
the close of the Second Punic War, were soon being celebrated with such licentious excesses and were accompanied by the plotting of so many crimes that the most
drastic action was taken by the senate and consuls in 186
to punish the guilty and prevent all further celebration of
the rites. An abstract of the decree passed by the senate
(the *Senatus Consultum de Bacchanalibus*), contained in an
official letter of the consuls to some local magistrates in
southern Italy, is still preserved on a bronze tablet and is
one of our earliest Latin documents. It appears in the

Dionysus and all the other things of like nature. And one will see among them, even though their manners are now corrupted, no ecstatic transports, no Corybantic frenzies, no begging under the colour of religion, no bacchanals [1] or secret mysteries, no all-night vigils of men and women together in the temples, nor any other mummery of this kind ; but alike in all their words and actions with respect to the gods a reverence is shown such as is seen among neither Greeks nor barbarians. And,—the thing which I myself have marvelled at most,—notwithstanding the influx into Rome of innumerable nations which are under every necessity of worshipping their ancestral gods according to the customs of their respective countries, yet the city has never officially adopted any of those foreign practices, as has been the experience of many cities in the past ; but, even though she has, in pursuance of oracles, introduced certain rites from abroad, she celebrates them in accordance with her own traditions, after banishing all fabulous clap-trap. The rites of the Idaean goddess [2] are a case in point ; for the praetors perform sacrifices and celebrate games in her honour every year according to the Roman customs, but the priest and priestess of the goddess are Phrygians, and it is they who carry her image in procession through

Corpus Inscript. Lat. i. 196 and x. 104, also in F. D. Allen's *Remnants of Early Latin*, pp. 28-31.

[2] The official title of Cybelê in Rome was *Mater Deum Magna Idaea*, commonly shortened to *Mater Magna* or *Mater Idaea*. The sacred black stone, which was her symbol, was brought from Pessinus in Asia Minor in 204 B.C., in response to a Sibylline oracle which declared that only thus could Hannibal be driven out of Italy. The games established in her honour were the Megalesia.

οὗτοι μητραγυρτοῦντες, ὥσπερ αὐτοῖς ἔθος, τύπους
τε περικείμενοι τοῖς στήθεσι καὶ καταυλούμενοι
πρὸς τῶν ἑπομένων τὰ μητρῷα μέλη καὶ τύμπανα
5 κροτοῦντες· Ῥωμαίων δὲ τῶν αὐθιγενῶν οὔτε
μητραγυρτῶν τις οὔτε καταυλούμενος πορεύεται
διὰ τῆς πόλεως ποικίλην ἐνδεδυκὼς στολὴν οὔτε
ὀργιάζει[1] τὴν θεὸν τοῖς Φρυγίοις ὀργιασμοῖς κατὰ
νόμον καὶ[2] ψήφισμα βουλῆς. οὕτως εὐλαβῶς ἡ
πόλις ἔχει πρὸς τὰ οὐκ ἐπιχώρια ἔθη περὶ θεῶν καὶ
πάντα ὀττεύεται τῦφον, ᾧ μὴ πρόσεστι τὸ εὐπρεπές.

XX. Καὶ μηδεὶς ὑπολάβῃ με ἀγνοεῖν ὅτι τῶν
Ἑλληνικῶν μύθων εἰσί τινες ἀνθρώποις χρήσιμοι,
οἱ μὲν ἐπιδεικνύμενοι τὰ τῆς φύσεως ἔργα δι' ἀλλη-
γορίας, οἱ δὲ παραμυθίας ἕνεκα συγκείμενοι τῶν
ἀνθρωπείων συμφορῶν, οἱ δὲ ταραχὰς ἐξαιρούμενοι
ψυχῆς καὶ δείματα καὶ δόξας καθαίροντες[3] οὐχ
ὑγιεῖς, οἱ δ' ἄλλης τινὸς ἕνεκα συμπλασθέντες
2 ὠφελείας. ἀλλὰ καίπερ ἐπιστάμενος ταῦτα οὐδενὸς
χεῖρον ὅμως εὐλαβῶς διάκειμαι πρὸς αὐτοὺς καὶ
τὴν Ῥωμαίων μᾶλλον ἀποδέχομαι θεολογίαν, ἐνθυμούμενος ὅτι τὰ μὲν ἐκ τῶν Ἑλληνικῶν μύθων
ἀγαθὰ μικρά τέ ἐστι καὶ οὐ πολλοὺς δυνάμενα
ὠφελεῖν, ἀλλὰ μόνους τοὺς ἐξητακότας ὧν ἕνεκα
γίνεται, σπάνιοι δ' εἰσὶν οἱ μετειληφότες ταύτης
τῆς φιλοσοφίας. ὁ δὲ πολὺς καὶ ἀφιλοσόφητος

---

[1] Ambrosch : ὀργιάζειν O.
[2] καὶ Kiessling : ἢ O.
[3] καθαίροντες A : καθαιροῦντες R, Jacoby.

the city, begging alms in her name according to their
custom, and wearing figures upon their breasts [1] and
striking their timbrels while their followers play
tunes upon their flutes in honour of the Mother
of the Gods. But by a law and decree of the senate
no native Roman walks in procession through the
city arrayed in a parti-coloured robe, begging alms
or escorted by flute-players, or worships the goddess
with the Phrygian ceremonies. So cautious are
they about admitting any foreign religious customs
and so great is their aversion to all pompous display
that is wanting in decorum.

XX Let no one imagine, however, that I am not
sensible that some of the Greek myths are useful to
mankind, part of them explaining, as they do, the
works of Nature by allegories, others being designed
as a consolation for human misfortunes, some freeing
the mind of its agitations and terrors and clearing
away unsound opinions, and others invented for
some other useful purpose. But, though I am
as well acquainted as anyone with these matters,
nevertheless my attitude toward the myths is one
of caution, and I am more inclined to accept the
theology of the Romans, when I consider that the
advantages from the Greek myths are slight and
cannot be of profit to many, but only to those who
have examined the end for which they are designed;
and this philosophic attitude is shared by few.
The great multitude, unacquainted with philosophy,

---

[1] Polybius twice (xxi. 6, 7 ; 37, 5) refers to the " figures
and pectorals " of the Galli, the priests of Cybelê ; but
we have no further information regarding them.

ὄχλος ἐπὶ τὰ χείρω λαμβάνειν φιλεῖ τοὺς περὶ αὐτῶν
λόγους καὶ δυεῖν πάσχει θάτερον, ἢ καταφρονεῖ τῶν
θεῶν ὡς ἐν πολλῇ κακοδαιμονίᾳ κυλινδουμένων, ἢ
τῶν αἰσχίστων τε καὶ παρανομωτάτων οὐδενὸς
ἀπέχεται θεοῖς αὐτὰ προσκείμενα ὁρῶν.

XXI. Ἀλλ' ὑπὲρ μὲν τούτων τοῖς αὐτὸ μόνον τὸ
θεωρητικὸν τῆς φιλοσοφίας μέρος ἀποτετμημένοις
ἀφείσθω σκοπεῖν, τῆς δ' ὑπὸ Ῥωμύλου κατασταθεί-
σης πολιτείας καὶ τάδε ἡγησάμην ἱστορίας ἄξια.
πρῶτον μέν, ὅτι πολλοῖς σώμασιν ἀπέδωκε θεραπεύειν τὸ δαιμόνιον. ἐν γοῦν ἄλλῃ πόλει νεοκτίστῳ
τοσούτους ἱερεῖς τε καὶ θεραπευτὰς θεῶν εὐθὺς ἀπο-
2 δειχθέντας οὐδεὶς ἂν εἰπεῖν ἔχοι. χωρὶς γὰρ τῶν
ἐχόντων τὰς συγγενικὰς ἱερωσύνας οἱ τὰ κοινὰ περὶ
τῆς πόλεως ἱερὰ συντελοῦντες κατὰ φυλάς τε καὶ
φράτρας ἑξήκοντα κατεστάθησαν ἐπὶ τῆς ἐκείνου
ἀρχῆς· λέγω δὲ ἃ Τερέντιος Οὐάρρων ἐν ἀρχαιολογίαις γέγραφεν, ἀνὴρ τῶν κατὰ τὴν αὐτὴν ἡλικίαν
3 ἀκμασάντων πολυπειρότατος. ἔπειτα, ὅτι τῶν
ἄλλων φαύλως πως καὶ ἀπερισκέπτως ὡς ἐπὶ τὸ[1]
πολὺ ποιουμένων τὰς αἱρέσεις τῶν ἐπιστησομένων
τοῖς ἱεροῖς καὶ τῶν μὲν ἀργυρίου τὸ τίμιον ἀξιούντων ἀποκηρύττειν, τῶν δὲ κλήρῳ διαιρούντων,[2] ἐκεῖνος οὔτε ὠνητὰς χρημάτων ἐποίησε τὰς ἱερωσύνας
οὔτε κλήρῳ μεριστάς, ἀλλ' ἐξ ἑκάστης φράτρας
ἐνομοθέτησεν ἀποδείκνυσθαι δύο τοὺς ὑπὲρ πεντήκοντα ἔτη γεγονότας γένει[3] τε προὔχοντας τῶν

---

[1] τὸ added by Kiessling.
[2] διαιρούντων B : διαιρούντων τοὺς ἱερεῖς R.

are prone to take these stories about the gods in the worse sense and to fall into one of two errors : they either despise the gods as buffeted by many misfortunes, or else refrain from none of the most shameful and lawless deeds when they see them attributed to the gods.

XXI. But let the consideration of these matters be left to those who have set aside the theoretical part of philosophy exclusively for their contemplation. To return to the government established by Romulus, I have thought the following things also worthy the notice of history. In the first place, he appointed a great number of persons to carry on the worship of the gods. At any rate, no one could name any other newly-founded city in which so many priests and ministers of the gods were appointed from the beginning. For, apart from those who held family priesthoods, sixty were appointed in his reign to perform by tribes and *curiae* the public sacrifices on behalf of the commonwealth ; I am merely repeating what Terentius Varro, the most learned man of his age, has written in his *Antiquities*. In the next place, whereas others generally choose in a careless and inconsiderate manner those who are to preside over religious matters, some thinking fit to make public sale of this honour and others disposing of it by lot, he would not allow the priesthoods to be either purchased for money or assigned by lot, but made a law that each *curia* should choose two men over fifty years of age, of distinguished birth and

---

³ γένει Kiessling : τοὺς γένει O, Jacoby.

ἄλλων καὶ ἀρετῇ διαφόρους καὶ χρημάτων περιουσίαν
ἔχοντας ἀρκοῦσαν καὶ μηδὲν ἠλαττωμένους τῶν περὶ
τὸ σῶμα· τούτους δὲ οὐκ εἰς ὡρισμένον τινὰ χρόνον
τὰς τιμὰς ἔταξεν ἔχειν, ἀλλὰ διὰ παντὸς τοῦ βίου,
στρατειῶν μὲν ἀπολελυμένους διὰ τὴν ἡλικίαν, τῶν
δὲ κατὰ τὴν πόλιν ὀχληρῶν διὰ τὸν νόμον.

XXII. Ἐπεὶ δὲ καὶ διὰ γυναικῶν ἔδει τινὰ ἱερὰ
συντελεῖσθαι καὶ διὰ παίδων ἀμφιθαλῶν ἕτερα, ἵνα
καὶ ταῦτα γένηται κατὰ τὸ κράτιστον, τάς τε
γυναῖκας ἔταξε τῶν ἱερέων τοῖς ἑαυτῶν ἀνδράσι
συνιερᾶσθαι, καὶ εἴ τι μὴ θέμις ἦν ὑπ' ἀνδρῶν
ὀργιάζεσθαι κατὰ νόμον τὸν ἐπιχώριον, ταύτας ἐπιτελεῖν καὶ παῖδας αὐτῶν τὰ καθήκοντα λειτουργεῖν·
τοῖς δὲ ἄπαισιν ἐκ τῶν ἄλλων οἴκων τοὺς χαριεστά-
τους καταλεγέντας ἐξ ἑκάστης φράτρας, κόρον καὶ
κόρην, τὸν μὲν ἕως ἥβης ὑπηρετεῖν ἐπὶ[1] τοῖς ἱεροῖς,
τὴν δὲ κόρην ὅσον ἂν ᾖ χρόνον ἁγνὴ γάμων· ἐκ
τῶν Ἑλληνικῶν νόμων καὶ ταῦτα μετενεγκάμενος,
2 ὡς ἐγὼ πείθομαι. ὅσα μὲν γὰρ αἱ κανηφόροι
καὶ ἀρρηφόροι[2] λεγόμεναι λειτουργοῦσιν ἐπὶ τῶν
Ἑλληνικῶν ἱερῶν, ταῦτα παρὰ Ῥωμαίοις αἱ προσ-
αγορευόμεναι τουτολᾶται[3] συντελοῦσι στεφάναις

---

[1] ἐπὶ A : om. B. [2] ἀρρηφόροι ABa : ἀρρητοφόροι Ba.
[3] τουτολᾶται Kiessling, τουτόλαι Köstlin : τοῦτο δὲ . . . A,
τοῦτο δὲ B.

---

[1] *Patrimi matrimique.* This requirement, very familiar
in Roman ritual, would not appear to have been so common
among the Greeks. Allusions to such a παῖς ἀμφιθαλής are
extremely rare, and then only in connexion with festivals
or, in one instance, a wedding.

exceptional merit, of competent fortune, and without any bodily defects; and he ordered that these should enjoy their honours, not for any fixed period, but for life, freed from military service by their age and from civil burdens by the law.

XXII. And because some rites were to be performed by women, others by children whose fathers and mothers were living,[1] to the end that these also might be administered in the best manner, he ordered that the wives of the priests should be associated with their husbands in the priesthood ; and that in the case of any rites which men were forbidden by the law of the country to celebrate, their wives should perform them and their children should assist as their duties required ; and that the priests who had no children should choose out of the other families of each *curia* the most beautiful boy and girl, the boy to assist in the rites till the age of manhood, and the girl so long as she remained unmarried. These arrangements also he borrowed, in my opinion, from the practices of the Greeks. For all the duties that are performed in the Greek ceremonies by the maidens whom they call *kanéphoroi* and *arrhéphoroi* [2] are performed by those whom the Romans call *tutulatae*,[3] who wear on their heads the same kind of

[2] The " basket-bearers " and the " bearers of the symbols (?) " of Athena Polias. But there is great dispute as regards both the spelling and the meaning of the second word.

[3] *Tutulatae* is due to Kiessling's conjecture. The feminine form does not occur elsewhere, but the masculine *tutulati* is attested by a gloss in Festus (pp. 354 f.). The word was descriptive of those who wore their hair plaited up in the shape of a cone (*tutulus*). This was an ancient style of arranging the hair, and was prescribed in the case of the *flaminica Dialis*.

κοσμούμεναι τὰς κεφαλάς, οἵαις κοσμεῖται τὰ
τῆς Ἐφεσίας Ἀρτέμιδος ἀφιδρύματα παρ' Ἕλλησιν.
ὅσα δὲ παρὰ Τυρρηνοῖς καὶ ἔτι πρότερον παρὰ
Πελασγοῖς ἐτέλουν ἐπί τε Κουρήτων καὶ μεγάλων
θεῶν ὀργιασμοῖς οἱ καλούμενοι πρὸς αὐτῶν κά-
δμιλοι,[1] ταῦτα κατὰ τὸν αὐτὸν τρόπον ὑπηρέτουν[2]
τοῖς ἱερεῦσιν οἱ λεγόμενοι νῦν ὑπὸ Ῥωμαίων κά-
3 μιλοι. ἔτι πρὸς τούτοις ἔταξε μάντιν ἐξ ἑκάστης
φυλῆς ἕνα παρεῖναι τοῖς ἱεροῖς, ὃν ἡμεῖς μὲν
ἱεροσκόπον καλοῦμεν, Ῥωμαῖοι δὲ ὀλίγον τι τῆς
ἀρχαίας φυλάττοντες ὀνομασίας ἀρούσπικα[3] προσαγορεύουσιν. ἅπαντας δὲ τοὺς ἱερεῖς τε καὶ
λειτουργοὺς τῶν θεῶν ἐνομοθέτησεν ἀποδείκνυσθαι
μὲν ὑπὸ τῶν φρατρῶν, ἐπικυροῦσθαι δὲ ὑπὸ τῶν
ἐξηγουμένων τὰ θεῖα διὰ μαντικῆς.

XXIII. Ταῦτα περὶ τῶν θρησκευόντων τοὺς
θεοὺς καταστησάμενος διῄρει πάλιν, ὡς ἔφην,
κατ' ἐπιτηδειότητα ταῖς φράτραις τὰ ἱερά, θεοὺς
ἀποδεικνὺς ἑκάστοις καὶ δαίμονας, οὓς ἔμελλον
ἀεὶ σέβειν, καὶ τὰς εἰς τὰ ἱερὰ δαπάνας ἔταξεν, ἃς
2 ἐχρῆν αὐτοῖς ἐκ τοῦ δημοσίου δίδοσθαι. συνέθυόν
τε τοῖς ἱερεῦσιν οἱ φρατριεῖς[4] τὰς ἀπομερισθείσας

---

[1] G. Voss : κάδωλοι O.   [2] ὑπηρετοῦσι Reiske.
[3] Lange emended to αὔσπικα.
[4] οἱ φρατριεῖς Kiessling : αἱ φράτραι εἰς O.

---

[1] *Cadmili* is another form resting on conjecture. Elsewhere the word occurs only in the singular, as a proper
name. Cadmilus (sometimes written Casmilus) was one
of the Cabeiri worshipped in Samothrace and was identified
with Hermes. The name was probably of Oriental origin.

crowns with which the statues of the Ephesian Artemis are adorned among the Greeks. And all the functions which among the Tyrrhenians and still earlier among the Pelasgians were performed by those they called *cadmili*[1] in the rites of the Curetes and in those of the Great Gods, were performed in the same manner by those attendants of the priests who are now called by the Romans *camilli*.[2] Furthermore, Romulus ordered one soothsayer out of each tribe to be present at the sacrifices. This soothsayer we call *hieroskopos* or " inspector of the vitals," and the Romans, preserving something of the ancient name, *aruspex*.[3] He also made a law that all the priests and ministers of the gods should be chosen by the *curiae* and that their election should be confirmed by those who interpret the will of the gods by the art of divination.

XXIII. After he had made these regulations concerning the ministers of the gods, he again, as I have stated,[4] assigned the sacrifices in an appropriate manner to the various *curiae*, appointing for each of them gods and genii whom they were always to worship, and determined the expenditures for the sacrifices, which were to be paid to them out of the public treasury. The members of each *curia* performed their appointed sacrifices together with their own

---

[2] The *camilli* were free-born youths who assisted in the sacrifices of the *flamen Dialis ;* in time, however, the term came to be applied to those assisting in other religious rites. The word was probably introduced from Etruria. Varro connected it with Casmilus (or Cadmilus), but most scholars to-day reject this derivation.

[3] *Aruspex* or, more properly, *haruspex*, meant " inspector of the entrails " ; but the element *haru-* is not, as Dionysius supposed, a corruption of *hiero-*.

[4] Chap. 21, 2-3.

αὐτοῖς θυσίας καὶ συνειστιῶντο κατὰ τὰς ἑορτὰς
ἐπὶ τῆς φρατριακῆς ἑστίας· ἑστιατόριον γὰρ ἦν
κατεσκευασμένον ἑκάστῃ φράτρᾳ καὶ ἐν αὐτῷ
καθωσίωτό τις, ὥσπερ ἐν τοῖς Ἑλληνικοῖς πρυ-
τανείοις, ἑστία κοινὴ τῶν φρατριέων.[1] ὄνομα δὲ
καὶ τοῖς ἑστιατορίοις ἦν, ὅπερ ταῖς φράτραις,
3 κουρίαι, καὶ μέχρις ἡμῶν οὕτω καλοῦνται. τοῦτο
τὸ πολίτευμα δοκεῖ μοι λαβεῖν ἐκ τῆς Λακεδαιμονίων ἀγωγῆς τῆς περὶ τὰ φιδίτια[2] κατ᾽ ἐκεῖνον
τὸν χρόνον ἐπιχωριαζούσης, ἣν Λυκοῦργος εἰση-
γήσασθαι δοκεῖ παρὰ Κρητῶν μαθών, καὶ μεγάλα
τὴν πόλιν ὠφελῆσαι ἐν εἰρήνῃ μὲν εἰς εὐτέλειαν
ἀγαγὼν[3] τοὺς βίους καὶ σωφροσύνην τῆς καθ᾽
ἡμέραν διαίτης, ἐν πολέμῳ δ᾽ εἰς αἰδῶ καὶ πρόνοιαν
καταστήσας ἕκαστον τοῦ μὴ καταλιπεῖν τὸν παρα-
στάτην, ᾧ καὶ συνέσπεισε καὶ συνέθυσε καὶ κοινῶν
4 ἱερῶν μετέσχεν. καὶ οὐ μόνον τῆς περὶ ταῦτα
σοφίας χάριν ἄξιος ἐπαινεῖσθαι ὁ ἀνήρ, ἀλλὰ καὶ
τῆς εὐτελείας τῶν θυσιῶν, αἷς γεραίρεσθαι τοὺς
θεοὺς ἐνομοθέτησεν, ὧν αἱ πλεῖσται διέμενον ἕως
τῆς καθ᾽ ἡμᾶς ἡλικίας, εἰ μὴ καὶ πᾶσαι, κατὰ
5 τὸν ἀρχαῖον ἐπιτελούμεναι τρόπον. ἐγὼ γοῦν
ἐθεασάμην ἐν ἱεραῖς οἰκίαις δεῖπνα προκείμενα
θεοῖς ἐπὶ τραπέζαις ξυλίναις ἀρχαϊκαῖς ἐν κάνησι
καὶ πινακίσκοις κεραμεοῖς, ἀλφίτων μάζας καὶ
πόπανα καὶ ζέας καὶ καρπῶν τινων ἀπαρχὰς καὶ
ἄλλα τοιαῦτα λιτὰ καὶ εὐδάπανα καὶ πάσης ἀπειρο-
καλίας ἀπηλλαγμένα· καὶ σπονδὰς εἶδον ἐγκεκρα-

[1] Grimm : φρατριῶν O, Jacoby.
[2] Gelenius : φιλίτια O.
[3] Bücheler : ἄγων B, Jacoby, ἀνάγων R.

priests, and on holy days they feasted together at
their common table. For a banqueting-hall had
been built for each *curia*, and in it there was consecrated, just as in the Greek *prytanea*, a common
table for all the members of the *curia*. These
banqueting-halls had the same name as the *curiae*
themselves, and are called so to our day. This
institution, it seems to me, Romulus took over from
the practice of the Lacedaemonians in the case of
their *phiditia*,[1] which were then the vogue. It
would seem that Lycurgus, who had learned the
institution from the Cretans, introduced it at Sparta
to the great advantage of his country ; for he thereby
in time of peace directed the citizens' lives toward
frugality and temperance in their daily repasts, and in
time of war inspired every man with a sense of shame
and concern not to forsake his comrade with whom
he had offered libations and sacrifices and shared
in common rites. And not alone for his wisdom
in these matters does Romulus deserve praise, but
also for the frugality of the sacrifices that he
appointed for the honouring of the gods, the greatest
part of which, if not all, remained to my day, being
still performed in the ancient manner. At any rate,
I myself have seen in the sacred edifices repasts
set before the gods upon ancient wooden tables,
in baskets and small earthen plates, consisting of
barley bread, cakes and spelt, with the first-offerings
of some fruits, and other things of like nature, simple,
cheap, and devoid of all vulgar display. I have
seen also the libation wines that had been mixed,

---

[1] The Spartan name for συσσίτια, the public messes.

μένας οὐκ ἐν ἀργυροῖς καὶ χρυσοῖς ἄγγεσιν, ἀλλ᾽
ἐν ὀστρακίναις κυλίσκαις[1] καὶ πρόχοις, καὶ πάνυ
ἠγάσθην τῶν ἀνδρῶν ὅτι διαμένουσιν ἐν τοῖς
πατρίοις ἔθεσιν οὐδὲν ἐξαλλάττοντες τῶν ἀρχαίων
6 ἱερῶν εἰς τὴν ἀλαζόνα πολυτέλειαν. ἔστι μὲν οὖν
ἃ καὶ Νόμας Πομπίλιος ὁ μετὰ Ῥωμύλον ἄρξας
τῆς πόλεως κατεστήσατο μνήμης ἄξια καὶ λόγου,
περιττὸς τὴν γνώμην ἀνὴρ καὶ τὰ θεῖα ἐξηγήσασθαι
σοφὸς ἐν ὀλίγοις, ὑπὲρ ὧν ὕστερον ἐρῶ, καὶ Τύλλος
Ὁστίλιος ὁ τρίτος ἀπὸ Ῥωμύλου βασιλεύσας καὶ
πάντες οἱ μετ᾽ ἐκεῖνον γενόμενοι βασιλεῖς· ἀλλ᾽ ὁ
τὰ σπέρματα καὶ τὰς ἀρχὰς αὐτοῖς παρασχὼν καὶ
τὰ κυριώτατα καταστησάμενος τῶν περὶ τὰ θεῖα
νομίμων Ῥωμύλος ἦν.

XXIV. Δοκεῖ δὲ καὶ τῆς ἄλλης εὐκοσμίας, ᾗ
χρώμενοι Ῥωμαῖοι διεφύλαξαν εὐδαιμονοῦσαν τὴν
πόλιν ἐπὶ πολλὰς γενεάς, ἐκεῖνος ἄρξαι νόμους κα-
λοὺς καὶ συμφέροντας, ἀγράφους μὲν τοὺς πλείστους,
ἔστι δ᾽ οὓς καὶ ἐν γράμμασι κειμένους καταστησάμενος, ὧν ἐγὼ τοὺς μὲν ἄλλους οὐδὲν δέομαι γράφειν, οὓς δὲ πάντων μάλιστα τεθαύμακα καὶ ἐξ
ὧν ὑπείληφα καταφανῆ καὶ τὴν ἄλλην τοῦ ἀνδρὸς
γενήσεσθαι νομοθεσίαν, ὡς αὐστηρὰ καὶ μισοπόνηρος
ἦν καὶ πολλὴν ἔχουσα πρὸς τοὺς ἡρωικοὺς βίους
2 ὁμοιότητα, δι᾽ ὀλίγης ὑπομνήσεως σημανῶ, τοσοῦτο
προειπών, ὅτι μοι δοκοῦσιν ἅπαντες οἱ διατάξαντες
τάς τε βαρβαρικὰς καὶ τὰς Ἑλληνικὰς πολιτείας τὸ
μὲν κοινὸν ὀρθῶς ἰδεῖν, ὅτι πόλιν ἅπασαν ἐκ πολλῶν

[1] κυλίσκαις B (but corrected to κύλιξι) : κυλικίσκαις A.

not in silver and gold vessels, but in little earthen cups and jugs, and I have greatly admired these men for adhering to the customs of their ancestors and not degenerating from their ancient rites into a boastful magnificence. There are, it is true, other institutions, worthy to be both remembered and related, which were established by Numa Pompilius, who ruled the city after Romulus, a man of consummate wisdom and of rare sagacity in interpreting the will of the gods, and of them I shall speak later ; and yet others were added by Tullus Hostilius, the second [1] king after Romulus, and by all the kings who followed him. But the seeds of them were sown and the foundations laid by Romulus, who established the principal rites of their religion.

XXIV. Romulus also seems to have been the author of that good discipline in other matters by the observance of which the Romans have kept their commonwealth flourishing for many generations ; for he established many good and useful laws, the greater part of them unwritten, but some committed to writing. There is no need for me to mention most of them, but I will give a short account of those which I have admired most of all and which I have regarded as suitable to illustrate the character of the rest of this man's legislation, showing how austere it was, how averse to vice, and how closely it resembled the life of the heroic age. However, I will first observe that all who have established constitutions, barbarian as well as Greek, seem to me to have recognized correctly the general principle that every State, since it consists of many

---

[1] Literally, the " third," counting inclusively.

οἴκων συνεστῶσαν ὀρθήν τε [1] πλεῖν εἰκὸς ὅταν οἱ
τῶν ἰδιωτῶν εὐσταθῶσι βίοι, καὶ χειμῶνα πολὺν
ἄγειν ὅταν κακῶς ἑκάστοις ἔχῃ τὰ ἴδια, καὶ ὅτι δεῖ
τὸν νοῦν ἔχοντα πολιτικόν, ἐάν τε νομοθέτης ἐάν τε
βασιλεὺς ᾖ, ταῦτα νομοθετεῖν, ἃ ποιήσει δικαίους
3 καὶ σώφρονας τοὺς τῶν ἰδιωτῶν βίους. ἐξ ὧν δ'
ἂν ἐπιτηδευμάτων καὶ δι' οἵων γένοιντο τοιοῦτοι
νόμων, οὐκέθ' ὁμοίως ἅπαντες δοκοῦσί μοι συνιδεῖν,
ἀλλ' ἔνιοί γε πολλοῦ καὶ τοῦ παντός, ὡς εἰπεῖν,
ἐν τοῖς κυριωτάτοις καὶ πρώτοις μέρεσι τῆς νο-
4 μοθεσίας ἁμαρτεῖν. αὐτίκα περὶ γάμων καὶ τῆς
πρὸς γυναῖκας ὁμιλίας, ἀφ' ἧς ἄρχεσθαι δεῖ τὸν
νομοθέτην, ὥσπερ καὶ ἡ φύσις ἁρμόττειν τοὺς βίους
ἡμῶν ἤρξατο, οἱ μὲν ἀπὸ τῶν θηρίων τὸ παράδειγμα
λαβόντες ἀφέτους καὶ κοινὰς τὰς μίξεις ἐποίησαν [2]
τῷ ἄρρενι πρὸς τὸ θῆλυ, ὡς ἐρωτικῶν τε οἴστρων
ἐλευθερώσοντες τοὺς βίους καὶ ζήλων ἀλληλοκτόνων
ἐξελούμενοι καὶ πολλῶν ἄλλων ἀπαλλάξοντες κακῶν,
ἃ καταλαμβάνει τούς τε ἰδίους οἴκους καὶ τὰς πόλεις
5 ὅλας διὰ γυναῖκας· οἱ δὲ ταύτας μὲν ἐξήλασαν ἐκ
τῶν πόλεων [3] τὰς ἀγερώχους καὶ θηριώδεις συνουσίας
ἄνδρα [4] συναρμόσαντες εἰς [5] γυναῖκα μίαν, περὶ δὲ
φυλακῆς γάμων καὶ σωφροσύνης γυναικῶν νομοθετεῖν οὔτε μεῖζον οὔτ' ἔλαττον οὐδὲν ἐπεχείρησαν,
6 ἀλλ' ὡς ἀδυνάτου πράγματος ἀπέστησαν· οἱ δὲ

---

[1] τε Bücheler : γε O.
[2] Kiessling : ἐποιήσαντο O.
[3] ἐκ τῶν πόλεων B : ἐκ τῆς πόλεως R.
[4] ἕνα ἄνδρα Kayser.
[5] εἰς O : πρὸς Reiske.

families, is most likely to enjoy tranquillity [1] when the lives of the individual citizens are untroubled, and to have a very tempestuous time when the private affairs of the citizens are in a bad way, and that every prudent statesman, whether he be a lawgiver or a king, ought to introduce such laws as will make the citizens just and temperate in their lives. Yet by what practices and by what laws this result may be accomplished they do not all seem to me to have understood equally well, but some of them seem to have gone widely and almost completely astray in the principal and fundamental parts of their legislation. For example, in the matter of marriage and commerce with women, from which the lawgiver ought to begin (even as Nature has begun thence to form our lives), some, taking their example from the beasts, have allowed men to have intercourse with women freely and promiscuously, thinking thus to free their lives from the frenzies of love, to save them from murderous jealousy, and to deliver them from many other evils which come upon both private houses and whole States through women. Others have banished this wanton and bestial intercourse from their States by joining a man to one woman ; and yet for the preservation of the marriage ties and the chastity of women they have never attempted to make even the slightest regulation whatsoever, but have given up the idea as something im-

---

[1] Literally, " to sail right," that is, on an even keel. Here, as often in Greek writers, the State is likened to a ship.

οὔτε ἀνεγγύους ἐποίησαν ὥσπερ ἔνιοι τῶν βαρβάρων
τὰς ἀφροδισίους μίξεις οὔτε ἀφῆκαν ὥσπερ Λακεδαιμόνιοι τὰς τῶν γυναικῶν φυλακάς, ἀλλὰ πολλοὺς
ἔθεσαν ἐπ' αὐταῖς νόμους σωφρονιστάς. εἰσὶ δ' οἳ
καὶ ἀρχήν τινα κατέστησαν ἐπιμελησομένην εὐκοσμίας γυναικῶν· οὐ μὴν ἀποχρῶσά γε ἡ πρόνοια
αὐτῶν τῆς τηρήσεως, ἀλλὰ μαλακωτέρα τοῦ δέοντος
ἐγένετο καὶ οὐχ ἱκανὴ τὴν[1] μὴ σπουδαίᾳ φύσει
κεκραμένην εἰς ἀνάγκην βίου σώφρονος ἀγαγεῖν.

XXV. Ὁ δὲ Ῥωμύλος οὔτε ἀνδρὶ κατὰ γυναικὸς
ἐγκλήματα δοὺς φθαρείσης ἢ τὸν οἶκον ἀδίκως
ἀπολιπούσης οὔτε γαμετῇ κατ' ἀνδρὸς αἰτιωμένῃ
κάκωσιν ἢ ἄδικον ἀπόλειψιν οὔτε περὶ προικὸς
ἀποδόσεως ἢ κομιδῆς νόμους θεὶς οὔτε ἄλλο τῶν
παραπλησίων τούτοις διορίσας οὐδ' ὁτιοῦν, ἕνα δὲ
νόμον[2] ὑπὲρ ἁπάντων εὖ ἔχοντα, ὡς αὐτὰ τὰ ἔργα
ἐδήλωσε, καταστησάμενος εἰς σωφροσύνην καὶ
2 πολλὴν εὐκοσμίαν[3] ἤγαγε τὰς γυναῖκας.[4] ἦν δὲ
τοιόσδε ὁ νόμος· γυναῖκα γαμετὴν τὴν κατὰ γάμους[5] ἱεροὺς συνελθοῦσαν ἀνδρὶ κοινωνὸν ἁπάντων
εἶναι χρημάτων τε καὶ ἱερῶν. ἐκάλουν δὲ τοὺς
ἱεροὺς καὶ νομίμους οἱ παλαιοὶ γάμους Ῥωμαϊκῇ
προσηγορίᾳ περιλαμβάνοντες φαρραχείους[6] ἐπὶ τῆς
κοινωνίας τοῦ φαρρός, ὃ καλοῦμεν ἡμεῖς ζέαν. αὕτη

---

[1] τὴν Ambrosch: τῷ B, τὸ A.
[2] νόμον Kiessling: μόνον O.
[3] εἰς εὐφροσύνην μᾶλλον δὲ σωφροσύνην καὶ πολλὴν εὐκοσμίαν
B, εἰς εὐκοσμίαν καὶ πολλὴν σωφροσύνην A.
[4] γυναῖκας B: γαμετάς R. [5] γάμους Sintenis: νόμους O.
[6] φαρραχίους A, φαρραγχείους B: φαρράκια Steph. The
correct form would seem to be either φαρρακίους or
φαρρακέους.

practicable. Others have neither permitted sexual intercourse without marriage, like some barbarians, nor neglected the guarding of their women, like the Lacedaemonians, but have established many laws to keep them within bounds. And some have even appointed a magistrate to look after the good conduct of women ; this provision, however, for their guarding was found insufficient and too weak to accomplish its purpose, being incapable of bringing the woman of unvirtuous nature to the necessity of a modest behaviour.

XXV. But Romulus, without giving either to the husband an action against his wife for adultery or for leaving his home without cause, or to the wife an action against her husband on the ground of ill-usage [1] or for leaving her without reason, and without making any laws for the returning or recovery of the dowry, or regulating anything of this nature, by a single law which effectually provides for all these things, as the results themselves have shown, led the women to behave themselves with modesty and great decorum. The law was to this effect, that a woman joined to her husband by a holy marriage should share in all his possessions and sacred rites. The ancient Romans designated holy and lawful marriages by the term " farreate," [2] from the sharing of *far*, which we call *zea* [3] ; for

---

[1] The term can also mean the mismanagement of her property.

[2] *Farracius* or *farraceus* is an adjective, " of spelt." It is not used by any extant writer in connexion with marriages ; but we do find the participles *farreatus* and *confarreatus* thus used, and especially the noun *confarreatio*. See note 2, p. 383.

[3] Both words mean " spelt," a coarse variety of wheat.

γὰρ ἦν ἀρχαία καὶ μέχρι πολλοῦ συνήθης ἅπασιν
αὐτοῖς ἡ τροφή· φέρει δὲ πολλὴν καὶ καλὴν ἡ Ῥωμαίων γῆ τὴν ζέαν.[1] καὶ ὥσπερ ἡμεῖς οἱ[2] Ἕλληνες
τὸν κρίθινον καρπὸν ἀρχαιότατον ὑπολαμβάνοντες
ἐπὶ τῶν θυσιῶν κριθαῖς καταρχόμεθα οὐλὰς[3] αὐτὰς
καλοῦντες, οὕτω Ῥωμαῖοι τιμιώτατόν τε καρπὸν
καὶ ἀρχαιότατον εἶναι νομίζοντες τὰς ζέας διὰ
τούτων ἁπάσης ἐμπύρου θυσίας κατάρχονται. μένει
γὰρ ἔτι καὶ οὐ μεταπέπτωκεν εἰς πολυτελεστέρας
3 ἀπαρχὰς[4] τὸ ἔθος. τὸ δὴ κοινωνοὺς τῆς ἱερωτάτης
τε καὶ πρώτης τροφῆς γενέσθαι γυναῖκας ἀνδράσι
καὶ ἐπὶ τῇ ὅλῃ[5] συνελθεῖν τύχῃ τὴν μὲν ἐπίκλησιν
τῆς κοινωνίας τοῦ φαρρὸς εἶχεν, εἰς σύνδεσμον δ'
ἀναγκαῖον οἰκειότητος ἔφερεν ἀδιαλύτου, καὶ τὸ
4 διαιρῆσον τοὺς γάμους τούτους οὐδὲν ἦν. οὗτος ὁ
νόμος τάς τε γυναῖκας ἠνάγκασε τὰς γαμετάς, οἷα
δὴ μηδεμίαν ἐχούσας ἑτέραν ἀποστροφήν, πρὸς ἕνα
τὸν τοῦ γεγαμηκότος ζῆν τρόπον, καὶ τοὺς ἄνδρας
ὡς ἀναγκαίου τε καὶ ἀναφαιρέτου κτήματος τῆς
5 γυναικὸς κρατεῖν. σωφρονοῦσα μὲν οὖν καὶ πάντα
τῷ γεγαμηκότι πειθομένη γυνὴ κυρία τοῦ οἴκου
τὸν αὐτὸν τρόπον ἦν, ὅνπερ[6] ὁ ἀνήρ, καὶ τελευτήσαντος ἀνδρὸς κληρονόμος ἐγίνετο τῶν χρημάτων,
ὡς θυγάτηρ πατρός, εἰ μὲν ἄπαις τε καὶ μηδὲν
διαθέμενος ἀποθάνοι πάντων οὖσα κυρία τῶν ἀπο-
λειφθέντων, εἰ δὲ γενεὰν ἔχοι τοῖς παισὶν ἰσόμοιρος

---

[1] τὴν ζέαν deleted by Reudler, Jacoby.
[2] ἡμεῖς οἱ added by Reiske.   [3] οὐλὰς B : ὀλὰς R.
[4] ἀπαρχὰς Steph. : ἀρχὰς O.
[5] τῇ ὅλῃ Reiske : πολλῇ O.

this was the ancient and, for a long time, the ordinary
food of all the Romans, and their country produces
an abundance of excellent spelt. And as we Greeks
regard barley as the most ancient grain, and for that
reason begin our sacrifices with barley-corns which
we call *oulai*, so the Romans, in the belief that spelt is
both the most valuable and the most ancient of grains,
in all burnt offerings begin the sacrifice with that.[1]
For this custom still remains, not having deteri-
orated into first-offerings of greater expense. The
participation of the wives with their husbands in
this holiest and first food and their union with them
founded on the sharing of all their fortunes took its
name [2] from this sharing of the spelt and forged the
compelling bond of an indissoluble union, and there
was nothing that could annul these marriages. This
law obliged both the married women, as having
no other refuge, to conform themselves entirely to
the temper of their husbands, and the husbands
to rule their wives as necessary and inseparable
possessions. Accordingly, if a wife was virtuous and
in all things obedient to her husband, she was mistress
of the house to the same degree as her husband was
master of it, and after the death of her husband she
was heir to his property in the same manner as
a daughter was to that of her father; that is, if
he died without children and intestate, she was
mistress of all that he left, and if he had children,
she shared equally with them. But if she did any

---

[1] The *mola salsa*.   [2] *Confarreatio.*

---

[6] ὅνπερ B : ὅνπερ καὶ R, Jacoby.

DIONYSIUS OF HALICARNASSUS

6 γινομένη. ἁμαρτάνουσα δέ τι δικαστὴν τὸν ἀδικού-
μενον ἐλάμβανε καὶ τοῦ μεγέθους τῆς τιμωρίας
κύριον. ταῦτα δὲ οἱ συγγενεῖς μετὰ τοῦ ἀνδρὸς
ἐδίκαζον ἐν οἷς ἦν φθορὰ σώματος καί, ὃ πάντων
ἐλάχιστον ἁμαρτημάτων Ἕλλησι δόξειεν ἂν ὑπάρχειν,
εἴ τις οἶνον εὑρεθείη πιοῦσα γυνή. ἀμφότερα γὰρ
ταῦτα θανάτῳ ζημιοῦν συνεχώρησεν ὁ Ῥωμύλος,
ὡς ἁμαρτημάτων γυναικείων ἔσχατα,[1] φθορὰν μὲν
7 ἀπονοίας ἀρχὴν νομίσας, μέθην δὲ φθορᾶς. καὶ
μέχρι πολλοῦ διέμεινε χρόνου ταῦτ' ἀμφότερα παρὰ
Ῥωμαίοις ἀπαραιτήτου τυγχάνοντα ὀργῆς. μάρτυς
δὲ τοῦ καλῶς ἔχειν τὸν περὶ τῶν γυναικῶν νόμον ὁ
πολὺς χρόνος. ὁμολογεῖται γὰρ ἐντὸς ἐτῶν εἴκοσι
καὶ πεντακοσίων μηδεὶς ἐν Ῥώμῃ λυθῆναι γάμος·
κατὰ δὲ τὴν ἑβδόμην ἐπὶ ταῖς τριάκοντα καὶ ἑκατὸν
ὀλυμπιάσιν ὑπατευόντων Μάρκου Πομπωνίου καὶ
Γαΐου Παπιρίου πρῶτος ἀπολῦσαι λέγεται τὴν
ἑαυτοῦ γυναῖκα Σπόριος Καρουΐλιος[2] ἀνὴρ οὐκ
ἀφανής, ἀναγκαζόμενος ὑπὸ τῶν τιμητῶν ὀμόσαι
τέκνων ἕνεκα γυναικὶ συνοικεῖν (ἦν δ' αὐτῷ στείρα
ἡ γυνή), ὃς ἐπὶ τῷ ἔργῳ τούτῳ καίτοι δι' ἀνάγκην
γενομένῳ μισούμενος ὑπὸ τοῦ δήμου διετέλεσεν.

---

[1] ἔσχατα O : αἴσχιστα Grasberger, Jacoby.
[2] Καρουΐλιος Ambrosch : καὶ ρουΐλιος AB.

---

[1] 231 B.C.
[2] Gellius (iv. 3), Valerius Maximus (ii. 1, 4) and Plutarch
(*Thes. et Rom.* 6) give this same tradition regarding
Carvilius, but differ widely as to his date. Gellius is in
virtual agreement with Dionysius, but Valerius gives

wrong, the injured party was her judge and determined the degree of her punishment. Other offences,
however, were judged by her relations together with
her husband ; among them was adultery, or where it
was found she had drunk wine—a thing which the
Greeks would look upon as the least of all faults.
For Romulus permitted them to punish both these
acts with death, as being the gravest offences women
could be guilty of, since he looked upon adultery as the
source of reckless folly, and drunkenness as the source
of adultery. And both these offences continued for
a long time to be punished by the Romans with
merciless severity. The wisdom of this law concerning wives is attested by the length of time it was in
force ; for it is agreed that during the space of five
hundred and twenty years no marriage was ever dis-
solved at Rome. But it is said that in the one
hundred and thirty-seventh Olympiad, in the consulship of Marcus Pomponius and Gaius Papirius,[1]
Spurius Carvilius, a man of distinction, was the
first to divorce his wife,[2] and that he was obliged
by the censors to swear that he had married for the
purpose of having children (his wife, it seems, was
barren) ; yet because of his action, though it was
based on necessity, he was ever afterwards hated
by the people.

604 B.C. and Plutarch 524. Moreover, Valerius states
elsewhere (ii. 9, 2) that L. Annius repudiated his wife in
307/6, a date confirmed by Livy (ix. 43, 25). It seems
most probable that Dionysius and Gellius are wrong in
their date. Scholars who accept this late date admit an
earlier voluntary dissolution of marriage or assume that
the ancient authors were thinking of different forms of
marriage or of different grounds for divorce.

XXVI. Ἃ μὲν οὖν εἰς γυναῖκας εὖ ἔχοντα ὁ
Ῥωμύλος ἐνομοθέτησεν, ἐξ ὧν κοσμιωτέρας περὶ
τοὺς ἄνδρας αὐτὰς ἀπειργάσατο, ταῦτ᾽ ἐστίν, ἃ δ᾽
εἰς αἰδῶ καὶ δικαιοσύνην παίδων, ἵνα σέβωσι τοὺς
πατέρας ἅπαντα πράττοντές τε καὶ λέγοντες ὅσα ἂν
ἐκεῖνοι κελεύωσιν, ἔτι τούτων ἦν σεμνότερα καὶ
μεγαλοπρεπέστερα καὶ πολλὴν ἔχοντα παρὰ τοὺς
2 ἡμετέρους νόμους διαφοράν. οἱ μὲν γὰρ τὰς Ἑλληνικὰς καταστησάμενοι πολιτείας βραχύν τινα
κομιδῇ χρόνον ἔταξαν ἄρχεσθαι τοὺς παῖδας ὑπὸ
τῶν πατέρων, οἱ μὲν ἕως τρίτον [1] ἐκπληρώσωσιν
ἀφ᾽ ἥβης ἔτος, οἱ δὲ ὅσον ἂν χρόνον ἠίθεοι μένωσιν,
οἱ δὲ μέχρι τῆς εἰς τὰ ἀρχεῖα τὰ δημόσια ἐγγραφῆς,
ὡς ἐκ τῆς Σόλωνος καὶ Πιττακοῦ καὶ Χαρώνδου
νομοθεσίας ἔμαθον, οἷς πολλὴ μαρτυρεῖται σοφία·
3 τιμωρίας τε κατὰ τῶν παίδων ἔταξαν, ἐὰν ἀπειθῶσι
τοῖς πατράσιν, οὐ βαρείας, ἐξελάσαι τῆς οἰκίας
ἐπιτρέψαντες αὐτοὺς καὶ χρήματα μὴ καταλιπεῖν,
περαιτέρω δὲ οὐδέν. εἰσὶ δ᾽ οὐχ ἱκαναὶ κατασχεῖν
ἄνοιαν νεότητος καὶ αὐθάδειαν τρόπων οὐδ᾽ εἰς τὸ
σῶφρον ἀγαγεῖν τοὺς ἠμεληκότας τῶν καλῶν αἱ
μαλακαὶ τιμωρίαι· τοιγάρτοι πολλὰ ἐν Ἕλλησιν
4 ὑπὸ τέκνων εἰς πατέρας ἀσχημονεῖται. ὁ δὲ τῶν
Ῥωμαίων νομοθέτης ἅπασαν ὡς εἰπεῖν ἔδωκεν
ἐξουσίαν πατρὶ καθ᾽ υἱοῦ καὶ παρὰ πάντα τὸν τοῦ
βίου χρόνον, ἐάν τε εἴργειν, ἐάν τε μαστιγοῦν, ἐάν
τε δέσμιον ἐπὶ τῶν κατ᾽ ἀγρὸν ἔργων κατέχειν,
ἐάν τε ἀποκτιννύναι προαιρῆται, κἂν τὰ πολιτικὰ
πράττων ὁ παῖς ἤδη τυγχάνῃ κἂν ἐν ἀρχαῖς ταῖς

[1] δεύτερον Bücheler.

XXVI. These, then, are the excellent laws which
Romulus enacted concerning women, by which he
rendered them more observant of propriety in relation to their husbands. But those he established
with respect to reverence and dutifulness of children
toward their parents, to the end that they should
honour and obey them in all things, both in their
words and actions, were still more august and of
greater dignity and vastly superior to our laws.
For those who established the Greek constitutions
set a very short time for sons to be under the rule
of their fathers, some till the expiration of the third
year after they reached manhood, others as long
as they continued unmarried, and some till their
names were entered in the public registers, as I
have learned from the laws of Solon, Pittacus and
Charondas, men celebrated for their great wisdom.
The punishments, also, which they ordered for dis-
obedience in children toward their parents were not
grievous : for they permitted fathers to turn their sons
out of doors and to disinherit them, but nothing
further. But mild punishments are not sufficient
to restrain the folly of youth and its stubborn ways
or to give self-control to those who have been heed-
less of all that is honourable ; and accordingly
among the Greeks many unseemly deeds are committed by children against their parents. But the
lawgiver of the Romans gave virtually full power
to the father over his son, even during his whole
life, whether he thought proper to imprison him, to
scourge him, to put him in chains and keep him at
work in the fields, or to put him to death, and this
even though the son were already engaged in public
affairs, though he were numbered among the highest

μεγίσταις ἐξεταζόμενος κἂν διὰ τὴν εἰς τὰ κοινὰ
5 φιλοτιμίαν ἐπαινούμενος. κατὰ τοῦτόν γέ τοι τὸν
νόμον ἄνδρες ἐπιφανεῖς δημηγορίας διεξιόντες ἐπὶ
τῶν ἐμβόλων ἐναντίας μὲν τῇ βουλῇ, κεχαρισμένας
δὲ τοῖς δημοτικοῖς, καὶ σφόδρα εὐδοκιμοῦντες ἐπὶ
ταύταις, κατασπασθέντες ἀπὸ τοῦ βήματος ἀπ-
ήχθησαν ὑπὸ τῶν πατέρων, ἣν ἂν ἐκείνοις φανῇ
τιμωρίαν ὑφέξοντες· οὓς ἀπαγομένους διὰ τῆς
ἀγορᾶς οὐδεὶς τῶν παρόντων ἐξελέσθαι δυνατὸς ἦν
οὔτε ὕπατος οὔτε δήμαρχος οὔτε ὁ κολακευόμενος
ὑπ᾽ αὐτῶν καὶ¹ πᾶσαν ἐξουσίαν ἐλάττω τῆς ἰδίας
6 εἶναι νομίζων ὄχλος. ἐῶ γὰρ λέγειν ὅσους ἀπέκτειναν οἱ πατέρες ἄνδρας ἀγαθοὺς ὑπ᾽ ἀρετῆς καὶ
προθυμίας ἕτερόν τι διαπράξασθαι γενναῖον ἔργον²
προαχθέντας ὃ μὴ προσέταξαν αὐτοῖς οἱ πατέρες,
καθάπερ ἐπὶ Μαλλίου Τορκουάτου καὶ πολλῶν
ἄλλων παρειλήφαμεν, ὑπὲρ ὧν κατὰ τὸν οἰκεῖον
καιρὸν ἐρῶ.

XXVII. Καὶ οὐδ᾽ ἐνταῦθα ἔστη τῆς ἐξουσίας ὁ
τῶν Ῥωμαίων νομοθέτης, ἀλλὰ καὶ πωλεῖν ἐφῆκε
τὸν υἱὸν τῷ πατρί, οὐδὲν ἐπιστραφεὶς εἴ τις ὠμὸν
ὑπολήψεται τὸ συγχώρημα καὶ βαρύτερον ἢ κατὰ
τὴν φυσικὴν συμπάθειαν. καὶ ὃ πάντων μάλιστα
θαυμάσειεν ἄν τις ὑπὸ τοῖς Ἑλληνικοῖς ἤθεσι τοῖς

¹ καὶ Reiske : κατὰ O.
² γενναῖον ἔργον R : ἔργον γενναῖον B, Jacoby.

---

¹ The son of the Manlius Torquatus who was consul in
340 B.C. Just before the battle with the Latins at the
foot of Mt. Vesuvius the consuls issued strict orders that
no Roman should engage in single combat with a Latin on

magistrates, and though he were celebrated for his zeal for the commonwealth. Indeed, in virtue of this law men of distinction, while delivering speeches from the rostra hostile to the senate and pleasing to the people, and enjoying great popularity on that account, have been dragged down from thence and carried away by their fathers to undergo such punishment as these thought fit; and while they were being led away through the Forum, none present, neither consul, tribune, nor the very populace, which was flattered by them and thought all power inferior to its own, could rescue them. I forbear to mention how many brave men, urged by their valour and zeal to perform some noble deed that their fathers had not ordered, have been put to death by those very fathers, as is related of Manlius Torquatus [1] and many others. But concerning them I shall speak in the proper place.

XXVII. And not even at this point did the Roman lawgiver stop in giving the father power over the son, but he even allowed him to sell his son, without concerning himself whether this permission might be regarded as cruel and harsher than was compatible with natural affection. And,—a thing which anyone who has been educated in the lax manners of the Greeks may wonder at above all things and

pain of death; but this youth could not resist the taunts of a Tusculan foe, and accepted his challenge. When he returned triumphantly with the spoils of his enemy, his father ordered his death. The portion of the *Antiquities* in which this incident was related is no longer extant.

ἐκλελυμένοις τραφεὶς ὡς πικρὸν καὶ τυραννικόν,
καὶ τοῦτο συνεχώρησε τῷ πατρί, μέχρι τρίτης
πράσεως ἀφ᾽ υἱοῦ χρηματίσασθαι, μείζονα δοὺς
ἐξουσίαν πατρὶ κατὰ παιδὸς ἢ δεσπότῃ κατὰ δού-
2 λων.¹ θεραπόντων μὲν γὰρ² ὁ πραθεὶς ἅπαξ,
ἔπειτα τὴν ἐλευθερίαν εὑρόμενος αὑτοῦ τὸ λοιπὸν
ἤδη κύριός ἐστιν, υἱὸς δὲ πραθεὶς ὑπὸ τοῦ πατρὸς
εἰ γένοιτο ἐλεύθερος ὑπὸ τῷ πατρὶ πάλιν ἐγίνετο,
καὶ³ τὸ δεύτερον ἀπεμποληθείς τε καὶ ἐλευθερωθεὶς
δοῦλος ὥσπερ ἐξ ἀρχῆς τοῦ πατρὸς ἦν· μετὰ δὲ
3 τὴν τρίτην πρᾶσιν ἀπήλλακτο τοῦ πατρός. τοῦτον
τὸν νόμον ἐν ἀρχαῖς μὲν οἱ βασιλεῖς ἐφύλαττον εἴτε
γεγραμμένον εἴτε ἄγραφον (οὐ γὰρ ἔχω τὸ σαφὲς
εἰπεῖν) ἁπάντων κράτιστον ἡγούμενοι νόμων.⁴ κατα-
λυθείσης δὲ τῆς μοναρχίας, ὅτε πρῶτον ἐφάνη
Ῥωμαίοις ἅπαντες τοὺς πατρίους ἐθισμούς τε καὶ
νόμους ἅμα τοῖς ἐπεισάκτοις ἐν ἀγορᾷ θεῖναι φανε-
ροὺς ἅπασι τοῖς πολίταις, ἵνα μὴ συμμεταπίπτῃ τὰ
κοινὰ δίκαια ταῖς τῶν ἀρχόντων ἐξουσίαις, οἱ λαβόντες παρὰ τοῦ δήμου τὴν ἐξουσίαν τῆς συναγωγῆς τε
καὶ ἀναγραφῆς αὐτῶν δέκα ἄνδρες ἅμα τοῖς ἄλλοις
ἀνέγραψαν νόμοις, καὶ ἔστιν ἐν τῇ τετάρτῃ τῶν
λεγομένων δώδεκα δέλτων, ἃς ἀνέθεσαν ἐν ἀγορᾷ.
4 ὅτι δ᾽ οὐχ οἱ δέκα ἄνδρες⁵ οἱ τριακοσίοις ἔτεσιν
ὕστερον ἀποδειχθέντες ἐπὶ τὴν ἀναγραφὴν τῶν νόμων
πρῶτοι τοῦτον εἰσηγήσαντο τὸν νόμον Ῥωμαίοις,
ἀλλ᾽ ἐκ πολλοῦ κείμενον παραλαβόντες οὐκ ἐτόλμησαν ἀνελεῖν, ἐκ πολλῶν μὲν καὶ ἄλλων κατα-

---

¹ δούλων B : δούλου A.　　　² γὰρ Reudler : γε O.
³ καὶ Kayser : κἂν O.　　　⁴ νόμων B : νόμον A, Jacoby.

390

look upon as harsh and tyrannical,—he even gave
leave to the father to make a profit by selling his
son as often as three times, thereby giving greater
power to the father over his son than to the master
over his slaves. For a slave who has once been sold
and has later obtained his liberty is his own master
ever after, but a son who had once been sold by
his father, if he became free, came again under his
father's power, and if he was a second time sold and
a second time freed, he was still, as at first, his
father's slave ; but after the third sale he was freed
from his father. This law, whether written or
unwritten, — I cannot say positively which, — the
kings observed in the beginning, looking upon it as
the best of all laws ; and after the overthrow of
the monarchy, when the Romans first decided to
expose in the Forum for the consideration of the
whole body of citizens all their ancestral customs
and laws, together with those introduced from
abroad, to the end that the rights of the people
might not be changed as often as the powers of
the magistrates, the decemvirs, who were authorized
by the people to collect and transcribe the laws,
recorded it among the rest, and it now stands on the
fourth of the Twelve Tables, as they are called, which
they then set up in the Forum. And that the decemvirs, who were appointed after three hundred
years to transcribe these laws, did not first introduce
this law among the Romans, but that, finding it
long before in use, they dared not repeal it, I infer
from many other considerations and particularly

---

⁵ οἱ δέκα ἄνδρες Cobet : οἱ ἄνδρες δέκα O.

λαμβάνομαι, μάλιστα δ' ἐκ τῶν Νόμα Πομπιλίου
τοῦ μετὰ Ῥωμύλον ἄρξαντος νόμων, ἐν οἷς καὶ οὗτος
γέγραπται· "'Εὰν πατὴρ υἱῷ συγχωρήσῃ γυναῖκα
ἀγαγέσθαι κοινωνὸν ἐσομένην ἱερῶν τε καὶ χρημάτων κατὰ τοὺς νόμους, μηκέτι τὴν ἐξουσίαν εἶναι
τῷ πατρὶ πωλεῖν τὸν υἱόν·" ὅπερ οὐκ ἂν ἔγραψεν εἰ
μὴ κατὰ τοὺς προτέρους νόμους ἅπαντας ἐξῆν τῷ
5 πατρὶ πωλεῖν τοὺς υἱούς. ἀλλ' ὑπὲρ μὲν τούτων
ἅλις, βούλομαι δὲ καὶ τὸν ἄλλον ἐπὶ κεφαλαίων [1]
διελθεῖν κόσμον, ᾧ τοὺς τῶν ἰδιωτῶν ὁ Ῥωμύλος
ἐκόσμησε βίους.

XXVIII. Ὁρῶν γὰρ ὅτι τὸ σωφρόνως ζῆν ἅπαντας καὶ τὰ δίκαια πρὸ τῶν κερδαλέων αἱρεῖσθαι
καρτερίαν τε τὴν παρὰ τοὺς πόνους ἀσκεῖν καὶ μηδὲν
ὑπολαμβάνειν χρῆμα τιμιώτερον ἀρετῆς οὐ λόγων
διδαχῇ παραγίνεσθαι τοῖς πολιτικοῖς πλήθεσι πέφυκεν, ἐν οἷς τὸ πλεῖόν ἐστι δυσάγωγον, ἀλλ' ἔργων
ἐθισμοῖς τῶν πρὸς ἑκάστην ἀρετὴν ἀγόντων, ὑπ'
ἀνάγκης τε μᾶλλον ἢ κατὰ γνώμην ἐπ' αὐτὰ τοὺς
πολλοὺς παραγινομένους,[2] εἰ δὲ μηδὲν εἴη τὸ κωλῦσον ἐπὶ τὴν φύσιν ὀλισθαίνοντας εἰδώς, ἐπιδιφρίους
μὲν καὶ βαναύσους καὶ προσαγωγοὺς ἐπιθυμιῶν
αἰσχρῶν τέχνας, ὡς ἀφανιζούσας καὶ λυμαινομένας
τά τε σώματα καὶ τὰς ψυχὰς τῶν μεταχειριζομένων,
δούλοις καὶ ξένοις ἀπέδωκε μεθοδεύειν· καὶ διέμεινεν ἕως πολλοῦ πάνυ χρόνου δι' αἰσχύνης ὄντα
Ῥωμαίοις τὰ τοιαῦτα ἔργα καὶ ὑπ' οὐδενὸς τῶν
2 αὐθιγενῶν ἐπιτηδευόμενα. δύο δὲ μόνα τοῖς ἐλευθέ-

---

[1] Sylburg : κεφαλαίῳ O.
[2] παραγομένους Kiessling, Hertlein.

from the laws of Numa Pompilius, the successor of Romulus, among which there is recorded the following: " If a father gives his son leave to marry a woman who by the laws is to be the sharer of his sacred rites and possessions, he shall no longer have the power of selling his son." Now he would never have written this unless the father had by all former laws been allowed to sell his sons. But enough has been said concerning these matters, and I desire also to give a summary account of the other measures by which Romulus regulated the lives of the private citizens.

XXVIII. Observing that the means by which the whole body of citizens, the greater part of whom are hard to guide, can be induced to lead a life of moderation, to prefer justice to gain, to cultivate perseverance in hardships, and to look upon nothing as more valuable than virtue, is not oral instruction, but the habitual practice of such employments as lead to each virtue, and knowing that the great mass of men come to practise them through necessity rather than choice, and hence, if there is nothing to restrain them, return to their natural disposition, he appointed slaves and foreigners to exercise those trades that are sedentary and mechanical and promote shameful passions, looking upon them as the destroyers and corruptors both of the bodies and souls of all who practise them ; and such trades were for a very long time held in disgrace by the Romans and were carried on by none of the native-born citizens. The only employments he left to free men were two,

ροις ἐπιτηδεύματα κατέλιπε τά τε κατὰ[1] γεωργίαν
καὶ τὰ κατὰ πολέμους, ὁρῶν ὅτι γαστρός τε ἄνθρωποι γίνονται διὰ τούτους τοὺς βίους ἐγκρατεῖς
ἀφροδισίοις τε ἧττον ἁλίσκονται παρανόμοις πλε-
ονεξίαν τε οὐ τὴν βλάπτουσαν ἀλλήλους διώκουσιν,
ἀλλὰ τὴν ἀπὸ τῶν πολεμίων περιποιουμένην τὰς
ὠφελείας. ἀτελῆ δὲ τούτων ἑκάτερον ἡγούμενος
εἶναι τῶν βίων χωριζόμενον θατέρου καὶ φιλαίτιον,
οὐχ ἑτέροις μέν τισιν ἀπέδωκεν ἐργάζεσθαι τὴν γῆν,
ἑτέροις δὲ τὰ πολεμίων φέρειν τε καὶ ἄγειν ὡς ὁ
παρὰ Λακεδαιμονίοις εἶχε νόμος, ἀλλὰ τοὺς αὐτοὺς
τόν τε πολεμικὸν καὶ τὸν γεωργικὸν ἔταξε βίον
3 ζῆν· εἰ μὲν εἰρήνην ἄγοιεν ἐπὶ τοῖς κατ' ἀγρὸν
ἔργοις ἐθίζων ἅπαντας μένειν, πλὴν εἴ ποτε δεηθεῖεν
ἀγορᾶς, τότε δ' εἰς ἄστυ συνιόντας ἀγοράζειν, ἐνάτην
ὁρίζων ἡμέραν ταῖς ἀγοραῖς· ὅτε δὲ πόλεμος κατα-
λάβοι στρατεύεσθαι διδάσκων καὶ μὴ παραχωρεῖν
ἑτέροις μήτε τῶν πόνων μήτε τῶν ὠφελειῶν. διῄρει
γὰρ αὐτοῖς ἐξ ἴσου γῆν τε ὅσην ἂν ἀφέλοιτο[2] πολεμίους καὶ ἀνδράποδα καὶ χρήματα, καὶ παρεσκεύαζεν
ἀγαπητῶς δέχεσθαι τὰς στρατείας.

XXIX. Τῶν δ' εἰς ἀλλήλους ἀδικημάτων οὐ
χρονίους ἀλλὰ ταχείας ἐποιεῖτο τὰς κρίσεις τὰ μὲν
αὐτὸς διαιτῶν, τὰ δ' ἄλλοις ἐπιτρέπων, καὶ τὰς

[1] κατέλιπε τά τε κατά Ambrosch : καταλείπεται τὰ κατὰ O
[2] ἀφέλοιτο B : ἀφέλοιτο R.

---

[1] The Spartan masters were the warrior class and the
Helots were primarily tillers of the soil. Nevertheless,
each Spartan soldier was accompanied to war by several
Helots, who fought as light-armed troops.

agriculture and warfare; for he observed that men
so employed become masters of their appetite, are
less entangled in illicit love affairs, and follow that
kind of covetousness only which leads them, not to
injure one another, but to enrich themselves at
the expense of the enemy. But, as he regarded
each of these occupations, when separate from the
other, as incomplete and conducive to fault-finding,
instead of appointing one part of the men to till
the land and the other to lay waste the enemy's
country, according to the practice of the Lacedaemonians,[1] he ordered the same persons to exercise
the employments both of husbandmen and soldiers.
In time of peace he accustomed them to remain
at their tasks in the country, except when it was
necessary for them to come to market, upon which
occasions they were to meet in the city in order to
traffic, and to that end he appointed every ninth [2]
day for the markets; and when war came he taught
them to perform the duties of soldiers and not to
yield to others either in the hardships or advantages
that war brought. For he divided equally among
them the lands, slaves and money that he took from
the enemy, and thus caused them to take part cheerfully in his campaigns.

XXIX. In the case of wrongs committed by
the citizens against one another he did not permit
the trials to be delayed, but caused them to be held
promptly, sometimes deciding the suits himself
and sometimes referring them to others; and he

---

[2] " Every ninth day," reckoning inclusively, means
every eighth day by modern reckoning. The name of
these market-days was *nundinae,* from *novem* and *dies.*

τιμωρίας αὐτῶν πρὸς τὰ μεγέθη τῶν ἁμαρτημάτων
ἐποιεῖτο ἀποτρέπειν τε ἀνθρώπους ἀπὸ παντὸς
ἔργου πονηροῦ τὸν φόβον μάλιστα δυνάμενον ὁρῶν
πολλὰ εἰς τοῦτο παρεσκευάσατο, χωρίον τε, ἐν ᾧ
καθεζόμενος ἐδίκαζεν, ἐν τῷ φανερωτάτῳ τῆς
ἀγορᾶς, καὶ στρατιωτῶν, οἳ παρηκολούθουν αὐτῷ
τριακόσιοι τὸν ἀριθμὸν ὄντες, καταπληκτικωτάτην
πρόσοψιν,[1] ῥάβδους τε καὶ πελέκεις ὑπ᾽ ἀνδρῶν
δώδεκα φερομένους, οἷς[2] τοὺς μὲν ἄξια μαστίγων
δεδρακότας ἔξαινον ἐν ἀγορᾷ, τῶν δὲ τὰ μέγιστα
ἠδικηκότων τοὺς τραχήλους ἀπέκοπτον ἐν τῷ
2 φανερῷ. τοιοῦτος μὲν δή τις ὁ κόσμος ἦν τῆς
κατασκευασθείσης ὑπὸ Ῥωμύλου πολιτείας· ἀπόχρη
γὰρ ἐκ τούτων καὶ περὶ τῶν ἄλλων εἰκάσαι.

XXX. Αἱ δὲ ἄλλαι πράξεις αἵ τε κατὰ τοὺς
πολέμους ὑπὸ τοῦ ἀνδρὸς γενόμεναι καὶ αἱ κατὰ
πόλιν,[3] ὧν ἄν τις καὶ λόγον[4] ποιήσαιτο ἐν ἱστορίας
2 γραφῇ, τοιαῦταί τινες παραδίδονται. πολλῶν
περιοικούντων τὴν Ῥώμην ἐθνῶν μεγάλων τε καὶ
τὰ πολέμια ἀλκίμων, ὧν οὐδὲν ἦν τοῖς Ῥωμαίοις
φίλιον, οἰκειώσασθαι ταῦτα βουληθεὶς ἐπιγαμίαις,
ὅσπερ ἐδόκει τοῖς παλαιοῖς τρόπος εἶναι βεβαιό-
τατος τῶν συναπτόντων φιλίας, ἐνθυμούμενος δὲ
ὅτι βουλόμεναι μὲν αἱ πόλεις οὐκ ἂν συνέλθοιεν
αὐτοῖς ἄρτι τε συνοικιζομένοις καὶ οὔτε χρήμασι
δυνατοῖς οὔτε λαμπρὸν ἔργον ἀποδεδειγμένοις[5]
οὐδέν, βιασθεῖσαι δὲ εἴξουσιν εἰ μηδεμία γένοιτο

---

[1] καταπληκτικωτάτην πρόσοψιν R : καταπληκτικώτατοι τὴν
πρόσοψιν B, Jacoby.
[2] οἷς B : οἱ R.
[3] κατὰ πόλιν O : κατὰ τὴν πόλιν Ambrosch, Jacoby.

proportioned the punishment to the magnitude of the crime. Observing, also, that nothing restrains men from all evil actions so effectually as fear, he contrived many things to inspire it, such as the place where he sat in judgment in the most conspicuous part of the Forum, the very formidable appearance of the soldiers who attended him, three hundred in number, and the rods and axes borne by twelve men,[1] who scourged in the Forum those whose offences deserved it and beheaded others in public who were guilty of the greatest crimes. Such. then, was the general character of the government established by Romulus; the details I have mentioned are sufficient to enable one to form a judgment of the rest.

XXX. The [2] other deeds reported of this man, both in his wars and at home, which may be thought deserving of mention in a history are as follows. Inasmuch as many nations that were both numerous and brave in war dwelt round about Rome and none of them was friendly to the Romans, he desired to conciliate them by intermarriages, which, in the opinion of the ancients, was the surest method of cementing friendships; but considering that the cities in question would not of their own accord unite with the Romans, who were just getting settled together in one city, and who neither were powerful by reason of their wealth nor had performed any brilliant exploit, but that they would yield to force

[1] The lictors; cf. Livy i. 8, 2-3.
[2] For chaps. 30-31 cf. Livy i. 9.

---

[4] καὶ λόγον Steph.: κατάλογον O.
[5] Garrer: ἐπιδεδειγμένοις O, Jacoby.

περὶ τὴν ἀνάγκην ὕβρις, γνώμην ἔσχεν, ᾗ καὶ
Νεμέτωρ ὁ πάππος αὐτοῦ προσέθετο, δι᾽ ἁρπαγῆς
παρθένων ἀθρόας γενομένης ποιήσασθαι τὰς ἐπι-
3 γαμίας. γνοὺς δὲ ταῦτα θεῷ μὲν εὐχὰς τίθεται
πρῶτον ἀπορρήτων βουλευμάτων ἡγεμόνι, ἐὰν ἡ
πεῖρα αὐτῷ χωρήσῃ κατὰ νοῦν θυσίας καὶ ἑορτὰς
ἄξειν καθ᾽ ἕκαστον ἐνιαυτόν· ἔπειτα τῷ συνεδρίῳ
τῆς γερουσίας ἀνενέγκας τὸν λόγον, ἐπειδὴ κἀκείνοις
τὸ βούλευμα ἤρεσκεν, ἑορτὴν προεῖπε καὶ πανήγυριν
ἄξειν Ποσειδῶνι καὶ περιήγγελλεν εἰς τὰς ἔγγιστα
πόλεις καλῶν τοὺς βουλομένους ἀγορᾶς τε μεταλαμ-
βάνειν καὶ ἀγώνων· καὶ γὰρ ἀγῶνας ἕξειν ἔμελλεν
4 ἵππων τε καὶ ἀνδρῶν παντοδαπούς. συνελθόντων
δὲ πολλῶν ξένων εἰς τὴν ἑορτὴν γυναιξὶν ἅμα
καὶ τέκνοις, ἐπειδὴ τάς τε θυσίας ἐπετέλεσε τῷ
Ποσειδῶνι καὶ τοὺς ἀγῶνας, τῇ τελευταίᾳ τῶν
ἡμερῶν, ᾗ διαλύσειν ἔμελλε τὴν πανήγυριν, παράγ-
γελμα δίδωσι τοῖς νέοις, ἡνίκ᾽ ἂν αὐτὸς ἄρῃ τὸ
σημεῖον ἁρπάζειν τὰς παρούσας ἐπὶ τὴν θέαν παρθένους, αἷς ἂν ἐπιτύχωσιν ἕκαστοι, καὶ φυλάττειν
ἁγνὰς ἐκείνην τὴν νύκτα, τῇ δ᾽ ἑξῆς ἡμέρᾳ πρὸς
5 ἑαυτὸν ἄγειν. οἱ μὲν δὴ νέοι διαστάντες κατὰ
συστροφάς, ἐπειδὴ τὸ σύνθημα ἀρθὲν εἶδον τρέπονται πρὸς τὴν τῶν παρθένων ἁρπαγήν, ταραχὴ
δὲ τῶν ξένων εὐθὺς ἐγένετο καὶ φυγὴ μεῖζόν τι
κακὸν ὑφορωμένων   τῇ δ᾽ ἑξῆς ἡμέρᾳ προαχθεισῶν
τῶν παρθένων, παραμυθησάμενος αὐτῶν τὴν ἀθυμίαν

if no insolence accompanied such compulsion, he deter
mined, with the approval of Numitor, his grand
father, to bring about the desired intermarriages by
a wholesale seizure of virgins. After he had taken
this resolution, he first made a vow to the god [1] who
presides over secret counsels to celebrate sacrifices
and festivals every year if his enterprise should succeed. Then, having laid his plan before the senate
and gaining their approval, he announced that he
would hold a festival and general assemblage in
honour of Neptune, and he sent word round about to
the nearest citics, inviting all who wished to do so to
be present at the assemblage and to take part in the
contests ; for he was going to hold contests of all
sorts, both between horses and between men. And
when many strangers came with their wives and
children to the festival, he first offered the sacrifices
to Neptune and held the contests ; then, on the last
day, on which he was to dismiss the assemblage, he
ordered the young men, when he himself should raise
the signal, to seize all the virgins who had come to the
spectacle, each group taking those they should first
encounter, to keep them that night without violating
their chastity and bring them to him the next day.
So the young men divided themselves into several
groups, and as soon as they saw the signal raised, fell
to seizing the virgins ; and straightway the strangers
were in an uproar and fled, suspecting some greater
mischief. The next day, when the virgins were
brought before Romulus, he comforted them in

[1] Consus. See p. 403 and note 1 (end).

ὁ 'Ρωμύλος, ὡς οὐκ ἐφ' ὕβρει τῆς ἁρπαγῆς ἀλλ' ἐπὶ
γάμῳ γενομένης, Ἑλληνικόν τε καὶ ἀρχαῖον ἀποφαίνων τὸ ἔθος καὶ τρόπον[1] συμπάντων καθ' οὓς
συνάπτονται γάμοι ταῖς γυναιξὶν ἐπιφανέστατον,
ἠξίου στέργειν τοὺς δοθέντας αὐταῖς ἄνδρας ὑπὸ
τῆς τύχης· καὶ μετὰ τοῦτο διαριθμήσας τὰς κόρας
ἑξακοσίας τε καὶ ὀγδοήκοντα καὶ τρεῖς εὑρεθείσας
κατέλεξεν αὖθις ἐκ τῶν ἀγάμων ἄνδρας ἰσαρίθμους,
οἷς αὐτὰς συνήρμοττε κατὰ τοὺς πατρίους ἑκάστης
ἐθισμούς, ἐπὶ κοινωνίᾳ πυρὸς καὶ ὕδατος ἐγγυῶν
τοὺς γάμους, ὡς καὶ μέχρι τῶν καθ' ἡμᾶς ἐπιτελοῦνται χρόνων.

XXXI. Ταῦτα δὲ γενέσθαι τινὲς μὲν γράφουσι
κατὰ τὸν πρῶτον ἐνιαυτὸν τῆς 'Ρωμύλου ἀρχῆς,
Γναῖος δὲ Γέλλιος κατὰ τὸν τέταρτον· ὃ καὶ μᾶλλον
εἰκός. νέον γὰρ οἰκιζομένης πόλεως ἡγεμόνα πρὶν
ἢ καταστήσασθαι τὴν πολιτείαν ἔργῳ τηλικούτῳ
ἐπιχειρεῖν οὐκ ἔχει[2] λόγον. τῆς δὲ ἁρπαγῆς τὴν
αἰτίαν οἱ μὲν εἰς σπάνιν γυναικῶν ἀναφέρουσιν,
οἱ δ' εἰς ἀφορμὴν πολέμου οἱ δὲ τὰ πιθανώτατα
γράφοντες, οἷς κἀγὼ συγκατεθέμην, εἰς τὸ συνάψαι
φιλότητα πρὸς τὰς πλησιοχώρους πόλεις ἀναγκαίαν.
2 τὴν δὲ τότε ὑπὸ 'Ρωμύλου[3] καθιερωθεῖσαν ἑορτὴν
ἔτι καὶ εἰς ἐμὲ ἄγοντες 'Ρωμαῖοι διετέλουν

---

[1] τρόπον A : τρόπων B, Jacoby.
[2] Bücheler : εἶχε O.
[3] ὑπὸ ῥωμύλου B : τῷ ῥωμύλῳ A.

their despair with the assurance that they had been
seized, not out of wantonness, but for the purpose
of marriage ; for he pointed out that this was an
ancient Greek custom [1] and that of all methods of
contracting marriages for women it was the most
illustrious, and he asked them to cherish those
whom Fortune had given them for their husbands.
Then counting them and finding their number to
be six hundred and eighty-three, he chose an equal
number of unmarried men to whom he united them
according to the customs of each woman's country.
basing the marriages on a communion of fire and
water, in the same manner as marriages are performed
even down to our times.

XXXI. Some state that these things happened
in the first year of Romulus' reign, but Gnaeus
Gellius says it was in the fourth, which is more
probable. For it is not likely that the head of a
newly-built city would undertake such an enterprise
before establishing its government. As regards the
reason for the seizing of the virgins, some ascribe
it to a scarcity of women, others to the seeking of a
pretext for war ; but those who give the most
plausible account—and with them I agree—attribute
it to the design of contracting an alliance with the
neighbouring cities, founded on affinity. And the
Romans even to my day continued to celebrate the
festival then instituted by Romulus, calling it the

[1] It is to be regretted that Dionysius did not see fit to
cite some specific instances of this practice from the Greek
world. But probably he merely inferred such an early
custom from some of the marriage rites of a later day, such
as the procedure of the Spartan bridegrooms described by
Plutarch (*Lycurg.* 15).

401

Κωνσουάλια καλοῦντες, ἐν ᾗ βωμός τε ὑπόγειος
ἱδρυμένος παρὰ τῷ μεγίστῳ τῶν ἱπποδρόμων
περισκαφείσης τῆς γῆς θυσίαις τε καὶ ὑπερπύροις
ἀπαρχαῖς γεραίρεται, καὶ δρόμος ἵππων ζευκτῶν τε
καὶ ἀζεύκτων ἐπιτελεῖται. καλεῖται δὲ ὁ θεός, ᾧ
ταῦτ᾽ ἐπιτελοῦσι, Κῶνσος ὑπὸ Ῥωμαίων, ὃν ἐξερμηνεύοντες εἰς τὴν ἡμετέραν γλῶτταν Ποσειδῶνα
Σεισίχθονά φασιν εἶναί τινες καὶ διὰ τοῦτο ὑπογείῳ
τετιμῆσθαι βωμῷ λέγουσιν, ὅτι τὴν γῆν ὁ θεὸς
3 οὗτος ἔχει. ἐγὼ δὲ καὶ ἕτερον οἶδα λόγον ἀκούων,
ὡς τῆς μὲν ἑορτῆς τῷ Ποσειδῶνι ἀγομένης καὶ τοῦ
δρόμου τῶν ἵππων[1] τούτῳ τῷ θεῷ γινομένου, τοῦ
δὲ καταγείου βωμοῦ δαίμονι ἀρρήτῳ τινὶ βουλευμάτων κρυφίων ἡγεμόνι καὶ φύλακι κατασκευασθέντος ὕστερον· Ποσειδῶνι γὰρ ἀφανῆ βωμὸν οὐδαμόθι
γῆς οὔθ᾽ ὑφ᾽ Ἑλλήνων οὔθ᾽ ὑπὸ βαρβάρων καθ-
ιδρῦσθαι· τὸ δ᾽ ἀληθὲς ὅπως ἔχει χαλεπὸν εἰπεῖν.

XXXII. Ὡς δὲ διεβοήθη τὰ περὶ τὴν ἁρπαγὴν
τῶν παρθένων καὶ τὰ περὶ τοὺς γάμους εἰς τὰς
πλησιοχώρους πόλεις, αἱ μὲν αὐτὸ τὸ πραχθὲν πρὸς
ὀργὴν ἐλάμβανον, αἱ δ᾽ ἀφ᾽ ἧς ἐπράχθη διαθέσεως

[1] ἵππων Sylburg : ἱππέων O.

---

[1] The Consualia was in origin a harvest festival held in
honour of Consus, an ancient Italic god of agriculture.
His altar was kept covered with earth except at these
festivals (cf. Plutarch, Rom. 14, 3), perhaps to commemo-
rate an ancient practice of storing the garnered grain underground or else to symbolize the secret processes of nature
in the production of crops. At the Consualia horses and
mules were given a holiday and crowned with flowers, as
we have already seen (i. 33, 2). Because of the races held

Consualia,[1] in the course of which a subterranean
altar, erected near the Circus Maximus, is un-
covered by the removal of the soil round about it
and honoured with sacrifices and burnt-offerings of
first-fruits and a course is run both by horses yoked
to chariots and by single horses. The god to whom
these honours are paid is called Consus by the
Romans, being the same, according to some who
render the name into our tongue, as Poseidon
Seisichthon or the " Earth-shaker " ; and they say
that this god was honoured with a subterranean
altar because he holds the earth.[2] I know also from
hearsay another tradition, to the effect that the
festival is indeed celebrated in honour of Neptune
and the horse-races are held in his honour, but
that the subterranean altar was erected later to a
certain divinity whose name may not be uttered,
who presides over and is the guardian of hidden
counsels ; for a secret altar has never been erected to
Neptune, they say, in any part of the world by either
Greeks or barbarians. But it is hard to say what
the truth of the matter is.

XXXII. When,[3] now, the report of the seizure of
the virgins and of their marriage was spread among
the neighbouring cities, some of these were incensed
at the proceeding itself, though others, considering

on his festival the god came to be identified with Poseidon
Hippios. The name Consus is evidently derived from the
verb *condere* (" to store up "); but the Romans connected it
with *consilium* and thought of him as a god of counsels
and secret plans.

[2] Or " upholds the earth." Compare his Greek epithet
Γαιήοχος (" Earth-upholding ").

[3] For chaps. 32-36 *cf.* Livy i. 10 ; 11, 1-5.

καὶ εἰς ὃ τέλος ἐχώρησεν ἀναλογιζόμεναι μετρίως
αὐτὸ ἔφερον, κατέσκηψε δ' οὖν ἀνὰ χρόνον εἰς
πολέμους τοὺς μὲν ἄλλους εὐπετεῖς, ἕνα δὲ τὸν
πρὸς Σαβίνους μέγαν καὶ χαλεπόν· οἷς ἅπασι τέλος
ἐπηκολούθησεν εὐτυχές, ὥσπερ αὐτῷ τὰ μαντεύματα
προεθέσπισε πρὶν ἐπιχειρῆσαι τῷ ἔργῳ, πόνους μὲν
καὶ κινδύνους μεγάλους προσημαίνοντα, τὰς δὲ
2 τελευτὰς αὐτῶν ἔσεσθαι καλάς. ἦσαν δὲ αἱ πρῶται
πόλεις ἄρξασαι τοῦ πρὸς αὐτὸν πολέμου Καινίνη
καὶ Ἄντεμνα καὶ Κρουστομερία, πρόφασιν μὲν
ποιούμεναι τὴν ἁρπαγὴν τῶν παρθένων καὶ τὸ μὴ
λαβεῖν ὑπὲρ αὐτῶν δίκας, ὡς δὲ τἀληθὲς εἶχεν
ἀχθόμεναι τῇ κτίσει τε καὶ αὐξήσει τῆς Ῥώμης δι'
ὀλίγου πολλῇ γενομένῃ καὶ οὐκ ἀξιοῦσαι περιιδεῖν
κοινὸν ἐπὶ τοῖς περιοίκοις ἅπασι κακὸν φυόμενον.
3 τέως μὲν οὖν πρὸς τὸ Σαβίνων ἔθνος ἀποστέλλουσαι
πρέσβεις ἐκείνους ἠξίουν τὴν ἡγεμονίαν τοῦ πολέμου
παραλαβεῖν ἰσχύν τε μεγίστην ἔχοντας καὶ χρήμασι
πλεῖστον [1] δυναμένους ἄρχειν τε ἀξιοῦντας τῶν
πλησιοχώρων καὶ οὐκ ἐλάχιστα τῶν ἄλλων περι-
υβρισμένους· τῶν γὰρ ἡρπασμένων αἱ πλείους ἦσαν
ἐκείνων.

XXXIII Ἐπεὶ δ' οὐδὲν ἐπέραινον ἀντικαθιστα-
μένων αὐταῖς τῶν παρὰ τοῦ Ῥωμύλου πρεσβειῶν
καὶ θεραπευουσῶν λόγοις τε καὶ ἔργοις τὸ ἔθνος,
ἀχθόμεναι τῇ τριβῇ τοῦ χρόνου, μελλόντων ἀεὶ τῶν
Σαβίνων καὶ ἀναβαλλομένων εἰς χρόνους μακροὺς

----

[1] πλεῖστον Cobet, πλεῖον Steph.[2]: πλείοσι O.

the motive from which it sprang and the outcome to which it led, bore it with moderation; but, at any rate, in the course of time it occasioned several wars, of which the rest were of small consequence, but that against the Sabines was a great and difficult one. All these wars ended happily, as the oracles had foretold to Romulus before he undertook the task, indicating as they did that the difficulties and dangers would be great but that their outcome would be prosperous. The first cities that made war upon him were Caenina, Antemnae and Crustumerium. They put forward as a pretext the seizure of the virgins and their failure to receive satisfaction on their account; but the truth was that they were displeased at the founding of Rome and at its great and rapid increase and felt that they ought not to permit this city to grow up as a common menace to all its neighbours. For the time being, then, these cities were sending ambassadors to the Sabines, asking them to take the command of the war, since they possessed the greatest military strength and were most powerful by reason of their wealth and were laying claim to the rule over their neighbours and inasmuch as they had suffered from the Romans' insolence quite as much as any of the rest; for the greater part of the virgins who had been seized belonged to them.

XXXIII. But when they found they were accomplishing nothing, since the embassies from Romulus opposed them and courted the Sabine people both by their words and by their actions, they were vexed at the waste of time—for the Sabines were forever affecting delays and putting off to distant

405

τὴν περὶ τοῦ πολέμου βουλήν, αὐταὶ καθ᾽ ἑαυτὰς
ἔγνωσαν τοῖς Ῥωμαίοις πολεμεῖν, ἀποχρῆν οἰόμεναι
τὴν οἰκείαν δύναμιν, εἰ καθ᾽ ἓν αἱ τρεῖς γένοιντο,
μίαν ἄρασθαι[1] πόλιν οὐ μεγάλην. ἐβουλεύσαντο
μὲν ταῦτα, συνελθεῖν δ᾽ οὐκ ἔφθησαν εἰς ἓν ἅπασαι
στρατόπεδον προεξαναστάντων προχειρότερον τῶν
ἐκ τῆς Καινίνης, οἵπερ καὶ μάλιστα ἐδόκουν τὸν
2 πόλεμον ἐνάγειν. ἐξεστρατευμένων δὲ τούτων καὶ
δῃούντων τὴν ὅμορον, ἐξαγαγὼν τὴν δύναμιν ὁ
Ῥωμύλος ἀφυλάκτοις οὖσιν ἔτι τοῖς πολεμίοις
ἀπροσδοκήτως ἐπιτίθεται καὶ τοῦ τε χάρακος
αὐτῶν ἀρτίως ἱδρυμένου γίνεται κύριος τοῖς τε
φεύγουσιν εἰς τὴν πόλιν ἐκ ποδὸς ἑπόμενος, οὐδέπω
τῶν ἔνδον πεπυσμένων τὴν περὶ τοὺς σφετέρους
συμφοράν, τεῖχός τε ἀφύλακτον εὑρὼν καὶ πύλας
ἀκλείστους αἱρεῖ τὴν πόλιν ἐξ ἐφόδου καὶ τὸν βασιλέα τῶν Καινινιτῶν ὑπαντήσαντα σὺν καρτερᾷ
χειρὶ μαχόμενος αὐτοχειρίᾳ κτείνει καὶ τὰ ὅπλα
ἀφαιρεῖται.

XXXIV. Τοῦτον δὲ τὸν τρόπον ἁλούσης τῆς
πόλεως τὰ ὅπλα παραδοῦναι τοὺς ἁλόντας κελεύσας
καὶ παῖδας εἰς ὁμηρείαν, οὓς ἐβούλετο, λαβὼν ἐπὶ
τοὺς Ἀντεμνάτας ἐχώρει. γενόμενος δὲ καὶ τῆς
ἐκείνων δυνάμεως ἐσκεδασμένης ἔτι κατὰ τὰς
προνομὰς τῇ παρ᾽ ἐλπίδας ἐφόδῳ καθάπερ καὶ
τῆς προτέρας ἐγκρατὴς καὶ τὰ αὐτὰ τοὺς ἁλόντας
διαθεὶς ἀπῆγεν ἐπ᾽ οἴκου τὴν δύναμιν, ἄγων σκῦλά

---

[1] ἄρασθαι Cobet: αἱρεῖσθαι A, αἱρῆισθαι Ba, αἱρήσειν Bb,
αἱρῆσαι R.

dates the deliberation concerning the war—and resolved to make war upon the Romans by themselves alone, believing that their own strength, if the three cities joined forces, was sufficient to conquer one inconsiderable city. This was their plan ; but they did not all assemble together promptly enough in one camp, since the Caeninenses, who seemed to be most eager in promoting the war. rashly set out ahead of the others. When these men, then, had taken the field and were wasting the country that bordered on their own, Romulus led out his army, and unexpectedly falling upon the enemy while they were as yet off their guard, he made himself master of their camp, which was but just completed. Then following close upon the heels of those who fled into the city, where the inhabitants had not as yet learned of the defeat of their forces, and finding the walls unguarded and the gates unbarred, he took the town by storm ; and when the king of the Caeninenses met him with a strong body of men, he fought with him, and slaying him with his own hands, stripped him of his arms.

XXXIV. The town being taken in this manner, he ordered the prisoners to deliver up their arms, and taking such of their children for hostages as he thought fit, he marched against the Antemnates. And having conquered their army also, in the same manner as the other, by falling upon them unexpectedly while they were still dispersed in foraging, and having accorded the same treatment to the prisoners, he led his army home, carrying with him

τε ἀπὸ τῶν πεπτωκότων¹ κατὰ τὴν μάχην καὶ
ἀκροθίνια λαφύρων θεοῖς, καὶ πολλὰς ἅμα τούτοις
2 θυσίας ἐποιήσατο. τελευταῖος δὲ τῆς πομπῆς αὐτὸς ἐπορεύετο ἐσθῆτα μὲν ἠμφιεσμένος ἁλουργῆ,
δάφνῃ δὲ κατεστεμμένος τὰς κόμας καί, ἵνα τὸ
βασίλειον ἀξίωμα σώζῃ, τεθρίππῳ παρεμβεβηκώς.
ἡ δ' ἄλλη δύναμις αὐτῷ παρηκολούθει πεζῶν τε
καὶ ἱππέων κεκοσμημένη κατὰ τέλη θεούς τε
ὑμνοῦσα πατρίοις ᾠδαῖς καὶ τὸν ἡγεμόνα κυδαί-
νουσα ποιήμασιν αὐτοσχεδίοις. οἱ δ' ἐκ τῆς
πόλεως ὑπήντων αὐτοῖς ἅμα γυναιξί τε καὶ τέκνοις
παρ' ἄμφω τὰ μέρη τῆς ὁδοῦ τῇ τε νίκῃ συνηδό-
μενοι καὶ τὴν ἄλλην ἅπασαν ἐνδεικνύμενοι φιλο-
φροσύνην. ὡς δὲ παρῆλθεν ἡ δύναμις εἰς τὴν πόλιν
κρατῆρσί τε ἐπετύγχανεν οἴνῳ κεκραμένοις καὶ
τραπέζαις τροφῆς παντοίας γεμούσαις, αἳ παρὰ τὰς
ἐπιφανεστάτας τῶν οἰκιῶν ἔκειντο, ἵνα ἐμφορεῖσθαι
3 τοῖς² βουλομένοις ᾖ. ἡ μὲν οὖν ἐπινίκιός τε καὶ
τροπαιοφόρος πομπὴ καὶ θυσία, ἣν καλοῦσι Ῥωμαῖοι
θρίαμβον, ὑπὸ Ῥωμύλου πρώτου κατασταθεῖσα
τοιαύτη τις ἦν ἐν δὲ τῷ καθ' ἡμᾶς βίῳ πολυτελὴς
γέγονε καὶ ἀλαζὼν εἰς πλούτου μᾶλλον ἐπίδειξιν ἢ
δόκησιν ἀρετῆς ἐπιτραγῳδουμένη καὶ καθ' ἅπασαν
4 ἰδέαν ἐκβέβηκε τὴν ἀρχαίαν εὐτέλειαν. μετὰ δὲ

¹ πεπτωκότων Bücheler, ἀποθανόντων or ἁλόντων Steph.²,
ἀπολωλότων Reiske, πεσόντων Kiessling: ἀποίκων O.
² ἐμφορεῖσθαι τοῖς Bücheler: τοῖς ἐμφορεῖσθαι O.

the spoils of those who had been slain in battle
and the choicest part of the booty as an offering
to the gods ; and he offered many sacrifices besides.
Romulus himself came last in the procession, clad
in a purple robe and wearing a crown of laurel
upon his head, and, that he might maintain the
royal dignity, he rode in a chariot drawn by four
horses.[1] The rest of the army, both foot and horse,
followed, ranged in their several divisions, praising
the gods in songs of their country and extolling
their general in improvised verses. They were met
by the citizens with their wives and children, who,
ranging themselves on each side of the road, con-
gratulated them upon their victory and expressed
their welcome in every other way. When the army
entered the city, they found mixing bowls filled to
the brim with wine and tables loaded down with all
sorts of viands, which were placed before the most
distinguished houses in order that all who pleased
might take their fill. Such was the victorious procession, marked by the carrying of trophies and
concluding with a sacrifice, which the Romans call
a triumph, as it was first instituted by Romulus.
But in our day the triumph has become a very
costly and ostentatious pageant, being attended
with a theatrical pomp that is designed rather as
a display of wealth than as the approbation of
valour, and it has departed in every respect from
its ancient simplicity. After the procession and the

---

[1] Plutarch (*Romulus* 16) corrects Dionysius on this point,
claiming that the first Tarquin, or, according to some,
Publicola, was the first to use a chariot in the triumphal
procession.

τῆι πομπήν τε καὶ θυσίαν νεὼν κατασκευάσας ὁ
Ῥωμύλος ἐπὶ τῆς κορυφῆς τοῦ Καπιτωλίου [1] Διός,
ὃν ἐπικαλοῦσι Ῥωμαῖοι Φερέτριον, οὗ μέγαν (ἔτι
γὰρ αὐτοῦ σώζεται τὸ ἀρχαῖον ἴχνος ἐλάττονας ἢ
πέντε ποδῶν καὶ δέκα τὰς μείζους πλευρὰς ἔχον),
ἐν τούτῳ καθιέρωσε τὰ σκῦλα τοῦ Καινινιτῶν
βασιλέως, ὃν αὐτοχειρίᾳ κατειργάσατο. τὸν δὲ
Δία τὸν Φερέτριον, ᾧ τὰ ὅπλα ὁ Ῥωμύλος
ἀνέθηκεν, εἴτε βούλεταί τις Τροπαιοῦχον εἴτε
Σκυλοφόρον καλεῖν ὡς ἀξιοῦσί τινες εἴθ', ὅτι
πάντων ὑπερέχει καὶ πᾶσαν ἐν κύκλῳ περιείληφε
τὴν τῶν ὄντων φύσιν τε καὶ κίνησιν, Ὑπερφερέτην,
οὐχ ἁμαρτήσεται τῆς ἀληθείας.

XXXV Ὡς δ' ἀπέδωκε τοῖς θεοῖς ὁ βασιλεὺς
τὰς χαριστηρίους θυσίας τε καὶ ἀπαρχάς, πρὶν ἢ
τῶν ἄλλων τι διαπράξασθαι βουλὴν ἐποιεῖτο περὶ
τῶν κρατηθεισῶν πόλεων, ὅντινα χρηστέον αὐταῖς
τρόπον, αὐτὸς ἦν ὑπελάμβανε κρατίστην εἶναι
2 γνώμην πρῶτος ἀποδειξάμενος. ὡς δὲ πᾶσι τοῖς
ἐν τῷ συνεδρίῳ παροῦσιν ἥ τε ἀσφάλεια τῶν
βουλευμάτων τοῦ ἡγεμόνος ἤρεσκε καὶ ἡ λαμπρό-
της τά τε ἄλλα ὅσα ἐξ αὐτῶν γενήσεται τῇ πόλει
χρήσιμα οὐκ ἐν τῷ παραχρῆμα μόνον ἀλλὰ καὶ
εἰς ἅπαντα τὸν ἄλλον χρόνον ἐπῃνεῖτο, συνελθεῖν
κελεύσας τὰς γυναῖκας ὅσαι τοῦ τε Ἀντεμνατῶν
καὶ τοῦ Καινινιτῶν ἐτύγχανον οὖσαι γένους, ἡρπα-
σμέναι δὲ ἅμα ταῖς ἄλλαις, ἐπεὶ δὲ [2] συνῆλθον ὀλοφυρό-
μεναί τε καὶ προκυλιόμεναι καὶ τὰς τῶν πατρίδων

---

[1] λόφου after Καπιτωλίου deleted by Kiessling.
[2] ἐπεὶ δὲ Kiessling : ἐπειδὴ O.

sacrifice Romulus built a small temple on the summit
of the Capitoline hill to Jupiter whom the Romans
call Feretrius ; indeed, the ancient traces of it still
remain, of which the longest sides are less than fifteen
feet. In this temple he consecrated the spoils of
the king of the Caeninenses, whom he had slain with
his own hand. As for Jupiter Feretrius, to whom
Romulus dedicated these arms, one will not err from
the truth whether one wishes to call him *Tropaiouchos*,
or *Skylophoros*, as some will have it, or, since he
excels all things and comprehends universal nature
and motion, *Hyperpheretês*.[1]

XXXV. After the king had offered to the gods
the sacrifices of thanksgiving and the first-fruits of
victory, before entering upon any other business,
he assembled the senate to deliberate with them in
what manner the conquered cities should be treated,
and he himself first delivered the opinion he thought
the best. When all the senators who were present
had approved of the counsels of their chief as both
safe and brilliant and had praised all the other advantages that were likely to accrue from them to the
commonwealth, not only for the moment but for
all future time, he gave command for the assembling
of all the women belonging to the race of the
Antemnates and of the Caeninenses who had been
seized with the rest. And when they had assembled,
lamenting, throwing themselves at his feet and
bewailing the calamities of their native cities, he

---

[1] These three Greek words mean, respectively, " Bearer
(or Receiver) of Trophies," " Bearer of Spoils," and
" Supreme." Dionysius obviously derived *Feretrius* from
ferre (" to bear "); but modern scholars agree with Propertius (iv. 10, 46) in connecting it with *ferire* (" to
strike ").

ἀνακλαίουσαι τύχας, ἐπισχεῖν τῶν ὀδυρμῶν καὶ
3 σιωπῆσαι κελεύσας ἔλεξε· " Τοῖς μὲν ὑμετέροις
πατράσι καὶ ἀδελφοῖς καὶ ὅλαις ταῖς πόλεσιν ὑμῶν
ἅπαντα τὰ δεινὰ ὀφείλεται παθεῖν, ὅτι πόλεμον
ἀντὶ φιλίας οὔτε ἀναγκαῖον οὔτε καλὸν ἀνείλοντο·
ἡμεῖς δὲ πολλῶν ἕνεκεν ἐγνώκαμεν μετρίᾳ χρήσασθαι γνώμῃ πρὸς αὐτοὺς θεῶν τε νέμεσιν ὑφορώ-
μενοι τὴν ἅπασι τοῖς ὑπερόγκοις ἐνισταμένην καὶ
ἀνθρώπων φθόνον δεδιότες ἔλεόν τε κοινῶν κακῶν
οὐ μικρὸν ἔρανον εἶναι νομίζοντες, ὡς κἂν[1] αὐτοί
ποτε τοῦ παρ' ἑτέρων δεηθέντες, ὑμῖν τε οὐ μεμπταῖς
ὑπαρχούσαις μέχρι τοῦδε περὶ τοὺς ἑαυτῶν ἄνδρας
οὐ μικρὰν οἰόμενοι ταύτην ἔσεσθαι τιμὴν καὶ χάριν.
4 παρίεμεν οὖν αὐτοῖς τὴν ἁμαρτάδα ταύτην ἀζήμιον
καὶ οὔτε ἐλευθερίαν οὔτε κτῆσιν οὔτ' ἄλλο τῶν
ἀγαθῶν οὐδὲν τοὺς πολίτας ὑμῶν ἀφαιρούμεθα.
ἐφίεμεν δὲ τοῖς τε μένειν γλιχομένοις ἐκεῖ καὶ τοῖς
μετενέγκασθαι βουλομένοις τὰς οἰκήσεις ἀκίνδυνόν
τε καὶ ἀμεταμέλητον τὴν αἵρεσιν. τοῦ δὲ μηδὲν
ἔτι αὐτοὺς ἐπεξαμαρτεῖν μηδ' εὑρεθῆναί τι χρῆμα,
ὃ ποιήσει τὰς πόλεις διαλύσασθαι τὴν πρὸς ἡμᾶς
φιλίαν, φάρμακον ἡγούμεθα κράτιστον εἶναι πρὸς
εὐδοξίαν τε καὶ πρὸς ἀσφάλειαν τὸ αὐτὸ χρήσιμον
ἀμφοτέροις, εἰ ποιήσαιμεν ἀποικίας τῆς Ῥώμης
τὰς πόλεις καὶ συνοίκους αὐταῖς πέμψαιμεν αὐτόθεν
τοὺς ἱκανούς. ἄπιτε οὖν ἀγαθὴν ἔχουσαι διάνοιαν
καὶ διπλασίως ἢ πρότερον ἀσπάζεσθε καὶ τιμᾶτε
τοὺς ἄνδρας, ὑφ' ὧν γονεῖς τε ὑμῶν ἐσώθησαν καὶ

---

[1] κἂν Kiessling: καὶ O.

412

commanded them to cease their lamentations and be silent, then spoke to them as follows : " Your fathers and brothers and your entire cities deserve to suffer every severity for having preferred to our friendship a war that was neither necessary nor honourable. We, however, have resolved for many reasons to treat them with moderation ; for we not only fear the vengeance of the gods, which ever threatens the arrogant, and dread the ill-will of men, but we also are persuaded that mercy contributes not a little to alleviate the common ills of mankind, and we realize that we ourselves may one day stand in need of that of others. And we believe that to you, whose behaviour towards your husbands has thus far been blameless, this will be no small honour and favour. We suffer this offence of theirs, therefore, to go unpunished and take from your fellow citizens neither their liberty nor their possessions nor any other advantages they enjoy ; and both to those who desire to remain there and to those who wish to change their abode we grant full liberty to make their choice, not only without danger but without fear of repenting. But, to prevent their ever repeating their fault or the finding of any occasion to induce their cities to break off their alliance with us, the best means, we consider, and that which will at the same time conduce to the reputation and security of both, is for us to make those cities colonies of Rome and to send a sufficient number of our own people from here to inhabit them jointly with your fellow citizens. Depart, therefore, with good courage ; and redouble your love and regard for your husbands, to whom your parents

5 ἀδελφοὶ καὶ πατρίδες ἐλεύθεραι ἀφίενται." αἱ μὲν
δὴ γυναῖκες ὡς ταῦτ' ἤκουσαν περιχαρεῖς γενόμεναι
καὶ πολλὰ δάκρυα ὑφ' ἡδονῆς ἀφεῖσαι μετέστησαν
ἐκ τῆς ἀγορᾶς, ὁ δὲ Ῥωμύλος τριακοσίους μὲν
ἄνδρας εἰς ἑκατέραν ἀποίκους ἀπέστειλεν, οἷς
ἔδοσαν αἱ πόλεις τρίτην κατακληρουχῆσαι μοῖραν
6 τῆς ἑαυτῶν γῆς. Καινινιτῶν δὲ καὶ Ἀντεμνατῶν
τοὺς βουλομένους μεταθέσθαι τὴν οἴκησιν εἰς
Ῥώμην γυναιξὶν ἅμα καὶ τέκνοις μετήγαγον κλήρους τε τοὺς ἑαυτῶν ἔχοντας καὶ χρήματα φερομένους ὅσα ἐκέκτηντο, οὓς εὐθὺς εἰς φυλὰς καὶ
φράτρας ὁ βασιλεὺς κατέγραψε,[1] τρισχιλίων οὐκ
ἐλάττους ὄντας, ὥστε τοὺς σύμπαντας ἑξακισχιλίους
πεζοὺς Ῥωμαίοις τότε πρῶτον ἐκ καταλόγου γε-
7 νέσθαι. Καινίνη μὲν δὴ καὶ Ἄντεμνα πόλεις οὐκ
ἄσημοι γένος ἔχουσαι τὸ Ἑλληνικόν, Ἀβοριγῖνες
γὰρ αὐτὰς ἀφελόμενοι τοὺς Σικελοὺς κατέσχον,
Οἰνώτρων μοῖρα τῶν ἐξ Ἀρκαδίας ἀφικομένων, ὡς
εἴρηταί μοι πρότερον, μετὰ τόνδε τὸν πόλεμον
ἀποικίαι Ῥωμαίων γεγένηντο.

XXXVI. Ὁ δὲ Ῥωμύλος ταῦτα διαπραξάμενος
ἐπὶ Κρουστομερίνους ἐξάγει τὴν στρατιὰν παρεσκευ-
ασμένους ἄμεινον τῶν προτέρων· οὓς ἐκ παρατάξεώς τε καὶ τειχομαχίας παραστησάμενος ἄνδρας
ἀγαθοὺς κατὰ τὸν ἀγῶνα γενομένους οὐδὲν ἔτι
διαθεῖναι κακὸν ἠξίωσεν, ἀλλὰ καὶ ταύτην ἐποίησεν
ἄποικον Ῥωμαίων τὴν πόλιν ὥσπερ τὰς προτέρας.
2 ἦν δὲ τὸ Κρουστομέριον Ἀλβανῶν ἀπόκτισις[2]

---

[1] Bücheler: κατέγραφε O.
[2] ἀπόκτισις ABa : ἀποίκησις Bb.

and brothers owe their preservation and your countries their liberty." The women, hearing this, were
greatly pleased, and shedding many tears of joy,
left the Forum ; but Romulus sent a colony of three
hundred men into each city, to whom these cities
gave a third part of their lands to be divided among
them by lot. And those of the Caeninenses and
Antemnates who desired to remove to Rome they
brought thither together with their wives and
children, permitting them to retain their allotments
of land and to take with them all their possessions ;
and the king immediately enrolled them, numbering
not less than three thousand, in the tribes and the
curiae, so that the Romans had then for the first
time six thousand foot in all upon the register. Thus
Caenina and Antemnae, no inconsiderable cities,
whose inhabitants were of Greek origin (for the
Aborigines had taken the cities from the Sicels and
occupied them, these Aborigines being, as I said
before, part of those Oenotrians who had come out
of Arcadia [1]), after this war became Roman colonies.

XXXVI. Romulus, having attended to these
matters, led out his army against the Crustumerians,
who were better prepared than the armies of the
other cities had been. And after he had reduced
them both in a pitched battle and in an assault upon
their city, although they had shown great bravery
in the struggle, he did not think fit to punish them
any further, but made this city also a Roman colony
like the two former. Crustumerium was a colony of

[1] i. 13.

πολλοῖς πρότερον τῆς Ῥώμης ἀποσταλεῖσα χρόνοις.
διαγγελλούσης δὲ τῆς φήμης πολλαῖς πόλεσι τήν τε
κατὰ πολέμους γενναιότητα τοῦ ἡγεμόνος καὶ τὴν¹
πρὸς τοὺς κρατηθέντας ἐπιείκειαν ἄνδρες τε αὐτῷ
προσετίθεντο πολλοὶ καὶ ἀγαθοὶ δυνάμεις ἀξιοχρέους
πανοικίᾳ μετανισταμένας ἐπαγόμενοι, ὧν ἐφ' ἑνὸς
ἡγεμόνος ἐκ Τυρρηνίας ἐλθόντος, ᾧ Καίλιος ὄνομα
ἦν, τῶν λόφων τις, ἐν ᾧ καθιδρύθη, Καίλιος εἰς
τόδε χρόνου καλεῖται· καὶ πόλεις ὅλαι παρεδίδοσαν
ἑαυτὰς ἀπὸ τῆς Μεδυλλίνων ἀρξάμεναι καὶ ἐγίνοντο
3 Ῥωμαίων ἀποικίαι. Σαβῖνοι δὲ ταῦτα ὁρῶντες
ἤχθοντο καὶ δι' αἰτίας ἀλλήλους εἶχον, ὅτι οὐκ
ἀρχομένην τὴν Ῥωμαίων ἰσχὺν ἐκώλυσαν, ἀλλ'
ἐπὶ μέγα προηκούσῃ συμφέρεσθαι ἔμελλον, ἐδόκει
τε αὐτοῖς ἐπανορθώσασθαι τὴν προτέραν ἄγνοιαν
ἀξιολόγου δυνάμεως ἀποστολῇ. καὶ μετὰ τοῦτο
ἀγορὰν ποιησάμενοι σύμπαντες ἐν τῇ μεγίστῃ τε
πόλει καὶ πλεῖστον ἀξίωμα ἐχούσῃ τοῦ ἔθνους, ᾗ
Κύρις ὄνομα ἦν, ψῆφον ὑπὲρ τοῦ πολέμου διήνεγκαν
ἀποδείξαντες ἡγεμόνα τῆς στρατιᾶς Τῖτον, ὃς ἐπεκαλεῖτο Τάτιος, βασιλέα Κυριτῶν. Σαβῖνοι μὲν
δὴ ταῦτα βουλευσάμενοι καὶ διαλυθέντες κατὰ τὰς
πόλεις τὰ πρὸς τὸν πόλεμον ηὐτρεπίζοντο, ὡς εἰς
νέωτα ἐπὶ τὴν Ῥώμην πολλῇ χειρὶ ἐλάσοντες.

XXXVII. Ἐν τούτῳ δὲ καὶ ὁ Ῥωμύλος ἀντι-
παρεσκευάζετο τὰ κράτιστα, ὡς ἀμυνούμενος ἄνδρας
τὰ πολέμια ἀλκίμους, τοῦ μὲν Παλατίου τὸ τεῖχος
ὡς ἀσφαλέστερον εἶναι τοῖς ἔνδον ὑψηλοτέροις ἐρύμασιν ἐγείρων, τοὺς δὲ παρακειμένους αὐτῷ λόφους

¹ τὴν Ambrosch : om. O, Jacoby.

the Albans sent out many years before the founding of Rome. The fame of the general's valour in war and of his clemency to the conquered being spread through many cities, many brave men joined him, bringing with them considerable bodies of troops, who migrated with their whole families. From one of these leaders, who came from Tyrrhenia and whose name was Caelius, one of the hills, on which he settled, is to this day called the Caelian. Whole cities also submitted to him, beginning with Medullia, and became Roman colonies. But the Sabines, seeing these things, were displeased and blamed one another for not having crushed the power of the Romans while it was in its infancy, instead of which they were now to contend with it when it was greatly increased. They determined, therefore, to make amends for their former mistake by sending out an army of respectable size. And soon afterwards, assembling a general council in the greatest and most famous city of the nation, called Cures they voted for the war and appointed Titus, surnamed Tatius, the king of that city, to be their general. After the Sabines had come to this decision, the assembly broke up and all returned home to their several cities, where they busied themselves with their preparations for the war, planning to advance on Rome with a great army the following year.

XXXVII. In the meantime Romulus also was making the best preparations he could in his turn, realizing that he was to defend himself against a warlike people. With this in view, he raised the wall of the Palatine hill by building higher ramparts upon it as a further security to the inhabitants. and fortified the adjacent hills—the

417

τόν τε Αὐεντῖνον καὶ τὸν Καπιτωλῖνον νῦν λεγόμενοι ἀποταφρεύων καὶ χαρακώμασι καρτεροῖς
περιλαμβάνων, ἐν οἷς τὰ ποίμνια καὶ τοὺς γεωργοὺς
αὐλίζεσθαι τὰς νύκτας ἐπέταξεν ἐχεγγύῳ φρουρᾷ
καταλαβὼν ἑκάτερον, καὶ εἴ τι ἄλλο χωρίον ἀσφάλειαν αὐτοῖς παρέξειν ἔμελλεν ἀποταφρεύων καὶ
2 περισταυρῶν καὶ διὰ φυλακῆς ἔχων. ἧκε δὲ αὐτῷ
Τυρρηνῶν ἐπικουρίαι ἱκανὴν ἄγων ἐκ Σολωνίου[1]
πόλεως ἀνὴρ δραστήριος καὶ τὰ πολέμια[2] διαφανής,
Λοκόμων ὄνομα, φίλος οὐ πρὸ πολλοῦ γεγονώς, καὶ
παρ' Ἀλβανῶν ἄνδρες, οὓς ὁ πάππος ἔπεμψεν αὐτῷ,
συχνοὶ στρατιῶται τε καὶ ὑπηρέται καὶ τεχνῖται
πολεμικῶν ἔργων, σῖτός τε καὶ ὅπλα καὶ ὅσα τούτοις πρόσφορα ἦν ἱκανῶς[3] ἅπαντα ἐπεχορηγεῖτο.
3 ἐπεὶ δ' ἐν ἑτοίμῳ τὰ πρὸς τὸν ἀγῶνα ἦι ἑκατέροις,
ἔαρος ἀρχομένου μέλλοντες ἐξάγειν οἱ Σαβῖνοι τὰς
δυνάμεις ἔγνωσαν ἀποστεῖλαι πρεσβείαν πρῶτον ὡς
τοὺς πολεμίους τάς τε γυναῖκας ἀξιώσουσαν ἀπολαβεῖν καὶ δίκας ὑπὲρ αὐτῶν αἰτήσουσαν τῆς
ἁρπαγῆς, ἵνα δὴ δι' ἀνάγκην δοκῶσιν ἀνειληφέναι
τὸν πόλεμον οὐ τυγχάνοντες τῶν δικαίων, καὶ τοὺς
4 κήρυκας ἔπεμπον ἐπὶ ταῦτα. Ῥωμύλου δὲ ἀξιοῦντος τὰς μὲν γυναῖκας. ἐπειδὴ οὐδ' αὐταῖς ἀκούσαις

---

[1] Οὐολσινίοι O. Müller. Οὐετολωνίου Cluver, Ποπλωνίου
Casaubon.
[2] ἔργα after πολέμια deleted by Ambrosch.
[3] ἱκανῶς Sintenis: καὶ οἷς AB.

418

Aventine and the one now called the Capitoline—
with ditches and strong palisades, and upon these
hills he ordered the husbandmen with their flocks
to pass the nights, securing each of them by a sufficient garrison ; and likewise any other place that
promised to afford them security he fortified with
ditches and palisades and kept under guard. In the
meantime there came to him a man of action and
reputation for military achievements, named Lucumo,
lately become his friend, who brought with him
from the city of Solonium [1] a considerable body of
Tyrrhenian mercenaries. There came to him also
from the Albans, sent by his grandfather, a goodly
number of soldiers with their attendants, and with
them artificers for making engines of war ; these
men were adequately supplied with provisions,
arms and all necessary equipment. When everything was ready for the war on both sides, the Sabines,
who planned to take the field at the beginning of
spring, resolved first to send an embassy to the
enemy both to ask for the return of the women and
to demand satisfaction for their seizure, just so
that they might seem to have undertaken the war
from necessity when they failed to get justice,
and they were sending the heralds for this purpose.
Romulus, however, asked that the women, since
they themselves were not unwilling to live with

---

[1] Solonium was an ancient city about twelve miles from
Rome, near the Ostian Way. It disappeared at an early
date, but its name survived in the *Solonius ager*. The
statement of Dionysius is confirmed by Propertius iv. 1,
31, where the latest editions, following the Neapolitan
MS., read *hinc Tities Ramnesque viri Luceresque Soloni*
(instead of *coloni*).

ὁ μετὰ τῶν ἀνδρῶν βίος ἦν, ἐὰν παρὰ τοῖς γεγαμη-
κόσι μένειν, εἰ δέ τινος ἄλλου δέονται, λαμβάνειν
ὡς παρὰ φίλων, πολέμου δὲ μὴ ἄρχειν, οὐδενὶ
τῶν ἀξιουμένων ὑπακούσαντες ἐξῆγον τὴν στρατιὰν
πεζοὺς μὲν ἄγοντες πεντακισχιλίους ἐπὶ δύο μυριά-
5 σιν, ἱππεῖς δὲ ὀλίγου δέοντας χιλίων. ἦν δὲ καὶ
ἡ[1] τῶν Ῥωμαίων δύναμις οὐ πολὺ τῆς Σαβίνων
ἀποδέουσα[2] δύο μὲν αἱ τῶν πεζῶν μυριάδες, ὀκτα-
κόσιοι δ' ἱππεῖς, καὶ προεκάθητο τῆς πόλεως διχῇ
διῃρημένη, μία μὲν μοῖρα τὸν Ἐσκυλῖνον κατέχουσα
λόφον, ἐφ' ἧς αὐτὸς ὁ Ῥωμύλος ἦν, ἑτέρα δὲ τὸν
Κυρίνιον οὔπω[3] ταύτην[4] ἔχοντα τὴν προσηγορίαν,
ἧς ὁ Τυρρηνὸς ἦν Λοκόμων ἡγεμών.

XXXVIII Μαθὼν δὲ τὴν παρασκευὴν αὐτῶν
Τάτιος[5] ὁ τῶν Σαβίνων βασιλεὺς νυκτὸς ἀναστήσας
τὸν στρατὸν ἦγε διὰ τῆς χώρας οὐδὲν σινόμενος[6]
τῶν κατὰ τοὺς ἀγροὺς καὶ πρὶν ἀνατεῖλαι τὸν
ἥλιον μεταξὺ τοῦ τε Κυρινίου καὶ τοῦ Καπιτωλίου
τίθησιν ἐν τῷ πεδίῳ τὸν χάρακα. ὁρῶν δὲ ἀσφαλεῖ
πάντα φυλακῇ κατεχόμενα πρὸς τῶν πολεμίων,
σφίσι δὲ οὐδὲν χωρίον ἀπολειπόμενον ὀχυρὸν εἰς
πολλὴν ἐνέπιπτεν ἀπορίαν οὐκ ἔχων ὅ τι χρήσεται
2 τῇ τριβῇ τοῦ χρόνου. ἀμηχανοῦντι δὲ αὐτῷ παρά-
δοξος εὐτυχία γίνεται παραδοθέντος τοῦ κρατίστου
τῶν ὀχυρωμάτων κατὰ τοιάνδε τινὰ συντυχίαν.
παρεξιόντας γὰρ τὴν ῥίζαν τοῦ Καπιτωλίου τοὺς
Σαβίνους εἰς ἐπίσκεψιν, εἴ τι μέρος εὑρεθείη τοῦ

---

[1] ἡ added by Ambrosch.   [2] Cobet: δέουσα O.
[3] οὔπω Ambrosch: οὔπω τὲ A, οὔποτε B.
[4] Sylburg: αὐτὴν O.
[5] Steph.: τάτις A τῖτος B (and so elsewhere).

their husbands, should be permitted to remain with them; but he offered to grant the Sabines anything else they desired, provided they asked it as from friends and did not begin war. Thereupon the others, agreeing to none of his proposals, led out their army, which consisted of twenty-five thousand foot and almost a thousand horse. And the Roman army was not much smaller than that of the Sabines, the foot amounting to twenty thousand and the horse to eight hundred; it was encamped before the city in two divisions, one of them, under Romulus himself, being posted on the Esquiline hill, and the other, commanded by Lucumo, the Tyrrhenian, on the Quirinal, which did not as yet have that name.

XXXVIII. Tatius,[1] the king of the Sabines, being informed of their preparations, broke camp in the night and led his army through the country, without doing any damage to the property in the fields, and before sunrise encamped on the plain that lies between the Quirinal and Capitoline hills. But observing all the posts to be securely guarded by the enemy and no strong position left for his army, he fell into great perplexity, not knowing what use to make of the enforced delay. While he was thus at his wit's end, he met with an unexpected piece of good fortune, the strongest of the fortresses being delivered up to him in the following circumstances. It seems that, while the Sabines were passing by the foot of the Capitoline to view the place and see whether any part

---

[1] For chaps. 38-44 cf. Livy i. 11, 6–12, 10.

[6] σινόμενος Bb : οἰνώμενος Ba, οἰόμενος A.

λόφου κλοπῇ ληφθῆναι δυνατὸν ἢ βίᾳ, παρθένος τις
ἀπὸ τοῦ μετεώρου κατεσκόπει, θυγάτηρ ἀνδρὸς
ἐπιφανοῦς, ᾧ προσέκειτο ἡ τοῦ χωρίου φυλακή,
3 Ταρπεία ὄνομα· καὶ αὐτήν, ὡς μὲν Φάβιός τε καὶ
Κίγκιος γράφουσιν, ἔρως εἰσέρχεται τῶν ψελλίων,[1]
ἃ περὶ τοῖς ἀριστεροῖς βραχίοσιν ἐφόρουν, καὶ τῶν
δακτυλίων· χρυσοφόροι γὰρ ἦσαν οἱ Σαβῖνοι τότε
καὶ Τυρρηνῶν οὐχ ἧττον ἁβροδίαιτοι· ὡς δὲ Πείσων
Λεύκιος ὁ τιμητικὸς ἱστορεῖ, καλοῦ πράγματος ἐπιθυμία, γυμνοὺς τῶν σκεπαστηρίων ὅπλων παρα-
4 δ᾿ εῖναι τοῖς πολίταις τοὺς πολεμίους. ὁπότερον δὲ
τούτων ἀληθέστερόν ἐστιν ἐκ τῶν ὕστερον γενομένων
ἔξεστιν εἰκάζειν. πέμψασα δ᾿ οὖν τῶν θεραπαινίδων
τινὰ διὰ πυλίδος, ἣν οὐδεὶς ἔμαθεν ἀνοιγομένην,
ἠξίου τὸν βασιλέα τῶν Σαβίνων ἐλθεῖν αὐτῇ δίχα
τῶν ἄλλων εἰς λόγους, ὡς ἐκείνῳ διαλεξομένη περὶ
πράγματος ἀναγκαίου καὶ μεγάλου. δεξαμένου δὲ
τοῦ Τατίου τὸν λόγον κατ᾿ ἐλπίδα προδοσίας καὶ
συνελθόντος εἰς τὸν ἀποδειχθέντα τόπον, προελ-
θοῦσα εἰς ἐφικτὸν ἡ παρθένος ἐξεληλυθέναι μὲν
νυκτὸς ἐκ τοῦ φρουρίου τὸν πατέρα αὐτῆς ἔφη
χρείας τινὸς ἕνεκα, τὰς δὲ κλεῖς αὐτὴ φυλάττειν
τῶν πυλῶν καὶ παραδώσειν αὐτοῖς τὸ ἔρυμα νυκτὸς
ἀφικομένοις μισθὸν τῆς προδοσίας λαβοῦσα τὰ
φορήματα τῶν Σαβίνων, ἃ περὶ τοῖς εὐωνύμοις

---

[1] ψελλίων Bb : ψαλίων ABa.

of the hill could be taken either by surprise or
by force, they were observed from above by a
maiden whose name was Tarpeia, the daughter of a
distinguished man who had been entrusted with the
guarding of the place. This maiden, as both Fabius
and Cincius relate, conceived a desire for the bracelets
which the men wore on their left arms and for their
rings ; for at that time the Sabines wore ornaments
of gold and were no less luxurious in their habits
than the Tyrrhenians.[1] But according to the account given by Lucius Piso, the ex-censor, she was
inspired by the desire of performing a noble deed,
namely, to deprive the enemy of their defensive
arms and thus deliver them up to her fellow citizens.
Which of these accounts is the truer may be conjectured by what happened afterwards. This girl,
therefore, sending out one of her maids by a little
gate which was not known to be open, desired the
king of the Sabines to come and confer with her in
private, as if she had an affair of necessity and importance to communicate to him. Tatius, in the
hope of having the place betrayed to him, accepted
the proposal and came to the place appointed ; and
the maiden, approaching within speaking distance,
informed him that her father had gone out of the
fortress during the night on some business, but that
she had the keys of the gates, and if they came in
the night, she would deliver up the place to them
upon condition that they gave her as a reward for
her treachery the things which all the Sabines wore

---

[1] It need hardly be pointed out how inconsistent this
description of the Sabines is with the traditional view of
their character as given below at the end of chapter 49.

5 εἶχον ἅπαντες βραχίοσιν. εὐδοκοῦντος δὲ τοῦ Τατίου λαβοῦσα τὰς πίστεις δι' ὅρκων παρ' αὐτοῦ καὶ αὐτὴ δοῦσα τοῦ μὴ ψεύδεσθαι τὰς ὁμολογίας τόπον τε ὁρίσασα, ἐφ' ὃν ἔδει τοὺς Σαβίνους ἐλθεῖν, τὸν ἐχυρώτατον[1] καὶ νυκτὸς ὥραν τὴν ἀφυλακτοτάτην ἀπήει καὶ τοὺς ἔνδον ἔλαθε.

XXXIX. Μέχρι μὲν δὴ τούτων συμφέρονται πάντες οἱ Ῥωμαίων συγγραφεῖς, ἐν δὲ τοῖς ὕστερον λεγομένοις οὐχ ὁμολογοῦσι. Πείσων γὰρ ὁ τιμητικός, οὗ καὶ πρότερον ἐμνήσθην, ἄγγελόν φησιν ὑπὸ τῆς Ταρπείας ἀποσταλῆναι νύκτωρ ἐκ τοῦ χωρίου δηλώσοντα τῷ Ῥωμύλῳ τὰς γενομένας τῇ κόρῃ πρὸς τοὺς Σαβίνους ὁμολογίας, ὅτι μέλλοι τὰ σκεπαστήρια παρ'[2] αὐτῶν αἰτεῖν ὅπλα διὰ τῆς κοινότητος τῶν ὁμολογιῶν παρακρουσαμένη, δύναμίν τε ἀξιώσοντα πέμπειν ἐπὶ τὸ φρούριον ἑτέραν νυκτός, ὡς αὐτῷ στρατηλάτῃ παραληψομένην[3] τοὺς πολεμίους γυμνοὺς τῶν ὅπλων· τὸν δὲ ἄγγελον αὐτομολήσαντα πρὸς τὸν ἡγεμόνα τῶν Σαβίνων κατήγορον γενέσθαι τῶν τῆς Ταρπείας βουλευμάτων. οἱ δὲ περὶ τὸν Φάβιόν τε καὶ Κίγκιον οὐδὲν τοιοῦτο γεγονέναι λέγουσιν, ἀλλὰ φυλάξαι τὴν κόρην διαβεβαιοῦνται τὰς περὶ τῆς προδοσίας συνθήκας.

2 τὰ δ' ἐξῆς ἅπαντες πάλιν ὁμοίως γράφουσι. φασὶ γὰρ ὅτι παραγενομένου σὺν τῷ κρατίστῳ τῆς στρατιᾶς μέρει τοῦ βασιλέως τῶν Σαβίνων φυλάττουσα τὰς ὑποσχέσεις ἡ Τάρπεια τοῖς μὲν πολεμίοις

---

[1] τὸν ἐχυρώτατον Kiessling : τῶν ἐχυρωτάτων AB.
[2] παρ' B : om. R.

on their left arms. And when Tatius consented to
this, she received his sworn pledge for the faithful
performance of the agreement and gave him hers.
Then having appointed, as the place to which the
Sabines were to repair, the strongest part of the
fortress, and the most unguarded hour of the night
as the time for the enterprise, she returned without
being observed by those inside.

XXXIX. So far all the Roman historians agree,
but not in what follows. For Piso, the ex-censor,
whom I mentioned before, says that a messenger
was sent out of the place by Tarpeia in the night to
inform Romulus of the agreement she had made
with the Sabines, in consequence of which she proposed, by taking advantage of the ambiguity of
the expression in that agreement, to demand their
defensive arms, and asking him at the same time to
send a reinforcement to the fortress that night,
so that the enemy together with their commander,
being deprived of their arms, might be taken
prisoners; but the messenger, he says, deserted
to the Sabine commander and acquainted him with
the designs of Tarpeia. Nevertheless, Fabius and
Cincius say that no such thing occurred, but they
insist that the girl kept her treacherous compact.
In what follows, however, all are once more in
agreement. For they say that upon the arrival
of the king of the Sabines with the flower of his
army, Tarpeia, keeping her promise, opened to the

---

[3] παραληψομένην Reiske (and Lapus in his translation):
παραληψόμενον O, Jacoby.

ἀνέῳξε τὴν συγκειμένην πυλίδα, τοὺς δ᾽ ἐν τῷ
χωρίῳ φύλακας ἀναστήσασα διὰ ταχέων σώζειν
ἑαυτοὺς ἠξίου καθ᾽ ἑτέρας ἐξόδους τοῖς πολεμίοις
ἀφανεῖς, ὡς κατεχόντων ἤδη τῶν Σαβίνων τὸ
3 φρούριον· διαφυγόντων δὲ τούτων τοὺς μὲν Σαβίνους ἀνεῳγμένας εὑρόντας τὰς πύλας κατασχεῖν
τὸ φρούριον ἔρημον τῶν φυλάκων, τὴν δὲ Τάρπειαν
ὡς τὰ παρ᾽ ἑαυτῆς ὅσα συνέθετο παρεσχημένην
ἀξιοῦν τοὺς μισθοὺς τῆς προδοσίας κατὰ τοὺς
ὅρκους ἀπολαβεῖν.

XL. Ἔπειτα πάλιν ὁ μὲν Πείσων φησὶ τῶν
Σαβίνων τὸν χρυσὸν ἑτοίμων ὄντων διδόναι τῇ κόρῃ
τὸν περὶ τοῖς ἀριστεροῖς βραχίοσι τὴν Τάρπειαν οὐ
τὸν κόσμον ἀλλὰ τοὺς θυρεοὺς παρ᾽ αὐτῶν αἰτεῖν.
Τατίῳ δὲ θυμόν τε εἰσελθεῖν ἐπὶ τῇ ἐξαπάτῃ καὶ
λογισμὸν τοῦ μὴ παραβῆναι τὰς ὁμολογίας. δόξαι
δ᾽ οὖν αὐτῷ δοῦναι μὲν τὰ ὅπλα, ὥσπερ ἡ παῖς
ἠξίωσε, ποιῆσαι δ᾽ ὅπως αὐτοῖς μηδὲν λαβοῦσα
χρήσεται,[1] καὶ αὐτίκα διατεινάμενον ὡς μάλιστα
ἰσχύος εἶχε ῥῖψαι τὸν θυρεὸν κατὰ τῆς κόρης καὶ
τοῖς ἄλλοις παρακελεύσασθαι ταὐτὸ[2] ποιεῖν. οὕτω
δὴ βαλλομένην πάντοθεν τὴν Τάρπειαν ὑπὸ πλήθους
τε καὶ ἰσχύος τῶν πληγῶν πεσεῖν καὶ περισωρευ-
2 θεῖσαν ὑπὸ τῶν θυρεῶν ἀποθανεῖν. οἱ δὲ περὶ τὸν
Φάβιον ἐπὶ τοῖς Σαβίνοις ποιοῦσι τὴν τῶν ὁμολογιῶν
ἀπάτην· δέον γὰρ αὐτοὺς τὸν χρυσόν, ὥσπερ ἡ
Τάρπεια ἠξίου, κατὰ τὰς ὁμολογίας ἀποδιδόναι,
χαλεπαίνοντας ἐπὶ τῷ μεγέθει τοῦ μισθοῦ τὰ
σκεπαστήρια κατ᾽ αὐτῆς βαλεῖν,[3] ὡς ταῦτα ὅτε

enemy the gate agreed upon, and rousing the garrison, urged them to save themselves speedily by other exits unknown to the enemy, as if the Sabines were already masters of the place ; that after the flight of the garrison the Sabines, finding the gates open, possessed themselves of the stronghold, now stripped of its guards, and that Tarpeia, alleging that she had kept her part of the agreement, insisted upon receiving the reward of her treachery according to the oaths.

XL. Here again Piso says that, when the Sabines were ready to give the girl the gold they wore on their left arms, Tarpeia demanded of them their shields and not their ornaments. But Tatius resented the imposition and at the same time thought of an expedient by which he might not violate the agreement. Accordingly, he decided to give her the arms as the girl demanded, but to contrive that she should make no use of them ; and immediately poising his shield, he hurled it at her with all his might, and ordered the rest to do the same ; and thus Tarpeia, being pelted from all sides, fell under the number and force of the blows and died, overwhelmed by the shields. But Fabius attributes this fraud in the performance of the agreement to the Sabines ; for they, being obliged by the agreement to give her the gold as she demanded, were angered at the magnitude of the reward and hurled their shields at her as if they had engaged themselves

---

[1] Meineke : χρήσηται O.   [2] Sylburg : τοῦτο O.
[3] βαλεῖν Reiske : βάλλειν O.

ὤμνυσαν αὐτῇ δώσειν ὑπεσχημένους. ἔοικε δὲ τὰ
μετὰ ταῦτα γενόμενα τὴν Πείσωνος ἀληθεστέραν
3 ποιεῖν ἀπόφασιν.¹ τάφου τε γὰρ ἔνθα ἔπεσεν
ἠξίωται τὸν ἱερώτατον τῆς πόλεως κατέχουσα λόφον, καὶ χοὰς αὐτῇ Ῥωμαῖοι καθ᾽ ἕκαστον ἐνιαυτὸν
ἐπιτελοῦσι (λέγω δὲ ἃ Πείσων γράφει), ὧν οὐδενὸς
εἰκὸς αὐτήν, εἰ προδιδοῦσα τὴν πατρίδα τοῖς πολεμίοις ἀπέθανεν, οὔτε παρὰ τῶν προδοθέντων οὔτε
παρὰ τῶν ἀποκτεινάντων τυχεῖν, ἀλλὰ καὶ εἴ τι
λείψανον αὐτῆς ἦν τοῦ σώματος ἀνασκαφὲν ἔξω
ῥιφῆναι σὺν χρόνῳ φόβου τε καὶ ἀποτροπῆς ² ἕνεκα
τῶν μελλόντων τὰ ὅμοια δρᾶν. ἀλλ᾽ ὑπὲρ μὲν
τούτων κρινέτω τις ὡς βούλεται.

XLI. Ὁ δὲ Τάτιος καὶ οἱ Σαβῖνοι φρουρίου
γενόμενοι καρτεροῦ κύριοι καὶ τὰ πλεῖστα τῆς
Ῥωμαίων ἀποσκευῆς ἀμοχθεὶ παρειληφότες ἐκ τοῦ
ἀσφαλοῦς ἤδη τὸν πόλεμον διέφερον. πολλαὶ μὲν
οὖν αὐτῶν ἐγίνοντο καὶ διὰ πολλὰς προφάσεις
παρεστρατοπεδευκότων ἀλλήλοις δι᾽ ὀλίγου πεῖραί
τε καὶ συμπλοκαὶ οὔτε κατορθώματα μεγάλα
ἑκατέρῳ φέρουσαι τῶν στρατευμάτων οὔτε ³ σφάλματα, μέγισται δ᾽ ἐκ παρατάξεως ὅλαις ταῖς
δυνάμεσι πρὸς ἀλλήλας μάχαι διτταὶ καὶ φόνος
2 ἑκατέρων πολύς· ἑλκομένου γὰρ ⁴ τοῦ χρόνου
γνώμην ἀμφότεροι τὴν αὐτὴν ἔσχον ὁλοσχερεῖ
κρῖναι τὸν ἀγῶνα μάχῃ, καὶ προελθόντες εἰς τὸ
μεταξὺ τῶν στρατοπέδων χωρίον ἡγεμόνες τε

¹ ἀπόφασιν L. Dindorf: ἀπόκρισιν O; om. Jacoby.
² ἀποτροπῆς Steph.: προτροπῆς O.
³ οὔτε Reudler: οὔτε τὰ O.
⁴ γὰρ Ambrosch, δὴ Kiessling, Jacoby: δὲ O.

by their oaths to give her these. But what followed gives the greater appearance of truth to the statement of Piso. For she was honoured with a monument in the place where she fell and lies buried on the most sacred hill of the city and the Romans every year perform libations to her (I relate what Piso writes); whereas, if she had died in betraying her country to the enemy, it is not to be supposed that she would have received any of these honours, either from those whom she had betrayed or from those who had slain her, but, if there had been any remains of her body, they would in the course of time have been dug up and cast out of the city, in order to warn and deter others from committing the like crimes. But let everyone judge of these matters as he pleases.

XLI. As for Tatius and the Sabines, having become masters of a strong fortress and having without any trouble taken the greatest part of the Romans' baggage, they carried on the war thereafter in safety. And as the armies lay encamped at a short distance from each other and many occasions offered, there were many essays and skirmishes, which were not attended with any great advantages or losses to either side, and there were also two very severe pitched battles, in which all the forces were opposed to each other and there was great slaughter on both sides. For, as the time dragged along, they both came to the same resolution, namely, to decide the issue by a general engagement. Whereupon leaders of both armies, who were masters of the art

ἄριστοι τὰ πολέμια καὶ στρατιῶται πολλῶν ἐθάδες
ἀγώνων ἄξια λόγου ἔργα ἀπεδείκνυντο ἐπιόντες
τ᾽[1] ἀλλήλοις καὶ τοὺς ἐπιόντας δεχόμενοι καὶ ἐξ
3 ὑποστροφῆς εἰς ἴσον αὖθις καθιστάμενοι. οἱ δ᾽
ἐπὶ τῶν ἐρυμάτων ἑστῶτες ἰσορρόπου θεαταὶ
ἀγῶνος καὶ θαμινὰ ἑκατέρωσε μεταπίπτοντος τῷ
μὲν κατορθοῦντι τῶν σφετέρων ἐπικελεύσει τε καὶ
παιανισμῷ πολλὴν ἐποίουν τὴν εἰς τὸ εὔψυχον
ἐπίδοσιν, τῷ δὲ κάμνοντι καὶ διωκομένῳ δεήσεις
τε καὶ οἰμωγὰς προϊέμενοι κωλυταὶ τοῦ εἰς τέλος
ἀνάνδρου ἐγίνοντο· ὑφ᾽ ὧν ἀμφοτέρων ἠναγκάζοντο
καὶ παρὰ δύναμιν ὑπομένειν τὰ δεινά. ἐκείνην μὲν
οὖν τὴν ἡμέραν οὕτω διενέγκαντες ἀγχωμάλως τὴν
μάχην, σκότους ὄντος ἤδη, ἄσμενοι εἰς τοὺς οἰκείους
ἑκάτεροι χάρακας ἀπηλλάσσοντο.

XLII. Ταῖς δ᾽ ἑξῆς ἡμέραις ταφὰς ποιησάμενοι
τῶν νεκρῶν καὶ τοὺς κεκμηκότας ὑπὸ τραυμάτων
ἀνακτησάμενοι δυνάμεις τε παρασκευάσαντες ἄλλας,
ἐπειδὴ ἔδοξεν αὐτοῖς αὖθις ἑτέραν συνάψαι μάχην,
εἰς τὸ αὐτὸ τῷ προτέρῳ χωρίον συνελθόντες ἄχρι
2 νυκτὸς ἐμάχοντο. ἐν ταύτῃ[2] τῇ μάχῃ Ῥωμαίων
ἀμφοτέροις ἐπικρατούντων τοῖς κέρασιν (εἶχε δὲ
τοῦ δεξιοῦ τὴν ἡγεμονίαν αὐτὸς ὁ Ῥωμύλος, τοῦ
δὲ ἀριστεροῦ Λοκόμων ὁ Τυρρηνός), τοῦ δὲ μέσου
μηδέπω κρίσιν ἔχοντος, ὁ κωλύσας τὴν εἰς τέλος
τῶν Σαβίνων ἧτταν καὶ εἰς ἀντίπαλα καταστήσας
αὖθις τὰ λειπόμενα τοῖς νικῶσιν εἷς ἀνὴρ ἐγένετο
Μέττιος[3] Κούρτιος ὄνομα ῥώμην τε σώματος

---

[1] τ᾽ added by Kiessling.

of war, as well as common soldiers, trained in many engagements, advanced into the plain that lay between the two camps and performed memorable feats both in attacking and receiving the enemy as well as in rallying and renewing the fight on equal terms. Those who from the ramparts were spectators of this doubtful battle, which, often varying, favoured each side in turn, when their own men had the advantage, inspired them with fresh courage by their exhortations and songs of victory, and when they were hard pressed and pursued, prevented them by their prayers and lamentations from proving utter cowards ; and thanks to these shouts of encouragement and entreaty the combatants were compelled to endure the perils of the struggle even beyond their strength. And so, after they had thus carried on the contest all that day without a decision, darkness now coming on, they both gladly retired to their own camps.

XLII. But on the following days they buried their dead, took care of the wounded and reinforced their armies ; then, resolving to engage in another battle, they met again in the same plain as before and fought till night. In this battle, when the Romans had the advantage on both wings (the right was commanded by Romulus himself and the left by Lucumo, the Tyrrhenian) but in the centre the battle remained as yet undecided, one man prevented the utter defeat of the Sabines and rallied their wavering forces to renew the struggle with the victors. This man, whose name was Mettius Curtius,

---

² Kiessling : αὐτῇ O.
³ Kiessling : μέττος A, μέστος (?) B.

πολὺς [1] καὶ κατὰ χεῖρα γενναῖος, μάλιστα δ' ἐπὶ
τῷ μηδένα ὀκνεῖν φόβον ἢ κίνδυνον εὐδοκιμῶν.
3 οὗτος δ' ἐτάχθη μὲν ἡγεῖσθαι τῶν κατὰ μέσην
ἀγωνιζομένων τὴν φάλαγγα καὶ τοὺς ἀντιτετα-
γμένους ἐνίκα, βουληθεὶς δὲ καὶ τὰ κέρατα τῶν
Σαβίνων μοχθοῦντα ἤδη καὶ ἐξωθούμενα εἰς τὸ
ἴσον καταστῆσαι,[2] παρακελευσάμενος τοῖς ἀμφ'
αὐτὸν ἐδίωκε τοὺς φεύγοντας τῶν πολεμίων ἐσκε-
δασμένους καὶ μέχρι τῶν πυλῶν αὐτοὺς ἤλασεν,
ὥστε ἠναγκάσθη καταλιπὼν ἡμιτελῆ τὴν νίκην ὁ
Ῥωμύλος ἐπιστρέψαι τε καὶ ἐπὶ τὰ νικῶντα τῶν
4 πολεμίων ὤσασθαι μέρη. τὸ μὲν δὴ κάμνον τῶν
Σαβίνων μέρος ἐν τῷ ἴσῳ πάλιν ἦν ἀπελθούσης
τῆς μετὰ Ῥωμύλου δυνάμεως, ὁ δὲ κίνδυνος ἅπας
περὶ τὸν Κούρτιον καὶ τοὺς σὺν ἐκείνῳ νικῶντας
ἐγεγόνει. χρόνον μὲν οὖν τινα οἱ Σαβῖνοι δεξά-
μενοι τοὺς Ῥωμαίους λαμπρῶς ἠγωνίσαντο, ἔπειτα
πολλῶν ἐπ' αὐτοὺς συνιόντων ἐνέκλινάν τε καὶ
διέσωζον ἑαυτοὺς ἐπὶ τὸν χάρακα, πολλὴν τοῦ
Κουρτίου παρέχοντος αὐτοῖς εἰς τὸ μὴ διώκεσθαι
τεταραγμένως [3] ἀλλὰ βάδην ἀποχωρεῖν ἀσφάλειαν.
5 αὐτὸς γὰρ εἰστήκει μαχόμενος καὶ τὸν Ῥωμύλον
ἐπιόντα ἐδέχετο,[4] γίνεταί τε τῶν ἡγεμόνων αὐτῶν
συμπεσόντων ἀλλήλοις μέγας καὶ καλὸς ἀγών.
ἔξαιμος δὲ ὢν ἤδη καὶ καταβελὴς ὁ Κούρτιος
ὑπῄει κατ' ὀλίγον, καὶ αὐτὸν ἐκ τῶν κατόπιν

---

[1] ἀνήρ after πολὺς deleted by Kiessling.
[2] Sylburg : καταστῆναι O.

was of great physical strength and courageous in
action, but he was famous especially for his contempt
of all fear and danger. He had been appointed to
command those fighting in the centre of the line and
was victorious over those who opposed him ; but
wishing to restore the battle in the wings also, where
the Sabine troops were by now in difficulties and
being forced back, he encouraged those about him,
and pursuing such of the enemy's forces as were
fleeing and scattered, he drove them back to the
gates of the city. This obliged Romulus to leave the
victory but half completed and to return and make
a drive against the victorious troops of the enemy.
Upon the departure of Romulus with his forces
those of the Sabines who had been in trouble were
once more upon equal terms with their opponents,
and the whole danger was now centred round Curtius
and his victorious troops. For some time the
Sabines received the onset of the Romans and
fought brilliantly, but when large numbers joined
in attacking them, they gave way and began to
seek safety in their camp, Curtius amply securing
their retreat, so that they were not driven back
in disorder, but retired without precipitation. For
he himself stood his ground fighting and awaited
Romulus as he approached ; and there ensued
a great and glorious engagement between the leaders
themselves as they fell upon each other. But at last
Curtius, having received many wounds and lost much
blood, retired by degrees till he came to a deep lake

ὑπεδέχετο λίμνη βαθεῖα, ἣν περιελθεῖν μὲν χαλεπὸν
ἦν περικεχυμένων πανταχόθεν τῶν πολεμίων, διελθεῖν δὲ ὑπό τε ἰλύος πλήθους, ἣν τὰ πέριξ τέλματα
εἶχε, καὶ βάθους ὕδατος τοῦ κατὰ μέσην αὐτὴν
6 συνεστῶτος ἄπορον. ταύτῃ πλησιάσας ἔρριψεν
ἑαυτὸν εἰς τὸ νᾶμα σὺν τοῖς ὅπλοις, καὶ ὁ Ῥωμύλος
ὡς αὐτίκα δὴ τοῦ ἀνδρὸς ἐν τῇ λίμνῃ διαφθαρη-
σομένου (καὶ ἅμα [1] ἀδύνατον ἦν κατὰ τέλματός τε
αὐτὸν καὶ δι' ὕδατος πολλοῦ διώκειν) ἐπὶ τοὺς
ἄλλους Σαβίνους τρέπεται· ὁ δὲ Κούρτιος πολλὰ
μοχθήσας σὺν χρόνῳ σώζεταί τε ἐκ τῆς λίμνης τὰ
ὅπλα ἔχων καὶ εἰς τὸν χάρακα ἀπάγεται. οὗτος
ὁ τόπος ἀνακέχωσται μὲν ἤδη, καλεῖται δ' ἐξ
ἐκείνου τοῦ πάθους Κούρτιος λάκκος, ἐν μέσῳ
μάλιστα ὢν τῆς Ῥωμαίων ἀγορᾶς.

XLIII. Ῥωμύλος δὲ τοὺς ἄλλους διώκων ἐγγὺς
γενόμενος τοῦ Καπιτωλίου καὶ πολλὰς ἐλπίδας ἔχων
αἱρήσειν τὸ φρούριον ἄλλοις τε πολλοῖς τραύμασι
καταπονηθεὶς καὶ δὴ καὶ λίθου πληγῇ ἐξαισίῳ κατὰ
κροτάφου ἐνεχθέντος ἐκ τῶν ἄνωθεν καρωθείς,[2]
αἴρεταί τε πρὸς τῶν παρόντων ἡμιθανὴς καὶ εἰς τὸ
2 τεῖχος ἀποφέρεται. τοῖς δὲ Ῥωμαίοις δέος ἐμ-
πίπτει τὸν ἡγεμόνα οὐκέτι ὁρῶσι, καὶ τρέπεται τὸ
δεξιὸν κέρας εἰς φυγήν· οἱ δ' ἐν τῷ εὐωνύμῳ
ταχθέντες ἅμα τῷ Λοκόμωνι τέως μὲν ἀντεῖχον
ὑπὸ τοῦ ἡγεμόνος ἀναθαρρυνόμενοι, λαμπροτάτου
τὰ πολέμια ἀνδρὸς καὶ πλεῖστα ἔργα κατὰ τοῦτον
τὸν πόλεμον ἀποδειξαμένου· ἐπεὶ δὲ κἀκεῖνος

---

[1] ἅμα B : ἅμα ἐπεὶ R.
[2] Naber : κακωθείς O, Jacoby.

in his rear which it was difficult for him to make his way round, his enemies being massed on all sides of it, and impossible to pass through by reason of the quantity of mud on the marshy shore surrounding it and the depth of water that stood in the middle. When he came to the lake, he threw himself into the water, armed as he was, and Romulus, supposing that he would immediately perish in the lake,— moreover, it was not possible to pursue him through so much mud and water,—turned upon the rest of the Sabines. But Curtius with great difficulty got safely out of the lake after a time without losing his arms and was led away to the camp. This place is now filled up, but it is called from this incident the Lacus Curtius, being about in the middle of the Roman Forum.[1]

XLIII. Romulus, while pursuing the others, had drawn near the Capitoline and had great hopes of capturing the stronghold, but being weakened by many other wounds and stunned by a severe blow from a stone which was hurled from the heights and hit him on the temple, he was taken up half dead by those about him and carried inside the walls. When the Romans no longer saw their leader, they were seized with fear and the right wing turned to flight; but the troops that were posted on the left with Lucumo stood their ground for some time, encouraged by their leader, a man most famous for his warlike prowess and who had performed many exploits during the course of this war. But when he in his

[1] *Cf.* Livy i. 13, 5.

ἐλαθεὶς διὰ τῶν πλευρῶν σαυνίῳ τῆς δυνάμεως
ὑπολιπούσης ἔπεσεν οὐδ᾽ αὐτοὶ διέμειναν, φυγὴ δὲ
μετὰ τοῦτο πάντων αὐτῶν ἐγίνετο, καὶ οἱ Σαβῖνοι
3 τεθαρρηκότες ἐδίωκον ἄχρι τῆς πόλεως. ἤδη δὲ
πλησιάζοντες ταῖς πύλαις ἀπηλαύνοντο τῆς νεότητος ἐπεξελθούσης αὐτοῖς ἀκραιφνοῦς, ᾗ τὰ τείχη
φυλάττειν ὁ βασιλεὺς ἐπέτρεψε, καὶ τοῦ ῾Ρωμύλου,
ῥᾷον γὰρ ἤδη εἶχεν ἐκ τοῦ τραύματος,[1] ἐκβοηθήσαν-
τος ὡς εἶχε τάχους, ἐγίνετό τε ἀγχίστροφος ἡ τοῦ
ἀγῶνος τύχη καὶ πολλὴν ἔχουσα τὴν ἐπὶ θάτερα
4 μεταβολήν. οἱ μέν γε φεύγοντες ὡς τὸν ἡγεμόνα
ἐκ τοῦ ἀπροσδοκήτου φανέντα εἶδον ἀναλαβόντες
ἑαυτοὺς ἐκ τοῦ προτέρου δέους εἰς τάξιν καθίσταντο
καὶ οὐκέτι ἀνεβάλλοντο μὴ οὐχ ὁμόσε τοῖς ἐχθροῖς
χωρεῖν· οἱ δὲ τέως κατείργοντες αὐτοὺς καὶ μηδεμίαν οἰόμενοι μηχανὴν εἶναι τὸ μὴ οὐ κατὰ κράτος
αὐτὴν[2] τὴν πόλιν ἁλῶναι, ἐπειδὴ τὸ αἰφνίδιόν τε
καὶ παράδοξον ἐθεάσαντο τῆς μεταβολῆς, περὶ
σωτηρίας αὐτοὶ τῆς ἑαυτῶν ἐσκόπουν. ἦν δὲ αὐτοῖς οὐκ[3] εὐπετὴς ἡ πρὸς τὸν χάρακα ἀναχώρησις
καθ᾽[4] ὑψηλοῦ τε χωρίου καὶ διὰ κοίλης ὁδοῦ
διωκομένοις, καὶ πολὺς αὐτῶν ὁ φόνος[5] ἐν ταύτῃ
5 γίνεται τῇ τροπῇ. ἐκείνην μὲν οὖν τὴν ἡμέραν
οὕτως ἀγχωμάλως ἀγωνισάμενοι καὶ εἰς τύχας
παραλόγους ἀμφότεροι καταστάντες ἡλίου περὶ
καταφορὰν ὄντος ἤδη διεκρίθησαν.

[1] ῥᾷον γὰρ ἤδη εἶχεν ἐκ τοῦ τραύματος Kiessling, ῥᾷον γὰρ ἤδη
ἐκ τοῦ τραύματος εἶχεν Sylburg: ῥᾷον γὰρ εἶχε τοῦ τραύματος B,
ῥᾴων ἦν γὰρ ἐκ τοῦ τραύματος A.
[2] αὐτὴν Kiessling: αὐτῶν B, τὴν πόλιν αὐτῶν R.
[3] οὐκ added by Casaubon.

turn was pierced through the side with a javelin and
fell through weakness, they also gave way ; and thereupon the whole Roman army was in flight, and the
Sabines, taking courage, pursued them up to the
city. But as they were already drawing near the
gates they were repulsed, when the youths whom
the king had appointed to guard the walls sallied
out against them with their forces fresh ; and
when Romulus, too, who by this time was in some
degree recovered of his wound, came out to their
assistance with all possible speed, the fortune of the
battle quickly turned and veered strongly to the
other side. For those who were fleeing recovered
themselves from their late fear on the unexpected
appearance of their leader, and reforming their lines,
no longer hesitated to come to blows with the enemy ;
while the latter, who but now had been driving the
fugitives into the city and thought there was nothing
that could prevent them from taking the city itself
by storm, when they saw this sudden and unexpected
change, took thought for their own safety. But
they found it no easy matter to retreat to their
camp, pursued as they were down from a height and
through a hollow way, and in this rout they sustained
heavy losses. And so, after they had thus fought
that day without a decision and both had met with
unexpected turns of fortune, the sun now being near
his setting, they parted.

---

[4] καθ' Casaubon, ἀπὸ Kiessling : ἀπὸ καθ' R, ἀπὸ . . . B.
[5] πολὺς αὐτῶν φόνος Ambrosch, πολὺς αὐτῶν ὁ φόνος Jacoby
(in note), οὐ πολὺς αὐτῶν φόνος Reiske, ὁ πολὺς αὐτῶν φόνος O.

XLIV. Ταῖς δ' ἑξῆς ἡμέραις οἵ τε Σαβῖνοι ἐν βουλῇ ἐγίνοντο πότερον ἀπάξουσιν[1] ἐπ' οἴκου τὰς δυνάμεις, ὅσα δύνανται τῆς χώρας τῶν πολεμίων κακώσαντες, ἢ προσμεταπέμψονται[2] στρατιὰν ἑτέραν οἴκοθεν καὶ προσμενοῦσι[3] λιπαροῦντες ἕως τὸ 2 κάλλιστον ἐπιθήσουσι τῷ πολέμῳ τέλος.[4] πονηρὸν δὲ αὐτοῖς καὶ τὸ ἀπιέναι μετ' αἰσχύνης τῆς ἀπράκτου ἀναχωρήσεως ἐφαίνετο εἶναι καὶ τὸ μένειν οὐδενὸς σφισι χωροῦντος κατ' ἐλπίδα. συμβάσεως δὲ πέρι τὸ[5] διαλέγεσθαι πρὸς τοὺς ἐχθρούς, ἥνπερ ἐδόκουν εἶναι μόνην εὐπρεπῆ τοῦ πολέμου ἀπαλλαγήν, οὐχ ἑαυτοῖς μᾶλλον ἢ Ῥωμαίοις ἁρμόττειν ὑπελάμ- 3 βανον. Ῥωμαῖοι δὲ οὐδὲν ἧττον ἀλλὰ καὶ μᾶλλον τῶν Σαβίνων εἰς πολλὴν ἀπορίαν ἐνέπιπτον ὅ τι χρήσαιντο τοῖς πράγμασιν. οὔτε γὰρ ἀποδιδόναι τὰς γυναῖκας ἠξίουν οὔτε κατέχειν· τῷ μὲν ἧτταν ὁμολογουμένην ἀκολουθεῖν οἰόμενοι καὶ ἀναγκαῖόν σφισιν ἐσόμενον πᾶν ὅ τι ἂν ἄλλο ἐπιταχθῶσιν ὑπομένειν, τῷ δὲ πολλὰ καὶ δεινὰ ἐπιδεῖν χώρας τε πορθουμένης καὶ νεότητος τῆς κρατίστης ἀπολ- λυμένης· περὶ φιλίας τε εἰ διαλέγοιντο πρὸς τοὺς Σαβίνους, οὐδενὸς ὑπελάμβανον τεύξεσθαι τῶν μετρίων διὰ πολλὰ μὲν καὶ ἄλλα, μάλιστα δ' ὅτι ταῖς αὐθαδείαις οὐ μετριότης γίνεται πρὸς τὸ ἀντί- παλον ἐπὶ θεραπείας τραπόμενον ἀλλὰ βαρύτης.

[1] ἀπάξουσιν Cobet, ἀπολύσουσιν Kiessling, ἀπίωσιν Naber: ἀποίσουσιν O, Jacoby.
[2] Sylburg: -πέμπονται O, -πέμπωνται Jacoby.
[3] Sylburg: -μείνωσι B (?), -μένωσι R (?), Jacoby.
[4] Kiessling: κράτος O.   [5] τὸ deleted by Reiske.

XLIV. But during the following days the Sabines were taking counsel whether they should lead their forces back home, after doing all possible damage to the enemy's country, or should send for another army from home and still hold out obstinately until they should put an end to the war in the most honourable manner. They considered that it would be a bad thing for them either to return home with the shame of having effected nothing or to stay there when none of their attempts succeeded according to their expectations. And to treat with the enemy concerning an accommodation, which they looked upon as the only honourable means of putting an end to the war, they conceived to be no more fitting for them than for the Romans. On the other side, the Romans were not less, but even more, perplexed than the Sabines what course to take in the present juncture. For they could not resolve either to restore the women or to retain them, believing that the former course involved an acknowledgment of defeat and that it would be necessary to submit to whatever else might be imposed upon them, and that the alternative course would necessitate their witnessing many terrible sights as their country was being laid waste and the flower of their youth destroyed; and, if they should treat with the Sabines for peace, they despaired of obtaining any moderate terms, not only for many other reasons, but chiefly because the proud and headstrong treat an enemy who resorts to courting them, not with moderation, but with severity.

XLV. Ἐν ᾧ δὲ ἀμφότεροι ταῦτα διαλογιζόμενοι
καὶ οὔτε μάχης ἄρχειν τολμῶντες οὔτε περὶ φιλίας
διαλεγόμενοι παρεῖλκον τὸν χρόνον, αἱ Ῥωμαίων
γυναῖκες ὅσαι τοῦ Σαβίνων ἐτύγχανον οὖσαι γένους,
δι᾽ ἃς ὁ πόλεμος συνειστήκει, συνελθοῦσαι δίχα τῶν
ἀνδρῶν εἰς ἓν χωρίον καὶ λόγον ἑαυταῖς δοῦσαι
γνώμην ἐποιήσαντο συμβατηρίων ἄρξαι πρὸς ἀμ-
2 φοτέρους αὐταὶ[1] λόγων. ἡ δὲ τοῦτο εἰσηγησαμένη
τὸ βούλευμα ταῖς γυναιξὶν Ἑρσιλία[2] μὲν ἐκαλεῖτο,
γένους δ᾽ οὐκ ἀφανοῦς ἦν ἐν Σαβίνοις. ταύτην δ᾽ οἱ
μέν φασι γεγαμημένην ἤδη σὺν ταῖς ἄλλαις ἁρ-
πασθῆναι κόραις ὡς παρθένον, οἱ δὲ τὰ πιθανώτατα γράφοντες ἑκοῦσαν ὑπομεῖναι λέγουσι μετὰ
θυγατρός ἁρπασθῆναι· γὰρ δὴ κἀκείνης θυγατέρα
3 μονογενῆ. ὡς δὲ ταύτην ἔσχοι τὴν γνώμην αἱ
γυναῖκες, ἧκοι ἐπὶ τὸ συνέδριον καὶ τυχοῦσαι λόγου
μακρὰς ἐξέτειναν δεήσεις, ἐπιτροπὴν ἀξιοῦσαι λαβεῖν τῆς πρὸς τοὺς συγγενεῖς ἐξόδου, πολλὰς καὶ
ἀγαθὰς ἐλπίδας ἔχειν λέγουσαι περὶ τοῦ συνάξειν
εἰς ἓν τὰ ἔθνη καὶ ποιήσειν φιλίαν.[3] ὡς δὲ ταῦτ᾽
ἤκουσαν οἱ συνεδρεύοντες τῷ βασιλεῖ σφόδρα τε
ἠγάσθησαν καὶ πόρον ὡς ἐν ἀμηχάνοις πράγμασι
4 τοῦτον ὑπέλαβον εἶναι μόνον. γίνεται δὴ μετὰ
τοῦτο δόγμα τοιόνδε βουλῆς· ὅσαι τοῦ Σαβίνων
γένους ἦσαν ἔχουσαι τέκνα, ταύταις ἐξουσίαν εἶναι
καταλιπούσαις τὰ τέκνα παρὰ τοῖς ἀνδράσι πρεσβεύειν ὡς τοὺς ὁμοεθνεῖς, ὅσαι δὲ πλειόνων παίδων

---

[1] Ambrosch: αὗται B, om. R.
[2] ἑρσιλία A ἑρσιλεία B (and so regularly).
[3] φιλίαν Bb: φιλια Ba, φίλια A.

XLV. While [1] both sides were consuming the time in these considerations, neither daring to renew the fight nor treating for peace, the wives of the Romans who were of the Sabine race and the cause of the war, assembling in one place apart from their husbands and consulting together, determined to make the first overtures themselves to both armies concerning an accommodation. The one who proposed this measure to the rest of the women was named Hersilia, a woman of no obscure birth among the Sabines. Some say that, though already married, she was seized with the others as supposedly a virgin ; but those who give the most probable account say that she remained with her daughter of her own free will, for according to them her only daughter was among those who had been seized. After the women had taken this resolution they came to the senate, and having obtained an audience, they made long pleas, begging to be permitted to go out to their relations and declaring that they had many excellent grounds for hoping to bring the two nations together and establish friendship between them. When the senators who were present in council with the king heard this, they were exceedingly pleased and looked upon it, in view of their present difficulties, as the only solution. Thereupon a decree of the senate was passed to the effect that those Sabine women who had children should, upon leaving them with their husbands, have permission to go as ambassadors to their countrymen, and that those who had several children should take along as many

---

[1] For chaps. 45-47 cf. Livy i. 13.

μητέρες ἦσαν ἐπάγεσθαι μοῖραν ἐξ αὐτῶν ὁσην-
δήτινα καὶ πράττειν ὅπως εἰς φιλίαν συνάξουσι τὰ
5 ἔθνη. μετὰ τοῦτο ἐξῄεσαν ἐσθῆτας ἔχουσαι πενθί-
μους, τινὲς δὲ αὐτῶν καὶ τέκνα νήπια ἐπαγόμεναι.
ὡς δ' εἰς τὸν χάρακα τῶν Σαβίνων προῆλθον ὀδυρό-
μεναί τε καὶ προσπίπτουσαι τοῖς τῶν ἀπαντώντων[1]
γόνασι πολὺν οἶκτον ἐκ τῶν ὁρώντων ἐκίνησαν, καὶ
6 τὰ δάκρυα κατέχειν οὐδεὶς ἱκανὸς ἦν. συναχθέντος
δὲ αὐταῖς τοῦ συνεδρίου τῶν προβούλων καὶ κελεύσαντος τοῦ βασιλέως ὑπὲρ ὧν ἥκουσι λέγειν ἡ τοῦ
βουλεύματος ἄρξασα καὶ τὴν ἡγεμονίαν ἔχουσα τῆς
πρεσβείας Ἑρσιλία μακρὰν καὶ συμπαθῆ διεξῆλθε
δέησιν, ἀξιοῦσα χαρίσασθαι τὴν εἰρήνην ταῖς δεομέ-
ναις ὑπὲρ τῶν ἀνδρῶν, δι' ἃς ἐξενηνέχθαι τὸν πόλεμον ἀπέφαινεν· ἐφ' οἷς δὲ γενήσονται δικαίοις αἱ
διαλύσεις, τοὺς ἡγεμόνας αὐτοὺς συνελθόντας ἐφ'
ἑαυτῶν διομολογήσασθαι πρὸς τὸ κοινῇ συμφέρον
ὁρῶντας.

XLVI. Τοιαῦτα εἰποῦσαι προὔπεσον ἅπασαι τῶν
τοῦ βασιλέως γονάτων ἅμα τοῖς τέκνοις καὶ διέμενον
ἐρριμμέναι τέως ἀνέστησαν αὐτὰς ἐκ τῆς γῆς οἱ
παρόντες ἅπαντα ποιήσειν τὰ μέτρια καὶ τὰ[2] δυ-
νατὰ ὑπισχνούμενοι. μεταστησάμενοι δὲ αὐτὰς
ἐκ τοῦ συνεδρίου καὶ βουλευσάμενοι καθ' ἑαυτοὺς
ἔκριναν ποιεῖσθαι τὰς διαλλαγάς. καὶ γίνονται τοῖς
ἔθνεσιν ἐκεχειρίαι μὲν πρῶτον· ἔπειτα συνελθόντων
2 τῶν βασιλέων συνθῆκαι περὶ φιλίας. ἦν δὲ τὰ
συνομολογηθέντα τοῖς ἀνδράσι, περὶ ὧν τοὺς ὅρκους

---

[1] τοῖς τῶν ἀπαντώντων Reiske : τοῖς ἀπάντων O.

of them as they wished and endeavour to reconcile the two nations. After this the women went out dressed in mourning, some of them also carrying their infant children. When they arrived in the camp of the Sabines, lamenting and falling at the feet of those they met, they aroused great compassion in all who saw them and none could refrain from tears. And when the councillors had been called together to receive them and the king had commanded them to state their reasons for coming, Hersilia, who had proposed the plan and was at the head of the embassy, delivered a long and pathetic plea, begging them to grant peace to those who were interceding for their husbands and on whose account, she pointed out, the war had been undertaken. As to the terms, however, on which peace should be made, she said the leaders, coming together by themselves, might settle them with a view to the advantage of both parties.

XLVI. After she had spoken thus, all the women with their children threw themselves at the feet of the king and remained prostrate till those who were present raised them from the ground and promised to do everything that was reasonable and in their power. Then, having ordered them to withdraw from the council and having consulted together, they decided to make peace. And first a truce was agreed upon between the two nations; then the kings met together and a treaty of friendship was concluded. The terms agreed upon by the two, which they confirmed by their oaths, were as

---

[2] τὰ added by Jacoby.

DIONYSIUS OF HALICARNASSUS

ἐποιήσαντο, τοιάδε· βασιλέας μὲν εἶναι Ῥωμαίων
Ῥωμύλον καὶ Τάτιον ἰσοψήφους ὄντας καὶ τιμὰς
καρπουμένους τὰς ἴσας, καλεῖσθαι δὲ τὴν μὲν πόλιν
ἐπὶ τοῦ κτίσαντος τὸ αὐτὸ φυλάττουσαν ὄνομα
Ῥώμην, καὶ ἕνα ἕκαστον τῶν ἐν αὐτῇ πολιτῶν
Ῥωμαῖον, ὡς πρότερον, τοὺς δὲ σύμπαντας ἐπὶ τῆς
Τατίου πατρίδος κοινῇ περιλαμβανομένους κλήσει
Κυρίτας· πολιτεύειν δὲ τοὺς βουλομένους Σαβίνων
ἐν Ῥώμῃ ἱερά τε συνενεγκαμένους καὶ εἰς φυλὰς
3 καὶ εἰς φράτρας ἐπιδοθέντας. ταῦτα ὀμόσαντες
καὶ βωμοὺς ἐπὶ τοῖς ὅρκοις[1] ἱδρυσάμενοι κατὰ
μέσην μάλιστα τὴν καλουμένην ἱερὰν ὁδὸν συνε-
κεράσθησαν ἀλλήλοις. καὶ οἱ μὲν ἄλλοι τὰς δυνάμεις ἀναλαβόντες ἡγεμόνες ἀπῆγον ἐπ᾽ οἴκου,
Τάτιος δὲ ὁ βασιλεὺς καὶ σὺν αὐτῷ τρεῖς ἄνδρες
οἴκων τῶν διαφανεστάτων ὑπέμειναν ἐν Ῥώμῃ καὶ
τιμὰς ἔσχον, ἃς τὸ ἀπ᾽ αὐτῶν ἐκαρποῦτο γένος,
Οὐόλοσσος[2] Οὐαλέριος καὶ Τάλλος Τυράννιος[3]
ἐπίκλησιν καὶ τελευταῖος Μέττιος Κούρτιος, ὁ τὴν
λίμνην σὺν τοῖς ὅπλοις διανηξάμενος, οἷς παρέμειναν
ἑταῖροί[4] τε καὶ συγγενεῖς καὶ πελάται, τῶν ἐπιχωρίων ἀριθμὸν οὐκ ἐλάττους.

XLVII. Καταστάντων δὲ τῶν πραγμάτων ἔδοξε
τοῖς βασιλεῦσιν, ἐπειδὴ πολλὴν ἐπίδοσιν εἰς ὄχλου
πλῆθος ἡ πόλις εἰλήφει, διπλάσιον τοῦ προτέρου

[1] Reiske proposed to read ὅρος, Naber ὁρίοις.
[2] Kiessling: βουλοσσός O; οὐόλεσσός early editors.
[3] Perizonius: τύραννος O. By a typographical error Jacoby cited and adopted Τυράννως as Perizonius' reading.
[4] ἑταῖροι Bb : ἕτεροι BaR.

444

follows: that Romulus and Tatius should be kings
of the Romans with equal authority and should
enjoy equal honours; that the city, preserving its
name, should from its founder be called Rome:
that each individual citizen should as before be
called a Roman, but that the people collectively
should be comprehended under one general appellation and from the city of Tatius [1] be called Quirites,
and that all the Sabines who wished might live in
Rome, joining in common rites with the Romans and
being assigned to tribes and *curiae*. After they had
sworn to this treaty and, to confirm their oaths,
had erected altars near the middle of the Sacred
Way, as it is called, they mingled together. And all
the commanders returned home with their forces
except Tatius, the king, and three persons of the
most illustrious families, who remained at Rome and
received those honours which their posterity after
them enjoyed; these were Volusus [2] Valerius and
Tallus, surnamed Tyrannius, with Mettius Curtius,
the man who swam cross the lake with his arms,
and with them there remained also their companions, relations and clients, no fewer in number
than the former inhabitants.

XLVII. Everything being thus settled, the kings
thought proper, since the city had received a great
increase of people, to double the number of the

---

[1] Cures; see chap. 36, 3; 48. Dionysius is giving the
ordinary Roman derivation of Quirites. The word may,
however, come directly from the Sabine *quiris* (chap. 48.
end) and mean the "spear men."

[2] The name should probably be Volesus, as spelled by
Livy (i. 58, 6; ii. 18, 6) and other Roman writers.

ποιῆσαι τὸν τῶν πατρικίων ἀριθμὸν προσκαταλέ-
ξαντας τοῖς [1] ἐπιφανεστάτοις οἴκοις ἐκ τῶν ὕστερον
ἐποικησάντων ἴσους τοῖς προτέροις, νεωτέρους οὓς
ἐκάλεσαν πατρικίους · ἐξ ὧν ἑκατὸν ἄνδρας, οὓς αἱ
φράτραι προεχειρίσαντο, τοῖς ἀρχαίοις βουλευταῖς
2 προσέγραψαν. περὶ μὲν οὖν τούτων ὀλίγου δεῖν
πάντες οἱ συγγράψαντες τὰς Ῥωμαϊκὰς ἱστορίας
συμπεφωνήκασιν, ὀλίγοι δέ τινες περὶ τοῦ πλήθους
τῶν προσκαταγραφέντων βουλευτῶν διαφέρονται.
οὐ γὰρ ἑκατὸν ἀλλὰ πεντήκοντα τοὺς ἐπεισελθόντας
3 εἰς τὴν βουλὴν ἀποφαίνουσι γενέσθαι. περὶ δὲ τῶν
τιμῶν, ἃς ταῖς γυναιξὶν οἱ βασιλεῖς ἀπέδοσαν, ὅτι
συνήγαγον αὐτοὺς εἰς φιλίαν, οὐχ ἅπαντες Ῥωμαίων
συγγραφεῖς συμφέρονται. τινὲς μὲν γὰρ αὐτῶν
γράφουσι τά τε ἄλλα πολλὰ καὶ μεγάλα δωρήσασθαι
ταῖς γυναιξὶ τοὺς ἡγεμόνας καὶ δὴ καὶ τὰς φράτρας
τριάκοντα οὔσας, ὥσπερ ἔφην, ἐπωνύμους τῶν γυναικῶν ποιῆσαι · τοσαύτας γὰρ εἶναι γυναῖκας τὰς
4 ἐπιπρεσβευσαμένας. Οὐάρρων δὲ Τερέντιος τοῦτ᾽
αὐτοῖς τὸ μέρος οὐχ ὁμολογεῖ παλαίτερον ἔτι λέγων
ταῖς [2] κουρίαις τεθῆναι τὰ ὀνόματα ὑπὸ τοῦ Ῥωμύλου
κατὰ τὴν πρώτην τοῦ πλήθους διαίρεσιν, τὰ μὲν ἀπ᾽
ἀνδρῶν ληφθέντα ἡγεμόνων, τὰ δ᾽ ἀπὸ πάγων · [3]
τάς τ᾽ ἐπὶ τὴν πρεσβείαν ἐξελθούσας γυναῖκας οὐ
τριάκοντα εἶναί φησιν, ἀλλὰ πεντακοσίας τε καὶ
τριάκοντα τριῶν δεούσας οἴεταί τε οὐδ᾽ εἰκὸς εἶναι
τοσούτων γυναικῶν τιμὴν ἀφελομένους τοὺς βασιλεῖς
ὀλίγαις ἐξ αὐτῶν δοῦναι μόναις. ἀλλ᾽ ὑπὲρ μὲν

patricians by adding to the most distinguished
families others from among the new settlers equal
in number to the old, and they called these " new
patricians." Of these a hundred persons, chosen by
the *curiae*, were enrolled with the original senators.
Concerning these matters almost all the writers of
Roman history agree. But some few differ regarding the number of the newly-enrolled senators,
for they say it was not a hundred, but fifty, that were
added to the senate. Concerning the honours,
also, which the kings conferred on the women
in return for having reconciled them, not all the
Roman historians agree ; for some write that,
besides many other signal marks of honour which
they bestowed upon them, they gave their names
to the *curiae*, which were thirty, as I have said, that
being the number of the women who went upon the
embassy. But Terentius Varro does not agree with
them in this particular, for he says that Romulus
gave the names to the *curiae* earlier than this, when
he first divided the people, some of these names
being taken from men who were their leaders and
others from districts ; and he says that the number
of the women who went upon the embassy was not
thirty, but five hundred and twenty-seven, and he
thinks it very improbable that the kings would have
deprived so many women of this honour to bestow
it upon only a few of them. But as regards these

---

¹ τοῖς Garrer : σὺν τοῖς O, Jacoby.
² ἔτι λέγων ταῖς Sylburg : τε λέγων ἐν ταῖς O.
³ ἀπὸ πάγων Kiessling : ἀπὸ πάντων BbR, ἐπὶ πάντων Ba.

τούτων οὔτε μηδένα ποιήσασθαι λόγον οὔτε πλείω
γράφειν τῶν ἱκανῶν ἐφαίνετό μοι.

XLVIII. Περὶ δὲ τῆς Κυριτῶν πόλεως, ἐξ ἧς
οἱ περὶ τὸν Τάτιον ἦσαν (ἀπαιτεῖ γὰρ ἡ διήγησις καὶ
περὶ τούτων, οἵτινές τε καὶ ὁπόθεν ἦσαν, εἰπεῖν)
τοσαῦτα παρελάβομεν. ἐν τῇ Ῥεατίνων χώρᾳ καθ'
ὃν χρόνον Ἀβοριγῖνες αὐτὴν κατεῖχον παρθένος τις
ἐπιχωρία τοῦ πρώτου γένους εἰς ἱερὸν ἦλθεν Ἐννα-
2 λίου χορεύσουσα [1] · τὸν δ' Ἐννάλιον οἱ Σαβῖνοι καὶ
παρ' ἐκείνων οἱ Ῥωμαῖοι μαθόντες Κυρῖνον ὀνομά-
ζουσιν, οὐκ ἔχοντες εἰπεῖν τὸ ἀκριβὲς εἴτε Ἄρης
ἐστὶν εἴτε ἕτερός τις ὁμοίας Ἄρει τιμὰς ἔχων. οἱ
μὲν γὰρ ἐφ' ἑνὸς οἴονται θεοῦ πολεμικῶν ἀγώνων
ἡγεμόνος ἑκάτερον τῶν ὀνομάτων κατηγορεῖσθαι,[2]
οἱ δὲ κατὰ δύο τάττεσθαι δαιμόνων πολεμιστῶν τὰ
3 ὀνόματα. ἐν δὴ [3] τοῦ θεοῦ τῷ τεμένει χορεύουσα
ἡ παῖς ἔνθεος ἄφνω γίνεται καὶ καταλιποῦσα τὸν
χορὸν εἰς τὸν σηκὸν εἰστρέχει τοῦ θεοῦ. ἔπειτα
ἐγκύμων ἐκ τοῦ δαίμονος, ὡς ἅπασιν ἐδόκει, γενομένη τίκτει παῖδα Μόδιον ὄνομα, Φαβίδιον ἐπίκλησιν, ὃς ἀνδρωθεὶς μορφήν τε οὐ κατ' ἄνθρωπον
ἀλλὰ δαιμόνιον ἴσχει, καὶ τὰ πολέμια πάντων γίνεται
λαμπρότατος · καὶ αὐτὸν εἰσέρχεται πόθος οἰκίσαι
4 πόλιν ἐφ' ἑαυτοῦ συναγαγὼν δὴ χεῖρα πολλὴν
τῶν περὶ ἐκεῖνα τὰ χωρία οἰκούντων ἐν ὀλίγῳ πάνυ
χρόνῳ κτίζει τὰς καλουμένας Κύρεις, ὡς μέν τινες
ἱστοροῦσιν ἐπὶ τοῦ δαίμονος, ἐξ οὗ γενέσθαι λόγος

---

[1] Reiske: χορεύουσα O.
[2] κατηγορεῖσθαι B: κατηγορῆσθαι A, Jacoby.
[3] δὴ Ambrosch: δὲ O.

matters, it has not seemed to me fitting either to omit all mention of them or to say more than is sufficient

XLVIII. Concerning the city of Cures from which Tatius and his followers came (for the course of my narrative requires that I should speak of them also, and say who they were and whence), we have received the following account. In the territory of Reate, when the Aborigines were in possession of it, a certain maiden of that country, who was of the highest birth, went into the temple of Enyalius to dance. The Sabines and the Romans, who have learned it from them, give to Enyalius the name of Quirinus, without being able to affirm for certain whether he is Mars or some other god who enjoys the same honours as Mars. For some think that both these names are used of one and the same god who presides over martial combats; others, that the names are applied to two different gods of war. Be that as it may, this maiden, while she was danc ing in the temple, was on a sudden seized with divine inspiration, and quitting the dance, ran into the inner sanctuary of the god; after which, being with child by this divinity, as everybody believed, she brought forth a son named Modius, with the surname Fabidius, who, being arrived at manhood, had not a human but a divine form and was re- nowned above all others for his warlike deeds. And conceiving a desire to found a city on his own account, he gathered together a great number of people of the neighbourhood and in a very short time built the city called Cures : he gave it this name, as some say, from the divinity whose son he was

αὐτὸν εἶχε, τοὔνομα τῇ πόλει θέμενος, ὡς δ' ἕτεροι γράφουσιν ἐπὶ τῆς αἰχμῆς· κύρεις γὰρ οἱ Σαβῖνοι τὰς αἰχμὰς καλοῦσιν. ταῦτα μὲν οὖν Τερέντιος Οὐάρρων γράφει.

XLIX. Ζηνόδοτος δ' ὁ[1] Τροιζήνιος, συγγραφεὺς . . . ,[2] Ὀμβρικοὺς ἔθνος αὐθιγενὲς[3] ἱστορεῖ τὸ μὲν πρῶτον οἰκῆσαι περὶ τὴν καλουμένην Ῥεατίνην· ἐκεῖθεν δὲ ὑπὸ Πελασγῶν ἐξελαθέντας εἰς ταύτην ἀφικέσθαι τὴν γῆν ἔνθα νῦν οἰκοῦσι καὶ μετα-βαλόντας ἅμα τῷ τόπῳ τοὔνομα Σαβίνους ἐξ
2 Ὀμβρικῶι προσαγορευθῆναι. Κάτων δὲ Πόρκιος τὸ μὲν ὄνομα τῷ Σαβίνων ἔθνει τεθῆναί φησιν ἐπὶ Σάβου[4] τοῦ Σάγκου δαίμονος ἐπιχωρίου, τοῦτον δὲ τὸι Σάγκοι ὑπό τινων Πίστιον καλεῖσθαι Δία. πρώτην δ' αὐτῶι οἴκησιν ἀποφαίνει γενέσθαι κώμην τινὰ καλουμένην Τεστρούναν ἀγχοῦ πόλεως Ἀμιτέρ-νης κειμένην, ἐξ ἧς ὁρμηθέντας τότε Σαβίνους εἰς τὴν Ῥεατίνην ἐμβαλεῖν Ἀβοριγίνων ἅμα Πελασγοῖς[5] κατοικούντων καὶ πόλιν αὐτῶν τὴν ἐπιφανεστάτην
3 Κοτυλίας[6] πολέμῳ χειρωσαμένους κατασχεῖν. ἐκ δὲ τῆς Ῥεατίνης ἀποικίας ἀποστείλαντας ἄλλας τε πόλεις κτίσαι πολλάς, ἐν αἷς οἰκεῖν ἀτειχίστοις, καὶ δὴ καὶ τὰς προσαγορευομένας Κύρεις· χώραν δὲ

[1] δ' (δὲ) ὁ Ambrosch : δὲ O.
[2] Lacuna recognized by Kiessling, who supplied παλαιὸς or λόγου ἄξιος.
[3] Ὀμβρικοὺς ἔθνος αὐθιγενὲς Reiske : ὀμβρικοῦ ἔθνους αὐθι-γενεῖς O.
[4] Sylburg : σαβίνου O.

reputed to be, or, as others state, from a spear, since the Sabines call spears *cures*.[1] This is the account given by Terentius Varro.

XLIX. But Zenodotus of Troezen, a . . . historian,[2] relates that the Umbrians, a native race, first dwelt in the Reatine territory, as it is called, and that, being driven from there by the Pelasgians, they came into the country which they now inhabit. and changing their name with their place of habitation, from Umbrians were called Sabines. But Porcius Cato says that the Sabine race received its name from Sabus. the son of Sancus. a divinity of that country, and that this Sancus was by some called Jupiter Fidius. He says also that their first place of abode was a certain village called Testruna, situated near the city of Amiternum ; that from there the Sabines made an incursion at that time into the Reatine territory, which was inhabited by the Aborigines together with the Pelasgians,[3] and took their most famous city, Cutiliae, by force of arms and occupied it ; and that, sending colonies out of the Reatine territory, they built many cities, in which they lived without fortifying them, among others the city called Cures. He further states that the

---

[1] Or *quires*. The Greek spelling can represent either form.
[2] The Greek text suggests the loss of an adjective or phrase qualifying " historian." See critical note.
[3] The word " Pelasgians " is due to Reiske. See critical note and i. 19 f.

---

[5] Πελασγοῖς added by Reiske ; Kiessling emended ἅμα to αὐτὴν.
[6] Gelenius : κοτύνας O.

κατασχεῖν τῆς μὲν Ἀδριανῆς θαλάττης ἀπέχουσαι
ἀμφὶ τοὺς ὀγδοήκοντα καὶ διακοσίους σταδίους
τῆς δὲ Τυρρηνικῆς τετταράκοντα πρὸς διακοσίοις·
μῆκος δὲ αὐτῆς εἶναι φησιν ὀλίγῳ μεῖον σταδίων
4 χιλίων. ἔστι δέ τις καὶ ἄλλος ὑπὲρ τῶν Σαβίνων
ἐν ἱστορίαις ἐπιχωρίοις λεγόμενος λόγος, ὡς Λακεδαιμονίων ἐποικησάντων αὐτοῖς καθ' ὃν χρόνον
ἐπιτροπεύων Εὔνομον τὸν ἀδελφιδοῦν Λυκοῦργος
ἔθετο τῇ Σπάρτῃ τοὺς νόμους. ἀχθομένους γάρ
τινας τῇ σκληρότητι τῆς νομοθεσίας καὶ διαστάντας
ἀπὸ τῶν ἑτέρων οἴχεσθαι τὸ παράπαν ἐκ τῆς πόλεως·
ἔπειτα διὰ πελάγους πολλοῦ φερομένους εὔξασθαι
τοῖς θεοῖς (πόθον γάρ τινα ὑπελθεῖν αὐτοὺς ὁποιασδήποτε γῆς) εἰς ἣν ἂν ἔλθωσι πρώτην, ἐν ταύτῃ [1]
5 κατοικήσειν. καταχθέντας δὲ τῆς Ἰταλίας περὶ τὰ
καλούμενα Πωμεντῖνα πεδία τό τε χωρίον, ἐν ᾧ
πρῶτον ὡρμίσαντο, Φορωνίαν [2] ἀπὸ τῆς πελαγίου
φορήσεως ὀνομάσαι καὶ θεᾶς ἱερὸν ἱδρύσασθαι
Φορωνίας, [3] ᾗ τὰς εὐχὰς ἔθεντο ἣν νῦν ἑνὸς ἀλλαγῇ
γράμματος Φερωνίαν καλοῦσιν. ἐκεῖθεν δ' ὁρμηθέντας αὐτῶν τινας συνοίκους τοῖς Σαβίνοις γενέσθαι καὶ διὰ τοῦτο πολλὰ τῶν νομίμων εἶναι
Σαβίνων [4] Λακωνικά, μάλιστα δὲ τὸ φιλοπόλεμόν
τε καὶ τὸ λιτοδίαιτον καὶ παρὰ πάντα τὰ ἔργα τοῦ

---

[1] ταύτῃ Reiske: αὐτῇ O.
[2] Ambrosch: φερωνείαν B, φερωνίαν R.
[3] Ambrosch: φορωνείας B, φερωνίας R.
[4] Σαβίνων B: om. R.

' The *Pomptinus ager* of Livy (ii. 34 ; iv. 25). The
marginal lands stretching round the Pontine marshes.

country they occupied was distant from the Adriatic
about two hundred and eighty stades and from the
Tyrrhenian Sea two hundred and forty, and that
its length was a little less than a thousand stades.
There is also another account given of the Sabines in the native histories, to the effect that a
colony of Lacedaemonians settled among them
at the time when Lycurgus, being guardian to his
nephew Eunomus, gave his laws to Sparta. For
the story goes that some of the Spartans, disliking
the severity of his laws and separating from the rest,
quitted the city entirely, and after being borne
through a vast stretch of sea, made a vow to the gods
to settle in the first land they should reach ; for
a longing came upon them for any land whatsoever.
At last they made that part of Italy which lies
near the Pomentine plains [1] and they called the
place where they first landed Foronia, in memory of
their being *borne* [2] through the sea, and built a temple
to the goddess Foronia, to whom they had addressed
their vows ; this goddess, by the alteration of one
letter, they now call Feronia. And some of them,
setting out from thence, settled among the Sabines.
It is for this reason, they say, that many of the
habits of the Sabines are Spartan, particularly their
fondness for war and their frugality and a severity

[2] One wonders why the author of this fanciful etymology
did not connect Feronia directly with the verb φέρεσθαι
("to be borne along "), instead of assuming an earlier
spelling Foronia, not otherwise attested, and deriving that
form from the abstract noun φόρησις. The name has not
as yet been satisfactorily explained.

βίου σκληρόν. ὑπὲρ μὲν δὴ τοῦ Σαβίνων γένους ταῦθ' ἱκανά.

L. Οἱ δὲ περὶ τὸν Ῥωμύλον καὶ Τάτιον τήν τε πόλιν εὐθὺς ἐποίουν μείζονα προσθέντες ἑτέρους αὐτῇ δύο λόφους, τόν τε Κυρίνιον κληθέντα καὶ τὸν Καίλιον, καὶ διελόμενοι τὰς οἰκήσεις χωρὶς ἀλλήλων δίαιταν ἐν τοῖς ἰδίοις ἑκάτεροι χωρίοις ἐποιοῦντο, Ῥωμύλος μὲν τὸ Παλάτιον κατέχων καὶ τὸ Καίλιον ὄρος (ἔστι δὲ τῷ Παλατίῳ προσεχές), Τάτιος δὲ τὸν Καπιτωλῖνον,[1] ὅνπερ ἐξ ἀρχῆς κατέσχε, καὶ τὸν 2 Κυρίνιον ὄχθον. τὸ δ' ὑποκείμενον τῷ Καπιτωλίῳ πεδίον ἐκκόψαντες τὴν ἐν αὐτῷ πεφυκυῖαν ὕλην καὶ τῆς λίμνης, ἣ δὴ διὰ τὸ κοῖλον εἶναι τὸ χωρίον ἐπλήθυε τοῖς κατιοῦσιν ἐκ τῶν ὀρῶν νάμασι, τὰ πολλὰ χώσαντες ἀγορὰν αὐτόθι κατεστήσαντο, ᾗ καὶ νῦν ἔτι χρώμενοι Ῥωμαῖοι διατελοῦσι, καὶ τὰς συνόδους ἐνταῦθα ἐποιοῦντο ἐν Ἡφαίστου χρηματί- ζοντες ἱερῷ μικρὸν ὑπερανεστηκότι[2] τῆς ἀγορᾶς. 3 ἱερά τε ἱδρύσαντο καὶ βωμοὺς καθιέρωσαν οἷς ηὔξαντο κατὰ τὰς μάχας θεοῖς, Ῥωμύλος μὲν Ὀρθωσίῳ Διὶ παρὰ ταῖς καλουμέναις Μουγωνίσι[3] πύλαις, αἳ φέρουσιν εἰς τὸ Παλάτιον ἐκ τῆς ἱερᾶς ὁδοῦ, ὅτι τὴν στρατιὰν αὐτοῦ φυγοῦσαν ἐποίησεν ὁ θεὸς ὑπακούσας ταῖς εὐχαῖς στῆναί τε καὶ πρὸς ἀλκὴν τραπέσθαι· Τάτιος δὲ Ἡλίῳ τε καὶ Σελήνῃ καὶ Κρόνῳ καὶ Ῥέᾳ, πρὸς δὲ τούτοις Ἑστίᾳ καὶ Ἡφαίστῳ καὶ Ἀρτέμιδι καὶ Ἐνναλίῳ καὶ ἄλλοις θεοῖς, ὧν χαλεπὸν ἐξειπεῖν Ἑλλάδι γλώττῃ τὰ

---

[1] Kiessling ; καπιτώλιον O.
[2] Ambrosch : ἐπανεστηκότι O, Jacoby.
[3] Μουγωνίσι Ambrosch: μουρωνίσι ABa. μυρωνίσι Bb.

in all the actions of their lives. But this is enough about the Sabine race.

L. Romulus and Tatius immediately enlarged the city by adding to it two other hills, the Quirinal, as it is called, and the Caelian; and separating their habitations, each of them had his particular place of residence. Romulus occupied the Palatine and Caelian hills, the latter being next to the Palatine, and Tatius the Capitoline hill, which he had seized in the beginning, and the Quirinal. And cutting down the wood that grew on the plain at the foot of the Capitoline and filling up the greatest part of the lake, which, since it lay in a hollow, was kept well supplied by the waters that came down from the hills, they converted this plain into a forum, which the Romans continue to use even now; there they held their assemblies, transacting their business in the temple of Vulcan, which stands a little above the Forum. They built temples also and consecrated altars to those gods to whom they had addressed their vows during their battles: Romulus to Jupiter Stator,[1] near the Porta Mugonia, as it is called, which leads to the Palatine hill from the Sacred Way, because this god had heard his vows and had caused his army to stop in its flight and to renew the battle; and Tatius to the Sun and Moon, to Saturn and to Rhea, and, besides these, to Vesta, Vulcan, Diana, Enyalius, and to other gods whose names are difficult to be expressed in the Greek language; and in every *curia*

[1] The " Stayer " of their flight.

ὀνόματα, ἐν ἁπάσαις τε ταῖς κουρίαις Ἥρᾳ τραπέζας ἔθετο Κυριτίδι [1] λεγομένῃ, αἳ καὶ εἰς τόδε χρόνου
4 κεῖνται. ἔτη μὲν οὖν πέντε συνεβασίλευσαν ἀλλήλοις ὑπὲρ οὐδενὸς διαφερόμενοι χρήματος, ἐν οἷς
κοινὴν πρᾶξιν ἀπεδείξαντο τὴν ἐπὶ Καμερίνους
στρατείαν. λῃστήρια γὰρ ἐκπέμποντες οἱ Καμερῖνοι
καὶ πολλὰ τὴν χώραν αὐτῶν κακοῦντες οὐ συν-
έβαινον ἐπὶ δίκην πολλάκις ὑπ' αὐτῶν καλούμενοι·
οὓς ἐκ παρατάξεώς τε νικήσαντες (ἐχώρησαν γὰρ
αὐτοῖς ὁμόσε) καὶ μετὰ ταῦτα ἐκ τειχομαχίας κατὰ
κράτος ἑλόντες ὅπλα μὲν ἀφείλοντο καὶ χώρας
ἐζημίωσαν τῇ τρίτῃ μερίδι· ἣν τοῖς σφετέροις
5 διεῖλον. τῶν δὲ Καμερίνων τοὺς ἐποίκους [2] λυμαινομένων [3] ἐπεξελθόντες καὶ τρεψάμενοι [4] αὐτούς,
τὰ μὲν αὐτῶν ἅπαντα τοῖς σφετέροις πολίταις
διεῖλον, αὐτοὺς δὲ τοὺς ἀνθρώπους ὁπόσοι ἐβούλοντο
ἐν Ῥώμῃ κατοικεῖν εἴασαν. ἐγένοντο δ' ὡς τετρα-
κισχίλιοι, οὓς ταῖς φράτραις ἐπεμέρισαν, καὶ τὴν
πόλιν αὐτῶν ἀποικίαν Ῥωμαίων ἐποίησαν. ἦν δὲ
Ἀλβανῶν ἀπόκτισις [5] ἡ Καμερία πολλοῖς χρόνοις
ἀποσταλεῖσα πρότερον τῆς Ῥώμης, τὸ δ' ἀρχαῖον
Ἀβοριγίνων οἴκησις ἐν τοῖς [6] πάνυ ἐπιφανής.

LI. Ἐνιαυτῷ δὲ ἕκτῳ περιίσταται πάλιν εἰς ἕνα
Ῥωμύλον ἡ τῆς πόλεως ἀρχὴ Τατίου τελευτήσαντος

[1] Schömann: κυριτίᾳ AB.
[2] The words τοῖς σφετέροις . . . ἐποίκους were supplied by
Kiessling (who used the form Καμεριναίων).
[3] τῇ τρίτῃ ἡμέρᾳ after λυμαινομένων deleted by Kiessling.
[4] τρεψάμενοι Kayser: τροπωσάμενοι O.
[5] ἀπόκτισις ABa: ἀποίκησις Bb.
[6] τοῖς Sintenis: ταῖς O.

he dedicated tables to Juno called Quiritis,[1] which remain even to this day. For five years, then, the kings reigned together in perfect harmony, during which time they engaged in one joint undertaking, the expedition against the Camerini ; for these people, who kept sending out bands of robbers and doing great injury to the country of the Romans, would not agree to have the case submitted to judicial investigation, though often summoned by the Romans to do so. After conquering the Camerini in a pitched battle (for they came to blows with them) and later besieging and taking their town by storm, they disarmed the inhabitants and deprived them of a third part of their land, which they divided among their own people.[2] And when the Camerini proceeded to harass the new settlers, they marched out against them, and having put them to flight, divided all their possessions among their own people, but permitted as many of the inhabitants as wished to do so to live at Rome. These amounted to about four thousand, whom they distributed among the *curiae*, and they made their city a Roman colony. Cameria was a colony of the Albans planted long before the founding of Rome, and anciently one of the most celebrated habitations of the Aborigines.

LI. But [3] in the sixth year, the government of the city devolved once more upon Romulus alone, Tatius

[1] The name also appears as Quiris, Curis and Cur(r)itis. It was variously derived from *currus* ("car"), from the Sabine *curis* ("spear") and from Cures, the city.

[2] More than an entire line is supplied here, following Kiessling's suggestion. See critical note.

[3] For chaps. 51-52 *cf*. Livy i. 14, 1-3.

ἐξ ἐπιβουλῆς, ἣν συνέστησαν ἐπ' αὐτῷ Λαουινιατῶν
οἱ κορυφαιότατοι συμφρονήσαντες ἀπὸ τοιαύτης
αἰτίας· τῶν ἑταίρων τινὲς τοῦ Τατίου ληστήριον
ἐξαγαγόντες εἰς τὴν Λαουινιατῶν χώραν χρήματά
τε αὐτῶν ἥρπασαν πολλὰ καὶ βοσκημάτων ἀπήλασαν
ἀγέλας, τῶν δ' ἐπιβοηθούντων οὓς μὲν ἀπέκτειναν,
2 οὓς δ' ἐτραυμάτισαν. ἀφικομένης δὲ πρεσβείας
παρὰ τῶν ἠδικημένων καὶ τὰ δίκαια ἀπαιτούσης ὁ
μὲν Ῥωμύλος ἐδικαίωσε παραδοῦναι τοὺς δράσαντας
τοῖς ἀδικηθεῖσιν ἀπάγειν, ὁ δὲ Τάτιος τῶν ἑταίρων
περιεχόμενος οὐκ ἠξίου πρὸ δίκης τινὰς ὑπ' ἐχθρῶν
ἄγεσθαι[1] καὶ ταῦτα πολίτας ὄντας ὑπὸ ξένων· δικά-
ζεσθαι δ' αὐτοῖς ἐκέλευε τοὺς ἠδικῆσθαι λέγοντας
3 εἰς Ῥώμην ἀφικομένους. οἱ μὲν δὴ πρέσβεις οὐδὲν
εὑρόμενοι τῶν δικαίων ἀγανακτοῦντες ἀπῄεσαν, ἀκο-
λουθήσαντες δ' αὐτοῖς τῶν Σαβίνων τινὲς ὑπ' ὀργῆς,
ἐσκηνωμένοις παρὰ τὴν ὁδόν (ἑσπέρα γὰρ αὐτοὺς
κατέλαβεν) ἐπιτίθενται καθεύδουσι καὶ τά τε χρή-
ματ' αὐτοὺς ἀφαιροῦνται καὶ ὁπόσους ἐν ταῖς κοίταις
ἔτι κατέλαβον ἀποσφάττουσιν, ὅσοις δὲ ταχεῖα τῆς
ἐπιβουλῆς αὐτῶν αἴσθησις ἐγένετο καὶ τοῦ διαφυγεῖν δύναμις εἰς τὴν πόλιν ἀφικνοῦνται. μετὰ
τοῦτο ἔκ τε Λαουινίου πρέσβεις ἀφικόμενοι καὶ ἐξ
ἄλλων πόλεων συχνῶν κατηγόρουν τῆς παρανομίας
καὶ πόλεμον παρήγγελλον εἰ μὴ τεύξονται τῆς
δίκης.

LII. Ῥωμύλῳ μὲν οὖν δεινόν, ὥσπερ ἦν, τὸ
περὶ τοὺς πρεσβευτὰς ἐφαίνετο πάθος καὶ ταχείας

---

[1] ἄγεσθαι Bb : ἐνάγεσθαι ABa ; ἀπάγεσθαι Bücheler.

having lost his life as the result of a plot which the principal men of Lavinium formed against him. The occasion for the plot was this. Some friends of Tatius had led out a band of robbers into the territory of the Lavinians, where they seized a great many of their effects and drove away their herds of cattle, killing or wounding those who came to the rescue. Upon the arrival of an embassy from the injured to demand satisfaction, Romulus decided that those who had done the injury should be delivered up for punishment to those they had wronged. Tatius, however, espousing the cause of his friends, would not consent that any persons should be taken into custody by their enemies before trial, and particularly Roman citizens by outsiders, but ordered those who complained that they had been injured to come to Rome and proceed against the others according to law. The ambassadors, accordingly, having failed to obtain any satisfaction, went away full of resentment ; and some of the Sabines, incensed at their action, followed them and set upon them while they were asleep in their tents, which they had pitched near the road when evening overtook them, and not only robbed them of their money, but cut the throats of all they found still in their beds ; those, however, who perceived the plot promptly and were able to make their escape got back to their city. After this ambassadors came both from Lavinium and from many other cities, complaining of this lawless deed and threatening war if they should not obtain justice.

LII. This violence committed against the ambassadors appeared to Romulus, as indeed it was, a

ἀφοσιώσεως δεόμενον, ὡς ἱεροῦ καταλελυμένου[1]
νόμου. καὶ οὐδὲν ἔτι διαμελλήσας, ὡς εἶδεν ὀλιγω-
ροῦντα τὸν Τάτιον αὐτὸς συνέλαβε τοὺς ἐνόχους τῷ
ἄγει καὶ δήσας παρέδωκε τοῖς πρεσβευταῖς ἀπάγειν.
2 Τατίῳ δὲ θυμός τε εἰσέρχεται τῆς ὕβρεως, ἣν ὑπὸ
τοῦ συνάρχοντος ᾐτιᾶτο ὑβρίσθαι κατὰ τὴν παρά-
δοσιν τῶν ἀνδρῶν, καὶ οἶκτος τῶν ἀπαγομένων (ἦν
γὰρ καὶ συγγενής τις αὐτοῦ τῷ ἄγει ἔνοχος) καὶ
αὐτίκα τοὺς στρατιώτας ἀναλαβὼν ἐβοήθει διὰ
τάχους ἐν ὁδῷ τε ὄντας τοὺς πρέσβεις καταλαβὼν
3 ἀφείλετο τοὺς ἀπαγομένους. χρόνου δὲ οὐ πολλοῦ
διελθόντος, ὡς μέν τινές φασιν, ἅμα Ῥωμύλῳ
παραγενόμενος εἰς τὸ Λαουίνιον ἕνεκα θυσίας, ἣν
ἔδει τοῖς πατρῴοις θεοῖς ὑπὲρ τῆς πόλεως θῦσαι
τοὺς βασιλεῖς, συστάντων ἐπ᾽ αὐτὸν τῶν ἑταίρων
τε καὶ γένει προσηκόντων τοῖς ἀνῃρημένοις πρέ-
σβεσιν ἐπὶ τῶν βωμῶν ταῖς μαγειρικαῖς σφαγίσι καὶ
4 τοῖς βουπόροις ὀβελοῖς παιόμενος ἀποθνήσκει. ὡς
δ᾽ οἱ περὶ Λικίννιον γράφουσιν οὐ μετὰ Ῥωμύλου
παραγενόμενος οὐδὲ χάριν ἱερῶν, ἀλλὰ μόνος ὡς
πείσων τοὺς ἀδικηθέντας ἀφεῖναι τοῖς δεδρακόσι
τὴν ὀργήν, ἀγανακτήσαντος τοῦ πλήθους ἐπὶ τῷ μὴ
παραδίδοσθαί σφισι τοὺς ἄνδρας, ὡς ὅ τε Ῥωμύλος
ἐδικαίωσε καὶ ἡ τῶν Ῥωμαίων ἔκρινε βουλή, καὶ
τῶν προσηκόντων τοῖς τεθνεῶσι κατὰ πλῆθος ὁρμη-
σάντων ἐπ᾽ αὐτόν, ἀδύνατος ὢν ἔτι διαφυγεῖν τὴν ἐκ
χειρὸς δίκην, καταλευσθεὶς ὑπ᾽ αὐτῶν ἀποθνήσκει.

---

[1] Bücheler: καταλυομένου O.

[1] Licinius Macer.

terrible crime and one calling for speedy expiation,
since it had been in violation of a sacred law ; and
finding that Tatius was making light of it, he himself,
without further delay, caused those who had been
guilty of the outrage to be seized and delivered up in
chains to the ambassadors to be led away. But Tatius
not only was angered at the indignity which he
complained he had received from his colleague in
the delivering up of the men, but was also moved
with compassion for those who were being led
away (for one of the guilty persons was actually a
relation of his) ; and immediately, taking his soldiers with him, he went in haste to their assistance,
and overtaking the ambassadors on the road, he
took the prisoners from them. But not long afterwards, as some say, when he had gone with Romulus
to Lavinium in order to perform a sacrifice which
it was necessary for the kings to offer to the ancestral
gods for the prosperity of the city, the friends and
relations of the ambassadors who had been murdered,
having conspired against him, slew him at the altar
with the knives and spits used in cutting up and
roasting the oxen. But Licinius [1] writes that he
did not go with Romulus nor, indeed, on account
of any sacrifices, but that he went alone, with the
intention of persuading those who had received
the injuries to forgive the authors of them, and that
when the people became angry because the men were
not delivered up to them in accordance with the
decision both of Romulus and of the Roman senate,
and the relations of the slain men rushed upon him
in great numbers, he was no longer able to escape
summary justice and was stoned to death by them.

5 Τάτιος μὲν οὖν τοιαύτης τελευτῆς ἔτυχε τρία μὲν
ἔτη πολεμήσας Ῥωμύλῳ, πέντε δὲ συνάρξας,
θάπτεται δ᾽ εἰς Ῥώμην κομισθεὶς ἐντίμῳ ταφῇ καὶ
χοὰς αὐτῷ καθ᾽ ἕκαστον ἐνιαυτὸν ἡ πόλις ἐπιτελεῖ
δημοσίᾳ.

LIII. Ῥωμύλος δὲ μόνος ἐπὶ τὴν ἀρχὴν τὸ δεύτερον καταστὰς τό τε ἄγος ἀφοσιοῦται τὸ περὶ τοὺς
πρέσβεις γενόμενον προειπὼν τοῖς ἐργασαμένοις τὸ
μύσος ὕδατος εἴργεσθαι καὶ πυρός (ἐπεφεύγεσαν
γὰρ ἐκ τῆς πόλεως ἅπαντες ἅμα τῷ τὸν Τάτιον
ἀποθανεῖν) καὶ τῶν Λαουινιατῶν τοὺς συστάντας
ἐπὶ τὸν Τάτιον δικαστηρίῳ παραδοὺς ἐκδοθέντας
ὑπὸ τῆς πόλεως, ἐπειδὴ δικαιότερα ἐδόκουν λέγειν
τὰ βίαια τιμωρησάμενοι τοῖς βιαίοις, ἀπέλυσε τῆς
2 αἰτίας. ταῦτα διαπραξάμενος ἐπὶ τὴν Φιδηναίων
ἐστράτευσε πόλιν ἀπὸ τετταράκοντα σταδίων τῆς
Ῥώμης κειμένην, μεγάλην τε καὶ πολυάνθρωπον
οὖσαν τότε. ἀγομένης γὰρ εἰς τὴν Ῥώμην ἀγορᾶς
ἐν σκάφαις ποταμηγοῖς, ἣν Κρουστομερῖνοι¹ πιεζομένοις ὑπὸ λιμοῦ Ῥωμαίοις ἀπέστειλαν, ὠσάμενοι
κατὰ πλῆθος ἐπὶ τὰς σκάφας οἱ Φιδηναῖοι τήν τε
ἀγορὰν διήρπασαν καὶ τῶν ἀνθρώπων τινὰς τῶν
ἐπιβοηθούντων ἀπέκτειναν αἰτούμενοί τε δίκας οὐχ
3 ὑπεῖχον. ἐφ᾽ οἷς ἀγανακτῶν ὁ Ῥωμύλος ἐνέβαλεν
εἰς τὴν χώραν αὐτῶν πολλῇ στρατιᾷ καὶ γενόμενος
ἀφθόνου λείας ἐγκρατὴς ἀπάγειν μὲν παρεσκευάζετο τὴν δύναμιν, ἐπεξελθόντων δὲ τῶν Φιδηναίων

¹ Ambrosch : κρουστομέριοι BbR, κροστομέρειοι Ba.

Such was the end to which Tatius came, after he had warred against Romulus for three years and had been his colleague for five. His body was brought to Rome, where it was given honourable burial ; and the city offers public libations to him every year.

LIII. But [1] Romulus, now established for the second time as sole ruler, expiated the crime committed against the ambassadors by forbidding those who had perpetrated the outrage the use of fire and water ; for upon the death of Tatius they had all fled from the city. After that, he brought to trial the Lavinians who had conspired against Tatius and who had been delivered up by their own city, and when they seemed to plead, with considerable justice, that they had but avenged violence with violence, he freed them of the charge. After he had attended to these matters, he led out his army against the city of Fidenae, which was situated forty stades from Rome and was at that time both large and populous. For on an occasion when the Romans were oppressed by famine and provisions which the people of Crustumerium had sent to them were being brought down the river in boats, the Fidenates crowded aboard the boats in great numbers, seized the provisions and killed some of the men who defended them, and when called upon to make satisfaction, they refused to do so. Romulus, incensed at this, made an incursion into their territory with a considerable force, and having possessed himself of a great quantity of booty, was preparing to lead his army home ; but when the Fidenates came out

[1] *Cf.* Livy i. 14, 4-11.

συνάπτει πρὸς αὐτοὺς μάχην. καρτεροῦ δὲ ἀγῶνος
γειομένου καὶ πολλῶν πεσόντων ἀφ' ἑκατέρων
ἡσσηθέντες οἱ Φιδηναῖοι τρέπονται πρὸς φυγήν, ὁ
δ' ἐκ ποδὸς συνακολουθῶν αὐτοῖς συνεισπίπτει τοῖς
4 φεύγουσιν εἰς τὸ τεῖχος. ἁλούσης δὲ τῆς πόλεως
ἐξ ἐφόδου τιμωρησάμενος ἐξ αὐτῶν ὀλίγους καὶ
φυλακὴν ἐν τῇ πόλει τριακοσίων ἀνδρῶν καταλιπὼν
τῆς τε χώρας μοῖραν ἀποτεμόμενος, ἣν τοῖς σφετέροις διεῖλεν, ἀποικίαν ἐποίησε Ῥωμαίων καὶ ταύτην
τὴν πόλιν. ἦν δὲ Ἀλβανῶν ἀπόκτισις κατὰ τὸν αὐτὸν
οἰκισθεῖσα Νωμεντῷ τε καὶ Κρουστομερίᾳ χρόνον,
τριῶν ἀδελφῶν τῆς ἀποικίας ἡγησαμένων, ὧν ὁ
πρεσβύτατος τὴν Φιδήνην ἔκτισεν.

LIV Μετὰ τοῦτον τὸν πόλεμον ἐπὶ Καμερίνους
ἐστράτευσει ἐπιθεμένους[1] τοῖς παρὰ σφίσιν ἐποίκοις, καθ' ὃν χρόνοι ἔκαμνεν ἡ Ῥωμαίων πόλις
ὑπὸ νόσου λοιμικῆς· ᾗ δὴ μάλιστα ἐπαρθέντες οἱ
Καμερῖνοι καὶ νομίσαντες ἄρδην τὸ Ῥωμαίων
διαφθαρήσεσθαι γένος ὑπὸ τῆς συμφορᾶς τοὺς μὲν
2 ἀπέκτειναν τῶν ἐποίκων, τοὺς δ' ἐξέβαλον. ἀνθ'
ὧν τιμωρούμενος αὐτοὺς ὁ Ῥωμύλος, ἐπειδὴ τὸ
δεύτερον ἐκράτησε τῆς πόλεως, τοὺς μὲν αἰτίους
τῆς ἀποστάσεως ἀπέκτεινε, τοῖς δὲ στρατιώταις
διαρπάσαι τὴν πόλιν ἐφῆκε, τῆς τε χώρας τὴν
ἡμίσειαν ἀποτεμόμενος ἔξω τῆς πρότερον τοῖς
κληρούχοις δοθείσης καὶ φρουρὰν ἀξιόχρεων καταλιπών, ὡς μηδὲν ἔτι παρακινῆσαι τοὺς ἔνδον,
ἀπῆγε τὴν δύναμιν. ἐκ ταύτης τῆς στρατείας καὶ[2]
δεύτερον θρίαμβον κατήγαγε καὶ ἀπὸ τῶν λαφύρων

---

[1] Bücheler: ἐπιτιθεμένους O.   [2] καὶ Bb : om. BaR.

against him, he gave them battle. After a severe struggle, in which many fell on both sides, the enemy were defeated and put to flight, and Romulus, following close upon their heels, rushed inside the walls along with the fugitives. When the city had been taken at the first assault, he punished a few of the citizens, and left a guard of three hundred men there; and taking from the inhabitants a part of their territory, which he divided among his own people, he made this city also a Roman colony. It had been founded by the Albans at the same time with Nomentum and Crustumerium, three brothers having been the leaders of the colony, of whom the eldest built Fidenae.

LIV. After this war Romulus undertook another against the Camerini, who had attacked the Roman colonists in their midst while the city of Rome was suffering from a pestilence; it was this situation in particular that encouraged the Camerini, and believing that the Roman nation would be totally destroyed by the calamity, they killed some of the colonists and expelled the rest. In revenge for this Romulus, after he had a second time made himself master of the city, put to death the authors of the revolt and permitted his soldiers to plunder the city; and he also took away half the land besides that which had been previously granted to the Roman settlers. And having left a garrison in the city sufficient to quell any future uprising of the inhabitants, he departed with his forces. As the result of this expedition he celebrated a second triumph, and out of the spoils he dedicated a chariot and four in

DIONYSIUS OF HALICARNASSUS

τέθριππον χαλκοῦν ἀνέθηκε τῷ Ἡφαίστῳ καὶ
παρ' αὐτῷ τὴν ἰδίαν ἀνέστησεν[1] εἰκόνα ἐπιγράψας
3 Ἑλληνικοῖς γράμμασι τὰς ἑαυτοῦ πράξεις. τρίτος
αὐτῷ συνέστη πόλεμος πρὸς ἔθνους Τυρρηνικοῦ τὴν
μεγίστην ἰσχὺν ἔχουσαν[2] τότε πόλιν, ἣ καλεῖται
μὲν Οὐιοί,[3] ἀπέχει δὲ τῆς Ῥώμης ἀμφὶ τοὺς ἑκατὸν
σταδίους, κεῖται δ' ἐφ' ὑψηλοῦ σκοπέλου καὶ περιρ-
ρῶγος μέγεθος ἔχουσα ὅσον Ἀθῆναι. ἐποιήσαντο
δ' οἱ Οὐιεντανοὶ τοῦ πολέμου πρόφασιν τὴν τῆς
Φιδήνης ἅλωσιν καὶ πρέσβεις ἀποστείλαντες ἐκέ-
λευον Ῥωμαίοις ἐξάγειν ἐκ τῆς πόλεως τὴν
φρουρὰν καὶ τὴν χώραν, ἣν κατεῖχον ἀφελόμενοι
τοὺς Φιδηναίους, ἀποδιδόναι τοῖς ἐξ ἀρχῆς κυρίοις.
ὡς δ' οὐκ ἔπειθον ἐλάσαντες πολλῇ στρατιᾷ
πλησίον τῆς Φιδήνης ἐν ἀπόπτῳ τίθενται τὸν
4 χάρακα. προεγνωκὼς δὲ αὐτῶν τὴν ἔξοδον ὁ
Ῥωμύλος ἐξεληλύθει τὴν κρατίστην δύναμιν ἔχων
καὶ ἦν ἐν τῇ πόλει τῶν Φιδηναίων εὐτρεπής. ἐπεὶ
δ' ἕτοιμα τὰ πρὸς τὸν ἀγῶνα ἦν, ἀμφότεροι προελθόντες εἰς τὸ πεδίον ἐμάχοντο καὶ διέμειναν ἄχρι
πολλῆς ὥρας ἐκθύμως ἀγωνιζόμενοι, ἕως[4] ἡ νὺξ
ἐπιλαβοῦσα διέκρινεν αὐτοὺς ἴσους κατὰ τὸν ἀγῶνα
γενομένους. καὶ ταύτην μὲν τὴν μάχην οὕτως
ἠγωνίσαντο·

LV. ἑτέρας δὲ μάχης μετ' οὐ πολὺ γενομένης,
ἐνίκων οἱ Ῥωμαῖοι σοφίᾳ τοῦ ἡγεμόνος ὄρος τι
καταλαβομένου νύκτωρ οὐ πολὺν τοῦ στρατοπέδου
τῶν πολεμίων τόπον ἀπέχον καὶ λοχίσαντος ἐν

---

[1] Jacoby: ἔστησεν O.

bronze to Vulcan, and near it he set up his own statue with an inscription in Greek characters setting forth his deeds. The[1] third war Romulus engaged in was against the most powerful city of the Tyrrhenian race at that time, called Veii, distant from Rome about a hundred stades ; it is situated on a high and craggy rock and is as large as Athens. The Veientes made the taking of Fidenae the pretext for this war, and sending ambassadors, they bade the Romans withdraw their garrison from that city and restore to its original possessors the territory they had taken from them and were now occupying. And when their demand was not heeded, they took the field with a great army and established their camp in a conspicuous place near Fidenae. Romulus, however, having received advance information of their march, had set out with the flower of his army and lay ready at Fidenae to receive them. When all their preparations were made for the struggle, both armies advanced into the plain and came to grips, and they continued fighting with great ardour for a long time, till the coming on of night parted them, after they had proved themselves evenly matched in the struggle. This was the course of the first battle.

LV. But in a second battle, which was fought not long afterwards, the Romans were victorious as the result of the strategy of their general, who had occupied in the night a certain height not far distant from the enemy's camp and placed there in

---

[1] For chap. 54, 3–55, 6 cf. Livy i. 15, 1-5.

[2] μεγίστην ἰσχὺν ἔχουσαν Kiessling : μεγίστην ἰσχύουσαν AB.
[3] Οὐιοί Sylburg : ἰοὶ A, ἴοι B.   [4] ἕως O : τέως Jacoby.

αὐτῷ τὴν ἀκμαιοτάτην τῶν ὕστερον ἀφικομένων
ἐκ τῆς πόλεως ἱππέων τε καὶ πεζῶν δύναμιν.
2 συνελθόντων δ᾽ εἰς τὸ πεδίον ἀμφοτέρων καὶ τὸν
αὐτὸν ἀγωνιζομένων τρόπον, ἐπειδὴ τὸ σύνθημα
ὁ Ῥωμύλος ἦρε τοῖς ἐπὶ τοῦ ὄρους, ἀλαλάξαντες
οἱ λοχῶντες ἔθεον ἐπὶ τοὺς Οὐιεντανοὺς ἐκ τῶν
κατόπιν καὶ προσπεσόντες ἀνθρώποις μεμοχθηκόσιν
αὐτοὶ ἀκμῆτες ὄντες οὐ σὺν πολλῷ τρέπουσι πόνῳ.¹
τῶν δ᾽ ὀλίγοι μέν τινες ἀποθνήσκουσι κατὰ τὴν
μάχην, οἱ δὲ πλείους εἰς τὸν Τέβεριν ποταμόν (ῥεῖ²
δὲ παρὰ τὴν Φιδήνην) ῥίψαντες ἑαυτούς, ὡς δια-
νηξόμενοι τὸ ῥεῦμα, διεφθάρησαν. τραυματίαι γὰρ
ὄντες καὶ βαρεῖς ὑπὸ κόπου ἀδύνατοι ἐγένοντο δια-
νήξασθαι· οἱ δὲ καὶ ἀπειρίᾳ τοῦ νεῖν, οὐ προϊόντες,³
ὑπὸ τοῦ δεινοῦ τὴν γνώμην ἐπιταραχθέντες, ἐν ταῖς
3 δίναις ἀπώλλυντο. εἰ μὲν οὖν συνέγνωσαν ἑαυτοῖς
Οὐιεντανοὶ κακῶς τὰ πρῶτα βεβουλευμένοις⁴ καὶ τὸ
λοιπὸν ἦγον ἡσυχίαν οὐδενὸς ἂν ἔτι μείζονος ἀπέ-
λαυσαν κακοῦ, νῦν δὲ ἀναμαχεῖσθαί τε τὰ πρότερα
σφάλματα ἐλπίσαντες καὶ εἰ μείζονι παρασκευῇ ἐπι-
βάλοιεν ῥᾳδίως ἐπικρατήσειν οἰόμενοι τῷ πολέμῳ,
πολλῇ στρατιᾷ τῇ τε ἐξ αὐτῆς τῆς πόλεως κατα-
γραφείσῃ καὶ τῇ⁵ ἐκ τῶν ὁμοεθνῶν κατὰ φιλίαν
παραγενομένῃ τὸ δεύτερον ἐπὶ τοὺς Ῥωμαίους
4 ἐλαύνουσι· καὶ γίνεται πάλιν αὐτῶν μάχη καρτερὰ

---

¹ οὐ σὺν πολλῷ τρέπουσι πόνῳ Sylburg, Casaubon, οὐ σὺν
πόνῳ τρέπουσι χρόνῳ Reiske : οὐ σὺν πολλῷ τρέπουσι χρόνῳ O,
Jacoby.
² ῥεῖ Kiessling, ἐκρεῖ Steph. : ἐκει O.
³ προιδόντες ABa : προειδότες Bb.

468

ambush the choicest both of the horse and foot that had come to him from Rome since the last action. The two armies met in the plain and fought in the same manner as before ; but when Romulus raised the signal to the troops that lay in ambush on the height, these, raising the battle cry, rushed upon the Veientes from the rear, and being themselves fresh while the enemy were fatigued, they put them to flight with no great difficulty. Some few of them were slain in battle, but the greater part, throwing themselves into the Tiber, which flows by Fidenae, with the intention of swimming across the river, were drowned ; for, being wounded and spent with labour, they were unable to swim across, while others, who did not know how to swim and had not looked ahead, having lost all presence of mind in face of the danger, perished in the eddies of the river. If, now, the Veientes had realized that their first plans had been ill-advised and had remained quiet after this, they would have met with no greater misfortune ; but, as it was, hoping to repair their former losses and believing that if they attacked with a larger force they would easily conquer in the war, they set out a second time against the Romans with a large army, consisting both of the levy from the city itself and of others of the same race [1] who in virtue of their league came to their assistance. Upon this, another severe battle was fought near

[1] *i.e.* Etruscans.

---

[4] βεβουλευμένοις Bb : βεβουλευμένοι Ba, βουλευόμενοι R.
[5] τῇ added by Kiessling.

τῆς Φιδήνης πλησίον, ἣν ἐνίκων Ῥωμαῖοι πολλοὺς
μὲν ἀποκτείναντες τῶν Οὐιεντανῶν, ἔτι δὲ πλείους
αἰχμαλώτους λαβόντες. ἑάλω δὲ καὶ ὁ χάραξ αὐτῶν
μεστὸς ὢν χρημάτων τε καὶ ὅπλων καὶ ἀνδραπόδων,
καὶ σκάφαι ποταμηγοὶ γέμουσαι πολλῆς ἀγορᾶς
ἐλήφθησαν, ἐν αἷς ὁ τῶν αἰχμαλώτων ὄχλος εἰς
5 τὴν Ῥώμην κατήγετο διὰ τοῦ ποταμοῦ. οὗτος
κατήχθη[1] τρίτος ὑπὸ Ῥωμύλου θρίαμβος μακρῷ
τῶν προτέρων ἐκπρεπέστερος. καὶ μετ' οὐ πολὺ
Οὐιεντανῶν πρεσβείας ἀφικομένης περὶ διαλύσεως
τοῦ πολέμου καὶ συγγνώμην τῶν ἁμαρτημάτωι
ἀξιούσης λαβεῖν δίκας ὁ Ῥωμύλος αὐτοῖς ἐπιτίθησι
τάσδε· χώραν τε παραδοῦναι Ῥωμαίοις τὴν προσ-
εχῆ τῷ Τεβέρει, τοὺς καλουμένους Ἑπτὰ πάγους,
καὶ τῶν ἁλῶν[2] ἀποστῆναι τῶν παρὰ ταῖς ἐκβολαῖς
τοῦ ποταμοῦ, τοῦ δὲ μηδὲν ἔτι νεωτερίσαι τὸ πιστὸν
6 παρασχεῖν ὅμηρα πεντήκοντα ἀγαγόντας. ὑπο-
μεινάντων δὲ Οὐιεντανῶν ἅπαντα ταῦτα σπονδὰς
ποιησάμενος πρὸς αὐτοὺς εἰς ἑκατὸν ἔτη στήλαις
ἐνεχάραξε τὰς ὁμολογίας. τῶν δ' αἰχμαλώτων
τοὺς μὲν ἀπιέναι βουλομένους ἀφῆκεν ἄνευ λύτρων,
τοὺς δ' αὐτοῦ μένειν προαιρουμένους πολλῷ πλείους
ὄντας τῶν ἑτέρων πολίτας ποιησάμενος ταῖς φράτραις ἐπιδιεῖλε καὶ κλήρους αὐτοῖς προσένειμε[3] ἐπὶ
τάδε τοῦ Τεβέριος.

LVI. Οὗτοι συνέστησαν οἱ πόλεμοι Ῥωμύλῳ
λόγου καὶ μνήμης ἄξιοι. τοῦ δὲ μηδὲν ἔτι τῶν

---

[1] κατήχθη Jacoby: ἤχθη O.
[2] ἁλῶν Gelenius, Sylburg: ἄλλων O.

Fidenae, in which the Romans were victorious, after killing many of the Veientes and taking more of them prisoners. Even their camp was taken, which was full of money, arms and slaves, and likewise their boats, which were laden with great store of provisions ; and in these the multitude of prisoners were carried down the river to Rome. This was the third triumph that Romulus celebrated. and it was much more magnificent than either of the former. And when, not long afterwards, ambassadors arrived from the Veientes to seek an end to the war and to ask pardon for their offences, Romulus imposed the following penalties upon them : to deliver up to the Romans the country adjacent to the Tiber, called the Seven Districts,[1] and to abandon the salt-works near the mouth of the river, and also to bring fifty hostages as a pledge that they would attempt no uprising in the future. When the Veientes submitted to all these demands, he made a treaty with them for one hundred years and engraved the terms of it on pillars. He then dismissed without ransom all the prisoners who desired to return home ; but those who preferred to remain in Rome—and these were far more numerous than the others—he made citizens, distributing them among the *curiae* and assigning to them allotments of land on this side of the Tiber.

LVI. These [2] are the memorable wars which Romulus waged. His failure to subdue any more

[1] Septem Pagi.   [2] *Cf.* Livy i. 16, 1-4.

---

[3] τοὺς after προσένειμε deleted by Jacoby ; Reiske emended to τῆς.

DIONYSIUS OF HALICARNASSUS

πλησίον ἐθνῶν ὑπαγαγέσθαι ταχεῖα ἡ τελευτὴ τοῦ
βίου συμβᾶσα ἔτι ἀκμάζοντι αὐτῷ τὰ πολέμια
πράττειν ἐν αἰτίᾳ γενέσθαι ἔδοξε· περὶ ἧς πολλοὶ
2 παραδέδονται λόγοι καὶ διάφοροι. οἱ μὲν οὖν
μυθωδέστερα τὰ περὶ αὐτοῦ ποιοῦντες ἐκκλησιά-
ζοντά φασιν αὐτὸν ἐπὶ στρατοπέδου ζόφου κατα-
σκήψαντος ἐξ αἰθρίας καὶ χειμῶνος μεγάλου καταρ-
ραγέντος ἀφανῆ γενέσθαι καὶ πεπιστεύκασιν ὑπὸ
3 τοῦ πατρὸς Ἄρεος τὸν ἄνδρα ἀνηρπάσθαι· οἱ δὲ
τὰ πιθανώτερα[1] γράφοντες πρὸς τῶν ἰδίων πολιτῶν
λέγουσιν αὐτὸν ἀποθανεῖν. αἰτίαν δὲ τῆς ἀναιρέ-
σεως αὐτοῦ φέρουσι τήν τε ἄφεσιν τῶν ὁμήρων,
οὓς παρὰ Οὐιεντανῶν ἔλαβεν, ἄνευ κοινῆς γνώμης
γενομένην παρὰ τὸ εἰωθός, καὶ τὸ[2] μηκέτι τὸν
αὐτὸν προσφέρεσθαι τρόπον τοῖς ἀρχαίοις[3] πολίταις καὶ τοῖς προσγράφοις, ἀλλὰ τοὺς μὲν ἐν τιμῇ
πλείονι ἄγειν, τῶν δ' ἐπεισαχθέντων ὑπερορᾶν, τό
τε ὠμὸν αὐτοῦ τὸ περὶ τὰς τιμωρίας τῶν ἐξαμαρτανόντων[4] (Ῥωμαίων γάρ τινας ἐπὶ λῃστείᾳ
τῶν πλησιοχώρων κατηγορηθέντας οὔτε ἀφανεῖς
ἄνδρας οὔτε ὀλίγους ἐκέλευσεν ὦσαι κατὰ τοῦ
κρημνοῦ τὴν δίκην αὐτὸς μόνος δικάσας), μάλιστα
δὲ ὅτι βαρὺς ἤδη καὶ αὐθάδης εἶναι ἐδόκει καὶ
τὴν ἀρχὴν οὐκέτι βασιλικῶς ἀλλὰ τυραννικώτερον
4 ἐξάγειν. διὰ ταύτας δὴ λέγουσι τὰς αἰτίας συστάντας ἐπ' αὐτῷ τοὺς πατρικίους βουλεῦσαι τὸν φόνον,

[1] πιθανώτερα A (?), Reiske: πιθανώτατα B.
[2] τὸ Steph.: om. AB.
[3] ἀρχαίοις (or ἀρχαιοτέροις) Reiske: ἀρχαιοτάτοις O.

472

of the neighbouring nations seems to have been due to
his sudden death, which happened while he was still
in the vigour of his age for warlike achievements.
There are many different stories concerning it. Those
who give a rather fabulous account of his life say
that while he was haranguing his men in the camp,
sudden darkness rushed down out of a clear sky
and a violent storm burst, after which he was
nowhere to be seen ; and these writers believe that
he was caught up into heaven by his father, Mars.
But those who write the more plausible accounts
say that he was killed by his own people ; and the
reason they allege for his murder is that he released
without the common consent, contrary to custom,
the hostages he had taken from the Veientes, and that
he no longer comported himself in the same manner
toward the original citizens and toward those who
were enrolled later, but showed greater honour
to the former and slighted the latter, and also because of his great cruelty in the punishment of de-
linquents (for instance, he had ordered a group of
Romans who were accused of brigandage against
the neighbouring peoples to be hurled down the
precipice [1] after he had sat alone in judgment upon
them, although they were neither of mean birth nor
few in number), but chiefly because he now seemed
to be harsh and arbitrary and to be exercising his
power more like a tyrant than a king. For these
reasons, they say, the patricians formed a conspiracy
against him and resolved to slay him ; and having

[1] The Tarpeian rock.

---

[4] καὶ αὔθαδες after ἐξαμαρτανόντων deleted by Bücheler
(note καὶ αὐθάδης four lines below).

πρᾶξαι δὲ τὸ ἔργον ἐν τῷ βουλευτηρίῳ καὶ διελόν-
τας τὸ σῶμα κατὰ μέρη χάριν τοῦ μὴ φανῆναι τὸν
νεκρὸν ἐξελθεῖν κρύπτοντας ὑπὸ ταῖς περιβολαῖς
ὅσον ἕκαστος εἶχεν αὐτοῦ μέρος καὶ μετὰ τοῦτο γῇ
5 κρύψαι κατὰ τὸ ἀφανές. οἱ δ' ἐκκλησιάζοντα μὲν
αὐτόν φασιν ὑπὸ τῶν νεοπολιτῶν Ῥωμαίων ἀναιρεθῆναι, ἐπιχειρῆσαι δ' αὐτοὺς τῷ φόνῳ καθ' ὃν
χρόνον ἡ ζάλη[1] καὶ τὸ σκότος ἐγένετο διασκεδα-
σθέντος ἐκ τῆς ἐκκλησίας τοῦ δήμου καὶ μονωθέντος
τῆς φυλακῆς τοῦ ἡγεμόνος. διὰ τοῦτο γοῦν φασι
τὴν ἡμέραν ἐν ᾗ τὸ πάθος ἐγένετο τῆς τροπῆς τοῦ
πλήθους ἐπώνυμον εἶναι καὶ μέχρι τῶν καθ' ἡμᾶς
6 χρόνων ὄχλου φυγὴν καλεῖσθαι. ἔοικε δ' οὐ μικρὰν
ἀφορμὴν παρέχειν τοῖς θεοποιοῦσι τὰ θνητὰ καὶ εἰς
οὐρανὸν ἀναβιβάζουσι τὰς ψυχὰς τῶν ἐπιφανῶν τὰ
συμβάντα ἐκ τοῦ θεοῦ περὶ τὴν σύγκρισιν τοῦ
ἀνδρὸς ἐκείνου καὶ τὴν διάκρισιν. ἔν τε γὰρ τῷ
βιασμῷ τῆς μητρὸς αὐτοῦ εἴθ' ὑπ' ἀνθρώπων τινὸς
εἴθ' ὑπὸ θεοῦ γενομένῳ τὸν ἥλιον ἐκλιπεῖν φασιν
ὅλον καὶ σκότος παντελῶς ὥσπερ ἐν νυκτὶ τὴν γῆν
κατασχεῖν ἔν τε τῇ τελευτῇ αὐτοῦ ταὐτὸ συμβῆναι
7 λέγουσι πάθος. ὁ μὲν δὴ κτίσας τὴν Ῥώμην καὶ
πρῶτος ἀποδειχθεὶς ὑπ' αὐτῆς βασιλεὺς Ῥωμύλος
τοιαύτης λέγεται τελευτῆς τυχεῖν, οὐδεμίαν ἐξ αὐτοῦ γενεὰν καταλιπών, ἑπτὰ μὲν ἔτη καὶ τριάκοντα
βασιλεύσας, πεντηκοστὸν δὲ καὶ πέμπτον ἔτος ἔχων

---

[1] ἡ ζάλη Kiessling (cf. Plut. Rom. 27), δὴ ζάλη Reiske:
δηλα ἡ O, Jacoby.

carried out the deed in the senate-house, they divided his body into several pieces, that it might not be seen, and then came out, each one hiding his part of the body under his robes, and afterwards burying it in secret.   Others say that while haranguing the people he was slain by the new citizens of Rome, and that they undertook the murder at the time when the rain and the darkness occurred, the assembly of the people being then dispersed and their chief left without his guard.   And for this reason, they say, the day on which this event happened got its name from the flight of the people and is called *Populifugia* [1] down to our times.   Be that as it may, the incidents that occurred by the direction of Heaven in connexion with this man's conception and death would seem to give no small authority to the view of those who make gods of mortal men and place the souls of illustrious persons in heaven.   For they say that at the time when his mother was violated, whether by some man or by a god, there was a total eclipse of the sun and a general darkness as in the night covered the earth, and that at his death the same thing happened. Such, then, is reported to have been the death of Romulus, who built Rome and was chosen by her citizens as their first king.   He left no issue, and after reigning thirty-seven years, died in the fifty-fifth

---

[1] Or *Poplifugia*.   The same explanation of the origin of this festival is given by Plutarch (*Rom.* 29), who also records the more common version that the original "flight of the people" occurred shortly after the departure of the Gauls, at a time when several Latin tribes suddenly appeared before the city.   According to a third view, found in Macrobius (iii. 2, 14), Etruscans were the invaders.

ἀπὸ γενεᾶς. νέος γὰρ δὴ παντάπασιν ἔτυχε τῆς
ἡγεμονίας ὀκτωκαιδεκαέτης ὤν,[1] ὡς ἅπαντες ὁμολογοῦσιν οἱ τὰς περὶ αὐτοῦ συγγράψαντες ἱστορίας.

LVII. Τῷ δ' ἑξῆς ἐνιαυτῷ βασιλεὺς μὲν οὐδεὶς
ἀπεδείχθη Ῥωμαίων, ἀρχὴ δέ τις, ἣν καλοῦσι
μεσοβασίλειον, ἐπεμελεῖτο τῶν κοινῶν τοιόνδε τινὰ
τρόπον ἀποδεικνυμένη· τῶν πατρικίων οἱ καταγραφέντες εἰς τὴν βουλὴν ὑπὸ Ῥωμύλου διακόσιοι
τὸν ἀριθμὸν ὄντες, ὥσπερ ἔφην, διενεμήθησαν εἰς
δεκάδας· ἔπειτα διακληρωσάμενοι τοῖς λαχοῦσι
δέκα πρώτοις ἀπέδωκαν ἄρχειν τῆς πόλεως τὴν
2 αὐτοκράτορα ἀρχήν. ἐκεῖνοι δ' οὐχ ἅμα πάντες
ἐβασίλευον, ἀλλ' ἐκ διαδοχῆς ἡμέρας πέντε ἕκαστος,
ἐν αἷς τάς τε ῥάβδους εἶχε καὶ τὰ λοιπὰ τῆς
βασιλικῆς ἐξουσίας σύμβολα. παρεδίδου δ' ὁ πρῶτος ἄρξας τῷ δευτέρῳ τὴν ἡγεμονίαν κἀκεῖνος τῷ
τρίτῳ καὶ τοῦτ' ἐγίνετο μέχρι τοῦ τελευταίου.
διεξελθούσης δὲ τοῖς πρώτοις δέκα[2] τῆς πεντηκον-
θημέρου προθεσμίας ἕτεροι δέκα τὴν ἀρχὴν παρ-
3 ελάμβανον καὶ παρ' ἐκείνων αὖθις ἄλλοι. ἐπεὶ δ'[3]
ἔδοξε τῷ δήμῳ παῦσαι τὰς δεκαδαρχίας[4] ἀχθομένῳ
ταῖς μεταβολαῖς τῶν ἐξουσιῶν διὰ τὸ μήτε προ-
αιρέσεις ἅπαντας ὁμοίας ἔχειν μήτε φύσεις, τότε
δὴ συγκαλέσαντες εἰς ἐκκλησίαν τὸ πλῆθος οἱ βου-
λευταὶ κατὰ φυλάς τε καὶ φράτρας ἀπέδωκαν αὐτῷ
περὶ τοῦ κόσμου τῆς πολιτείας σκοπεῖν, εἴτε βασιλεῖ

---

[1] ὤν added by Ambrosch.
[2] βασιλεῦσι after δέκα deleted by Bücheler; Reiske emended
to μεσοβασιλεῦσι.
[3] ἐπεὶ δ' Reiske: ἔπειτα O.
[4] δεκαδαρχίας B: δεκαρχίας R.

year of his age ; for he was very young when he
obtained the rule, being no more than eighteen
years old, as is agreed by all who have written
his history.

LVII. The[1] following year there was no king
of the Romans elected, but a certain magistracy,
called by them an interregnum, had the oversight of
public affairs, being created in much the following
manner : The patricians who had been enrolled
in the senate under Romulus, being, as I have
said,[2] two hundred in number, were divided into
decuriae;[3] then, when lots had been cast, the first
ten persons upon whom the lot fell were invested
by the rest with the absolute rule of the State.
They did not, however, all reign together, but suc-
cessively, each for five days, during which time they
had both the rods and the other insignia of the royal
power.   The first, after his power had expired,
handed over the government to the second, and he
to the third, and so on to the last.   After the first ten
had reigned their appointed time of fifty days, ten
others received the rule from them, and from those
in turn others.   But presently the people decided
to abolish the rule of the *decuriae*, being irked
by the changes of power, since the men did not all
have either the same purposes or the same natural
abilities.   Thereupon the senators, calling the people
together in assembly by tribes and *curiae*, permitted
them to consider the form of government and determine whether they wished to entrust the public

---

[1] For chaps. 57-58 *cf.* Livy i. 17 ; 18, 1 and 5.
[2] Chap. 47, 1.   [3] Groups of ten.

βούλεται τὰ κοινὰ ἐπιτρέπειν εἴτε ἀρχαῖς ἐνιαυσίοις.
4 οὐ μὴν ὅ γε δῆμος ἐφ' ἑαυτῷ τὴν αἵρεσιν ἐποίησεν,
ἀλλ' ἀπέδωκε τοῖς βουλευταῖς τὴν διάγνωσιν, ὡς
ἀγαπήσων ὁποτέραν ἂν ἐκεῖνοι δοκιμάσωσι τῶν
πολιτειῶν· τοῖς δὲ βασιλικὴν μὲν ἐδόκει καταστήσασθαι πολιτείαν ἅπασι, περὶ δὲ τοῦ μέλλοντος
ἄρξειν στάσις ἐνέπιπτεν ἐξ ὁποτέρας ἔσται τάξεως.
οἱ μὲν γὰρ ἐκ τῶν ἀρχαίων βουλευτῶν ᾤοντο δεῖν
ἀποδειχθῆναι τὸν ἐπιτροπεύσοντα τὴν πόλιν, οἱ δ'
ἐκ τῶν ὕστερον ἐπεισαχθέντων, οὓς νεωτέρους
ἐκάλουν.

LVIII. Ἑλκομένης δ' ἐπὶ πολὺ τῆς φιλονεικίας
τελευτῶντες ἐπὶ τούτῳ συνέβησαν τῷ δικαίῳ, ὥστε
δυεῖν θάτερον, ἢ τοὺς πρεσβυτέρους βουλευτὰς ἀποδεῖξαι βασιλέα σφῶν μὲν αὐτῶν μηδένα, τῶν δ'
ἄλλων ὃν ἂν ἐπιτηδειότατον εἶναι νομίσωσιν, ἢ
τοὺς νεωτέρους τὸ αὐτὸ ποιῆσαι τοῦτο. δέχονται
τὴν αἵρεσιν οἱ πρεσβύτεροι καὶ πολλὰ ἐπὶ σφῶν
αὐτῶν βουλευσάμενοι τάδε ἔγνωσαν· ἐπειδὴ τῆς
ἡγεμονίας αὐτοὶ κατὰ τὰς συνθήκας ἀπηλαύνοντο
μηδὲ[1] τῶν ἐπεισαχθέντων βουλευτῶν[2] μηδενὶ προσ-
θεῖναι τὴν ἀρχήν, ἀλλ' ἐπακτόν τινα ἔξωθεν ἄνδρα
καὶ μηδ' ὁποτέροις προσθησόμενον, ὡς ἂν μάλιστα
ἐξαιρεθείη τὸ στασιάζον, ἐξευρόντες ἀποδεῖξαι
2 βασιλέα. ταῦτα βουλευσάμενοι προὐχειρίσαντο
ἄνδρα γένους μὲν τοῦ Σαβίνων, υἱὸν δὲ Πομπιλίου

---

[1] μηδὲ Bücheler, Sintenis : μήγε A, μήτε B.
[2] τῶν ἐπεισαχθέντων βουλευτῶν Cary, τῶν ἐπεισελθόντων
βουλευτῶν Jacoby, τῶν νεωστὶ βουλευόντων Sintenis, τῶν
βουλευτῶν Kiessling, τῶν ἑτέρων βουλευτῶν Garrer : τῶν
ἐπιβουλευόντων O.

interests to a king or to annual magistrates. The
people, however, did not take the choice upon themselves, but referred the decision to the senators. in
timating that they would be satisfied with whichever
form of government the others should approve. The
senators all favoured establishing a monarchical form
of government, but strife arose over the question
from which group the future king should be chosen.
For some thought that the one who was to govern
the commonwealth ought to be chosen from among
the original senators, and others that he should be
chosen from among those who had been admitted
afterwards and whom they called new senators.

LVIII. The contest being drawn out to a great
length, they at last reached an agreement on the
basis that one of two courses should be followed—
either the older senators should choose the king,
who must not, however, be one of themselves, but
might be anyone else whom they should regard as
most suitable, or the new senators should do the same.
The older senators accepted the right of choosing,
and after a long consultation among themselves
decided that, since by their agreement they themselves were excluded from the sovereignty, they
would not confer it on any of the newly-admitted
senators, either, but would find some man from outside who would espouse neither party, and declare
him king, as the most effectual means of putting an
end to party strife. After they had come to this resolution, they chose a man of the Sabine race, the son
of Pompilius Pompon, a person of distinction, whose

479

Πόμπωνος ἀνδρὸς ἐπιφανοῦς ὄνομα[1] Νόμαν,[2] ἡλικίας
τε τῆς φρονιμωτάτης ὄντα, τετταρακονταετίας γὰρ
3 οὐ πολὺ ἀπεῖχε, καὶ ἀξιώσει μορφῆς βασιλικόν. ἦν
δὲ αὐτοῦ καὶ κλέος μέγιστον οὐ παρὰ Κυρίταις μόνον, ἀλλὰ καὶ παρὰ τοῖς περιοίκοις ἐπὶ σοφίᾳ. ὡς
δὲ τοῦτ᾽ ἔδοξεν αὐτοῖς συγκαλοῦσι τὸ πλῆθος εἰς
ἐκκλησίαν, καὶ παρελθὼν ἐξ αὐτῶν ὁ τότε μεσο-
βασιλεὺς εἶπεν, ὅτι κοινῇ δόξαν ἅπασι τοῖς βουλευταῖς βασιλικὴν καταστήσασθαι πολιτείαν, κύριος
γεγονὼς αὐτὸς τῆς[3] διαγνώσεως τοῦ παραληψο-
μένου τὴν ἀρχὴν βασιλέα τῆς πόλεως αἱρεῖται
Νόμαν Πομπίλιον. καὶ μετὰ τοῦτο πρεσβευτὰς
ἀποδείξας ἐκ τῶν πατρικίων ἀπέστειλε τοὺς παρα-
ληψομένους τὸν ἄνδρα ἐπὶ τὴν ἀρχὴν ἐνιαυτῷ τρίτῳ
τῆς ἑκκαιδεκάτης ὀλυμπιάδος, ἣν[4] ἐνίκα στάδιον
Πυθαγόρας[5] Λάκων.

LIX. Μέχρι μὲν δὴ τούτων οὐδὲν ἀντειπεῖν ἔχω
πρὸς τοὺς ἐκδεδωκότας τὴν περὶ τὸν ἄνδρα τοῦτον
ἱστορίαν, ἐν δὲ τοῖς ἑξῆς ἀπορῶ τι ποτε χρὴ λέγειν.
πολλοὶ μὲν γάρ εἰσιν οἱ γράψαντες[6] ὅτι Πυθαγόρου
μαθητὴς ὁ Νόμας ἐγένετο καὶ καθ᾽ ὃν χρόνον ὑπὸ
τῆς Ῥωμαίων πόλεως ἀπεδείχθη βασιλεὺς φιλο-
σοφῶν ἐν Κρότωνι διέτριβεν, ὁ δὲ χρόνος τῆς
2 Πυθαγόρου ἡλικίας μάχεται πρὸς τὸν λόγον. οὐ

[1] κατ before ὄνομα deleted by Kiessling.
[2] After Νόμαν the MSS. have χρὴ δὲ τὴν δευτέραν συλλαβὴν
ἐκτείνοντας βαρυτονεῖν, rejected by Portus.
[3] τῆς added by Kiessling.   [4] ἣν Jacoby: ἐν ᾗ O.

name was Numa. He was in that stage of life, being near forty, in which prudence is the most conspicuous, and of an aspect full of royal dignity; and he enjoyed the greatest renown for wisdom, not only among the citizens of Cures, but among all the neighbouring peoples as well. After reaching this decision the senators assembled the people, and that one of their number who was then the interrex, coming forward, told them that the senators had unanimously resolved to establish a monarchical form of government and that he, having been empowered to decide who should succeed to the rule, chose Numa Pompilius as king of the State. After this he appointed ambassadors from among the patricians and sent them to conduct Numa to Rome that he might assume the royal power. This happened in the third year of the sixteenth Olympiad,[1] at which Pythagoras, a Lacedaemonian, won the foot-race.

LIX. Up[2] to this point, then, I have nothing to allege in contradiction to those who have published the history of this man; but in regard to what follows I am at a loss what to say. For many have written that Numa was a disciple of Pythagoras and that when he was chosen king by the Romans he was studying philosophy at Croton. But the date of Pythagoras contradicts this account, since he was

[1] 713 B.C.   [2] Cf. Livy i. 18, 2-4.

---

[5] Steph.: πισαμόρας ABa, πεισαγόρας Bb.
[6] εἰσιν οἱ γράψαντες Jacoby: οἱ γράψαντες O; ἔγραψαν Bücheler.

γὰρ ὀλίγοις ἔτεσιν, ἀλλὰ καὶ τέτταρσι γενεαῖς ὅλαις
ὕστερος ἐγένετο Πυθαγόρας Νόμα, ὡς ἐκ τῶν
κοινῶν παρειλήφαμεν ἱστοριῶν. ὁ μὲν γὰρ ἐπὶ τῆς
ἑκκαιδεκάτης ὀλυμπιάδος μεσούσης τὴν Ῥωμαίων
βασιλείαν παρέλαβε, Πυθαγόρας δὲ μετὰ τὴν πεντη-
3 κοστὴν ὀλυμπιάδα διέτριψεν ἐν Ἰταλίᾳ. τούτου
δ᾽ ἔτι μεῖζον ἔχω τεκμήριον εἰπεῖν ὑπὲρ τοῦ μὴ
συμφωνεῖν τοὺς χρόνους ταῖς παραδεδομέναις ὑπὲρ
τοῦ ἀνδρὸς ἱστορίαις, ὅτι καθ᾽ ὃν χρόνον ὁ Νόμας
ἐπὶ τὴν βασιλείαν ἐκαλεῖτο ὑπὸ Ῥωμαίων οὔπω
πόλις ἦν ἡ Κρότων· τέτταρσι γὰρ ὅλοις ὕστερον
ἔτεσιν ἢ Νόμαν ἄρξαι Ῥωμαίων Μύσκελος αὐτὴν
ἔκτισεν ἐνιαυτῷ τρίτῳ τῆς ἑπτακαιδεκάτης ὀλυμπιάδος. οὔτε δὲ Πυθαγόρᾳ τῷ Σαμίῳ συμφιλο-
σοφῆσαι τῷ μετὰ τέτταρας ἀκμάσαντι γενεὰς
δυνατὸν ἦν τὸν Νόμαν οὔτ᾽ ἐν Κρότωνι διατρίβειν,
ὅτ᾽ αὐτὸν ἐκάλουν ἐπὶ τὴν βασιλείαν Ῥωμαῖοι, τῇ
4 μήπω τότ᾽ οὔσῃ πόλει. ἀλλ᾽ ἐοίκασιν οἱ τὰ ὑπὲρ
αὐτοῦ γράψαντες, εἰ χρὴ δόξαν ἰδίαν ἀποφήνασθαι,
δύο ταῦτα λαβόντες ὁμολογούμενα, τήν τε Πυθαγόρου διατριβὴν τὴν γενομένην ἐν Ἰταλίᾳ καὶ τὴν
Νόμα σοφίαν (ὡμολόγηται[1] γὰρ ὑπὸ πάντων ὁ ἀνὴρ
γενέσθαι σοφός) ἐπισυνάψαι ταῦτα καὶ ποιῆσαι
Πυθαγόρου μαθητὴν τὸν Νόμαν οὐκέτι τοὺς βίους
αὐτῶν ἐξετάσαντες, εἰ κατὰ τοὺς αὐτοὺς ἤκμασαν
ἀμφότεροι χρόνους, ὅπερ ἐγὼ πεποίηκα νῦν· εἰ μή
τις ἄρα Πυθαγόραν ἕτερον ὑποθήσεται πρὸ τοῦ
Σαμίου γεγονέναι παιδευτὴν σοφίας, ᾧ συνδιέτριψεν

---

[1] ὡμολόγηται Bb : ὁμολογεῖται BaR.

not merely a few years younger than Numa, but
actually lived four whole generations later, as we
learn from universal history ; for Numa succeeded
to the sovereignty of the Romans in the middle of
the sixteenth Olympiad, whereas Pythagoras resided
in Italy after the fiftieth Olympiad.[1] But I can
advance yet a stronger argument to prove that the
chronology is incompatible with the reports handed
down about Numa, and that is, that at the time
when he was called to the sovereignty by the Romans
the city of Croton did not yet exist ; for it was not
until four whole years after Numa had begun to
rule the Romans that Myscelus founded this city,
in the third year of the seventeenth Olympiad.[2]
Accordingly, it was impossible for Numa either to
have studied philosophy with Pythagoras the
Samian, who flourished four generations after him,
or to have resided in Croton, a city not as yet
in existence when the Romans called him to the
sovereignty. But if I may express my own opinion,
those who have written his history seem to have
taken these two admitted facts, namely, the residence of Pythagoras in Italy and the wisdom of
Numa (for he has been allowed by everybody to
have been a wise man), and combining them, to have
made Numa a disciple of Pythagoras, without going
on to inquire into their lives, as I have now done,
to discover whether they both flourished at the same
period—unless, indeed, one is going to assume that
there was another Pythagoras who taught philosophy
before the Samian, and that with him Numa

[1] 580/79 B.C.   [2] 709 B.C.

ὁ Νόμας. τοῦτο δ' οὐκ οἶδ' ὅπως ἂν ἀποδεῖξαι
δύναιτο μηδενὸς τῶν ἀξιολόγων μήτε Ῥωμαίου
μήθ' Ἕλληνος, ὅσα κἀμὲ[1] εἰδέναι, παραδεδωκότος
ἐν ἱστορίᾳ. ἀλλὰ περὶ μὲν τούτων ἅλις.

LX. Ὁ δὲ Νόμας ἀφικομένων ὡς αὐτὸν τῶν[2]
καλούντων ἐπὶ τὴν ἡγεμονίαν, τέως μὲν ἀντέλεγε
καὶ μέχρι πολλοῦ διέμεινεν ἀπομαχόμενος μὴ λαβεῖν
τὴν ἀρχήν, ὡς δὲ οἵ τε ἀδελφοὶ προσέκειντο λιπαροῦντες καὶ τελευτῶν ὁ πατὴρ οὐκ ἠξίου τηλικαύτην
τιμὴν διδομένην ἀπωθεῖσθαι, συνέγνω γενέσθαι βα-
2 σιλεύς· τοῖς δὲ Ῥωμαίοις πυθομένοις ταῦτα παρὰ
τῶν πρεσβευτῶν, πρὶν ὄψει τὸν ἄνδρα ἰδεῖν πολὺς
αὐτοῦ παρέστη πόθος, ἱκανὸν ἡγουμένοις τεκμήριον
εἶναι τῆς σοφίας, εἰ τῶν ἄλλων ὑπὲρ τὸ μέτριον
ἐκτετιμηκότων βασιλείαν καὶ τὸν εὐδαίμονα βίον ἐν
ταύτῃ[3] τιθεμένων μόνος ἐκεῖνος ὡς φαύλου τινὸς καὶ
οὐκ ἀξίου σπουδῆς πράγματος καταφρονεῖ, παρα-
γενομένῳ τε ὑπήντων ἔτι καθ' ὁδὸν ὄντι σὺν ἐπαίνῳ
πολλῷ καὶ ἀσπασμοῖς καὶ ταῖς ἄλλαις τιμαῖς παρα-
3 πέμποντες εἰς τὴν πόλιν. ἐκκλησίας δὲ μετὰ τοῦτο
συναχθείσης, ἐν ᾗ διήνεγκαν ὑπὲρ αὐτοῦ τὰς ψήφους
αἱ φυλαὶ κατὰ φράτρας καὶ τῶν πατρικίων ἐπικυ-
ρωσάντων τὰ δόξαντα τῷ πλήθει καὶ τελευταῖον
ἔτι τῶν ὀρνιθοσκόπων αἴσια τὰ παρὰ τοῦ δαιμονίου
σημεῖα ἀποφηνάντων παραλαμβάνει τὴν ἀρχήν.
4 τοῦτον τὸν ἄνδρα Ῥωμαῖοί φασι στρατείαν μηδεμίαν ποιήσασθαι, θεοσεβῆ δὲ καὶ δίκαιον γενόμενον
ἐν εἰρήνῃ πάντα τὸν τῆς ἀρχῆς χρόνον διατελέσαι

────────

[1] ὅσα κἀμὲ B : ὅσους με R.

associated. But I do not know how this could be proved, since it is not supported, so far as I know, by the testimony of any author of note, either Greek or Roman. But I have said enough on this subject.

LX. When the ambassadors came to Numa to invite him to the sovereignty, he for some time refused it and long persisted in his resolution not to accept the royal power. But when his brothers kept urging him insistently and at last his father argued that the offer of so great an honour ought not to be rejected, he consented to become king. As soon as the Romans were informed of this by the ambassadors, they conceived a great yearning for the man before they saw him, esteeming it a sufficient proof of his wisdom that, while the others had valued sovereignty beyond measure, looking upon it as the source of happiness, he alone despised it as a paltry thing and unworthy of serious attention. And when he approached the city, they met him upon the road and with great applause, salutations and other honours conducted him into the city. After that, an assembly of the people was held, in which the tribes by *curiae* gave their votes in his favour ; and when the resolution of the people had been confirmed by the patricians, and, last of all, the augurs had reported that the heavenly signs were auspicious, he assumed the office. The Romans say that he undertook no military campaign, but that, being a pious and just man, he passed the whole period of his reign in peace and caused the

---

² αὐτὸν τῶν Kiessling : αὐτὸν τούτων τῶν O.
³ ἐν ταύτῃ B : ἐνταῦθα R.

καὶ τὴν πόλιν ἄριστα πολιτευομένην παρασχεῖν,
λόγους τε ὑπὲρ αὐτοῦ πολλοὺς καὶ θαυμαστοὺς
λέγουσιν ἀναφέροντες τὴν ἀνθρωπίνην σοφίαν εἰς
5 θεῶν ὑποθήκας. νύμφην γάρ τινα μυθολογοῦσιν
Ἡγερίαν φοιτᾶν πρὸς αὐτὸν ἑκάστοτε διδάσκουσαν
τὴν βασιλικὴν σοφίαν, ἕτεροι δὲ οὐ νύμφην, ἀλλὰ
τῶν Μουσῶν μίαν. καὶ τοῦτό φασι γενέσθαι πᾶσι
φανερόν. ἀπιστούντων γάρ, ὡς ἔοικε, τῶν ἀνθρώπων κατ' ἀρχὰς καὶ πεπλάσθαι νομιζόντων τὸν
περὶ τῆς θεᾶς λόγον, βουλόμενον αὐτὸν ἐπιδείξασθαι
τοῖς ἀπιστοῦσιν ἐναργές τι μήνυμα τῆς πρὸς τὴν
δαίμονα ὁμιλίας¹ διδαχθέντα ὑπ' αὐτῆς ποιῆσαι
6 τάδε· καλέσαντα Ῥωμαίων πολλοὺς καὶ ἀγαθοὺς
εἰς τὴν οἰκίαν, ἐν ᾗ διαιτώμενος ἐτύγχανεν, ἔπειτα
δείξαντα τοῖς ἐλθοῦσι τὰ ἔνδον τῇ τε ἄλλῃ κατασκευῇ φαύλως κεχορηγημένα καὶ δὴ καὶ τῶν εἰς
ἑστίασιν ὀχλικὴν ἐπιτηδείων ἄπορα, τότε μὲν ἀπαλ-
λάττεσθαι κελεύειν, εἰς ἑσπέραν δὲ καλεῖν αὐτοὺς
7 ἐπὶ τὸ δεῖπνον· παραγενομένοις δὲ κατὰ τὴν ἀπο-
δειχθεῖσαν ὥραν ἐπιδεῖξαι στρωμνάς τε πολυτελεῖς
καὶ τραπέζας ἐκπωμάτων γεμούσας πολλῶν καὶ
καλῶν ἑστίασίν τε αὐτοῖς παραθεῖναι κατακλιθεῖσιν
ἁπάσης ἐδωδῆς, ἣν οὐδ' ἂν ἐκ πολλοῦ πάνυ χρόνου
παρασκευάσασθαί τινι τῶν τότε ἀνθρώπων ῥᾴδιον
ἦν. τοῖς δὲ Ῥωμαίοις κατάπληξίν τε πρὸς ἕκαστον
τῶν ὁρωμένων ὑπελθεῖν καὶ δόξαν ἐξ ἐκείνου τοῦ
χρόνου παραστῆναι βέβαιον, ὅτι θεά τις αὐτῷ συνῆν.

LXI. Οἱ δὲ τὰ μυθώδη πάντα περιαιροῦντες ἐκ
τῆς ἱστορίας πεπλάσθαι φασὶν ὑπὸ τοῦ Νόμα τὸν

¹ καὶ after ὁμιλίας deleted by Reiske.

State to be most excellently governed.[1] They relate also many marvellous stories about him, attributing his human wisdom to the suggestions of the gods. For they fabulously affirm that a certain nymph, Egeria, used to visit him and instruct him on each occasion in the art of reigning, though others say that it was not a nymph, but one of the Muses. And this, they claim, became clear to every one; for, when people were incredulous at first, as may well be supposed, and regarded the story concerning the goddess as an invention, he, in order to give the unbelievers a manifest proof of his converse with this divinity, did as follows, pursuant to her instructions. He invited to the house where he lived a great many of the Romans, all men of worth, and having shown them his apartments, very meanly provided with furniture and particularly lacking in everything that was necessary to entertain a numerous company, he ordered them to depart for the time being, but invited them to dinner in the evening. And when they came at the appointed hour, he showed them rich couches and tables laden with a multitude of beautiful cups, and when they were at table, he set before them a banquet consisting of all sorts of viands, such a banquet, indeed, as it would not have been easy for any man in those days to have prepared in a long time. The Romans were astonished at everything they saw, and from that time they entertained a firm belief that some goddess held converse with him.

LXI. But those who banish everything that is fabulous from history say that the report concerning

---

[1] For §§ 4-7 *cf.* Livy i. 19, 1-5.

περὶ τῆς Ἡγερίας λόγον, ἵνα ῥᾷον αὐτῷ προσ-
έχωσιν οἱ τὰ θεῖα δεδιότες καὶ προθύμως δέχωνται
τοὺς ὑπ᾽ αὐτοῦ τιθεμένους νόμους, ὡς παρὰ θεῶν
2 κομιζομένους. λαβεῖν δὲ αὐτὸν τὴν τούτων μίμησιν
ἀποφαίνουσιν ἐκ τῶν Ἑλληνικῶν παραδειγμάτων
ζηλωτὴν γενόμενον τῆς τε Μίνω τοῦ Κρητὸς καὶ
τῆς Λυκούργου τοῦ Λακεδαιμονίου σοφίας· ὧν ὁ
μὲν ὁμιλητὴς ἔφη γενέσθαι τοῦ Διὸς καὶ φοιτῶν
εἰς τὸ Δικταῖον ὄρος, ἐν ᾧ τραφῆναι τὸν Δία μυθολογοῦσιν οἱ Κρῆτες ὑπὸ τῶν Κουρήτων νεογνὸν
ὄντα, κατέβαινεν εἰς τὸ ἱερὸν ἄντρον καὶ τοὺς
νόμους ἐκεῖ συντιθεὶς ἐκόμιζεν, οὓς ἀπέφαινε παρὰ
τοῦ Διὸς λαμβάνειν· ὁ δὲ Λυκοῦργος εἰς Δελφοὺς
ἀφικνούμενος ὑπὸ τοῦ Ἀπόλλωνος ἔφη διδάσκεσθαι
3 τὴν νομοθεσίαν. τὸ μὲν οὖν ἀκριβολογεῖσθαι περὶ
τῶν μυθικῶν ἱστορημάτων καὶ μάλιστα τῶν εἰς
θεοὺς ἀναφερομένων μακρῶν λόγων δεόμενον ὁρῶν
ἐάσω, ἃ δέ μοι δοκοῦσιν ἀγαθὰ Ῥωμαῖοι λαβεῖν
ἐκ τῆς ἐκείνου τοῦ ἀνδρὸς ἀρχῆς, ὡς ἐκ τῶν ἐπιχωρίων ἔμαθον ἱστοριῶν ἀφηγήσομαι, προειπὼν ἐν
οἵαις ἐτύγχανε ταραχαῖς τὰ πράγματα τῆς πόλεως
ὄντα, πρὶν ἐκεῖνον ἐπὶ τὴν βασιλείαν παρελθεῖν.

LXII. Μετὰ τὴν Ῥωμύλου τελευτὴν ἡ βουλὴ
τῶν κοινῶν γενομένη κυρία καὶ χρόνον ἐνιαύσιον,
ὥσπερ ἔφην, κατασχοῦσα τὴν δυναστείαν διαφέρε-
σθαι καὶ στασιάζειν αὐτὴ πρὸς ἑαυτὴν ἤρξατο περὶ
τοῦ πλείονός τε καὶ ἴσου. ὅσον μὲν γὰρ αὐτῆς
μέρος Ἀλβανῶν ἦν ἀπὸ τῶν ἅμα Ῥωμύλῳ τὴν

---

[1] Chap. 57.

Egeria was invented by Numa, to the end that, when once the people were possessed with a fear of the gods, they might more readily pay regard to him and willingly receive the laws he should enact, as coming from the gods. They say that in this he followed the example of the Greeks, emulating the wisdom both of Minos the Cretan and of Lycurgus the Lacedaemonian. For the former of these claimed to hold converse with Zeus, and going frequently to the Dictaean mountain, in which the Cretan legends say that the new-born Zeus was brought up by the Curetes, he used to descend into the holy cave ; and having composed his laws there, he would produce them, affirming that he had received them from Zeus. And Lycurgus, paying visits to Delphi, said he was forming his code of laws under the instruction of Apollo. But, as I am sensible that to give a particular account of the legendary histories, and especially of those relating to gods, would require a long discussion, I shall omit doing so, and shall relate instead the benefits which the Romans seem to me to have received from this man's rule, according to the information I have derived from their own histories. But first I will show in what confusion the affairs of the State were before he came to the throne.

LXII. After the death of Romulus the senate, being now in full control of the government and having held the supreme power for one year, as I have related,[1] began to be at odds with itself and to split into factions over questions of pre-eminence and equality. For the Alban element, who together with Romulus had planted the colony,

ἀποικίαν στειλάντων, γνώμης τε ἄρχειν ἠξίου καὶ
τιμῶν τὰς μεγίστας λαμβάνειν καὶ θεραπεύεσθαι
2 πρὸς τῶν ἐπηλύδων· οἱ δ' ὕστερον εἰς τοὺς πατρικίους καταγραφέντες ἐκ τῶν ἐποίκων οὐδεμιᾶς
ᾤοντο δεῖν ἀπελαύνεσθαι τιμῆς οὐδὲ μειονεκτεῖν
τῶν ἑτέρων, μάλιστα δ' ὅσοι τοῦ Σαβίνων ἐτύγχανον ὄντες γένους καὶ κατὰ τὰς συνθήκας τὰς
γενομένας Ῥωμύλῳ πρὸς Τάτιον ἐπὶ τοῖς ἴσοις[1]
μετειληφέναι τῆς πόλεως παρὰ τῶν ἀρχαίων οἰκητόρων καὶ[2] τὴν αὐτὴν χάριν ἐκείνοις αὐτοὶ δεδω-
3 κέναι ἐδόκουν.[3] ἅμα δὲ τῷ τὴν βουλὴν διαστῆναι
καὶ τὸ τῶν πελατῶν πλῆθος διχῇ μερισθὲν ἑκατέρᾳ
συνέβαινε τῶν στάσεων. ἦν δέ τι τοῦ δημοτικοῦ
μέρος οὐκ ὀλίγον ἐκ τῶν νεωστὶ προσεληλυθότων
τῇ πολιτείᾳ ὃ διὰ τὸ μηδενὸς συνάρασθαι τῷ
Ῥωμύλῳ πολέμου παρημελημένον ὑπὸ τοῦ ἡγεμόνος οὔτε γῆς εἰλήφει μοῖραν οὔτε ὠφελείας.[4]
τοῦτο ἀνέστιον καὶ πτωχὸν ἀλώμενον ἐχθρὸν ἐκ
τοῦ ἀναγκαίου τοῖς κρείττοσιν ἦν καὶ νεωτερίζειν
4 ἑτοιμότατον. ἐν τοιούτῳ δὴ κλύδωνι τὰ πράγματα
τῆς πόλεως σαλεύοντα ὁ Νόμας καταλαβών, πρῶτον
μὲν τοὺς ἀπόρους τῶν δημοτῶν ἀνέλαβε διανείμας
αὐτοῖς ἀφ' ἧς Ῥωμύλος ἐκέκτητο χώρας καὶ ἀπὸ
τῆς δημοσίας μοῖράν τινα ὀλίγην· ἔπειτα τοὺς
πατρικίους οὐδὲν μὲν ἀφελόμενος ὧν οἱ κτίσαντες
τὴν πόλιν εὕροντο, τοῖς δ' ἐποίκοις ἑτέρας τινὰς

---

[1] γενόμενοι after ἴσοις deleted by Bücheler: emended
εὐχόμενοι by Portus.
[2] καὶ Sylburg: ἢ AB.

claimed the right, not only of delivering their opinions first and enjoying the greatest honours, but also of being courted by the newcomers. Those, on the other hand, who had been admitted afterwards into the number of the patricians from among the new settlers thought that they ought not to be excluded from any honours or to stand in an inferior position to the others. This was felt particularly by those who were of the Sabine race and who, in virtue of the treaty made by Romulus with Tatius, supposed they had been granted citizenship by the original inhabitants on equal terms, and that they had shown the same favour to the former in their turn. The senate being thus at odds, the clients also were divided into two parties and each joined their respective factions. There were, too, among the plebeians not a few, lately admitted into the number of the citizens, who, having never assisted Romulus in any of his wars, had been neglected by him and had received neither a share of land nor any booty. These, having no home, but being poor and vagabonds, were by necessity enemies to their superiors and quite ripe for revolution. So Numa, having found the affairs of the State in such a raging sea of confusion, first relieved the poor among the plebeians by distributing to them some small part of the land which Romulus had possessed and of the public land ; and afterwards he allayed the strife of the patricians, not by depriving them of anything the founders of the city had gained, but by bestowing

---

[3] ἐδόκουν added by Kiessling.
[4] οὔτ᾽ ἄλλας ὠφελείας Reiske, οὔτε λείας Kiessling.

DIONYSIUS OF HALICARNASSUS

5 ἀποδοὺς τιμάς, ἔπαυσε διαφερομένους. ἁρμοσά-
μενος δὲ τὸ πλῆθος ἅπαν ὥσπερ ὄργανον πρὸς ἕνα
τὸν τοῦ κοινῇ¹ συμφέροντος λογισμὸν καὶ τῆς
πόλεως τὸν περίβολον αὐξήσας τῷ Κυρινίῳ λόφῳ
(τέως γὰρ ἔτι ἀτείχιστος ἦν) τότε τῶν ἄλλων
πολιτευμάτων ἥπτετο δύο ταῦτα πραγματευόμενος,
οἷς κοσμηθεῖσαν ὑπελάμβανεν² τὴν πόλιν εὐδαίμονα
γενήσεσθαι καὶ μεγάλην· εὐσέβειαν μὲν πρῶτον,
διδάσκων τοὺς ἀνθρώπους ὅτι παντὸς ἀγαθοῦ θεοὶ
δοτῆρές εἰσι τῇ θνητῇ φύσει καὶ φύλακες, ἔπειτα
δικαιοσύνην, δι' ἣν καὶ τὰ παρὰ τῶν θεῶν ἀπ-
έφαινεν ἀγαθὰ καλὰς τὰς ἀπολαύσεις φέροντα τοῖς
κτησαμένοις.

LXIII. Ἐξ ὧν δὲ διεπράξατο νόμων τε καὶ πολιτευμάτων ἑκάτερον τούτων εἰς μεγάλην ἐπίδοσιν
προελθεῖν ἅπαντα μὲν οὐκ ἀξιῶ γράφειν, τὸ μῆκος
ὑφορώμενος τοῦ λόγου καὶ ἅμα οὐδ' ἀναγκαίαν
ὁρῶν τὴν ἀναγραφὴν³ αὐτῶν Ἑλληνικαῖς ἱστορίαις,
αὐτὰ δὲ τὰ κυριώτατα καὶ φανερὰν δυνάμενα
ποιῆσαι πᾶσαν τὴν προαίρεσιν τοῦ ἀνδρὸς ἐπὶ
κεφαλαίων ἐρῶ, τὴν ἀρχὴν ἀπὸ τῆς περὶ τὰ θεῖα
2 διακοσμήσεως ποιησάμενος. ὅσα μὲν οὖν ὑπὸ
Ῥωμύλου ταχθέντα ἐν ἐθισμοῖς τε καὶ νόμοις
παρέλαβεν, ἀπὸ τοῦ κρατίστου τετάχθαι πάντα
ἡγησάμενος εἴα κατὰ χώραν μένειν, ὅσα δ' ὑπ'
ἐκείνου παραλελεῖφθαι ἐδόκει, ταῦτα προσετίθει
πολλὰ μὲν ἀποδεικνὺς τεμένη τοῖς μήπω τιμῶν

¹ κοινῇ Kiessling: κοινοῦ O.
² ἂν after ὑπελάμβανεν deleted by Bücheler, Meineke.
³ Kiessling: γραφὴν O.

492

some other honours on the new settlers. And having attuned the whole body of the people, like a musical instrument, to the sole consideration of the public good and enlarged the circuit of the city by the addition of the Quirinal hill (for till that time it was still without a wall), he then addressed himself to the other measures of government, labouring to inculcate these two things by the possession of which he conceived the State would become prosperous and great : first, piety, by informing his subjects that the gods are the givers and guardians of every blessing to mortal men, and, second, justice, through which, he showed them, the blessings also which the gods bestow bring honest enjoyment to their possessors.

LXIII. As regards the laws and institutions by which he made great progress in both these directions, I do not think it fitting that I should enter into all the details, not only because I fear the length of such a discussion but also because I do not regard the recording of them as necessary to a history intended for Greeks ; but I shall give a summary account of the principal measures, which are sufficient to reveal the man's whole purpose, beginning with his regulations concerning the worship of the gods. I should state, however, that all those rites which he found established by Romulus, either in custom or in law, he left untouched, looking upon them all as established in the best possible manner. But whatever he thought had been overlooked by his predecessor, he added, consecrating many precincts to those gods who had

τυγχάνουσι θεοῖς, πολλοὺς δὲ βωμοὺς καὶ ναοὺς
ἱδρυόμενος ἑορτάς τε ἑκάστῳ αὐτῶν ἀπονέμων
καὶ τοὺς ἐπιμελησομένους αὐτῶν ἱερεῖς καθιστὰς
ἁγνείας τε καὶ θρησκείας καὶ καθαρμοὺς καὶ τὰς
ἄλλας θεραπείας καὶ τιμὰς πάνυ πολλὰς νομοθετῶν,
ὅσας οὔθ' Ἑλληνὶς οὔτε βάρβαρος ἔχει πόλις οὐδ'
3 αἱ μέγιστον ἐπ' εὐσεβείᾳ φρονοῦσαί ποτε· αὐτόν
τε τὸν Ῥωμύλον ὡς κρείττονα γενόμενον ἢ κατὰ
τὴν θνητὴν φύσιν ἱεροῦ κατασκευῇ καὶ θυσίαις
διετησίοις ἔταξε Κυρῖνον ἐπονομαζόμενον γεραίρεσθαι. ἔτι γὰρ ἀγνοούντων τὸν ἀφανισμὸν αὐτοῦ
Ῥωμαίων εἴτε κατὰ δαίμονος πρόνοιαν εἴτ' ἐξ ἐπιβουλῆς ἀνθρωπίνης ἐγένετο, παρελθών τις εἰς τὴν
ἀγορὰν Ἰούλιος ὄνομα τῶν ἀπ' Ἀσκανίου γεωργι-
κὸς ἀνὴρ καὶ τὸν βίον ἀνεπίληπτος, οἷος μηδὲν ἂν
ψεύσασθαι κέρδους ἕνεκεν [1] οἰκείου, ἔφη παραγιγνό-
μενος ἐξ ἀγροῦ Ῥωμύλον ἰδεῖν ἀπιόντα ἐκ τῆς
πόλεως ἔχοντα τὰ ὅπλα, καὶ ἐπειδὴ ἐγγὺς ἐγένετο
4 ἀκοῦσαι ταῦτα αὐτοῦ λέγοντος· "Ἄγγελλε Ῥωμαίοις, Ἰούλιε, τὰ παρ' ἐμοῦ, ὅτι με ὁ λαχὼν ὅτ'
ἐγενόμην δαίμων εἰς θεοὺς ἄγεται τὸν θνητὸν
ἐκπληρώσαντα αἰῶνα· εἰμὶ δὲ Κυρῖνος." περι-
λαβὼν δὲ ἅπασαν τὴν περὶ τὰ θεῖα νομοθεσίαν
γραφαῖς διεῖλεν εἰς ὀκτὼ μοίρας, ὅσαι τῶν ἱερῶν
ἦσαν αἱ συμμορίαι.

LXIV. Ἀπέδωκε δὲ μίαν μὲν ἱερουργιῶν διά-
ταξιν τοῖς τριάκοντα κουρίωσιν, οὓς ἔφην τὰ κοινὰ

---

[1] ἕνεκεν Jacoby in note: ἕνεκα O, Jacoby in text.

494

hitherto received no honours, erecting many altars and temples, instituting festivals in honour of each, and appointing priests to have charge of their sanctuaries and rites, and enacting laws concerning purifications, ceremonies, expiations and many other observances and honours in greater number than are to be found in any other city, either Greek or barbarian, even in those that have prided themselves the most at one time or another upon their piety. He also ordered that Romulus himself, as one who had shown a greatness beyond mortal nature, should be honoured, under the name of Quirinus, by the erection of a temple and by sacrifices throughout the year. For [1] while the Romans were yet in doubt whether divine providence or human treachery had been the cause of his disappearance, a certain man, named Julius, descended from Ascanius, who was a husbandman and of such a blameless life that he would never have told an untruth for his private advantage, arrived in the Forum and said that, as he was coming in from the country, he saw Romulus departing from the city fully armed and that, as he drew near to him, he heard him say these words : " Julius, announce to the Romans from me, that the genius to whom I was allotted at my birth is conducting me to the gods, now that I have finished my mortal life, and that I am Quirinus." Numa, having reduced his whole system of religious laws to writing, divided them into eight parts, that being the number of the different classes of religious ceremonies.

LXIV. The first division of religious rites he assigned to the thirty *curiones*, who, as I have stated,[2]

---

[1] *Cf.* Livy i. 16, 5-8.   [2] Chap. 23, 1-2.

2 θύειν ὑπὲρ τῶν φρατριῶν[1] ἱερά. τὴν δὲ δευτέραν
τοῖς καλουμένοις ὑπὸ μὲν Ἑλλήνων στεφανηφόροις,[2]
ὑπὸ δὲ Ῥωμαίων φλάμισιν,[3] οὓς ἐπὶ τῆς φορήσεως
τῶν πίλων[4] τε καὶ στεμμάτων, ἃ καὶ νῦν ἔτι φοροῦσι
3 † φλάμα[5] καλοῦντες, οὕτω προσαγορεύουσι. τὴν
δὲ τρίτην τοῖς ἡγεμόσι τῶν κελερίων, οὓς ἔφην
ἱππεῖς τε καὶ πεζοὺς στρατευομένους φύλακας ἀποδείκνυσθαι τῶν βασιλέων, καὶ γὰρ οὗτοι τεταγμένας
4 τινὰς ἱερουργίας ἐπετέλουν. τὴν δὲ τετάρτην τοῖς
ἐξηγουμένοις τὰ θεόπεμπτα σημεῖα καὶ διαιροῦσι
τίνων ἐστὶ μηνύματα πραγμάτων ἰδίᾳ τε καὶ δημοσίᾳ, οὓς ἀφ' ἑνὸς εἴδους τῶν θεωρημάτων τῆς
τέχνης Ῥωμαῖοι καλοῦσιν αὔγορας, ἡμεῖς δ' ἂν
εἴποιμεν οἰωνοπόλους, ἁπάσης τῆς μαντικῆς παρ'
αὐτοῖς ὄντας ἐπιστήμονας τῆς τε περὶ τὰ οὐράνια
5 καὶ τὰ μετάρσια καὶ τὰ ἐπίγεια. τὴν δὲ πέμπτην
ταῖς φυλαττούσαις τὸ ἱερὸν πῦρ παρθένοις, αἳ
καλοῦνται πρὸς αὐτῶν ἐπὶ τῆς θεᾶς ἣν θεραπεύ-

---

[1] φρατριῶν Bb : φρατριέων A.   [2] Steph. : στεφηφόροις O.
[3] Steph. : φλάμοσιν AB, Jacoby.
[4] πιλῶν . . . B : πιλωτῶν R.
[5] The word is corrupt : φιλάμινα was proposed by Turne-
bus, φλάμεα by Scaliger. But the word really wanted here
is φῖλα ; this could easily have been changed to φλάμα by a
scribe who saw no connexion between φῖλα and φλάμονες.

---

[1] *Stephanēphoros* was a title given in various Greek states
to magistrates entitled to wear a crown as a symbol of
their office ; here the word is used as the best Greek
equivalent for "wearers of the fillet."

perform the public sacrifices for the *curiae.* The second, to those called by the Greeks *stephanéphoroi* [1] or " wearers of the crown " and by the Romans *flamines;* [2] they are given this name from their wearing of caps and fillets, called † *flama,* [3] which they continue to wear even to this day. The third, to the commanders of the *celeres,* who, as I have stated, [4] were appointed to be the body-guards of the kings and fought both as cavalry and infantry ; for these also performed certain specified religious rites. The fourth, to those who interpret the signs sent by the gods and determine what they portend both to private persons and to the public ; these, from one branch of the speculations belonging to their art, the Romans call augurs, and we should call them *oiônopoloi* or " soothsayers by means of birds " ; they are skilled in all sorts of divination in use among the Romans, whether founded on signs appearing in the heavens, in mid-air or on the earth. The fifth he assigned to the virgins who are the guardians of the sacred fire and who are called Vestals by the

[2] *Cf.* Livy i. 20, 2.

[3] An error for *fila* ? Dionysius is here giving the usual Roman etymology of *flamen,* which is preserved to us by Varro (*de Ling. Lat.* v. 84) and by Festus (p. 87). Both authorities state that these priests got their name from the *filum,* the fillet of wool which they wore round about the top of their caps. It is hard to believe that our author could have confused *filum* with *flammeum,* the bridal veil ; see the critical note. The true etymology of *flamen* is disputed ; but there is much to be said in favour of deriving it from *flare* (" to blow "), since one of the first duties of a priest would be to blow up the fire for the sacrifices.

[4] Chap. 13.

ουσιν ἑστιάδες, αὐτὸς πρῶτος ἱερὸν ἱδρυσάμενος
Ῥωμαίοις Ἑστίας καὶ παρθένους ἀποδείξας αὐτῇ
θυηπόλους· ὑπὲρ ὧν ὀλίγα καὶ αὐτὰ τἀναγκαιό-
τατα τῆς ὑποθέσεως ἀπαιτούσης ἀναγκαῖον εἰπεῖν.
ἔστι γὰρ ἃ καὶ ζητήσεως ἠξίωται[1] παρὰ πολλοῖς
τῶν Ῥωμαϊκῶν συγγραφέων κατὰ τὸν τόπον τοῦτον, ὧν[2] οἱ τὰς αἰτίας οὐκ ἐξητακότες ἐπιμελῶς
εἰκαιοτέρας ἐξήνεγκαν τὰς γραφάς.

LXV. Τὴν γοῦν ἵδρυσιν τοῦ ἱεροῦ Ῥωμύλῳ τινὲς
ἀνατιθέασι, τῶν ἀμηχάνων νομίζοντες εἶναι πόλεως
οἰκιζομένης ὑπ' ἀνδρὸς ἐμπείρου μαντικῆς μὴ
κατασκευασθῆναι πρῶτον ἑστίαν κοινὴν τῆς πόλεως, καὶ ταῦτα ἐν Ἄλβᾳ τοῦ κτίστου τραφέντος,
ἐν ᾗ παλαιὸν ἐξ οὗ τὸ τῆς θεᾶς ταύτης ἱερὸν
ἱδρυμένον ἦν, καὶ τῆς μητρὸς αὐτοῦ θυηπόλου
γενομένης τῇ θεῷ· διαιρούμενοί τε διχῇ τὰ ἱερὰ
καὶ τὰ μὲν αὐτῶν κοινὰ ποιοῦντες καὶ πολιτικά,
τὰ δὲ ἴδια καὶ συγγενικά, δι' ἄμφω ταῦτά φασι
πολλὴν ἀνάγκην εἶναι τῷ Ῥωμύλῳ ταύτην σέβειν
2 τὴν θεόν. οὔτε γὰρ ἀναγκαιότερον ἀνθρώποις
οὐδὲν εἶναι τῆς κοινῆς ἑστίας οὔτε τῷ Ῥωμύλῳ
κατὰ διαδοχὴν γένους οὐδὲν οἰκειότερον, προγόνων
μὲν ὑπάρχοντι τῶν ἐξ Ἰλίου τὰ τῆς θεᾶς ἱερὰ
μετενεγκαμένων, μητρὸς δὲ ἱερείας. ἐοίκασι δ' οἱ
διὰ ταῦτα τὴν ἵδρυσιν τοῦ ἱεροῦ Ῥωμύλῳ μᾶλλον

[1] καὶ after ἠξίωται deleted by Ambrosch.
[2] ὑπὲρ before ὧν deleted by Ambrosch.

---

[1] Cf. Livy i. 20, 3.
[2] The word ἑστία means, as a common noun, "hearth,"
and, as a proper noun, Hestia, the hearth-goddess, corresponding to the Roman Vesta.

Romans, after the goddess whom they serve, he himself having been the first to build a temple at Rome to Vesta and to appoint virgins to be her priestesses.[1] But concerning them it is necessary to make a few statements that are most essential, since the subject requires it ; for there are problems that have been thought worthy of investigation by many Roman historians in connexion with this topic and those authors who have not diligently examined into the causes of these matters have published rather worthless accounts.

LXV. At any rate, as regards the building of the temple of Vesta, some ascribe it to Romulus, looking upon it as an inconceivable thing that, when a city was being founded by a man skilled in divination, a public hearth[2] should not have been erected first of all, particularly since the founder had been brought up at Alba, where the temple of this goddess had been established from ancient times, and since his mother had been her priestess. And recognizing two classes of religious ceremonies—the one public and common to all the citizens, and the other private and confined to particular families—they declare that on both these grounds Romulus was under every obligation to worship this goddess. For they say that nothing is more necessary for men than a public hearth, and that nothing more nearly concerned Romulus, in view of his descent, since his ancestors had brought the sacred rites of this goddess from Ilium and his mother had been her priestess. Those, then, who for these reasons ascribe the building of the temple to Romulus rather than to Numa

ἀνατιθέντες ἢ Νόμᾳ τὸ μὲν κοινὸν ὀρθῶς λέγειν,
ὅτι πόλεως οἰκιζομένης ἑστίαν πρῶτον ἔδει ἱδρυθῆ-
ναι καὶ ταῦτα ὑπ' ἀνδρὸς οὐκ ἀπείρου τῆς περὶ τὰ
θεῖα σοφίας, τὰ δὲ κατὰ μέρος ὑπέρ τε τῆς κατασκευῆς τοῦ νῦν ὄντος ἱεροῦ καὶ τῶν θεραπευουσῶν
3 τὴν θεὸν παρθένων ἠγνοηκέναι. οὔτε γὰρ τὸ χωρίον
τοῦτο ἐν ᾧ τὸ ἱερὸν φυλάττεται πῦρ Ῥωμύλος ἦν
ὁ καθιερώσας τῇ θεῷ (μέγα δὲ τούτου τεκμήριον
ὅτι τῆς τετραγώνου καλουμένης Ῥώμης ἦν ἐκεῖνος
ἐτείχισεν ἐκτός ἐστιν, ἑστίας δὲ κοινῆς ἱερὸν ἐν τῷ
κρατίστῳ μάλιστα καθιδρύονται τῆς πόλεως ἅπαντες, ἔξω δὲ τοῦ τείχους οὐδείς) οὔτε διὰ παρθένων
τὰς θεραπείας κατεστήσατο τῇ θεῷ, μεμνημένος
ὡς ἐμοὶ δοκεῖ τοῦ περὶ τὴν μητέρα πάθους, ᾗ
συνέβη θεραπευούσῃ τὴν θεὸν τὴν παρθενίαν ἀπο-
βαλεῖν, ὡς οὐχ ἱκανὸς ἐσόμενος, ἐάν τινα τῶν
θυηπόλων εὕρῃ διεφθαρμένην, κατὰ τοὺς πατρίους
τιμωρήσασθαι νόμους διὰ τὴν ἐπὶ ταῖς οἰκείαις
1 συμφοραῖς ἀνάμνησιν. διὰ ταῦτα μὲν δὴ κοινὸν
ἱερὸν οὐ κατεσκευάσατο τῆς Ἑστίας οὐδὲ ἱερείας
ἔταξεν αὐτῇ παρθένους, ἐν ἑκάστῃ δὲ τῶν τριάκοντα
φρατριῶν ἱδρυσάμενος ἑστίαν, ἐφ' ἧς ἔθυον οἱ φρατριεῖς, θυηπόλους αὐτῶν ἐποίησε τοὺς τῶν κουριῶν
ἡγεμόνας, τὰ παρ' Ἕλλησιν ἔθη μιμησάμενος, ἅπερ
ἐν[1] ταῖς ἀρχαιοτάταις τῶν πόλεων ἔτι γίγνεται.
τά γέ τοι καλούμενα πρυτανεῖα παρ' αὐτοῖς Ἑστίας[2]

---

[1] ἅπερ ἐν Sintenis: ἃ παρὰ O, Jacoby.
[2] Ἑστίας added by Reiske.

seem to be right, in so far as the general principle
is concerned that, when a city was being founded,
it was necessary for a hearth to be established first
of all, particularly by a man who was not unskilled
in matters of religion; but of the details relating
to the building of the present temple and to the
virgins who are in the service of the goddess they
seem to have been ignorant. For, in the first place,
it was not Romulus who consecrated to the goddess
this place where the sacred fire is preserved (a strong
proof of this is that it is outside of what they call
Roma Quadrata,[1] which he surrounded with a wall,
whereas all men place the shrine of the public hearth
in the best part of a city and nobody outside of the
walls); and, in the second place, he did not appoint
the service of the goddess to be performed by virgins,
being mindful, I believe, of the experience that had
befallen his mother, who while she was serving the
goddess lost her virginity; for he doubtless felt
that the remembrance of his domestic misfortunes
would make it impossible for him to punish according
to the traditional laws any of the priestesses he
should find to have been violated. For this reason,
therefore, he did not build a common temple of Vesta
nor did he appoint virgins to be her priestesses;
but having erected a hearth in each of the thirty
curiae on which the members sacrificed, he appointed
the chiefs of the *curiae* to be the priests of those
hearths, therein imitating the customs of the
Greeks that are still observed in the most ancient
cities. At any rate, what are called *prytanea* among

---

[1] A later name for the old Palatine city, which, according
to the theory of the augurs, was quadrangular.

ἐστὶν ἱερά, καὶ θεραπεύεται πρὸς τῶν ἐχόντων τὸ
μέγιστον ἐν ταῖς πόλεσι κράτος.

LXVI. Νόμας δὲ τὴν ἀρχὴν παραλαβὼν τὰς μὲν
ἰδίας οὐκ ἐκίνησε τῶν φρατριῶν ἑστίας, κοινὴν δὲ
κατεστήσατο πάντων μίαν ἐν τῷ μεταξὺ τοῦ τε
Καπιτωλίου καὶ τοῦ Παλατίου χωρίῳ, συμπεπολισμένων ἤδη τῶν λόφων ἑνὶ περιβόλῳ καὶ μέσης
ἀμφοῖν οὔσης τῆς ἀγορᾶς, ἐν ᾗ κατεσκεύασται τὸ
ἱερόν, τήν τε φυλακὴν τῶν ἱερῶν κατὰ τὸν πάτριον
τῶν Λατίνων νόμον διὰ παρθένων ἐνομοθέτησε
2 γίνεσθαι· ἔχει δέ τινας ἀπορίας καὶ τὸ φυλαττόμενον ἐν τῷ ἱερῷ τί δήποτέ ἐστι καὶ διὰ τί
πρόσκειται παρθένοις. τινὲς μὲν οὖν οὐδὲν ἔξω
τοῦ φανεροῦ πυρὸς εἶναί φασι τὸ τηρούμενον, τὴν
δὲ φυλακὴν αὐτοῦ παρθένοις ἀνακεῖσθαι μᾶλλον ἢ
ἀνδράσι ποιοῦνται κατὰ τὸ εἰκός, ὅτι πῦρ μὲν
ἀμίαντον, παρθένος δ' ἄφθαρτον, τῷ δ' ἁγνοτάτῳ
τῶν θείων τὸ [1] καθαρώτατον τῶν θνητῶν φίλον.
3 Ἑστίᾳ δ' ἀνακεῖσθαι τὸ πῦρ νομίζουσιν, ὅτι γῆ τε
οὖσα ἡ θεὸς καὶ τὸν μέσον κατέχουσα τοῦ κόσμου
τόπον τὰς ἀνάψεις τοῦ μεταρσίου ποιεῖται πυρὸς
ἀφ' ἑαυτῆς. εἰσὶ δέ τινες οἵ φασιν ἔξω τοῦ πυρὸς
ἀπόρρητα τοῖς πολλοῖς ἱερὰ κεῖσθαί τινα ἐν τῷ

[1] τὸ O : τὸν Jacoby (typographical error ?).

---

[1] Apparently each capital city among the Greeks had a
prytaneum, containing the common hearth of the State,
where the sacred fire was kept burning. This building
would serve naturally as the headquarters of the chief
magistrates (though in Athens the archons removed at an

them are temples of Hestia, and are served by the
chief magistrates of the cities.[1]

LXVI. Numa, upon taking over the rule, did not
disturb the individual hearths of the *curiae*, but
erected one common to them all in the space between the Capitoline and the Palatine (for these
hills had already been united by a single wall into
one city, and the Forum, in which the temple is
built, lies between them), and he enacted, in accordance with the ancestral custom of the Latins, that
the guarding of the holy things should be committed
to virgins. There is some doubt, however, what it is
that is kept in this temple and for what reason the
care of it has been assigned to virgins, some affirming
that nothing is preserved there but the fire, which
is visible to everybody. And they very reasonably
argue that the custody of the fire was committed to
virgins, rather than to men, because fire is incorrupt
and a virgin is undefiled, and the most chaste of
mortal things must be agreeable to the purest of those
that are divine. And they regard the fire as consecrated to Vesta because that goddess, being the
earth[2] and occupying the central place in the
universe, kindles the celestial fires from herself.
But there are some who say that besides the fire
there are some holy things in the temple of the
goddess that may not be revealed to the public,

early date to the Thesmotheteum and the *prytaneis* took
their meals in the Tholos); and here were entertained
foreign ambassadors and also citizens who had deserved
well of the State.

[2] Vesta is similarly identified with the earth by Ovid,
Fasti vi. 267. See Sir James Frazer's instructive note on
that passage (vol. iv. pp. 201 f.).

τεμένει τῆς θεᾶς, ὧν οἵ τε ἱεροφάνται τὴν γνῶσιν
ἔχουσι καὶ αἱ παρθένοι, τεκμήριον οὐ μικρὸν παρ-
εχόμενοι τοῦ λόγου τὸ συμβὰν περὶ τὴν ἔμπρησιν
τοῦ ἱεροῦ κατὰ τὸν Φοινικικὸν πόλεμον τὸν πρῶτον συστάντα Ῥωμαίοις πρὸς Καρχηδονίους περὶ
4 Σικελίας. ἐμπρησθέντος γὰρ τοῦ τεμένους καὶ
τῶν παρθένων φευγουσῶν ἐκ τοῦ πυρὸς τῶν ἱεροφαντῶν τις Λεύκιος Καικίλιος ὁ καλούμενος Μέ-
τελλος ἀνὴρ ὑπατικός, ὁ τὸν ἀοίδιμον ἐκ Σικελίας
ἀπὸ Καρχηδονίων καταγαγὼν ὀκτὼ καὶ τριάκοντα
καὶ ἑκατὸν ἐλεφάντων θρίαμβον, ὑπεριδὼν τῆς ἰδίας
ἀσφαλείας τοῦ κοινῇ συμφέροντος ἕνεκα παρεκιν-
δύνευσεν εἰς τὰ καιόμενα βιάσασθαι καὶ τὰ κατα-
λειφθέντα ὑπὸ τῶν παρθένων ἁρπάσας ἱερὰ διέσωσεν ἐκ τοῦ πυρός· ἐφ' ᾧ τιμὰς παρὰ τῆς πόλεως
ἐξηνέγκατο μεγάλας, ὡς ἡ τῆς εἰκόνος αὐτοῦ τῆς ἐν
5 Καπιτωλίῳ κειμένης[1] ἐπιγραφὴ μαρτυρεῖ. τοῦτο
δὴ λαβόντες ὁμολογούμενον ἐπισυνάπτουσιν αὐτοὶ
στοχασμούς τινας ἰδίους, οἱ μὲν ἐκ τῶν ἐν Σαμο-
θρᾴκῃ λέγοντες ἱερῶν μοῖραν εἶναί τινα φυλαττομένην τὴν ἐνθάδε, Δαρδάνου μὲν εἰς τὴν ὑφ' ἑαυτοῦ
κτισθεῖσαν πόλιν ἐκ τῆς νήσου τὰ ἱερὰ μετενεγ-
καμένου, Αἰνείου δέ, ὅτ' ἔφυγεν ἐκ τῆς Τρωάδος
ἅμα τοῖς ἄλλοις καὶ ταῦτα κομίσαντος εἰς Ἰταλίαν,
οἱ δὲ τὸ διοπετὲς Παλλάδιον ἀποφαίνοντες εἶναι τὸ
παρ' Ἰλιεῦσι γενόμενον, ὡς Αἰνείου κομίσαντος
αὐτὸ δι' ἐμπειρίαν, Ἀχαιῶν δὲ τὸ μίμημα αὐτοῦ
λαβόντων κλοπῇ· περὶ οὗ πολλοὶ σφόδρα εἴρηνται
6 ποιηταῖς τε καὶ συγγραφεῦσι λόγοι. ἐγὼ δὲ τὸ

---

[1] κειμένης Bücheler, ἀνακειμένης Reiske: γενομένης O.

of which only the pontiffs and the virgins have knowledge. As a strong confirmation of this story they cite what happened at the burning of the temple during the First Punic War between the Romans and the Carthaginians over Sicily. For when the temple caught fire and the virgins fled from the flames, one of the pontiffs, Lucius Caecilius, called Metellus, a man of consular rank, the same who exhibited a hundred and thirty-eight elephants in the memorable triumph which he celebrated for his defeat of the Carthaginians in Sicily,[1] neglecting his own safety for the sake of the public good, ventured to force his way into the burning structure, and, snatching up the holy things which the virgins had abandoned, saved them from the fire ; for which he received great honours from the State, as the inscription upon his statue on the Capitol testifies. Taking this incident, then, as an admitted fact, they add some conjectures of their own. Thus, some affirm that the objects preserved here are a part of those holy things which were once in Samothrace ; that Dardanus removed them out of that island into the city which he himself had built, and that Aeneas, when he fled from the Troad, brought them along with the other holy things into Italy. But others declare that it is the Palladium that fell from Heaven, the same that was in the possession of the people of Ilium ; for they hold that Aeneas, being well acquainted with it, brought it into Italy, whereas the Achaeans stole away the copy,— an incident about which many stories have been related both by poets and by historians. For my part,

---

[1] At Panormus, in 250. The temple of Vesta was burned in 241.

505

μὲν εἶναί τινα τοῖς πολλοῖς ἄδηλα ἱερὰ φυλαττόμενα
ὑπὸ τῶν παρθένων καὶ οὐ τὸ πῦρ μόνον ἐκ πολλῶν
πάνυ καταλαμβάνομαι, τίνα δὲ ταῦτ' ἔστιν οὐκ
ἀξιῶ πολυπραγμονεῖν οὔτ' ἐμαυτὸν οὔτε ἄλλον
οὐδένα τῶν βουλομένων τὰ πρὸς θεοὺς ὅσια τηρεῖν.

LXVII. Αἱ δὲ θεραπεύουσαι τὴν θεὸν παρθένοι
τέτταρες μὲν ἦσαν κατ' ἀρχὰς τῶν βασιλέων αὐτὰς
αἱρουμένων ἐφ' οἷς κατεστήσατο δικαίοις ὁ Νόμας,
ὕστερον δὲ διὰ πλῆθος τῶν ἱερουργιῶν ἃς ἐπιτελοῦ-
σιν ἓξ γενόμεναι μέχρι τοῦ καθ' ἡμᾶς διαμένουσι
χρόνου, δίαιταν ἔχουσαι παρὰ τῇ θεῷ, ἔνθα δι'
ἡμέρας μὲν οὐδεὶς ἀπείργεται τῶν βουλομένων
εἰσιέναι, νύκτωρ δὲ οὐδενὶ τῶν ἀρρένων ἐναυλίσα-
2 σθαι θέμις. χρόνον δὲ τριακονταετῆ μένειν αὐτὰς
ἀναγκαῖον ἁγνὰς γάμων θυηπολούσας τε καὶ τἆλλα
θρησκευούσας κατὰ νόμον, ἐν ᾧ δέκα μὲν ἔτη μαν-
θάνειν αὐτὰς ἔδει, δέκα δ' ἐπιτελεῖν τὰ ἱερά, τὰ δὲ
λοιπὰ δέκα διδάσκειν ἑτέρας. ἐκπληρωθείσης δὲ
τῆς τριακονταετίας οὐδὲν ἦν τὸ κωλῦσον τὰς βουλο-
μένας ἀποθείσας τὰ στέμματα καὶ τὰ λοιπὰ παρά-
σημα τῆς ἱερωσύνης γαμεῖσθαι. καὶ ἐποίησάν τινες
τοῦτο πάνυ ὀλίγαι, αἷς ἄζηλοι συνέβησαν αἱ τελευταὶ
τῶν βίων καὶ οὐ πάνυ εὐτυχεῖς, ὥστε δι' οἰωνοῦ
λαμβάνουσαι τὰς ἐκείνων συμφορὰς αἱ λοιπαὶ παρθένοι μένουσι παρὰ τῇ θεῷ μέχρι θανάτου, τότε δὲ
εἰς τὸν τῆς ἐκλιπούσης ἀριθμὸν ἑτέρα πάλιν ὑπὸ
3 τῶν ἱεροφαντῶν ἀποδείκνυται. τιμαὶ δὲ αὐταῖς

I find from very many evidences that there are indeed some holy things, unknown to the public, kept by the virgins, and not the fire alone ; but what they are I do not think should be inquired into too curiously, either by me or by anyone else who wishes to observe the reverence due to the gods.

LXVII. The virgins who serve the goddess were originally four and were chosen by the kings according to the principles established by Numa, but afterwards, from the multiplicity of the sacred rites they perform, their number was increased to six, and has so remained down to our time. They live in the temple of the goddess, into which none who wish are hindered from entering in the daytime, whereas it is not lawful for any man to remain there at night. They were required to remain undefiled by marriage for the space of thirty years, devoting themselves to offering sacrifices and performing the other rites ordained by law. During the first ten years their duty was to learn their functions, in the second ten to perform them, and during the remaining ten to teach others. After the expiration of the term of thirty years nothing hindered those who so desired from marrying, upon laying aside their fillets and the other insignia of their priesthood. And some, though very few, have done this ; but they came to ends that were not at all happy or enviable. In consequence, the rest, looking upon their misfortunes as ominous, remain virgins in the temple of the goddess till their death, and then once more another is chosen by the pontiffs to supply the vacancy. Many high honours have been granted

ἀποδέδονται παρὰ τῆς πόλεως πολλαὶ καὶ καλαί,
δι' ἃς οὔτε παίδων αὐταῖς ἐστι πόθος οὔτε γάμων,
τιμωρίαι τε ἐπὶ τοῖς ἁμαρτανομένοις κεῖνται μεγάλαι, ὧν ἐξετασταί τε καὶ κολασταὶ κατὰ νόμον
εἰσὶν οἱ ἱεροφάνται, τὰς μὲν ἄλλο τι τῶν ἐλαττόνων
ἁμαρτανούσας ῥάβδοις μαστιγοῦντες, τὰς δὲ φθα-
ρείσας αἰσχίστῳ τε καὶ ἐλεεινοτάτῳ παραδιδόντες
4 θανάτῳ. ζῶσαι γὰρ ἔτι πομπεύουσιν ἐπὶ κλίνης
φερόμεναι τὴν ἀποδεδειγμένην τοῖς νεκροῖς ἐκφοράν,
ἀνακλαιομένων αὐτὰς καὶ προπεμπόντων φίλων τε
καὶ συγγενῶν, κομισθεῖσαι δὲ μέχρι τῆς Κολλίνης
πύλης, ἐντὸς τείχους[1] εἰς σηκὸν ὑπὸ γῆς κατεσκευασμένον ἅμα τοῖς ἐνταφίοις κόσμοις τίθενται
καὶ οὔτ' ἐπιστήματος οὔτ' ἐναγισμῶν οὔτ' ἄλλου
5 τῶν νομίμων οὐδενὸς τυγχάνουσι. πολλὰ μὲν οὖν
καὶ ἄλλα δοκεῖ μηνύματα εἶναι τῆς οὐχ ὁσίως
ὑπηρετούσης τοῖς ἱεροῖς, μάλιστα δὲ ἡ σβέσις τοῦ
πυρός, ἣν ὑπὲρ ἅπαντα τὰ δεινὰ Ῥωμαῖοι δεδοί-
κασιν ἀφανισμοῦ τῆς πόλεως σημεῖον ὑπολαμβάνοντες, ἀφ' ἧς ποτ' ἂν αἰτίας γένηται, καὶ
πολλαῖς αὐτὸ θεραπείαις ἐξιλασκόμενοι κατάγουσι
πάλιν εἰς τὸ ἱερόν· ὑπὲρ ὧν κατὰ τὸν οἰκεῖον
καιρὸν ἐρῶ.

LXVIII. Πάνυ δ' ἄξιον καὶ τὴν ἐπιφάνειαν
ἱστορῆσαι τῆς θεᾶς, ἣν ἐπεδείξατο ταῖς ἀδίκως
ἐγκληθείσαις παρθένοις· πεπίστευται γὰρ ὑπὸ Ῥωμαίων, εἰ καὶ παράδοξά ἐστι, καὶ πολὺν πεποίηνται
2 λόγον ὑπὲρ αὐτῶν οἱ συγγραφεῖς. ὅσοι μὲν οὖν

---

[1] τείχους B : τοῦ τείχους R.

them by the commonwealth, as a result of which they feel no desire either for marriage or for children ; and severe penalties have been established for their misdeeds. It is the pontiffs who by law both inquire into and punish these offences ; those Vestals who are guilty of lesser misdemeanours they scourge with rods, but those who have suffered defilement they deliver up to the most shameful and the most miserable death. For while they are yet alive they are carried upon a bier with all the formality of a funeral, their friends and relations attending them with lamentations, and after being brought as far as the Colline Gate, they are placed in an underground cell prepared within the walls, clad in their funeral attire ; but they are not given a monument or funeral rites or any other customary solemnities. There are many indications, it seems, when a priestess is not performing her holy functions with purity, but the principal one is the extinction of the fire, which the Romans dread above all misfortunes, looking upon it, from whatever cause it proceeds, as an omen that portends the destruction of the city ; and they bring fire again into the temple with many supplicatory rites, concerning which I shall speak on the proper occasion.[1]

LXVIII. However, it is also well worth relating in what manner the goddess has manifested herself in favour of those virgins who have been falsely accused. For these things, however incredible they may be, have been believed by the Romans and their historians have related much about them.

[1] This promise is not fulfilled in the extant portions of the history.

509

τὰς ἀθέους ἀσκοῦσι φιλοσοφίας, εἰ δὴ καὶ φιλοσοφίας αὐτὰς δεῖ καλεῖν, ἁπάσας διασύροντες τὰς
ἐπιφανείας τῶν θεῶν τὰς παρ' Ἕλλησιν ἢ βαρβάροις γενομένας καὶ ταύτας εἰς γέλωτα πολὺν
ἄξουσι τὰς ἱστορίας ἀλαζονείαις ἀνθρωπίναις αὐτὰς
ἀνατιθέντες, ὡς οὐδενὶ θεῶν μέλον ἀνθρώπων οὐδενός.
ὅσοι δ' οὐκ ἀπολύουσι τῆς ἀνθρωπίνης ἐπιμελείας
τοὺς θεούς, ἀλλὰ καὶ τοῖς ἀγαθοῖς εὐμενεῖς εἶναι
νομίζουσι καὶ τοῖς κακοῖς δυσμενεῖς διὰ πολλῆς
ἐληλυθότες ἱστορίας, οὐδὲ ταύτας ὑπολήψονται τὰς
3 ἐπιφανείας εἶναι ἀπίστους. λέγεται δή ποτε τοῦ
πυρὸς ἐκλιπόντος δι' ὀλιγωρίαν τινὰ τῆς τότε αὐτὸ
φυλαττούσης Αἰμιλίας, ἑτέρᾳ παρθένῳ τῶν νεωστὶ
κατειλεγμένων καὶ ἄρτι μανθανουσῶν παραδούσης
τὴν ἐπιμέλειαν, ταραχὴ πολλὴ γενέσθαι κατὰ τὴν
πόλιν ὅλην καὶ ζήτησις ὑπὸ τῶν ἱεροφαντῶν, μή τι
μίασμα περὶ τὸ πῦρ τῆς ἱερείας ἐτύγχανε γεγονός·
ἔνθα δή φασι τὴν Αἰμιλίαν ἀναίτιον μὲν οὖσαν,
ἀπορουμένην δ' ἐπὶ τῷ συμβεβηκότι παρόντων τῶν
ἱερέων καὶ τῶν ἄλλων παρθένων τὰς χεῖρας ἐπὶ τὸν
4 βωμὸν ἐκτείνασαν εἰπεῖν· "'Εστία, τῆς Ῥωμαίων
πόλεως φύλαξ, εἰ μὲν ὁσίως καὶ δικαίως ἐπι-
τετέλεκά[1] σοι τὰ ἱερὰ χρόνον ὀλίγου[2] δέοντα
τριακονταετοῦς καὶ ψυχὴν ἔχουσα καθαρὰν καὶ
σῶμα ἁγνόν, ἐπιφάνηθί μοι καὶ βοήθησον[3] καὶ μὴ
περιίδῃς τὴν σεαυτῆς ἱέρειαν τὸν οἴκτιστον μόρον
ἀποθανοῦσαν· εἰ δὲ ἀνόσιόν τι πέπρακταί μοι, ταῖς

---

[1] Kiessling: τετέλεκα O.   [2] Kiessling: ὀλίγῳ O.
[3] βοήθησον Reiske: βοήθησόν τε Aa, βοήθησόν γε Ab,
βοήθησον .. B.

To be sure, the professors of the atheistic philosophies,—if, indeed, their theories deserve the name of philosophy,—who ridicule all the manifestations of the gods which have taken place among either the Greeks or barbarians, will also laugh these reports to scorn and attribute them to human imposture, on the ground that none of the gods concern themselves in anything relating to mankind. Those, however, who do not absolve the gods from the care of human affairs, but, after looking deeply into history, hold that they are favourable to the good and hostile to the wicked, will not regard even these manifestations as incredible. It is said, then, that once, when the fire had been extinguished through some negligence on the part of Aemilia, who had the care of it at the time and had entrusted it to another virgin, one of those who had been newly chosen and were then learning their duties, the whole city was in great commotion and an inquiry was made by the pontiffs whether there might not have been some defilement of the priestess to account for the extinction of the fire. Thereupon, they say, Aemilia, who was innocent, but distracted at what had happened, stretched out her hands toward the altar and in the presence of the priests and the rest of the virgins cried : " O Vesta, guardian of the Romans' city, if, during the space of nearly thirty years, I have performed the sacred offices to thee in a holy and proper manner, keeping a pure mind and a chaste body, do thou manifest thyself in my defence and assist me and do not suffer thy priestess to die the most miserable of all deaths ; but if I have been guilty of any impious deed, let my punishment

ἐμαῖς τιμωρίαις τὸ τῆς πόλεως ἄγος ἀφάγνισον."[1]
5 ταῦτ' εἰποῦσαν καὶ περιρρήξασαν ἀπὸ τῆς καρπασί-
νης ἐσθῆτος, ἣν ἔτυχεν ἐνδεδυκυῖα, βαλεῖν τὸν
τελαμῶνα ἐπὶ τὸν βωμὸν μετὰ τὴν εὐχὴν λέγουσι
καὶ ἐκ τῆς κατεψυγμένης πρὸ πολλοῦ καὶ οὐδένα
φυλαττούσης σπινθῆρα τέφρας ἀναλάμψαι φλόγα
πολλὴν διὰ τῆς καρπάσου, ὥστε μηδὲν ἔτι δεῆσαι
τῇ πόλει μήτε ἁγνισμῶν μήτε νέου πυρός.

LXIX. Ἔτι δὲ τούτου θαυμασιώτερόν ἐστι καὶ
μύθῳ μᾶλλον ἐοικὸς ὃ μέλλω λέγειν. κατηγορῆσαί
τινά φασιν ἀδίκως μιᾶς τῶν παρθένων τῶν ἱερῶν
Τυκκίας[2] ὄνομα, ἀφανισμὸν μὲν πυρὸς οὐκ ἔχοντα
προφέρειν, ἄλλας δέ τινας ἐξ εἰκότων τεκμηρίων
καὶ μαρτυριῶν ἀποδείξεις φέροντα οὐκ ἀληθεῖς.
κελευσθεῖσαν δ' ἀπολογεῖσθαι τὴν παρθένον τοσοῦτο[3]
μόνον εἰπεῖν, ὅτι τοῖς ἔργοις ἀπολύσεται τὰς δια-
2 βολάς· ταῦτα δ' εἰποῦσαν καὶ τὴν θεὸν ἐπικαλεσα-
μένην ἡγεμόνα τῆς ὁδοῦ γενέσθαι προάγειν ἐπὶ τὸν
Τέβεριν ἐπιτρεψάντων μὲν αὐτῇ τῶν ἱεροφαντῶν,
τοῦ δὲ κατὰ τὴν πόλιν ὄχλου συμπροπέμποντος·
γενομένην δὲ τοῦ ποταμοῦ πλησίον τὸ παροιμιαζό-
μενον ἐν τοῖς πρώτοις τῶν ἀδυνάτων τόλμημα ὑπομεῖναι, ἀρυσαμένην ἐκ τοῦ ποταμοῦ κοσκίνῳ[4] καὶ
μέχρι τῆς ἀγορᾶς ἐνέγκασαν παρὰ τοὺς πόδας
3 τῶν ἱεροφαντῶν ἐξεράσαι τὸ ὕδωρ. καὶ μετὰ
ταῦτά φασι τὸν κατήγορον αὐτῆς πολλῆς ζητήσεως
γενομένης μήτε ζῶντα εὑρεθῆναι μήτε νεκρόν.
ἀλλ' ὑπὲρ μὲν τῶν ἐπιφανειῶν τῆς θεᾶς ἔχων ἔτι

---

[1] ἀφάγνισον B : ἀφάγνισαι A ; ἀφάνισαι Steph.
[2] Kiessling : τυγκίας O.

expiate the guilt of the city." Having said this, she tore off the band of the linen garment she had on and threw it upon the altar, they say, following her prayer; and from the ashes, which had been long cold and retained no spark, a great flame flared up through the linen, so that the city no longer required either expiations or a new fire.

LXIX. But what I am going to relate is still more wonderful and more like a myth. They say that somebody unjustly accused one of the holy virgins, whose name was Tuccia, and although he was unable to point to the extinction of the fire as evidence, he advanced false arguments based on plausible proofs and depositions; and that the virgin, being ordered to make her defence, said only this, that she would clear herself from the accusation by her deeds. Having said this and called upon the goddess to be her guide, she led the way to the Tiber, with the consent of the pontiffs and escorted by the whole population of the city; and when she came to the river, she was so hardy as to undertake the task which, according to the proverb, is among the most impossible of achievement: she drew up water from the river in a sieve, and carrying it as far as the Forum, poured it out at the feet of the pontiffs. After which, they say, her accuser, though great search was made for him, could never be found either alive or dead. But, though I have yet many other things to say concerning the

---

[3] τοσοῦτο Jacoby in note : τοῦτο O, Jacoby in text.
[4] καινῷ before κοσκίνῳ deleted by Jacoby ; emended to κενῷ by Steph.

πολλὰ λέγειν καὶ ἄλλα,[1] ταῦτα ἱκανὰ εἰρῆσθαι
νομίζω.

LXX. Ἕκτη δὲ μοῖρα τῆς περὶ τὰ θεῖα νομοθεσίας ἦν ἡ προσνεμηθεῖσα τοῖς καλουμένοις ὑπὸ
Ῥωμαίων Σαλίοις, οὓς αὐτὸς ὁ Νόμας ἀπέδειξεν ἐκ
τῶν πατρικίων δώδεκα τοὺς εὐπρεπεστάτους ἐπιλεξάμενος νέους, ὧν ἐν Παλατίῳ κεῖται τὰ ἱερὰ
καὶ αὐτοὶ καλοῦνται Παλατῖνοι. οἱ μὲν γὰρ
Ἀγωναλεῖς, ὑπὸ δέ τινων Κολλῖνοι καλούμενοι
Σάλιοι, ὧν τὸ ἱεροφυλάκιόν ἐστιν ἐπὶ τοῦ Κυρινίου [2]
λόφου, μετὰ Νόμαν ἀπεδείχθησαν ὑπὸ βασιλέως
Ὁστιλίου κατ᾽ εὐχήν, ἣν ἐν τῷ πρὸς Σαβίνους εὔξατο
πολέμῳ. οὗτοι πάντες οἱ Σάλιοι χορευταί τινές
2 εἰσι καὶ ὑμνηταὶ τῶν ἐνόπλων [3] θεῶν. ἑορτὴ δ᾽
αὐτῶν ἐστι περὶ τὰ Παναθήναια τῷ [4] καλουμένῳ
Μαρτίῳ μηνὶ δημοτελὴς ἐπὶ πολλὰς ἡμέρας ἀγο-
μένη, ἐν αἷς διὰ τῆς πόλεως ἄγουσι τοὺς χοροὺς
εἴς τε τὴν ἀγορὰν καὶ τὸ Καπιτώλιον καὶ πολλοὺς
ἄλλους ἰδίους τε καὶ δημοσίους τόπους, χιτῶνας
ποικίλους χαλκαῖς μίτραις κατεζωσμένοι καὶ τη-
βέννας ἐμπεπορπημένοι περιπορφύρους φοινικοπαρύ-
φους, ἃς καλοῦσι τραβέας (ἔστι δ᾽ ἐπιχώριος αὕτη
Ῥωμαίοις ἐσθὴς ἐν τοῖς πάνυ τιμία) καὶ τὰς καλου-

---

[1] ἄλλα Bücheler : om. O, Jacoby.
[2] Κυρινίου Cary : κολλίνου O, Jacoby.
[3] ἐνόπλων Bb : ἐνοπλίων BaR.
[4] τῷ O : ἐν τῷ Ambrosch, Jacoby.

---

[1] Cf. Livy i. 20, 4.   [2] Usually called *Agonenses*.
[3] "Colline hill," the absurd reading of the MSS. and
editors, cannot be from the hand of Dionysius.

manifestations of this goddess, I regard what has already been said as sufficient.

LXX. The sixth division of his religious institutions was devoted to those the Romans call *Salii*. whom Numa himself appointed out of the patricians, choosing twelve young men of the most graceful appearance.[1] These are the *Salii* whose holy things are deposited on the Palatine hill and who are themselves called the (*Salii*) *Palatini*; for the (*Salii*) Agonales,[2] by some called the *Salii Collini*, the repository of whose holy things is on the Quirinal hill,[3] were appointed after Numa's time by King Hostilius, in pursuance of a vow he had made in the war against the Sabines. All these *Salii* are a kind of dancers and singers of hymns in praise of the gods of war. Their festival falls about the time of the Panathenaea,[4] in the month which they call March, and is celebrated at the public expense for many days, during which they proceed through the city with their dances to the Forum and to the Capitol and to many other places both private and public. They wear embroidered tunics girt about with wide girdles of bronze, and over these are fastened, with brooches, robes striped with scarlet and bordered with purple, which they call *trabeae*; this garment is peculiar to the Romans and a mark of the greatest honour.

[4] "Panathenaea" does not here mean the well-known Athenian festival (which took place in August), but the Quinquatria, the Roman festival in honour of Minerva (March 19–23). The principal celebration of the *Salii* began on the first of March and continued until at least the 24th; Polybius (xxi. 10, 12) gives the total period as thirty days.

μένας ἄπικας ἐπικείμενοι ταῖς κεφαλαῖς, πίλους
ὑψηλοὺς εἰς σχῆμα συναγομένους κωνοειδές, ἃς
3 Ἕλληνες προσαγορεύουσι κυρβασίας. παρέζωσται
δ' ἕκαστος αὐτῶν ξίφος καὶ τῇ μὲν δεξιᾷ χειρὶ
λόγχην ἢ ῥάβδον ἤ τι τοιοῦθ' ἕτερον κρατεῖ, τῇ
δ' εὐωνύμῳ κατέχει πέλτην Θρακίαν· ἡ δ' ἐστὶ
ῥομβοειδεῖ θυρεῷ στενωτέρας ἔχοντι τὰς λαγόνας
ἐμφερής, οἵας λέγονται φέρειν οἱ τὰ Κουρήτων
4 παρ' Ἕλλησιν ἐπιτελοῦντες ἱερά. καί εἰσιν οἱ
Σάλιοι κατὰ γοῦν τὴν ἐμὴν γνώμην [1] Ἑλληνικῷ
μεθερμηνευθέντες ὀνόματι Κουρῆτες, ὑφ' ἡμῶν μὲν
ἐπὶ τῆς ἡλικίας οὕτως ὠνομασμένοι παρὰ τοὺς
κούρους, ὑπὸ δὲ Ῥωμαίων ἐπὶ τῆς συντόνου κινή-
σεως. τὸ γὰρ ἐξάλλεσθαί τε καὶ πηδᾶν σαλίρε ὑπ'
αὐτῶν λέγεται. ἀπὸ δὲ τῆς αὐτῆς αἰτίας καὶ τοὺς
ἄλλους ἅπαντας ὀρχηστάς, ἐπεὶ κἂν τούτοις πολὺ
τὸ ἅλμα καὶ σκίρτημα ἔνεστι, παράγοντες ἀπὸ τῶν
5 Σαλίων τοὔνομα σαλτάτωρας [2] καλοῦσιν. εἰ δὲ
ὀρθῶς ὑπείληφα ταύτην αὐτοῖς τὴν προσηγορίαν
ἀποδιδοὺς ἐκ τῶν γιγνομένων ὑπ' αὐτῶν ὁ βουλόμενος συμβαλεῖ. κινοῦνται γὰρ πρὸς αὐλὸν ἐν
ῥυθμῷ τὰς ἐνοπλίους κινήσεις τοτὲ μὲν ὁμοῦ, τοτὲ
δὲ παραλλάξ, καὶ πατρίους τινὰς ὕμνους ᾄδουσιν
ἅμα ταῖς χορείαις. χορείαν δὲ καὶ κίνησιν ἐνό-
πλιον καὶ τὸν ἐν ταῖς ἀσπίσιν ἀποτελούμενον ὑπὸ
τῶν ἐγχειριδίων ψόφον, εἴ τι δεῖ τοῖς ἀρχαίοις

---

[1] γνώμην Kiessling: γνῶσιν Bb, om. ABa.
[2] Portus: σαλάτορας AB.

On their heads they wear *apices*, as they are called, that is, high caps contracted into the shape of a cone, which the Greeks call *kyrbasiai*. They have each of them a sword hanging at their girdle and in their right hand they hold a spear or a staff or something else of the sort, and on their left arm a Thracian buckler, which resembles a lozenge-shaped shield with its sides drawn in,[1] such as those are said to carry who among the Greeks perform the sacred rites of the Curetes. And, in my opinion at least, the *Salii*, if the word be translated into Greek, are Curetes, whom, because they are *kouroi* or " young men," we call by that name from their age, whereas the Romans call them *Salii* from their lively motions. For to leap and skip is by them called *salire ;* and for the same reason they call all other dancers *saltatores*, deriving their name from the *Salii*, because their dancing also is attended by much leaping and capering. Whether I have been well advised or not in giving them this appellation, anyone who pleases may gather from their actions. For they execute their movements in arms, keeping time to a flute, sometimes all together, sometimes by turns, and while dancing sing certain traditional hymns. But this dance and exercise performed by armed men and the noise they make by striking their bucklers with their daggers, if we may base any conjectures on the ancient accounts,

[1] " Lozenge-shaped " here doubtless means oval. What have been identified as these sacred *ancilia* are seen depicted on a few ancient coins and gems. They are of the shape often called " figure of eight." This was not the shape of the Thracian buckler, which is described as crescent-shaped.

τεκμηριοῦσθαι λόγοις, Κουρῆτες ἦσαν οἱ πρῶτοι
καταστησάμενοι. τὸν δὲ περὶ αὐτῶν μῦθον οὐδὲν
δέομαι πρὸς εἰδότας ὀλίγου δεῖν πάντας γράφειν.

LXXI. Ἐν δὲ ταῖς πέλταις, ἃς οἵ τε Σάλιοι
φοροῦσι καὶ ἃς ὑπηρέται τινὲς αὐτῶν ἠρτημένας
ἀπὸ κανόνων κομίζουσι, πολλαῖς πάνυ οὔσαις μίαν
εἶναι λέγουσι διοπετῆ, εὑρεθῆναι δ᾽ αὐτήν φασιν
ἐν τοῖς βασιλείοις τοῖς Νόμα, μηδενὸς ἀνθρώπων
εἰσενέγκαντος μηδ᾽ ἐγνωσμένου πρότερον ἐν Ἰταλοῖς
τοιούτου σχήματος, ἐξ ὧν ἀμφοτέρων ὑπολαβεῖν
2 Ῥωμαίους θεόπεμπτον εἶναι τὸ ὅπλον. βουληθέντα
δὲ τὸν Νόμαν τιμᾶσθαί τε αὐτὸ φερόμενον ὑπὸ τῶν
κρατίστων νέων ἐν ἱεραῖς ἡμέραις ἀνὰ τὴν πόλιν
καὶ θυσιῶν ἐπετείων τυγχάνειν, δεδοικότα δὲ ἐπι-
βουλάς τε τὰς ἀπ᾽ ἐχθρῶν καὶ ἀφανισμὸν αὐτοῦ
κλοπαῖον, ὅπλα λέγουσι πολλὰ κατασκευάσασθαι
τῷ διοπετεῖ παραπλήσια, Μαμορίου τινὸς δημιουρ-
γοῦ τὸ ἔργον ἀναδεξαμένου, ὥστε ἄσημον γενέσθαι
καὶ δυσδιάγνωστον τοῖς μέλλουσιν ἐπιβουλεύειν
τὴν τοῦ θεοπέμπτου φύσιν διὰ τὴν ἀπαράλλακτον
3 τῶν ἀνθρωπείων ἔργων ὁμοιότητα. ἐπιχώριον δὲ
Ῥωμαίοις καὶ πάνυ τίμιον ὁ κουρητισμός, ὡς ἐκ
πολλῶν μὲν καὶ ἄλλων ἐγὼ συμβάλλομαι, μάλιστα
δ᾽ ἐκ τῶν περὶ τὰς πομπὰς τάς τε ἐν ἱπποδρόμῳ
4 καὶ τὰς ἐν τοῖς θεάτροις γινομένας · ἐν ἁπάσαις γὰρ

---

[1] The legend that made them the protectors of the infant
Zeus in the island of Crete; see chap. 61, 2. They were

was originated by the Curetes. I need not mention the legend [1] which is related concerning them, since almost everybody is acquainted with it.

LXXI. Among the vast number of bucklers which both the *Salii* themselves bear and some of their servants carry suspended from rods, they say there is one that fell from heaven and was found in the palace of Numa, though no one had brought it thither and no buckler of that shape had ever before been known among the Italians; and that for both these reasons the Romans concluded that this buckler had been sent by the gods. They add that Numa, desiring that it should be honoured by being carried through the city on holy days by the most distinguished young men and that annual sacrifices should be offered to it, but at the same time being fearful both of the plots of his enemies and of its disappearance by theft, caused many other bucklers to be made resembling the one which fell from heaven, Mamurius, an artificer, having undertaken the work; so that, as a result of the perfect resemblance of the man-made imitations, the shape of the buckler sent by the gods was rendered inconspicuous and difficult to be distinguished by those who might plot to possess themselves of it. This dancing after the manner of the Curetes was a native institution among the Romans and was held in great honour by them, as I gather from many other indications and especially from what takes place in their processions both in the Circus and in the theatres. For

said to have clashed their spears against their shields in order to drown the cries of the infant Zeus, lest his whereabouts should be discovered.

ταύταις¹ πρόσηβοι κόροι χιτωνίσκους ἐνδεδυκότες
ἐκπρεπεῖς κράνη καὶ ξίφη καὶ πάρμας ἔχοντες
στοιχηδὸν πορεύονται, καί εἰσιν οὗτοι τῆς πομπῆς
ἡγεμόνες καλούμενοι πρὸς αὐτῶν ἐπὶ τῆς παιδιᾶς
τῆς ὑπὸ Λυδῶν ἐξευρῆσθαι δοκούσης λυδίωνες,
εἰκόνες ὡς ἐμοὶ δοκεῖ τῶν Σαλίων, ἐπεὶ τῶν γε
Κουρητικῶν οὐδὲν ὥσπερ οἱ Σάλιοι δρῶσιν οὔτ᾽ ἐν
ὕμνοις οὔτ᾽ ἐν ὀρχήσει. χρῆν δὲ τούτους² ἐλευθέρους τε εἶναι καὶ αὐθιγενεῖς καὶ ἀμφιθαλεῖς, οἱ δ᾽
εἰσὶν ἐξ ὁποιασδήποτε τύχης. τί γὰρ δεῖ τὰ πλείω
περὶ αὐτῶν γράφειν ;

LXXII. Ἡ δὲ ἑβδόμη μοῖρα τῆς ἱερᾶς νομοθεσίας τῷ συστήματι προσετέθη τῶν καλουμένων φη-
τιαλίων.³ οὗτοι δ᾽ ἂν εἴησαν κατὰ τὴν Ἑλληνικὴν
καλούμενοι διάλεκτον εἰρηνοδίκαι. εἰσὶ δ᾽ ἐκ τῶν
ἀρίστων οἴκων ἄνδρες ἐπίλεκτοι διὰ παντὸς ἱερώ-
μενοι τοῦ βίου, Νόμα τοῦ βασιλέως πρώτου καὶ
τοῦτο Ῥωμαίοις τὸ ἱερὸν ἀρχεῖον καταστησαμένου·
2 εἰ μέντοι παρὰ τῶν καλουμένων Αἰκικλῶν⁴ τὸ
παράδειγμα ἔλαβεν ὥσπερ οἴονταί τινες, ἢ παρὰ
τῆς Ἀρδεατῶν πόλεως ὡς γράφει Γέλλιος οὐκ ἔχω
λέγειν, ἀπόχρη δὲ μοι τοσοῦτο μόνον εἰπεῖν, ὅτι πρὸ
τῆς Νόμα ἀρχῆς οὔπω τὸ τῶν εἰρηνοδικῶν σύστημα

¹ ταύταις Garrer : αὐταῖς O.
² τούτους Ambrosch : αὐτοὺς O.
³ φητιαλίων Kiessling, φετιαλίων Steph., Jacoby : φιτιαλίων
A (?), φιτιάλων B.
⁴ Cluver : ἐκικλῶν AB.

in all of them young men clad in handsome tunics, with helmets, swords and bucklers, march in file. These are the leaders of the procession and are called by the Romans, from a game of which the Lydians seem to have been the inventors, *ludiones ;* [1] they show merely a certain resemblance, in my opinion, to the *Salii*, since they do not, like the *Salii*, do any of the things characteristic of the Curetes, either in their hymns or dancing. And it was necessary that the *Salii* should be free men and native Romans and that both their fathers and mothers should be living; whereas the others are of any condition whatsoever. But why should I say more about them ?

LXXII. The seventh division of his sacred institutions was devoted to the college of the *fetiales* [2]; these may be called in Greek *eirênodikai* or " arbiters of peace." They are chosen men, from the best families, and exercise their holy office for life ; King Numa was also the first who instituted this holy magistracy among the Romans. But whether he took his example from those called the Aequicoli,[3] according to the opinion of some, or from the city of Ardea, as Gellius writes, I cannot say. It is sufficient for me to state that before Numa's reign the college of the *fetiales* did not exist among the

[1] From the well-known chapter (vii. 2) in which Livy describes the beginnings of drama at Rome we learn that these *ludiones* or " players " were at first mere dancers and only later pantomimists.

[2] *Cf.* Livy i. 24 and 32. Livy does not mention the *fetiales* until the reign of Numa's successor, Tullus Hostilius.

[3] Another name for the Aequi ; but in time the word seems to have been interpreted as meaning " lovers of justice " (from *aequum* and *colere*).

3 παρὰ ῾Ρωμαίοις ἦν. κατεστήσατο δ᾽ αὐτὸ Νόμας ὅτε Φιδηνάταις ἔμελλε πολεμεῖν ληστείας καὶ καταδρομὰς τῆς χώρας αὐτοῦ ποιησαμένοις, εἰ βούλοιντο συμβῆναι δίχα πολέμου πρὸς αὐτόν, ὅπερ εἰς ἀνάγκην καταστάντες ἐποίησαν. οἴομαι δέ, ἐπειδήπερ οὐκ ἔστιν ἐπιχώριον ῞Ελλησι τὸ περὶ τοὺς εἰρηνοδίκας ἀρχεῖον, ἀναγκαῖον εἶναί μοι πόσων καὶ πηλίκων ἐστὶ πραγμάτων κύριον διελθεῖν, ἵνα τοῖς ἀγνοοῦσι τὴν ῾Ρωμαίων εὐσέβειαν, ἣν οἱ τότε[1] ἄνδρες ἐπετήδευον, μὴ παράδοξον εἶναι φανῇ τὸ πάντας αὐτοῖς τὸ κάλλιστον λαβεῖν τοὺς πολέμους τέλος.

4 ἁπάντων γὰρ αὐτῶν τὰς ἀρχὰς καὶ τὰς ὑποθέσεις εὐσεβεστάτας φανήσονται ποιησάμενοι καὶ διὰ τοῦτο μάλιστα τοὺς θεοὺς ἐσχηκότες ἐν τοῖς κινδύνοις εὐμενεῖς. ἅπαντα μὲν οὖν ὅσα ἀνάκειται τούτοις τοῖς εἰρηνοδίκαις ἐπελθεῖν διὰ πλῆθος οὐ ῥᾴδιον, κεφαλαιώδει δ᾽ ὑπογραφῇ δηλῶσαι τοιάδ᾽ ἐστί· φυλάττειν ἵνα μηδένα ῾Ρωμαῖοι πόλεμον ἐξενέγκωσι κατὰ μηδεμιᾶς ἐνσπόνδου πόλεως ἄδικον, ἀρξάντων δὲ παρασπονδεῖν εἰς αὐτοὺς ἑτέρων πρεσβεύεσθαί τε καὶ τὰ δίκαια πρῶτον αἰτεῖν λόγῳ, ἐὰν δὲ μὴ πείθωνται τοῖς ἀξιουμένοις, τότ᾽ ἐπικυροῦν τὸν

5 πόλεμον. ὁμοίως δὲ κἂν ἀδικεῖσθαί τινες ὑπὸ ῾Ρωμαίων ἔνσπονδοι λέγοντες τὰ δίκαια αἰτῶσι, τούτους διαγινώσκειν τοὺς ἄνδρας εἴ τι πεπόνθασιν ἔκσπονδον, καὶ ἐὰν δόξωσι τὰ προσήκοντα ἐγκαλεῖν, τοὺς ἐνόχους ταῖς αἰτίαις συλλαβόντας ἐκδότους τοῖς ἀδικηθεῖσι παραδιδόναι, τά τε περὶ τοὺς

---

[1] τότε Bb : τε ABa.

Romans. It was instituted by Numa when he was
upon the point of making war on the people of
Fidenae, who had raided and ravaged his territories,
in order to see whether they would come to an accommodation with him without war ; and that is what
they actually did, being constrained by necessity.
But since the college of the *fetiales* is not in use
among the Greeks, I think it incumbent on me to
relate how many and how great affairs fall under its
jurisdiction, to the end that those who are unacquainted with the piety practised by the Romans
of those times may not be surprised to find that
all their wars had the most successful outcome ; for
it will appear that the origins and motives of them
all were most holy, and for this reason especially
the gods were propitious to them in the dangers
that attended them. The multitude of duties, to be
sure, that fall within the province of these *fetiales*
makes it no easy matter to enumerate them all ; but
to indicate them by a summary outline, they are as
follows : It is their duty to take care that the
Romans do not enter upon an unjust war against
any city in alliance with them, and if others begin
the violation of treaties against them, to go as ambassadors and first make formal demand for justice,
and then, if the others refuse to comply with their
demands, to sanction war. In like manner, if any
people in alliance with the Romans complain of
having been injured by them and demand justice,
these men are to determine whether they have suffered anything in violation of their alliance ; and
if they find their complaints well grounded, they are
to seize the accused and deliver them up to the
injured parties. They are also to take cognizance

DIONYSIUS OF HALICARNASSUS

πρεσβευτὰς ἀδικήματα δικάζειν καὶ τὰ περὶ τὰς
συνθήκας ὅσια φυλάττειν εἰρήνην τε ποιεῖσθαι
καὶ γεγενημένην, ἐὰν μὴ κατὰ τοὺς ἱεροὺς δόξῃ
πεπρᾶχθαι νόμους, ἀκυροῦν καὶ τὰς τῶν στρατηγῶν παρανομίας, ὅσαι περί τε ὅρκους καὶ σπονδὰς
ἐπιτελοῦνται, διαγινώσκοντας ἀφοσιοῦσθαι, περὶ ὧν
κατὰ τοὺς οἰκείους καιροὺς ποιήσομαι τὸν λόγον.
6 τὰ δὲ περὶ τὰς ἐπικηρυκείας ὑπ' αὐτῶν γινόμενα,
ὅτε τὴν δόξασαν ἀδικεῖν πόλιν αἰτοῖεν δίκας (ἄξιον
γὰρ μηδὲ ταῦτ' ἀγνοεῖν κατὰ πολλὴν φροντίδα τῶν
ὁσίων καὶ δικαίων γινόμενα) τοιαῦτα παρέλαβον·
εἷς μὲν ἐκ τῶν εἰρηνοδικῶν, ὃν οἱ λοιποὶ προχειρί-
σαιντο, κεκοσμημένος ἐσθῆτι καὶ φορήμασιν ἱεροῖς,
ἵνα διάδηλος ᾖ παρὰ τοὺς ἄλλους, εἰς τὴν τῶν
ἀδικούντων παρεγίνετο πόλιν· ἐπιστὰς δὲ τοῖς
ὁρίοις τόν τε Δία καὶ τοὺς ἄλλους ἐπεκαλεῖτο
θεοὺς μαρτυρόμενος ὅτι δίκας αἰτῶν ἥκει ὑπὲρ[1]
7 τῆς Ῥωμαίων πόλεως· ἔπειτα ὀμόσας ὅτι πρὸς
ἀδικοῦσαν ἔρχεται πόλιν καὶ ἀρὰς τὰς μεγίστας εἰ
ψεύδοιτο ἐπαρασάμενος ἑαυτῷ τε καὶ τῇ Ῥώμῃ,
τότ' ἐντὸς ᾔει τῶν ὅρων· ἔπειτα ὅτῳ πρώτῳ περι-
τύχοι τοῦτον ἐπιμαρτυράμενος, εἴτε τῶν ἀγροίκων
εἴτε τῶν πολιτικῶν εἴη, καὶ τὰς αὐτὰς προσθεὶς
ἀρὰς πρὸς τὴν πόλιν ᾤχετο, κᾆτα πρὶν εἰς τὴν
πόλιν παρελθεῖν τὸν πυλωρὸν ἢ τὸν πρῶτον ἀπαν-
τήσαντα ἐν ταῖς πύλαις τὸν αὐτὸν τρόπον ἐπιμαρτυράμενος εἰς τὴν ἀγορὰν προῄει· ἐκεῖ δὲ

---

[1] ὑπὲρ Hertlein, following Reiske; παρὰ Kiessling: περὶ
O, Jacoby.

524

of the crimes committed against ambassadors, to take care that treaties are religiously observed, to make peace, and if they find that peace has been made otherwise than is prescribed by the holy laws, to set it aside; and to inquire into and expiate the transgressions of the generals in so far as they relate to oaths and treaties, concerning which I shall speak in the proper places. As to the functions they performed in the quality of heralds when they went to demand justice of any city thought to have injured the Romans (for these things also are worthy of our knowledge, since they were carried out with great regard to both religion and justice), I have received the following account: One of these *fetiales*, chosen by his colleagues, wearing his sacred robes and insignia to distinguish him from all others, proceeded towards the city whose inhabitants had done the injury; and, stopping at the border, he called upon Jupiter and the rest of the gods to witness that he was come to demand justice on behalf of the Roman State. Thereupon he took an oath that he was going to a city that had done an injury; and having uttered the most dreadful imprecations against himself and Rome, if what he averred was not true, he then entered their borders. Afterwards, he called to witness the first person he met, whether it was one of the countrymen or one of the townspeople, and having repeated the same imprecations, he advanced towards the city. And before he entered it he called to witness in the same manner the gatekeeper or the first person he met at the gates, after which he proceeded to the forum; and taking his

καταστὰς τοῖς ἐν τέλει περὶ ὧν ἥκοι διελέγετο
πανταχῆ τούς τε ὅρκους καὶ τὰς ἀρὰς προστιθείς.
8 εἰ μὲν οὖν ὑπέχοιεν τὰς δίκας παραδιδόντες τοὺς ἐν
ταῖς αἰτίαις, ἀπῄει τοὺς ἄνδρας ἀπάγων φίλος τε
ἤδη γεγονὼς καὶ παρὰ φίλων· εἰ δὲ χρόνον εἰς
βουλὴν αἰτήσαιντο δέκα διδοὺς ἡμέρας παρεγίνετο
πάλιν καὶ μέχρι τρίτης αἰτήσεως ἀνεδέχετο. διελ-
θουσῶν δὲ τῶν τριάκοντα ἡμερῶν, εἰ μὴ παρεῖχεν
αὐτῷ τὰ δίκαια ἡ πόλις, ἐπικαλεσάμενος τούς τε
οὐρανίους καὶ καταχθονίους θεοὺς ἀπῄει, τοσοῦτο
μόνον εἰπὼν ὅτι βουλεύσεται περὶ αὐτῶν ἡ Ῥω-
9 μαίων πόλις ἐφ᾽ ἡσυχίας. καὶ μετὰ τοῦτο ἀπέ-
φαινεν εἰς τὴν βουλὴν ἅμα τοῖς ἄλλοις εἰρηνοδίκαις
παραγενόμενος ὅτι πέπρακται πᾶν αὐτοῖς ὅσον ἦν
ὅσιον ἐκ τῶν ἱερῶν νόμων καὶ εἰ βούλοιντο ψηφί-
ζεσθαι πόλεμον οὐδὲν ἔσται τὸ κωλῦσον ἀπὸ θεῶν.
εἰ δέ τι μὴ γένοιτο τούτων οὔτε ἡ βουλὴ κυρία ἦν
ἐπιψηφίσασθαι πόλεμον οὔτε ὁ δῆμος. περὶ μὲν
οὖν τῶν εἰρηνοδικῶν τοσαῦτα παρελάβομεν.

LXXIII. Τελευταῖος δ᾽ ἦν τῆς Νόμα διατάξεως
μερισμὸς ὑπὲρ τῶν ἱερῶν, ὧν ἔλαχον οἱ τὴν μεγίστην
παρὰ Ῥωμαίοις ἱερατείαν καὶ ἐξουσίαν ἔχοντες.
οὗτοι κατὰ μὲν τὴν ἑαυτῶν διάλεκτον ἐφ᾽ ἑνὸς τῶν
ἔργων ὃ πράττουσιν ἐπισκευάζοντες τὴν ξυλίνην
γέφυραν ποντίφικες προσαγορεύονται, εἰσὶ δὲ τῶν

---

[1] Cf. Livy i. 20, 5–7.
[2] According to Dionysius himself (iii. 45) the *pons
sublicius* was built by Ancus Marcius ; but it will be noted

stand there, he discussed with the magistrates the reasons for his coming, adding everywhere the same oaths and imprecations. If, then, they were disposed to offer satisfaction by delivering up the guilty, he departed as a friend taking leave of friends, carrying the prisoners with him. Or, if they desired time to deliberate, he allowed them ten days, after which he returned and waited till they had made this request three times. But after the expiration of the thirty days, if the city still persisted in refusing to grant him justice, he called both the celestial and infernal gods to witness and went away, saying no more than this, that the Roman State would deliberate at its leisure concerning these people. Afterwards he, together with the other *fetiales*, appeared before the senate and declared that they had done everything that was ordained by the holy laws, and that, if the senators wished to vote for war, there would be no obstacle on the part of the gods. But if any of these things was omitted, neither the senate nor the people had the power to vote for war. Such, then, is the account we have received concerning the *fetiales*.

LXXIII. The last branch of the ordinances of Numa related to the sacred offices allotted to those who held the highest priesthood and the greatest power among the Romans.[1] These, from one of the duties they perform, namely, the repairing of the wooden bridge,[2] are in their own language called *pontifices;* but they have jurisdiction over the most

that he does not say explicitly that these priests bore the name *pontifices* from the first.

2 μεγίστων πραγμάτων κύριοι. καὶ γὰρ δικάζουσιν
οὗτοι τὰς ἱερὰς δίκας ἁπάσας ἰδιώταις τε καὶ
ἄρχουσι καὶ λειτουργοῖς θεῶν καὶ νομοθετοῦσιν
ὅσα τῶν ἱερῶν, ἄγραφα ὄντα καὶ ἀνέθιστα,[1] ἐπιτή-
δεια τυγχάνειν αὐτοῖς φανείη νόμων τε καὶ ἐθισμῶν ·
τάς τε ἀρχὰς ἁπάσας, ὅσαις θυσία τις ἢ θεραπεία
θεῶν ἀνάκειται, καὶ τοὺς ἱερεῖς ἅπαντας ἐξετά-
ζουσιν, ὑπηρέτας τε αὐτῶν καὶ λειτουργούς, οἷς
χρῶνται πρὸς τὰ ἱερά, οὗτοι φυλάττουσι μηδὲν
ἐξαμαρτάνειν περὶ[2] τοὺς ἱεροὺς νόμους · τοῖς τε
ἰδιώταις ὁπόσοι μὴ ἴσασι τοὺς περὶ τὰ θεῖα ἢ
δαιμόνια σεβασμούς, ἐξηγηταὶ γίνονται καὶ προ-
φῆται · καὶ εἴ τινας αἴσθοιντο μὴ πειθομένους
ταῖς ἐπιταγαῖς αὐτῶν, ζημιοῦσι πρὸς ἕκαστον
χρῆμα ὁρῶντες, εἰσί τε ἀνυπεύθυνοι πάσης δίκης
τε καὶ ζημίας οὔτε βουλῇ λόγον ἀποδιδόντες οὔτε
3 δήμῳ, περὶ γοῦν[3] τῶν ἱερῶν[4] · ὥστε εἰ βούλεταί
τις αὐτοὺς ἱεροδιδασκάλους καλεῖν εἴτε ἱερονόμους
εἴτε ἱεροφύλακας εἴτε, ὡς ἡμεῖς ἀξιοῦμεν, ἱεροφάν-
τας, οὐχ ἁμαρτήσεται τοῦ ἀληθοῦς. ἐκλιπόντος
δέ τινος αὐτῶν τὸν βίον ἕτερος εἰς τὸν ἐκείνου
καθίσταται τόπον οὐχ ὑπὸ τοῦ δήμου αἱρεθείς,
ἀλλ' ὑπ' αὐτῶν ἐκείνων, ὃς ἂν ἐπιτηδειότατος εἶναι
δοκῇ τῶν πολιτῶν · παραλαμβάνει δὲ τὴν ἱερατείαν

---

[1] κρίνοντες ἃ ἂν after ἀνέθιστα deleted by Kiessling. Reiske
rejected κρίνοντες, reading ἀνέθιστα νομίζωσιν ἀποδοχῆς ἄξια
εἶναι ἀκυροῦσι δὲ ἃ ἂν ἀνεπιτήδεια κ.τ.έ. Jacoby retained
κρίνοντες ἃ ἂν, indicating a lacuna before these words.
[2] περὶ Ab : παρὰ AaB.   [3] γοῦν Kiessling : οὖν O.
[4] ἱερῶν Kiessling : ἱερέων O.

weighty matters. For they are the judges in all religious causes wherein private citizens, magistrates or the ministers of the gods are concerned ; they make laws for the observance of any religious rites, not established by written law or by custom, which may seem to them worthy of receiving the sanction of law and custom ; they inquire into the conduct of all magistrates to whom the performance of any sacrifice or other religious duty is committed, and also into that of all the priests ; they take care that their servants and ministers whom they employ in religious rites commit no error in the matter of the sacred laws ; to the laymen who are unacquainted with such matters they are the expounders and interpreters of everything relating to the worship of the gods and genii ; and if they find that any disobey their orders, they inflict punishment upon them with due regard to every offence ; moreover, they are not liable to any prosecution or punishment, nor are they accountable to the senate or to the people, at least concerning religious matters. Hence, if anyone wishes to call them *hierodidaskaloi, hieronomoi, hierophylakes,* or, as I think proper, *hierophantai,*[1] he will not be in error. When one of them dies, another is appointed in his place, being chosen, not by the people, but by the *pontifices* themselves, who select the person they think best qualified among their fellow citizens ; and the one thus

---

[1] These words mean respectively "teachers of religion," "supervisors of religion," "guardians of religion" and "interpreters of religion." The last is the term regularly employed by Dionysius when he translates the word *pontifices.*

ὁ δοκιμασθείς, ἐὰν εὐόρνιθες αὐτῷ τύχωσιν οἰωνοὶ
4 γενόμενοι. τὰ μὲν δὴ περὶ τὸ θεῖον νομοθετηθέντα
ὑπὸ τοῦ Νόμα καὶ διαιρεθέντα κατὰ τὰς συμμορίας
τῶν ἱερῶν, ἐξ ὧν εὐσεβεστέραν συνέβη γενέσθαι
τὴν πόλιν, πρὸς τοῖς ἄλλοις ἐλάττοσι τὰ μέγιστα
καὶ φανερώτατα ταῦτ' ἦν.

LXXIV. Τὰ δ' εἰς εὐτέλειάν τε καὶ σωφροσύνην
ἄγοντα τὸν ἑκάστου βίον καὶ εἰς ἐπιθυμίαν καταστήσαντα τῆς φυλαττούσης ἐν ὁμονοίᾳ τὴν πόλιν
δικαιοσύνης πλεῖστα ὅσα, τὰ μὲν ἐγγράφοις περιλη-
φθέντα νόμοις, τὰ δ' ἔξω γραφῆς εἰς ἐπιτηδεύσεις
ἀχθέντα καὶ συνασκήσεις χρονίους· ὑπὲρ ὧν ἁπάντων μὲν πολὺ ἂν ἔργον εἴη λέγειν, ἀρκέσει δὲ δύο
τὰ μεγίστης μνήμης τυχόντα τεκμήρια καὶ τῶν
2 ἄλλων γενέσθαι· τῆς μὲν αὐταρκείας καὶ τοῦ μηδένα τῶν ἀλλοτρίων ἐπιθυμεῖν ἡ περὶ τοὺς ὁρισμοὺς
τῶν κτήσεων νομοθεσία. κελεύσας γὰρ ἑκάστῳ
περιγράψαι τὴν ἑαυτοῦ κτῆσιν καὶ στῆσαι λίθους
ἐπὶ τοῖς ὅροις ἱεροὺς ἀπέδειξεν Ὁρίου Διὸς τοὺς
λίθους, καὶ θυσίας ἔταξεν αὐτοῖς ἐπιτελεῖν ἅπαντας
ἡμέρᾳ τακτῇ καθ' ἕκαστον ἐνιαυτὸν ἐπὶ τὸν τόπον
συνερχομένους, ἑορτὴν ἐν τοῖς [1] πάνυ τιμίαν [2] τὴν
3 τῶν ὁρίων θεῶν καταστησάμενος. ταύτην Ῥωμαῖοι
Τερμινάλια καλοῦσιν ἐπὶ τῶν τερμόνων καὶ τοὺς
ὅρους αὐτοὺς ἑνὸς ἀλλαγῇ γράμματος παρὰ τὴν
ἡμετέραν διάλεκτον ἐκφέροντες τέρμινας [3] προσα-

---

[1] τοῖς Meineke : ταῖς O.
[2] καὶ after τιμίαν deleted by Bücheler.
[3] τέρμινας B, τερμῖνας A ; probably an error for τέρμινα or τερμίνους.

approved of receives the priesthood, provided the
omens are favourable to him. These—not to speak
of others less important—are the greatest and the
most notable regulations made by Numa concerning
religious worship and divided by him according
to the different classes of sacred rites; and through
these it came about that the city increased in
piety.

LXXIV. His regulations, moreover, that tended
to inspire frugality and moderation in the life of
the individual citizen and to create a passion for
justice, which preserves the harmony of the State,
were exceedingly numerous, some of them being
comprehended in written laws, and others not written
down but embodied in custom and long usage. To
treat of all these would be a difficult task; but
mention of the two of them which have been most
frequently cited will suffice to give evidence of the
rest. First, to the end that people should be content with what they had and should not covet what
belonged to others, there was the law that appointed
boundaries to every man's possessions. For, having
ordered every one to draw a line around his own land
and to place stones on the bounds, he consecrated
these stones to Jupiter Terminalis and ordained
that all should assemble at the place every year on
a fixed day and offer sacrifices to them; and he
made the festival in honour of these gods of
boundaries among the most dignified of all. This
festival the Romans call Terminalia, from the
boundaries, and the boundaries themselves, by the
change of one letter as compared with our language,

531

γορεύουσιν. εἰ δέ τις ἀφανίσειεν ἢ μεταθείη τοὺς
ὅρους, ἱερὸν ἐνομοθέτησεν εἶναι τοῦ θεοῦ τὸν τούτων τι διαπραξάμενον, ἵνα τῷ βουλομένῳ κτείνειν
αὐτὸν ὡς ἱερόσυλον ἥ τε ἀσφάλεια καὶ τὸ καθαρῷ
4 μιάσματος εἶναι προσῇ. τοῦτο δ᾽ οὐκ ἐπὶ τῶν
ἰδιωτικῶν κατεστήσατο μόνον κτήσεων τὸ δίκαιον,
ἀλλὰ καὶ ἐπὶ τῶν δημοσίων, ὅροις κἀκείνας περι-
λαβών, ἵνα καὶ τὴν Ῥωμαίων γῆν ἀπὸ τῆς ἀστυγεί-
τονος ὅριοι διαιρῶσι θεοὶ καὶ τὴν κοινὴν ἀπὸ τῆς
ἰδίας. τούτου[1] μέχρι τῶν καθ᾽ ἡμᾶς χρόνων
φυλάττουσι Ῥωμαῖοι μνημεῖα[2] τῆς ὁσίας αὐτῆς
ἕνεκα. θεούς τε γὰρ ἡγοῦνται τοὺς τέρμονας καὶ
θύουσιν αὐτοῖς ὁσέτη, τῶν μὲν ἐμψύχων οὐδέν (οὐ
γὰρ ὅσιον αἱμάττειν τοὺς λίθους), πελάνους δὲ δη-
5 μητρίους[3] καὶ ἄλλας τινὰς καρπῶν ἀπαρχάς. ἐχρῆν
δὲ καὶ τὸ ἔργον ἔτι φυλάττειν αὐτούς, οὗ[4] χάριν
θεοὺς ἐνόμισε[5] τοὺς τέρμονας ὁ Νόμας,[6] ἱκανουμέ-
νους τοῖς ἑαυτῶν κτήμασι, τῶν δ᾽ ἀλλοτρίων μήτε

---

[1] τούτου Schmitz: τοῦτο O, Jacoby.
[2] Before μνημεῖα the MSS. have τοῦ χρόνου, deleted, however, in B. Casaubon regarded these words as corrupt;
Reiske emended to τοῦ ἀρχαίου or τοῦ τότε χρόνου, Bücheler
to τοῦ νόμου.
[3] Meineke: δήμητρος O.
[4] αὐτούς, οὗ Canter, αὐτούς, ὅτου Portus, αὐτό, οὗ Sylburg,
ἅπαντας, οὗ Reiske, πιστὸν αὐτούς, οὗ Jacoby, ἀπὸ τοῦ ἴσου, οὗ
Ambrosch, Sintenis: ἀπυτονάσου A, ἀπαυτου .. ου B (but last
ου changed to οὗ by Bb).
[5] ἐνόμισε Bücheler: ἐνόμισαν O.
[6] ὁ Νόμας Bücheler: ὀνομάσαι Ba, ὀνομάσαι BbR.

they call *termines*.[1] He also enacted that, if any
person demolished or displaced these boundary stones
he should be looked upon as devoted to the god, to
the end that anyone who wished might kill him as
a sacrilegious person with impunity and without
incurring any stain of guilt. He established this
law with reference not only to private possessions
but also to those belonging to the public; for he
marked these also with boundary stones, to the
end that the gods of boundaries might distinguish
the lands of the Romans from those of their neighbours, and the public lands from such as belonged
to private persons. Memorials of this custom are observed by the Romans down to our times, purely
as a religious form. For they look upon these boundary stones as gods and sacrifice to them yearly,
offering up no kind of animal (for it is not lawful
to stain these stones with blood), but cakes made
of cereals and other first-fruits of the earth. But
they ought still to observe the motive, as well,
which led Numa to regard these boundary stones
as gods and content themselves with their own
possessions without appropriating those of others

[1] When Dionysius says that the Latin and Greek words
differ by only one letter he is almost certainly referring
to the stem (*termin-* : τερμον-) or to the nominative singular (*termen* : τέρμων); he would naturally disregard
the case-endings, since he regularly inflects Latin words
as if they were Greek. The form τέρμινας, *i.e. terminēs*,
can hardly be from the hand of Dionysius, who must have
known that most nouns terminating in -*men* were neuter
(compare his κάρμινα, *carmina*, in i. 31). The true form
here should evidently be either τέρμινα or τερμίνους, *i.e.
termina* or *termini* (to cite them in the nominative).

DIONYSIUS OF HALICARNASSUS

βίᾳ σφετεριζομένους μηδὲν μήτε δόλῳ. νῦν δ' οὐχ
ὡς ἄμεινον οὐδ' ὡς οἱ πρόγονοι παρέδοσαν ὁρίζουσί
τινες ἀπὸ τῶν ἀλλοτρίων τὰ οἰκεῖα, ἀλλ' ἔστιν αὐτοῖς ὅρος τῶν κτήσεων οὐχ ὁ νόμος, ἀλλ' ἡ πάντων
ἐπιθυμία, πρᾶγμα οὐ καλόν. ἀλλ' ὑπὲρ μὲν τούτων
ἑτέροις[1] παρίεμεν σκοπεῖν.

LXXV. Ὁ δὲ Νόμας εἰς μὲν εὐτέλειαν καὶ
σωφροσύνην διὰ τοιούτων συνέστειλε[2] νόμων τὴν
πόλιν, εἰς δὲ τὴν περὶ τὰ συμβόλαια δικαιοσύνην
ὑπηγάγετο πρᾶγμα ἐξευρὼν ἠγνοημένον ὑπὸ πάντων τῶν καταστησαμένων τὰς ἐλλογίμους πολιτείας.
ὁρῶν γὰρ ὅτι τῶν συμβολαίων τὰ μὲν ἐν φανερῷ
καὶ μετὰ μαρτύρων πραττόμενα ἡ τῶν συνόντων
αἰδὼς φυλάττει, καὶ σπάνιοί τινές εἰσιν οἱ περὶ τὰ
τοιαῦτα ἀδικοῦντες, τὰ δὲ ἀμάρτυρα πολλῷ πλείω
τῶν ἑτέρων ὄντα μίαν ἔχει φυλακὴν τὴν τῶν συμ-
βαλόντων πίστιν, περὶ ταύτην ᾤετο δεῖν σπουδάσαι
παντὸς ἄλλου μάλιστα καὶ ποιῆσαι θείων σεβασμῶν
2 ἀξίαν. Δίκην μὲν γὰρ καὶ Θέμιν καὶ Νέμεσιν καὶ
τὰς καλουμένας παρ' Ἕλλησιν Ἐρινύας καὶ ὅσα
τούτοις ὅμοια ὑπὸ τῶν πρότερον ἀποχρώντως ἐκ-
τεθειῶσθαί τε καὶ καθωσιῶσθαι ἐνόμισε, Πίστιν
δέ, ἧς οὔτε μεῖζον οὔτε ἱερώτερον πάθος ἐν ἀνθρώποις οὐδέν, οὔπω σεβασμῶν τυγχάνειν οὔτ' ἐν τοῖς
κοινοῖς τῶν πόλεων πράγμασιν οὔτ' ἐν τοῖς ἰδίοις.
3 ταῦτα δὴ διανοηθεὶς πρῶτος ἀνθρώπων ἱερὸν
ἱδρύσατο Πίστεως δημοσίας καὶ θυσίας αὐτῇ κατεστήσατο, καθάπερ καὶ τοῖς ἄλλοις θεοῖς, δημο-

---

[1] Steph.: ἐν ἑτέροις AB.
[2] συνέστειλε B : συνέστησε R.

534

either by violence or by fraud ; whereas now there are some who, in disregard of what is best and of the example of their ancestors, instead of distinguishing that which is theirs from that which belongs to others, set as bounds to their possessions, not the law, but their greed to possess everything, —which is disgraceful behaviour. But we leave the considerations of these matters to others.

LXXV. By such laws Numa brought the State to frugality and moderation. And in order to encourage the observance of justice in the matter of contracts, he hit upon a device which was unknown to all who have established the most celebrated constitutions. For, observing that contracts made in public and before witnesses are, out of respect for the persons present, generally observed and that few are guilty of any violation of them, but that those which are made without witnesses—and these are much more numerous than the others—rest on no other security than the faith of those who make them, he thought it incumbent on him to make this faith the chief object of his care and to render it worthy of divine worship. For he felt that Justice, Themis, Nemesis, and those the Greeks call Erinyes, with other concepts of the kind, had been sufficiently revered and worshipped as gods by the men of former times, but that Faith, than which there is nothing greater nor more sacred among men, was not yet worshipped either by states in their public capacity or by private persons. As the result of these reflexions he, first of all men, erected a temple to the Public Faith and instituted sacrifices in her honour at the public expense in the same manner as

τελεῖς. ἔμελλε δὲ ἄρα σὺν χρόνῳ τὸ κοινὸν τῆς
πόλεως ἦθος πιστὸν καὶ βέβαιον πρὸς ἀνθρώπους
γενόμενον τοιούτους ἀπεργάσασθαι καὶ τοὺς τῶν
ἰδιωτῶν τρόπους. οὕτω γοῦν σεβαστόν τι πρᾶγμα
καὶ ἀμίαντον ἐνομίσθη τὸ πιστόν, ὥστε ὅρκον τε
μέγιστον γενέσθαι τὴν ἰδίαν ἑκάστῳ πίστιν καὶ
μαρτυρίας συμπάσης ἰσχυροτάτην, καὶ ὁπότε ὑπὲρ
ἀμαρτύρου συναλλάγματος ἀμφίλογόν τι γένοιτο ἑνὶ
πρὸς ἕνα, ἡ διαιροῦσα τὸ νεῖκος καὶ προσωτέρω
χωρεῖν οὐκ ἐῶσα τὰς φιλονεικίας ἡ θατέρου τῶν
διαδικαζομένων αὐτῶν πίστις ἦν, αἵ τε ἀρχαὶ καὶ
4 τὰ δικαστήρια τὰ πλεῖστα τῶν ἀμφισβητημάτων
τοῖς ἐκ τῆς πίστεως ὅρκοις διῆτων. τοιαῦτα[1] μὲν
δὴ σωφροσύνης τε παρακλητικὰ καὶ δικαιοσύνης
ἀναγκαστήρια ὑπὸ τοῦ Νόμα τότε ἐξευρεθέντα
κοσμιωτέραν οἰκίας τῆς κράτιστα οἰκουμένης τὴν
Ῥωμαίων πόλιν ἀπειργάσατο.

LXXVI. Ἃ δὲ μέλλω νῦν λέγειν ἐπιμελῆ τε
αὐτὴν ἀπέδωκε τῶν ἀναγκαίων καὶ τῶν ἀγαθῶν
ἐργάτιν. ἐνθυμούμενος γὰρ ὁ ἀνήρ, ὅτι πόλιν τὴν
μέλλουσαν ἀγαπήσειν τὰ δίκαια καὶ μενεῖν[2] ἐν τῷ
σώφρονι βίῳ τῆς ἀναγκαίου δεῖ χορηγίας εὐπορεῖν,
διεῖλε τὴν χώραν ἅπασαν εἰς τοὺς καλουμένους
πάγους καὶ κατέστησεν ἐφ' ἑκάστου τῶν πάγων
ἄρχοντα ἐπίσκοπόν τε καὶ περίπολον τῆς ἰδίας
2 μοίρας. οὗτοι γὰρ περιόντες θαμινὰ τοὺς εὖ τε

[1] διῆτων. τοιαῦτα Kiessling: διητωντο · ταῦτα B, διῆτων·
ταῦτα R.
[2] μενεῖν Kiessling: μένειν O.

to the rest of the gods.[1] And in truth the result was bound to be that this attitude of good faith and constancy on the part of the State toward all men would in the course of time render the behaviour of the individual citizens similar. In any case, so revered and inviolable a thing was good faith in their estimation, that the greatest oath a man could take was by his own faith, and this had greater weight than all the testimony taken together. And if there was any dispute between one man and another concerning a contract entered into without witnesses, the faith of either of the parties was sufficient to decide the controversy and prevent it from going any farther. And the magistrates and courts of justice based their decisions in most causes on the oaths of the parties attesting by their faith. Such regulations, devised by Numa at that time to encourage moderation and enforce justice, rendered the Roman State more orderly than the best regulated household.

LXXVI. But the measures which I am now going to relate made it both careful to provide itself with necessaries and industrious in acquiring the advantages that flow from labour. For this man, considering that a State which was to love justice and to continue in the practice of moderation ought to abound in all things necessary to the support of life, divided the whole country into what are called *pagi* or " districts," and over each of these districts he appointed an official whose duty it was to inspect and visit the lands lying in his own jurisdiction. These men, going their rounds frequently, made a

[1] *Cf.* Livy i. 21, 1 and 4.

καὶ κακῶς εἰργασμένους τῶν ἀγρῶν ἀπεγράφοντο
καὶ πρὸς τὸν βασιλέα ἀπέφαινον, ὁ δὲ τοὺς μὲν
ἐπιμελεῖς γεωργοὺς ἐπαίνοις τε καὶ φιλανθρωπίαις
ἀνελάμβανε, τοὺς δὲ ἀργοὺς[1] ὀνειδίζων τε καὶ
ζημιῶν ἐπὶ τὸ θεραπεύειν ἄμεινον τὴν γῆν προὔ-
τρέπετο. τοιγάρτοι πολέμων τε ἀπηλλαγμένοι καὶ
τῶν κατὰ πόλιν πραγμάτων σχολὴν πολλὴν ἄγοντες
ἀργίας τε καὶ βλακείας σὺν αἰσχύνῃ τίνοντες δίκας
αὐτουργοὶ πάντες ἐγίνοντο καὶ τὸν ἐκ γῆς πλοῦτον
ἁπάντων ὄντα[2] δικαιότατον τῆς στρατιωτικῆς καὶ
οὐκ ἐχούσης τὸ βέβαιον εὐπορίας γλυκύτερον ἐτί-
3 θεντο. τῷ δὲ Νόμα περιῆν ἐκ τούτων φιλεῖσθαι
μὲν ὑπὸ τῶν ἀρχομένων, ζηλοῦσθαι δ᾽ ὑπὸ τῶν
περιοίκων, μνημονεύεσθαι δ᾽ ὑπὸ τῶν ἐπιγινομένων·
δι᾽ ὧν οὔτε στάσις ἐμφύλιος τὴν πολιτικὴν ἔλυσεν
ὁμόνοιαν, οὔτε πόλεμος ἀλλοεθνὴς ἐκ τῶν κρατίστων καὶ θαυμασιωτάτων τὴν πόλιν ἐπιτηδευμάτων
ἐκίνησε. τοσοῦτον γὰρ ἀπέσχον οἱ περίοικοι τὴν
ἀπόλεμον ἡσυχίαν Ῥωμαίων ἀφορμὴν τῆς κατ᾽
αὐτῶν ἐπιθέσεως ὑπολαβεῖν, ὥστε καὶ εἴ τις αὐτοῖς πρὸς ἀλλήλους συνέστη πόλεμος διαλλακτῆρας
ἐποιοῦντο Ῥωμαίους καὶ ἐπὶ διαιτητῇ Νόμα τὰς
4 ἔχθρας διαλύειν ἠξίουν. τοῦτον οὖν[3] οὐκ ἂν
αἰσχυνθείην ἐγὼ τὸν ἄνδρα τῶν ἐπ᾽ εὐδαιμονίᾳ
διαβοηθέντων ἐν τοῖς πρώτοις καταριθμεῖν. γένους
τε γὰρ ἔφυ βασιλείου καὶ μορφῆς ἀπέλαυσε βασιλικῆς παιδείαν τε οὐ τὴν περὶ λόγους[4] ἄχρηστον

---

[1] γεωργοὺς after ἀργοὺς deleted by Meineke, Bücheler.
[2] πλούτων after ὄντα deleted by Kiessling.
[3] οὖν added by Steph.².   [4] λόγους Steph.: λόγον O.

record of the lands that were well and ill cultivated and laid it before the king, who repaid the diligence of the careful husbandmen with commendations and favours, and by reprimanding and fining the slothful encouraged them to cultivate their lands with greater attention. Accordingly, the people, being freed from wars and exempt from any attendance on the affairs of the State, and at the same time being disgraced and punished for idleness and sloth, all became husbandmen and looked upon the riches which the earth yields and which of all others are the most just as more enjoyable than the precarious affluence of a military life. And by the same means Numa came to be beloved of his subjects, the example of his neighbours, and the theme of posterity. It was owing to these measures that neither civil dissension broke the harmony of the State nor foreign war interrupted the observance of his most excellent and admirable institutions. For their neighbours were so far from looking upon the peaceful tranquillity of the Romans as an opportunity for attacking them, that, if at any time they were at war with one another, they chose the Romans for mediators and wished to settle their enmities under the arbitration of Numa. This man, therefore, I should take no shame in placing among the foremost of those who have been celebrated for their felicity in life. For he was of royal birth and of royal appearance ; and he pursued an education which was not the kind of useless training that deals only with words,[1] but a discipline that taught

---

[1] A thrust at the sophists or rhetoricians.

DIONYSIUS OF HALICARNASSUS

ἤσκησεν, ἀλλ' ἐξ ἧς εὐσεβεῖν ἔμαθε καὶ τὰς ἄλλας
5 ἐπιτηδεύειν ἀρετάς. ἡγεμονίαν δὲ τὴν Ῥωμαίων
παραλαβεῖν ἠξιώθη νέος ὢν κατὰ κλέος ἀρετῆς ὑπ'
αὐτῶν ἐπίκλητος ἀχθεὶς καὶ διετέλεσε πειθομένοις
ἅπαντα τὸν βίον τοῖς ἀρχομένοις χρώμενος · ἡλικίας
δ' ἐπὶ μήκιστον ἤλασεν ὁλόκληρος οὐδὲν ὑπὸ τῆς
τύχης κακωθεὶς καὶ θανάτων τὸν ῥᾷστον ἐτελεύ-
τησεν ὑπὸ γήρως μαρανθείς, ὁμοίου παραμείναντος
αὐτῷ τοῦ συγκληρωθέντος ἐξ ἀρχῆς δαίμονος ἕως
ἐξ ἀνθρώπων ἠφανίσθη, βιώσας μὲν ὑπὲρ ὀγδοήκοντα ἔτη, βασιλεύσας δὲ τρία καὶ τετταράκοντα,
γενεὰν δὲ καταλιπών, ὡς μὲν οἱ πλείους γράφουσιν,
υἱοὺς τέτταρας καὶ θυγατέρα μίαν, ὧν ἔτι σώζεται
τὰ γένη, ὡς δὲ Γέλλιος Γναῖος ἱστορεῖ, θυγατέρα
μόνην, ἐξ ἧς ἐγένετο Ἄγκος Μάρκιος ὁ τρίτος ἀπ'
6 ἐκείνου γενόμενος Ῥωμαίων βασιλεύς. τελευτήσαντι δ' αὐτῷ πένθος μέγα προύθετο ἡ πόλις καὶ
ταφὰς ἐποιήσατο λαμπροτάτας. κεῖται δ' ἐν
Ἰανίκλῳ πέραν τοῦ Τεβέριος ποταμοῦ. καὶ τὰ
μὲν περὶ Πομπιλίου Νόμα τοσαῦτα παρελάβομεν.

him to practise piety and every other virtue. When
he was young he was thought worthy to assume the
sovereignty over the Romans, who had invited him
to that dignity upon the reputation of his virtue;
and he continued to command the obedience of
his subjects during his whole life. He lived to a
very advanced age without any impairment of
his faculties and without suffering any blow at
Fortune's hands; and he died the easiest of all
deaths, being withered by age, the genius who had
been allotted to him from his birth having continued
the same favour to him till he disappeared from
among men. He lived more than eighty years and
reigned forty-three, leaving behind him, according to
most historians, four sons and one daughter, whose
posterity remain to this day; but according to
Gnaeus Gellius he left only one daughter, who was
the mother of Ancus Marcius, the second [1] king
of the Romans after him. His death was greatly
lamented by the state, which gave him a most
splendid funeral. He lies buried upon the Janiculum,
on the other side of the river Tiber. Such is the account we have received concerning Numa Pompilius.

[1] Literally, "the third," counting inclusively.

INDEX

ABORIGINES, origin of, 31-43, 307, 415 ; cities of, 43-49, 51-55, 61, 449, 451, 457, cf. 65 f. ; unite with Pelasgians, 55, 61-67, 69, 75, 83, 315, 451 ; early dwellers on site of Rome, 29, 99, 109, 125, 129, 307, 313 f. ; under rule of Faunus, 101, 139, 141, 143 ; under Latinus, 143, 189 f., 195-201, 209, 239, 241 : called Latins, 31, 201.

Acallaris, ancestress of Aeneas, 207.

Acarnanians, 165, 169 and notes.

Achaeans, take Troy, 145-51, 157, 173, 193, 209, 229, 237, 505.

—— a nation in the Peloponnesus, 83 ; cf. 309.

—— a tribe on the eastern shore of the Euxine, 309.

Achaeus, son of Poseidon, 57.

Achaia, in the Peloponnesus, 35, 83.

—— in Thessaly, 57.

Achilles, 157, 173.

Actê, peninsula of Chalcidicê, 81.

Actium, 165.

Adriatic sea, 9, 453.

Aegesta (Segesta), city in Sicily, 173 f.

Aegestus, a Trojan, 151, 171-75.

—— a priest at Lavinium, 221.

—— son of Numitor, 253.

Aelii, the, 25 and n. 2.

Aemilia, a Vestal, 511.

Aeneas, ancestry of, 207, cf. 201 f. ; at fall of Troy, 147-51, 157 ; leads Trojans to Italy, 143 f., 153-201, 209 f., 317, 505, cf. 219, 237, 241 f. ; death of, 211 f. ; shrines and monuments to, 167, 175, 179 f., 213.

—— (different from preceding), leads Trojans to Italy, 177.

—— son of Silvius, Alban king, 233.

Aeneia, town in Thrace, 161 f., cf. 179.

—— town in Latium, 243.

Aeneias, cult-title of Aphroditê, 165, 175.

Aequicoli, Italian tribe, 521.

Aeschylus, tragic poet (525-456), 137.

Aetolians, 57, 169.

Aezeians, earlier name of Oenotrians, 37.

Aezeius, early king in Peloponnesus. 35, 37.

Agathocles, tyrant of Syracuse, 239.

Agathyllus, Arcadian poet, 159, 237.

Agylla, earlier name of Caere, 65.

Alba, Alban king, 233.

Alba Longa, 145, 217 f., 243, 275, 277, 295, 297.

Alban district, 119, 219.

Albans, found Rome, 235, 243, 315 ; found other cities, 417, 457, 465 ; other allusions to, 253, 255, 317, 419, cf. 489.

Albula, old name for the Tiber, 233.

Alcmena, mother of Hercules, 131.

Alcyonê, priestess at Argos, 71.

Alexander (Paris), 157.

—— the Great, 9, 163.

—— father of Dionysius, 27.

Alimentus, L. Cincius (fl. ca. 210), Roman annalist, 21, 245, 263, 423 f.

Allodius, Alban king, 233.

Alpheus, river in Peloponnesus, 111.

Alps, 31, 137.

Alsium, ancient city on coast of Etruria, 67.

Aluntium, town in Sicily, 169.

Amata, wife of Latinus, 211.

Ambracia, 165 f.

Ambracian gulf, 165.

Ambrax, king of Ambracia, 165.

Amiternum, old Sabine town, 49, 451.

Amulius, Alban king, 235, 253-63, 277-87, 289-93.

Amyntor, grandson of Pelasgus, 91.

543

INDEX

Anactorium, city in Acarnania, 169.
Anaximenes, historian (fourth cent.), 3.
Anchisa, town in Italy, 243.
Anchises, father of Aeneas, 141, 155, 167, 177, 207, 213, 243, 317; cf. 149, 153.
—— Harbour of, in Epirus, 167.
Ancus Marcius. See Marcius.
Anius, king of Delos, 163, 197.
Antemnae, town in Latium, 55, 405, 415.
Antemnates, inhabitants of Antemnae, 407, 411-15.
Anthemonê, wife of Aeneas, 159.
Anteias, founder of Antium, 241.
Antenoridae, treachery of, 147.
Antias, Valerius, historian (early first cent.), 25, 349.
Antigonus, historian (date unknown), 19.
Antiochus of Syracuse, historian (late fifth cent.), 39, 73, 113 f., 243 f.
Antium, town in Latium, 241, n. 1.
Apennine mountains, 29, 43.
Aphroditê, 155, 161-67, 177, 207, 317; surnamed Aeneias, 165, 175.
Apollo, 75, 489; cf. 61, 63.
Arcadia, original home (a) of Oenotrians, 35, 41, 313 f., 415; (b) of Evander and his company, 99, 315; (c) of Trojans, 201-05; Aeneias in, 159, 179.
Arcadians, in the Peloponnesus, 35, 43, 83, 163; in Italy with Evander, 99-109, 129-33, 139, 143, 145, 267, 289, 307, 315 f.
Arctinus, epic poet, 225, 227.
Ardea, town in Latium, 521; cf. 241, n. 1.
Ardeias, founder of Ardea, 241.
Argos, 55, 67, 71, 83, 125, 135, 141; cf. 307.
Ariaethus (or Araethus), Arcadian historian (?), 159.
Aristotle, philosopher (fourth cent.), 237 f.
Artemis, 373.
Ascanian lake, in Asia Minor, 153.
Ascanius, son of Aeneas, 153, 177 f., 213-17, 229 f., 237, 241, 329, 495; cf. 149.
Asia, 7, 57, 85, 89, 203 f., 225.
Asies, brother of Atys, 87.

Assaracus, son of Tros, 207.
Assyrians, 7.
Athena, 107, 225 f.
Athenians, 9, 207, 335, 339, 359.
Athens, 83, 93, 235, 247 f., 251.
Atlas, first king of Arcadia, 163, 201 f.
Atthides, histories of Attica, 27; cf. 205, n. 1.
Attica, 27, 205.
Atys, Lydian king, 87, 89.
Augustus Caesar, 23, 231, n. 1.
Auronissi (error for Aurunci ?), tribe in Campania, 67.
Aurunci, 67 and note.
Ausonia, Greek name for Italy, 115.
Ausonian sea, 37.
Ausonians, 71, 93.
Aventine hill, 103, 235, 271, 289, 297, 419.
Aventinus Alban king, 235.

BABYLONIA, 117.
Bateia, wife of Dardanus, 163, 207.
Batia, town of the Aborigines, 47.
Bebrycia, district on the Hellespont, 179.
Boeotia, 57.
Bruttians, 307.
Brutus, L. Junius (cos. 507), 247.
Buthrotum, town in Epirus, 167.

CABEIRI, divinities worshipped in Samothrace and neighbouring regions, 77.
Cacus, a robber, 127 f., 137 f.
Caelian hill, 417, 455.
Caelius, an Etruscan, 417.
Caelus (Uranus), 363.
Caenina, town in Latium, 273, 405, 415.
Caeninenses, inhabitants of Caenina, 407, 411-15.
Caere, city in Etruria, 65.
Caesar, Augustus, 23, 231, n. 1.
—— Julius, 231, n. 1.
Caieta, Italian promontory, 175.
Callias of Syracuse, historian (*fl. ca.* 300), 239.
Callirrhoê, daughter of Oceanus, 85.
—— daughter of Scamander, 207.
Callistratus, Domitius, historian (date uncertain), 225.
Callithea, mother of Tyrrhenus, 87.

544

INDEX

INDEX

DAICLES, Olympic victor, 235.

Damastes of Sigeum, genealogist and geographer (*fl. ca.* 400), 237.

Dardanidae, 317.

Dardanus, ancestor of Aeneas, 163, 203 f., 207, 225 f., 505.

—— city in the Troad, 147, 151, 201, 205.

Dascylitis, district on the Propontis, 152.

Daunians, 119.

Deïanira, wife of Pelasgus, 35, 41.

Deimas, son of Dardanus, 203.

Delians, 197.

Delos, 163.

Delphi, 61, 489.

Demagoras of Samos, writer on Trojan or Samothracian antiquities (date unknown), 237.

Demeter, 39, 205.

Deucalion, son of Prometheus, 57.

Dexamenus, son of Herakles, 165.

Diadochi, the "Successors" of Alexander the Great, 9, 163 ; *cf.* 19, n. 1.

Diana, 455.

Dictê, mountain in Crete, 489.

Diomed, 227.

Dionysius of Chalcis, historian (fourth cent.), 241.

—— of Halicarnassus, historian (late first cent.), 27.

Dionysus, 365.

Dioryctus, place on canal near Leucas, 165 and note.

Dodona, city in Epirus, 49, 59, 63, 167.

Dorians, 91.

Drepana, town in western Sicily, 171.

ECHINADES, islands off coast of Acarnania, 169.

Egeria, a nymph, 487 f.

Egypt, 9, 117.

Eleans, 111, 309 and note.

Electra, daughter of Atlas, 163, 203.

Elis, 111, 315 f.

Elyma, city in Sicily, 173 and note.

Elymians, a people in Sicily, 71, 175, 209.

Elymus, a Trojan, 151, 171-75.

—— mountain in Sicily, 175 ; *cf.* 173, n. 3.

Emathion, father of Romus, 241.

Ennius, Roman poet (239-169), 111, n. 1.

Enyalius, 449, 455.

Epeans, ancient people of Elis, 111, 139, 201, 315 f.

Epigoni, sons of the Diadochi, 19 and note.

Epirus, 19, 167.

Eratosthenes, Greek scientific writer (third cent.), 247.

Erichthonius, son of Dardanus, 163 f., 207.

Erinyes, 535.

Erytheia, island near Spain, 125, 315.

Erythrae, Sibyl of, 183 and note.

Eryx, city and mountain in Sicily, 173, n. 3.

Esquiline hill 421.

Etruria and Etruscans. See **Tyrrhenia** and **Tyrrhenians**.

Euboea, 57.

Eumedes, ancestor of Aeneas, 207.

Eunomus, nephew of Lycurgus, 453.

Europe, 7 f., 43, 117, 153, 181, 203.

Euryleon, earlier name of Ascanius, 213 ; or brother of Ascanius, 237.

Eurystheus, king of Mycenae, 125.

Euxenus (?), unknown mythographer, 111 and note.

Euxine sea, 11, 309.

Evander, 99, 103, 129 f., 139, **141**, 201, 267, 273, 289, 307, 315.

FABIDIUS, Modius, founder of Cures, 449.

Fabius Maximus Servilianus, Q. (cos. 142), author of a work on religious antiquities and a history (?), 25 and n. 1.

—— Pictor, Q., first Roman annalist (late second cent.), 21, 245, 263, 275, 423, 425, 427.

Faith, Public, divine honours paid to, 535 f.

Falerii, city in Etruria, 67.

Falernian district, in north-west corner of Campania, 119 · *cf.* 219.

Faunus, king of the Aborigines, 101, 139 f., 143.

Faustinus, brother of Faustulus, 289.

Faustulus, foster-father of Romulus and Remus, 269, 275 f., 283 f., 289 f., 301.

546

INDEX

547

INDEX

548

INDEX

549

INDEX

INDEX

Etruscan city, 93 ; in reality a Greek city, 17, 305-11 ; named after (*a*) Romulus, 31, 145, 319, (*b*) Romus, 241, 243 and note, or (*c*) Romê, 237, 239 ; extent of its dominion, 11, 29, 101, 187.

Romê, one of the Trojan women with Aeneas, 237, 239.

Romulus, son of Aeneas, 159, 237, 241 f. ; son of Ilia, the Vestal, 255 f., 261 ; early life of, 263-77, 281-93 ; founds Rome, 31, 145, 235, 243, 249 f., 293-305, 317-23 ; chosen king, 325-29 ; political, religious and social institutions of, 329-401, 411-15, 445 f., 455 f., 499 f., *cf.* 459-63 ; wars of, 403-11, 415-445, 457, 463-71 ; death of, 471-477 ; worshipped under name of Quirinus, 495 ; other allusions to, 249 f., 477, 489 f., 493.

Romus, founder of Rome in Greek traditions, 237 and n. 2, 239 f., 243, n. 1.

Rutulians, ancient people of Latium, 141, 189, 197, 211.

SABINE women, seized by Roman youths, 399-405 ; effect peace between the two peoples, 441 f.

Sabines, early history of, 451-55, *cf.* 49 ; make war upon Rome, 405 f., 417-41, 515 ; conclude peace, 443 f.

Sabus, eponymous hero of the Sabines, 451.

Sal(l)entine promontory, in Calabria, 169.

Salii, dancing priests, 515-21.

Samnites, 307.

Samon, son of Hermes, 203.

Samothrace, 203, 225 and n. 2, 505.

Samothracians, 225, 229.

Sancus, Sabine divinity, 451.

Sardinia, 359.

Saturn, 111 f., 115, 121 f., 363, 455. See also Cronus.

Saturnia, old name for Italy, 59, 113, 115 ; *cf.* 63.

—— town founded on Capitoline by Peloponnesian followers of Hercules, 145, 295. See also Saturnian hill.

—— town in Etruria, 65.

Saturnian hill (old name for Capitoline), settled by Peloponnesians, 109, 113, 123, 143, 307, 315.

Satyrus, mythographer (date unknown), 225.

Scamander, grandfather of Tros, 207.

Scamandrius, son of Hector, 153.

Scylacian bay, in southern Italy, 113.

Segesta, city in Sicily, 173, n. 2.

Sempronius, C. See Tuditanus.

Septem Aquae, lake in Reatine territory, 47.

Septem Pagi, region surrendered by Veientes to Rome, 471.

Servius Tullius, sixth king of Rome, 251.

Sibyl of Erythrae, on Mount Ida, 183 and n. 2.

Sibylline oracles, 113, 161, 183.

Sicania, earlier name for Sicily, 71.

Sicanians, 69 f., 171.

Sicels, early inhabitants of Italy, 29, 41, 51, 55, 63-69, 201, 313, 415 ; migrate to Sicily, 69-73, 173.

Sicelus, early Italian king, 41, 71 f., 245.

Sicilian quarter, in Tibur, 55.

—— strait, 39, 69, 115, 171.

Sicily, 39, 69-73, 115, 143, 169, 171-75, 179, 209, 359, 505.

Silenus, historian (end of third cent.), 19.

Silvia, Rhea. See Ilia.

Silvius, posthumous son of Aeneas, 229-33.

Solon, 387.

Solonium, ancient town in Latium, 419.

Sophocles, tragic poet (495-406), 39, 83, 155 f.

Spain, 109, 135, 141, 359.

Sparta, 453.

Spartans, 359.

Spina, town at mouth of Po, 61.

Spinetic mouth of Po, 59, 91.

Straton, leader of Sicels, 73.

Suesbola (Suessula ?), city of the Aborigines, 45.

Sun, as a god, 181, 455.

Suna, city of the Aborigines, 45.

TALLUS TYRANNIUS, a Sabine, 445.
Tarentum, 245, 313.

551

INDEX

INDEX